Philosophy
for a New
Generation

Philosophy for a New Generation

Third Edition

A. K. Bierman
San Francisco State College

James A. Gould
University of South Florida

Macmillan Publishing Co., Inc.
New York

Macmillan Publishing Co., Inc.
866 Third Avenue, New York, New York 10022

Collier Macmillan Canada, Ltd.

Library of Congress Cataloging in Publication Data

Bierman, Arthur Kalmer, (date)   comp.
   Philosophy for a new generation.

   Includes bibliographies.
   1. Philosophy—Addresses, essays, lectures.
2. Violence—Moral and religious aspects—Addresses,
essays, lectures. 3. Technology and civilization—
Addresses, essays, lectures. 4. Self (Philosophy)—
Addresses, essays, lectures. I. Gould,
James A., (date)   II. Title.
B29.B52 1977   108   76–12091
ISBN 0–02–309790–6

Printing: 12345678   Year: 7890123

In memory of my union brothers Al Anderson, Sidney Zink, Chuck Tyner, Paul Hayner, Ernesto Lombardi, Floyd Cave, Sam Pollach, and Herb Williams, who, while they were in the world, were also of it.

A. K. B.

For Arthur K. Bierman, whose successful fights for the unions and against HUAC were inspirations for the old and new generations alike.

J. A. G.

In part, the problems of philosophy are unchanging; in part, they vary from age to age, according to the special characteristics of human life and thought at the time; and in the best philosophers of every age these two parts are so interwoven that the permanent problems appear sub specie saeculi, *and the special problems of the age* sub specie aeternitatis.

R. G. Collingwood
The Idea of History

Preface to the Third Edition

Although this edition continues the life-pertinent orientation of the previous two editions, it is by two thirds a new book. For those of you who have used the book before, it will be a chance to vary your routine. We have retained the articles that almost universally were thought to be the "core" essays; we have added some central traditional material, but most of the thirty-nine new articles out of a total of sixty-three were selected for their timeliness, liveliness, philosophic content, and readability for beginning students.

For both those who have and those who have not used the book before, we point out that it, unlike the previous two editions, can serve as the sole text for an introductory course. This is because it now covers all the traditional fields of philosophy save logic. We have added chapters on the theory of knowledge and philosophy of art and culture while retaining chapters on morality and ethics, political philosophy, metaphysics, philosophy of religion, and the meaning of life.

Given the present and anticipated economic situation, every instructor will welcome a shortening of the book's length, enabling us to hedge book inflation. The price will enable instructors to tailor their course with supplementary books without unduly burdening the student financially.

Peter Radcliff, our publisher's reader, was unusually helpful with his criticism and suggestions; we hereby acknowledge and warmly thank him for his contribution to the betterment of this edition. We also express our thanks to Ken Scott, philosophy editor at Macmillan, for his ideas and for helping to secure the ideas of others. We should be and are grateful for the thoughtful comments, largely uniform it turned out, of Arvid Adell, Robert Arrigon, Robert Baird, Otto Begus, Richard Doherty, Elmer Duncan, Daniel Herman, Michael Hoffman, Van Pernis, and an anonymous respondent.

We hope you profit from and enjoy the book.

A. K. B.

J. A. G.

Preface to the First Edition

There are so many excellent introductory philosophy books available that we owe philosophy students and instructors a justification for adding another one. We would not have presumed to edit the book if it were to be only a variation on a familiar theme. On the contrary, we have tried to produce a book that will fill an obvious gap in the literature. There is at present no philosophy anthology that meets the rising student and faculty demand for "relevance." Although "relevance" is a word that has been so tirelessly repeated that it has become tiresome, the hunger for relevance is not tiresome, and we shall probably not be spared the repetition of "relevance" until the demand is met. This anthology is designed for students of philosophy living in the 1970's.

In selecting material for this book, we kept the following in mind:

1. We tried to identify the fields of human interest and endeavor that are of high moment to young people today. These fields determined the choice of chapters.

2. We kept in mind the fact that most students who take an introductory course in philosophy will not take another or will take at most one other. Consequently, this anthology is not designed as an introduction solely for students who will major in philosophy.

3. Although philosophy is not a literary subject, it is a field in which, like any other, good writing promotes comprehension. For this reason, the writing merits of a piece had to be as prominent as its philosophical merits before it was accepted by us.

4. The essays were chosen with an eye for stimulating class discussion and for helping the student to improve his own philosophizing. This anthology is a survey neither of the great philosophers in history nor of the problems that have occupied the interest of prominent modern philosophers or well-known ancient philosophers.

5. We have been very concerned that philosophy not degenerate into a static, fusty exhibit in some mausoleum of ideas. One way of avoiding that is to spur a two-way influence between the practical and the intellectual worlds. We have been partial to essays that stimulate that influence.

Since the scope of the material that we have made eligible for selection is wider than is customary, we cannot pretend to have looked at all of it nor always to have picked the best available on a given topic. If this book merits subsequent editions, they will be improved by comments, references, and recommendations from teachers and students. We welcome your communications.

Many people have already given us generously of their time, their very life substance, and in gratitude we hereby acknowledge their help. Among those who gave us advice on selections are Jack Alexis, Anatole Anton, L. W. Beals, Russell Kahl, Mike Lerner, Jacob Needleman, Roberto Rivera, Peter Radcliff, and Eric Solomon.

Rudolph Weingartner set a high standard for publishers' readers by his measured assessment and fruitful suggestions. He escorted us back to the book, prepared for an improved effort.

Priscilla Johnson, Judy Barkan, and Rider Cooey, please accept our thanks for helping us wrestle a recalcitrant manuscript into a civil state.

A. K. B.

J. A. G.

Contents

Two

THE NOW AND FUTURE GENERATIONS: THE MORAL USE OF TECHNOLOGY 137

Three

THE ARTS AND MASS CULTURE: SHAPING CONSCIOUSNESS 213

Four

REFLECTIONS ON HUMAN KNOWLEDGE   269

Five

CRIME AND PUNISHMENT   335

Six
FREEDOM AND LIBERATION   415

Philosophy
for a New
Generation

Introduction: The Fire and the Stone

Howe canne won gett on sanss fylosoufee? Porley.

—Fanebius Perlyng

Anyone who believes the statement "Not everyone philosophizes" is one who takes the "high road" to philosophy. When he comes to number the philosophers, he would think of Socrates, Plato, Aristotle, Alfarabi, Spinoza, Hume, Locke, Kant, Hegel, Bradley, Wittgenstein, Russell, Moore, and Carnap. These are honored names. According to the high road, one who has no knowledge of philosophers like these knows little or nothing of philosophy.

So, what should we say of two men in a bar arguing whether a man, Tristan, who knew his death was near, is to be considered a suicide because he subsequently cut off his oxygen supply in order to provide his heart for a transplant? Are they philosophizing or not? They are not famous philosophers, perhaps only famous drinkers. One man says Tristan is a suicide because by his own hand he brought on his death by casting off his oxygen supply. The other avers that Tristan is no suicide, because he died of natural causes; under oxygen he had only an artificial life. The first rejoins that it would not be suicide if a man severed his oxygen supply accidentally, but in this case it was a deliberate act calculated to end his life; hence, suicide. Intent is all. To this, the second replies that since by his act Tristan gave another person prolonged life, Tristan is not to be considered a suicide but a donor. To call him a suicide is to condemn him; we should praise him instead, and because of that it is morally wrong to call him a suicide. The bartender keeps a discreet silence throughout, but when they leave, he remarks to the remaining customers, "Those two guys are always philosophizing." That is the "low road."

In this anthology we take both the low road and the high road. Philosophy is not something that occurs only in the books of great philosophers. It occurs whenever and wherever men ponder, discuss, or argue over the use, application, limits, or meaning of important ideas. The two men in the bar were arguing about the application of the idea of suicide to the man who

1

cut off his oxygen supply; suicide is an important idea; therefore, the two men were philosophizing.

The low road to philosophy is a broader, more generous way. We have all traveled the low road. For anyone editing an anthology, the decision to include the low road as well as the high road broadens the scope of his choice. He is no longer confined to making selections from historically great philosophers or from contemporary, famous, or fashionable ones.

This is a consequence that we, the editors, sought, for it freed us to choose material about ideas that are more directly and obviously important to you. We believe that an introductory philosophy course should begin where you are rather than where past thinkers were. This does not mean that past philosophers or contemporary professional philosophers have nothing relevant to say about the ideas you are interested in. They often do, and some of their works are included in this anthology, but we believe that you will profit most from them if you start philosophizing from where you are and think your way to where they were or are.

When we say philosophy is concerned with "important ideas," we introduce an element into our definition of philosophy that is subject to variance. An idea that is important to one man may not be important to another; an idea may be important to many people at one time and not at another; what may be important to healthy, young people may not be important to sick, old people; and so forth. We must not assume uncritically that there is an unchanging stock of ideas with which philosophy always has, is now, and always will be concerned. That gives one the impression that philosophy endures because it possesses the unchanging permanence of stone.

We could make a case that philosophy is more like fire than like stone. The stock of ideas with which philosophers have wrestled has continually changed; this stock has been as restless as flame. And like fire, philosophy's continued existence is assured only if it is fed fresh fuel. The universe of ideas is not static. Notice how delightfully archaic is the discussion between Mr. Square and Mr. Thwackum, the philosopher and the divine, respectively, in Henry Fielding's *Tom Jones* (Book III, Chapter III):

> After this short introduction, the reader will be pleased to remember that the parson had concluded his speech with a triumphant question, to which he had apprehended no answer, viz., Can any honour exist independent of religion?
>
> To this Square answered, that it was impossible to discourse philosophically concerning words till their meaning was first established: that there were scarce any two words of a more vague and uncertain signification than the two he had mentioned, for that there were almost as many different opinions concerning honour as concerning religion. "But," says he, "if by honour you mean the true natural beauty of virtue, I will maintain it may exist independent of any religion whatever. Nay," added he, "you yourself will allow it may exist independent of all but one: so will a Mahometan, a Jew, and all the maintainers of all the different sects in the world."
>
> Thwackum replied, this was arguing with the usual malice of all the enemies of the true Church. . . . When I mention religion I mean the Christian religion; and

not the Christian religion, but the Protestant religion; and not only the Protestant religion, but the Church of England.

Fielding may have raised the question in order to take a sly poke at Thwackum-type divines, but still it is not the kind of question that is likely to have been raised by you or your friends, either in jest or in earnest. The idea of honor is not in vogue at this time; we rarely see or discuss it. It was a prominent idea during the days of chivalry. Now there is an air of nostalgia about it: we think of World War I and von Richthofen and other aces when we think of honor. It may be popular again some day.

Here are some of the outmoded ideas that were once an important part of the stock-in-trade of professional philosophers: perfection, forgiveness, soul, substance, love, innocence, sin, fate, harmony, sublimity, conation, wisdom, authority, will, novelty, analysis, imagination, evolution, the artificial, ideals, dignity, friendship, passion, power, spirit, judgment, intuition, happiness, charity, adultery, obedience, simony, slavery, and immortality.

Why do the ideas that concern philosophers change? There are several explanations. To claim that ideas float in and out of the modish stock just as hemlines and necklines float up and down with the fashion is to make philosophical change appear too arbitrary. Still, there is some truth in it—a truth that should not be harshly condemned. Some people think fashion changes are frivolous and that the people who are influenced by them are weak-willed, wasteful conformists. Yet in a visit to an art museum, these same people will look at several paintings, instead of devoting all their time to one, no matter how "great" it may be. Why? Because they have got all they want out of the picture, are bored looking at it, are curious about the next one, or want to refresh their lagging spirit. The same reasons can be given for approving fashion changes—and for approving philosophical changes.

Changing social and political conditions also explain why some ideas gain importance and others lose it. Consider the effects of the civil rights movement. The ideas of equality, justice, prejudice, discrimination, segregation, and civil disobedience came to the fore. The wave of activism in the colleges and universities has cast up the ideas of participation, freedom, radicalism, relevance, revolution, power, respect, involvement, repression, and confrontation. The hippie and drug culture levitated, perhaps only momentarily, the ideas of love, religion, meditation, leisure, community, festival, tribe, and identity. Opposition to the Vietnam war has revived the ideas of pacifism, conscience and the law, dissent, and imperialism. Black militancy has spotlighted the ideas of oppression, violence, race, and rights.

We are living in a time of social ferment; changes are occurring at a dizzying pace. This has radically altered the stock of ideas with which we comprehend and advocate social change. Although most of the ideas we listed have never been totally eliminated from professional philosophers' stock of ideas, neither have most of them been of central concern. If the social changes that have made them prominent do not subside too soon, these ideas will in time receive greater attention from the professional philosophers. However, that does not dictate that we should wait to philosophize about them; because they are important, we are bound to philosophize about them—now. This anthology is designed to recognize the resurgence of these ideas, the need to philosophize about them, and the value of relating previous philosophizing to the newly prominent ideas.

It is difficult for anyone to get excited about ideas they think unimportant. To force you to "ponder, discuss, or argue over" ideas that are unimportant to you is to force you into juiceless exercises. Perhaps that would introduce you to a history of philosophical doctrines, but it would not help you learn to philosophize—and there is nothing sweeter, more satisfying, or more exhilarating when it is important to *you*.

Social change is not the only kind of change that shakes up our stock of ideas; technological and scientific change also does this. The idea of death has become prominent with the advent of heart transplants. The "pill" challenges our idea of right insofar as it bears on sexual conduct. New "bugging" devices make us anxious enough to think again about the idea of privacy. A Leningrad professor discovered a drug, phenigama, which combats the effect of "mechanization" of industrial work; the idea of social engineering, made so notorious by Aldous Huxley in *Brave New World,* is here! Soma has arrived.

The technologically possible prospect of preserving our bodies indefinitely by sudden freezing and of subsequently reviving them by thawing jeopardizes our idea of mortality, of wills and inheritance, and of divorce (one might just freeze himself until the spouse passes away). Although all these conceptual cramps may be uncomfortable, they at least make us rethink some ideas we had taken for granted.

Our concept of man as a unique, thinking, rational creature has been a source of pride to us. Thinking is man's glory, but the emergence of sophisticated computers that "calculate," "remember," "design" other computers, "follow" directions, and "communicate" casts a shadow on that pride. If machines can do all that, aren't they thinking? Can it be that man is only a supersophisticated machine? Our advances in technology have made us question our concept of man.

Automation has already made us think anew about the ideas of work, labor, and leisure. Since these ideas are not isolated, thinking about and discussing them pull other ideas into our current stock. For example, the shifting amount of work we will do in our life in ratio to the amount of leisure we will have makes a thoughtful person reassess his idea of education. Is a college education to be designed primarily to prepare us for work or for leisure?

So far, our main emphasis has been on matters that support the fire image of philosophy. We have taken the side of Heracleitus, the ancient Greek philosopher who thought that all things in the universe were in motion. "You cannot step twice into the same river," he said. Of the four elements that Greek cosmologists thought the world might be composed (earth, air, fire, and water), Heracleitus thought it to be fire. Fire symbolizes ceaseless change. If philosophy is like fire, then its incessant change continually introduces new ideas to philosophize about. In this case, nothing of past philosophy is relevant to the present or future; you cannot step twice into the same philosophy!

This is an extreme doctrine, although in part true. Its opposite extreme is the stone image of philosophy. Parmenides, another ancient Greek philosopher, claimed that there is no motion in the universe. If philosophy is like stone, then its stock of ideas does not change.

Our anthology represents a compromise. Philosophy is in part like fire and in part like stone. After all, there are some ideas that have formed an unchanging core in the stock of ideas. Philosophers have long and steadily contended with the concepts of good, truth, knowledge, evil, mind, matter, quality, quantity, and ideas. The fire part of philosophy led us to incorporate some essays outside the "classical" corpus, and the stone part led us to select some "classical" material; the compromise led us to relate classical material to current issues. The pedagogical justification for our stand is stated very nicely by William Paley in the preface to *The Principles of Moral and Political Philosophy* (1785, first edition):

> An experience of nine years in the office of a public tutor in one of the universities, and in that department of education to which these chapters relate, afforded me frequent occasion to observe, that in discoursing to young minds upon topics of morality, it required much more pains to make them perceive the difficulty, than to understand the solution: that, unless the subject was so drawn up to a point, as to exhibit the full force of an object, or the exact place of a doubt, before any explanation was entered upon—in other words, unless some curiosity was excited before it was attempted to be satisfied, the labour of the teacher was lost. When information was not desired, it was seldom, I found, retained. I have made this observation my guide in the following work: that is, upon each occasion I have endeavored, before I suffered myself to proceed in the disquisition, to put the reader in complete possession of the question, and to do it in the way I thought most likely to stir up his doubts and solicitude about it.

One

Morality: Old and New

> The supreme principle of all moral judgment lies in the understanding: that of the moral incentive to action lies in the heart. This motive is moral feeling. We must guard against confusing the principle of the judgment with the principle of the motive. The first is the norm; the second the incentive. The motive cannot take the place of the rule. Where the motive is wanting, the error is practical; but when the judgment fails the error is theoretical.
> —Immanuel Kant
> *Lectures on Ethics*
> "The Supreme Principle of Morality"

Introduction

Three important moral questions are:

What ought I to do?

What is morally good?

Why should I be moral?

In asking what we ought to do, we are asking which of the several actions open to us to perform on some occasion is the one that is morally obligatory. We contrast "obligatory" to "right" because, although there might be two (or more) right acts to perform on an occasion, only one may be obligatory—the one that is more right. For example, performing one act might be right because it fulfills a promise, and performing another act might be right because it aids someone in distress; however, the same act might not both fulfill a promise and aid the distressed, and we might not be able to perform both. Therefore, we have to choose sometimes between two rights, only one of them being our obligation. Since our moral obligation is to perform the act that is more right, we have to determine degree of rightness.

In answering the question "What ought I to do?" the natural response is to answer with a *maxim:* we ought to keep our promises; we ought to help those in distress; we ought to be fair; we ought to respect other persons' rights; we ought to honor our father and our mother; we ought not to despoil the environment; and so forth. When we refer to persons' morals, often we mean to refer to the set of maxims that they believe specify which acts humans ought and ought not perform. These maxims are also called "norms," "imperatives," "rules," or "standards." The third section of this chapter concentrates on moral maxims.

In asking what is morally good, we are asking what kinds of things have moral merit. The things that we judge to be morally good are *ends* that we think are worth striving for and attaining. Among the moral ends that have been advocated, we include a good life, a good character, a good experience. Kant thought only one thing to be morally good: a good will.

Aristotle thought that the supreme end for which we strive is happiness; the good life is a life of happiness, which we attain by living in accordance with virtue. Some have thought that the good life is one spent in contemplation of God. Others think the primary aim of life is to develop our potential as humans.

As for moral character, one could claim that we should strive to be honest, kind, generous, and cheerful. Should we add "to be just?" How about "humble?" Or is a proud (not to be confused with arrogant) character morally better than a humble one? The second section of this chapter concentrates on moral ends.

Some people think the chief ends at which we aim are pleasure, satisfaction of desires, or fulfillment of needs. It is true that we strive for them, because generally we prefer pleasant to unpleasant experiences, satisfaction to frustration, fulfillment to disappointment. Ethical hedonism, for example, is the view that we ought to maximize our or others' pleasant experiences. You may have some doubt that pleasure in itself (or satisfaction or fulfillment) is *morally* good. It may be a good, but you may wonder if it is a "moral" good. Is the enjoyment of a good steak a moral occasion?

Suppose that the steak were a gift from a person grateful for an act of kindness you performed. Enjoying the steak might then be a moral occasion, not because of the pleasure itself but because it is a reward. Or, suppose you stole the steak from a poor, dying woman who was going to celebrate her last birthday. In this case, enjoying the steak would be morally wrong, not because of the pleasure but because the wrong person is enjoying it. Here it appears that it is the deservedness or undeservedness of the pleasure rather than the pleasure itself that gives pleasant experience its moral nature, which brings us to the third important moral question.

In asking why we should be moral, we could be interpreted as asking for the motive or incentive for performing obligatory acts or for pursuing morally good ends. Kant, in the quote at the head of this introduction, distinguishes between the *judgment* that something is morally right or good and the *motive* for performing right acts or pursuing good ends. Pleasure, satisfaction, and fulfillment, and their opposites, pain, frustration, and disappointment, may be seen as morally relevant because they may, respectively, be rewards for moral behavior and punishments for immoral behavior. Rewards and punishments are incentives. In answer to "Why should I keep my promises?" we might say "Because you will be rewarded with pleasure from the trust others develop in you." In answer to "Why shouldn't I despoil my environment?" we might say "Because you will be punished with ugliness and diminished crops if you do."

Pleasure, satisfaction, and fulfillment are morally relevant because by being conferred they are rewards and by being withheld they are punishments. They are rewards when conferred because we prefer them to their opposites. Because we prefer them, they may serve as motivations or incentives.

"Because," then, is ambiguous; it may signal either a reason or a motive.

"Why should I give this ten dollars to Virginia?" *"Because* you promised to repay her." In this instance, "because" gives us the *reason* why this is an act we ought to perform; what follows the "because" is a maxim.

"Why should I keep my promise to Virginia?" *"Because* if you don't, no one will trust you hereafter and you will suffer the pain of isolation." In this instance, "because" gives us a *motive* why this is an act you ought to perform; what follows the "because" is an incentive.

We want now to show why these three questions lead to philosophy, why we cannot avoid philosophizing about morals. The occasion for philosophizing arises when we find ourselves in problematic situations. Problematic situations occur when we find an incompatibility in beliefs, either between ours and others or between our own, and when the incompatible beliefs each has *prima facie* plausibility because there are plausible arguments for each. If we consider persons' morals to consist of the set of maxims they believe, the set of moral ends they believe should be pursued, and the beliefs about human motivations, then we have several possibilities for incompatible morals. Maxims may be incompatible with each other, goals may be incompatible with each other, maxims and goals may be incompatible, maxims may be incompatible with motives, goals may be incompatible with motives, and motives may be incompatible with each other.

Incompatibility of beliefs can be resolved only by giving up one or both of the beliefs. To make a rational resolution of incompatibility requires thinking about and evaluating the reasons for each belief and finding their connections with other beliefs; that is, a rational resolution requires philosophizing. Let's consider some of these incompatibilities.

Incompatible maxims present us with the problem of deciding which one we ought to use as our guide to moral action; a choice is sometimes forced on us by circumstances—they might be life-and-death circumstances. Consider X Liberation Front, whose members believe that a government is unjust, cruelly exploitative, and oppressive to many of its citizens; they believe and act on the maxims that such governments should not continue to rule, that it is a moral person's duty to overthrow such governments, and that random acts of violence, such as bombing, are the right acts to perform when other avenues of action are foreclosed.

You, on the other hand, may disagree with the third maxim, although you agree with the first two; you may hold the maxim that it is not right to do violence in pursuit of political ends to any person who is not a member of the government and, so, not responsible for its policy decisions and/or acts. You may hold, also, the maxim that anyone guilty of such violence should be executed if caught and convicted.

One evening there is a loud, urgent knock on your door. You open it to find your sister; she asks you to hide her because the police are looking for her as one of the bombers at an airport. What do you do? Hide her, turn her in, or refuse her admittance while keeping your silence? It may be difficult to decide because you discover how strongly you hold the maxim that you should be loyal to your family members. To decide requires reflection on some important ideas; that is, it calls for philosophizing.

We may have incompatible moral goals. You may believe in the Christian virtue of humility, a part of what Friedrich Nietzsche called a slave morality. Someone else may believe this is not a trait of a good moral character. Humility makes a person into a doormat, they might argue. Being a doormat to someone else leads to a passivity, which, in turn, leads people to obey immoral edicts of dictators; humble people may torture, gas, and persecute so-called "enemies of the state." Perhaps a better moral goal is to become nobly self-assertive. In thinking about which kind of character we should pursue, we would be philosophizing.

There may also be a conflict between the maxims we hold and the ends we pursue. Consider the well-known phrase "The ends justify the means." Suppose there is a crime wave in your community; to stop the contagion, it is believed necessary that someone be imprisoned, tried, and convicted in order that law and order be restored. Stopping the crime wave is a good, moral goal. It may even be achieved just as well by convicting innocent persons who appear to be guilty as by convicting the guilty. Does this end justify that means? You probably hold the maxim that innocent persons ought not to be punished. Here a good end is incompatible with this moral maxim. Which one is to be chosen? It is not enough to say that a good end does not justify an immoral means because the good end may take moral precedence over a moral maxim; to claim otherwise requires reasoning about some important ideas; that is, it requires philosophizing.

One of the most frequently experienced moral incompatibilities occurs between our maxims and our motives. I may have promised Esther I would help her move on Saturday and then find that the opera I've always wanted to see is playing for the last and only time on Saturday and I cannot reach Esther because she has had her phone taken out. My desire is to see the opera, and I'm not at all keen on carrying furniture; however, I do hold the maxim that I should keep my promises. What should I do? Do what I ought to do or do what I desire to do? Is duty always to be chosen over desire? This takes a little "low road" philosophizing.

We also find problematic situations when we find an incompatibility between our moral goals and our motives. For example, I may have the goal of achieving an honest character. This commits me to telling the truth; but when I think of all the things I would have to say to my friends, work associates, and family to achieve this kind of character, I shudder at the distress I would cause in others and in myself, distress I devoutly want to avoid. This leads me, and most other people, to all shades of white lies to avoid the distress and embarrassment. Philosophize about that for a while.

An interesting philisophical problem arises when we consider the limits of motivating persons to act morally. Suppose it is agreed on all hands that Jessup is obliged to perform an act A; but we know Jessup will balk at performing it, not having any incentive to perform A. We who are knowledgeable about the springs of human action know that we can get Jessup to perform *A* by making him think he is performing some other act, *B*, which we know he is motivated to perform. For example, Jessup does not want to split his deceased parents' estate with his sister, act *A*, but we can get him to do this by pointing out that he can increase his own inheritance if he is taxed on only one half of the estate rather than the whole of it. Are we justified in manipulating Jessup to perform an act even if we thereby get him to perform the act he is obliged to perform? We may not have any doubt about condemning human manipulation when sex images are used to induce persons to buy unnecessary and/or harmful products. But in this case the manipulation has for its end the performing of an obligation, which is surely a good end. Still there may be some motives we should not use in order to get someone to perform his duty. This incompatibility is something to philosophize about.

We have suggested that the occurrence of incompatible morals creates problematic situations that call for resolution. And we have suggested that philosophizing is one way of reaching resolution. We should recognize that there are nonphilosophical ways of achieving resolution. An extreme way is to kill the person whose morals are incompatible with yours; in the event that it is your own morals that are incompatible, you can commit suicide. Another way is to exercise enough threat backed by enough force to frighten the other person into silence or to deter him or her from acting in accord with his or her morals. A typical way of handling incompatibilities in your own morals is to pretend they do not exist; of course, this may lead to a little hypocrisy; you may profess one maxim or espouse one end on some occasion but act in accord with another, incompatible, maxim or end; you will get used to being hypocritical after a while.

However, if neither murder, suicide, threats, self-pretense, nor hypocrisy is palatable to you, you could try philosophizing with yourself and others instead. The point of philosophizing about morals is to think your way past unreflective incompatible morals to a moral *system* that we can all share.

Such a moral system should have at least these three properties: (1) No part of the morals (maxims, ends, motives) may be incompatible with any other part; that is, the morals should be consistent. (2) The set of morals should be comprehensive; it should be a system covering every moral situation or provide a means of generating whatever additional morals are needed. (3) The set should be integrated; every part of the system should be related to every other part either directly or indirectly.

Integration. A set of morals should be integrated; each part should be related to every other part; otherwise, we will not be able to detect if each part is compatible with every other part of the system. Suppose that one's moral set contains the two maxims that one should not commit adultery and that one should repay loans. Are they compatible? We could integrate them, showing that they are indirectly related to each other by showing that each is related in the same way to a third maxim. The argument might go like this. Adultery is breaking a promise of fidelity; not repaying a loan is breaking a promise to repay; thus, both maxims are instances of the maxim that one should keep promises. Further, since the promise maxim is self-consistent, the adultery and loan maxims are shown to be compatible. Knowing that the adultery and loan maxims are compatibly integrated with the promise maxim, we are able to produce an argument showing that they are compatible with each other.

The feature of *generality* enables us to integrate morals. In our example, the promise maxim is more general than either the adultery or the loan maxim. By making use of generality, we can proceed to integrate our morals. We may establish that there are some moral parts that are of lowest generality, say, level one; then they might be integrated under other parts of higher generality, say, level two, and so forth, until, finally, we find a single maxim of the highest generality under which all the remaining parts of the various levels are integrated. (Those which are not so integrable are suspect because they are not shown to be compatible.) All the parts would have been shown indirectly to be integrated with each other because every part is integrated directly under one and the same maxim. Utilitarianism, represented in the second section of this chapter by Bentham, is an example of a moral philosophy that tries to achieve integration by proposing a single, highest-level maxim: We ought to do that which will produce the greatest good for the greatest number.

Integration by generality is not by itself sufficient to attain integration, however. Consider the following case. Quimby owes Snavely money; Quimby is married; hers is not an open marriage; Quimby has no money and the note is due. Snavely offers Quimby the opportunity to repay him by having sex with him ten times. This poses the following incompatibility for Quimby. She should repay Snavely the loan according to the promise maxim, but if she repays him as Snavely suggests, and it is the only way open to her, she will break her promise of fidelity to Mr. Quimby. In this case, the two maxims, although they are both integrated under the higher-level promise maxim, are incompatible; if she does have sex with Snavely, she has performed both an obligatory act and a forbidden act; if she does not have sex with Snavely, she will have failed in one obligation but will have kept the other.

In order to escape this kind of dilemma, we have to supplement generality with *priority;* when two parts of a morals are incompatible, as for Quimby, we have to give one of the parts priority over the other. This, of course, requires a bit of philosophizing. One particularly important priority issue is whether moral maxims take precedence over moral ends. Those who give moral ends priority are called teleologists and those who give moral maxims priority are called deontologists. We will have more to say on this issue in the introductions of the second and third sections of this chapter.

Comprehensiveness. Comprehensiveness is a necessary property of a set of morals if it is to be a system of morals, because without it neither of the other two criteria—consistency and integration—can be shown to have been met. If a maxim for some moral situation is not included in our system, we will not have related a needed maxim to other maxims in the system, and hence will not have shown the set to be integrated. And if it is not shown to be integrated, it will not have been shown that the missing maxim is compatibly related to the other maxims in the set.

So far we have indicated the major moral questions, examined the notions of problematic situations and moral incompatibility, discussed how the various parts of morals may be incompatible, and distinguished between morals and a moral system. We have shown why we want philosophically to advance from morals to a moral system; we have specified three properties of a moral system: consistency, integration, and comprehensiveness; and we have explained how generality and priority serve to help integrate the parts of a set of morals into a moral system.

We distinguish, now, between a moral system and an ethical theory. A moral system is a set of maxims, ends, and a view of human nature that are consistent, integrated, and comprehensive. An ethical theory is a theory *about* morals and *about* a moral system or systems. It consists of reasoned answers to such questions as: Is there a single moral system with the three properties we talked about? Or are there several possible moral systems? If there are several, is it possible to evaluate rationally and choose from among them? Suppose that we have two moral systems, each with a single, different, highest-generality maxim; is there a rational way of choosing one of them? Of showing that one is better than the other? You already have been immersed in ethical theory, because our discussion of the properties of a moral system is a discussion *about* morals and a moral system.

Answers to these ethical theory questions have popularly been divided into two kinds, conventionally labeled "relativistic" and "absolutistic." The first section in this chapter contains essays that deal with relativism, and, by implication, absolutism also, because it is an opposite of relativism.

Relativism

Could it be brought home to people that there is no absolute standard in morality, they would perhaps be somewhat more tolerant in their judgments, and more apt to listen to the voice of reason.

—Edward A. Westermarck

Relativism has seemed to many a plausible ethical theory because they have observed variability of morals, a variability of morals between persons, between social classes, between nations, between historical periods, between "primitive" and "civilized" cultures, and so forth.

Luther Binkley, in this section's first essay, reviews some of the factors and persons to which he thinks we can attribute the presently prevailing relativistic view of ethics. He points out that to many people relativism is synonymous with arbitrary and irrational value choices; this means that if one holds to relativism, one believes there is no rational way of choosing from among the variable morals with which we are confronted. Variability of morals is not by itself relativism; relativism is variability plus the denial that there is a rational way of showing that one of the variable morals is morally better than any others.

Binkley does not subscribe to this version of relativism. He notes that "The theatre of the absurd is an attempt to portray the nature of human life when one comes to accept the belief that there are no values which are better than any others, that all life is therefore senseless and meaningless." Although this is an unacceptable form of life for him Binkley acknowledges that we have to distinguish between values and facts; that science is the study of facts; and that no amount of scientific knowledge about the facts of persons' behavior will tell us how persons *ought* to behave; thus, there can be no way of showing that one value choice is better than another in the way that we can show that one statement of fact is true and its contradictory is false. Nevertheless, he claims "that one's decision is not completely arbitrary, for reasons can be given for making the value judgment." He points out that in choosing between buying a book and going to a play we consider how many books we have bought and read, the nature of the book and the play, and so forth. These are factors in rational deliberation; the choice is not arbitrary as a toss of the coin would be; we have reasons for choosing, say, the play over the book.

Failure to distinguish between variability and relativism occurs often enough to bear repeating: The two are not identical. The two often are not distinguished because the phrase "relative to" is often used to express both these ideas, as in "Morals are relative to culture." If "relative to" is taken in one sense, that remark may obviously be true; it may be a mere statement of fact that culture A has one set of morals and culture B has another set of morals, and that members of each culture favor their morals and/or think their culture's morals are superior to those of the other. This use of "relative to," although referring only to variability, may lead the careless to slip into the belief that one also holds a relativistic theory of ethics. However, this would not be correct. To be a relativist requires also holding that there is no way of showing that one set of morals or one moral system is the correct or the true one.

Carl Wellman, in this section's third essay, shows that the variability sense of "relative" does not by itself establish the case for a relativistic ethical theory. He shows this of several moral variables in turn; these include mores, social institutions, human nature, acts, goals, value experiences, moral emotions (compare his remarks with those in Westermarck's essay), moral concepts, moral judgments, and moral reasoning. From Wellman, you will learn that it is not as easy to prove that a relativistic ethical theory is correct as you might have thought, especially once you keep the distinction beween variability and relativistic in mind.

In the introduction to this chapter, we talked about incompatible morals. "Incompatible" is a logical term; it designates a relation between statements; two statements are incompatible just in the case when not both of them may be true. A relativist such as **Edward A. Westermarck** denies that morals are incompatible. Nor will he allow that they are compatible. They are neither, because moral claims are neither true nor false.

Westermarck is the author of *The Origin and Development of the Moral Ideas,* a two-volume, 1,400-page examination of the various morals found in a large number of cultures. His opening remarks explain why he began his extensive investigation of morals: He "was once discussing with some friends the point how far a bad man ought to be treated with kindness. The opinions were divided, and, in spite of much deliberation, unanimity could not be attained." Westermarck was baffled by his and his friends' failure to reach agreement by rational deliberation. This needed explaining.

Obviously, the failure to find a rational way of reaching agreement does not prove that no rational solution exists; the most that it proves is that no rational solution has been found. You are familiar with the difficulty of finding the proof for geometrical or algebraic theorems; you do not conclude out of your despair that there is no proof. Westermarck realizes he can't establish relativism in this negative way; he knows that he must generate an ethical theory that demonstrates that no rational way of reaching moral agreement is possible. That is the burden of his essay in this book.

We can build some background for understanding Westermarck's positive theory by reflecting on what a rational method of reaching agreement would be like. Morals is not the only place where difference of opinion occurs; it occurs also in science and mathematics. When two differing scientific opinions are put forward, we assume that not both of them are true. We also assume that truth is relative only to the facts, not to person, time, place, culture, or circumstance. A factual statement is true or false regardless of who stated it or regardless of the culture in which the person who stated it lives. And we assume, further, that we agree on the means of discovering the facts and that these means of discovery are uniform for almost everyone.

That there are, for example, ten people in a room can be determined because we share the technique of counting, because we agree on what are and what are not persons, and because normal eyes have uniform capabilities.

In essence, Westermarck's argument that there can be no rational means for reaching unanimity, and that neither compatibility nor incompatibility holds between moral claims, rests on the view that "there can be no moral truth in the sense in which this term is generally understood. The ultimate reason for this is that the moral concepts are based upon emotions and that the contents of emotion fall entirely outside the category of truth." The means we use to settle differing scientific opinions are, therefore, not applicable to differing moral claims because the former have a truth property, whereas moral claims do not.

"Relativism" is an elusive term; Westermarck's relativism is only one of several kinds. It will help us to capture the various relativisms if we approach the topic somewhat more systematically now that we have located its habitat.

"Relative to" is the basic phrase. Morals are said to be "relative to" persons, time, place, circumstance, social class, culture, and so forth. One meaning of "relative to," as indicated before, is that moral choices and judgments—about moral maxims and moral goods—*vary* with respect to persons, time, place, social class, and so forth. This may be true, and often is, but in itself it is not disquieting because we notice variability among factual, nonmoral judgments also. Variability of factual judgments involves the same kind of factors that variability in moral judgments does, but they do not generally lead persons who embrace moral relativism into accepting factual relativism.

Consider "The cloth is blue." Norma might make this judgment but Diffton might have a different opinion, say, "The cloth is green." Well, is the cloth blue or green? We assume that it has to be one or the other, even though it appears blue to Norma and green to Diffton, and the appearance is the only evidence that either has. We might discount Diffton's evidence because we determine that he has defective eyesight while Norma's eyesight is normal. Here color judgment varies with persons.

Again, the judgment that even normal-sighted persons make could vary with the kind of light in which the cloth is seen. If it is seen under fluorescent light, Norma might say "The cloth is green." When we buy clothes in stores with fluorescent lighting, we often take them into sunlight to determine their colors. We consider sunlight to be the standard light.

Colors vary sometimes depending upon the surrounding colors. Seen in one setting, we might say "The cloth is blue" and, seen in another setting, we might say "The cloth is green." To settle the cloth's color, we could specify that it has the color that it appears to have against a standard white background, for example.

Despite these variability factors, we isolate the "fact." It is a "fact" that the cloth is blue, not green; that is, we affirm that "The cloth is blue" is true and affirm that "The cloth is green" is false. We establish that these two statements are incompatible because not both may be true; that are incompatible, unlike the two statements, "The cloth appears blue to me" and "The cloth appears green to me."

What makes it possible to move from differing "appearances" of color to the single fact "The cloth is blue"? As you have probably noted, our specification of "standard" or "normal" eyesight, light, and background enables us to overcome the variability factors. Standardizing enables us to isolate the single "fact." It is the singleness of the "fact" that makes "is blue" and "is green" incompatible; the *one* fact excludes the cloth from being *two* colors. Factual relativism is avoided by standardizing variability factors, even though what color the cloth "appears" to have is "relative to" a person's kind of eyesight, "relative to" the light in which the cloth is seen, and "relative to" the background in which the cloth is placed. Here we can understand that "relative to" could be paraphrased as "in relation to." "In relation to normal eyesight, sunlight, and white background, the cloth appears to be blue; in relation to these standard conditions, we can truly say that "The cloth *is* blue."

Now, consider "Sexism is right" and "Sexism is wrong." An "absolutist" would maintain that these two statements are incompatible; they are incompatible because one of them is true and the other is false. The "relativist" would deny that they have truth value, and so cannot be incompatible or compatible. They cannot have truth value because, unlike the color case, we cannot standardize the variability factors; without such standardization, we cannot move from "Sexism *seems* (appears) wrong to me" to "Sexism *is* wrong." Standardization is a necessary feature of a rational procedure for determining the "facts." This being absent in morals, we cannot overcome moral relativism as we overcame factual relativism.

Relativists' first point is that in moral as in color judgments we have to consider that our judgment is "relative to" various factors. Sexism may appear or seem wrong to the one who suffers from it while it may seem to be right to the one who benefits from it. Judgments about the morality of sexism vary with the person.

They may also vary with the culture. In relation to one way of conducting social life, sexism may seem right to persons in that culture; we can imagine that in relation to another culture, it may seem wrong.

Judgments about the morality of sexism obviously vary over time. A few years ago, few were even conscious of sexism being a moral issue, let alone thinking it was wrong; now there are few who are unconscious of it, and if some still think it right, they are beginning to be on the defensive.

There are other variability factors, such as social class and dominant religion, that could be cited here, but the point has been sufficiently made to allow us to proceed to relativists' second point.

Relativists' second point is that there is no way of standardizing these variability factors in morality as we did in color vision. Suppose that a race of creatures, Revers, obviously intelligent, although distinct from human beings, happen to be so constructed that what gives us pleasure gives them pain and what gives us pain gives them pleasure. We suppose further that Revers pain–pleasure reversal is of survival value to them. We make many of our moral judgments on the basis of the pain and/or pleasure that our acts cause in others, even though it may not be the sole basis. We think we ought to refrain from torture because of the pain it causes in others. However, torturing Revers is beneficial to them and so need not be forbidden. Given these suppositions, we cannot say flat out that "Torture is wrong" or "Torture is right." Absolutism would be a mistaken position to take.

One might try to save absolutism by citing human beings as the "normal" ones; this would allow us to isolate the single "fact" that would enable us to move from "Torture seems wrong to humans" to "Torture is wrong;" it makes "Torture is right" false, and so incompatible with "Torture is wrong." That torture seems right to the Revers does not provide evidence that it really is right, because they are abnormal observers such as Diffton was in relation to color.

But which race is the "normal" one? Human beings or Revers? Relativists deny that it is possible to pick out the normal or standard one. To pick out one as normal is to favor one race over the other; this is already making a moral judgment; thus, the standardization of observers that is needed to get a factlike condition begs the moral question; to get a moral fact presupposes making a prior moral judgment which is not a fact.

It is possible that you might think the following move helps to settle our problem. Why not, you might think, say that "Torture *is* wrong for humans" and "Torture *is* right for Revers?" Both of these are true and so not incompatible. There are normal humans and there are normal Revers; what *seems* wrong and right to them, respectively, *is* wrong and right *to them* (relative to them). This way we can have true moral claims and do not have to concede the relativists' position; and, simultaneously, we have got rid of incompatibility.

This will not work, relativists' may argue, because, perhaps, you are supposing that these two races do not have to live together. They might point out that we do not need to make fanciful suppositions about a "reversed" race of creatures in order to show that it is not possible to specify a "normal" moral observer. Those who are victims and those who are beneficiaries of sexism are such reverse "races." Which one are we to pick as the "normal" one? Obviously the victims and the beneficiaries would have rather varying views of this; and in the absence of any "standardization," there is no way to determine the moral "fact." Additionally, because they have to live together, the move to saying "Sexism is right for the beneficiaries" and "Sexism is wrong for the victims" is not a solution to the problem. The beneficiary of sexism will not be a beneficiary unless he or she makes someone a victim of sexism; with benefits go victims and vice versa. And here we are back to conflict. Having no standardized conditions, we have no moral facts; having no moral facts, we have no rational way of deciding on the truth or falsity of moral statements; having no truth or falsity, we have no incompatibilities.

If the relativists are correct in their claims and you think that sexism *is* wrong—for both victims and beneficiaries—then you have a philosophical task cut out for yourself.

We are now in a position to see why there are several kinds of relativists.

According to relativists', moral judgments are more complicated than we might have thought. We cannot say simply "Sexism is right" or "Sexism is wrong"; we have to say that it *seems* right or wrong in relation to (relative to) a number of variable factors. Thus, "Sexism seems wrong to Quimby at this time, in this place, under these circumstances, in this culture, and so forth." There can be as many kinds of relativism as there are the number of kinds of variable factors that are built into moral claims when properly set out. A "cultural relativist" is one who emphasizes the role of culture in making sexism seem right or wrong; a "subjective relativist" is one who emphasizes the factor of person in viewing sexism, sexism appearing differently to a victim person than it does to a beneficiary person.

Westermarck might be called an "emotive relativist" because he emphasizes the emotional response—approval or indignation—which a person makes to an act or goal. Of course, one might be a more complicated relativist by claiming that more than one variable factor is incapable of being standardized or normalized.

After this discussion, you might be wondering about Binkley's essay. He talks about relativists' claim that moral judgments and choices are arbitrary and irrational; we have examined this and traced it to the claim that standardization is not possible. On the other hand, Binkley claims that we do not need to surrender to this version of relativism because we do give reasons for our choice; rational deliberation is part of our normal choice procedure. These seem to be two different positions; if there really are reasons, then relativism in any "version" is false. How are we to make sense of Binkley's essay?

One might think of internal reasons and external reasons. Given that a person holds to particular maxims, pursues particular moral goals, and believes certain propositions about human motivations, then relative to this intellectual background, normal for him, he can give reasons for a choice or a judgment; these reasons are internal to this background. But when two persons have different intellectual backgrounds, the reasons they give each other for differing moral judgments are external to each other's intellectual backgrounds; sharing no intellectual "normality," the reasons of the other are arbitrary and irrational. Whether we can distinguish between internal and external reasons is, obviously, an interesting philosophical question.

The Age of Relativism

LUTHER BINKLEY

Luther J. Binkley (1925–   ) is professor and chairman of the department of philosophy and director of the humanities program at Franklin and Marshall College. His
interests are in the fields of ethics, religion, and philosophy of law. Among his books
are *Contemporary Ethical Theories* (1961) and the *Mercersburg Theology* (1953).

. . .

The Age of Relativism

Our age has often been called an age of relativism. During the so-called Jazz
Age of the Twenties Walter Lippmann observed that "the acids of modernity"
had dissolved the religious certainties of the past. The influence of the scientific
method and the growth of industrial and urban society were largely responsible,
he believed, for the loss of faith in absolutes. Even in the realm of morals the
codes we had inherited from the Hebrews of the Old Testament were beginning
to dissolve in the spirit of a new age.[1] Lippman's insights were confirmed by
the findings of many social scientists who found in their studies that different
cultures professed radically different values, thus suggesting that there was no
justification for our traditional belief that our values were the only ones which
sane men could adopt.

The most sustained treatment of relativism in ethics was by Edward Westermarck, whose studies show a blend of anthropological, sociological and philosophical interests. In the *Origin and Development of Moral Ideas* (1906) and
Ethical Relativity (1932) he shows the great diversity among the moral judgments of different societies and individuals. Some of these differences in moral
standards may be accounted for by differences in environment, in religion, and
in beliefs, but many of them represented what he considered to be unresolvable
moral differences. In providing examples of the latter type of moral differences,
he referred to the various concepts held by different societies and by individuals as to how widely within or beyond the group the principles of morality
apply, and what should be done when one's interests clash with those of others.
These differences in moral judgment led Westermarck to conclude that ethics
is based on emotional reactions in which there is a basic impulse to repay the
good or evil that has been done to oneself. Westermarck held an individualistic
theory of ethics to the extent that he maintained that what one calls good is
that which arouses in him the emotion of approval, while that is considered
bad which arouses the emotion of disapproval. He did point out, however, that

---

[1] Walter Lippman, *A Preface to Morals* (New York: Macmillan, 1929), *passim*.

Source: Luther J. Binkley, *Conflict of Ideals* (New York, 1969), pp. 2–11. Copyright © 1969
by Litton Educational Publishing, Inc. Reprinted by permission of D. Van Nostrand Company.

no one can develop arbitrarily his own emotions of approval or disapproval. They are really conditioned to a great extent by the moral emotions held in the particular age and locality in which the person is living. Thus, moral standards were found to vary from age to age as well as from culture to culture.[2] Because Westermarck supported his conclusions with a wealth of historical data, his theory of moral relativism seemed to many minds convincing.

In addition to the monumental study of morals in various societies by Westermarck, several other scholars tended to support his findings. Emile Durkheim, who was primarily interested in sociology, in studying primitive societies suggested that the facts of human behavior were more important than ethical theories. One had first to understand how men did in fact act, before one could say anything meaningful about how they ought to act. Herein, he asserted, was one of the great mistakes made by most philosophers. They had pronounced their ideal ethical codes with little reference to the actual nature of man and his behavior. Durkheim stressed more than Westermarck did the role of society in forming one's moral standards. The feelings of approval or disapproval which characterize good and bad conduct, he suggested, are determined by the opinions of society as a unit rather than by the individuals of the society. For Durkheim the supreme authority concerning moral values is the particular society in which one happens to live. The peculiar urgency which attaches to moral commands is due to the fact that they originate in the society and not simply in individuals. But these commands are relativistic, on the basis of this kind of analysis, for they have no validity beyond the particular societies in which they appear.[3]

William Graham Sumner, the first significant American sociologist, also contributed to the belief that moral values are relative in maintaining that moral judgments were accurately described as non-rational manifestations of social forces. Moral values, according to him, are part of the folkways of a given society. Folkways are the customary ways by which man seeks to satisfy his basic needs. When folkways have a certain coerciveness about them, and when the implication is drawn that obeying them is good for the society which developed them, then they have become *mores*. That which we call good is, according to this view, only that to which we refer when we are expressing in forceful language the prevailing customs of our present society. But he also found that these customs varied from society to society, and that they tended to change within any given society from time to time. Philosophy and ethics then become nothing more than attempts to give some rational order to the prevailing folkways, and the reason for each age having its own distinctive philosophy is simply that each age attempts anew to rationalize its favorite customs, folkways and mores. No man can lift himself outside of the mores of his group, and Sumner insisted that the religious prophet or the social reformer was no exception to this rule. For Sumner morals are simply social customs

---

[2] Edward Westermarck, *Ethical Relativity* (Paterson, N.J.: Littlefield, Adams & Co., 1960), *passim*.

[3] Emile Durkheim, *The Elementary Forms of the Religious Life,* trans. by Joseph Ward Swain (New York: Collier Books, 1961), *passim*.

which are more rigidly fixed and enforced than are such customs as styles in dress.[4]

Karl Mannheim has gone even further and has maintained that modes of thought are always conditioned by their social origins. All our ways of thinking are ideologies, according to Mannheim, even though we usually reserve the word to refer disparagingly to views with which we are in disagreement. As he puts it, the ethical system of any country at any time is simply an ideological expression by the prevailing group in power regarding the conduct it values as socially useful. All moral values and norms are then relative; an absolute standard is unobtainable. In fact, Mannheim maintained that even the very concepts of good and of right are purely ideological. It is true that he admitted that for a particular culture one ideology may be practicably more useful than another, but he found no way to stand apart from all ideologies so as to find a universal value.[5]

We might cite many more writers who have contributed to the prevailing relativistic climate in this century, but we have probably already made clear the converging lines of evidence from the social sciences which seem to suggest that "all values are relative."[6] We take for granted today that there are different patterns of culture; not all societies have adopted the same basic values as traditional Western civilization. What remains to be done, however, is to point out that there are conflicting judgments as to what relativism in morals implies.

One popular interpretation of the belief that all values are relative holds then that all values become equally arbitrary and irrational. According to this view, there is no rational justification for any act that an individual does; to save a human life is as irrational as to commit murder. One author has summarized this position as follows:

> It all depends on where you are,
> It all depends on when you are,
> It all depends on what you feel,
> It all depends on how you feel.
> It all depends on how you're raised,
> It all depends on what is praised,
> What's right today is wrong tomorrow,
> Joy in France, in England sorrow.
> It all depends on point of view,
> Australia or Timbuctoo,
> In Rome do as the Romans do.
> If tastes just happen to agree,
> Then you have morality.

[4] William Graham Sumner, *Folkways: A Study of the Sociological Importance of Usages, Manners, Customs, Mores, and Morals* (New York: The New American Library of World Literature, Inc., 1960).

[5] Karl Mannheim, *Ideology and Utopia: An Introduction to the Sociology of Knowledge,* trans. by Louis Wirth and Edward Shils (New York: A Harvest Book, Harcourt, Brace & World, Inc., 1936).

[6] Among works which have appeared recently, the reader might be interested in referring to Ruth Benedict, *Patterns of Culture* (Boston: Houghton Mifflin Co., 1934), and the numerous anthropological writings of Margaret Mead.

> But where they are conflicting trends,
> It all depends, it all depends. . . .[7]

Sometimes, this interpretation of relativism is used to justify one's own conduct, even if it harms other people. If all values are relative, and I "get my kicks" in a different way than you, then it is claimed that you have no right to object to my behavior. Thus, "All values are relative" is often used as an emotive justification of any conduct whatsoever. As the hero of John Barth's novel *The Floating Opera* puts it: "The reasons for which people assign value to things are always ultimately (though not necessarily immediately) arbitrary, irrational."[8]

The logical conclusion of this kind of an interpretation of relativism is found in the contemporary Theatre of the Absurd. The plays of Samuel Beckett, Eugène Ionesco, and Jean Genet reflect the breakdown of the belief in rationality and in the traditional Hebraic-Christian values which marked the recent past. The drama of the absurd not only deals with the futility and uselessness of the ordinary activities of men, but also with the emptiness in men's hearts resulting from the loss of the traditional values of Western civilization. In Beckett's *Waiting for Godot* the main characters, Estragon and Vladimir, carry on meaningless conversations in order to pass the time. Day after day they wait for Godot, who never arrives, and yet they continue to wait, despite the absurdity of their behavior. One day is like any other day, and there is no sense of purpose or meaning to their lives. They discuss separating from each other, hanging themselves, moving to some other spot, but reject all these possibilities. To do anything at all is absurd, and so they might just as well continue in their senseless and eternal waiting. Their constant chatter and antics seem to have only one justification:

VLADIMIR: That passed the time.
ESTRAGON: It would have passed in any case.
VLADIMIR: Yes, but not so rapidly.
        Pause.
ESTRAGON: What do we do now?
VLADIMIR: I don't know.
ESTRAGON: Let's go.
VLADIMIR: We can't.
ESTRAGON: Why not?
VLADIMIR: We're waiting for Godot.
ESTRAGON: (*despairingly*) Ah![9]

Another aspect often present in the drama of the absurd stresses the overwhelming horror individuals face in having to cope with a vast world in the

---

[7] Quoted in Abraham Edel, *Ethical Judgment: The Use of Science in Ethics* (New York: The Free Press, A Division of The Macmillan Co., 1955), p. 16. Edel himself does not subscribe to this kind of an interpretation of ethical relativity; in fact his book is an excellent attempt to find a common human basis for morality.

[8] John Barth, *The Floating Opera* (New York: An Avon Library Book, 1956), p. 216.

[9] Samuel Beckett, *Waiting for Godot: A Tragicomedy in Two Acts* (New York: Grove Press, Inc., 1954), pp. 31–32.

face of the impossibility of really having authentic communication with anyone else. In Ionesco's *The Chairs* an old married couple in their nineties await the arrival of a distinguished crowd of people who have been invited to hear the message which the old man will deliver at the end of his life. But since the old man is no orator, he has hired a professional orator to deliver his message. The guests arrive but are never seen or heard; instead the two old people fill the stage with chairs to seat them and carry on endless polite conversation with the empty chairs. The absurdity of attempting to communicate one's wisdom with other human beings is nicely satirized by the spectacle of the empty chairs on the stage. But the ending of the play portrays an even greater absurdity. The old man, convinced that the orator will deliver his message, jumps into the sea, followed by his wife. The professional orator faces the crowd of empty chairs, and prepares to speak. However, he is deaf and dumb and hence makes only an inarticulate gurgling noise. He then attempts to write something on a blackboard, but this is nothing more than a jumble of meaningless letters. Obviously, both in form and content, this play shows the ultimate meaninglessness and absurdity of man's existence.[10]

Jean Genet's plays attack the traditional values of Western civilization head on. All of us are protrayed as actors playing roles, and each role is shown to be empty, absurd, and meaningless. In *The Balcony* the scene is set in a fetishistic house of ill-repute, where people go in order to enact the roles which they really would prefer to play in the society in which they live. Despite a violent revolution being waged outside in the "real world" the clients, including the chief of police, continue to come to this establishment where they can act out whatever roles they desire. Ironically, the leader of the revolutionary band comes to the brothel to enact the role of chief of police. The mirrors in the house reflect the false images which men assume in their roles of fantasy, but Genet suggests that these images are not any more unreal than the roles most men actually perform in the outside world. Irma, proprietress of the house of illusions, makes this point in her speech to the audience at the end of the play: "You must now go home, where everything—you can be quite sure—will be even falser than here."[11]

The connection between the absurd and man's loss of belief in the traditional values of the past was clearly expressed by Albert Camus in *The Myth of Sisyphus*:

A world that can be explained even with bad reasons is a familiar world. But, on the other hand, in a universe suddenly divested of illusions and lights, man feels an alien, a stranger. His exile is without remedy since he is deprived of the memory of a lost home or the hope of a promised land. This divorce between man and his life, the actor and his setting, is properly the feeling of absurdity.[12]

[10] Eugène Ionesco, *Four Plays: The Bald Soprano, The Lesson, Jack or the Submission, The Chairs, trans.* by Donald M. Allen (New York: Grove Press, Inc., 1958).

[11] Jean Genet, *The Balcony,* trans. by Bernard Frechtman (New York: Grove Press, Inc., 1958), p. 115.

[12] Albert Camus, *The Myth of Sisyphus and Other Essays,* trans. by Justin O'Brien (New York: Vintage Books, Inc., Random House, 1959), p. 5.

The theatre of the absurd is an attempt to portray the nature of human life when one comes to accept the belief that there are no values which are better than any others, that all life is therefore senseless and meaningless. It is an attempt to force man to confront his life with full awareness of the reality of arbitrary and irrational choices. If one is outraged and shocked by the themes and devices of the theatre of the absurd, one should recall that these dramatists believe that only by a new kind of play can we be awakened from our present conformism and moral insensibility. As Ionesco put it: "To tear ourselves away from the everyday, from habit, from mental laziness which hides from us the strangeness of reality, we must receive something like a real bludgeon blow."[13] The theatre of the absurd has sought to accomplish this mission; to reveal to the audience the absurdity of all value commitments if one believes that all values are equally irrational and arbitrary.

There is, however, a more justifiable interpretation of relativism than the one which we have discussed. This view maintains that moral judgments are relative to something or to some persons; they are not merely irrational and arbitrary whims. This kind of interpretation does not deny the findings of the social scientists for it recognizes that moral standards have in fact varied from culture to culture, from era to era, and even among the individuals in a particular society. In our own society, for example, it is clear that not all people hold the same moral judgments concerning euthanasia or birth control. But to maintain that moral evaluations are relative to our time in history and to the culture of which we are a part is not, according to this interpretation, to disparage morals but rather to help us to formulate more coherent and consistent basic principles for acting in our modern world. Just as science is relative to the age in which it is formulated, so quite naturally are our moral standards and judgments. Everyone knows that the physical sciences have changed radically in their basic principles since the time of their founding several centuries ago, and many scientists expect that similar changes are quite likely to occur in the future. What is not so often recognized is that no one argues that since science has changed so radically in several hundred years, any one is justified in holding arbitrary and irrational beliefs about scientific issues since all such beliefs are relative to the time in which they are formulated. Our understanding of human behavior and of the nature of man has also changed radically in the past several centuries, but this is no reason to maintain that therefore all values are equally absurd, arbitrary and irrational.

It is important that we do not mislead the reader to believe that this second interpretation of the significance of relativism rests on the assumption that moral values are exactly like scientific theories. Far from it, for while this kind of interpretation of relativism does call attention to the fact that scientific theories change and are in that sense relative to the age in which they are proclaimed, it also recognizes that there are crucial differences between believing in a scientific theory and committing oneself to a value judgment. The crucial tests for subscribing to a scientific theory depend upon the ability to explain

<hr>

[13] Eugène Ionesco, "Discovering the Theatre," in *Theatre in the Twentieth Century*, ed. by Robert W. Corrigan (New York: Grove Press, Inc., 1965), p. 86.

observable events in terms of the theory, and to permit predictions of how similar events will occur in the future. A scientific theory concerning human behavior would attempt to explain man's actions in terms of a general theory, and then the theory would be accepted or rejected according to its success in predicting future behavior. We have no over-arching general scientific theory of human behavior as yet, although many social scientists claim that we know enough about man for some general explanations and predictions to be made. B. F. Skinner, the Harvard psychologist, has made some extremely penetrating generalizations about human behavior as a result of his experimentation with positive reinforcement as a factor in human conditioning.[14] But while this may tell us how man in fact behaves, and what techniques we can use to condition him to behave in other ways, this scientific study does not tell us how man *ought* to behave. Whenever we ask such questions as "What ought I to do?" we have gone beyond the facts and scientific theories and are asking for a value judgment.

To clarify the distinction we are drawing between facts and values let us consider an example from our own day. The mass media, such as television, have profited from the social scientists' study of human behavior. It is not by accident that television commercials seek to associate their products with the things which most men enjoy or desire. If we can be made to associate a particular brand of cigarettes with the virility of the cowboys of the old West, then we may be conditioned into not only smoking but also into purchasing that particular brand. Even more effective, however, will be to have the cowboy offer one of his cigarettes to a beautiful woman. The appeal will then be made to both the desire of males to be virile, strong he-men, and to the females to be feminine and beautiful. Advertising tries to find out what most people like, and then it seeks for ways by means of which it can associate the products of its clients with these human desires. The degree of success of these conditioning procedures can be determined by any one of you. Do you buy any cola beverage, any brand of aspirin? Or do you ask for a particular brand? If you ask for a particular brand, did you ever try to find out why? Does that brand of cola really taste better? Is that particular brand of aspirin any better than any other brand? Or have you been conditioned by the mass media to associate cola and aspirin with particular brands?

The reader will probably grant that the mass media do indeed condition us to behave in certain ways, but he might ask "Is it right for them to do so?" In the light of the evidence which suggests that there is a connection between the smoking of cigarettes and cancer, should not cigarette manufacturers discontinue their advertising campaigns? Is it right for them to continue to associate cigarette smoking with relaxation and pleasure, with really being a mature man? When questions such as these are raised we have entered the area of value judgments. Notice, however, that not every one would say that cigarette manufacturers should discontinue their advertising. An appeal could well be made for the right of the individual to make his own choice as to whether or

[14] B. F. Skinner, *Science and Human Behavior* (New York: The Free Press, A Division of Macmillan Publishing Co., 1965), *passim*.

not he wished to smoke. One might even argue that the states need the tax dollars which they get from the sale of cigarettes, or that the stockholders in the cigarette companies have a right to expect these companies to do everything they can to show a profit. Indeed, would not preventing cigarette companies from engaging in advertising campaigns be a violation of their rights in a free enterprise economy? This issue raises some very basic questions about values. Are economic values to be considered as more important than those of the health of the general populace? Is pleasure of the moment to be valued higher than a long life? Does a state have the right to prohibit its citizens from obtaining pleasure in the ways they choose, if some of their chosen behavior may be injurious to their health or welfare? Who is ultimately to make these decisions? The individual himself? The state, acting for the individual through the representatives he has elected to Congress?

It is possible to reply that a rational man who understands the techniques employed in advertising can resist the pressures brought to bear upon him to use certain products. Furthermore, there are many conflicting voices raised, and we have the opportunity to choose from among them the ones which we believe to be correct. And, of course, each one of us likes to think of himself as one of those rational individuals who makes his own decisions. Suppose, however, that we had been reared in a society like that described by Skinner in *Walden Two*. Frazier, the head of Walden Two, uses his knowledge of human conditioning to train all the inhabitants of this utopian community to cooperate with each other. Competition is unheard of. All the frustrations and conflicts which we experience in our present world are eliminated. The conditioning process has been so thorough that none of the inhabitants raise any questions about the goals of this "ideal" community. Frazier invites some scholars from the outside world to his Walden Two so that they can observe how well he has succeeded. In a discussion with the philosopher in the group of visitors, Frazier proclaims:

> "This *is* the Good Life. We know it. It's a fact, not a theory. It has an experimental justification, not a rational one. As for your conflict of principles, that's an experimental question, too. We don't puzzle our little minds over the outcome of Love versus Duty. We simply arrange a world in which serious conflicts occur as seldom as possible or, with a little luck, not at all."[15]

But the philosopher's main reservation about Walden Two was not grasped by Frazier. Clearly it was a fact that he had conditioned the people in this community to respond in far more cooperative and peaceful ways than they do in our contemporary world. The philosopher, however, asked in effect, "Is this really the Good Life? Ought man to be conditioned into behaving docilely? Is the absence of all competition and conflict a good thing? How would it ever be possible for a genius or an exceptionally creative man to develop in Walden Two? Is not a genius, who rejects the values of his day, of more worth than thousands of conforming robot-like men? Why should Frazier determine the values to which the entire community would be conditioned to conform? What right did any man have to so completely determine the lives of others?" These

[15] B. F. Skinner, *Walden Two* (New York: Macmillan, 1962), p. 161.

were questions concerning values, not concerning facts and scientific theories.

The reader should now understand that to make a value judgment is to express a preference; it is to make an estimation of worth. We all make value judgments every day of our lives. In such a simple act as choosing to spend ten dollars to see a play, rather than to buy a book, one is expressing the belief that at that particular time seeing that particular play will be more worthwhile than buying that particular book. Furthermore, in such an act, we also can see what this second kind of interpretation of relativism maintains. One is not maintaining that it is always better to see a play than to buy a book; to do so would be to subscribe to an absolute value judgment. Rather, one's judgment is based upon the comparison of a particular play with a particular book at a particular time. If one had not recently bought a great many books, one might have chosen to buy a particular novel instead of going to the play. If one has been reading a great deal lately, and desires some form of relaxing entertainment, he might very well choose to see a particular musical comedy. Clearly, one would not maintain that everyone ought to make exactly the same choice as he made, but notice also that one's decision is not completely arbitrary, for reasons can be given for making the value judgment.

Our concern here, however, will be with more basic and general value commitments, rather than with particular decisions. What do I most want out of Life? Is my personal integrity of greater value to me than success? Should I always be oriented so as to seek my own welfare, even if it is at the expense of others? Should my values not happen to agree with those generally held by my society, ought I to follow my own convictions anyway? These and many other questions like them raise general questions concerning one's basic values in terms of which many of one's everyday choices are made. This second interpretation of relativism, which we have been considering, reminds us that even these more basic commitments are related to specific persons who are living in a particular period of history. We must, therefore, not become the slaves of the principles of the past, but rather seek honestly for the most rationally defensible values which will assist in making our world a more humane one in which to live. Moral values then are not arbitrary; they are relative to man.

Relativism in moral theory need not, therefore, lead one into despair and absurdity; rather it may be seen as a liberating force requiring that each man make a serious effort to choose those values which he finds to be most meaningful for himself and society. John Barth has the hero of *The Floating Opera* reject the view he held earlier concerning the absurdity of values. After many years of thought and life he realizes:

> If there are no absolutes, then a value is no less authentic, no less genuine, no less compelling, no less "real," for its being relative! It is one thing to say "Values are *only* relative"; quite another, and more thrilling, to remove the pejorative adverb and assert "There *are* relative values!" These, at least, we have, and if they are all we have, then *in no way whatsoever* are they inferior.[16]

We shall examine in later chapters the positions adopted concerning moral relativism by the proponents of different value orientations for our century.

---

[16] Barth, *The Floating Opera*, p. 271.

We shall find that some of these writers, such as Marx, Nietzsche and Freud, fully accept moral relativism as an inevitable fact in the modern world; while others, such as Kierkegaard and Fromm, attempt to defend a commitment to absolute or objective values. That we live in an age of pluralism will become quite apparent when we examine the views of contemporary theologians, some of whom frankly call for a new morality based on relativism. But we must not get ahead of our story. In addition to our century being called an age of relativism, we are often told that it is an age dominated by pragmatism. Let us see what this suggests about our contemporary moral climate.

The Relativity of Ethics

EDWARD A. WESTERMARCK

Edward A. Westermarck (1862–1939), the Danish author of *The Origin and Development of Moral Ideas* (1924–1926), was a leading ethical relativist.

The main object of this book [from which this essay is taken] will perhaps be best explained by a few words concerning its origin.

Its author was once discussing with some friends the point how far a bad man ought to be treated with kindness. The opinions were divided, and, in spite of much deliberation, unanimity could not be attained. It seemed strange that the disagreement should be so radical, and the question arose, Whence this diversity of opinion? Is it due to defective knowledge, or has it a merely sentimental origin? And the problem gradually expanded. Why do the moral ideas in general differ so greatly? And, on the other hand, why is there in many cases such a wide agreement? Nay, why are there any moral ideas at all?

Since then many years have passed, spent by the author in trying to find an answer to these questions. The present work is the result of his researches and thoughts.

The first part of it will comprise a study of the moral concepts: right, wrong, duty, justice, virtue, merit, &c. Such a study will be found to require an examination into the moral emotions, their nature and origin, as also into the relations between these emotions and the various moral concepts. There will then be a discussion of the phenomena to which such concepts are applied—the subjects of moral judgments. The general character of these phenomena will be scrutinised, and an answer sought to the question why facts of a certain type are matters of moral concern, while other facts are not. Finally, the most important of these phenomena will be classified, and the moral ideas relating to each class will be stated, and, so far as possible, explained.

An investigation of this kind cannot be confined to feelings and ideas prevalent in any particular society or at any particular stage of civilisation. Its

Source: Edward A. Westermarck, *The Origin and Development of Moral Ideas* (1924–1926), Intro. and Chap. 1. Reprinted by permission of the estate of Edward A. Westermarck.

subject-matter is the moral consciousness of mankind at large. It consequently involves the survey of an unusually rich and varied field of research—psychological, ethnographical, historical, juridical, theological. In the present state of our knowledge, when monographs on most of the subjects involved are wanting, I presume that such an undertaking is, strictly speaking, too big for any man; at any rate it is so for the writer of this book. Nothing like completeness can be aimed at. Hypotheses of varying degrees of probability must only too often be resorted to. Even the certainty of the statements on which conclusions are based is not always beyond a doubt. But though fully conscious of the many defects of his attempt, the author nevertheless ventures to think himself justified in placing it before the public. It seems to him that one of the most important objects of human speculation cannot be left in its present state of obscurity; that at least a glimpse of light must be thrown upon it by researches which have extended over some fifteen years; and that the main principles underlying the various customs of mankind may be arrived at even without subjecting these customs to such a full and minute treatment as would be required of an anthropological monograph.

Possibly this essay, in spite of its theoretical character, may even be of some practical use. Though rooted in the emotional side of our nature, our moral opinions are in a large measure amenable to reason. Now in every society the traditional notions as to what is good or bad, obligatory or indifferent, are commonly accepted by the majority of people without further reflection. By tracing them to their source it will be found that not a few of these notions have their origin in sentimental likings and antipathies, to which a scrutinising and enlightened judge can attach little importance; whilst, on the other hand, he must account blameable many an act and omission which public opinion, out of thoughtlessness, treats with indifference. It will, moreover, appear that a moral estimate often survives the cause from which it sprang. And no unprejudiced person can help changing his views if he be persuaded that they have no foundation in existing facts.

The Emotional Origin of Moral Judgments

That the moral concepts are ultimately based on emotions either of indignation or approval, is a fact which a certain school of thinkers have in vain attempted to deny. The terms which embody these concepts must originally have been used—indeed they still constantly are so used—as direct expressions of such emotions with reference to the phenomena which evoked them. Men pronounced certain acts to be good or bad on account of the emotions those acts aroused in their minds, just as they called sunshine warm and ice cold on account of certain sensations which they experienced, and as they named a thing pleasant or painful because they felt pleasure or pain. But to attribute a quality to a thing is never the same as merely to state the existence of a particular sensation or feeling in the mind which perceives it. Such an attribution must mean that the thing, under certain circumstances, makes a certain impression on the mind. By calling an object warm or pleasant, a person asserts that it is apt to produce in him a sensation of heat or a feeling of pleasure.

Similarly, to name an act good or bad, ultimately implies that it is apt to give rise to an emotion of approval or disapproval in him who pronounces the judgment. Whilst not affirming the actual existence of any specific emotion in the mind of the person judging or of anybody else, the predicate of a moral judgment attributes to the subject a tendency to arouse an emotion. The moral concepts, then, are essentially generalisations of tendencies in certain phenomena to call forth moral emotions.

However, as is frequently the case with general terms, these concepts are mentioned without any distinct idea of their contents. The relation in which many of them stand to the moral emotions is complicated; the use of them is often vague; and ethical theorisers, instead of subjecting them to a careful analysis, have done their best to increase the confusion by adapting the meaning of the terms to fit their theories. Very commonly, in the definition of the goodness or badness of acts, reference is made, not to their tendencies to evoke emotions of approval or indignation, but to the causes of these tendencies, that is, to those qualities in the acts which call forth moral emotions. Thus, because good acts generally produce pleasure and bad acts pain, goodness and badness have been identified with the tendencies of acts to produce pleasure or pain. The following statement of Sir James Stephen is a clearly expressed instance of this confusion, so common among utilitarians: "Speaking generally, the acts which are called right do promote or are supposed to promote general happiness, and the acts which are called wrong do diminish or are supposed to diminish it. I say, therefore, that this is what the words 'right' and 'wrong' mean, just as the words 'up' and 'down' mean that which points from or towards the earth's centre of gravity, though they are used by millions who have not the least notion of the fact that such is their meaning, and though they were used for centuries and millenniums before any one was or even could be aware of it."[1] So, too, Bentham maintained that words like "ought," "right," and "wrong" have no meaning unless interpreted in accordance with the principle of utility;[2] and James Mill was of the opinion that "the very morality" of the act lies, not in the sentiments raised in the breast of him who perceives or contemplates it, but in "the consequences of the act, good or evil, and their being within the intention of the agent."[3] He adds that a rational assertor of the principle of utility approves of an action "because it is good," and calls it good "because it conduces to happiness."[4] This, however, is to invert the sequence of the facts, since, properly speaking, an act is called good because it is approved of, and is approved of by an utilitarian in so far as it conduces to happiness.

Such confusion of terms cannot affect the real meaning of the moral concepts. It is true that he who holds that "actions are right in proportion as they tend to promote happiness, wrong as they tend to produce the reverse of happiness,"[5] may, by a merely intellectual process, pass judgment on the moral character of

---

[1] Stephen, *Liberty, Equality, Fraternity,* p. 338.
[2] Bentham, *Principles of Morals and Legislation,* p. 4.
[3] James Mill, *Fragment on Mackintosh,* pp. 5, 376.
[4] Ibid., p. 368.
[5] Stuart Mill, *Utilitarianism,* p. 9 sq.

particular acts; but, if he is an utilitarian from conviction, his first principle, at least, has an emotional origin. The case is similar with many of the moral judgments ordinarily passed by men. They are applications of some accepted general rule: conformity or non-conformity to the rule decides the rightness or wrongness of the act judged. But whether the rule be the result of a person's independent deductions, or be based upon authority, human or divine, the fact that his moral consciousness recognises it as valid implies that it has an emotional sanction in his own mind.

Whilst the import of the predicate of a moral judgment may thus in every case be traced back to an emotion in him who pronounces the judgment, it is generally assumed to possess the character of universality or "objectivity" as well. The statement that an act is good or bad does not merely refer to an individual emotion; as will be shown subsequently, it always has reference to an emotion of a more public character. Very often it even implies some vague assumption that the act must be recognised as good or bad by everybody who possesses a sufficient knowledge of the case and of all attendant circumstances, and who has a "sufficiently developed" moral consciousness. We are not willing to admit that our moral convictions are a mere matter of taste, and we are inclined to regard convictions differing from our own as errors. This characteristic of our moral judgments has been adduced as an argument against the emotionalist theory of moral origins, and has led to the belief that the moral concepts represent qualities which are discerned by reason.

Cudworth, Clarke, Price, and Reid are names which recall to our mind a theory according to which the morality of actions is perceived by the intellect, just as are number, diversity, causation, proportion. "Morality is eternal and immutable," says Richard Price. "Right and wrong, it appears, denote what actions are. Now whatever any thing is, that it is, not by will, or decree, or power, but by nature and necessity. Whatever a triangle or circle is, that it is unchangeably and eternally. . . . The same is to be said of right and wrong, of moral good and evil, as far as they express real characters of actions. They must immutably and necessarily belong to those actions of which they are truly affirmed."[6] And as having a real existence outside the mind, they can only be discerned by the understanding. It is true that this discernment is accompanied with an emotion: "Some impressions of pleasure or pain, satisfaction or disgust, generally attend our perceptions of virtue and vice. But these are merely their effects and concomitants, and not the perceptions themselves, which ought no more to be confounded with them, than a particular truth (like that for which Pythagoras offered a hecatomb) ought to be confounded with the pleasure that may attend the discovery of it."[7]

According to another doctrine, the moral predicates, though not regarded as expressions of "theoretical" truth, nevertheless derive all their import from reason—from "practical" or "moral" reason, as it is variously called. Thus Professor Sidgwick holds that the fundamental notions represented by the word "ought" or "right," which moral judgments contain expressly or by implication,

[6] Price, *Review of the Principal Questions in Morals,* pp. 63, 74 sq.
[7] Ibid., p. 63.

are essentially different from all notions representing facts of physical or psychical experience, and he refers such judgments to the "reason," understood as a faculty of cognition. By this he implies "that what ought to be is a possible object of knowledge, *i.e.,* that what I judge ought to be, must, unless I am in error, be similarly judged by all rational beings who judge truly of the matter." The moral judgments contain moral *truths,* and "cannot legitimately be interpreted as judgments respecting the present or future existence of human feelings or any facts of the sensible world."[8]

Yet our tendency to objectivise the moral judgments is not sufficient ground for referring them to the province of reason. If, in this respect, there is a difference between these judgments and others that are rooted in the subjective sphere of experience, it is, largely, a difference in degree rather than in kind. The aesthetic judgments, which indisputably have an emotional origin, also lay claim to a certain amount of "objectivity." By saying of a piece of music that it is beautiful, we do not merely mean that it gives ourselves aesthetic enjoyment, but we make a latent assumption that it must have a similar effect upon everybody who is sufficiently musical to appreciate it. This objectivity ascribed to judgments which have a merely subjective origin springs in the first place from the similarity of the mental constitution of men, and, generally speaking, the tendency to regard them as objective is greater in proportion as the impressions vary less in each particular case. If "there is no disputing of tastes," that is because taste is so extremely variable; and yet even in this instance we recognise a certain "objective" standard by speaking of a "bad" and a "good" taste. On the other hand, if the appearance of objectivity in the moral judgments is so illusive as to make it seem necessary to refer them to reason, that is partly on account of the comparatively uniform nature of the moral consciousness.

Society is the school in which men learn to distinguish between right and wrong. The headmaster is Custom, and the lessons are the same for all. The first moral judgments were pronounced by public opinion; public indignation and public approval are the prototypes of the moral emotions. As regards questions of morality, there was, in early society, practically no difference of opinion; hence a character of universality, or objectivity, was from the very beginning attached to all moral judgments. And when, with advancing civilisation, this unanimity was to some extent disturbed by individuals venturing to dissent from the opinions of the majority, the disagreement was largely due to facts which in no way affected the moral principle, but had reference only to its application.

Most people follow a very simple method in judging of an act. Particular modes of conduct have their traditional labels, many of which are learnt with language itself; and the moral judgment commonly consists simply in labelling the act according to certain obvious characteristics which it presents in common with others belonging to the same group. But a conscientious and intelligent judge proceeds in a different manner. He carefully examines all the details connected with the act, the external and internal conditions under which it was performed, its consequences, its motive; and, since the moral estimate in a

---

[8] Sidgwick, *Methods of Ethics,* pp. 25, 33 sq.

large measure depends upon the regard paid to these circumstances, his judgment may differ greatly from that of the man in the street, even though the moral standard which they apply be exactly the same. But to acquire a full insight into all the details which are apt to influence the moral value of an act is in many cases anything but easy, and this naturally increases the disagreement. There is thus in every advanced society a diversity of opinion regarding the moral value of certain modes of conduct which results from circumstances of a purely intellectual character—from the knowledge of ignorance of positive facts—and involves no discord in principle.

Now it has been assumed by the advocates of various ethical theories that all the differences of moral ideas originate in this way, and that there is some ultimate standard which must be recognised as authoritative by everybody who understands it rightly. According to Bentham, the rectitude of utilitarianism has been contested only by those who have not known their own meaning: "When a man attempts to combat the principle of utility . . . his arguments, if they prove anything, prove not that the principle is wrong, but that, according to the applications he supposes to be made of it, it is misapplied."[9] Mr. Spencer, to whom good conduct is that "which conduces to life in each and all," believes that he has the support of "the true moral consciousness," or "moral consciousness proper," which, whether in harmony or in conflict with the "pro-ethical" sentiment, is vaguely or distinctly recognised as the rightful ruler.[10] Samuel Clarke, the intuitionist, again, is of the opinion that if a man endowed with reason denies the eternal and necessary moral differences of things, it is the very same "as if a man that has the use of his sight, should at the same time that he beholds the sun, deny that there is any such thing as light in the world; or as if a man that understands Geometry or Arithmetic should deny the most obvious and known proportions of lines or numbers."[11] In short, all disagreement as to questions of morals is attributed to ignorance or misunderstanding.

The influence of intellectual considerations upon moral judgments is certainly immense. We shall find that the evolution of the moral consciousness to a large extent consists in its development from the unreflecting to the reflecting, from the unenlightened to the enlightened. All higher emotions are determined by cognitions; they arise from "the presentation of determinate objective conditions;"[12] and moral enlightenment implies a true and comprehensive presentation of those objective conditions by which the moral emotions, according to their very nature, are determined. Morality may thus in a much higher degree than, for instance, beauty be a subject of instruction and of profitable discussion, in which persuasion is carried by the representation of existing data. But although in this way many differences may be accorded, there are points in which unanimity cannot be reached even by the most accurate presentation of facts or the subtlest process of reasoning.

Whilst certain phenomena will almost of necessity arouse similar moral

---

[9] Bentham, *Principles of Morals and Legislation*, p. 4 sq.

[10] Spencer, *Principles of Ethics*, i. 45, 337 sq.

[11] Clarke, *Discourse concerning the Unchangeable Obligations of Natural Religion*, p. 179.

[12] Marshall, *Pain, Pleasure, and Aesthetics*, p. 83.

emotions in every mind which perceives them clearly, there are others with which the case is different. The emotional constitution of man does not present the same uniformity as the human intellect. Certain cognitions inspire fear in nearly every breast; but there are brave men and cowards in the world, independently of the accuracy with which they realise impending danger. Some cases of suffering can hardly fail to awaken compassion in the most pitiless heart; but the sympathetic dispositions of men vary greatly, both in regard to the beings with whose sufferings they are ready to sympathise, and with reference to the intensity of the emotion. The same holds good for the moral emotions. The existing diversity of opinion as to the rights of different classes of men, and of the lower animals, which springs from emotional differences, may no doubt be modified by a clearer insight into certain facts, but no perfect agreement can be expected as long as the conditions under which the emotional dispositions are formed remain unchanged. Whilst an enlightened mind *must* recognize the complete or relative irresponsibility of an animal, a child, or a madman, and *must* be influenced in its moral judgment by the motives of an act—no intellectual enlightenment, no scrutiny of facts, can decide how far the interests of the lower animals should be regarded when conflicting with those of men, or how far a person is bound, or allowed, to promote the welfare of his nation, or his own welfare, at the cost of that of other nations or other individuals. Professor Sidgwick's well-known moral axiom, "I ought not to prefer my own lesser good to the greater good of another,"[13] would, if explained to a Fuegian or a Hottentot, be regarded by him, not as self-evident, but as simply absurd; nor can it claim general acceptance even among ourselves. Who is that "Another" to whose greater good I ought not to prefer my own lesser good? A fellow-countryman, a savage, a criminal, a bird, a fish—all without distinction? It will, perhaps, be argued that on this, and on all other points of morals, there would be general agreement, if only the moral consciousness of men were sufficiently developed.[14] But then, when speaking of a "sufficiently developed" moral consciousness (beyond insistence upon a full insight into governing facts of each case), we practically mean nothing else than agreement with our own moral convictions. The expression is faulty and deceptive, because, if intended to mean anything more, it presupposes an objectivity of the moral judgments which they do not possess, and at the same time seems to be proving what it presupposes. We may speak of an intellect as sufficiently developed to grasp a certain truth, because truth is objective; but it is not proved to be objective by the fact that it is recognised as true by a "sufficiently developed" intellect. The objectivity of truth lies in the recognition of facts as true by all who understand them *fully*, whilst the appeal to a *sufficient* knowledge assumes their objectivity. To the verdict of a perfect intellect, that is, an intellect which knows everything existing, all would submit; but we can form no idea of a moral consciousness which could lay claim to a similar authority. If the believers in an all-good God, who has revealed his will to mankind, maintain that they in

[13] Sidgwick, op. cit., p. 383.
[14] This, in fact, was the explanation given by Professor Sidgwick himself in a conversation which I had with him regarding his moral axioms.

this revelation possess a perfect moral standard, and that, consequently, what is in accordance with such a standard must be objectively right, it may be asked what they mean by an "all-good" God. And in their attempt to answer this question, they would inevitably have to assume the objectivity they wanted to prove.

The error we commit by attributing objectivity to moral estimates becomes particularly conspicuous when we consider that these estimates have not only a certain quality, but a certain quantity. There are different degrees of badness and goodness, a duty may be more or less stringent, a merit may be smaller or greater.[15] These quantitative differences are due to the emotional origin of all moral concepts. Emotions vary in intensity almost indefinitely, and the moral emotions form no exception to this rule. Indeed, it may be fairly doubted whether the same mode of conduct ever arouses exactly the same degree of indignation or approval in any two individuals. Many of these differences are of course too subtle to be manifested in the moral judgment; but very frequently the intensity of the emotion is indicated by special words, or by the way in which the judgment is pronounced. It should be noticed, however, that the quantity of the estimate expressed in a moral predicate is not identical with the intensity of the moral emotion which a certain mode of conduct arouses on a special occasion. We are liable to feel more indignant if an injury is committed before our eyes than if we read of it in a newspaper, and yet we admit that the degree of wrongness is in both cases the same. The quantity of moral estimates is determined by the intensity of the emotions which their objects tend to evoke under exactly similar external circumstances.

Besides the relative uniformity of moral opinions, there is another circumstance which tempts us to objectivise moral judgments, namely, the authority which, rightly or wrongly, is ascribed to moral rules. From our earliest childhood we are taught that certain acts *are* right and that others *are* wrong. Owing to their exceptional importance for human welfare, the facts of the moral consciousness are emphasised in a much higher degree than any other subjective facts. We are allowed to have our private opinions about the beauty of things, but we are not so readily allowed to have our private opinions about right and wrong. The moral rules which are prevalent in the society to which we belong are supported by appeals not only to human, but to divine, authority, and to call in question their validity is to rebel against religion as well as against public opinion. Thus the belief in a moral order of the world has taken hardly less firm hold of the human mind than the belief in a natural order of things. And the moral law has retained its authoritativeness even when the appeal to an external authority has been regarded as inadequate. It filled Kant with the same awe as the star-spangled firmament. According to Butler, conscience is "a faculty in kind and in nature supreme over all others, and which bears its own authority of being so."[16] Its supremacy is said to be

---

[15] It will be shown in a following chapter why there are no degrees of rightness. This concept implies accordance with the moral law. The adjective "right" means that duty is fulfilled.

[16] Butler, 'Sermon II.–Upon Human Nature,' in *Analogy of Religion, &c.* p. 403.

"felt and tacitly acknowledged by the worst no less than by the best of men."[17] Adam Smith calls the moral faculties the "viceregents of God within us," who "never fail to punish the violation of them by the torments of inward shame and self-condemnation; and, on the contrary, always reward obedience with tranquillity of mind, with contentment, and self-satisfaction."[18] Even Hutcheson, who raises the question why the moral sense should not vary in different men as the palate does, considers it "to be naturally destined to command all the other powers."[19]

Authority is an ambiguous word. It may indicate knowledge of truth, and it may indicate a rightful power to command obedience. The authoritativeness attributed to the moral law has often reference to both kinds of authority. The moral lawgiver lays down his rules in order that they should be obeyed, and they are authoritative in so far as they have to be obeyed. But he is also believed to know what is right and wrong, and his commands are regarded as expressions of moral truths. As we have seen, however, this latter kind of authority involves a false assumption as to the nature of the moral predicates, and it cannot be justly inferred from the power to command.

In spite of all this, however, the supreme authority assigned to the moral law is not altogether an illusion. It really exists in the minds of the best, and is nominally acknowledged by the many. By this I do not refer to the universal admission that the moral law, whether obeyed or not, ought under all circumstances to be obeyed; for this is the same as to say that what ought to be ought to be. But it is recognised, in theory at least, that morality, either alone or in connection with religion, possesses a higher value than anything else; that rightness and goodness are preferable to all other kinds of mental superiority, as well as of physical excellence. If this theory is not more commonly acted upon, that is due to its being, in most people, much less the outcome of their own feelings than of instruction from the outside. It is ultimately traceable to some great teacher whose own mind was ruled by the idea of moral perfection, and whose words became sacred on account of his supreme wisdom, like Confucius or Buddha,[20] or on religious grounds, like Jesus. The authority of the moral law is thus only an expression of a strongly developed, overruling moral consciousness. It can hardly, as Mr. Sidgwick maintains, be said to "depend upon" the conception of the objectivity of duty.[21] On the contrary, it must be regarded as a cause of this conception—not only, as has already been pointed out, where it is traceable to some external authority, but where it results from the strength of the individual's own moral emotions. As clearness and distinctness of the conception of an object easily produce the belief in its truth, so the intensity of a moral emotion makes him who feels it disposed to

[17] Dugald Stewart, *Philosophy of the Active and Moral Powers of Man,* i. 302.

[18] Adam Smith, *Theory of Moral Sentiments,* p. 235.

[19] Ziegler, *Social Ethics,* p. 103.

[20] Besides the ideal king, the personification of Power and Justice, another ideal has played an important part in the formation of early Buddhist ideas regarding their Master. . . . It was the ideal of a perfectly Wise Man, the personification of Wisdom, the Buddha." (Rhys Davids, *Hibbert Lectures on Some Points in the History of Buddhism,* p. 141.)

[21] Sidgwick, op. cit., p. 104.

objectivise the moral estimate to which it gives rise, in other words, to assign to it universal validity. The enthusiast is more likely than anybody else to regard his judgments as true, and so is the moral enthusiast with reference to his moral judgments. The intensity of his emotions makes him the victim of an illusion.

The presumed objectivity of moral judgments thus being a chimera, there can be no moral truth in the sense in which this term is generally understood. The ultimate reason for this is that the moral concepts are based upon emotions, and that the contents of an emotion fall entirely outside the category of truth. But it may be true or not that we have a certain emotion, it may be true or not that a given mode of conduct has a tendency to evoke in us moral indignation or moral approval. Hence a moral judgment is true or false according as its subject has or has not that tendency which the predicate attributes to it. If I say that it is wrong to resist evil, and yet resistance to evil has no tendency whatever to call forth in me an emotion of moral disapproval, then my judgment is false.

If there are no general moral truths, the object of scientific ethics cannot be to fix rules for human conduct, the aim of all science being the discovery of some truth. It has been said by Bentham and others that moral principles cannot be proved because they are first principles which are used to prove everything else.[22] But the real reason for their being inaccessible to demonstration is that, owing to their very nature, they can never be true. If the word "Ethics," then, is to be used as the name for a science, the object of that science can only be to study the moral consciousness as a fact.[23]

Ethical subjectivism is commonly held to be a dangerous doctrine, destructive to morality, opening the door to all sorts of libertinism. If that which appears to each man as right or good stands for that which is right or good; if he is allowed to make his own law, or to make no law at all; then, it is said, everybody has the natural right to follow his caprice and inclinations, and to hinder him from doing so is an infringement on his rights, a constraint with which no one is bound to comply provided that he has the power to evade it. This inference was long ago drawn from the teaching of the Sophists,[24] and it will no doubt be still repeated as an argument against any theorist who dares to assert that nothing can be said to be truly right or wrong.

To this argument may, first, be objected that a scientific theory is not invalidated by the mere fact that it is likely to cause mischief. The unfortunate circumstance that there do exist dangerous things in the world proves that something may be dangerous and yet true. Another question is whether any scientific truth really is mischievous on the whole, although it may cause much discomfort to certain people. I venture to believe that this, at any rate, is not the case with that form of ethical subjectivism which I am here advocating.

[22] Bentham, *Principles of Morals and Legislation*, p. 4. Höffding, *Etik*, p. 43.

[23] Cf. Simmel, *Einleitung in die Moralwissenschaft*, i. p. iii. sq.; Westermarck, 'Normative und psychologische Ethik,' in *Dritter Internationaler Congress für Psychologie in München*, p. 428 sqq.

[24] Zeller, *History of Greek Philosophy*, ii. 475.

The charge brought against the Sophists does not at all apply to it. I do not even subscribe to that beautiful modern sophism which admits every man's conscience to be an infallible guide. If we had to recognise, or rather if we did recognise, as right everything which is held to be right by anybody, savage or Christian, criminal or saint, morality would really suffer a serious loss. But we do not, and we cannot, do so. My moral judgments are my own judgments; they spring from my own moral consciousness; they judge of the conduct of other men not from their point of view, but from mine, not with primary reference to their opinions about right and wrong, but with reference to my own. Most of us indeed admit that, when judging of an act, we also ought to take into consideration the moral conviction of the agent, and the agreement or disagreement between his doing and his idea of what he ought to do. But although we hold it to be wrong of a person to act against his conscience, we may at the same time blame him for having such a conscience as he has. Ethical subjectivism covers all such cases. It certainly does not allow everybody to follow his own inclinations; nor does it lend sanction to arbitrariness and caprice. Our moral consciousness belongs to our mental constitution, which we cannot change as we please. We approve and we disapprove because we cannot do otherwise. Can we help feeling pain when the fire burns us? Can we help sympathising with our friends? Are these phenomena less necessary, less powerful in their consequences, because they fall within the subjective sphere of experience? So, too, why should the moral law command less obedience because it forms part of our own nature?

Far from being a danger, ethical subjectivism seems to me more likely to be an acquisition for moral practice. Could it be brought home to people that there is no absolute standard in morality, they would perhaps be somewhat more tolerant in their judgments, and more apt to listen to the voice of reason. If the right has an objective existence, the moral consciousness has certainly been playing at blindman's buff ever since it was born, and will continue to do so until the extinction of the human race. But who does admit this? The popular mind is always inclined to believe that it possesses the knowledge of what *is* right and wrong, and to regard public opinion as the reliable guide of conduct. We have, to be sure, no reason to regret that there are men who rebel against the established rules of morality; it is more deplorable that the rebels are so few, and that, consequently, the old rules change so slowly. Far above the vulgar idea that the right is a settled something to which everybody has to adjust his opinions, rises the conviction that it has its existence in each individual mind, capable of any expansion, proclaiming its own right to exist, if needs be, venturing to make a stand against the whole world. Such a conviction makes for progress.

The Ethical Implications of Cultural Relativity

CARL WELLMAN

Carl Wellman (1926–   ) teaches at Washington University in St. Louis and is the author of *The Language of Ethics* (1961) and numerous journal articles.

It is often thought that the discoveries of anthropology have revolutionary implications for ethics. Readers of Sumner, Benedict, and Herskovits are apt to come away with the impression that the only moral obligation is to conform to one's society, that polygamy is as good as monogamy, or that no ethical judgment can be rationally justified. While these anthropologists might complain that they are being misinterpreted, they would not deny that their real intent is to challenge the traditional view of morals. Even the anthropologist whose scientific training has made him skeptical of sweeping generalities and wary of philosophical entanglements is inclined to believe that the scientific study of cultures has undermined the belief in ethical absolutes of any kind.

Just what has been discovered that forces us to revise our ethics? Science has shown that certain things that were once thought to be absolute are actually relative to culture. Something is relative to culture when it varies with and is causally determined by culture. Clearly, nothing can be both relative to culture and absolute, for to be absolute is to be fixed and invariable, independent of man and the same for all men.

Exactly which things are relative and in what degree is a question still being debated by cultural anthropologists. Important as this question is, I do not propose to discuss it. It is the empirical scientists who must tell us which things vary from culture to culture and to what extent each is causally determined by its culture. It is not for me to question the findings of the anthropologists in this area. Instead, let me turn to the philosophical problem of the implications of cultural relativity. Assuming for the moment that cultural relativity is a fact, what follows for ethics?

What follows depends in part upon just what turns out to be relative. Anthropologists are apt to use the word "values" to refer indiscriminately to the things which have value, the characteristics which give these things their value, the attitudes of the persons who value these things, and the judgments of those people that these things have value. Similarly, one finds it hard to be sure whether "morals" refers to the mores of a people, the set of principles an observer might formulate after observing their conduct, the practical beliefs the people themselves entertain, or the way they feel about certain kinds of

Source: Carl Wellman, "The Ethical Implications of Cultural Relativity," *Journal of Philosophy,* Vol. LX, No. 7 (March 1963), pp. 169–184. Reprinted by permission of the Journal and the author.

conduct. Until such ambiguities are cleared up, one hardly knows what is being asserted when it is claimed that "values" or "morals" are relative.

It seems to me there are at least ten quite different things of interest to the ethicist that the anthropologist might discover to be relative to culture: mores, social institutions, human nature, acts, goals, value experiences, moral emotions, moral concepts, moral judgments, and moral reasoning. Since I can hardly discuss all the ethical conclusions that various writers have tried to draw from these different facts of cultural relativity, what I propose to do is to examine critically the reasoning by which one ethical conclusion might be derived from each of them.

I

It has long been recognized that mores are relative to culture. Mores are those customs which are enforced by social pressure. They are established patterns of action to which the individual is expected to conform and from which he deviates only at the risk of disapproval and punishment. It seems clear that mores vary from society to society and that the mores of any given society depend upon its culture. What does this imply for ethics?

The conclusion most frequently drawn is that what is right in one society may be wrong in another. For example, although it would be wrong for one of us to kill his aged parents, this very act is right for an Eskimo. This is because our mores are different from those of Eskimo society, and it is the mores that make an act right or wrong.

Let us grant, for the sake of discussion, that different societies do have different mores. Why should we grant that the mores make an act right or wrong? It has been claimed that this is true by definition. "Right" simply means according to the mores, and "wrong" means in violation of the mores. There is something to be said for this analysis of our concepts of right and wrong. It seems to explain both the imperativeness and the impersonality of obligation.

The "ought" seems to tell one what to do and yet to be more than the command of any individual; perhaps its bindingness lies in the demands of society. Attractive as this interpretation appears at first glance, I cannot accept it. It can be shown that no naturalistic analysis of the meaning of ethical words is adequate. In addition, this particular analysis is objectionable in that it makes it self-contradictory to say that any customary way of acting is wrong. No doubt, social reformers are often confused, but they are not always inconsistent.

If the view that the mores make an act right or wrong is not true by definition, it amounts to the moral principle that one ought always to conform to the mores of his society. None of the ways in which this principle is usually supported is adequate. (a) Any society unconsciously develops those mores which are conducive to survival and well-being under its special circumstances. Each individual ought to obey the mores of his society because this is the best way to promote the good life for the members of that society. I admit that there is a tendency for any society to develop those mores which fit its special circumstances, but I doubt that this is more than a tendency. There is room for reform in most societies, and this is particularly true when conditions are changing for one reason or another. (b) One ought to obey the mores of his society because disobedience would tend to destroy those mores. Without mores any society would lapse into a state of anarchy that would be intolerable for its members. It seems to me that this argument deserves to be taken seriously, but it does not prove that one ought always to obey the mores of his society. What it does show is that one ought generally to obey the mores of his society and that whenever he considers disobedience, he should give due weight to the effects of his example upon social stability. (c) One ought to obey the mores of his society because disobedience tends to undermine their existence. It is important to preserve the mores, not simply to avoid anarchy, but because it is their mores which give shape and meaning to the life of any people. I grant that the individual does tend to think of his life in terms of the mores of his group and that anything which disrupts those mores tends to rob his life of significance. But once again, all this shows is that one should conform to the mores of his society on the whole. Although there is some obligation to conformity, this is not the only nor the most important obligation on the member of any society.

Therefore, it does not seem to me that one can properly say that the mores make an act right or wrong. One cannot define the meaning of these ethical words in terms of the mores, nor can one maintain the ethical principle that one ought always to obey the mores of his society. If the mores do not make acts right or wrong, the fact that different societies have different mores does not imply that the same kind of act can be right in one society and wrong in another.

II

Cultural relativity seems to apply to institutions as well as to mores. A social institution is a type of organization; it involves a pattern of activity in which two or more people play recognized roles. The family, the church, the government, the liberal arts college, the bridge club are all social institutions. Institutions can be classified more or less specifically. Thus monogamy, polygamy, and polyandry are specific institutions which fall under the generic institution of the family. Since the specific form an institution takes seems to vary from society to society depending upon the culture of that society, let us grant that social institutions are relative to culture. What does this imply for ethics?

A conclusion that is sometimes drawn is that we should never try to adopt an institution from another society or seek to impose one of our institutions upon another people. The main argument for this view is that each institution is an expression of the total culture of which it is a part. To try to take an institution out of its cultural environment is sure to maim or even kill it; to try to bring an institution into an alien culture is likely to disorganize and even destroy that cultural pattern. Thus the attempt to transport an institution from one society to another will fail to achieve its intended result and will produce many unintended and socially undesirable effects.

No doubt the attempt to import or export a social institution is often a dismal failure. The transported institution becomes a mere caricature of its former self, and the society into which it is introduced becomes demoralized or even destroyed. Extreme caution is certainly necessary. But is it not incautious to conclude that the attempt will always fail? The most glaring examples of cultural demoralization and destruction, such as the intervention of the white man in Africa, have involved much more than the imposition of one or two institutions. Moreover, some institutions may be less alien to a given culture than others. If so, there might be some institutions that the society could adopt with only minor modifications. In fact, societies seem to have been borrowing from one another for centuries. While the effects of this borrowing have often been bad, they have not always been totally destructive or even grossly demoralizing. Occasionally they may have been beneficial. It seems unnecessary to conclude that we should never import or export an institution from the fact that social institutions are culturally relative.

III

Another thing which may be relative to culture is human nature. As soon as one ponders the differences between the Chinese aristocrat and the Australian bushman, the American tycoon and the Indian yogi, one finds it hard to believe that there is anything basic to human nature which is shared by all men. And reflection upon the profound effects of enculturation easily leads one to the conclusion that what a man is depends upon the society in which he has been brought up. Therefore, let us assume that human nature is culturally relative and see what this implies.

This seems to imply that no kind of action, moral character, or social institution is made inevitable by human nature. This conclusion is important because it cuts the ground out from under one popular type of justification in ethics. For example, capitalism is sometimes defended as an ideal on the grounds that this is the only economic system that is possible in the light of man's greedy and competitive nature. Or it might be claimed that adultery is permissible because the ideal of marital fidelity runs counter to man's innate drives or instincts. If there is no fixed human nature, such arguments are left without any basis.

One may wonder, however, whether the only alternatives are an entirely fixed and an entirely plastic human nature. It might be that enculturation could mold a human being but only within certain limits. These limits might exist either because certain parts of human nature are not at all plastic or because all parts are only moderately plastic. For example, it might turn out that the need for food and the tendency to grow in a certain way cannot be modified at all by enculturation, or it might turn out that every element in human nature can be modified in some ways but not in others. In either case, what a man becomes would depend partly upon enculturation and partly upon the nature of the organism being enculturated.

Thus cultural relativity may be a matter of degree. Before we can decide just what follows from the fact that human nature is relative to culture, we must know how far and in what ways it is relative. If there are certain limits to the plasticity of human nature, these do rule out some kinds of action, character, or institution. But anthropology indicates that within any such limits a great many alternatives remain. Human nature may make eating inevitable, but what we eat and when we eat and how we eat is up to us. At least we can say that to the degree that human nature is relative to culture no kind of action, moral character, or social institution is made possible by human nature.

IV

It has been claimed that acts are also relative to culture. This is to say that the same general type of action may take on specific differences when performed in different societies because those societies have different cultures. For example, it is one thing for one of us to kill his aged parent; it is quite a different thing for an Eskimo to do such an act. One difference lies in the consequences of these two acts. In our society, disposing of old and useless parents merely allows one to live in greater luxury; to an Eskimo this act may mean the difference between barely adequate subsistence and malnutrition for himself and his family. What are we to make of this fact that the nature of an act is culturally relative?

One possible conclusion is that the same kind of act may be right in one society and wrong in another. This presupposes that the rightness of an act depends upon its consequences and that it consequences may vary from society to society. Since I accept these presuppositions, I agree that the rightness or wrongness of an act is relative to its social context.

It is important, however, to distinguish this conclusion from two others with which it is often confused. To say that the rightness of an act is relative to the society in which it is performed is not to say that exactly the same sort of act can be both right and wrong. It is because the social context makes the acts different in kind that one can be right while the other is wrong. Compare an act of infanticide in our society with an act of infanticide in some South Seas society. Are these two acts the same or different? They are of the same kind inasmuch as both are acts of killing an infant. On the other hand, they are different in that such an act may be necessary to preserve the balance between family size and food resources in the South Seas while this is not the case in our society. These two acts are generically similar but specifically different; that is, they belong to different species of the same genus. Therefore, the conclusion that the same kind of act may be right in one society and wrong in another does not amount to saying that two acts which are precisely the same in every respect may differ in rightness or wrongness.

Neither is this conclusion to be confused with the view that acts are made right or wrong by the mores of society. No doubt our society disapproves of infanticide and some South Seas societies approve of it, but it is not *this* which makes infanticide wrong for us and right for them. If infanticide is wrong for us and right for them, it is because acts of infanticide have very different consequences in our society and in theirs, not because the practice is discouraged here and customary there.

V

The goals that individuals or groups aim for also seem relative to culture. What objects people select as goals varies from society to society depending upon the cultures of those societies. One group may strive for social prestige and the accumulation of great wealth, another may aim at easy comfort and the avoidance of any danger, a third may seek military glory and the conquest of other peoples. What follows from this fact of cultural relativity?

This fact is often taken as a basis for arguing that it is impossible to compare the value of acts, institutions, or total ways of life belonging to different societies. The argument rests on the assumptions that acts, institutions, and ways of life are means directed at certain ends, that means can be evaluated only in terms of their ends, and that ends are incommensurable with respect to value.

Granted these assumptions, the argument seems a good one, but I doubt that ends are really incommensurable. It seems to me that we can recognize that certain ends are more worth while than others, for example that pleasure is intrinsically better than pain. I may be mistaken, but until this has been shown, the conclusion that it is impossible to compare the value of acts, institutions, or ways of life belonging to different societies has not been established.

VI

People from different societies apparently experience the same object or situation in quite different ways depending upon the cultural differences between their societies. The satisfying experience that a cultured Chinese might derive from eating bird's nest soup would be diametrically opposed to the experience I would undergo if I forced myself to gulp down my helping of that exotic dish out of politeness. Again, an experience which I would greatly value, sitting in the bleachers watching the Red Sox clinch the pennant, would be nothing but a boring observation of meaningless motions accompanied by the sensations of scorching sun, trickling sweat, and unyielding benches to a Hottentot visitor. In large measure the nature of any experience is determined by the process of enculturation that the experiencer has undergone. Thus, value experiences are also relative to culture.

It might seem to follow that the same experience could be good to one person and bad to another, but this is just what does *not* follow. The difference in value stems from the fact that, although confronted with similar objects or situations, the two people have very different experiences. The nature of a person's experience depends upon the kind of person he has become through the process of enculturation as much as upon the external stimulus. It would be a mistake to conclude that qualitatively identical experiences are good to me and bad to the Hottentot. Although he and I are in the same ballpark watching the same game, we are having very different experiences.

What one should conclude is that the same kind of object or situation can have different values to people from different societies. This follows from the fact that the nature of a person's experience depends in large measure upon the way in which he has been enculturated, together with the assumption that the value of any object or situation depends upon its effects on experience. Since my ethical view is that the value of objects and situations is derived from their impact upon experience, I accept the conclusion that the same kind of object or situation can have very different values to people who come from different cultures.

VII

It appears that moral emotions are also relative to culture. What a person desires, approves, or feels guilty about seems to vary from society to society depending upon the cultural differences between those societies. What does the fact that moral emotions are culturally relative imply for ethics?

One possible conclusion would be that the same kind of act or person can be morally good in one society and morally bad in another. This is supposed to follow from the fact that the same kind of act or person can be approved in one society and disapproved in another together with the view that to be morally good or bad is simply to be approved or disapproved.

That infanticide is approved in certain South Seas societies and disapproved in ours need not be doubted. That infanticide constitutes exactly the same kind of act in the two societies is, as we have seen, more dubious. But even if it did, I would not accept the conclusion in question; for I would not admit that the moral value of any act or person depends upon whether it is approved or disapproved. That the grounds for moral evaluation lie outside the moral emotions can be seen by the fact that it always makes sense to ask someone *why* he approves or disapproves of something. If approving or disapproving made its object morally good or bad, there would be no need of such justification. Thus, the fact that moral emotions are culturally relative does not prove that identical acts or persons can be morally good in one society and morally bad in another.

VIII

Both linguistic and psychological studies have suggested that people living in different societies conceptualize their experience in different ways. Probably, moral concepts vary from society to society depending upon the cultural backgrounds from which they arise. The ancient Greek thought of virtue quite differently from the modern American; the Christian conception of obligation is probably absent from the mind of the African who has escaped the influence of any missionary. What are we to conclude from the fact that moral concepts are relative to culture?

The obvious implication appears to be that people of different cultural backgrounds are almost sure to disagree on any ethical questions. Obvious as it may seem, this is not implied at all. In fact, people using different concepts could never disagree, for disagreement presupposes that both parties are thinking in the same terms. For one thing, on what question are they supposed to be disagreeing? If each person is using his own set of concepts, each person formulates his own question in his own terms. And if the two persons do not have any common set of ethical concepts there is no way for formulating a single question that will be intelligible to both of them. Again, in what sense do their respective answers disagree? When an American says that Poland is undemocratic and a Russian insists that it is a fine example of democracy, it appears that they are disagreeing. No doubt they do disagree in many ways, but not in their utterances. Their statements are quite compatible, for they are using the word "democracy" in different senses. Similarly, people of different cultures would only seem to disagree if they attached different concepts to their ethical words.

The proper conclusion to draw is that any comparison between the ethical views of the members of different cultures can be only partial. As long as each view is stated only in its own terms, there can be no comparison between them; comparison becomes possible only when they are stated in the same set of concepts. But if the sets of concepts are not identical, any translation of one view into the language of the other or of both into some neutral language will be approximate at best. Even where something approaching adequate translation is possible, some of the meaning will be lost or something will be added that was not in the original concept. For this reason, any claim that the ethical views of people in different societies are either identical or contradictory is likely to tell only part of the story. To some extent, at least, the ethics of different cultures are incommensurate.

IX

The aspect of cultural relativity most often emphasized is that pertaining to moral judgments. Objects that the members of one society think to be good are considered bad by another group; acts considered wrong in one society are thought of as right in another. Moreover, these differences in judgments of value and obligation seem to reflect cultural differences between the respective societies. There is a great deal of evidence to suggest that ethical judgments are relative to culture.

To many anthropologists and philosophers it is a corollary of this fact that one of a set of contrary ethical judgments is no more valid than another, or, put positively, that all ethical judgments are equally valid. Unfortunately, there is a crucial ambiguity lurking in this epistemological thicket. Ethical judgments might have equal validity either because all are valid or because none are: similarly, one ethical judgment might be no more valid than another either because both are equally valid or because both are equally lacking in validity. Since these two interpretations are quite different, let us consider them separately.

On the first interpretation, the conclusion to be drawn from the fact that ethical judgments are relative to culture is that every moral judgment is valid for the society in which it is made. Instead of denying the objective validity of ethical judgments, this view affirms it, but in a qualified form which will allow for the variations in ethical belief.

There seem to be three main ways of defending this position. (a) Ethical judgments have objective validity because it is possible to justify them rationally. However, this validity is limited to a given society because the premises used in such justification are those which are agreed upon in that society. Since there are no universally accepted premises, no universal validity is possible. I would wish to deny that justification is real if it is limited in this way. If all our reasoning really does rest on certain premises which can be rejected by others without error, then we must give up the claim to objective validity. When I claim validity for ethical judgments, I intend to claim more than that it is possible to support them with logical arguments; I also claim that it is incorrect to deny the premises of such arguments. (b) Any ethical judgment is an expression of a total pattern of culture. Hence it is possible to justify any single judgment in terms of its coherence with the total cultural configuration of the judger. But one cannot justify the culture as a whole, for it is not part of a more inclusive pattern. Therefore, ethical judgments have objective validity, but only in terms of a given cultural pattern. I would make the same objection to this view as to the preceding one. Since it allows justification to rest upon an arbitrary foundation, it is inadequate to support any significant claim to objective validity. (c) Any ethical judgment has objective validity because it is an expression of a moral code. The validity of a moral code rests on the fact that without conformity to a common code social cohesion breaks down, leading to disastrous results. Since any given moral code provides cohesion for one and only one society, each ethical judgment has validity for a single society. There are at least two difficulties with this defense of objectivity. Surely one could deny some ethical judgments without destroying the entire moral code they reflect; not every judgment could be shown to be essential to social stability. Moreover, the argument seems to rest on the ethical judgment that one ought not to contribute to the breakdown of social stability. How is this judgment to be shown to be valid? One must either appeal to some other basis of validity or argue in a circle. None of these arguments to show that every moral judgment is valid for the society in which it is made is adequate.

On the second interpretation, the conclusion to be drawn from the fact that moral judgments are relative to culture is that moral judgments have no objective validity. This amounts to saying that the distinction between true and false, correct and incorrect, does not apply to such judgments. This conclusion obviously does not follow simply from the fact that people disagree about ethical questions. We do not deny the objective validity of scientific judgments either on the grounds that different scientists propose alternative theories or on the grounds that the members of some societies hold fast to many unscientific beliefs.

Why, then, does the fact that moral judgments are relative to culture imply that they have no objective validity? (a) Individuals make different ethical judgments because they judge in terms of different frames of reference, and they adopt these frames of reference uncritically from their cultures. Since ethical judgments are the product of enculturation rather than reasoning, they cannot claim rational justification. I do not find this argument convincing, for it seems to confuse the origin of a judgment with its justification. The causes of a judgment are one thing; the reasons for or against it are another. It remains to be shown that any information about what causes us to judge as we do has any bearing on the question of whether or not our judgments are correct. (b) It is impossible to settle ethical questions by using the scientific method. Therefore, there is no objective way to show that one ethical judgment is any more correct than another, and, in the absence of any method of establishing the claim to objective validity, it makes no sense to continue to make the claim. I will concede that, if there is no rational method of establishing ethical judgments, then we might as well give up the claim to objective validity. And if the scientific method is restricted to the testing of hypotheses by checking the predictions they imply against the results of observation and experiment, it does seem to be inapplicable to ethical questions. What I will not concede is the tacit assumption that the scientific method is the only method of establishing the truth. Observation and experimentation do not figure prominently in the method used by mathematicians. I even wonder whether the person who concludes that ethical judgments have no objective validity can establish *this* conclusion by using the scientific method. The fact that ethical judgments cannot be established scientifically does not by itself prove that they cannot be established by any method of reasoning. (c) There might be some method of settling ethical disputes, but it could not be a method of reasoning. Any possible reasoning would have to rest upon certain premises. Since the members of different societies start from different premises, there is no basis for argument that does not beg the question. I suspect, however, that we have been looking for our premises in the wrong place. The model of deduction tempts us to search for very general premises from which all our more specific judgments can be deduced. Unfortunately, it is just in this area of universal moral principles that disagreement seems most frequent and irremedial. But suppose that these ethical generalizations are themselves inductions based upon particular moral judgments. Then we could argue for or against them in terms of relatively specific ethical judgments and the factual judgments that are in turn relevant to these. Until this possibility is explored further, we need not admit that there is no adequate basis for ethical reasoning. Thus it appears that none of these refutations of the objective validity of ethical judgments is really conclusive.

The fact that ethical judgments are relative to culture is often taken to prove that no ethical judgment can claim to be any more valid than any of its contraries. I have tried to show that on neither of the two possible interpretations of this conclusion does the conclusion necessarily follow from the fact of cultural relativity.

X

Finally, moral reasoning might turn out to be relative to culture. When some ethical statement is denied or even questioned, the person who made the statement is apt to leap to its defense. He attempts to justify his statement by producing reasons to support it. But speakers from different societies tend to justify their statements in different ways. The difference in their reasoning may be of two kinds. Either their reasoning may rest on different assumptions or they may draw inferences in a different manner. That is, the arguments they advance may either start from different premises or obey different logics. We can ignore the former case here; for it boils down to a difference in their judgments, and we have discussed that at length in the preceding section. Instead let us assume that people who belong to different societies tend to draw their moral conclusions according to different logics depending upon their respective cultures. What difference would it make if moral reasoning were thus culturally relative?

The most interesting conclusion that might be drawn from the fact that moral reasoning is relative to culture is that it has no objective validity. The claim to objective validity is empty where it cannot be substantiated. But how could one justify the claim that any given kind of moral reasoning is valid? To appeal to the same kind of reasoning would be circular. To appeal to some other kind of reasoning would not be sufficient to justify this kind; for each kind of reasoning involves principles of inference which go beyond, and therefore cannot be justified by appealing to, any other kind.

I find this line of argument inconclusive for several reasons. First, it is not clear that a given kind of reasoning cannot be justified by appealing to a different kind of reasoning. In fact, this seems to be a fairly common practice in logic. Various forms of syllogistic arguments can be shown to be valid by reducing them to arguments of the form Barbara. Again, a logician will sometimes justify certain rules for natural deduction by an involved logical argument which does not itself use these same rules. Second, in what sense is it impossible to show another person that my moral arguments are valid? I can show him that the various moral arguments I advance conform to the principles of my logic. If he does not accept these principles, he will remain unconvinced. This may show that I cannot persuade him that my arguments are valid, but does it show that I have not proved that they are? It is not obvious that persuading a person and proving a point are identical. Third, is the claim to objective validity always empty in the absence of any justification for it? Perhaps some reasoning is ultimate in that it requires no further justification. To assume the opposite seems to lead to an infinite regress. If every valid justification stands in need of further justification, no amount of justification would ever be sufficient.

I do not claim to have established the objective validity of moral reasoning. I am not even sure how that validity might be established or even whether it needs to be established. All I have been trying to do is to suggest that such validity is not ruled out by the fact, if it is a fact, that moral reasoning is relative to culture.

No doubt the reader will wish to challenge my acceptance or rejection of this or that particular conclusion. Quite apart from such specific ethical questions, however, there are certain over-all logical conclusions which seem to me inevitable. (1) What conclusions one can legitimately draw from the facts of cultural relativity will depend upon *which* facts one starts from. It is worth distinguishing between the relativity of mores, social institutions, human nature, acts, goals, value experiences, moral emotions, moral concepts, moral judgments, and moral reasoning; for each of these has different implications for ethics. (2) By themselves the facts of cultural relativity do not imply anything for ethics. Any argument that is both interesting and valid requires additional premises. Thus it is only in conjunction with certain statements that go beyond anthropology that the findings of anthropology have any bearing at all on ethics. (3) What conclusions one should draw will obviously depend upon which of these additional premises one accepts. Therefore, one's ethical and epistemological theory will determine the significance one will attach to cultural relativity. (4) Before we can criticize or even understand the arguments by which ethical conclusions are derived from the facts of such relativity, we must make these additional premises explicit and see what can be said for or against them. My main purpose in this paper has been to make a start in this complicated yet crucial task.

SUGGESTED READINGS

1. "Is Ethical Relativity Necessary? A Symposium," *Proceedings of the Aristotelian Society*, Supp. Vol. 17, London (1938).
2. RADER, MELVIN, *Ethics and Society* (New York: Holt, 1950), Ch. 5.
3. SAVERY, B., "Relativity Versus Absolutism in Value-Theory," *The Journal of Philosophy*, Vol. 34 (Feb. 18, 1937), 85–93.
4. STACE, WALTER, *The Concept of Morals* (New York: Macmillan, 1937), Chs. 1, 2. One of the best discussions.

Egoism, Hedonism, and Beyond

> Humility, as something beyond the real demand of correct self-appraisal, was specially a Christian virtue because it involved subservience to God. In a secular context it can only represent subservience to other men and their projects.
>
> —Bernard Williams

Earlier, in the introduction to this chapter, we pointed out that we can use the difference in generality of moral maxims to help systematize our morals. We illustrated this with the promise maxim; because the maxim "One should keep his promises" is more general than either of two instances of it (practicing fidelity to one's spouse and paying off one's loans), it enables us to integrate the two less general maxims. Now, as a prelude to the introduction of another issue in ethical theory, we will discuss other examples of the use of generality in trying to systematize morals.

Think of a maxim we learned as children, "You should divide the dessert evenly," and of a maxim attaining wider currency day by day, "Husbands and wives should take turns doing dishes (and other chores)." These are maxims of lower generality than "You should act fairly," which covers the other two.

The two relatively general maxims about promise keeping and acting fairly are not as general as it is possible for moral maxims to be. Just as they are more general than other maxims, so there are maxims more general than they. Logically, however, there must be a most general maxim, the highest maxim on the moral maxim pyramid. It seems as if the most general maxim would be "You should do that which is right," because no moral concept dealing with acts is more general than "right" is, except "wrong," which is equally general.

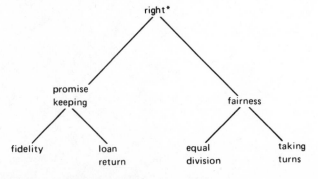

* Nothing is implied here about the number of levels nor about whether between the levels shown there are other levels.

"Right" and "wrong" are the moral concepts we use to talk about human acts. "Good" and "bad" are also moral words; we use them to talk about experiences, human character, and things and their properties and relations. "Good" and "bad," too, are the most general of another set of concepts.

It has been claimed that having enough food to eat and having the respect of others are instances of the relatively more general good of satisfying our needs, in this instance, psychological and physical needs, and that obtaining an education and being free to make our own decisions are instances of the relatively more general good of realizing our human potentiality. Satisfying our needs and realizing our human potential are, in turn, instances of the most general concept of "good" itself.

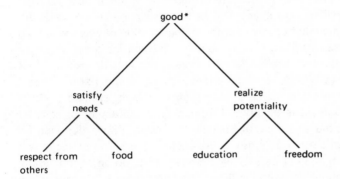

We can raise, now, the ethical theory question: What is the relation between the two general concepts the "right" and the "good?"

Teleologists hold the view that good is the more basic concept. In moral thinking we first must determine what is morally good, determine what moral goods we think worth pursuing; once we have determined this, we have a standard by which to judge the rightness of an act. An act will be right if it contributes to the attainment of what is morally good; and that act will be more right that makes the greater contribution.

For teleologists, then, the most important moral task is to determine what things are morally good. The three essays in this section address themselves to that task.

One issue that is germane to deciding what is morally good is: Whose good do we have to consider in thinking about what is morally good? **James Rachels,** in the section's first essay, discusses egoism; he distinguishes psychological from ethical or moral egoism. "Psychological egoism is the view that all men are selfish in everything that they do, that is, that the only motive from which anyone ever acts is self-interest." Psychological egoists, then, confine considerations of what is morally good to what each agent considers good for him or her without regard to what is good for other agents. Note that Rachels uses the term "motive," as is proper in considering "psychological" egoism. Psychological egoism is related to the third important moral question we listed at the beginning of the introduction to this chapter: "Why should I be moral?" Rachels argues that psychological egoism is false and exposes some confusions that have led many persons to think that it is true.

Rachels properly addresses himself to psychological egoism before ethical egoism because if the former is true, the latter is empty. "Ethical egoism is a normative view about how men *ought* to act." If, in fact, we do always act in our own interest; and if the psychological motive springs of human nature are so constituted that we cannot do otherwise, it would be empty to say that we *ought* to act always in our own interest. It would be empty to say we ought to act as ethical egoists. It is empty to tell a person that he or she ought to act in his or her own interests if they are motivated to do that anyway and cannot act in any other way.

Rachels believes that there is no way to *logically* refute ethical egoists, but we can answer them. He says "The egoist challenge to our ordinary moral convictions amounts to a demand for an explanation of why we should adopt certain policies of action, namely policies in which the good of others is given importance." The answer to "Why shouldn't you do actions that will harm others?" is "Because doing those actions would harm others." Rachels denies that this is a "piece of philosophical sleight-of-hand." "What we have come up against is simply a fundamental requirement of rational action, namely, that the existence of reasons for action always depends on the prior existence of certain attitudes in the agent. . . . So a nonegoist will accept 'It would harm another person' as a reason not to do an action simply because he cares about what happens to that other person." In our introduction we distinguished between "reasons" and "motives" and pointed out that "because" is ambiguous, sometimes being a reason and sometimes being a motive. In Rachels' answer to the egoist, do you think that the "because" in "Because doing those actions would harm others" is a reason "because" as he says it is or do you think it is a motive "because?" Does it tell us why others' welfare is a moral good or does it tell us under what conditions others' welfare is a motive for action?

Jeremy Bentham, in this section's second essay, is a hedonist; for him, pleasure and the absence of pain are the only goods we have to consider as being morally relevant. He is a teleologist. In determining what acts are right, we determine their utility in producing a greater balance of pleasure over pain; that act which has the greatest utility is the act we ought to perform; it is the most right act. Because Bentham and his associates and followers used the term "utility" in stating their teleological position, they are usually called "Utilitarians."

Bentham is a universalistic utilitarian; he believes, unlike the egoist teleologist, that the rightness of an act should be determined by counting *every* affected persons' pleasure and pain, not merely the agent's own pleasure or pain. Ratting on your Underground cell may have good consequences for you because the "feds" promise to give you immunity, but it may have bad consequences for the other members of your cell. Bentham thinks that in calculating the rightness or wrongness of ratting we should include the consequences to you, to the members of your cell, and to all other members of society who might be affected by the cell members' acts.

In our culture we tend to disapprove of ratting, snitching, informing, and betraying. We tend to believe we are obligated to be loyal to and to expect loyalty from our immediate friends and associates; our morality resembles or, perhaps, is a gang morality. As children we tended to form gangs as a sort of protective agency against parents, teachers, and other adults. We saw our gang as a mutual interest group and, in determining the morality of loyally not ratting on our gang, we generally counted the consequences to ourselves and our fellow gang members and did not count the consequences to people who are not in the gang. Children and gangsters are somewhat limited utilitarians, "gang utilitarians." People who carry this morality into adulthood, as most of us do, carry a gang morality with them.

A gang morality may seem morally more defensible to us than it should because we have an unexamined belief in the morality of loyalty. A universalistic utilitarian such as Bentham could argue that loyalty is not the morally defensible virtue that many think it is. Suppose that a member of the Underground cell changes her views. She finds that acts of terrorism and violence are producing bad consequences for people outside the cell, and, further, she changes from a limited to a universalistic utilitarianism. Then, considering the painful consequences for those affected directly and indirectly by the terrorist acts, and finding that these painful consequences considerably outweigh the good consequences, she finds that the only morally right act for her to perform is to rat on her fellow Underground members; in this way, she can help stop these horrible acts. If you have some reservations about morally condemning ratting, snitching, informing, and betraying and also hold a utilitarian moral theory, you have to produce an argument showing why limited utilitarianism is better than universalistic utilitarianism, why loyalty to our cell, family and friends comes before loyalty to the humanity that is not in your cell, family, or circle of friends.

Loyalty sometimes parades under other names, for example, "patriotism," which is loyalty to a large gang, the members of your nation. Patriotism is just a form of gang loyalty. Patriots hope their side beats up on the other side. "My country right or wrong?"

Utilitarianism is an attractive ethical position. It takes generality to its limit with its principle of the greatest good for the greatest number; it provides a single test for the multitude of moral phenomena and situations; it seems right to say that an acts' consequences shed light on its morality; even if one were not a hedonist, that is, did not confine one's moral goods to pleasure alone, at least utilitarianism takes account of human responses to events and objects; it is down-to-earth.

Despite these attractive features, utilitarianism may be an ethical theory unequal to its task. **Bernard Williams** thinks it is. In this section's third essay, Williams proceeds to try to show that it is unable to make intelligible the value of integrity.

As Williams uses the term "integrity," it is a profound value and central to a moral outlook on life. Its meaning for him goes beyond its typical meaning as in "She is a woman of integrity"; in this context, to have integrity means to be honest, steadfast to one's principles, not bribeable, a person who acts on professed principles undeterred by proffered personal advantages that would accrue if one did not consistently follow through with previous commitments.

"Integrity" is related to "integrated"; to be integrated is to be whole, every part hanging together with every other part. For Williams a person "is identified with his actions as flowing from projects and attitudes which in some cases he takes seriously at the deepest level, as what his life is about. . . ." A person is also identified with his or her moral feelings and commitments. If a person is cut off from, alienated from, his or her projects, actions, commitments, feelings by following a utilitarian ethic, then a person loses integrity; having lost integrity, one loses moral identity, and so has lost the most basic factor in our human identity. Any ethical theory, including utilitarian ethics, that leads to such an outcome is unacceptable, according to Williams. Integrity is a moral good too central and important to be lost.

Williams explains how utilitarianism alienates persons from their moral feelings. He gives the example of Jim, who is given the honor of shooting one of twenty Indians in a South American country; by doing so, the other nineteen will be spared by Pedro, the captain of soldiers. What should Jim do? A Utilitarian considers the consequences of the act, balances the good against the bad; since acts have both immediate and remote consequences, presumably all of them have to be used in calculating the rightness of the act, with due regard for our lesser knowledge about the remote ones. Among the immediate consequences will be the psychological effect of the decision on the agent; in Jim's case, he may anticipate a very strong psychological shock upon shooting an unknown, innocent person. Is this consequence to be counted among those put into the utilitarian balance? If one has determined on utilitarian grounds that the right action is to kill one of the Indians, then to balk at the action could be considered self-indulgent squeamishness. The squeamishness is out of place if the utilitarian theory is right, because the squeamishness could justifiably occur only if Jim thought he was doing the wrong thing, which, contrariwise, he could not be doing if the utilitarian theory is correct. But if he were boldly to seize the rightness of his utilitarian authorized act, he would be alienated from his moral feeling of repugnance at shooting an innocent person. "Because our moral relation to the world is partly given by such feelings, and by a sense of what we can or cannot 'live with,' to come to regard these feelings from a purely utilitarian point of view, that is to say, as happenings outside one's moral self, is to lose a sense of one's moral identity; to lose, in the most literal way, one's integrity."

Williams explains how utilitarianism may alienate us from our actions as well. Our actions grow out of our projects, projects such as obtaining things for ourselves, our families, our friends; pursuing intellectual, cultural, and creative interests; we may have causes, such as Zionism or abolishing chemical and biological warfare; we have projects growing out of commitments—to a person, a cause, an institution, one's own genius. While the utilitarian's project is the purusit of happiness, this higher-level project would be empty except for such lower-level projects as mentioned above. A utilitarian, then, has to decide which projects are to be included among those lower-level projects whose fulfillment will constitute his happiness. This will include considering the extent to which we will give up our own projects when they conflict with someone else's projects. For the utilitarian, the determination of which projects are to be sanctioned will involve calculating and balancing the satisfactions to the parties of fulfilling their projects. But, wonders Williams, can this be a reasonable answer for those projects we call "commitments?" "How can a man, as a utilitarian agent, come to regard as one satisfaction among others, and a dispensable one, a project or attitude around which he has built his life, just because someone else's projects have so structured the causal scene that that is how the utilitarian sum comes out?" If Jim had all his life directed his actions from the central commitment that he would never lend his agency to any act that harmed, much less killed, any other person, should he give up this commitment because Pedro's project has structured the situation in which he has found himself?

Williams says, "The point is that he [each person] is identified with his actions as flowing from projects and attitudes which in some cases he takes seriously at the deepest level, as what his life is about. . . . It is absurd to demand of such a man, when the sums come in from the utility network which the projects of others have in part determined, that he should just step aside from his own project. . . ." The utility calculation "is to alienate him in a real sense from his actions and the source of his action in his own convictions. . . . It is thus, in the most literal sense, an attack on his integrity."

The facile way that utilitarianism has with coordinating projects becomes even more doubtful for Williams in the political context. The utilitarian ethic is also designed for political decisions; indeed, that was the original purpose of Bentham; note the title from which our selection is taken includes *Principles of . . . Legislation.*" But while utilitarians are technically and intellectually sophisticated, they seem to be simple-minded because their view "runs against the complexities of moral thought. . . ."

Utilitarianism is challenged, then, by Williams, because it may not be equal to its teleological task. If integrity is one of our moral goods which the utilitarian theory prevents us from attaining, then, on teleological grounds, we have to reject this teleological theory.

The Psychological and Ethical Egoism

JAMES RACHELS

James Rachels (1941–   ), professor of philosophy at the University of Miami, writes in the areas of ethics and philosophy of action. Among his publications is *Moral Problems* (1971).

1. Our ordinary thinking about morality is full of assumptions that we almost never question. We assume, for example, that we have an obligation to consider the welfare of other people when we decide what actions to perform or what rules to obey; we think that we must refrain from acting in ways harmful to others, and that we must respect their rights and interests as well as our own. We also assume that people are in fact capable of being motivated by such considerations, that is, that people are not wholly selfish and that they do sometimes act in the interests of others.

Both of these assumptions have come under attack by moral sceptics, as long ago as by Glaucon in Book II of Plato's *Republic*. Glaucon recalls the legend of Gyges, a shepherd who was said to have found a magic ring in a fissure opened by an earthquake. The ring would make its wearer invisible and thus would enable him to go anywhere and do anything undetected. Gyges used the power of the ring to gain entry to the Royal Palace where he seduced the Queen, murdered the King, and subsequently seized the throne. Now Glaucon asks us to determine that there are two such rings, one given to a man of virtue and one given to a rogue. The rogue, of course, will use his ring unscrupulously and do anything necessary to increase his own wealth and power. He will recognize no moral constraints on his conduct, and, since the cloak of invisibility will protect him from discovery, he can do anything he pleases without fear of reprisal. So, there will be no end to the mischief he will do. But how will the so-called virtuous man behave? Glaucon suggests that he will behave no better than the rogue: "No one, it is commonly believed, would have such iron strength of mind as to stand fast in doing right or keep his hands off other men's goods, when he could go to the market-place and fearlessly help himself to anything he wanted, enter houses and sleep with any woman he chose, set prisoners free and kill men at his pleasure, and in a word go about among men with the powers of a god. He would behave no better than the other; both would take the same course."[1] Moreover, why shouldn't he? Once he is freed from the fear of reprisal, why shouldn't a man simply do

[1] *The Republic of Plato,* translated by F. M. Cornford (Oxford, 1941), p. 45.

Source: James Rachels, "Egoism and Moral Scepticism," *Ethics,* pp. 423–434. Reprinted by permission of the author.

what he pleases, or what he thinks is best for himself? What reason is there for him to continue being "moral" when it is clearly not to his own advantage to do so?

These sceptical views suggested by Glaucon have come to be known as *psychological egoism* and *ethical egoism* respectively. Psychological egoism is the view that all men are selfish in everything that they do, that is, that the only motive from which anyone ever acts is self-interest. On this view, even when men are acting in ways apparently calculated to benefit others, they are actually motivated by the belief that acting in this way is to their own advantage, and if they did not believe this, they would not be doing that action. Ethical egoism is, by contrast, a normative view about how men *ought* to act. It is the view that, regardless of how men do in fact behave, they have no obligation to do anything except what is in their own interests. According to the ethical egoist, a person is always justified in doing whatever is in his own interests, regardless of the effect on others.

Clearly, if either of these views is correct, then "the moral institution of life" (to use Butler's well-turned phrase) is very different than what we normally think. The majority of mankind is grossly deceived about what is, or ought to be, the case, where morals are concerned.

2. Psychological egoism seems to fly in the face of the facts. We are tempted to say: "Of course people act unselfishly all the time. For example, Smith gives up a trip to the country, which he would have enjoyed very much, in order to stay behind and help a friend with his studies, which is a miserable way to pass the time. This is a perfectly clear case of unselfish behavior, and if the psychological egoist thinks that such cases do not occur, then he is just mistaken." Given such obvious instances of "unselfish behavior," what reply can the egoist make? There are two general arguments by which he might try to show that all actions, including those such as the one just outlined, are in fact motivated by self-interest. Let us examine these in turn:

a. The first argument goes as follows. If we describe one person's action as selfish, and another person's action as unselfish, we are overlooking the crucial fact that in both cases, assuming that the action is done voluntarily, *the agent is merely doing what he most wants to do.* If Smith stays behind to help his friend, that only shows that he wanted to help his friend more than he wanted to go to the country. And why should he be praised for his "unselfishness" when he is only doing what he most wants to do? So, since Smith is only doing what he wants to do, he cannot be said to be acting unselfishly.

This argument is so bad that it would not deserve to be taken seriously except for the fact that so many otherwise intelligent people have been taken in by it. First, the argument rests on the premise that people never voluntarily do anything except what they want to do. But this is patently false; there are at least two classes of actions that are exceptions to this generalization. One is the set of actions which we may not want to do, but which we do anyway as a means to an end which we want to achieve; for example, going to the dentist in order to stop a toothache, or going to work every day in order to be able to draw our pay at the end of the month. These cases may be regarded as consistent with the spirit of the egoist argument, however, since the ends mentioned are wanted by the agent. But the other set of actions are those which we do, not because we want to, nor even because there is an end which we want to achieve, but because we feel ourselves *under an obligation* to do them. For example, someone may do something because he has promised to do it, and thus feels obligated, even though he does not want to do it. It is sometimes suggested that in such cases we do the action because, after all, we want to keep our promises; so, even here, we are doing what we want. However, this dodge will not work: if I have promised to do something, and if I do not want to do it, then it is simply false to say that I want to keep my promise. In such cases we feel a conflict precisely because we do *not* want to do what we feel obligated to do. It is reasonable to think that Smith's action falls roughly into this second category: he might stay behind, not because he wants to, but because he feels that his friend needs help.

But suppose we were to concede, for the sake of the argument, that all voluntary action is motivated by the agent's wants, or at least that Smith is so motivated. Even if this were granted, it would not follow that Smith is acting selfishly or from self-interest. For if Smith wants to do something that will help his friend, even when it means forgoing his own enjoyments, that is precisely what makes him *un*selfish. What else could unselfishness be, if not wanting to help others? Another way to put the same point is to say that it is the *object* of a want that determines whether it is selfish or not. The mere fact that I am acting on *my* wants does not mean that I am acting selfishly; that depends on *what it is* that I want. If I want only my own good, and care nothing for others, then I am selfish; but if I also want other people to be well-off and happy, and if I act on *that* desire, then my action is not selfish. So much for this argument.

b. The second argument for psychological egoism is this. Since so-called unselfish actions always produce a sense of self-satisfaction in the agent,[2] and since this sense of satisfaction is a pleasant state of consciousness, it follows that the point of the action is really to achieve a pleasant state of consciousness, rather than to bring about any good for others. Therefore, the action is "unselfish" only at a superficial level of analysis. Smith will feel much better with himself for having stayed to help his friend—if he had gone to the country, he would have felt terrible about it—and that is the real point of the action. According to a well-known story, this argument was once expressed by Abraham Lincoln:

> Mr. Lincoln once remarked to a fellow-passenger on an old-time mud-coach that all men were prompted by selfishness in doing good. His fellow-passenger was antagonizing this position when they were passing over a corduroy bridge that spanned a slough. As they crossed this bridge they espied an old razor-backed sow on the bank making a terrible noise because her pigs had got into the slough and were in danger of drowning. As the old coach began to climb the hill, Mr. Lincoln called out, "Driver, can't you stop just a moment?" Then Mr. Lincoln jumped out, ran

---

[2] Or, as it is sometimes said, "It gives him a clear conscience," or "He couldn't sleep at night if he had done otherwise," or "He would have been ashamed of himself for not doing it," and so on.

back, and lifted the little pigs out of the mud and water and placed them on the bank. When he returned, his companion remarked: "Now, Abe, where does selfishness come in on this little episode?" "Why, bless your soul, Ed, that was the very essence of selfishness. I should have had no peace of mind all day had I gone on and left that suffering old sow worrying over those pigs. I did it to get peace of mind, don't you see?"[3]

This argument suffers from defects similar to the previous one. Why should we think that merely because someone derives satisfaction from helping others this makes him selfish? Isn't the unselfish man precisely the one who *does* derive satisfaction from helping others, while the selfish man does not? If Lincoln "got peace of mind" from rescuing the piglets, does this show him to be selfish, or, on the contrary, doesn't it show him to be compassionate and good-hearted? (If a man were truly selfish, why should it bother his conscience that *others* suffer—much less pigs?) Similarly, it is nothing more than shabby sophistry to say, because Smith takes satisfaction in helping his friend, that he is behaving selfishly. If we say this rapidly, while thinking about something else, perhaps it will sound all right; but if we speak slowly, and pay attention to what we are saying, it sounds plain silly.

Moreover, suppose we ask *why* Smith derives satisfaction from helping his friend. The answer will be, it is because Smith cares for him and wants him to succeed. If Smith did not have these concerns, then he would take no pleasure in assisting him; and these concerns, as we have already seen, are the marks of unselfishness, not selfishness. To put the point more generally: if we have a positive attitude toward the attainment of some goal, then we may derive satisfaction from attaining that goal. But the *object* of our attitude is *the attainment of that goal;* and we must want to attain the goal *before* we can find any satisfaction in it. We do not, in other words, desire some sort of "pleasurable consciousness" and then try to figure out how to achieve it; rather, we desire all sorts of different things—money, a new fishing-boat, to be a better chess-player, to get a promotion in our work, etc.—and because we desire these things, we derive satisfaction from attaining them. And so, if someone desires the welfare and happiness of another person, he will derive satisfaction from that; but this does not mean that this satisfaction is the object of his desire, or that he is in any way selfish on account of it.

It is a measure of the weakness of psychological egoism that these insupportable arguments are the ones most often advanced in its favor. Why, then, should anyone ever have thought it a true view? Perhaps because of a desire for theoretical simplicity: In thinking about human conduct, it would be nice if there were some simple formula that would unite the diverse phenomena of human behavior under a single explanatory principle, just as simple formulae in physics bring together a great many apparently different phenomena. And since it is obvious that self-regard is an overwhelmingly important factor in motivation, it is only natural to wonder whether all motivation might not be explained in these terms. But the answer is clearly No; while a great many

---

[3] Frank C. Sharp, *Ethics* (New York, 1928), pp. 74–75. Quoted from the Springfield (Ill.) *Monitor* in the *Outlook*, vol. 56, p. 1059.

human actions are motivated entirely or in part by self-interest, only by a deliberate distortion of the facts can we say that all conduct is so motivated. This will be clear, I think, if we correct three confusions which are commonplace. The exposure of these confusions will remove the last traces of plausibility from the psychological egoist thesis.

The first is the confusion of selfishness with self-interest. The two are clearly not the same. If I see a physician when I am feeling poorly, I am acting in my own interest but no one would think of calling me "selfish" on account of it. Similarly, brushing my teeth, working hard at my job, and obeying the law are all in my self-interest but none of these are examples of selfish conduct. This is because selfish behavior is behavior that ignores the interests of others, in circumstances in which their interests ought not to be ignored. This concept has a definite evaluative flavor; to call someone "selfish" is not just to describe his action but to condemn it. Thus, you would not call me selfish for eating a normal meal in normal circumstances (although it may surely be in my self-interest); but you would call me selfish for hoarding food while others about are starving.

The second confusion is the assumption that every action is done *either* from self-interest or from other-regarding motives. Thus, the egoist concludes that if there is no such thing as genuine altruism then all actions must be done from self-interest. But this is certainly a false dichotomy. The man who continues to smoke cigarettes, even after learning about the connection between smoking and cancer, is surely not acting from self-interest, not even by his own standards—self-interest would dictate that he quit smoking at once—and he is not acting altruistically either. He *is*, no doubt, smoking for the pleasure of it, but all that this shows is that undisciplined pleasure-seeking and acting from self-interest are very different. This is what led Butler to remark that "The thing to be lamented is, not that men have so great regard to their own good or interest in the present world, for they have not enough."[4]

The last two paragraphs show (*a*) that it is false that all actions are selfish, and (*b*) that it is false that all actions are done out of self-interest. And it should be noted that these two points can be made, and were, without any appeal to putative examples of altruism.

The third confusion is the common but false assumption that a concern for one's own welfare is incompatible with any genuine concern for the welfare of others. Thus, since it is obvious that everyone (or very nearly everyone) does desire his own well-being, it might be thought that no one can really be concerned with others. But again, this is false. There is no inconsistency in desiring that everyone, including oneself *and* others, be well-off and happy. To be sure, it may happen on occasion that our own interests conflict with the interests of others, and in these cases we will have to make hard choices. But even in these cases we might sometimes opt for the interests of others, especially when

---

[4] *The Works of Joseph Butler,* edited by W. E. Gladstone (Oxford, 1896), vol. II, p. 26. It should be noted that most of the ponits I am making against psychological egoism were first made by Butler. Butler made all the important points; all that is left for us is to remember them.

the others involved are our family or friends. But more importantly, not all cases are like this: sometimes we are able to promote the welfare of others when our own interests are not involved at all. In these cases not even the strongest self-regard need prevent us from acting considerately toward others.

Once these confusions are cleared away, it seems to me obvious enough that there is no reason whatever to accept psychological egoism. On the contrary, if we simply observe people's behavior with an open mind, we may find that a great deal of it is motivated by self-regard, but by no means all of it; and that there is no reason to deny that "the moral institution of life" can include a place for the virtue of beneficence.[5]

3. The ethical egoist would say at this point, "Of course it is possible for people to act altruistically, and perhaps many people do act that way—but there is no reason why they *should* do so. A person is under no obligation to do anything except what is in his own interests."[6] This is really quite a radical doctrine. Suppose I have an urge to set fire to some public building (say, a department store) just for the fascination of watching the spectacular blaze: according to this view, the fact that several people might be burned to death provides no reason whatever why I should not do it. After all, this only concerns *their* welfare, not my own, and according to the ethical egoist the only person I need think of is myself.

Some might deny that ethical egoism has any such monstrous consequences. They would point out that it is really to my own advantage not to set fire—for, if I do that I may be caught and put into prison (unlike Gyges, I have no magic ring for protection). Moreover, even if I could avoid being caught it is still to my advantage to respect the rights and interests of others, for it is to my advantage to live in a society in which people's rights and interests are respected. Only in such a society can I live a happy and secure life; so, in acting kindly toward others, I would merely be doing my part to create and maintain the sort of society which it is to my advantage to have.[7] Therefore, it is said, the egoist would not be such a bad man; he would be as kindly and considerate as anyone else, because he would see that it is to his own advantage to be kindly and considerate.

This is a seductive line of thought, but it seems to me mistaken. Certainly it is to everyone's advantage (including the egoist's) to preserve a stable society where people's interests are generally protected. But there is no reason for the egoist to think that merely because *he* will not honor the rules of the social game, decent society will collapse. For the vast majority of people are not egoists, and there is no reason to think that they will be converted by his

---

[5] The capacity for altruistic behavior is not unique to human beings. Some interesting experiments with rhesus monkeys have shown that these animals will refrain from operating a device for securing food if this causes other animals to suffer pain. See Masserman, Wechkin, and Terris, " 'Altruistic' Behavior in Rhesus Monkeys," *The American Journal of Psychiatry*, vol. 121 (1964), 584–585.

[6] I take this to be the view of Ayn Rand, in so far as I understand her confusing doctrine.

[7] Cf. Thomas Hobbes, *Leviathan* (London, 1651), chap. 17.

example—especially if he is discreet and does not unduly flaunt his style of life. What this line of reasoning shows is not that the egoist himself must act benevolently, but that he must encourage *others* to do so. He must take care to conceal from public view his own self-centered method of decision-making, and urge others to act on precepts very different from those on which he is willing to act.

The rational egoist, then, cannot advocate that egoism be universally adopted by everyone. For he wants a world in which his own interests are maximized; and if other people adopted the egoistic policy of pursuing their own interests to the exclusion of his interests, as he pursues his interests to the exclusion of theirs, then such a world would be impossible. So he himself will be an egoist, but he will want others to be altruists.

This brings us to what is perhaps the most popular "refutation" of ethical egoism current among philosophical writers—the argument that ethical egoism is at bottom inconsistent because it cannot be universalized.[8] The argument goes like this:

To say that any action or policy of action is *right* (or that it *ought* to be adopted) entails that it is right for *anyone* in the same sort of circumstances. I cannot, for example, say that it is right for me to lie to you, and yet object when you lie to me (provided, of course, that the circumstances are the same). I cannot hold that it is all right for me to drink your beer and then complain when you drink mine. This is just the requirement that we be consistent in our evaluations; it is a requirement of logic. Now it is said that ethical egoism cannot meet this requirement because, as we have already seen, the egoist would not want others to act in the same way that he acts. Moreover, suppose he *did* advocate the universal adoption of egoistic policies: he would be saying to Peter, "You ought to pursue your own interests even if it means destroying Paul"; and he would be saying to Paul, "You ought to pursue your own interest even if it means destroying Peter." The attitudes expressed in these two recommendations seem clearly inconsistent—he is urging the advancement of Peter's interest at one moment, and countenancing their defeat at the next. Therefore, the argument goes, there is no way to maintain the doctrine of ethical egoism as a consistent view about how we ought to act. We will fall into inconsistency whenever we try.

What are we to make of this argument? Are we to conclude that ethical egoism has been refuted? Such a conclusion, I think, would be unwarranted; for I think that we can show, contrary to this argument, how ethical egoism can be maintained consistently. We need only to interpret the egoist's position in a sympathetic way: we should say that he has in mind a certain kind of world which he would prefer over all others; it would be a world in which his own interests were maximized, regardless of the effects on other people. The egoist's primary policy of action, then, would be to act in such a way as to bring about, as nearly as possible, this sort of world. Regardless of however morally

[8] See, for example, Brian Medlin, "Ultimate Principles and Ethical Egoism," *Australasian Journal of Philosophy,* vol. 35 (1957), 111–118; and D. H. Monro, *Empiricism and Ethics* (Cambridge, 1967), chap. 16.

reprehensible we might find it, there is nothing *inconsistent* in someone's adopting this as his ideal and acting in a way calculated to bring it about. And if someone did adopt this as his ideal, then he would not advocate universal egoism; as we have already seen, he would want other people to be altruists. So, if he advocates any principles of conduct for the general public, they will be altruistic principles. This would not be inconsistent; on the contrary, it would be perfectly consistent with his goal of creating a world in which his own interests are maximized. To be sure, he would have to be deceitful; in order to secure the good will of others, and a favorable hearing for his exhortations to altruism, he would have to pretend that he was himself prepared to accept altruistic principles. But again, that would be all right; from the egoist's point of view, this would merely be a matter of adopting the necessary means to the achievement of his goal—and while we might not approve of this, there is nothing inconsistent about it. Again, it might be said: "He advocates one thing, but does another. Surely *that's* inconsistent." But it is not; for what he advocates and what he does are both calculated as means to an end (the *same* end, we might note); and as such, he is doing what is rationally required in each case. Therefore, contrary to the previous argument, there is nothing inconsistent in the ethical egoist's view. He cannot be refuted by the claim that he contradicts himself.

Is there, then, no way to refute the ethical egoist? If by "refute" we mean show that he has made some *logical* error, the answer is that there is not. However, there is something more that can be said. The egoist challenge to our ordinary moral convictions amounts to a demand for an explanation of why we should adopt certain policies of action, namely policies in which the good of others is given importance. We can give an answer to this demand, albeit an indirect one. The reason one ought not to do actions that would hurt other people is: other people would be hurt. The reason one ought to do actions that would benefit other people is: other people would be benefited. This may at first seem like a piece of philosophical sleight-of-hand, but it is not. The point is that the welfare of human beings is something that most of us value *for its own sake,* and not merely for the sake of something else. Therefore, when *further* reasons are demanded for valuing the welfare of human beings, we cannot point to anything further to satisfy this demand. It is not that we have no reason for pursuing these policies, but that our reason *is* that these policies are for the good of human beings.

So: if we are asked "Why shouldn't I set fire to this department store?" one answer would be "Because if you do, people may be burned to death." This is a complete, sufficient reason which does not require qualification or supplementation of any sort. If someone seriously wants to know why this action shouldn't be done, that's the reason. If we are pressed further and asked the sceptical question "But why shouldn't I do actions that will harm others?" we may not know what to say—but this is because the questioner has included in his question the very answer we would like to give: "Why shouldn't you do actions that will harm others? Because, doing those actions would harm others."

The egoist, no doubt, will not be happy with this. He will protest that *we* may accept this as a reason, but *he* does not. And here the argument stops: there are limits to what can be accomplished by argument, and if the egoist really doesn't care about other people—if he honestly doesn't care whether they are helped or hurt by his actions—then we have reached those limits. If we want to persuade him to act decently toward his fellow humans, we will have to make our appeal to such other attitudes as he does possess, by threats, bribes, or other cajolery. That is all that we can do.

Though some may find this situation distressing (we would like to be able to show that the egoist is just *wrong*), it holds no embarrassment for common morality. What we have come up against is simply a fundamental requirement of rational action, namely, that the existence of reasons for action always depends on the prior existence of certain attitudes in the agent. For example, the fact that a certain course of action would make the agent a lot of money is a reason for doing it only if the agent wants to make money; the fact that practicing at chess makes one a better player is a reason for practicing only if one wants to be a better player; and so on. Similarly, the fact that a certain action would help the agent is a reason for doing the action only if the agent cares about his own welfare, and the fact that an action would help others is a reason for doing it only if the agent cares about others. In this respect ethical egoism and what we might call ethical altruism are in exactly the same fix: both require that the agent *care* about himself, or about other people, before they can get started.

So a nonegoist will accept "It would harm another person" as a reason not to do an action simply because he cares about what happens to that other person. When the egoist says that he does *not* accept that as a reason, he is saving something quite extraordinary. He is saying that he has no affection for friends or family, that he never feels pity or compassion, that he is the sort of person who can look on scenes of human misery with complete indifference, so long as he is not the one suffering. Genuine egoists, people who really don't care at all about anyone other than themselves, are rare. It is important to keep this in mind when thinking about ethical egoism; it is easy to forget just how fundamental to human psychological makeup the feeling of sympathy is. Indeed, a man without any sympathy at all would scarcely be recognizable as a man; and that is what makes ethical egoism such a disturbing doctrine in the first place.

4. There are, of course, many different ways in which the sceptic might challenge the assumptions underlying our moral practice. In this essay I have discussed only two of them, the two put forward by Glaucon in the passage that I cited from Plato's *Republic*. It is important that the assumptions underlying our moral practice should not be confused with particular judgments made within that practice. To defend one is not to defend the other. We may assume—quite properly, if my analysis has been correct—that the virtue of beneficence does, and indeed should, occupy an important place in "the moral institution of life"; and yet we may make constant and miserable errors when it comes to judging when and in what ways this virtue is to be exercised. Even worse, we may often be able to make accurate moral judgments, and know what we ought to do, but not do it. For these ills, philosophy alone is not the cure.

Utility, Pleasure, and the Good

JEREMY BENTHAM

Jeremy Bentham (1748–1832) was the leading figure in the early phase of the British Utilitarian Movement in philosophy and politics. He was primarily interested in legal reform and constantly sought a philosophical basis for the reforms he advocated. In this connection he wrote highly influential works on the theory of law and on ethics.

Of the Principle of Utility

1. Nature has placed mankind under the governance of two sovereign masters, *pain* and *pleasure*. It is for them alone to point out what we ought to do, as well as to determine what we shall do. On the one hand the standard of right and wrong, on the other the chain of causes and effects, are fastened to their throne. They govern us in all we do, in all we say, in all we think: every effort we can make to throw off our subjection will serve but to demonstrate and confirm it. In words a man may pretend to abjure their empire; but in reality he will remain subject to it all the while. The *principle of utility* recognises this subjection, and assumes it for the foundation of that system, the object of which is to rear the fabric of felicity by the hands of reason and of law. Systems which attempt to question it, deal in sounds instead of sense, in caprice instead of reason, in darkness instead of light.

But enough of metaphor and declamation: it is not by such means that moral science is to be improved.

II. The principle of utility is the foundation of the present work: it will be proper therefore at the outset to give an explicit and determinate account of what is meant by it. By the principle of utility is meant that principle which approves or disapproves of every action whatsoever, according to the tendency which it appears to have to augment or diminish the happiness of the party whose interest is in question: or, what is the same thing in other words, to promote or to oppose that happiness. I say of every action whatsoever; and therefore not only of every action of a private individual, but of every measure of government.

III. By utility is meant that property in any object, whereby it tends to produce benefit, advantage, pleasure, good, or happiness (all this in the present case comes to the same thing) or (what comes again to the same thing) to prevent the happening of mischief, pain, evil, or unhappiness to the party whose interest is considered: if that party be the community in general, then the happiness of the community: if a particular individual, then the happiness of that individual.

IV. The interest of the community is one of the most general expressions that

Source: Jeremy Bentham, *An Introduction to the Principles of Morals and Legislation* (1780).

can occur in the phraseology of morals: no wonder that the meaning of it is often lost. When it has a meaning, it is this. The community is a fictitious *body,* composed of the individual persons who are considered as constituting as it were its *members.* The interest of the community then is, what?—the sum of the interests of the several members who compose it.

V. It is in vain to talk of the interest of the community, without understanding what is the interest of the individual. A thing is said to promote the interest, or to be *for* the interest, of an individual, when it tends to add to the sum total of his pleasures: or, what comes to the same thing, to diminish the sum total of his pains.

VI. An action then may be said to be conformable to the principle of utility, or, for shortness sake, to utility (meaning with respect to the community at large) when the tendency it has to augment the happiness of the old community is greater than any it has to diminish it.

VII. A measure of government (which is but a particular kind of action, performed by a particular person or persons) may be said to be conformable to or dictated by the principle of utility, when in like manner the tendency which it has to augment the happiness of the community is greater than any which it has to diminish it.

VIII. When an action, or in particular a measure of government, is supposed by a man to be conformable to the principle of utility, it may be convenient, for the purposes of discourse to imagine a kind of law or dictate, called a law or dictate of utility: and to speak of the action in question, as being conformable to such law or dictate.

IX. A man may be said to be a partizan of the principle of utility, when the approbation or disapprobation he annexes to any action, or to any measure, is determined by and proportioned to the tendency which he conceives it to have to augment or to diminish the happiness of the community: or in other words, to its conformity or unconformity to the laws or dictates of utility.

X. If an action that is conformable to the principle of utility one may always say either that it is one that ought to be done, or at least that it is no one that ought not to be done. One may say also, that it is right it should be done; at least that it is not wrong it should be done: that it is a right action; at least that it is not a wrong action. When thus interpreted, the words *ought,* and *right* and *wrong,* and others of that stamp, have a meaning: when otherwise, they have none.

XI. Has the rectitude of this principle been ever formally contested? It should seem that it had, by those who have not known what they are meaning. Is it susceptible of any direct proof? It should seem not: for that which is used to prove every thing else, cannot itself be proved: a chain of proofs must have their commencement somewhere. To give such a proof is as impossible as it is needless.

XII. Not that there is or ever has been that human creature breathing, however stupid or perverse, who has not on many, perhaps on most occasions of his life, deferred to it. By the natural constitution of the human frame, on most occasions of their lives men in general embrace this principle, without thinking of it: if not for the ordering of their own actions, yet for the trying of their own actions, as well as of those of other men. There have been, at the same time, not many, perhaps, even of the most intelligent, who have been disposed to embrace it purely and without reserve. There are even few who have not taken some occasion or other to quarrel with it, either on account of their not understanding always how to apply it, or on account of some prejudice or other which they were afraid to examine into, or could not bear to part with. For such is the stuff that man is made of: in principle and in practise, in a right track and in a wrong one, the rarest of all human qualities is consistency.

XIII. When a man attempts to combat the principle of utility, it is with reasons drawn, without his being aware of it, from that very principle itself. His arguments, if they prove any thing, prove not that the principle is *wrong,* but that, according to the applications he supposes to be made of it, it is *misapplied.* Is it possible for a man to move the earth? Yes; but he must find out another earth to stand upon.

XIV. To disprove the propriety of it by arguments is impossible; but, from the causes that have been mentioned, or from some confused or partial view of it, a man may happen to be disposed not to relish it. Where this is the case, if he thinks the settling of his opinions on such a subject worth the trouble, let him take the following steps, and at length, perhaps, he may come to reconcile himself to it.

1. Let him settle with himself, whether he would wish to discard this principle altogether; if so, let him consider what it is that all his reasonings (in matters of politics especially) can amount to?

2. If we would, let him settle with himself, whether he would judge and act without any principle, or whether there is any other he would judge and act by?

3. If there be, let him examine and satisfy himself whether the principle he thinks he has found is really any separate intelligible principle; or whether it be not a mere principle in words, a kind of phrase, which at bottom expresses neither more nor less than the mere averment of his own unfounded sentiments; that is, what in another person he might be apt to call caprice?

4. If he is inclined to think that his own approbation and disapprobation, annexed to the idea of an act, without any regard to its consequences, is a sufficient foundation for him to judge and act upon, let him ask himself whether his sentiment is to be a standard of right and wrong, with respect to every other man, or whether every man's sentiment has the same privilege of being a standard to itself?

5. In the first case, let him ask himself whether his principle is not despotical, and hostile to all the rest of the human race?

6. In the second case, whether it is not anarchial, and whether at this rate there are not as many different standards of right and wrong as there are men? and whether even to the same man, the same thing, which is right to-day, may not (without the least change in its nature) be wrong to-morrow? and whether the same thing is not right and wrong in the same place at the same time? and in either case, whether all argument is not at an end? and whether, when two men have said, "I like this," and "I don't like it," they can (upon such principle) have anything more to say?

7. If he should have said to himself, No: for that the sentiment which he proposes as a standard must be grounded on reflection, let him say on what

particulars the reflection is to turn? If on particulars having relation to the utility of the act, then let him say whether this is not deserting his own principle and borrowing assistance from that very one in opposition to which he sets it up: or if not on those particulars, on what other particulars?

8. If he should be for compounding the matter, and adopting his own principle in part, and the principle of utility in part, let him say how far he will adopt it?

9. When he has settled with himself where he will stop, then let him ask himself how he justifies to himself adopting it so far? and why he will not adopt it any farther?

10. Admitting any other principle than the principle of utility to be a right principle, a principle that it is right for a man to pursue; admitting (what is not true) that the word *right* can have a meaning without reference to utility, let him say whether there is any such thing as a *motive* than a man can have to pursue the dictates of it: if there is, let him say what that motive is, and how it is to be distinguished from those which enforce the dictates of utility: if not, then lastly let him say what it is this other principle can be good for?

Of the Four Sanctions or Sources of Pain and Pleasure

I. It has been shown that the happiness of the individuals, of whom a community is composed, that is, their pleasures and their security, is the end and the sole end which the legislator ought to have in view: the sole standard, in conformity to which each individual ought, as far as depends upon the legislator, to be *made* to fashion his behaviour. But whether it be this or any thing else that is to be *done*. there is nothing by which a man can ultimately be *made* to do it, but either pain or pleasure. Having taken a general view of these two grand objects (*viz.* pleasure, and what comes to the same thing, immunity from pain) in the character of *final*.causes: it will be necessary to take a view of pleasure and pain itself, in the character of *efficient* causes or means.

II. There are four distinguishable sources from which pleasure and pain are in use to flow: considered separately, they may be termed the *physical,* the *political,* the *moral,* and the *religious:* and inasmuch as the pleasures and pains belonging to each of them are capable of giving a binding force to any law or rule of conduct, they may all of them be termed *sanctions.*

III. If it be in the present life, and from the ordinary course of nature, not purposely modified by the interposition of the will of any human being, nor by any extraordinary interposition of any superior invisible being, that the pleasure or the pain takes place or is expected, it may be said to issue from or to belong to the *physical sanction.*

IV. If at the hands of a *particular* person or set of persons in the community, who under names correspondent to that of *judge,* are chosen for the particular purpose of dispensing it, according to the will of the sovereign or supreme ruling power in the state, it may be said to issue from the *political sanction.*

V. If at the hands of such *chance* persons in the community, as the party in question may happen in the course of his life to have concerns with, according to each man's spontaneous disposition, and not according to any settled or concerted rule, it may be said to issue from the *moral or popular sanction*.

VI. If from the immediate hand of a superior invisible being, either in the present life, or in a future, it may be said to issue from the *religious sanction*.

VII. Pleasures or pains which may be expected to issue from the *physical, political,* or *moral* sanctions, must all of them be expected to be experienced, if ever, in the *present* life: those which may be expected to issue from the *religious* sanction, may be expected to be experienced either in the *present* life or in a *future*.

VIII. Those which can be experienced in the present life, can of course be no others than such as human nature in the course of the present life is susceptible of: and from each of these sources may flow all the pleasures or pains of which, in the course of the present life, human nature is susceptible. With regard to these then (with which alone we have in this place any concern) those of them which belong to any one of the other three: the only difference there is among them lies in the circumstances that accompany their production. A suffering which befalls a man in the natural and spontaneous course of things, shall be styled, for instance, a *calamity;* in which case, if it be supposed to befall him through any imprudence of his, it may be styled a punishment issuing from the physical sanction. Now this same suffering, if inflicted by the law, will be what is commonly called a *punishment;* if incurred for want of any friendly assistance, which the misconduct, or supposed misconduct, of the sufferer has occasioned to be withholden, a punishment issuing from the *moral* sanction; if through the immediate interposition of a particular providence, a punishment issuing from the religious sanction.

IX. A man's goods, or his person, are consumed by fire. If this happened to him by what is called an accident, it was a calamity: if by reason of his own imprudence (for instance, from his neglecting to put his candle out) it may be styled a punishment of the physical sanction: if it happened to him by the sentence of the political magistrate, a punishment belonging to the political sanction; that is, what is commonly called a punishment: if for want of any assistance which his *neighbour* withheld from him out of some dislike to his *moral* character, a punishment of the *moral* sanction: if by an immediate act of *God's* displeasure, manifested on account of some *sin* committed by him, or through any distraction of mind, occasioned by the dread of such displeasure, a punishment of the *religious* sanction.

X. As to such of the pleasures and pains belonging to the religious sanction, as regard a future life, of what kind these may be we cannot know. These lie not open to our observation. During the present life they are matter only of expectation: and, whether that expectation be derived from natural or revealed religion, the particular kind of pleasure or pain, if it be different from all those which lie open to our observation, is what we can have no idea of. The best ideas we can obtain of such pains and pleasures are altogether unliquidated in point of quality. In what other respects our ideas of them *may* be liquidated will be considered in another place.

XI. Of these four sanctions the physical is altogether, we may observe, the ground-work of the political and the moral: so is it also of the religious, in as far as the latter bears relation to the present life. It is included in each of those other three. This may operate in any case (that is, any of the pains or pleasures belonging to it may operate) independently of *them:* none of *them* can operate but by means of this. In a word, the powers of nature may operate of themselves; but neither the magistrate, nor men at large, *can* operate, nor is God in the case in question *supposed* to operate, but through the powers of nature.

XII. For these four objects, which in their nature have so much in common, it seemed of use to find a common name. It seemed of use, in the first place, for the convenience of giving a name to certain pleasures and pains, for which a name equally characteristic could hardly otherwise have been found: in the second place, for the sake of holding up the efficacy of certain moral forces, the influence of which is apt not to be sufficiently attended to. Does the political sanction exert an influence over the conduct of mankind? The moral, the religious sanctions do so too. In every inch of his career are the operations of the political magistrate liable to be aided or impeded by these two foreign powers: who, one or other of them, or both, are sure to be either his rivals or his allies. Does it happen to him to leave them out in his calculations? he will be sure almost to find himself mistaken in the result. Of all this we shall find abundant proofs in the sequel of this work. It behoves him, therefore, to have them continually before his eyes; and that under such a name as exhibits the relation they bear to his own purposes and designs.

Value of a Lot of Pleasure or Pain, How To Be Measured

I. Pleasures then, and the avoidance of pains, are the *ends* which the legislator has in view: it behoves him therefore to understand their *value.* Pleasures and pains are the *instruments* he has to work with: it behoves him therefore to understand their force, which is again, in other words, their value.

II. To a person considered *by himself,* the value of a pleasure or pain considered *by itself,* will be greater or less, according to the four following circumstances[1]:

1. Its *intensity.*
2. Its *duration.*
3. Its *certainty* or *uncertainty.*
4. Its *propinquity* or *remoteness.*

---

[1] These circumstances have since been denominated *elements* or *dimensions* of *value* in a pleasure or a pain.

Not long after the publication of the first edition, the following memoriter verses were framed, in the view of lodging more effectually, in the memory, these points, on which the whole fabric of morals and legislation may be seen to rest.

> Intense, long, certain, speedy, fruitful, pure—
> Such marks in *pleasures* and in *pains* endure.
> Such pleasures seek if *private* be thy end:
> If it be *public,* wide let them *extend.*
> Such *pains* avoid, whichever be thy view:
> If pains *must* come, let them *extend* to few.

III. These are the circumstances which are to be considered in estimating a pleasure or a pain considered each of them by itself. But when the value of any pleasure or pain is considered for the purpose of estimating the tendency of any *act* by which it is produced, there are two other circumstances to be taken into the account; these are,

5. Its *fecundity,* or the chance it has of being followed by sensations of the *same* kind: that is, pleasures, if it be a pleasure: pains, if it be a pain.

6. Its *purity,* or the chance it has of *not* being followed by sensations of the *opposite* kind: that is, pains, if it be a pleasure: pleasure, if it be a pain.

These two last, however, are in strictness scarcely to be deemed properties of the pleasure or the pain itself; they are not, therefore, in strictness to be taken into the account of the value of that pleasure or that pain. They are in strictness to be deemed properties only of the act, or other event, by which such pleasure or pain has been produced; and accordingly are only to be taken into the account of the tendency of such act or such event.

IV. To a *number* of persons, with reference to each of whom the value of a pleasure or a pain is considered, it will be greater or less, according to seven circumstances: to wit, the six preceding ones; *viz.*

1. Its *intensity.*
2. Its *duration.*
3. Its *certainty* or *uncertainty.*
4. Its *propinquity* or *remoteness.*
5. Its *fecundity.*
6. Its *purity.*

And one other; to wit:

7. Its *extent;* that is, the number of persons to whom it *extends;* or (in other words) who are affected by it.

V. To take an exact account then of the general tendency of any act, by which the interests of a community are affected, proceed as follows. Begin with any one person of those whose interests seem most immediately to be affected by it: and take an account,

1. Of the value of each distinguishable *pleasure* which appears to be produced by it in the *first* instance.

2. Of the value of each *pain* which appears to be produced by it in the *first* instance.

3. Of the value of each pleasure which appears to be produced by it *after* the first. This constitutes the *fecundity* of the first *pleasure* and the *impurity* of the first *pain.*

4. Of the value of each *pain* which appears to be produced by it after the first. This constitutes the *fecundity* of the first *pain,* and the *impurity* of the first pleasure.

5. Sum up all the values of all the *pleasures* on the one side, and those of all the pains on the other. The balance, if it be on the side of pleasure, will give the *good* tendency of the act upon the whole, with respect to the interests of that *individual* person; if on the side of pain, the *bad* tendency of it upon the whole.

6. Take an account of the *number* of persons whose interests appear to be concerned; and repeat the above process with respect to each. *Sum up* the num-

bers expressive of the degrees of *good* tendency, which the act has, with respect to each individual, in regard to whom the tendency of it is *good* upon the whole: do this again with respect to each individual, in regard to whom the tendency of it is *good* upon the whole: do this again with respect to each individual, in regard to whom the tendency of it is *bad* upon the whole. Take the *balance;* which, if on the side of *pleasure,* will give the general *good tendency* of the act, with respect to the total number or community of individuals concerned; if on the side of pain, the general *evil tendency,* with respect to the same community.

VI. It is not to be expected that this process should be strictly pursued previously to every moral judgment, or to every legislative or judicial operation. It may, however, be always kept in view: and as near as the process actually pursued on these occasions approaches to it, so near will such process approach to the character of an exact one.

VII. The same process is alike applicable to pleasure and pain, in whatever shape they appear: and by whatever denomination they are distinguished: to pleasure, whether it be called *good* (which is properly the cause or instrument of pleasure) or *profit* (which is distant pleasure, or the cause or instrument of distant pleasure) or *convenience,* or *advantage, benefit, emolument, happiness,* and so forth: to pain, whether it be called *evil* (which corresponds to *good*) or *mischief,* or *inconvenience,* or *disadvantage,* or *loss,* or *unhappiness,* and so forth.

VIII. Nor is this a novel and unwarranted, any more than it is a useless theory. In all this there is nothing but what the practice of mankind, wheresoever they have a clear view of their own interest, is perfectly conformable to. An article of property, and estate in land, for instance, is valuable, on what account? On account of the pleasures of all kinds which it enables a man to produce, and what comes to the same thing the pains of all kinds which it enables him to avert. But the value of such an article of property is universally understood to rise or fall according to the length or shortness of the time which a man had in it: the certainty or uncertainty of its coming into possession: and the nearness or remoteness of the time at which, if at all, it is to come into possession. As to the *intensity* of the pleasures which a man may derive from it, this is never thought of, because it depends upon the use which each particular person may come to make of it; which cannot be estimated till the particular pleasures he may come to derive from it, or the particular pains he may come to exclude by means of it, are brought to view. For the same reason, neither does he think of the *fecundity* or *purity* of those pleasures.

Thus much for pleasure and pain, happiness and unhappiness, in *general.*

A Critique of Utilitarianism

BERNARD WILLIAMS

Bernard Williams (1929–   ) is professor of philosophy at Cambridge University, Cambridge, England. Among his books are *Morality* (1972) and *Problems of the Self* (1973).

. . .

Now, however, let us look more concretely at two examples, to see what utilitarianism might say about them, what we might say about utilitarianism and, most importantly of all, what would be implied by certain ways of thinking about the situations. The examples are inevitably schematized, and they are open to the objection that they beg as many questions as they illuminate. There are two ways in particular in which examples in moral philosophy tend to beg important questions. One is that, as presented, they arbitrarily cut off and restrict the range of alternative courses of action—this objection might particularly be made against the first of my two examples. The second is that they inevitably present one with the situation as a going concern, and cut off questions about how the agent got into it, and correspondingly about moral considerations which might flow from that: this objection might perhaps specially arise with regard to the second of my two situations. These difficulties, however, just have to be accepted, and if anyone finds these examples cripplingly defective in this sort of respect, then he must in his own thought rework them in richer and less question-begging form. If he feels that no presentation of any imagined situation can ever be other than misleading in morality, and that there can never be any substitute for the concrete experienced complexity of actual moral situations, then this discussion, with him, must certainly grind to a halt: but then one may legitimately wonder whether every discussion with him about conduct will not grind to a halt, including any discussion about the actual situations, since discussion about how one would think and feel about situations somewhat different from the actual (that is to say, situations to that extent imaginary) plays an important role in discussion of the actual.

1. George, who has just taken his Ph.D. in chemistry, finds it extremely difficult to get a job. He is not very robust in health, which cuts down the number of jobs he might be able to do satisfactorily. His wife has to go out to work to keep them, which itself causes a great deal of strain, since they have small children and there are severe problems about looking after them. The results of all this, especially on the children, are damaging. An older chemist, who knows about this situation, says that he can get George a decently paid job in a certain laboratory, which pursues research into chemical and biological

Source: Bernard Williams, "A Critique of Utilitarianism," in J. J. C. Smart and Bernard Williams, *Utilitarianism For and Against* (New York, 1973), pp. 96–118. Reprinted by permission of Cambridge University Press.

warfare. George says that he cannot accept this, since he is opposed to chemical and biological warfare. The older man replies that he is not too keen on it himself, come to that, but after all George's refusal is not going to make the job or the laboratory go away; what is more, he happens to know that if George refuses the job, it will certainly go to a contemporary of George's who is not inhibited by any such scruples and is likely if appointed to push along the research with greater zeal than George would. Indeed, it is not merely concern for George and his family, but (to speak frankly and in confidence) some alarm about this other man's excess of zeal, which has led the older man to offer to use his influence to get George the job . . . George's wife, to whom he is deeply attached, has views (the details of which need not concern us) from which it follows that at least there is nothing particularly wrong with research into CBW. What should he do?

2. Jim finds himself in the central square of a small South American town. Tied up against the wall are a row of twenty Indians, most terrified, a few defiant, in front of them several armed men in uniform. A heavy man in a sweat-stained khaki shirt turns out to be the captain in charge and, after a good deal of questioning of Jim which establishes that he got there by accident while on a botanical expedition, explains that the Indians are a random group of the inhabitants who, after recent acts of protest against the government, are just about to be killed to remind other possible protestors of the advantages of not protesting. However, since Jim is an honoured visitor from another land, the captain is happy to offer him a guest's privilege of killing one of the Indians himself. If Jim accepts, then as a special mark of the occasion, the other Indians will be let off. Of course, if Jim refuses, then there is no special occasion, and Pedro here will do what he was about to do when Jim arrived, and kill them all. Jim, with some desperate recollection of schoolboy fiction, wonders whether if he got hold of a gun, he could hold the captain, Pedro and the rest of the soldiers to threat, but it is quite clear from the set-up that nothing of that kind is going to work: any attempt at that sort of thing will mean that all the Indians will be killed, and himself. The men against the wall, and the other villagers, understand the situation, and are obviously begging him to accept. What should he do?

To these dilemmas, it seems to me that utilitarianism replies, in the first case, that George should accept the job, and in the second, that Jim should kill the Indian. Not only does utilitarianism give these answers but, if the situations are essentially as described and there are no further special factors, it regards them, it seems to me, as *obviously* the right answers. But many of us would certainly wonder whether, in (1), that could possibly be the right answer at all; and in the case of (2), even one who came to think that perhaps that was the answer, might well wonder whether it was obviously the answer. Nor is it just a question of the rightness or obviousness of these answers. It is also a question of what sort of considerations come into finding the answer. A feature of utilitarianism is that it cuts out a kind of consideration which for some others makes a difference to what they feel about such cases: a consideration involving the idea, as we might first and very simply put it, that each of us is specially responsible for what *he* does, rather than for what other people do. This is an idea closely connected with the value of integrity. It is often suspected that utilitarianism, at least in its direct forms, makes integrity as a value more or less unintelligible. I shall try to show that this suspicion is correct. Of course, even if that is correct, it would not necessarily follow that we should reject utilitarianism; perhaps, as utilitarians sometimes suggest, we should just forget about integrity, in favour of such things as a concern for the general good. However, if I am right, we cannot merely do that, since the reason why utilitarianism cannot understand integrity is that it cannot coherently describe the relations between a man's projects and his actions.

Two Kinds of Remoter Effect

A lot of what we have to say about this question will be about the relations between my projects and other people's projects. But before we get on to that, we should first ask whether we are assuming too hastily what the utilitarian answers to the dilemmas will be. In terms of more direct effects of the possible decisions, there does not indeed seem much doubt about the answer in either case; but it might be said that in terms of more remote or less evident effects counterweights might be found to enter the utilitarian scales. Thus the effect on George of a decision to take the job might be invoked, or its effect on others who might know of his decision. The possibility of there being more beneficent labours in the future from which he might be barred or disqualified, might be mentioned; and so forth. Such effects—in particular, possible effects on the agent's character, and effects on the public at large—are often invoked by utilitarian writers dealing with problems about lying or promise-breaking, and some similar considerations might be invoked here.

There is one very general remark that is worth making about arguments of this sort. The certainty that attaches to these hypotheses about possible effects is usually pretty low; in some cases, indeed, the hypothesis invoked is so implausible that it would scarcely pass if it were not being used to deliver the respectable moral answer, as in the standard fantasy that one of the effects of one's telling a particular lie is to weaken the disposition of the world at large to tell the truth. The demands on the certainty or probability of these beliefs as beliefs about particular actions are much milder than they would be on beliefs favouring the unconventional course. It may be said that this is as it should be, since the presumption must be in favour of the conventional course: but that scarcely seems a *utilitarian* answer, unless utilitarianism has already taken off in the direction of not applying the consequences to the particular act at all.

Leaving aside that very general point, I want to consider now two types of effect that are often invoked by utilitarians, and which might be invoked in connexion with these imaginary cases. The attitude or tone involved in invoking these effects may sometimes seem peculiar; but that sort of peculiarity soon becomes familiar in utilitarian discussions, and indeed it can be something of an achievement to retain a sense of it.

First, there is the psychological effect on the agent. Our descriptions of these situations have not so far taken account of how George or Jim will be after they have taken the one course or the other; and it might be said that if they take the course which seemed at first the utilitarian one, the effects on them will be in fact bad enough and extensive enough to cancel out the initial utilitarian advantages of that course. Now there is one version of this effect in which, for a utilitarian, some confusion must be involved, namely that in which the agent feels bad, his subsequent conduct and relations are crippled and so on, *because he thinks that he has done the wrong thing*—for if the balance of outcomes was as it appeared to be *before* invoking this effect, then he has not (from the utilitarian point of view) done the wrong thing. So that version of the effect, for a rational and utilitarian agent, could not possibly make any difference to the assessment of right and wrong. However, perhaps he is not a thoroughly rational agent, and is disposed to have bad feelings, whichever he decided to do. Now such feelings, which are from a strictly utilitarian point of view irrational— nothing, a utilitarian can point out, is advanced by having them—cannot, consistently, have any great weight in a utilitarian calculation. I shall consider in a moment an argument to suggest that they should have no weight at all in it. But short of that, the utilitarian could reasonably say that such feelings should not be encouraged, even if we accept their existence, and that to give them a lot of weight is to encourage them. Or, at the very best, even if they are straightforwardly and without any discount to be put into the calculation, their weight must be small: they are after all (and at best) one man's feelings.

That consideration might seem to have particular force in Jim's case. In George's case, his feelings represent a larger proportion of what is to be weighed, and are more commensurate in character with other items in the calculation. In Jim's case, however, his feelings might seem to be of very little weight compared with other things that are at stake. There is a powerful and recognizable appeal that can be made on this point: as that a refusal by Jim to do what he has been invited to do would be a kind of self-indulgent squeamishness. That is an appeal which can be made by other than utilitarians—indeed, there are some uses of it which cannot be consistently made by utilitarians, as when it essentially involves the idea that there is something dishonourable about such self-indulgence. But in some versions it is a familiar, and it must be said a powerful, weapon of utilitarianism. One must be clear, though, about what it can and cannot accomplish. The most it can do, so far as I can see, is to invite one to consider how seriously, and for what reasons, one feels that what one is invited to do is (in these circumstances) wrong, and in particular, to consider that question from the utilitarian point of view. When the agent is not seeing the situation from a utilitarian point of view, the appeal cannot force him to do so; and if he does come round to seeing it from a utilitarian point of view, there is virtually nothing left for the appeal to do. If he does not see it from a utilitarian point of view, he will not see his resistance to the invitation, and the unpleasant feelings he associates with accepting it, *just* as disagreeable experiences of his; they figure rather as emotional expressions of a thought that to accept would be wrong. He may be asked, as by the appeal, to consider whether he is right, and indeed whether he is fully serious, in thinking that. But the assertion of the appeal, that he is being self-indulgently squeamish, will not itself answer that question, or even help to answer it, since it essentially tells him to regard his feelings just as unpleasant experiences of his, and he cannot, by doing that, answer the question they pose when they are precisely not so regarded, but are regarded as indications[1] of what he thinks is right and wrong. If he does come round fully to the utilitarian point of view then of course he will regard these feelings just as unpleasant experiences of his. And once Jim—at least—has come to see them in that light, there is nothing left for the appeal to do, since *of course* his feelings, so regarded, are of virtually no weight at all in relation to the other things at stake. The "squeamishness" appeal is not an argument which adds in a hitherto neglected consideration. Rather, it is an invitation to consider the situation, and one's own feelings, from a utilitarian point of view.

The reason why the squeamishness appeal can be very unsettling, and one can be unnerved by the suggestion of self-indulgence in going against utilitarian considerations, is not that we are utilitarians who are uncertain what utilitarian value to attach to our moral feelings, but that we are partially at least not utilitarians, and cannot regard our moral feelings merely as objects of utilitarian value. Because our moral relation to the world is partly given by such feelings, and by a sense of what we can or cannot "live with," to come to regard those feelings from a purely utilitarian point of view, that is to say, as happenings outside one's moral self, is to lose a sense of one's moral identity; to lose, in the most literal way, one's integrity. At this point utilitarianism alienates one from one's moral feelings; we shall see a little later how, more basically, it alienates one from one's actions as well.

If, then, one is really going to regard one's feelings from a strictly utilitarian point of view, Jim should give very little weight at all to his; it seems almost indecent, in fact, once one has taken that point of view, to suppose that he should give any at all. In George's case one might feel that things were slightly different. It is interesting, though, that one reason why one might think that— namely that one person principally affected is his wife—is very dubiously available to a utilitarian. George's wife has some reason to be interested in George's integrity and his sense of it; the Indians, quite properly, have no interest in Jim's. But it is not at all clear how utilitarianism would describe that difference.

There is an argument, and a strong one, that a strict utilitarian should give not merely small extra weight, in calculations of right and wrong, to feelings of this kind, but that he should give absolutely no weight to them at all. This is based on the point, which we have already seen, that if a course of action is, before taking these sorts of feelings into account, utilitarianly preferable, then bad feelings about that kind of action will be from a utilitarian point of view irrational. Now it might be thought that even if that is so, it would not mean that in a utilitarian calculation such feelings should not be taken into account; it is after all a well-known boast of utilitarianism that it is a realistic outlook which seeks the best in the world as it is, and takes any form of happiness or unhappiness into account. While a utilitarian will no doubt seek to diminish the incidence of feelings which are utilitarianly irrational—or at least of disagreeable feelings which are so—he might be expected to take them into account while

---

[1] On the non-cognitivist meta-ethic in terms of which Smart presents his utilitarianism, the term "indications" here would represent an understatement.

they exist. This is without doubt classical utilitarian doctrine, but there is good reason to think that utilitarianism cannot stick to it without embracing results which are startlingly unacceptable and perhaps self-defeating.

Suppose that there is in a certain society a racial minority. Considering merely the ordinary interests of the other citizens, as opposed to their sentiments, this minority does no particular harm; we may suppose that it does not confer any very great benefits either. Its presence is in those terms neutral or mildly beneficial. However, the other citizens have such prejudices that they find the sight of this group, even the knowledge of its presence, very disagreeable. Proposals are made for removing in some way this minority. If we assume various quite plausible things (as that programmes to change the majority sentiment are likely to be protracted and ineffective) then even if the removal would be unpleasant for the minority, a utilitarian calculation might well end up favouring this step, especially if the minority were a rather small minority and the majority were very severely prejudiced, that is to say, were made very severely uncomfortable by the presence of the minority.

A utilitarian might find that conclusion embarrassing; and not merely because of its nature, but because of the grounds on which it is reached. While a utilitarian might be expected to take into account certain other sorts of consequences of the prejudice, as that a majority prejudice is likely to be displayed in conduct disagreeable to the minority, and so forth, he might be made to wonder whether the unpleasant experiences of the prejudiced people should be allowed, *merely as such,* to count. If he does count them, merely as such, then he has once more separated himself from a body of ordinary moral thought which he might have hoped to accommodate; he may also have started on the path of defeating his own view of things. For one feature of these sentiments is that they are from the utilitarian point of view itself irrational, and a thoroughly utilitarian person would either not have them, or if he found that he did tend to have them, would himself seek to discount them. Since the sentiments in question are such that a rational utilitarian would discount them in himself, it is reasonable to suppose that he should discount them in his calculations about society; it does not seem quite unreasonable for him to give just as much weight to feelings—considered just in themselves, one must recall, as experiences of those that have them—which are essentially based on views which are from a utilitarian point of view irrational, as to those which accord with utilitarian principles. Granted this idea, it seems reasonable for him to rejoin a body of moral thought in other respects congenial to him, and discount those sentiments, just considered in themselves, totally, on the principle that no pains or discomforts are to count in the utilitarian sum which their subjects have just because they hold views which are by utilitarian standards irrational. But if he accepts that, then in the cases we are at present considering no extra weight at all can be put in for bad feelings of George or Jim about their choices, if those choices are, leaving out those feelings, on the first round utilitarianly rational.

The psychological effect on the agent was the first of two general effects considered by utilitarians, which had to be discussed. The second is in general a more substantial item, but it need not take so long, since it is both clearer and has little application to the present cases. This is the *precedent effect.* As Burke rightly emphasized, this effect can be important: that one morally *can* do what someone has actually done, is a psychologically effective principle, if not a deontically valid one. For the effect to operate, obviously some conditions must hold on the publicity of the act and on such things as the status of the agent (such considerations weighed importantly with Sir Thomas More); what these may be will vary evidently with circumstances.

In order for the precedent effect to make a difference to a utilitarian calculation, it must be based upon a confusion. For suppose that there is an act which would be the best in the circumstances, except that doing it will encourage by precedent other people to do things which will not be the best things to do. Then the situation of those other people must be relevantly different from that of the original agent; if it were not, then in doing the same as what would be the best course for the original agent, they would necessarily do the best thing themselves. But if the situations are in this way relevantly different, it must be a confused perception which takes the first situation, and the agent's course in it, as an adequate precedent for the second.

However, the fact that the precedent effect, if it really makes a difference, is in this sense based on a confusion, does not mean that it is not perfectly real, nor that it is to be discounted: social effects are by their nature confused in this sort of way. What it does emphasize is that calculations of the precedent effect have got to be realistic, involving considerations of how people are actually likely to be influenced. In the present examples, however, it is very implausible to think that the precedent effect could be invoked to make any difference to the calculation. Jim's case is extraordinary enough, and it is hard to imagine who the recipients of the effect might be supposed to be; while George is not in a sufficiently public situation or role for the question to arise in that form, and in any case one might suppose that the motivations of others on such an issue were quite likely to be fixed one way or another already.

No appeal, then, to these other effects is going to make a difference to what the utilitarian will decide about our examples. Let us now look more closely at the structure of those decisions.

Integrity

The situations have in common that if the agent does not do a certain disagreeable thing, someone else will, and in Jim's situation at least the result, the state of affairs after the other man has acted, if he does, will be worse than after Jim has acted, if Jim does. The same, on a smaller scale, is true of George's case. I have already suggested that it is inherent in consequentialism that it offers a strong doctrine of negative responsibility: if I know that if I do X, O_1 will eventuate, and if I refrain from doing X, O_2 will, and that O_2 is worse than O_1, then I am responsible for O_2 if I refrain voluntarily from doing X. 'You could have prevented it', as will be said, and truly, to Jim, if he refuses, by the relatives of the other Indians. (I shall leave the important question, which is to the side of the present issue, of the obligations, if any, that nest round the world "know": how far does one, under utilitarianism, have to research into the possibilities of maximally beneficent action, including prevention?)

In the present cases, the situation of O_2 includes another agent bringing about results worse than O_1. So far as O_2 has been identified up to this point—merely as the worse outcome which will eventuate if I refrain from doing X—we might equally have said that what that other brings about is O_2; but that would be to underdescribe the situation. For what occurs if Jim refrains from action is not solely twenty Indians dead, but *Pedro's killing twenty Indians,* and that is not a result which Pedro brings about, though the death of the Indians is. We can say: what one does is not included in the outcome of what one does, while what another does can be included in the outcome of what one does. For that to be so, as the terms are now being used, only a very weak condition has to be satisfied: for Pedro's killing the Indians to be the outcome of Jim's refusal, it only has to be causally true that if Jim had not refused, Pedro would not have done it.

That may be enough for us to speak, in some sense, of Jim's responsibility for that outcome, if it occurs; but it is certainly not enough, it is worth noticing, for us to speak of Jim's *making* those things happen. For granted this way of their coming about, he could have made them happen only by making Pedro shoot, and there is no acceptable sense in which his refusal makes Pedro shoot. If the captain had said on Jim's refusal, "you leave me with no alternative," he would have been lying, like most who use that phrase. While the deaths, and the killing, may be the outcome of Jim's refusal, it is misleading to think, in such a case, of Jim having an *effect* on the world through the medium (as it happens) of Pedro's acts; for this is to leave Pedro out of the picture in his essential role of one who has intentions and projects, projects for realizing which Jim's refusal would leave an opportunity. Instead of thinking in terms of supposed effects of Jim's projects on Pedro, it is more revealing to think in terms of the effects of Pedro's projects on Jim's decision. This is the direction from which I want to criticize the notion of negative responsibility.

There are of course other ways in which this notion can be criticized. Many have hoped to discredit it by insisting on the basic moral relevance of the distinction between action and inaction, between intervening and letting things take their courses. The distinction is certainly of great moral significance, and indeed it is not easy to think of any moral outlook which could get along without making some use of it. But it is unclear, both in itself and in its moral applications, and the unclarities are of a kind which precisely cause it to give way when, in very difficult cases, weight has to be put on it. There is much to be said in this area, but I doubt whether the sort of dilemma we are considering is going to be resolved by a simple use of this distinction. Again, the issue of negative responsibility can be pressed on the question of how limits are to be placed on one's apparently boundless obligation, implied by utilitarianism, to improve the world. Some answers are needed to that, too—and answers which stop short of relapsing into the bad faith of supposing that one's responsibilities could be adequately characterized just by appeal to one's roles.[2] But, once again, while that is a real question, it cannot be brought to bear directly on the present

[2] For some remarks bearing on this, see *Morality,* the section on "Goodness and roles," and Cohen's article there cited.

kind of case, since it is hard to think of anyone supposing that in Jim's case it would be an adequate response for him to say that it was none of his business.

What projects does a utilitarian agent have? As a utilitarian, he has the general project of bringing about maximally desirable outcomes; how he is to do this at any given moment is a question of what causal levers, so to speak, are at that moment within reach. The desirable outcomes, however, do not just consist of agents carrying out *that* project; there must be other more basic or lower-order projects which he and other agents have, and the desirable outcomes are going to consist, in part, of the maximally harmonious realization of those projects ("in part," because one component of a utilitarianly desirable outcome may be the occurrence of agreeable experiences which are not the satisfaction of anybody's projects). Unless there were first-order projects, the general utilitarian project would have nothing to work on, and would be vacuous. What do the more basic or lower-order projects comprise? Many will be the obvious kinds of desires for things for oneself, one's family, one's friends, including basic necessities of life, and in more relaxed circumstances, objects of taste. Or there may be pursuits and interests of an intellectual, cultural or creative character. I introduce those as a separate class not because the objects of them lie in a separate class, and provide—as some utilitarians, in their churchy way, are fond of saying—"higher" pleasures. I introduce them separately because the agent's identification with them may be of a different order. It does not have to be: cultural and aesthetic interests just belong, for many, along with any other taste; but some people's commitment to these kinds of interests just is at once more thoroughgoing and serious than their pursuit of various objects of taste, while it is more individual and permeated with character than the desire for the necessities of life.

Beyond these, someone may have projects connected with his support of some cause: Zionism, for instance, or the abolition of chemical and biological warfare. Or there may be projects which flow from some more general disposition towards human conduct and character, such as a hatred of injustice, or of cruelty, or of killing.

It may be said that this last sort of disposition and its associated project do not count as (logically) "lower-order" relative to the higher-order project of maximizing desirable outcomes; rather, it may be said, it is itself a "higher-order" project. The vital question is not, however, how it is to be classified, but whether it and similar projects are to count among the projects whose satisfaction is to be included in the maximizing sum, and, correspondingly, as contributing to the agent's happiness. If the utilitarian says "no" to that, then he is almost certainly committed to a version of utilitarianism as absurdly superficial and shallow as Benthamite versions have often been accused of being. For this project will be discounted, presumably, on the ground that it involves, in the specification of its object, the mention of other people's happiness or interests: thus it is the kind of project which (unlike the pursuit of food for myself) presupposes a reference to other people's projects. But that criterion would eliminate any desire at all which was not blankly and in the most straightforward sense egoistic.[3] Thus we should be reduced to frankly egoistic first-order projects, and—for all essential purposes—the one second-order utilitarian project of maximally satisfying first-order projects. Utilitarianism has a tendency to slide in this direction, and to leave a vast hole in the range of human desires, between egoistic inclinations and necessities at one end, and impersonally benevolent happiness-management at the other. But the utilitarianism which has to leave this hole is the most primitive form, which offers a quite rudimentary account of desire. Modern versions of the theory are supposed to be neutral with regard to what sorts of things make people happy or what their projects are. Utilitarianism would do well then to acknowledge the evident fact that among the things that make people happy is not only making other people happy, but being taken up or involved in any of a vast range of projects, or—if we waive the evangelical and moralizing associations of the word—commitments. One can be committed to such things as a person, a cause, an institution, a career, one's own genius, or the pursuit of danger.

Now none of these is itself the *pursuit of happiness:* by an exceedingly ancient platitude, it is not at all clear that there could be anything which was just that, or at least anything that had the slightest chance of being successful. Happiness, rather, requires being involved in, or at least content with, something else.[4] It is not impossible for utilitarianism to accept that point: it does not have to be saddled with a naïve and absurd philosophy of mind about the relation between desire and happiness. What it does have to say is that if such commitments are worth while, then pursuing the projects that flow from them, and realizing some of those projects, will make the person for whom they are worth while, happy. It may be that to claim that is still wrong: it may well be that a commitment can make sense to a man (can make sense of his life) without his supposing that it will make him *happy*.[5] But that is not the present point; let us grant to utilitarianism that all worthwhile human projects must conduce, one way or another, to happiness. The point is that even if that is true, it does not follow, nor could it possibly be true, that those projects are themselves projects of pursuing happiness. One has to believe in, or at least want, or quite minimally, be content with, other things, for there to be anywhere that happiness can come from.

Utilitarianism, then, should be willing to agree that its general aim of maximizing happiness does not imply that what everyone is doing is just pursuing happiness. On the contrary, people have to be pursuing other things. What

[3] On the subject of egoistic and non-egoistic desires, see "Egoism and altruism," in *Problems of the Self* (Cambridge University Press, London, 1973).

[4] This does not imply that there is no such thing as the project of pursuing pleasure. Some writers who have correctly resisted the view that all desires are desires for pleasure, have given an account of pleasure so thoroughly adverbial as to leave it quite unclear how there could be a distinctively hedonist way of life at all. Some room has to be left for that, though there are important difficulties both in defining it and living it. Thus (particularly in the case of the very rich) it often has highly ritual aspects, apparently part of a strategy to counter boredom.

[5] For some remarks on this possibility, see *Morality,* section on "What is morality about?"

those other things may be, utilitarianism, sticking to its professed empirical stance, should be prepared just to find out. No doubt some possible projects it will want to discourage, on the grounds that their being pursued involves a negative balance of happiness to others: though even there, the unblinking accountant's eye of the strict utilitarian will have something to put in the positive column, the satisfactions of the destructive agent. Beyond that, there will be a vast variety of generally beneficent or at least harmless projects; and some no doubt, will take the form not just of tastes or fancies, but of what I have called "commitments." It may even be that the utilitarian researcher will find that many of those with commitments, who have really identified themselves with objects outside themselves, who are thoroughly involved with other persons, or institutions, or activities or causes, are actually happier than those whose projects and wants are not like that. If so, that is an important piece of utilitarian empirical lore.

When I say "happier" here, I have in mind the sort of consideration which any utilitarian would be committed to accepting: as for instance that such people are less likely to have a break-down or commit suicide. Of course that is not all that is actually involved, but the point in this argument is to use to the maximum degree utilitarian notions, in order to locate a breaking point in utilitarian thought. In appealing to this strictly utilitarian notion, I am being more consistent with utilitarianism than Smart is. In his struggles with the problem of the brain-electrode man, Smart (p. 22) commends the idea that "happy" is a partly evaluative term, in the sense that we call "happiness" those kinds of satisfaction which, as things are, we approve of. But *by what standard* is this surplus element of approval supposed, from a utilitarian point of view, to be allocated? There is no source for it, on a strictly utilitarian view, except further degrees of satisfaction, but there are none of those available, or the problem would not arise. Nor does it help to appeal to the fact that we dislike in prospect things which we like when we get there, for from a utilitarian point of view it would seem that the original dislike was merely irrational or based on an error. Smart's argument at this point seems to be embarrassed by a well-known utilitarian uneasiness, which comes from a feeling that it is not respectable to ignore the "deep," while not having anywhere left in human life to locate it.[6]

Let us now go back to the agent as utilitarian, and his higher-order project of maximizing desirable outcomes. At this level, he is committed only to that: what the outcome will actually consist of will depend entirely on the facts, on what persons with what projects and what potential satisfactions there are within calculable reach of the causal levers near which he finds himself. His own substantial projects and commitments come into it, but only as one lot among others—they potentially provide one set of satisfactions among those which he may be able to assist from where he happens to be. He is the agent of the satisfaction system who happens to be at a particular point at a particular

---

[6] One of many resemblances in spirit between utilitarianism and high-minded evangelical Christianity.

time: in Jim's case, our man in South America. His own decisions as a utilitarian agent are a function of all the satisfactions which he can affect from where he is: and this means that the projects of others, to an indeterminately great extent, determine his decision.

This may be so either positively or negatively. It will be so positively if agents within the causal field of his decision have projects which are at any rate harmless, and so should be assisted. It will equally be so, but negatively, if there is an agent within the causal field whose projects are harmful, and have to be frustrated to maximize desirable outcomes. So it is with Jim and the soldier Pedro. On the utilitarian view, the undesirable projects of other people as much determine, in this negative way, one's decisions as the desirable ones do positively: if those people were not there, or had different projects, the causal nexus would be different, and it is the actual state of the causal nexus which determines the decision. The determination to an indefinite degree of my decisions by other people's projects is just another aspect of my unlimited responsibility to act for the best in a causal framework formed to a considerable extent by their projects.

The decision so determined is, for utilitarianism, the right decision. But what if it conflicts with some project of mine? This, the utilitarian will say, has already been dealt with: the satisfaction to you of fulfilling your project, and any satisfactions to others of your so doing, have already been through the calculating device and have been found inadequate. Now in the case of many sorts of projects, that is a perfectly reasonable sort of answer. But in the case of projects of the sort I have called "commitments," those with which one is more deeply and extensively involved and identified, this cannot just by itself be an adequate answer, and there may be no adequate answer at all. For, to take the extreme sort of case, how can a man, as a utilitarian agent, come to regard as one satisfaction among others, and a dispensable one, a project or attitude round which he has built his life, just because someone else's projects have so structured the causal scene that that is how the utilitarian sum comes out?

The point here is not, as utilitarians may hasten to say, that if the project or attitude is that central to his life, then to abandon it will be very disagreeable to him and great loss of utility will be involved. I have already argued in section 4 that it is not like that; on the contrary, once he is prepared to look at it like that, the argument in any serious case is over anyway. The point is that he is identified with his actions as flowing from projects and attitudes which in some cases he takes seriously at the deepest level, as what his life is about (or, in some cases, this section of his life—seriousness is not necessarily the same as persistence). It is absurd to demand of such a man, when the sums come in from the utility network which the projects of others have in part determined, that he should just step aside from his own project and decision and acknowledge the decision which utilitarian calculation requires. It is to alienate him in a real sense from his actions and the source of his action in his own convictions. It is to make him into a channel between the input of everyone's projects, including his own, and an output of optimistic decision; but this is to neglect the extent to which *his* actions and *his* decisions have to be seen as the actions and decisions which flow from the projects and attitudes with which he is most closely identified. It is thus, in the most literal sense, an attack on his integrity.[7]

These sorts of considerations do not in themselves give solutions to practical dilemmas such as those provided by our examples; but I hope they help to provide other ways of thinking about them. In fact, it is not hard to see that in George's case, viewed from this perspective, the utilitarian solution would be wrong. Jim's case is different, and harder. But if (as I suppose) the utilitarian is probably right in this case, that is not to be found out just by asking the utilitarian's questions. Discussions of it—and I am not going to try to carry it further here—will have to take seriously the distinction between my killing someone, and its coming about because of what I do that someone else kills them: a distinction based, not so much on the distinction between action and inaction, as on the distinction between my projects and someone else's projects. At least it will have to start by taking that seriously, as utilitarianism does not; but then it will have to build out from there by asking why that distinction seems to have less, or a different, force in this case than it has in George's. One question here would be how far one's powerful objection to killing people just is, in fact, an application of a powerful objection to their being killed. Another dimension of that is the issue of how much it matters that the people at risk are actual, and there, as opposed to hypothetical, or future, or merely elsewhere.[8]

There are many other considerations that could come into such a question, but the immediate point of all this is to draw one particular contrast with utilitarianism: that to reach a grounded decision in such a case should not be regarded as a matter of just discounting one's reactions, impulses and deeply held projects in the face of the pattern of utilities, nor yet merely adding them in—but in the first instance of trying to understand them.

Of course, time and circumstances are unlikely to make a grounded decision, in Jim's case at least, possible. It might not even be decent. Instead of thinking in a rational and systematic way either about utilities or about the value of human life, the relevance of the people at risk being present, and so forth, the presence of the people at risk may just have its effect. The significance of the immediate should not be underestimated. Philosophers, not only utilitarian ones, repeatedly urge one to view the world *sub specie aeternitatis*,[9] but for most human purposes that is not a good *species* to view it under. If we are not agents

---

[7] Interestingly related to these notions is the Socratic idea that courage is a virtue particularly connected with keeping a clear sense of what one regards as most important. They also centrally raise questions about the value of pride. Humility, as something beyond the real demand of correct self-appraisal, was specially a Christian virtue because it involved subservience to God. In a secular context it can only represent subservience to other men and their projects.

[8] For a more general discussion of this issue see Charles Fried, *An Anatomy of Values* (Harvard University Press, Cambridge, Mass., 1970), Part Three.

[9] Cf. Smart, p. 63.

of the universal satisfaction system, we are not primarily janitors of any system of values, even our own: very often, we just act, as a possibly confused result of the situation in which we are engaged. That, I suspect, is very often an exceedingly good thing. To what extent utilitarians regard it as a good thing is an obscure question. To that sort of question I now turn.

Rules and Duties

It is the *shamefulness* of vice, not its *harmfulness* (to the agent himself) that must be emphasized above all. For unless the dignity of virtue is exalted above everything else in actions, then the concept of duty itself vanishes and dissolves into mere pragmatic precepts, since man's consciousness of his nobility then disappears and he is for sale and can be bought for a price that seductive inclinations offer him.

—Immanuel Kant

A rather forbidding name, "deontologists," has been given to the thinkers who disagree with Bentham and other teleologists. Deontologists do not believe that the concept of "right" can be derived from the concept of "good." This section has essays by two of the greatest and best-known deontologists, Immanuel Kant and W. D. Ross.

The fourth essay in this section, by **Jonathan Bennett,** sets the contrast that provides the best entreé into the mind of the deontologist. This is the contrast between inclination and reason.

A predominant number of teleologists find the origin of human goods in our inclinations—our feelings, emotions, desires, wants, needs. Inclinations are the possession of all sentient beings, animals as well as humans; persons who believe that inclinations are the source of value are called "naturalists" in value theory. Unless there were pleasures, sexual desires, needs for such things as food, security, and love, feelings of repugnance and delight, anger, envy, and other emotions, there would be no such thing as value in the world; without value, there would be no goods, including moral goods; and, hence, no such thing as morality, moral right being dependent upon moral good.

Bennett concentrates on a specific inclination, sympathy for the plight of others. We saw that this inclination played a central role in Rachels' answer to egoism. Bennett plays sympathy off against morality, a morality most of us would agree is a bad morality. What makes Bennett's essay relevant for our topic is that he shows by some interesting cases how the inclination of sympathy is in conflict with moral principles (maxims of duty). Further, these principles are products of conscientious thought, and this is what makes the contrast, because feeling and thought traditionally have been contrasted as providing opposite directives for decision and action. Should we follow our heart or our mind? Should we be guided by our feelings, such as sympathy, or by the dictates of reason's principles? Deontologists have advocated reason over feeling, while teleologists, typically, have given pride of place to feeling, although giving priority to feeling does not mean that reason, reflection, or thought have no role to play.

Bennett's essay is instructive here because the ancient opposition between feeling and reason, teleologists and deontologists, is stated with force and with the use of clear, interesting examples. The fact that he illustrates a conflict between feeling and *bad* morality does not justify concluding that feeling is a better touchstone of morality than reason, and that, therefore, the deontologists' advocacy of reason ought to be rejected by us. That Huck Finn's inherited morality was bad, that Hitler and Himmler's morality was bad, that Jonathan Edwards morality was bad is assumed by Bennett, and he assumes that we will agree. However, the badness of these principles is not shown by the fact that they conflict with the inclination of sympathy. As Bennett points out, our feelings of sympathy also conflict with good principles, as in the case where a mother's sympathy for her child's fright at the doctor does not lead her to conclude that it is morally bad for her to put her child in the doctor's hands and care. Thus, that a morality is bad might be determined on some other grounds than its conflict with sympathy; it might be determined on the basis of reason, which is the deontologist's position.

As Bennett says, "I don't give my sympathies a blank check in advance. In a conflict between principle and sympathy, principles ought sometimes to win." Which times? On what basis? The question is still open. The question is still open because it does not occur only with fictional characters, remote ones such as Edwards, or pathological ones like Himmler. Consider the following remark of Dr. Jerome Jaffe, who was the White House staff psychiatrist from 1971 to 1973. "The [Nixon] administration admired people who could be cold and dispassionate in making personnel decisions. To make concessions to people's feeling, to recognize that a particular objective was not worth destroying people in the process of its attainment, was not something that elicited any admiration. Such a concern was viewed as a fatal flaw." In this case, we can agree that a morality such as Nixon's was bad even in the absence of an opposing sympathy on their part and agree that they, too, ought to have known that even though they did not have any such natural sympathy.

The question that is still open is: "What makes right acts right?"

W. D. Ross, in this section's second essay, raises this ethical theory question. Negatively, deontologists such as Ross deny that it is the good consequences of an act that make it right, contrary to teleologists' claim. Positively, according to Ross, an act is right because it falls under a moral principle, and general moral principles or maxims or duties are seen by our reason to be *prima facie* right. "When we have reached sufficient mental maturity and have given sufficient attention to the proposition it is evident without any need of proof, or of evidence beyond itself. It is self-evident just as a mathematical axiom, or the validity of a form of inference, is evident."

Suppose that we have constructed a moral system; this will include a set of compatible, comprehensive, integrated maxims, with the most general maxim, "You should do what is right," covering all the rest. If someone asks us "what makes a right act right?" we can say that what makes it right is that it is an instance of an act of a certain kind that falls under some maxim. If someone were to ask us what makes husbands and wives taking turns doing the dishes right, we can answer, "Because it is an instance of a maxim that we ought to treat people fairly." If we are asked what makes fair treatment right, we can reply, "Because it is an instance of the maxim that we should deal justly with people." But then we may be asked what makes dealing justly with people right, and we, moving ever upward in the moral maxim pyramid, finally reach the top and say, "Because it is an instance of doing what is right." If our questioner persists and asks, "What makes doing what is right right?" what are we to answer? We could just say that it is obvious that what is right is right. We have no other maxim to appeal to; we have run out of maxims; after all, there is an end to maxims.

At this point, though, we might recognize that, while we have run out of moral system because we have run out of maxims, we have run into an ethical theory question. It is here that the issue between teleologists and deontologists is joined. The teleologist may claim that he does not have to resort to the "obvious" answer that "right is right" because his ethical theory is able to supply a further answer that is unavailable to the deontologist. Because teleologists hold the ethical theory position that "right" can be derived from "good," they may claim they can explain that what makes doing what is right right is that it produces a greater balance of good over bad than any other act open to the agent. Deontologists' general maxim "You should do what is right" is transformed by teleologists into the general maxim "You should do what produces a greater balance of good over bad" because they substitute "what produces a greater balance of good over bad" for "what is right." They make this substitution because they believe "right" is derivable from "good."

It is this substitution that deontologists such as Ross and Kant deny can be made. We will not recount the arguments that Ross gives for his position. You can read them yourself. But there is a possible confusion to which we alert you.

Do not confuse a moral issue with an ethical theory issue. "You should do what produces a greater balance of good over bad" is one thing considered as a moral maxim and another thing considered as an answer to the ethical theory question "What makes right acts right?" Deontologists do not reject this as a moral maxim; they do reject it as an answer to the ethical theory question. They reject it because they think they can ask "What makes an act that produces a greater balance of good over bad right?" If we can ask that ethical theory question about the teleological maxim itself, then we cannot give that maxim as an answer to the ethical theory question "What ultimately makes right acts right?" The ethical theory question is *about* the maxims; therefore, you cannot use one of the maxims themselves to answer the question. Do not fall into that confusion.

The answer to Ross's question is not of mere theoretical interest. Ethical theory is not sealed off from moral practice. Different answers to Ross's question will produce different life-styles because the answers will sanction different moral systems, some of them incompatible with each other. Suppose that someone is an egoistic teleologist, and suppose he thinks that what makes right acts right is their being to the advantage of the agent. In considering what maxims he is going to include in his system, he will have to exclude the universalistic teleological maxim "You should do what produces a greater balance of good over bad *regardless of whose good or bad it is."* Since acts done in accord with the universalistic maxim cannot always be shown to be to the agent's advantage, acts done in accord with it cannot be shown to be egoistically right; hence, it should not be included in the egoist's moral system. The racist in a racist society may find it is to his advantage to be a racist. An egoistic teleological answer to "What makes right acts right?" would sanction his racism. If you think racism is wrong, you must give a different answer to Ross's question than the egoist teleologist gives.

According to deontologists, turning to universalistic teleology to answer the racist is unsatisfactory. Your appeal to the racist to include in his calculations the bad that happens to the victims of racism as well as the good that happens to him will be met with the following question from him: "What makes acts with a balance of good consequences, considering all persons affected, right?" Perhaps your need for an answer to this challenge will motivate you to read Ross with some interest.

We have said that the deontologist comes down on the side of reason rather than inclination. Morally right acts are those done in accordance with maxims; these maxims are selected by the operation of our reason; for Ross, these maxims are self-evident to a fully matured, thoughtful human. So far we have looked rather cooly at the position of the deontologists, as if it were merely a result of a disinterested, disembodied mind at work. There is something much more profound driving them. We find this in Kant's ethics.

Immanuel Kant was intensely, unremittingly interested in human nobility, dignity, and respect. These are central concepts for his morality. What kind of things are due respect, have dignity? Rational beings. Why? Because "Rational beings alone have the faculty of acting according *to the conception of laws*—that is, according to principles, that is, have a *will."* This remark is best understood by contrasting human beings with other animals. Most of us think of ourselves as having more worth than other animals; given a choice between the life of an animal and a human being, most of us would unhesitatingly choose the life of a human being. John Stuart Mill asked whether it is better to be a pig satisfied than Socrates dissatisfied. Even if we knew that we were to live unhappily as human beings, most of us would choose to be human. The worth of human beings, then, does not lie in our happiness.

What is the significant difference between human beings and other animals that leads us to choose being human? According to Kant, it is that human beings have rationality and animals do not. Being rational gives us the possibility of conceiving of laws, maxims, principles, rules, imperatives, commands; being able to conceive of and acting according to laws gives us another source of action other than inclinations. Animals are confined to act according to laws of inclination, that is, according to psychological and physiological laws that determine their existence. Take the extreme case of water. The direction it runs is determined by natural laws. Being unable to conceive and formulate laws for itself, water acts in accord solely with natural law; it cannot conceive and choose its laws by rational reflection.

Kant thinks that animals are as locked into their actions by natural laws as water is; but human beings are not, and this is the source of our dignity: We have rationality and, therefore, can act according to practical reason, that is, act willfully.

We have put it as acting "willfully" rather than having "a will" because the latter suggests too strongly that we are dealing with a mysterious, separate faculty. Kant is not always easy to interpret; we are suggesting that Kant thinks of reason as having a power to move us and that "will" is a short term for "practical reason" rather than the name of a separate faculty able to move the body according to the dictates of reason. Acting "willfully" is acting as our reason determines; this is acting according to a principle or rule to which our reason gives assent.

Kant recognizes that we do not always act in accord with our rationally chosen principles; that is, we do not always act "willfully"; sometimes we are overcome by inclination, as Huck Finn was. Reason is not always sufficient to determine how we will act; we have impulses and inclinations pulling us to act contrary to our principles. This is what makes it difficult to be moral; we often know what we ought to do but often fail to do it because we follow our desires instead.

Given that "will," understood as interpreted above, is what distinguishes human beings from other animals, and that this is what gives human beings their dignity and makes them worthy of respect, we can understand Kant's opening remark, "Nothing can possibly be conceived in the world, or even out of it, which can be called good without qualification, except a *good will.*" By "good" here he means "morally good." There are other kinds of goods and he immediately lists some after the opening remark, but none of them have moral goodness, because none of them constitute our *moral* nature; none of them are the basis for human dignity or respect. That a person wants to be happy, desires health, and so forth are what we naturally expect of any human being; there is nothing remarkable about these desires or wants and their objects. How absurd it sounds to say "I respect Jocko because he wants to be happy." Your remark would be "Who doesn't want to be happy? This doesn't make Jocko so special." The only thing that could be morally good is what makes morality possible, namely, a will; therefore, to be morally *good* is to have a morally *good* will. Of course, even the morally evil are worthy of respect simply because they have a will, that is, can act according to principle even if they do not do so. We are to treat criminals as human beings and with dignity because they are human; evil human beings are treated differently from animals because, although evil, they remain human; that is, they retain the capability of being moral, a capability that animals never possess.

Kant's way of marking off the moral from the nonmoral realm leads him to formulate a narrow notion of a "moral act." At the beginning of our selection, he sets out three features of moral acts.

First, an act is a moral one if it is done from a sense of duty and duty alone. An act done from inclination has no moral merit. Recall that Rachels answered the egoist by remarking that we find it reasonable to benefit others because of the "prior existence" of an inclination or "attitude" in the agent of caring for others. This teleological condition is of no moral moment for Kant. He says, "There are many minds so sympathetically constituted that, without any other motive of vanity or self-interest, they find a pleasure in spreading joy around them, and can take delight in the satisfaction of others so far as it is their own work. But I maintain that in such a case an action of this kind, however proper, however amiable it may be, has nevertheless no true moral worth, but is on a level with other inclinations. . . ."

Second, the worth of a moral act is judged on the basis of the agent's volition. Since, according to the first point, only acts done from duty are moral acts, the volition of a moral act cannot be our inclination for what we think we can attain by our act. The only basis on which it is proper to praise an agent for his or her act is if it is done *just because* it is in accord with a maxim. Ends in view are not moral volitions, contrary to the teleological view. This means, also, that even though an agent fails to bring about the results intended by the act, if it is done from a sense of duty, the agent is morally worthy of praise.

Third, in acting out of a sense of duty and duty alone, exclusive of inclination, we are acting morally because of our *pure respect* for the law. Nothing should remain to determine our will to act in a certain way except this respect. This is the subjective side to deontology. Carrying deontology this far may seem extreme to you; however, there is a way of thinking about it that may help you resist thinking of Kant as a "rule mad" philosopher. In a teleological world, which our modern moral world seems to be, the moral task is somehow so to arrange human relations that we maximally coordinate and satisfy persons' inclinations; something for everyone, but, preferably, everything for everyone. One can look on ours as the mad world of the moral optimist. A realistic, if not pessimistic, estimate of the mad teleologist's chances for success leads one to acknowledge that they are small. Facing this prospect could plunge one into a hopeless depression. Life is not a comedy; it never ends happily. But if one takes Kant's viewpoint, at least we are saved by turning failed comedy into tragedy. We may salvage dignity and respect from a world of frayed ends. We can do this by concentrating on moral volition rather than teleological success; sure, we human beings will fail to maximally coordinate and satisfy our inclinations, but if we judge ourselves on the basis of willfully living according to rational, self-given laws, not all is lost. Human beings may yet be seen as noble creatures even though we are fated for an unhappy end.

You may say that this is all well and good, this acting according to duty, out of respect for law, but how shall we find such a law? It is one thing to talk about such a law and another thing to produce it. Kant recognizes the fairness of this challenge: "But what sort of law can that be the conception of which must determine the will, even without paying any regard to the effect expected from it, in order that this will may be called good absolutely and without qualification?"

It is the categorical imperative.

An imperative is a sentence containing an "ought" or a "shall." A hypothetical imperative is not what Kant is looking for. It states a condition, "If . . ." and is followed by a "then . . ." clause, which contains the "ought." Typically what goes into the "If . . ." clause is a statement of an outcome that may be desired; for example, "If (you do not wish to be hungry)" or "If (you want to be loved)." The "then . . ." clause is a statement telling you what act you ought to perform in order to satisfy your wish or want; for example, "then (eat food)" or "then (treat other persons kindly)." But hypothetical imperatives will obviously not do as laws for the will because they are based on inclinations. What is wanted is a categorical imperative, that is, an imperative that states an ought unconditionally, leaving off the "If . . ."s of inclinations.

Kant formulates the categorical imperative in three ways in our selection. It is not perfectly clear that he intends to say the same thing in three different ways or that he intends to make three different but logically connected statements.

The first formulation of the categorical imperative requires of any moral maxim that it be universal; it should be a maxim that is applicable to everyone at every time in every place to act upon when the circumstances make it appropriate. Kant tells us to act only on that maxim whereby one can at the same time will that it should become a universal law. He gives four instances of maxims that fail this test; in each case, they fail because universalizing them as demanded by the first imperative would produce a contradiction. Recall that Kant is looking for a categorical imperative for rational beings, for a law that such beings can respect; it must, consequently, set a logically respectable criterion for maxims.

The categorical imperative is the highest principle from which maxims of actions can be "deduced" or "derived." "Deduced" is too strong a term, perhaps; let's say that the categorical imperative sets the standard or criterion by which we judge whether a proposed maxim is one that we ought to legislate for ourselves and to follow. What makes right acts right is that they are instances of a maxim; and what makes a maxim right is that it is in accord with the categorical imperative.

The four maxims that fail to pass the universalization test are those covering acts of suicide, failing to keep a promise, indulging in pleasure rather than developing a culturally useful talent, and neglecting those in need of help. These maxims fail because when stated as universal maxims, they would be contradictory. Critics of Kant's ethical theory often dispute the claim that such maxims would be contradictory.

The second formulation of the categorical imperative makes Kant sound as if he were a teleologist. "Now that which serves the will as the objective ground of its self-determination is the *end,* and if this is assigned by reason alone, it must hold for all rational beings." Notice that Kant says "objective" ground; he contrasts this to "subjective" grounds, which are those given by our desires and which he calls the "springs" of volition; an "objective" ground he calls the "motive" of volition, a use of "motive" different from the way we used it earlier. Our use of "motive" was similar to Kant's use of "spring."

What would be an end that serves as the objective ground for moral volition? They cannot be the *effects* of persons' actions as teleologists claim; because these are only relative, varying from person to person and occasion to occasion, they do not hold categorically for all rational beings. Kant maintains that the only end "whose existence has in itself an absolute worth," something which is "an end in itself," is man and any rational being. Rational beings are not "things"; they are "persons." This distinction reflects that they are beings which are objects of respect; as objects of respect universally, they are the objective grounds of moral volition. Persons, unlike things, are to be treated with respect; it is morally indifferent if we saw boards with which to make something; but not if we saw the top off a person's head to make ashtrays. Persons are to be treated as ends, not as means, which essentially requires that we restrict the freedom of our action; we restrict our acts on human beings in ways that we do not with things. This shows our respect. Kant puts the second formulation as: "So act as to treat humanity, whether in thine own person or in that of any other, in every case as an end withal, never as means only."

Give the notion of "end" as an object of respect which restricts our freedom of action, you can see that Kant is not a teleologist even though his talk about "ends" may initially suggest it. The objective ground of all acts is the person; every moral act's effects are undertaken to serve the person as end; and, of course, "end" does not mean here "effect" as it does for the teleologist.

The third formulation of the categorical imperative is that: Every human will is a will which in all its maxims gives universal laws. That is, every rational being is self-legislating. The dignity of rational beings, we said, lies in their ability to think; this means thinking for yourself and giving yourself laws, laws fit for every rational being. If others were to give you maxims, you would be a subject and subject to their laws; maximally, the slave is in this position; anyone who condones slavery has to think of slaves as less than human, as partial persons, because they do not give slaves the respect of allowing them to legislate their own actions; the master legislates for the slave. (On this topic, Kelsey's essay in Chapter Eight is quite interesting and useful). As Kant says at the end of our selection, some things have market value, things that are objects of inclinations and wants; some things have fancy value, objects of taste such as art works; but human beings have dignity. In the event you get somewhat confused while studying Kant, keep this central point about human dignity and respect in mind as the hub around which to organize your Kantian thoughts.

In **D. Thomas O'Connor's** essay in this section, keep in mind that it turns importantly on a distinction made by Ross. The distinction is between a general principle or maxim and its application. While general principles are self-evidently right, what Ross calls *prima facie* duties, their application to actual situations, are not. In thinking about what we ought to do on any given occasion, we have to have knowledge of the surrounding circumstances because we have to identify the maxim that appropriately applies in this case. On some occasions, two or more maxims might apply. Ross says, "Every act therefore, viewed in some aspects, will be *prima facie* right, and viewed in others, *prima facie* wrong. . . ." Deontologists recognize that morality is not merely the abstract business of rationally considering maxims; it is also the difficult business of applying maxims to our complex, often muddled, and intertwined existence. O'Connor's essay on the *prima facie* rules of war bring this out clearly in relation to an enormously complex and important set of acts—acts of war. He discusses five rules of a so-called just war: (1) It must be for a just cause; (2) it must be carried out with the right attitude—in terms of rationality, a basic respect for moral principles, and a commitment to seek and apply knowledge; (3) it must be conducted by a legitimate authority; (4) the means of war must be proportional to the moral and political ends sought; and (5) there must be discrimination as to who is to be considered a combatant.

The Categorical Imperative

IMMANUEL KANT

Immanuel Kant (1724–1804) is recognized as one of the greatest philosophers of all times. All of his well-ordered life was spent in Königsberg, East Prussia, where he was a professor of philosophy. In *The Critique of Pure Reason* (1781), Kant developed his Critical Philosophy, an ingenious synthesis of rationalism and empiricism. He believed it to be a revolution in the theory of knowledge as significant as that of Copernicus in astronomy. Kant made significant and highly original contributions to cosmology, ethics, aesthetics, jurisprudence, and the philosophy of religion as well as to theory of knowledge.

Nothing can possibly be conceived in the world, or even out of it, which can be called good without qualification, except a *good will.* Intelligence, wit, judgment, and other *talents* of the mind, however they may be named, or courage, resolution, perseverance, as qualities of temperament, are undoubtedly good and desirable in many respects; but these gifts of nature may also become extremely bad and mischievous if the will which is to make use of them, and which, therefore, constitutes what is called *character,* is not good. It is the same with the *gifts of fortune.* Power, riches, honor, even health, and the general well-being and contentment with one's condition which is called *happiness,* inspire pride, and often presumption, if there is not a good will to correct the influence of these on the mind, and with this also to rectify the whole principle of acting, and adapt it to its end. The sight of a being who is not adorned

Source: Immanuel Kant, *Fundamental Principles of the Metaphysics of Morals,* trans. by T. K. Abbott (1907).

with a single feature of a pure and good will, enjoying unbroken prosperity, can never give pleasure to an impartial rational spectator. Thus a good will appears to constitute the indispensable condition even of being worthy of happiness.

There are even some qualities which are of service to this good will itself, and may facilitate its action, yet which have no intrinsic unconditional value, but always presuppose a good will, and this qualifies the esteem that we justly have for them, and does not permit us to regard them as absolutely good. Moderation in the affections and passions, self-control, and calm deliberation are not only good in many respects, but even seem to constitute part of the intrinsic worth of the person; but they are far from deserving to be called good without qualification, although they have been so unconditionally praised by the ancients. For without the principles of a good will, they may become extremely bad; and the coolness of a villain not only makes him far more dangerous, but also directly makes him more abominable in our eyes than he would have been without it.

A good will is good not because of what it performs or effects, not by its aptness for the attainment of some proposed end, but simply by virtue of the volition—that is, it is good in itself, and considered by itself is to be esteemed much higher than all that can be brought about by it in favor of any inclination, nay, even of the sum-total of all inclinations. Even if it should happen that, owing to special disfavor of fortune, or the niggardly provision of a stepmotherly nature, this will should wholly lack power to accomplish its purpose, if with its greatest efforts it should yet achieve nothing, and there should remain only the good will (not, to be sure, a mere wish, but the summoning of all means in our power), then, like a jewel, it would still shine by its own light, as a thing which has its whole value in itself. Its usefulness or fruitlessness can neither add to nor take away anything from this value. It would be, as it were, only the setting to enable us to handle it the more conveniently in common commerce, or to attract to it the attention of those who are not yet connoisseurs, but not to recommend it to true connoisseurs, or to determine its value. . . .

We have then to develop the notion of a will which deserves to be highly esteemed for itself, and is good without a view to anything further, a notion which exists already in the sound natural understanding, requiring rather to be cleared up than to be taught, and which in estimating the value of our actions always takes the first place and constitutes the condition of all the rest. In order to do this, we will take the notion of duty, which includes that of a good will, although implying certain subjective restrictions and hindrances. These, however, far from concealing it or rendering it unrecognizable, rather bring it out by contrast and make it shine forth so much the brighter.

I omit here all actions which are already recognized as inconsistent with duty, although they may be useful for this or that purpose, for with these the question whether they are done *from duty* cannot arise at all, since they even conflict with it. I also set aside those actions which really conform to duty, but to which men have *no* direct *inclination,* performing them because they are impelled thereto by some other inclination. For in this case we can readily distinguish whether the action which agrees with duty is done *from duty* or from a selfish view. It is much harder to make this distinction when the action accords with duty, and the subject has besides a *direct* inclination to it. For example, it is always a matter of duty that a dealer should not over-charge an inexperienced purchaser; and wherever there is much commerce the prudent tradesman does not overcharge, but keeps a fixed price for everyone, so that a child buys of him as well as any other. Men are thus *honestly* served; but this is not enough to make us believe that the tradesman has so acted from duty and from principles of honesty; his own advantage required it; it is out of the question in this case to suppose that he might besides have a direct inclination in favor of the buyers, so that, as it were, from love he should give no advantage to one over another. Accordingly the action was done neither from duty nor from direct inclination, but merely with a selfish view.

On the other hand, it is a duty to maintain one's life; and, in addition, everyone has also a direct inclination to do so. But on this account the often anxious care which most men take for it has no intrinsic worth, and their maxim has no moral import. They preserve their life as *duty requires,* no doubt, but not *because duty requires.* On the other hand, if adversity and hopeless sorrow have completely taken away the relish for life, if the unfortunate one, strong in mind, indignant at his fate rather than desponding or dejected, wishes for death, and yet preserves his life without loving it—not from inclination or fear, but from duty—then his maxim has a moral worth.

To be beneficent when we can is a duty; and besides this, there are many minds so sympathetically constituted that, without any other motive of vanity or self-interest, they find a pleasure in spreading joy around them, and can take delight in the satisfaction of others so far as it is their own work. But I maintain that in such a case an action of this kind, however proper, however amiable it may be, has nevertheless no true moral worth, but is on a level with other inclinations, for example, the inclination to honor, which, if it is happily directed to that which is in fact of public utility and accordant with duty, and consequently honorable, deserves praise and encouragement, but not esteem. For the maxim lacks the moral import, namely, that such actions be done *from duty,* not from inclination. Put the case that the mind of that philanthropist was clouded by sorrow of his own, extinguishing all sympathy with the lot of others, and that while he still has the power to benefit others in distress, he is not touched by their trouble because he is absorbed with his own; and now suppose that he tears himself out of this dead insensibility and performs the action without any inclination to it, but simply from duty, then first has his action its genuine moral worth. Further still, if nature has put little sympathy in the heart of this or that man, if he, supposed to be an upright man, is by temperament cold and indifferent to the sufferings of others, perhaps because in respect of his own he is provided with the special gift of patience and fortitude, and supposes, or even requires, that others should have the same—and such a man would certainly not be the meanest product of nature—but if nature had not specially framed him for a philanthropist, would he not still find in himself a source from whence to give himself a far higher worth than that of a good-natured temperament could be? Unquestionably. It is just in this that the moral worth of the character is brought out which is incomparably the highest of all, namely, that he is beneficient, not from inclination, but from duty.

To secure one's own happiness is a duty, at least indirectly; for discontent with one's condition, under a pressure of many anxieties and amidst unsatisfied wants, might easily become a great *temptation to transgression of duty*. But here again, without looking to duty, all men have already the strongest and most intimate inclination to happiness, because it is just in this idea that all inclinations are combined in one total. But the precept of happiness is often of such a sort that it greatly interferes with some inclinations, and yet a man cannot form any definite and certain conception of the sum of satisfaction of all of them which is called happiness. It is not then to be wondered at that a single inclination, definite both as to what it promises and as to the time within which it can be gratified, is often able to overcome such a fluctuating idea, and that a gouty patient, for instance, can choose to enjoy what he likes, and to suffer what he may, since, according to his calculation, on this occasion at least, he has [only] not sacrificed the enjoyment of the present moment to a possibly mistaken expectation of a happiness which is supposed to be found in health. But even in this case, if the general desire for happiness did not influence his will, and supposing that in his particular case health was not a necessary element in this calculation, there yet remains in this, as in all other cases, this law—namely, that he should promote his happiness not from inclination but from duty, and by this would his conduct first acquire true moral worth.

It is in this manner, undoubtedly, that we are to understand those passages of Scripture also in which we are commanded to love our neighbor, even our enemy. For love, as an affection, cannot be commanded, but beneficence for duty's sake may, even though we are not impelled to it by any inclination—nay, are even repelled by a natural and unconquerable aversion. This is *practical* love, and not *pathological*—a love which is seated in the will, and not in the propensions of sense—in principles of action and not of tender sympathy; and it is this love alone which can be commanded.

The second[1] proposition is: That an action done from duty derives its moral worth, *not from the purpose* which is to be attained by it, but from the maxim by which it is determined, and therefore does not depend on the realization of the object of the action, but merely on the *principle of volition* by which the action has taken place, without regard to any object of desire. It is clear from what precedes that the purposes which we may have in view in our actions, or their effects regarded as ends and springs of the will, cannot give to actions any unconditional or moral worth. In what, then, can their worth lie if it is not to consist in the will and in reference to its expected effect? It cannot lie anywhere but in the *principle of the will* without regard to the ends which can be attained by the action. For the will stands between its *a priori*

---

[1] The first proposition was that to have moral worth an action must be done from duty. Translator's footnote.

principle, which is formal, and its *a posteriori* spring, which is material, as between two roads, and as it must be determined by something, it follows that it must be determined by the formal principle of volition when an action is done from duty, in which case every material principle has been withdrawn from it.

The third proposition, which is a consequence of the two preceding, I would express thus: *Duty is the necessity of acting from respect for the law.* I may have *inclination* for an object as the effect of my proposed action, but I cannot have *respect* for it just for this reason that it is an effect and not an energy of will. Similarly, I cannot have respect for inclination, whether my own or another's; I can at most, if my own, approve it; if another's, sometimes even love it, that is, look on it as favorable to my own interest. It is only what is connected with my will as a principle, by no means as an effect—what does not subserve my inclination, but overpowers it, or at least in case of choice excludes it from its calculation—in other words, simply the law of itself, which can be an object of respect, and hence a command. Now an action done from duty must wholly exclude the influence of inclination, and with it every object of the will, so that nothing remains which can determine the will except objectively the *law,* and subjectively *pure respect* for this practical law, and consequently the maxim that I should follow this law even to the thwarting of all my inclinations.

Thus the moral worth of an action does not lie in the effect expected from it, nor in any principle of action which requires to borrow its motive from this expected effect. For all these effects—agreeableness of one's condition, and even the promotion of the happiness of others—could have been also brought about by other causes, so that for this there would have been no need of the will of a rational being; whereas it is in this alone that the supreme and unconditional good can be found. The pre-eminent good which we call moral can therefore consist in nothing else than *the conception of law* in itself, *which certainly is only possible in a rational being,* in so far as this conception, and not the expected effect, determines the will. This is a good which is already present in the person who acts accordingly, and we have not to wait for it to appear first in the result.

But what sort of law can that be the conception of which must determine the will, even without paying any regard to the effect expected from it, in order that this will may be called good absolutely and without qualification? As I have deprived the will of every impulse which could arise to it from obedience to any law, there remains nothing but the universal conformity of its actions to law in general, which alone is to serve the will as a principle, that is, I am never to act otherwise than so *that I could also will that my maxim should become a universal law*. Here, now, it is the simple conformity to law in general, without assuming any particular law applicable to certain actions, that serves the will as its principle, and must so serve it if duty is not to be a vain delusion and a chimerical notion. The common reason of men in its practical judgments perfectly coincides with this, and always has in view the principle here suggested. Let the question be, for example: May I when in distress make a promise with the intention not to keep it? I readily distinguish here between the two significations which the question may have: whether it is prudent or whether it is right to make a false promise? The former may undoubtedly often be the case. I see clearly indeed that it is not enough to extricate myself from a present difficulty by means of this subterfuge, but it must be well considered whether there may not hereafter spring from this lie much greater inconvenience than that from which I now free myself, and as, with all my supposed *cunning,* the consequences cannot be so easily foreseen but that credit once lost may be much more injurious to me than any mischief which I seek to avoid at present, it should be considered whether it would not be more *prudent* to act herein according to a universal maxim, and to make it a habit to promise nothing except with the intention of keeping it. But it is soon clear to me that such a maxim will still only be based on the fear of consequences. Now it is a wholly different thing to be truthful from duty, and to be so from apprehension of injurious consequences. In the first case, the very notion of the action already implies a law for me; in the second case, I must first look about elsewhere to see what results may be combined with it which would affect myself. For to deviate from the principle of duty is beyond all doubt wicked; but to be unfaithful to my maxim of prudence may often be very advantageous to me, although to abide by it is certainly safer. The shortest way, however, and an unerring one, to discover the answer to this question whether a lying promise is consistent with duty, is to ask myself, Should I be content that my maxim (to extricate myself from difficulty by a false promise) should hold good as a universal law, for myself as well as for others; and should I be able to say to myself, "Every one may make a deceitful promise when he finds himself in a difficulty from which he cannot otherwise extricate himself"? Then I presently become aware that, while I can will the lie, I can by no means will that lying should be a universal law. For with such a law there would be no promises at all, since it would be in vain to allege my intention in regard to my future actions to those who would not believe this allegation, or if they over-hastily did so, would pay me back in my own coin. Hence my maxim, as soon as it should be made a universal law, would necessarily destroy itself.

I do not, therefore, need any far-reaching penetration to discern what I have to do in order that my will may be morally good. Inexperienced in the course of the world, incapable of being prepared for all its contingencies, I only ask myself: Canst thou also will that thy maxim should be a universal law? If not, then it must be rejected, and that not because of a disadvantage accruing from it to myself or even to others, but because it cannot enter as a principle into a possible universal legislation, and reason extorts from me immediate respect for such legislation. I do not indeed as yet *discern* on what this respect is based (this the philosopher may inquire), but at least I understand this—that it is an estimation of the worth which far outweighs all worth of what is recommended by inclination, and that the necessity of acting from *pure* respect for the practical law is what constitutes duty, to which every other motive must give place because it is the condition of a will being good *in itself,* and the worth of such a will is above everything. . . .

Everything in nature works according to laws. Rational beings alone have the faculty of acting according *to the conception* of laws—that is, according to principles, that is, have a *will*. Since the deduction of actions from principles requires *reason,* the will is nothing but practical reason. If reason infallibly determines the will, then the actions of such a being which are recognized as objectively necessary are subjectively necessary also, that is, the will is a faculty to choose *that only* which reason independent of inclination recognizes as practically necessary, that is, as good. But if reason of itself does not sufficiently determine the will, if the latter is subject also to subjective conditions (particular impulses) which do not always coincide with the objective conditions, in a word, if the will does not *in itself* completely accord with reason (which is actually the case with men), then the actions which objectively are recognized as necessary are subjectively contingent, and the determination of such a will according to objective laws is *obligation,* that is to say, the relation of the objective laws to a will that is not thoroughly good is conceived as the determination of the will of a rational being by principles of reason, but which the will from its nature does not of necessity follow.

The conception of an objective principle, in so far as it is obligatory for a will, is called a command (of reason), and the formula of the command is called an Imperative.

All imperatives are expressed by the word *ought* [or *shall*], and thereby indicate the relation of an objective law of reason to a will which from its subjective constitution is not necessarily determined by it (an obligation). They say that something would be good to do or to forbear, but they say it to a will which does not always do a thing because it is conceived to be good to do it. That is practically *good,* however, which determines the will by means of the conceptions of reason, and consequently not from subjective causes, but objectively, that is, on principles which are valid for every rational being as such. It is distinguished from the *pleasant* as that which influences the will only by means of sensation from merely subjective causes, valid only for the sense of this or that one, and not as a principle of reason which holds for every one.

A perfectly good will would therefore be equally subject to objective laws (viz., laws of good), but could not be conceived as *obliged* thereby to act lawfully, because of itself from its subjective constitution it can only be determined by the conception of good. Therefore no imperatives hold for the Divine will, or in general for a *holy* will; *ought* is here out of place because the volition is already of itself necessarily in unison with the law. Therefore imperatives are only formulae to express the relation of objective laws of all volition to the subjective imperfection of the will of this or that rational being, for example, the human will.

Now all *imperatives* command either *hypothetically* or *categorically.* The former represent the practical necessity of a possible action as means to something else that is willed (or at least which one might possibly will). The categorical imperative would be that which represented an action as necessary of itself without reference to another end, that is, as objectively necessary.

Since every practical law represents a possible action as good, and on this account, for a subject who is practically determinable by reason as necessary, all imperatives are formulae determining an action which is necessary according to the principle of a will good in some respects. If now the action is good only as a means *to something else,* then the imperative is *hypothetical;* if it is conceived as good *in itself* and consequently as being necessarily the principle of a will which of itself conforms to reason, then it is *categorical.*

Thus the imperative declares what action possible by me would be good, and presents the practical rule in relation to a will which does not forthwith perform an action simply because it is good, whether because the subject does not always know that it is good, or because, even if it know this, yet its maxims might be opposed to the objective principles of practical reason.

Accordingly the hypothetical imperative only says that the action is good for some purpose, *possible* or *actual.* In the first case it is a *problematical,* in the second an *assertorial* practical principle. The categorical imperative which declares an action to be objectively necessary in itself without reference to any purpose, that is, without any other end, is valid as an *apodictic* (practical) principle.

Whatever is possible only by the power of some rational being may also be conceived as a possible purpose of some will; and therefore the principles of action as regards the means necessary to attain some possible purpose are in fact infinitely numerous. All sciences have a practical part consisting of problems expressing that some end is possible for us, and of imperatives directing how it may be attained. These may, therefore, be called in general imperatives of *skill.* Here there is no question whether the end is rational and good, but only what one must do in order to attain it. The precepts for the physician to make his patient thoroughly healthy, and for a poisoner to ensure certain death, are of equal value in this respect, that each serves to effect its purpose perfectly. Since in early youth it cannot be known what ends are likely to occur to us in the course of life, parents seek to have their children taught a *great many things,* and provide for their *skill* in the use of means for all sorts of arbitrary ends, of none of which can they determine whether it may not perhaps hereafter be an object to their pupil, but which it is at all events *possible* that he might aim at; and this anxiety is so great that they commonly neglect to form and correct their judgment on the value of the things which may be chosen as ends.

There is *one* end, however, which may be assumed to be actually such to all rational beings (so far as imperatives apply to them, viz., as dependent beings), and, therefore, one purpose which they not merely *may* have, but which we may with certainty assume that they all actually *have* by a natural necessity, and this is *happiness.* The hypothetical imperative which expresses the practical necessity of an action as means to the advancement of happiness is *assertorial.* We are not to present it as necessary for an uncertain and merely possible purpose, but for a purpose which we may presuppose with certainty and *a priori* in every man, because it belongs to his being. Now skill in the choice of means to his own greatest well-being may be called *prudence,* in the narrowest sense. And thus the imperative which refers to the choice of means to one's own happiness, that is, the precept of prudence, is still always *hypothetical;* the action is not commanded absolutely, but only as means to another purpose.

Finally, there is an imperative which commands a certain conduct immediately, without having as its condition any other purpose to be attained by it. This imperative is *categorical.* It concerns not the matter of the action, or its intended result, but its form and the principle of which it is itself a result; and what is essentially good in it consists in the mental disposition, let the consequence be what it may. This imperative may be called that of *morality.* . . .

When I conceive a hypothetical imperative, in general I do not know beforehand what it will contain until I am given the condition. But when I conceive a categorical imperative, I know at once what it contains. For as the imperative contains besides the law only the necessity that the maxims[2] shall conform to this law, while the law contains no conditions restricting it, there remains nothing but the general statement that the maxim of the action should conform to a universal law, and it is this conformity alone that the imperative properly represents as necessary.

There is therefore but one categorical imperative, namely, this: *Act only on that maxim whereby thou canst at the same time will that it should become a universal law.*

Now if all imperatives of duty can be deduced from this one imperative as from their principle, then, although it should remain undecided whether what is called duty is not merely a vain notion, yet at least we shall be able to show what we understand by it and what this notion means.

Since the universality of the law according to which effects are produced constitutes what is properly called *nature* in the most general sense (as to form) —that is, the existence of things so far as it is determined by general laws—the imperative of duty may be expressed thus: *Act as if the maxim of thy action were to become by thy will a universal law of nature.*

We will now enumerate a few duties, adopting the usual division of them into duties to ourselves and to others, and into perfect and imperfect duties.

1. A man reduced to despair by a series of misfortunes feels wearied of life, but is still so far in possession of his reason that he can ask himself whether it would not be contrary to his duty to himself to take his own life. Now he inquires whether the maxim of his action could become a universal law of nature. His maxim is: From self-love I adopt it as a principle to shorten my life when its longer duration is likely to bring more evil than satisfaction. It is asked then simply whether this principle founded on self-love can become a universal law of nature. Now we see at once that a system of nature of which it should be a law to destroy life by means of the very feeling whose special nature it is to impel to the improvement of life would contradict itself, and

---

[2] A "maxim" is a subjective principle of action, and must be distinguished from the *objective principle,* namely, practical law. The former contains the practical rule set by reason according to the conditions of the subject (often its ignorance or its inclinations), so that it is the principle on which the subject *acts;* but the law is the objective principle valid for every rational being, and is the principle on which it *ought to act*—that is, an imperative.

therefore could not exist as a system of nature; hence that maxim cannot possibly exist as a universal law of nature, and consequently would be wholly inconsistent with the supreme principle of all duty.

2. Another finds himself forced by necessity to borrow money. He knows that he will not be able to repay it, but sees also that nothing will be lent to him unless he promises stoutly to repay it in a definite time. He desires to make this promise, but he has still so much conscience as to ask himself: Is it not unlawful and inconsistent with duty to get out of a difficulty in this way? Suppose, however, that he resolves to do so, then the maxim of his action would be expressed thus: When I think myself in want of money, I will borrow money and promise to repay it, although I know that I never can do so. Now this principle of self-love or of one's own advantage may perhaps be consistent with my whole future welfare; but the question now is, Is it right? I change then the suggestion of self-love into a universal law, and state the question thus: How would it be if my maxim were a universal law? Then I see at once that it could never hold as a universal law of nature, but would necessarily contradict itself. For supposing it to be a universal law that everyone when he thinks himself in a difficulty should be able to promise whatever he pleases, with the purpose of not keeping his promise, the promise itself would become impossible, as well as the end that one might have in view in it, since no one would consider that anything was promised to him, but would ridicule all such statements as vain pretenses.

3. A third finds in himself a talent which with the help of some culture might make him a useful man in many respects. But he finds himself in comfortable circumstances and prefers to indulge in pleasure rather than to take pains in enlarging and improving his happy natural capacities. He asks, however, whether his maxim of neglect of his natural gifts, besides agreeing with his inclination to indulgence, agrees also with what is called duty. He sees then that a system of nature could indeed subsist with such a universal law, although men (like the South Sea islanders) should let their talents rest and resolve to devote their lives merely to idleness, amusement, and propagation of their species—in a word, to enjoyment: but he cannot possibly *will* that this should be a universal law of nature, or be implanted in us as such by a natural instinct. For, as a rational being, he necessarily wills that his faculties be developed, since they serve him, and have been given him, for all sorts of possible purposes.

4. A fourth, who is in prosperity, while he sees that others have to contend with great wretchedness and that he could help them, thinks: What concern is it of mine? Let everyone be as happy as Heaven pleases, or as he can make himself; I will take nothing from him nor even envy him, only I do not wish to contribute anything to his welfare or to his assistance in distress! Now no doubt, if such a mode of thinking were a universal law, the human race might very well subsist, and doubtless even better than in a state in which everyone talks of sympathy and good-will, or even takes care occasionally to put it into practice, but, on the other side, also cheats when he can, betrays the rights of men, or otherwise violates them. But although it is possible that a universal law of nature might exist in accordance with that maxim, it is im-

possible to *will* that such a principle should have the universal validity of a law of nature. For a will which resolved this would contradict itself, inasmuch as many cases might occur in which one would have need of the love and sympathy of others, and in which, by such a law of nature, sprung from his own will, he would deprive himself of all hope of the aid he desires.

These are a few of the many actual duties, or at least what we regard as such, which obviously fall into two classes on the one principle that we have laid down. We must be *able to will* that a maxim of our action should be a universal law. This is the canon of the moral appreciation of the action generally. Some actions are of such a character that their maxim cannot without contradiction be even *conceived* as a universal law of nature, far from it being possible that we should *will* that it *should* be so. In others, this intrinsic impossibility is not found, but still it is impossible to *will* that their maxim should be raised to the universality of a law of nature, since such a will would contradict itself. It is easily seen that the former violate strict or rigorous (inflexible) duty; the latter only laxer (meritorious) duty. Thus it has been completely shown by these examples how all duties depend as regards the nature of the obligation (not the object of the action) on the same principle.

If now we attend to ourselves on occasion of any transgression of duty, we shall find what we in fact do not will that our maxim should be a universal law, for that is impossible for us; on the contrary, we will that the opposite should remain a universal law, only we assume the liberty of making an *exception* in our own favor or (just for this time only) in favor of our inclination. Consequently, if we considered all cases from one and the same point of view, namely, that of reason, we should find a contradiction in our own will, namely, that a certain principle should be objectively necessary as a universal law, and yet subjectively should not be universal, but admit of exceptions. As, however, we at one moment regard our action from the point of view of a will wholly conformed to reason, and then again look at the same action from the point of view of a will affected by inclination, there is not really any contradiction, but an antagonism of inclination to the precept of reason, whereby the universality of the principle is changed into a mere generality, so that the practical principle of reason shall meet the maxim half way. Now, although this cannot be justified in our own impartial judgment, yet it proves that we do really recognize the validity of the categorical imperative and (with all respect for it) only allow ourselves a few exceptions which we think unimportant and forced from us. . . .

The will is conceived as a faculty of determining oneself to action *in accordance with the conception of certain laws*. And such a faculty can be found only in rational beings. Now that which serves the will as the objective ground of its self-determination is the *end,* and if this is assigned by reason alone, it must hold for all rational beings. On the other hand, that which merely contains the ground of possibility of the action of which the effect is the end, this is called the *means*. The subjective ground of the desire is the *spring,* the objective ground of the volition is the *motive;* hence the distinction between subjective ends which rest on springs, and objective ends which depend on motives valid for every rational being. Practical principles are *formal* when they abstract from all subjective ends; they are *material* when they assume these, and therefore particular, springs of action. The ends which a rational being proposes to himself at pleasure as *effects* of his actions (material ends) are all only relative, for it is only their relation to the particular desires of the subject that gives them their worth, which therefore cannot furnish principles universal and necessary for all rational beings and for every volition, that is to say, practical laws. Hence all these relative ends can give rise only to hypothetical imperatives.

Supposing, however, that there were something *whose existence* has *in itself* an absolute worth, something which, being *an end in itself,* could be a source of definite laws, then in this and this alone would lie the source of a possible categorical imperative, that is, a practical law.

Now I say: man and generally any rational being *exists* as an end in himself, *not merely as a means* to be arbitrarily used by this or that will, but in all his actions, whether they concern himself or other rational beings, must be always regarded at the same time as an end. All objects of the inclinations have only a conditional worth; for if the inclinations and the wants founded on them did not exist, then their object would be without value. But the inclinations themselves, being sources of want, are so far from having an absolute worth for which they should be desired that, on the contrary, it must be the universal wish of every rational being to be wholly free from them. Thus the worth of any object which is *to be acquired* by our action is always conditional. Beings whose existence depends not on our will but on nature's, have nevertheless, if they are not rational beings, only a relative value as means, and are therefore called *things;* rational beings, on the contrary, are called *persons,* because their very nature points them out as ends in themselves, that is, as something which must not be used merely as means, and so far therefore restricts freedom of action (and is an object of respect). These, therefore, are not merely subjective ends whose existence has a worth *for us* as an effect of our action, but *objective ends,* that is, things whose existence is an end in itself—an end, moreover, for which no other can be substituted, which they should subserve *merely* as means, for otherwise nothing whatever would possess *absolute worth;* but if all worth were conditioned and therefore contingent, then there would be no supreme practical principle of reason whatever.

If then there is a supreme practical principle or, in respect of the human will, a categorical imperative, it must be one which, being drawn from the conception of that which is necessarily an end for everyone because it is *an end in itself,* constitutes an *objective* principle of will, and can therefore serve as a universal practical law. The foundation of this principle is: *rational nature exists as an end in itself.* Man necessarily conceives his own existence as being so; so far then this is a *subjective* principle of human actions. But every other rational being regards its existence similarly, just on the same rational principle that holds for me; so that it is at the same time an objective principle from which as a supreme practical law all laws of the will must be capable of being deduced. Accordingly the practical imperative will be as follows: *So act as to treat humanity, whether in thine own person or in that of any other, in every case as an end withal, never as means only.* We will now inquire whether this can be practically carried out.

To abide by the previous examples:

First, under the head of necessary duty to oneself: He who contemplates suicide should ask himself whether his action can be consistent with the idea of humanity *as an end in itself.* If he destroys himself in order to escape from painful circumstances, he uses a person merely as *a mean* to maintain a tolerable condition up to the end of life. But a man is not a thing, that is to say, something which can be used merely as means, but must in all his actions be always considered as an end in himself. I cannot, therefore, dispose in any way of a man in my own person so as to mutilate him, to damage or kill him. (It belongs to ethics proper to define this principle more precisely, so as to avoid all misunderstanding, for example, as to the amputation of the limbs in order to preserve myself; as to exposing my life to danger with a view to preserve it, etc. This question is therefore omitted here.)

Secondly, as regards necessary duties, or those of strict obligation, towards others: He who is thinking of making a lying promise to others will see at once that he would be using another man *merely as a mean,* without the latter containing at the same time the end in himself. For he whom I propose by such a promise to use for my own purposes cannot possibly assent to my mode of acting towards him, and therefore cannot himself contain the end of this action. This violation of the principle of humanity in other men is more obvious if we take in examples of attacks on the freedom and property of others. For then it is clear that he who transgresses the rights of men intends to use the person of others merely as means, without considering that as rational beings they ought always to be esteemed also as ends, that is, as beings who must be capable of containing in themselves the end of the very same action.

Thirdly, as regards contingent (meritorious) duties to oneself: It is not enough that the action does not violate humanity in our own person as an end in itself, it must also *harmonize with it.* Now there are in humanity capacities of greater perfection which belong to the end that nature has in view in regard to humanity in ourselves as the subject; to neglect these might perhaps be consistent with the *maintenance* of humanity as an end in itself, but not with the *advancement* of this end.

Fourthly, as regards meritorious duties towards others: The natural end which all men have is their own happiness. Now humanity might indeed subsist although no one should contribute anything to the happiness of others, provided he did not intentionally withdraw anything from it; but after all, this would only harmonize negatively, not positively, with *humanity as an end in itself,* if everyone does not also endeavor, as far as in him lies, to forward the ends of others. For the ends of any subject which is an end in himself ought as far as possible to be *my* ends also, if that conception is to have its *full* effect with me.

This principle that humanity and generally every rational nature is *an end in itself* (which is the supreme limiting condition of every man's freedom of action), is not borrowed from experience, *first,* because it is universal, applying as it does to all rational beings whatever, and experience is not capable of determining anything about them; *secondly,* because it does not present humanity as an end to men (subjectively), that is, as an object which men do of themselves actually adopt as an end; but as an objective end which must as a law constitute the supreme limiting condition of all our subjective ends, let them be what we will; it must therefore spring from pure reason. In fact the objective principle of all practical legislation lies (according to the first principle) in *the rule* and its form of universality which makes it capable of being a law (say, for example, a law of nature); but the *subjective* principle is in the *end;* now by the second principle, the subject of all ends is each rational being inasmuch as it is an end in itself. Hence follows the third practical principle of the will, which is the ultimate condition of its harmony with the universal practical reason, viz., the idea of *the will of every rational being as a universally legislative will.*

On this principle all maxims are rejected which are inconsistent with the will being itself universal legislator. Thus the will is not subject to the law, but so subject that it must be regarded *as itself giving the law,* and on this ground only subject to the law (of which it can regard itself as the author).

In the previous imperatives, namely, that based on the conception of the conformity of actions to general laws, as in a *physical system of nature,* and that based on the universal *prerogative* of rational beings as *ends* in themselves —these imperatives just because they were conceived as categorical excluded from any share in their authority all admixture of any interest as a spring of action, they were, however, only *assumed* to be categorical, because such an assumption was necessary to explain the conception of duty. But we could not prove independently that there are practical propositions which command categorically, nor can it be proved in this section; one thing, however, could be done, namely, to indicate in the imperative itself, by some determinate expression, that in the case of volition from duty all interest is renounced, which is the specific criterion of categorical as distinguished from hypothetical imperatives. This is done in the present (third) formula of the principle, namely, in the idea of the will of every rational being as a *universally legislating will.*

For although a will *which is subject to laws* may be attached to this law by means of an interest, yet a will which is itself a supreme lawgiver, so far as it is such, cannot possibly depend on any interest, since a will so dependent would itself still need another law restricting the interest of its self-love by the condition that it should be valid as universal law.

Thus the *principle* that every human will is *a will which in all its maxims gives universal laws,*[3] provided it be otherwise justified, would be very *well adapted* to be the categorical imperative, in this respect, namely, that just because of the idea of universal legislation it is *not based on any interest,* and therefore it alone among all possible imperatives can be *unconditional.* Or

---

[3] I may be excused from adducing examples to elucidate this principle, as those which have already been used to elucidate the categorical imperative and its formula would all serve for the like purpose here.

still better, converting the proposition, if there is a categorical imperative (that is, a law for the will of every rational being), it can only command that everything be done from maxims of one's will regarded as a will which could be at the same time will that it should itself give universal laws, for in that case only the practical principle and the imperative which it obeys are unconditional, since they cannot be based on any interest. . . .

The conception of every rational being as one which must consider itself as giving in all the maxims of its will universal laws, so as to judge itself and its actions from this point of view—this conception leads to another which depends on it and is very fruitful, namely, that of a *kingdom of ends.*

By a "kingdom" I understand the union of different rational beings in a system by common laws. Now since it is by laws that ends are determined as regards their universal validity, hence, if we abstract from the personal differences of rational beings, and likewise from all the content of their private ends, we shall be able to conceive all ends combined in a systematic whole (including both rational beings as ends in themselves, and also the special ends which each may propose to himself), that is to say, we can conceive a kingdom of ends, which on the preceding principles is possible.

For all rational beings come under the *law* that each of them must treat itself and all others *never merely as means,* but in every case *at the same time as ends in themselves.* Hence results a systematic union of rational beings by common objective laws, that is, a kingdom which may be called a kingdom of ends, since what these laws have in view is just the relation of these beings to one another as ends and means. It is certainly only an ideal.

A rational being belongs as a *member* to the kingdom of ends when, although giving universal laws in it, he is also himself subject to these laws. He belongs to it *as sovereign* when, while giving laws, he is not subject to the will of any other.

A rational being must always regard himself as giving laws either as member or as sovereign in a kingdom of ends which is rendered possible by the freedom of will. He cannot, however, maintain the latter position merely by the maxims of his will, but only in case he is a completely independent being without wants and with unrestricted power adequate to his will.

Morality consists then in the reference of all action to the legislation which alone can render a kingdom of ends possible. This legislation must be capable of existing in every rational being, and of emanating from his will, so that the principle of this will is never to act on any maxim which could not without contradition be also a universal law, and accordingly always so to act *that the will could at the same time regard itself as giving in its maxims universal laws.* If now the maxims of rational beings are not by their own nature coincident with this objective principle, then the necessity of acting on it is called practical necessitation that is, *duty.*

The practical necessity of acting on this principle, that is, duty, does not rest at all on feelings, impulses, or inclinations, but solely on the relation of rational beings to one another, a relation in which the will of a rational being must always be regarded as *legislative,* since otherwise it could not be conceived as *an end in itself*. Reason then refers every maxim of the will, regarding it as legislating universally, to every other will and also to every action towards oneself: and this not on account of any other practical motive or any future advantage, but from the idea of the *dignity* of a rational being, obeying no law but that which he himself also gives.

Whatever has reference to the general inclinations and wants to mankind has a *market value;* whatever, without presupposing a want, corresponds to a certain taste, that is, to a satisfaction in the mere purposeless play of our faculties, has a *fancy value;* but that which constitutes the condition under which alone anything can be an end in itself, this has not merely a relative worth, that is, value, but an intrinsic worth, that is, *dignity*.

Duties and the Right

W. D. ROSS

William David Ross (1877–   ) was born in Scotland and educated in the Edinburgh and Oxford Universities. He taught for many years at Oxford and served as its vice-chancellor. He is the author of important works in the history of philosophy and is the editor of the Oxford edition of Aristotle, Ross having translated the *Ethics* and *Metaphysics* himself. In *The Right and the Good* (1930) and *Foundations of Ethics* (1939), he presents his own theory of ethics.

The real point at issue between hedonism and utilitarianism on the one hand and their opponents on the other is not whether "right" means "productive of so and so"; for it cannot with any plausibility be maintained that it does. The point at issue is that to which we now pass, viz. whether there is any general character which makes right acts right, and if so, what it is. Among the main historical attempts to state a single characteristic of all right actions which is the foundation of their rightness are those made by egoism and utilitarianism. But I do not propose to discuss these, not because the subject is unimportant, but because it has been dealt with so often and so well already, and because there has come to be so much agreement among moral philosophers that neither of these theories is satisfactory. A much more attractive theory has been put forward by Professor [G. E.] Moore: that what makes actions right is that they are productive of more *good* than could have been produced by any other action open to the agent.[1]

This theory is in fact the culmination of all the attempts to base rightness on productivity of some sort of result. The first form this attempt takes is the attempt to base rightness on productivity of some sort of result. The first form

[1] I take the theory which, as I have tried to show, seems to be put forward in *Ethics* rather than the earlier and less plausible theory put forward in *Principia Ethica*.

Source: W. D. Ross, *The Right and the Good* (Oxford, 1930), pp. 16–20, 29–33, 41–44. Reprinted by permission of The Clarendon Press.

this attempt takes is the attempt to base rightness on conduciveness to the advantage or pleasure of the agent. This theory comes to grief over the fact, which stares us in the face, that a great part of duty consists in an observance of the rights and a furtherance of the interests of others, whatever the cost to ourselves may be. Plato and others may be right in holding that a regard for the rights of others never in the long run involves a loss of happiness for the agent, that "the just life profits a man." But this, even if true, is irrelevant to the rightness of the act. As soon as a man does an action *because* he thinks he will promote his own interests thereby, he is acting not from a sense of its rightness but from self-interest.

To the egoistic theory, hedonistic utilitarianism supplies a much-needed amendment. It points out correctly that the fact that a certain pleasure will be enjoyed by the agent is no reason why he *ought* to bring it into being rather than an equal or greater pleasure to be enjoyed by another, though, human nature being what it is, it makes it not unlikely that he *will* try to bring it into being. But hedonistic utilitarianism in its turn needs a correction. On reflection it seems clear that pleasure is not the only thing in life that we think good in itself, that for instance we think the possession of a good character, or an intelligent understanding of the world, as good or better. A great advance is made by the substitution of "productive of the greatest good" for "productive of the greatest pleasure."

Not only is this theory more attractive than hedonistic utilitarianism, but its logical relation to that theory is such that the latter could not be true unless *it* were true, while it might be true though hedonistic utilitarianism were not. It is in fact one of the logical bases of hedonistic utilitarianism. For the view that what produces the maximum pleasure is right has for its bases the views (1) that what produces the maximum good is right, and (2) that pleasure is the only thing good in itself. If they were not assuming that what produces the maximum *good* is right, the utilitarians' attempt to show that pleasure is the only thing good in itself, which is in fact the point they take most pains to establish, would have been quite irrelevant to their attempt to prove that only what produces the maximum *pleasure* is right. If, therefore, it can be shown that productivity of the maximum good is not what makes all right actions right, we shall *a fortiori*[2] have refuted hedonistic utilitarianism.

When a plain man fulfils a promise because he thinks he ought to do so, it seems clear that he does so with no thought of its total consequences, still less with any opinion that these are likely to be the best possible. He thinks in fact much more of the past than of the future. What makes him think it right to act in a certain way is the fact that he has promised to do so—that and, usually, nothing more. That his act will produce the best possible consequences is not his reason for calling it right. What lends colour to the theory we are examining, then, is not the actions (which form probably a great majority of our actions) in which some such reflections as "I have promised" is the only reason we give ourselves for thinking a certain action right, but the exceptional cases in which the consequences of fulfilling a promise (for instance) would be so disastrous

---

[2] [With stronger reason.—Eds.]

to others that we judge it right not to do so. It must of course be admitted that such cases exist. If I have promised to meet a friend at a particular time for some trivial purpose, I should certainly think myself justified in breaking my engagement if by doing so I could prevent a serious accident or bring relief to the victims of one. And the supporters of the view we are examining hold that my thinking so is due to my thinking that shall bring more good into existence by the one action than by the other. A different account may, however, be given of the matter, an account which will, I believe, show itself to be the true one. It may be said that besides the duty of fulfilling promises, I have and recognize a duty of relieving distress,[3] and that when I think it right to do the latter at the cost of not doing the former, it is not because I think I shall produce more good thereby but because I think it the duty which is in the circumstances more of a duty. This account surely corresponds much more closely with what we really think in such a situation. If, so far as I can see, I could bring equal amounts of good into being by fulfilling my promise and by helping some one to whom I had made no promise, I should not hesitate to regard the former as my duty. Yet on the view that what is right is right because it is productive of the most good, I should not so regard it.

There are two theories, each in its way simple, that offer a solution of such cases of conscience. One is the view of Kant, that there are certain duties of perfect obligation, such as those of fulfilling promises, of paying debts, of telling the truth, which admit of no exception whatever in favour of duties of imperfect obligation, such as that of relieving distress. The other is the view of, for instance, Professor Moore and Dr. [H.] Rashdall, that there is only the duty of producing good, and that all "conflicts of duties" should be resolved by asking "by which action will most good be produced?" But it is more important that our theory fit the facts than that it be simple, and the account we have given above corresponds (it seems to me) better than either of the simpler theories with what we really think, viz. that normally promise-keeping, for example, should come before benevolence, but that when and only when the good to be produced by the benevolent act is very great and the promise comparatively trivial, the act of benevolence becomes our duty.

In fact the theory of "ideal utilitarianism," if I may for brevity refer so to the theory of Professor Moore, seems to simplify unduly our relations to our fellows. It says, in effect, that the only morally significant relation in which my neighbors stand to me is that of being possible beneficiaries by my action.[4] They do stand in this relation to me, and this relation is morally significant. But they may also stand to me in the relation of promisee to promiser, of creditor to debtor, of wife to husband, of child to parent, of friend to friend, of fellow countryman to fellow countryman, and the like; and each of these relations is the foundation of a *prima facie* duty, which is more or less in-

---

[3] These are not, strictly speaking, duties, but things that tend to be our duty, or *prima facie* duties. Cf. pp. 19–20, *The Right and the Good*.

[4] Some will think it, apart from other considerations, a sufficient refutation of this view to point out that I also stand in that relation to myself, so that for this view the distinction of oneself from others is morally insignificant.

cumbent on me according to the circumstances of the case. When I am in a situation, as perhaps I always am, in which more than one of these *prima facie* duties is incumbent on me, what I have to do is to study the situation as fully as I can until I form the considered opinion (it is never more) that in the circumstances one of them is more incumbent than any other; then I am bound to think that do this *prima facie* duty is my duty *sans phrase* in the situation.

I suggest *"prima facie* duty" or "conditional duty" as a brief way of referring to the characteristic (quite distinct from that of being a duty proper) which an act has, in virtue of being of a certain kind (e.g. the keeping of a promise), of being an act which would be a duty proper if it were not at the same time of another kind which is morally significant. Whether an act is a duty proper or actual duty depends on *all* the morally significant kinds it is an instance of.

It is necessary to say something by way of clearing up the relation between *prima facie* duties and the actual or absolute duty to do one particular act in particular circumstances. If, as almost all moralists except Kant are agreed, and as most plain men think, it is sometimes right to tell a lie or to break a promise, it must be maintained that there is a difference between *prima facie* duty and actual or absolute duty. When we think ourselves justified in breaking, and indeed morally obliged to break, a promise, in order to relieve some one's distress, we do not for a moment cease to recognize a *prima facie* duty to keep our promise, and this leads us to feel, not indeed shame or repentance, but certainly compunction, for behaving as we do; we recognize, further, that it is our duty to make up somehow to the promisee for the breaking of the promise. We have to distinguish from the characteristic of being our duty that of tending to be our duty. Any act that we do contains various elements in virtue of which it falls under various categories. In virtue of being the breaking of a promise, for instance, it tends to be wrong; in virtue of being an instance of relieving distress it tends to be right. Tendency to be one's duty may be called a parti-resultant attribute, i.e., one which belongs to an act in virtue of some one component in its nature. *Being* one's duty is a toti-resultant attribute, one which belongs to an act in virtue of its whole nature and of nothing less than this. This distinction between parti-resultant and toti-resultant attributes is one which we shall meet in another context also.

Something should be said of the relation between our apprehension of the *prima facie* rightness of certain types of act and our mental attitude towards particular acts. It is proper to use the word "apprehension" in the former case and not in the latter. That an act, *qua* fulfilling a promise, or *qua* effecting a just distribution of good, or *qua* returning services rendered, or *qua* promoting the good of others, or *qua* promoting the virtue or insight of the agent, is *prima facie* right, is self-evident; not in the sense that it is evident from the beginning of our lives, or as soon as we attend to the proposition for the first time, but in the sense that when we have reached sufficient mental maturity and have given sufficient attention to the proposition it is evident without any need of proof, or of evidence beyond iself. It is self-evident just as a mathematical axiom, or the validity of a form of inference, is evident. The moral order expressed in these propositions is just as much part of the fundamental nature of the universe (and, we may add, of any possible universe in which there were moral agents at all) as is the spatial or numerical structure expressed in the axioms of geometry or arithmetic. In our confidence that these propositions are true there is involved the same trust in our reason that is involved in our confidence in mathematics; and we should have no justification for trusting it in the latter sphere and distrusting it in the former. In both cases we are dealing with propositions that cannot be proved, but that just as certainly need no proof.

Our judgements about our actual duty in concrete situations have none of the certainty that attaches to our recognition of the general principles of duty. A statement is certain, i.e. is an expression of knowledge, only in one or other of two cases: when it is either self-evident, or a valid conclusion from self-evident premises. And our judgements about our particular duties have neither of these characters. (1) They are not self-evident. Where a possible act is seen to have two characteristics, in virtue of one of which it is *prima facie* right, and in virtue of the other *prima facie* wrong, we are (I think) well aware that we are not certain whether we ought or ought not to do it; that whether we do it or not, we are taking a moral risk. We come in the long run, after consideration, to think one duty more pressing than the other, but we do not feel certain that it is so. And though we do not always recognize that a possible act has two such characteristics, and though there *may* be cases in which it has not, we are never certain that any particular possible act has not, and therefore never certain that it is right, nor certain that it is wrong. For, to go no further in the analysis, it is enough to point out that any particular act will in all probability in the course of time contribute to the bringing about of good or of evil for many human beings, and thus have a *prima facie* rightness or wrongness of which we know nothing. (2) Again, our judgements about our particular duties are not logical conclusions from self-evident premises. The only possible premises would be the general principles stating their *prima facie* rightness or wrongness *qua* having the different characteristics they do have; and even if we could (as we cannot) apprehend the extent to which an act will tend on the one hand, for example, to bring about advantages for our benefactors, and on the other hand to bring about disadvantages for fellow men who are not our benefactors, there is no principle by which we can draw the conclusion that it is on the whole right or on the whole wrong. In this respect the judgement as to the rightness of a particular act is just like the judgement as to the beauty of a particular natural object or work of art. A poem is, for instance, in respect of certain qualities beautiful and in respect of certain others not beautiful; and our judgement as to the degree of beauty it possesses on the whole is never reached by logical reasoning from the apprehension of its particular beauties or particular defects. Both in this and in the moral case we have more or less probable opinions which are not logically justified conclusions from the general principles that are recognised as self-evident.

There is therefore much truth in the description of the right act as a fortunate act. If we cannot be certain that it is right, it is our good fortune if the act we do is the right act. This consideration does not, however, make the doing of our duty a mere matter of chance. There is a parallel here between the doing of duty and the doing of what will be to our personal advantage. We never *know* what act will in the long run be to our advantage. Yet it is certain that we are more likely in general to secure our advantage if we estimate to the best of our ability the probable tendencies of our actions in this respect, than if we act on caprice. And similarly we are more likely to do our duty if we reflect to the best of our ability on the *prima facie* rightness or wrongness of various possible acts in virtue of the characteristics we perceive them to have, than if we act without reflection. With this greater likelihood we must be content.

The general principles of duty are obviously not self-evident from the beginning of our lives. How do they come to be so? The answer is that they come to be self-evident to us just as mathematical axioms do. We find by experience that this couple of matches and that couple make four matches, that this couple of balls on a wire and that couple make four balls; and by reflection on these and similar discoveries we come to see that it is of the nature of two and two to make four. In a precisely similar way, we see the *prima facie* rightness of an act which would be the fulfilment of a particular promise, and of another which would be the fulfilment of another promise, and when we have reached sufficient maturity to think in general terms, we apprehend *prima facie* rightness to belong to the nature of any fulfilment of promise. What comes first in time is the apprehension of the self-evident *prima facie* rightness of an individual act of a particular type. From this we come by reflection to apprehend the self-evident general principle of *prima facie* duty. From this, too, perhaps along with the apprehension of the self-evident *prima facie* rightness of the same act in virtue of its having another characteristic as well, and perhaps in spite of the apprehension of its *prima facie* wrongness in virtue of its having some third characteristic, we come to believe something not self-evident at all, but an object of probable opinion, viz. that this particular act is (not *prima facie* but) actually right.

It is worth while to try to state more definitely the nature of the acts that are right. We may try to state first what (if anything) is the universal nature of *all* acts that are right. It is obvious that any of the acts that we do has countless effects, directly or indirectly, on countless people, and the probability is that any act, however right it be, will have adverse effects (though these may be very trivial) on some innocent people. Similarly, any wrong act will probably have beneficial effects on some deserving people. Every act therefore, viewed in some aspects, will be *prima facie* right, and viewed in others, *prima facie* wrong, and right acts can be distinguished from wrong acts only as being those which, of all those possible for the agent in the circumstances, have the greatest balance of *prima facie* rightness, in those respects in which they are *prima facie* right, over their *prima facie* wrongness, in those respects in which they are *prima facie* wrong—*prima facie* rightness and wrongness being understood in the sense previously explained. For the estimation of the comparative stringency of these *prima facie* obligations no general rules can, so far as I can see, be laid down. We can only say that a great deal of stringency belongs to the duties of "perfect obligation"—the duties of keeping our promises, of repairing wrongs we have done, and of returning the equivalent of services we have received. For the rest, ἐν τῇ αἰσθήσει ἡ ξίσις.[5] This sense of our particular duty in particular circumstances, preceded and informed by the fullest reflection we can bestow on the act in all its bearings, is highly fallible, but it is the only guide we have to our duty.

When we turn to consider the nature of individual right acts, the first point to which attention should be called is that any act may be correctly described in an indefinite, and in principle infinite, number of ways. An act is the production of a change in the state of affairs (if we ignore, for simplicity's sake, the comparatively few cases in which it is the maintenance of an existing state of affairs; cases which, I think, raise no special difficulty). Now, the only changes we can *directly* produce are changes in our own bodies or in our own minds. But these are not, as such, what as a rule we think it our duty to produce. Consider some comparatively simple act, such as telling the truth or fulfilling a promise. In the first case what I produce directly is movements of my vocal organs. But what I think it my duty to produce is a true view in some one else's mind about some fact, and between my movement of my vocal organs and this result there intervenes a series of physical events and events in his mind. Again, in the second case, I may have promised, for instance, to return a book to a friend. I may be able, by a series of movements of my legs and hands, to place it in his hands. But what I am just as likely to do, and to think I have done my duty in doing, is to send it by a messenger or to hand it to his servant or to send it by post; and in each of these cases what I *do* directly is worthless in itself and is connected by a series of intermediate links with what I have promised to return to him. This being so, it *seems* as if what I *do* has no obligatoriness in itself and as if one or other of three accounts should be given of the matter, each of which makes rightness not belong to what I do, considered in its own nature.

(1) One of them would be that what is obligatory is not *doing* anything in the natural sense of producing any change in the state of affairs, but *aiming at* something—at, for instance, my friend's reception of the book. But this account will not do. For (*a*) to aim at something is to act from a motive consisting of the wish to bring that thing about. But we have seen that motive never forms part of the content of our duty; if anything is certain about morals, that, I think, is certain. And (*b*) if I have promised to return the book to my friend. I obviously do not fulfil my promise and do my duty merely by aiming at his receiving the book; I must see that he actually receives it. (2) A more plausible account is that which says I must do that which is likely to produce the result. But this account is open to the second of these objections, and probably also to the first. For in the first place, however likely my act may seem, even on careful consideration, and even however likely it may in fact be, to produce the result, if it does not produce it, I have not done what I promised to do, i.e. have not done my duty. And secondly, when it is said that I ought to do what is likely to produce the result, what is *probably* meant is that I ought to do a certain thing as a result of the wish to produce a certain result, and of the thought that my act is likely to produce it; and this again introduces motive

---

[5] "The decision rests with perception." Arist. *Nic. Eth.* 1109 b 23, 1126b 4.

into the content of duty. (3) Much the most plausible of the three accounts is that which says, "I ought to do that which will actually produce a certain result." This escapes objection (*b*). Whether it escapes objection (*a*) or not depends on what exactly is meant. If it is meant that I ought to do a certain thing from the wish to produce a certain result and the thought that it will do so, the account is still open to objection (*a*). But if it is meant simply that I ought to do a certain thing, and that the reason why I ought to do it is that it will produce a certain result, objection (*a*) is avoided. Now this account in its second form is that which utilitarianism gives. It says what is right is certain acts, not certain acts motivated in a certain way; and it says that acts are never right by their own nature but by virtue of the goodness of their actual results. And this account is, I think, clearly nearer the truth than one which makes the rightness of an act depend on the goodness of either the *intended* or the *likely* results.

Nevertheless, this account appears not to be the true one. For it implies that what we consider right or our duty is what we do *directly*. It is this, e.g. the packing up and posting of the book, that derives its moral significance not from its own nature but from its consequences. But this is *not* what we should describe, strictly, as our duty; our duty is to fulfil our promise, i.e. to put the book into our friend's possession. This we consider obligatory in its own nature, just because it is a fulfilment of promise, and not because of *its* consequences. But, it might be replied by the utilitarian, I do not do this; I only do something that leads up to this, and what I do has no moral significance in itself but only because of its consequences. In answer to this, however, we may point out that a cause produces not only its immediate, but also its remote consequences, and the latter no less than the former. I, therefore, not only produce the immediate movements of parts of my body but also my friend's reception of the book, which results from these. Or, if this be objected to on the grounds that I can hardly be said to have produced my friend's reception of the book when I have packed and posted it, owing to the time that has still to elapse before he receives it, and that to say I have produced the result hardly does justice to the part played by the Post Office, we may at least say that I have *secured* my friend's reception of the book. What I do is as truly describable in this way as by saying that it is the packing and posting of a book. (It is equally truly describable in many other ways; e.g. I have provided a few moments' employment for Post Office officials. But this is irrelevant to the argument.) And if we ask ourselves whether it is *qua* the packing and posting of a book, or *qua* the securing of my friend's getting what I have promised to return to him, that my action is right, it is clear that it is in the second capacity that it is right; and in this capacity, the only capacity in which it is right, it is right by its own nature and not because of its consequences.

The Prima Facie Rules of War

D. THOMAS O'CONNOR

Thomas O'Connor (1932–   ) is professor of philosophy at Marietta College. He writes about the philosophical basis of contemporary moral issues.

Moral decision making in respect to war is so problematic that one is tempted either to damn all wars as immoral or to declare that only "might makes right" in war. The former solution to the dilemma of war is often a moral commitment worthy of respect. Individual conscientious objectors and the various pacifist organizations exert a humanizing influence upon society by keeping the evils of war before the public conscience. It is doubtful, however, that pacifism is a fully adequate social ethic in circumstances where crucial values can be preserved only by the exercise of physical force. The latter alternative—"might makes right" in war—does not resolve the ambiguity of war but rather abandons the ethical task altogether.

A more fruitful approach holds that relative moral judgments in respect to war are both possible and necessary. But how does one provide a suitable framework for moral reflection on war? This essay suggests one possible basis by reexamining the traditional rules of just warfare in the light of the contemporary world situation.[1] In my judgment, the just-war tradition is best understood as various prima facie moral principles which emerged from both religious and secular reflection throughout the course of Western history. These moral guidelines gained a measure of public acceptance because they reflect human sensibilities about the need to limit warfare to potentially moral purposes. The rules of just warfare are prima facie duties because they define abstract moral obligations. Thus, a nation ought not to violate a principle of just warfare unless a more important principle takes precedence. As W. D. Ross insisted, moral rules define abstract rights or duties; whether an actual right or duty exists can be determined only by examining all of the relevant facts and principles in a given moral context.[2]

Understanding the just-war tradition in terms of prima facie duty provides both structure and flexibility for viewing war in a moral perspective. Since the rules of just warfare admittedly conflict, they cannot be applied apart from a full understanding of the moral context. Moreover, these rules cannot be traced to one absolute, higher principle without unduly narrowing or oversimplifying

---

[1] The presentation of these rules is adapted from the treatment in Edward L. Long, *War and Conscience in America* (Philadelphia: Westminster Press, 1968), pp. 24–30. The explanation and modern interpretation of these principles are my own.

[2] W. D. Ross, *Foundations of Ethics,* Gifford Lectures, 1935–1936 (Oxford: Clarendon Press, 1939), pp. 313ff.

Source: D. Thomas O'Connor, "A Reappraisal of the Just War Tradition," *Ethics,* Vol. 84, No. 2 (January 1974), pp. 167–173. Reprinted by permission of The University of Chicago Press and the author.

the scope of this moral tradition. Finally, since the rules of just warfare are not abstract, timeless absolutes, they must be subjected to reexamination and reinterpretation in each historical era.

The first rule of just warfare is that war must be conducted for a just cause. This provision recognizes that great evils attend any war and that only very grave reasons can morally justify the decision to go to war. In traditional just-war theory, it is not the overall justice of a regime that determines whether a just cause exists; rather, a specific incident or unjust action provides the occasion for a just declaration of war. The just warring power, therefore, serves a judicial function in punishing a wayward nation. The modern view, however, correctly understands international conflict as a long-term process; the specific "cause" leading to an outbreak of hostilities may be less important than the underlying circumstances in the relationship between the warring nations.[3]

The "just cause" stipulation of the just-war tradition assumes that nations have a prima facie right to self-defense. Usually, unprovoked aggression provides a just cause for a declaration of war by the victim. But even the basic right of self-defense cannot be held absolutely. For example, it is doubtful that an attack upon the United States by an enemy using conventional weapons would morally justify a nuclear response on the basis of self-defense. It cannot even be stated in advance that a nuclear attack upon the United States would always justify nuclear retaliation. The principle of self-defense might be overruled by the principle of proportionality (discussed more fully below), which requires that military means be related to rational political ends. The right of self-defense remains a prima facie principle, however, and provides legitimacy for the defense efforts of all nations.

The just-cause principle involves determinations of relative justice which are especially important in moral judgments concerning revolution. On the one hand, an existing government's claim to legitimacy entitles it to wield the right of self-defense against both external threats and internal disruptions. On the other hand, a regime may be so corrupt or unjust that one is morally impelled to bring about its downfall. In the latter instance, valid appeals can also be made to the criterion of just cause. Although decisions in this area are unavoidably relative, one must consider such factors as the potential for political change short of revolution, the degree to which the present government is repressive, unjust, or dehumanizing, and the prospects for creating and maintaining a better social order.

Judgments of relative justice are also important in evaluating various causes in international conflict. It is no easy task to determine which side of a conflict has the greater measure of justice. But this uncertainty is present in all moral judgments involving a conflict of principles or factual disagreements. Despite these obvious limitations, it still makes sense to argue, for example, that the Allies of World War II fought for a just cause. It is interesting that all papers on this question presented at the 1970 meeting of the American Political Science Association reached this conclusion, although the authors approached this issue

---

[3] Joseph D. Stamey, "Christian Ethics and Violent Conflict: The 'Just War' as an Ethical Model" (Ph.D. diss., Boston University Graduate School, 1968), p. 393.

from different ethical perspectives.[4] Such a judgment would necessarily consider arguments in support of the Nazi cause, such as the injustices perpetrated against Germany by the Treaty of Versailles, but it would insist that the aggression against Czechoslovakia, Poland, Holland, Belgium, et al., and the Nazi commitment to genocide, were evils of such enormity that the Allies were morally justified in opposing the Nazi regime by military force. To deny the possibility of such judgments of relative justice is to deny the possibility of moral judgments altogether.

The just-cause criterion limits the ends for which men are morally permitted to fight. While the application of this principle is regrettably inexact, the just-cause rule is an indispensable ingredient of the just-war legacy. It acknowledges the evils of war, insists that war is justified only for grave reasons, and makes the moral claim that might is not the sole determinant of right in international conflict. This principle provides an important basis for our own moral judgments about the rightness or wrongness of a particular war.

The second traditional rule of just warfare is that war must be carried out with a right attitude. In Saint Augustine's original formulation of this principle, the understanding of right attitude was highly subjective. Augustine insisted that war could be conducted with a loving, Christian disposition, since the guilty nation was only being punished for its own good.[5]

A right attitude in war, however, does not consist of sincere beliefs or pious intentions. Indeed, ideology founded on either a religious or secular basis is a dangerous ingredient in warfare. A just war becomes a "holy crusade" precisely at the point where ideology replaces a more rational, balanced perspective. A right attitude toward war is both realistic and rational. It recognizes the great evils which accompany even a just war, it acknowledges the need to limit objectives and to anticipate the needs for order and stability once a war is concluded. Of course, war invariably generates passion. But if passion is unchecked, both the means and ends of war become total. The first requirement for a right attitude, therefore, is a calm, reasonable outlook which is never completely engulfed by a tide of emotion.

A second ingredient of right attitude is a basic respect for moral principles. Despite serious ideological differences, there are moral principles embodied in the United Nations Charter, for example, which almost all of the nations of the world acknowledge. Although selfish motives are often decisive, a nation's intent in waging war should include a commitment to support or advance the cause of justice. This provision of right attitude allows for the criticism of one's own government, as well as the enemy, whenever the moral limits of war are violated.

A third ingredient of right attitude concerns the factual dimensions of belief. While attitudes are subjectively held beliefs, they are often subject to verification or falsification. For example, right-wing attitudes toward communism are usually

---

[4] Richard S. Hartigan, "Aggression, Justice and the Second World War"; Michael Walzer, "World War II: Why Was This War Different?"; Richard A. Falk, "On Just Wars: The Case of World War II" (papers delivered at the Sixty-sixth Annual Meeting of the American Political Science Association, Biltmore Hotel, Los Angeles, Calif., September 8–12, 1970).

[5] Herbert A. Deane, *The Political and Social Ideas of St. Augustine* (New York and London: Columbia University Press, 1963), p. 164.

based on the belief that communism is a monolithic, irredeemably evil threat. If empirical evidence suggests that communism is a pluralistic phenomenon which embodies possibilities for change, the right-winger's willingness to oppose communism everywhere, regardless of the cost, is seen to be based upon a wrong attitude.

Thus if "right attitude" is defined in terms of rationality, a basic respect for the moral principles, and a commitment to seek and apply knowledge, it becomes a flexible but important principle for viewing war in a moral perspective. After all, it is on the grounds of right attitude that some of the most incisive criticisms of the United States' involvement in Vietnam have been made. To the extent that the United States was committed to a containment of communism, regardless of the consequences for the Vietnamese people themselves, its motive stemmed from an immoral, and hence, wrong attitude. If factual errors were involved in estimating the danger to world security posed by Communist insurgency in Vietnam, then a wrong attitude of fear and hostility was needlessly generated. Like the principle of "just cause," the requirement of "right attitude" is relevant to present moral judgments in war.

The third prima facie principle is that war must be conducted by a legitimate authority. This principle—like the previous two—must be reinterpreted to serve our present needs. The traditional statement of this principle left the relationship of power and authority largely unexamined: the ruler was the legitimate authority simply because he was the ruler.[6] In democratic theory, however, power is dependent upon such diverse elements as physical force, charisma, and consensus. Authority is never simply a given quality; it must be supported by various forms of power.

The principle of legitimate authority in a democracy requires that government leaders maintain a reasonable consensus for their military policies. Lyndon Johnson's tragedy resulted, in part, from insufficient authority in the sense of congressional support and public opinion. To be sure, certain key decisions were made with considerable congressional and public approval (e.g., the Gulf of Tonkin Resolution), but the desired consensus was superficial and short-lived. Errors of judgment were made both as to the determination of the enemy and the staying power of the American people.

Although a democratic regime's inability to maintain a consistent effort in an unpopular war is sometimes viewed as a foreign-policy liability, the concern that an elected official must show for his base of authority provides a needed check against unwise and immoral military involvements. Congressional revocation of the Gulf of Tonkin Resolution may be understood as an application of the "legitimate authority" provision of just-war theory. A claim was made that the ultimate locus of authority in a democracy resides with the people, hence, wars which are not supported by a fair spectrum of the population are not conducted by right authority.

A second modern application of the principle of legitimate authority concerns revolution in the developing world. Civil war, even when aided by outside powers, is fundamentally a struggle for power and authority. It is difficult, for

---

[6] Stamey, p. 393.

example, to identify the locus of authority in South Vietnam, since both the Republic of South Vietnam and the National Liberation Front claim to be rightful heirs to political power. Essentially, this conflict must be resolved before a right authority can be designated.

The principle of self-determination insists that nations have the right to resolve their own power struggles unless other circumstances are sufficiently important to outweigh this prima facie right. On the basis of this principle, local insurgents may claim greater moral justification than foreign counter-insurgents who have no real stake in the society in which they fight. Of course, it is not always wrong for a nation to intervene in a revolutionary situation. Before a nation intervenes, however, it should understand that the question of legitimate authority is not usually settled by an imposition of external force.[7] More often than not, intervention proves to be both morally unjustified and pragmatically unwise.

The fourth principle of just warfare is that military means must be carefully related to the moral and political ends being sought. This is the rule of proportionality which has played such a significant role in the discussions of war in the nuclear age. Many persons have become nuclear pacifists by concluding that no political ends—even the preservation of freedom and democracy—are worth a possible extinction of the human race resulting from a nuclear holocaust. This argument carries a great deal of weight, even among those who cannot commit themselves to unilateral disarmament. As distasteful as the prospects of living under a dictatorship may seem, the utter destruction of Western civilization would be immeasurably worse.

Since today's means of warfare are so destructive, formerly good reasons for war are often invalidated on the grounds of proportionality. Indeed, the overriding moral obligation of leaders today is to prevent the just cause from occurring by exercising great caution and moderation in the pursuit of foreign-policy goals.[8] Present efforts to encourage rapprochement between East and West seem to be a strategy required, in part, by the rule of proportionality.

The final rule of the just-war tradition is the principle of discrimination. Paul Ramsey, who has devoted much attention to just-war theory in recent years, elevates this principle above all others and declares that a direct attack upon noncombatants is absolutely prohibited.[9] In my judgment, Ramsey is mistaken in absolutizing one principle from the just-war tradition. Like the four principles discussed above, the principle of discrimination is a prima facie duty only. It should not be applied in an abstract manner without fully considering the moral context.

Since the present nuclear deterrence strategy of both the United States and the Soviet Union includes a commitment to bomb cities in retaliation to a nuclear strike, some moralists have declared that either the principle of dis-

[7] Eqbal Ahmad, *No More Vietnams?* ed. Richard M. Pfeffer (New York: Harper & Row, 1968), p. 236.

[8] Lynn H. Miller, "The Contemporary Significance of the Doctrine of Just War," *World Politics* 16 (January 1964): 283.

[9] Paul Ramsey, *War and the Christian Conscience* (Durham, N.C.: Duke University Press, 1961), pp. 34–59.

crimination or the strategy of deterrence must be abandoned. When the principle of discrimination is viewed as a moral absolute, this choice seems inevitable. But there is surely a relevant moral distinction between the intention to bomb non-combatants in some conceivable circumstances and the actual decision to proceed with the bombing. Both commitments are abstractly wrong, but the latter step involves a decision to actualize what is forbidden on a prima facie basis.

My judgment is that the strategy of deterrence must be morally tolerated while the present efforts toward arms control continue. This position stems from a belief that sudden abandonment of nuclear deterrence by the United States would endanger national security and create international instability. Yet the failure of deterrence remains a disturbing possibility. In the event of a first strike against the United States, it is doubtful that the right of self-defense would be sufficient to outweigh the principles of discrimination and proportionality.

The principle of discrimination is also important for moral judgments about insurgency warfare. This rule serves in a revolutionary situation primarily to prohibit indiscriminate terror and killing. Moral judgments on the Vietnam war have depended largely on determining which mode of warfare is most indiscriminate: the terror tactics of the insurgents or the modern fire power of the counterinsurgents. For example, Paul Ramsey condemns the terror tactics of the Viet Cong as violations of the principle of noncombatant immunity.[10] In my judgment, however, the weight of evidence suggests that United States' reliance on bombing and village pacification is a more serious violation of this principle.

The principle of discrimination serves with the principle of proportionality to reinforce a new implicit moral understanding among the superpowers: *No preventive wars and no first use of nuclear weapons.*[11] To be sure, these rules are supported by self-interest, since initiating a nuclear war would invite retaliation. But they also reflect moral sensibilities shared by Communist and capitalist alike. Thus far the moral ban against using nuclear weapons has remained in force. It is in the interest of all nations to maintain this implicit understanding.

The conclusion of this essay is simply that the rules of just warfare provide a rational framework for moral reflections on war. My approach to just-war theory has been pragmatic rather than formalistic, since no certain formula is offered for balancing the various principles. The limitations of this moral tradition are quite apparent: These rules are seldom consciously observed in practice and they are difficult to apply in ambiguous circumstances. Indeed, nuclear power may have introduced a qualitatively new era which will eventually require the elimination of military conflict altogether. But the just-war rules are presently necessary, if not sufficient, in a world where there is still war and rumors of war.

[10] Paul Ramsey, *The Just War* (New York: Charles Scribner's Sons, 1968), pp. 502–503.

[11] Sylvester P. Theisen, "Man and Nuclear Weapons," in *Moral Issues and Christian Responses,* ed. Paul T. Jersild and Dale A. Johnson (New York: Holt, Rinehart & Winston, 1971), pp. 322–323; and Richard A. Falk, *Law, Morality, and War in the Contemporary World,* Princeton Studies in World Politics (New York: Frederick A. Praeger, Inc., 1963), p. 15.

The Conscience of Huck Finn

JONATHAN BENNETT

Jonathan Bennett (1930–   ), professor of philosophy at the University of British Columbia, has authored many books, including *Rationality* (1964), *Kant's Analytic* (1966), and *Kant's Dialectic* (1974).

In this paper, I shall present not just the conscience of Huckleberry Finn but two others as well. One of them is the conscience of Heinrich Himmler. He became a Nazi in 1923; he served drably and quietly, but well, and was rewarded with increasing responsibility and power. At the peak of his career he held many offices and commands, of which the most powerful was that of leader of the S.S.—the principal police force of the Nazi regime. In this capacity, Himmler commanded the whole concentration-camp system, and was responsible for the execution of the so-called "final solution of the Jewish problem." It is important for my purposes that this piece of social engineering should be thought of not abstractly but in concrete terms of Jewish families being marched to what they think are bath-houses, to the accompaniment of loud-speaker renditions of extracts from *The Merry Widow* and *Tales of Hoffman,* there to be choked to death by poisonous gases. Altogether, Himmler succeeded in murdering about four and a half million of them, as well as several million gentiles, mainly Poles and Russians.

The other conscience to be discussed is that of the Calvinist theologian and philosopher Jonathan Edwards. He lived in the first half of the eighteenth century, and has a good claim to be considered America's first serious and considerable philosophical thinker. He was for many years a widely-renowned preacher and Congregationalist minister in New England; in 1748 a dispute with his congregation led him to resign (he couldn't accept their view that unbelievers should be admitted to the Lord's Supper in the hope that it would convert them); for some years after that he worked as a missionary, preaching to Indians through an interpreter; then in 1758 he accepted the presidency of what is now Princeton University, and within two months died from a smallpox inoculation. Along the way he wrote some first-rate philosophy: his book attacking the notion of free will is still sometimes read. Why I should be interested in Edwards' *conscience* will be explained in due course.

I shall use Heinrich Himmler, Jonathan Edwards and Huckleberry Finn to illustrate different aspects of a single theme, namely the relationship between *sympathy* on the one hand and *bad morality* on the other.

All that I can mean by a 'bad morality' is a morality whose principles I deeply disapprove of. When I call a morality bad, I cannot prove that mine is better;

Source: Jonathan Bennett, "The Conscience of Huckleberry Finn," *Philosophy,* Vol. 49 (1974), pp. 123–134. Reprinted by permission of The Royal Institute of Philosophy and the author.

but when I here call any morality bad, I think you will agree with me that it is bad; and that is all I need.

There could be dispute as to whether the springs of someone's actions constitute a *morality*. I think, though, that we must admit that someone who acts in ways which conflict grossly with our morality may nevertheless have a morality of his own—a set of principles of action which he sincerely assents to, so that for him the problem of acting well or rightly or in obedience to conscience is the problem of conforming to *those* principles. The problem of conscientiousness can arise as acutely for a bad morality as for any other: rotten principles may be as difficult to keep as decent ones.

As for "sympathy": I use this term to cover every sort of fellow-feeling, as when one feels pity over someone's loneliness, or horrified compassion over his pain, or when one feels a shrinking reluctance to act in a way which will bring misfortune to someone else. These *feelings* must not be confused with *moral judgments*. My sympathy for someone in distress may lead me to help him, or even to think that I ought to help him; but in itself it is not a judgment about what I ought to do but just a *feeling* for him in his plight. We shall get some light on the difference between feelings and moral judgments when we consider Huckleberry Finn.

Obviously, feelings can impel one to action, and so can moral judgments; and in a particular case sympathy and morality may pull in opposite directions. This can happen not just with bad moralities, but also with good ones like yours and mine. For example, a small child, sick and miserable, clings tightly to his mother and screams in terror when she tries to pass him over to the doctor to be examined. If the mother gave way to her sympathy, that is to her feeling for the child's misery and fright, she would hold it close and not let the doctor come near; but don't we agree that it might be wrong for her to act on such a feeling? Quite generally, then, anyone's moral principles may apply to a particular situation in a way which runs contrary to the particular thrusts of fellow-feeling that he has in that situation. My immediate concern is with sympathy in relation to bad morality, but not because such conflicts occur only when the morality is bad.

Now, suppose that someone who accepts a bad morality is struggling to make himself act in accordance with it in a particular situation where his sympathies pull him another way. He sees the struggle as one between doing the right, conscientious thing, and acting wrongly and weakly, like the mother who won't let the doctor come near her sick, frightened baby. Since we don't accept this person's morality, we may see the situation very differently, thoroughly disapproving of the action he regards as the right one, and endorsing the action which from his point of view constitutes weakness and backsliding.

Conflicts between sympathy and bad morality won't always be like this, for we won't disagree with every single dictate of a bad morality. Still, it can happen in the way I have described, with the agent's right action being our wrong one, and vice versa. That is just what happens in a certain episode in chapter 16 of *The Adventures of Huckleberry Finn*, an episode which brilliantly illustrates how fiction can be instructive about real life.

Huck Finn has been helping his slave friend Jim to run away from Miss Watson, who is Jim's owner. In their raft-journey down the Mississippi river, they are near to the place at which Jim will become legally free. Now let Huck take over the story:

Jim said it made him all over trembly and feverish to be so close to freedom. Well, I can tell you it made me all over trembly and feverish, too, to hear him, because I begun to get it through my head that he *was* most free—and who was to blame for it? Why, *me*. I couldn't get that out of my conscience, no how nor no way. . . . It hadn't ever come home to me, before, what this thing was that I was doing. But now it did; and it stayed with me, and scorched me more and more. I tried to make out to myself that *I* warn't to blame, because *I* didn't run Jim off from his rightful owner; but it warn't no use, conscience up and say, every time: "But you knowed he was running for his freedom, and you could a paddled ashore and told some-body." That was so—I couldn't get around that, no way. That was where it pinched. Conscience says to me: "What had poor Miss Watson done to you, that you could see her nigger go off right under your eyes and never say one single word? What did that poor old woman do to you, that you could treat her so mean? . . ." I got to feeling so mean and so miserable I most wished I was dead.

Jim speaks of his plan to save up to buy his wife, and then his children, out of slavery; and he adds that if the children cannot be bought he will arrange to steal them. Huck is horrified:

Thinks I, this is what comes of my not thinking. Here was this nigger which I had as good as helped to run away, coming right out flat-footed and saying he would steal his children—children that belonged to a man I didn't even know; a man that hadn't ever done me no harm.

I was sorry to hear Jim say that, it was such a lowering of him. My conscience got to stirring me up hotter than ever, until at last I says to it: "Let up on me—it ain't too late, yet—I'll paddle ashore at first light, and tell." I felt easy, and happy, and light as a feather, right off. All my troubles was gone.

This is bad morality all right. In his earliest years Huck wasn't taught any principles, and the only ones he has encountered since then are those of rural Missouri, in which slave-owning is just one kind of ownership and is not subject to critical pressure. It hasn't occurred to Huck to question those principles. So the action, to us abhorrent, of turning Jim in to the authorities presents itself *clearly* to Huck as the right thing to do.

For us, morality and sympathy would both dictate helping Jim to escape. If we felt any conflict, it would have both these on one side and something else on the other—greed for a reward, or fear of punishment. But Huck's morality conflicts with his sympathy, that is, with his unargued, natural feeling for his friend. The conflict starts when Huck sets off in the canoe towards the shore, pretending that he is going to reconnoitre, but really planning to turn Jim in:

As I shoved off, [Jim] says: "Pooty soon I'll be a-shout'n for joy, en I'll say, it's all on accounts o' Huck I's a free man . . . Jim won't ever forget you, Huck; you's de bes' fren' Jim's ever had; en you's de *only* fren' old Jim's got now."

I was paddling off, all in a sweat to tell on him; but when he says this, it seemed to kind of take the tuck all out of me. I went along slow then, and I warn't right down certain whether I was glad I started or whether I warn't. When I was fifty yards off, Jim says:

"Dah you goes, de ole true Huck; de on'y white genlman dat ever kep' his promise to ole Jim." Well, I just felt sick. But I says, I *got* to do it—I can't get *out* of it.

In the upshot, sympathy wins over morality. Huck hasn't the strength of will to do what he sincerely thinks he ought to do. Two men hunting for runaway slaves ask him whether the man on his raft is black or white:

I didn't answer up prompt. I tried to, but the words wouldn't come. I tried, for a second or two, to brace up and out with it, but I warn't man enough—hadn't the spunk of a rabbit. I see I was weakening; so I just give up trying, and up and says: "He's white."

So Huck enables Jim to escape, thus acting weakly and wickedly—he thinks. In this conflict between sympathy and morality, sympathy wins.

One critic has cited this episode in support of the statement that Huck suffers "excruciating moments of wavering between honesty and respectability." That is hopelessly wrong, and I agree with the perceptive comment on it by another critic, who says:

The conflict waged in Huck is much more serious: he scarcely cares for respectability and never hesitates to relinquish it, but he does care for honesty and gratitude—and both honesty and gratitude require that he should give Jim up. It is not, in Huck, honesty at war with respectability but love and compassion for Jim struggling against his conscience. His decision is for Jim and hell: a right decision made in the mental chains that Huck never breaks. His concern for Jim is and remains *irrational*. Huck finds many reasons for giving Jim up and none for stealing him. To the end Huck sees his compassion for Jim as a weak, ignorant, and wicked felony.[1]

That is precisely correct—and it can have that virtue only because Mark Twain wrote the episode with such unerring precision. The crucial point concerns *reasons,* which all occur on one side of the conflict. On the side of conscience we have principles, arguments, considerations, ways of looking at things:

"It hadn't ever come home to me before what I was doing"
"I tried to make out that I warn't to blame"
"Conscience said 'But you knowed . . .'—I couldn't get around that"
"What had poor Miss Watson done to you?"
"This is what comes of my not thinking"
". . . children that belonged to a man I didn't even know."

On the other side, the side of feeling, we get nothing like that. When Jim rejoices in Huck, as his only friend, Huck doesn't consider the claims of friendship or have the situation "come home" to him in a different light. All that happens is: 'When he says this, it seemed to kind of take the tuck all out of me.

[1] M. J. Sidnell, "Huck Finn and Jim," *The Cambridge Quarterly,* vol. 2, pp. 205–206.

I went along slow then, and I warn't right down certain whether I was glad I started or whether I warn't.' Again, Jim's words about Huck's "promise" to him don't give Huck any *reason* for changing his plan: in his morality promises to slaves probably don't count. Their effect on him is of a different kind: "Well, I just felt sick." And when the moment for final decision comes, Huck doesn't weigh up pros and cons: he simply *fails* to do what he believes to be right—he isn't strong enough, hasn't "the spunk of a rabbit." This passage in the novel is notable not just for its finely wrought irony, with Huck's weakness of will leading him to do the right thing, but also for its masterly handling of the difference between general moral principles and particular unreasoned emotional pulls.

Consider now another case of bad morality in conflict with human sympathy the case of the odious Himmler. Here, from a speech he made to some S.S. generals, is an indication of the content of his morality:

> What happens to a Russian, to a Czech, does not interest me in the slightest. What the nations can offer in the way of good blood of our type, we will take, if necessary by kidnapping their children and raising them here with us. Whether nations live in prosperity or starve to death like cattle interests me only in so far as we need them as slaves to our *Kultur;* otherwise it is of no interest to me. Whether 10,000 Russian females fall down from exhaustion while digging an antitank ditch interests me only in so far as the antitank ditch for Germany is finished.[2]

But has this a moral basis at all? And if it has, was there in Himmler's own mind any conflict between morality and sympathy? Yes there was. Here is more from the same speech:

> . . . I also want to talk to you quite frankly on a very grave matter . . . I mean . . . the extermination of the Jewish race. . . . Most of you must know what it means when 100 corpses are lying side by side, or 500, or 1,000. To have stuck it out and at the same time—apart from exceptions caused by human weakness—to have remained decent fellows, that is what has made us hard. This is a page of glory in our history which has never been written and is never to be written.

Himmler saw his policies as being hard to implement while still retaining one's human sympathies—while still remaining a "decent fellow." He is saying that only the weak take the easy way out and just squelch their sympathies, and is praising the stronger and more glorious course of retaining one's sympathies while acting in violation of them. In the same spirit, he ordered that when executions were carried out in concentration camps, those responsible "are to be influenced in such a way as to suffer no ill effect in their character and mental attitude." A year later he boasted that the S.S. had wiped out the Jews

[2] Quoted in William L. Shirer, *The Rise and Fall of the Third Reich* (New York, 1960), pp. 937–938. Next quotation: Ibid., p. 966. All further quotations relating to Himmler are from Roger Manwell and Heinrich Fraenkel, *Heinrich Himmler* (London, 1965), pp. 132, 197, 184 (twice), 187.

without our leaders and their men suffering any damage in their minds and souls. The danger was considerable, for there was only a narrow path between the Scylla of their becoming heartless ruffians unable any longer to treasure life, and the Charybdis of their becoming soft and suffering nervous breakdowns.

And there really can't be any doubt that the basis of Himmler's policies was a set of principles which constituted his morality—a sick, bad, wicked *morality*. He described himself as caught in 'the old tragic conflict between will and obligation.' And when his physician Kersten protested at the intention to destroy the Jews, saying that the suffering involved was "not to be contemplated," Kersten reports that Himmler replied:

> He knew that it would mean much suffering for the Jews. . . . "It is the curse of greatness that it must step over dead bodies to create new life. Yet we must . . . cleanse the soil or it will never bear fruit. It will be a great burden for me to bear."

This, I submit, is the language of morality.

So in this case, tragically, bad morality won out over sympathy. I am sure that many of Himmler's killers did extinguish their sympathies, becoming "heartless ruffians" rather than "decent fellows"; but not Himmler himself. Although his policies ran against the human grain to a horrible degree, he did not sandpaper down his emotional surfaces so that there was no grain there, allowing his actions to slide along smoothly and easily. He did, after all, bear his hideous burden, and even paid a price for it. He suffered a variety of nervous and physical disabilities, including nausea and stomach-convulsions, and Kersten was doubtless right in saying that these were "the expression of a psychic division which extended over his whole life."

This same division must have been present in some of those officials of the Church who ordered heretics to be tortured so as to change their theological opinions. Along with the brutes and the cold careerists, there must have been some who cared, and who suffered from the conflict between their sympathies and their bad morality.

In the conflict between sympathy and bad morality, then, the victory may go to sympathy as in the case of Huck Finn, or to morality as in the case of Himmler.

Another possiblity is that the conflict may be avoided by giving up, or not ever having, those sympathies which might interfere with one's principles. That seems to have been the case with Jonathan Edwards. I am afraid that I shall be doing an injustice to Edwards' many virtues, and to his great intellectual energy and inventiveness; for my concern is only with the worst thing about him—namely his morality, which was worse than Himmler's.

According to Edwards, God condemns some men to an eternity of unimaginably awful pain, though he arbitrarily spares others—"arbitrarily" because none deserve to be spared:

> Natural men are held in the hand of God over the pit of hell; they have deserved the fiery pit, and are already sentenced to it; and God is dreadfully provoked, his

anger is as great towards them as to those that are actually suffering the executions of the fierceness of his wrath in hell . . . ; the devil is waiting for them, hell is gaping for them, the flames gather and flash about them, and would fain lay hold on them . . . ; and . . . there are no means within reach that can be any security to them. . . . All that preserves them is the mere arbitrary will, and uncovenanted unobliged forebearance of an incensed God.[3]

Notice that he says "they have deserved the fiery pit." Edwards insists that men *ought* to be condemned to eternal pain; and his position isn't that this is right because God wants it, but rather that God wants it because it is right. For him, moral standards exist independently of God, and God can be assessed in the light of them (and of course found to be perfect). For example, he says:

They deserve to be cast into hell; so that . . . justice never stands in the way, it makes no objection against God's using his power at any moment to destroy them. Yea, on the contrary, justice calls aloud for an infinite punishment of their sins.

Elsewhere, he gives elaborate arguments to show that God is acting justly in damning sinners. For example, he argues that a punishment should be exactly as bad as the crime being punished; God is infinitely excellent; so any crime against him is infinitely bad; and so eternal damnation is exactly right as a punishment—it is infinite, but, as Edwards is careful also to say, it is "no more than infinite."

Of course, Edwards himself didn't torment the damned; but the question still arises of whether his sympathies didn't conflict with his *approval* of eternal torment. Didn't he find it painful to contemplate any fellow-human's being tortured for ever? Apparently not:

The God that holds you over the pit of hell, much as one holds a spider or some loathsome insect over the fire, abhors you, and is dreadfully provoked; . . . he is of purer eyes than to bear to have you in his sight; you are ten thousand times so abominable in his eyes as the most hateful venomous serpent is in ours.

When God is presented as being as misanthropic as that, one suspects misanthropy in the theologian. This suspicion is increased when Edwards claims that "the saints in glory will . . . understand how terrible the sufferings of the damned are; yet . . . will not be sorry for [them]."[4] He bases this partly on a view of human nature whose ugliness he seems not to notice:

The seeing of the calamities of others tends to heighten the sense of our own enjoyments. When the saints in glory, therefore, shall see the doleful state of the damned, how will this heighten their sense of the blessedness of their own state.

[3] Vergilius Ferm (ed.), *Puritan Sage: Collected Writings of Jonathan Edwards* (New York, 1953), p. 370. Next three quotations: Ibid., p. 366, p. 294 ("no more than infinite"), p. 372.

[4] This and the next two quotations are from "The End of the Wicked Contemplated by the Righteous: or, The Torments of the Wicked in Hell, no Occasion of Grief to the Saints in Heaven," from *The Works of President Edwards* (London, 1817), vol. IV, pp. 507–508, 511–512, and 509 respectively.

> . . . When they shall see how miserable others of their fellow-creatures are . . . ;
> when they shall see the smoke of their torment, . . . and hear their dolorous
> shrieks and cries, and consider that they in the mean time are in the most blissful
> state, and shall surely be in it to all eternity; how they will rejoice!

I hope this is less than the whole truth! His other main point about why the
saints will rejoice to see the torments of the damned is that it is *right* that they
should do so:

> The heavenly inhabitants . . . will have no love nor pity to the damned. . . .
> [This will not show] a want of a spirit of love in them . . . ; for the heavenly in-
> habitants will know that it is not fit that they should love [the damned] because
> they will know then, that God has no love to them, nor pity for them.

The implication that *of course* one can adjust one's feelings of pity so that they
conform to the dictates of some authority—doesn't this suggest that ordinary
human sympathies played only a small part in Edwards' life?

Huck Finn, whose sympathies are wide and deep, could never avoid the
conflict in that way; but he is determined to avoid it, and so he opts for the
only other alternative he can see—to give up morality altogether. After he has
tricked the slave-hunters, he returns to the raft and undergoes a peculiar crisis:

> I got aboard the raft, feeling bad and low, because I knowed very well I had done
> wrong, and I see it warn't no use for me to try to learn to do right; a body that
> don't get *started* right when he's little, ain't got no show—when the pinch comes
> there ain't nothing to back him up and keep him to his work, and so he gets beat.
> Then I thought a minute, and says to myself, hold on—s'pose you'd a done right
> and give Jim up; would you feel better than what you do now? No, says I, I'd
> feel bad—I'd feel just the same way I do now. Well, then, says I, what's the use
> you learning to do right, when it's troublesome to do right and ain't no trouble to
> do wrong, and the wages is just the same? I was stuck. I couldn't answer that. So
> I reckoned I wouldn't bother no more about it, but after this always do whichever
> come handiest at the time.

Huck clearly cannot conceive of having any morality except the one he has
learned—too late, he thinks—from his society. He is not entirely a prisoner of
that morality, because he does after all reject it; but for him that is a decision
to relinquish morality as such; he cannot envisage revising his morality, altering
its content in face of the various pressures to which it is subject, including
pressures from his sympathies. For example, he does not begin to approach the
thought that slavery should be rejected on moral grounds, or the thought that
what he is doing is not theft because a person cannot be owned and therefore
cannot be stolen.

The basic trouble is that he cannot or will not engage in abstract intellectual
operations of any sort. In chapter 33 he finds himself "feeling to blame, somehow" for something he knows he had no hand in; he assumes that this feeling
is a deliverance of conscience; and this confirms him in his belief that conscience
shouldn't be listened to:

It don't make no difference whether you do right or wrong, a person's conscience ain't got no sense, and just goes for him *anyway*. If I had a yaller dog that didn't know no more than a person's conscience does, I would poison him. It takes up more than all the of a person's insides, and yet ain't no good, nohow.

That brisk, incurious dismissiveness fits well with the comprehensive rejection of morality back on the raft. But this is a digression.

On the raft, Huck decides not to live by principles, but just to do whatever "comes handiest at the time"—always acting according to the mood of the moment. Since the morality he is rejecting is narrow and cruel, and his sympathies are broad and kind, the results will be good. But moral principles are good to have, because they help to protect one from acting badly at moments when one's sympathies happen to be in abeyance. On the highest possible estimate of the role one's sympathies should have, one can still allow for principles as embodiments of one's best feelings, one's broadest and keenest sympathies. On that view, principles can help one across intervals when one's feelings are at less than their best, i.e. through periods of misanthropy or meanness or self-centredness or depression or anger.

What Huck didn't see is that one can live by principles and yet have ultimate control over their content. And one way such control can be exercised is by checking of one's principles in the light of one's sympathies. This is sometimes a pretty straightforward matter. It can happen that a certain moral principle becomes untenable—meaning literally that one cannot hold it any longer—because it conflicts intolerably with the pity or revulsion or whatever that one feels when one sees what the principle leads to. One's experience may play a large part here: experiences evoke feelings, and feelings force one to modify principles. Something like this happened to the English poet Wilfred Owen, whose experiences in the First World War transformed him from an enthusiastic soldier into a virtual pacifist. I can't document his change of conscience in detail; but I want to present something which he wrote about the way experience can put pressure on morality.

The Latin poet Horace wrote that it is sweet and fitting (or right) to die for one's country—*dulce et decorum est pro patria mori*—and Owen wrote a fine poem about how experience could lead one to relinquish that particular moral principle.[5] He describes a man who is too slow donning his gas mask during a gas attack—"As under a green sea I saw him drowning," Owen says. The poem ends like this:

> In all my dreams before my helpless sight
> He plunges at me, guttering, choking, drowning.
> If in some smothering dreams, you too could pace
> Behind the wagon that we flung him in,
> And watch the white eyes writhing in his face,
> His hanging face, like a devil's sick of sin;

[5] I am grateful to the Executors of the Estate of Harold Owen, and to Chatto and Windus Ltd., for permission to quote from Wilfred Owen's "Dulce et Decorum Est" and "Insensibility."

If you could hear, at every jolt, the blood
Come gargling from the froth-corrupted lungs,
Bitter as the cud
Of vile, incurable sores on innocent tongues,—
My friend, you would not tell with such high zest
To children ardent for some desperate glory,
The old Lie: Dulce et decorum est
Pro patria mori.

There is a difficulty about drawing from all this a moral for ourselves. I imagine that we agree in our rejection of slavery, eternal damnation, genocide, and uncritical patriotic self-abnegation; so we shall agree that Huck Finn, Jonathan Edwards, Heinrich Himmler, and the poet Horace would all have done well to bring certain of their principles under severe pressure from ordinary human sympathies. But then we can say this because we can say that all those are bad moralities, whereas we cannot look at our own moralities and declare them bad. This is not arrogance: it is obviously incoherent for someone to declare the system of moral principles that he *accepts* to be *bad,* just as one cannot coherently say of anything that one *believes* it but it is *false.*

Still, although I can't point to any of my beliefs and say "That is false," I don't doubt that some of my beliefs *are f*alse; and so I should try to remain open to correction. Similarly, I accept every single item in my morality—that is inevitable—but I am sure that my morality could be improved, which is to say that it could undergo changes which I should be glad of once I had made them. So I must try to keep my morality open to revision, exposing it to whatever valid pressures there are—including pressures from my sympathies.

I don't give my sympathies a blank cheque in advance. In a conflict between principle and sympathy, principles ought sometimes to win. For example, I think it was right to take part in the Second World War on the allied side; there were many ghastly individual incidents which might have led someone to doubt the rightness of his participation in that war; and I think it would have been right for such a person to keep his sympathies in a subordinate place on those occasions, not allowing them to modify his principles in such a way as to make a pacifist of him.

Still, one's sympathies should be kept as sharp and sensitive and aware as possible, and not only because they can sometimes affect one's principles or one's conduct or both. Owen, at any rate, says that feelings and sympathies are vital even when they can do nothing but bring pain and distress. In another poem he speaks of the blessings of being numb in one's feelings: "Happy are the men who yet before they are killed/Can let their veins run cold," he says. These are the ones who do not suffer from any compassion which, as Owen puts it, "makes their feet/Sore on the alleys cobbled with their brothers." He contrasts these "happy" ones, who "lose all imagination," with himself and others "who with a thought besmirch/Blood over all our soul." Yet the poem's verdict goes against the "happy" ones. Owen does not say that they will act worse than the others whose souls are besmirched with blood because of their keen awareness of human suffering. He merely says that they are the losers because they have cut themselves off from the human condition:

By choice they made themselves immune
To pity and whatever moans in man
Before the last sea and the hapless stars;
Whatever mourns when many leave these shores;
Whatever shares
The eternal reciprocity of tears.[6]

[6] This paper began life as the Potter Memorial Lecture, given at Washington State University in Pullman, Washington, in 1972.

Two

The Now and Future Generations: The Moral Use of Technology

> The morality of an act is a function of the state of the system at the time it is performed.
>
> —Garrett Hardin

Introduction

In our introduction to Chapter One we distinguished among morals, a moral system, and a theory of ethics. A moral system is what morals become when as a result of reflection our morals become consistent, integrated, and comprehensive. An ethical theory is the product of reflection about morals and moral systems.

We raised some ethical theory issues in the previous chapter—egoism, relativism, whether right or good is the primary moral concept, and the content of a moral system. We said that the content of a moral system consists of three parts, claims about moral goods, maxims of action, and the nature of human beings. In this chapter we consider technology and its impact on morals and moral systems. We pointed out in the introduction to Chapter One that to be comprehensive a moral system has to be capable of generating new morals to cover new types of situations. Because technology is a major contributor to the spawning of new moral situations, it forces us to consider anew the content of our morals; new types of events call for new judgments about moral goodness or badness, new maxims of action, and, with the advent of computers and biomedicine, perhaps new ideas about the nature of human beings.

Technology is not new to human beings, but according to a prevalent anthropological view, is as old as we are. Some anthropologists distinguish human beings from other creatures by their ability to manufacture and use tools. Tools are instruments that enable us to magnify our own powers to shape the material world for our ends; the lever and steam engine magnify our physical powers; slide rules and computers magnify our mental powers.

Technology is the application of our growing knowledge to the manufacture of tools. A growing technology poses growing moral challenges to the now and future generations. We have chosen essays for this chapter that deal with the impact of industrial technology on our life-sustaining environment (Hardin, Naess, McGinn, and Passmore); the impact of prying technology on our public and private lives (Bierman); the impact of biomedical technology on our physical and mental well-being (Kass); and the impact of the capitalist social structure, generated by the Industrial Revolution, on our collective life (Marx).

Our ethical theory reflections on relativism in Chapter One will help us to understand why the changes brought about by technology force us to think anew about our morals.

We suggested that "relative to" be interpreted as "in relation to." Thus, instead of saying that morals are relative, one should say that morals are relative to such and such, which, in turn, is better interpreted as saying that moral judgments are made in relation to such-and-such variable factors. To schematize a bit: In relation to $factor_1$, $factor_2$, $factor_3$, act A is judged wrong. But in relation to $factor_1$, $factor_3$, $factor_4$, act A is judged right. Changing the variable factors may lead to a change in the moral judgment.

With this interpretation of relativism, we recognize that in our moral reflections we have to consider a complex of factors; this is so whether we are considering the moral goodness of an act's consequences, the maxims under which an act or contemplated act falls, or the identification of what is distinctively human. Given that moral thinking has to deal with a complex of factors, and that these factors are variable, we can appreciate the impact that technology has on moral thinking when we realize that it is a major producer of new factors. Given new factors, we have a new complex situation to consider; a new judgment is up for consideration. To take an example, think of the technology that we now have for supporting life—heart fibrilators, lung respirators, kidney dialysis machines, and so forth. This has had an impact on the maxim "To take human life deliberately is wrong," on the claim that "Human life is good," and on the ancient definition that "Human beings are rational animals."

Is human life good under conditions where life continues only by being attached to these life-support systems? Always? Some do not think so and wish to die in a "dignified way." We have been forced to ask anew when a human body is a human being; technology to register brain waves supposedly enables us to know when significant brain activity has ceased; if there is no longer brain activity of a certain level, the body may no longer be rational, and by the ancient definition, may no longer be human. This leads to a challenge to the maxim formerly applied to doctors' acts when they deliberately unhooked life-support systems; formerly to unhook was to take human life, a forbidden act; if brain activity is the way of identifying human life, then unhooking life-support systems upon the cessation of significant brain activity is not taking human life and so is not a forbidden act.

In short, life-support technology has introduced new circumstances; this has introduced new factors "in relation to" which our former judgments and maxims and definitions may no longer be fully appropriate: they require modifying statements. In relation to such-and-such brain activity, this is not a rational being, that is, is not human; in relation to such-and-such brain activity, this life is not good; in relation to such-and-such brain activity, it is not wrong to end this life.

Altering our moral judgments and decisions with varying circumstances is nothing new; it is typical. Consider the following act performed innumerable times over the centuries: One person shoving another. Holding to an absolutist maxim "It is wrong to shove another" is conceiving morals too simplistically. There could be differing circumstances, differing factors, "in relation to" which our judgment about the act of shoving would vary.

Suppose you come around the corner of a building and observe Rock shoving Philo. Right or wrong?

Factor 1: A car was about to hit Philo. Right or wrong to shove? Clearly, the act is right.

Factor 2: Philo has threatened physical violence to Rock. Right or wrong? Pretty clearly, right.

Factor 3: Philo and Rock are old football buddies and this is their rather physical way of greeting one another. Right or wrong? Pretty clearly, not wrong.

Factor 4: Philo has insulted Rock. Right or wrong? Pretty clearly, wrong.

Factor 4 & 5: Philo has insulted Rock; this is the tenth time in as many days, each insult growing more unspeakable. Right or wrong? Wrong, but not as clearly wrong as for factor 4 alone.

Our shoving example illustrates how varying factors lead us to different moral judgments about it. But in each case, we do not have to introduce any new morality because we already have enough moral maxims to handle the differing factors. What makes technology morally interesting is that the factors it introduces may be new in kind, and, being so, may require new morals. We turn, now, to the essays in this chapter and point out some new factors the authors think challenge the old morals. The factors we pick out do not necessarily exhaust what the authors write about, but the ones we select should help you to identify others, which you may want to discuss in your classes.

Garrett Hardin concentrates on three concepts and their interrelation: population, pollution, and freedom. By considering the consequences of unbridled growth in population and consequent growth in pollution, he is led to challenge an old maxim: People should be free to have as many children as they wish.

He is led to challenge the old maxim by developing an argument based on an analogy with a commons. A commons is a pasture shared by inhabitants of a village; each puts a cow to graze on the commons. Each person may reason that by putting another cow to graze he or she will realize a benefit from it. But if each person did that, the commons would be destroyed and each would lose by putting another cow to graze. For mutual benefit, there needs to be a curtailment of the freedom to place cows in the commons; the new circumstance forces us to reject any earlier maxim about freedom. Pollution is just the reverse of the grazing problem; where grazing takes matter out of the commons, pollution puts matter in.

Technological advances have made an increase in population a new moral factor, and pollution as well. This new factor should, according to Hardin, lead to legislating a law that curtails the former moral maxim giving persons the freedom to breed without restraints other than their own. You might ask yourself what other moral maxims Hardin assumes in order to draw his conclusion that freedom to breed should be curtailed; and you might ask yourself whether or not these other moral maxims are old ones or new ones.

Arne Naess, in this brief, densely packed essay, points out that the additional factors modifying our moral scene are more extensive than usually represented by "shallow" ecologists. Much more than pollution and resource depletion are involved in rethinking our new moral circumstances; this rethinking needs to be more extensive and radical than we allow ourselves to acknowledge. To emphasize the nature of this "deeper" ecological movement, he suggests a new name for it, "ecophilosophical." Ecology is limited *science;* it excludes what has traditionally been a philosophical goal, namely, *wisdom.* "Sophia," in "philo-sophia," is the Greek word for wisdom. Wisdom differs from scientific knowledge in that it frankly contains a normative element; one who seeks wisdom does not just search for the facts but also for values.

We call your attention here to Naess's first set of remarks on the deep ecology movement, where he replaces the factor of man-in-environment with "the relational, total-field image." He proposes that ecophilosophy forces us to reconsider the nature of man. Basically, Naess is pointing out that nothing is a thing-in-itself; the nature of everything depends on the relations that it has to other things; thus, we should speak of things-in-relations. This is particularly true of human beings considered in the moral context. If you think of yourself and what you are, one of the things characterizing you is that you are a child or, perhaps, a parent. This feature is not something you have in-yourself; it is something you have in-relation to other persons—your parents or children. Our moral obligations to another person vary depending upon our relation to that person; if she is our mother, we have a different moral obligation than if she is unknown to us and an inhabitant of another part of the world. Naess's remarks make us rethink the nature of human beings; thinking of ourselves as in-relation in a total field may lead us to reconceive the extensiveness of our moral obligations; we need a total-field concept of morals. Naess follows up this total-field concept by his remarks on anthropocentrism, biospherical egalitarianism, preservation of diversity, exploitation of others by class division, failure to systematize our knowledge of the various life factors, and the decentralization of government to preserve autonomy. (For a fuller discussion of the concept of people as beings-in-relation, see Bierman's essay in Chapter Seven.)

We make three sets of comments on **Thomas McGinn's** essay. First, briefly, he expands on many of Naess's deep-ecology topics; he discusses anthropocentrism, the extensiveness of our moral responsibility, the unity of ecological systems and of our knowledge of them, value egalitarianism, and the exploitation of others by favored classes and affluent societies.

Second, and perhaps most interestingly, he is led by ecological considerations to challenge Kant's central point. Kant maintained that human beings, unlike things, should be treated as ends; persons differ from things; things may be treated as means. For Kant, the only entities to which the categorical imperative applies are human beings. McGinn suggests that "the life world and the planetary order *must be willed as ends along with man.*" The ecology-related factors which our wide use of technology has generated forces us to rethink our notions of what deserves moral respect.

Third, McGinn recognizes that because our technology may make such long-lasting changes in our world, we have to consider some factors that we did not consider before, factors that should modify our usual moral maxims. Our usual maxims cover acts to the extent that they allow for effects likely to occur in our own lifetime; but if the effects are going to alter the lives of future generations, these new factors may lead us to alter our maxims. The old morals—a this-generation egoism—may have to give way to a new morals—future-generations altruism.

John Passmore knocks the stuffing out of some windy, sentimental, half-baked, and inflated movements that have feasted on the rise in ecological consciousness. You will enjoy his essay even though you may also be punctured by it.

Passmore directly addresses the question about the need for a new morality now that our technology has changed our relation to nature. He says, "That, I think, is not entirely wrong-headed. During most of the West's history, its moral philosophers, Stoic or Christian, denied that man's relationship with nature is governed by any moral considerations whatsoever. From Montaigne onwards, however, to say nothing of his neo-Platonic predecessors, sceptics and humanists took a different view. And by the end of the eighteenth century even Christians began to argue, although often against fierce opposition from their co-religionists, that callousness towards animal suffering was morally wrong." Passmore agrees with McGinn and with the view we expressed in relation to Naess that a new relationship calls for a new moral orientation.

But, Passmore qualifies this agreement in two ways. The first is indicated in the quote above; the "new" morals is not entirely new; the history of controversy about the treatment of animals shows this. The second qualification is his defense of his "human chauvinism," of which he reports being accused. Even though our moral responsibilities extend beyond humans to the land and the plants and animals growing on it, an ethics dealing with them "would have to be justified by reference to human interests." Human beings, still, are of paramount value. Much of a "new ethic" is not needed because simple adherence to a perfectly familiar ethic is sufficient. "The land which a bad farmer allows to slip into a river did not have a "right" to stay where it was. The supposition that anything but a human being has "rights" is, or so I have suggested, quite untenable." Passmore thus supports Kant and opposes McGinn.

Two areas of technology have forced an expansion in our moral reflections on the importance of privacy. One area is the expansion of tools to gather information about persons without their awareness; this includes listening devices, recording instruments, and electronic interceptive capacities. The second area is information recovery; with computers, a huge mass of information is manageable because it is so easy to recover. Keeping paper files in drawers is one thing; being able to store information electronically and to recover it with a few typed directions is something else. Improved recovery techniques is a factor that makes information gathering a different moral problem than it was.

Many persons do not realize the extent to which their privacy has been lost. They may not think the FBI, the CIA, the IRS, or the local police intelligence unit has bothered to plug in on them because they "have nothing to hide" and so nothing worth finding out about. But credit bureaus do have an interest in them and each person may indeed have something to hide; almost everybody buys some things on credit. What do "they" know about your financial "profile"? If you do not know what they know about you, you do not know you have nothing to fear from privacy invasion. Blissful, ignorant world, undisturbed ethics. Hardly anyone wants the big brother, "1984" society; this extreme is easily rejected. But what degree of approach to it is tolerable? And do you have a clear idea of what degree of approach we now suffer?

Persons who acknowledge that they voice unpopular and unconventional views are often those most concerned with privacy. They recognize that capability to invade privacy has a chilling effect on speech, which in turn restricts freedom of collective, political action because such action depends on communication. Citizens who are afraid to speak and to act soon find themselves living in a society that cannot deal with the problems it faces. Without full discussion of, for example, the Vietnam war and Watergate, those problems would not have been addressed, nor war and spying activities halted.

Complacency about invasion of privacy by government agencies is often fostered by the belief that one does not have unpopular and unconventional views. However, the person spied upon is generally not the one to define what is "unpopular and unconventional." This is in the hands of the spy, whose political views may be quite different and more extreme than the person spied upon. You need only read about the Huston Plan in **A. K. Bierman's** essay in order to appreciate how the spy master defines what is worth finding out about.

Frequently, the justification for invasion of privacy turns on "national security." The implication is that privacy is invaded only for purposes of thwarting external enemies. The Huston Plan, however, shows how many "internal" citizens could be linked with external enemies. Even if the original intent in gathering intelligence information is to concentrate on "foreign" sources, once the machinery is in operation it poses a threat to citizens. Senator Frank Church, who chaired a Senate Committee investigating intelligence gathering remarked on the capability of intercepting messages that it could "at any time be turned around on the American people, and no American would have any privacy left, such is the capability to monitor everything, telephone conversations, telegrams, it does not matter. There would be no place to hide. If this government ever became a tyranny, if a dictator ever took charge in this country, the technological capacity that the intelligence community has given the government could enable it to impose total tyranny and there would be no way to fight back."

Even if you do not consider yourself "political," you probably do contemplate having some sex in your life. You may also contemplate working for the government. In case you think your sex life is your own business, that you "have nothing to hide," and that no one has a right to invade your "sexual" privacy, you should rethink your morals about privacy. FBI, Economic Opportunity, Postal, National Aeronautics and Space Administration, and IRS employees are known to have been dismissed because of information gathered about their sex lives. The sexual activities for which they were dismissed may not be "unconventional" by your standards, but as we remarked before, the one spied upon is not the one to define its conventionality. The spy defines the activity as "unconventional or unpopular." Do you consider living out of wedlock with a person of the opposite sex "unconventional"? Some people were fired for that reason.

In his essay, Bierman claims that there is an important connection between our thinking about the morals of privacy and the ethical theory question about the primacy of right or good. He points out that the usual "liberal" ethical theory may be inadequate to defend the right of privacy. In this case a teleological theory may not be as defensible as a deontological theory; in defending the right of privacy right may have to be considered the primary concept and good the subsidiary one rather than the other way around as teleological liberals would have it. Technological advances, thus, force us to rethink not only our morals and moral systems but also our ethical theory; Bierman's article shows that morals and ethical theory, although distinguishable, are not sealed off from one another.

Leon R. Kass fully appreciates how technology initiates new moral thinking. He raises some questions about moral goods. "A *full* understanding of the new technology of man requires an exploration of ends, values, standards. What ends will or should the new techniques serve? What values should guide society's adjustments? By what standards should the assessment agencies assess? Behind these questions lie others: what is a good man, what is a good life for man, what is a good community?"

Biomedical technology is different from other technologies because "biomedical technology works to change the user himself." It may change the nature of humans, the third part of moral content. This makes questions "about ends and ultimate ends" more important and more relevant than ever. We are now dealing with "social engineering." Kass points out that we are dealing with ethical theory questions as well as moral system questions because human engineering forces us to think about the kind of "utilitarian calculus" advocated by Bentham and other Utilitarians. Kass says, "we weigh "benefits" against "risks," and we weigh them for both the individual and "society." We often ignore the fact that the very definitions of "a benefit" and "a risk" are themselves based upon judgments about value. . . . The very pragmatism that makes us sensitive to considerations of economic cost often blinds us to the larger social costs exacted by biomedical advances." Kass then points out that our need for theorizing is generated by incompatible morals, a topic we discussed in the introduction to Chapter One. Faced with incompatible moral values, we have to rethink them. He gives two examples of moral "conflict." On the one hand, we seek to control population growth by lowering fertility; on the other hand, we develop techniques to enable every infertile woman to bear a child. On the one hand, we try to extend the lives of individuals with genetic disease; on the other, we wish to eliminate deleterious genes from the human population. Technology introduces new possibilities for changing humans; these new possibilities require value decisions that may conflict with old value decisions.

Kass recognizes another ethical theory question; he wonders whether it is possible to settle rationally a value conflict. "Problems of distributive justice are frequently mentioned and discussed, but they are hard to resolve in a rational manner. We find them especially difficult because of the enormous range of conflicting values and interests that characterizes our pluralistic society." Do interests and values have a nonrational source? If they do, we find ourselves forced to inquire about the extent to which rational thought is able to alter values and interests, which is a very basic ethical theory question.

For more on the relation between biomedical technology and ethics, you can look at your library's journal collection, which should include *The Hastings Center Report,* a report published by the Institute of Society, Ethics and the Life Sciences.

One final remark about Kass's rich essay. Biomedical technology poses a threat to Kant's concept of human beings as ends. Kass remarks, "We are witnessing the erosion, perhaps the final erosion, of the idea of man as something splendid or divine, and its replacement with a view that sees man, no less than nature, as simply more raw material for manipulation and homogenization. Hence, our peculiar moral crisis."

Karl Marx distinguished between productive relations, how society is organized to produce its material goods, and social relations, how society is organized legally, politically, artistically, religiously, and philosophically. He maintained that the social relations essentially serve the productive relations and that, therefore, social relations are formed by the productive relations in a society. When societies are basically agricultural productive societies, feudal social relations are appropriate. Clearly, the industrial revolution brought enormous changes in productive relations, which generated capitalist social relations, and the industrial revolution was possible because of a quantum jump in technology. Thus, for Marx, changes in technology directly change productive relations and indirectly change social relations.

Changes in social relations lag behind changes in productive relations; this gives rise to a tension or a contradiction between the two sets of relations, which is resolved only when a revolution occurs that changes the social relations. Marx, then, clearly set out a theory pertinent to our chapter; changes in technology force us to think about and to change our social, that is, our moral, relations with each other.

In the famous essay in this chapter, Marx concentrates on capitalist social relations. Capitalist productive arrangements have had a deleterious effect on humans and their social relations. Capitalism has alienated or estranged human beings from their products, their own activity, from others, and from their "species life." Alienation is an unwanted human condition because it runs athwart of the essential human nature. We have said that beliefs about human nature form the third part of a moral system; Marx's essay addresses itself to this issue. A main factor causing alienation from our essential nature is private property. Until the productive relations change, of which private property is a central part, we will be unable to change the social relations and eliminate alienation.

To help you understand Marx's essay, we summarize his statement of the four alienations—from products, from our activity, from others, and from our species life—and their connections.

Persons are alienated from their products when they realize a disparity in their own and their products' value. In a capitalist economy, products increase in value while the value of persons decreases. The value disparity leads us to see our product as alien to us because it has power that is independent of us. Because the product is alien and because our own work activity is embedded in the object, we come to realize that our own activity is also alien to us. We work in a capitalist economy not because it is a fulfillment of our essential nature but because we are forced to work merely as a means of bodily survival; work has become an externally imposed activity, not our own, self-imposed activity.

Workers' alienation from their products and from their own activity is closely tied to the alienation from their species life. Human beings are the only entities that have a species life because they are the only creatures who are conscious of themselves. Man is conscious of himself in that "his own life is an object for him." Every kind of thing in the world has an essence; that is what makes it that kind of thing and what makes it differ from other kinds of things. The essence of a chair is different from the essence of a book or of an elephant or of a human. Human beings, in being their own objects, are aware of their own essence. Hence, human beings are aware of themselves as a species, for this essence is what defines the species "human."

For Marx, the essence or nature of human beings, what makes us different from other kinds of things, is that we are capable of free, conscious activity. We literally objectify our own essence by freely making objects, intellectual and material; we contemplate ourselves when we contemplate the products we have made; in those products we have deposited ourselves, and we can contemplate ourselves, *provided* that we see them as our own. But this is precisely what we cannot do if we are alienated from our products and our own activities. Thus, our alienation from our species life follows from our alienation from our own activities. We are alienated from our own activities because, as we saw, we are forced to work; being forced to work, we no longer work freely according to our essence, and this alienates us from our species life.

Because each person *qua* species bears the same essence, essence being universal in human beings, when a person is alienated from his or her own essence or species life, he or she is, thereby, also alienated from other persons who bear that same essence. In this alienated condition, workers are divorced from and lose their own reality (their products, their activities, their essence). By consenting to our alienated condition, we workers create our own domination in that someone else comes to possess that from which we workers have been alienated. This dominating possessor is the one who holds private property. Alienation has been shown, Marx believes, to be the expression of private property. If his analysis is correct, quite obviously, our alienated condition cannot be eliminated until private property disappears.

The Tragedy of the Commons

GARRETT HARDIN

Garrett Hardin (1921–   ) teaches at the University of California at Santa Barbara, where he is professor of biology. He is the author of *Biology: Its Principles and Implications* (1966), a collection of readings, and is editor of *Population, Evolution, and Birth Control* (1964) and *Nature and Man's Fate* (1959).

What Shall We Maximize?

Population, as Malthus said, naturally tends to grow "geometrically," or, as we would now say, exponentially. In a finite world this means that the per capita share of the world's goods must steadily decrease. Is ours a finite world?

A fair defense can be put forward for the view that the world is infinite; or that we do not know that it is not. But, in terms of the practical problems that we must face in the next few generations with the foreseeable technology, it is clear that we will greatly increase human misery if we do not, during the immediate future, assume that the world available to the terrestrial human population is finite. "Space" is no escape.[1]

A finite world can support only a finite population; therefore, population growth must eventually equal zero. (The case of perpetual wide fluctuations above and below zero is a trivial variant that need not be discussed.) When this

[1] Garrett Hardin, *Journal of Heredity,* Vol. 50 (1959), p. 68; S. von Hoerner, *Science,* Vol. 137 (1962), p. 18.

Source: Garrett Hardin, "The Tragedy of the Commons," *Science,* Vol. 162 (December 13, 1968), pp. 1243–1248. Copyright © 1968 by the American Association for the Advancement of Science. Reprinted by permission of *Science* and the author.

condition is met, what will be the situation of mankind? Specifically, can Bentham's goal of "the greatest good for the greatest number" be realized?

No—for two reasons, each sufficient by itself. The first is a theoretical one. It is not mathematically possible to maximize for two (or more) variables at the same time. This was clearly stated by von Neumann and Morgenstern,[2] but the principle is implicit in the theory of partial differential equations, dating back at least to D'Alembert (1717–1783).

The second reason springs directly from biological facts. To live, any organism must have a source of energy (for example, food). This energy is utilized for two purposes: mere maintenance and work. For man, maintenance of life requires about 1600 kilo-calories a day ("maintenance calories"). Anything that he does over and above merely staying alive will be defined as work, and is supported by "work calories" which he takes in. Work calories are used not only for what we call work in common speech; they are also required for all forms of enjoyment, from swimming and automobile racing to playing music and writing poetry. If our goal is to maximize population it is obvious what we must do: We must make the work calories per person approach as close to zero as possible. No gourmet meals, no vacations, no sports, no music, no literature, no art. . . . I think that everyone will grant, without argument or proof, that maximizing population does not maximize goods. Bentham's goal is impossible.

.   .   .

We can make little progress in working toward optimum population size until we explicitly exorcize the spirit of Adam Smith in the field of practical demography. In economic affairs, *The Wealth of Nations* (1776) popularized the "invisible hand," the idea that an individual who "intends only his own gain," is, as it were, "led by an invisible hand to promote . . . the public interest."[3] Adam Smith did not assert that this was invariably true, and perhaps neither did any of his followers. But he contributed to a dominant tendency of thought that has ever since interfered with positive action based on rational analysis, namely, the tendency to assume that decisions reached individually will, in fact, be the best decisions for an entire society. If this assumption is correct it justifies the continuance of our present policy of laissez-faire in reproduction. If it is correct we can assume that men will control their individual fecundity so as to produce the optimum population. If the assumption is not correct, we need to reexamine our individual freedoms to see which ones are defensible.

Tragedy of Freedom in a Commons

The rebuttal of the invisible hand in population control is to be found in a scenario first sketched in a little-known pamphlet[4] in 1833 by a mathematical

---

[2] J. von Neumann and O. Morgenstern, *Theory of Games and Economic Behavior* (Princeton, N.J.: Princeton University Press, 1947), p. 11.

[3] Adam Smith, *The Wealth of Nations* (New York: Modern Library, 1937), p. 423.

[4] William Forster Lloyd, *Two Lectures on the Checks to Population* (Oxford: Oxford University Press, 1833), reprinted (in part) in *Population, Evolution, and Birth Control*, Garrett Hardin, ed. (San Francisco: Freeman, 1964), p. 37.

amateur named William Forster Lloyd (1794–1852). We may well call it "the tragedy of the commons," using the word "tragedy" as the philosopher Whitehead used it:[5] "The essence of dramatic tragedy is not unhappiness. It resides in the solemnity of the remorseless working of things." He then goes on to say, "This inevitableness of destiny can only be illustrated in terms of human life by incidents which in fact involve unhappiness. For it is only by them that the futility of escape can be made evident in the drama."

The tragedy of the commons develops in this way. Picture a pasture open to all. It is to be expected that each herdsman will try to keep as many cattle as possible on the commons. Such an arrangement may work reasonably satisfactorily for centuries because tribal wars, poaching, and disease keep the numbers of both man and beast well below the carrying capacity of the land. Finally, however, comes the day of reckoning, that is, the day when the long-desired goal of social stability becomes a reality. At this point, the inherent logic of the commons remorselessly generates tragedy.

As a rational being, each herdsman seeks to maximize his gain. Explicitly or implicitly, more or less consciously, he asks: "What is the utility *to me* of adding one more animal to my herd?" This utility has one negative and one positive component.

1. The positive component is a function of the increment of one animal. Since the herdsman receives all the proceeds from the sale of the additional animal, the positive utility is nearly $+1$.

2. The negative component is a function of the additional overgrazing created by one more animal. Since, however, the effects of overgrazing are shared by all the herdsmen, the negative utility for any particular decision-making herdsman is only a fraction of -1.

Adding together the component partial utilities, the rational herdsman concludes that the only sensible course for him to pursue is to add another animal to his herd. And another; and another. . . . But this is the conclusion reached by each and every rational herdsman sharing a commons. Therein is the tragedy. Each man is locked into a system that compels him to increase his herd without limit—in a world that is limited. Ruin is the destination toward which all men rush, each pursuing his own best interest in a society that believes in the freedom of the commons. Freedom in a commons brings ruin to all.

. . .

Pollution

In a reverse way, the tragedy of the commons reappears in problems of pollution. Here it is not a question of taking something out of the commons, but of putting something in—sewage, or chemical, radioactive, and heat wastes into water; noxious and dangerous fumes into the air; and distracting and unpleasant advertising signs into the line of sight. The calculations of utility are much the same as before. The rational man finds that his share of the cost of the wastes he

---

[5] Alfred North Whitehead, *Science and the Modern World* (New York: Mentor Books, 1948), p. 17.

discharges into the commons is less than the cost of purifying his wastes before releasing them. Since this is true for everyone, we are locked into a system of "fouling our own nest," so long as we behave only as independent, rational, free-enterprisers.

· · ·

The pollution problem is a consequence of population. It did not much matter how a lonely American frontiersman disposed of his waste. "Flowing water purifies itself every 10 miles," my grandfather used to say, and the myth was near enough to the truth when he was a boy, for there were not too many people. But as population became denser, the natural chemical and biological recycling processes became overloaded, calling for a redefinition of property rights.

How to Legislate Temperance?

Analysis of the pollution problem as a function of population density uncovers a not generally recognized principle of morality, namely: *the morality of an act is a function of the state of the system at the time it is performed.*[6] Using the commons as a cesspool does not harm the general public under frontier conditions, because there is no public; the same behavior in a metropolis is unbearable. A hundred and fifty years ago a plainsman could kill an American bison, cut out only the tongue for his dinner, and discard the rest of the animal. He was not in any important sense being wasteful. Today, with only a few thousand bison left, we would be appalled at such behavior.

· · ·

That morality is system-sensitive escaped the attention of most codifiers of ethics in the past. "Thou shalt not . . ." is the form of traditional ethical directives which make no allowance for particular circumstances. The laws of our society follow the pattern of ancient ethics, and therefore are poorly suited to governing a complex, crowded, changeable world. Our epicyclic solution is to augment statutory law with administrative law. Since it is practically impossible to spell out all the conditions under which it is safe to burn trash in the back yard or to run an automobile without smog-control, by law we delegate the details to bureaus. The result is administrative law, which is rightly feared for an ancient reason—*Quis custodiet ipsos custodes?*—"Who shall watch the watchers themselves?" John Adams said that we must have "a government of laws and not men." Bureau administrators, trying to evaluate the morality of acts in the total system, are singularly liable to corruption, producing a government by men, not laws.

· · ·

Freedom to Breed Is Intolerable

The tragedy of the commons is involved in population problems in another way. In a world governed solely by the principle of "dog eat dog"—if indeed there ever was such a world—how many children a family had would not be a

[6] J. Fletcher, *Situation Ethics* (Philadelphia: Westminster, 1966).

matter of public concern. Parents who bred too exuberantly would leave fewer descendants, not more, because they would be unable to care adequately for their children. David Lack and others have found that such a negative feedback demonstrably controls the fecundity of birds.[7] But men are not birds, and have not acted like them for millenniums, at least.

If each human family were dependent only on its own resources; *if* the children of improvident parents starved to death; *if,* thus, overbreeding brought its own "punishment" to the germ line—*then* there would be no public interest in controlling the breeding of families. But our society is deeply committed to the welfare state,[8] and hence is confronted with another aspect of the tragedy of the commons.

In a welfare state, how shall we deal with the family, the religion, the race, or the class (or indeed any distinguishable and cohesive group) that adopts overbreeding as a policy to secure its own aggrandizement?[9] To couple the concept of freedom to breed with the belief that everyone born has an equal right to the commons is to lock the world into a tragic course of action.

Unfortunately this is just the course of action that is being pursued by the United Nations. In late 1967, some 30 nations agreed to the following.[10]

The Universal Declaration of Human Rights describes the family as the natural and fundamental unit of society. It follows that any choice and decision with regard to the size of the family must irrevocably rest with the family itself, and cannot be made by anyone else.

. . .

Conscience Is Self-Eliminating

It is a mistake to think that we can control the breeding of mankind in the long run by an appeal to conscience. Charles Galton Darwin made this point when he spoke on the centennial of the publication of his grandfather's great book. The argument is straightforward and Darwinian.

People vary. Confronted with appeals to limit breeding, some people will undoubtedly respond to the plea more than others. Those who have more children will produce a larger fraction of the next generation than those with more susceptible consciences. The difference will be accentuated, generation by generation.

In C. G. Darwin's words: "It may well be that it would take hundreds of generations for the progenitive instinct to develop in this way, but if it should do so, nature would have taken her revenge, and the variety *Homo contracipiens* would become extinct and would be replaced by the variety *Homo progenitivus.*"[11]

. . .

[7] David Lack, *The Natural Regulation of Animal Numbers* (Oxford: Clarendon Press, 1954).

[8] H. Girvetz, *From Wealth to Welfare* (Stanford, Calif.: Stanford University Press, 1950).

[9] Garrett Hardin, *Perspectives in Biological Medicine,* Vol. 6 (1963), p. 366.

[10] U Thant, *International Planned Parenthood News,* No. 168 (Feb. 1968), p. 3.

[11] *Evolution After Darwin,* Vol. 2, S. Tax, ed. (Chicago: University of Chicago Press, 1960), p. 469.

Pathogenic Effects of Conscience

The long-term disadvantage of an appeal to conscience should be enough to condemn it; but it has serious short-term disadvantages as well. If we ask a man who is exploiting a commons to desist "in the name of conscience," what are we saying to him? What does he hear?—not only at the moment but also in the wee small hours of the night when, half asleep, he remembers not merely the words we used but also the nonverbal communication cues we gave him unawares? Sooner or later, consciously or subconsciously, he senses that he has received two communications, and that they are contradictory: (1) (intended communication) "If you don't do as we ask, we will openly condemn you for not acting like a responsible citizen"; (2) (the unintended communication) "If you *do* behave as we ask, we will secretly condemn you for a simpleton who can be shamed into standing aside while the rest of us exploit the commons."

. . .

Mutual Coercion Mutually Agreed Upon

The social arrangements that produce responsibility are arrangements that create coercion, of some sort. Consider bank-robbing. The man who takes money from a bank acts as if the bank were a commons. How do we prevent such action? Certainly not by trying to control his behavior solely by a verbal appeal to his sense of responsibility. Rather than rely on propaganda we follow Frankel's lead and insist that a bank is not a commons; we seek the definite social arrangements that will keep it from becoming a commons. That we thereby infringe on the freedom of would-be robbers we neither deny nor regret.

The morality of bank-robbing is particularly easy to understand because we accept complete prohibition of this activity. We are willing to say "Thou shalt not rob banks," without providing for exceptions. But temperance also can be created by coercion. Taxing is a good coercive device. To keep downtown shoppers temperate in their use of parking space we introduce parking meters for short periods, and traffic fines for longer ones. We need not actually forbid a citizen to park as long as he wants to; we need merely make it increasingly expensive for him to do so. Not prohibition, but carefully biased options are what we offer him. A Madison Avenue man might call this persuasion; I prefer the greater candor of the word coercion.

Coercion is a dirty word to most liberals now, but it need not forever be so. As with the four-letter words, its dirtiness can be cleansed away by exposure to the light, by saying it over and over without apology or embarrassment. To many, the word coercion implies arbitrary decisions of distant and irresponsible bureaucrats; but this is not a necessary part of its meaning. The only kind of coercion I recommend is mutual coercion, mutually agreed upon by the majority of the people affected.

To say that we mutually agree to coercion is not to say that we are required to enjoy it, or even pretend to enjoy it. Who enjoys taxes? We all grumble about them. But we accept compulsory taxes because we recognize that voluntary taxes would favor the conscienceless. We institute and (grumblingly) support taxes and other coercive devices to escape the horror of the commons.

. . .

Recognition of Necessity

Perhaps the simplest summary of this analysis of man's population problems is this: the commons, if justifiable at all, is justifiable only under conditions of low-population density. As the human population has increased, the commons has had to be abandoned in one aspect after another.

First we abandoned the commons in food gathering, enclosing farm land and restricting pastures and hunting and fishing areas. These restrictions are still not complete throughout the world.

Somewhat later, we saw that the commons as a place for waste disposal would also have to be abandoned. Restrictions on the disposal of domestic sewage are widely accepted in the Western world; we are still struggling to close the commons to pollution by automobiles, factories, insecticide sprayers, fertilizing operations, and atomic energy installations.

In a still more embryonic state is our recognition of the evils of the commons in matters of pleasure. There is almost no restriction on the propagation of sound waves in the public medium. The shopping public is assaulted with mindless music, without its consent. Our government is paying out billions of dollars to create supersonic transport which will disturb 50,000 people for every one person who is whisked from coast to coast 3 hours faster. Advertisers muddy the airwaves of radio and television and pollute the view of travelers. We are a long way from outlawing the commons in matters of pleasure. Is this because our Puritan inheritance makes us view pleasure as something of a sin, and pain (that is, the pollution of advertising) as the sign of virtue?

Every new enclosure of the commons involve the infringement of somebody's personal liberty. Infringements made in the distant past are accepted because no contemporary complains of a loss. It is the newly proposed infringements that we vigorously oppose; cries of "rights" and "freedom" fill the air. But what does "freedom" mean? When men mutually agreed to pass laws against robbing, mankind became more free, not less so. Individuals locked into the logic of the commons are free only to bring on universal ruin; once they see the necessity of mutual coercion, they become free to pursue other goals. I believe it was Hegel who said, "Freedom is the recognition of necessity."

The most important aspect of necessity that we must now recognize, is the necessity of abandoning the commons in breeding. No technical solution can rescue us from the misery of overpopulation. Freedom to breed will bring ruin to all. At the moment, to avoid hard decisions many of us are tempted to propagandize for conscience and responsible parenthood. The temptation must be resisted, because an appeal to independently acting consciences selects for the disappearance of all conscience in the long run, and an increase in anxiety in the short.

The only way we can preserve and nurture other and more precious freedoms is by relinquishing the freedom to breed, and that very soon. "Freedom is the recognition of necessity"—and it is the role of education to reveal to all the necessity of abandoning the freedom to breed. Only so, can we put an end to this aspect of the tragedy of the commons.

The Shallow and the Deep, Long-Range Ecology Movement

ARNE NAESS

Arne Naess (1925–   ), professor of philosophy at the University of Oslo, has written on the contemporary linguistic movement in philosophy and is the author of several books in the area of ethics.

Ecologically responsible policies are concerned only in part with pollution and resource depletion. There are deeper concerns which touch upon principles of diversity, complexity, autonomy, decentralization, symbiosis, egalitarianism, and classlessness.

The emergence of ecologists from their former relative obscurity marks a turning-point in our scientific communities. But their message is twisted and misused. A shallow, but presently rather powerful movement, and a deep, but less influential movement, compete for our attention. I shall make an effort to characterize the two.

1. *The Shallow Ecology movement:*

Fight against pollution and resource depletion. Central objective: the health and affluence of people in the developed countries.

2. *The Deep Ecology movement:*

a. Rejection of the man-in-environment image in favour of *the relational, total-field image.* Organisms as knots in the biospherical net or field of intrinsic relations. An intrinsic relation between two things A and B is such that the relation belongs to the definitions or basic constitutions of A and B, so that without the relation, A and B are no longer the same things. The total-field model dissolves not only the man-in-environment concept, but every compact thing-in-milieu concept—except when talking at a superficial or preliminary level of communication.

b. *Biospherical egalitarianism*—in principle. The 'in principle' clause is inserted because any realistic praxis necessitates some killing, exploitation, and suppression. The ecological field-worker acquires a deep-seated respect, or even veneration, for ways and forms of life. He reaches an understanding from within, a

Source: Arne Naess, "The Shallow and the Deep, Long-Range Ecology Movement. A Summary," *Inquiry,* Vol. 16 (1973), pp. 95–100. Reprinted by permission of Universitetsforlaget, Oslo, and the author.

kind of understanding that others reserve for fellow men and for a narrow section of ways and forms of life. To the ecological field-worker, *the equal right to live and blossom* is an intuitively clear and obvious value axiom. Its restriction to humans is an anthropocentrism with detrimental effects upon the life quality of humans themselves. This quality depends in part upon the deep pleasure and satisfaction we receive from close partnership with other forms of life. The attempt to ignore our dependence and to establish a master–slave role has contributed to the alienation of man from himself.

Ecological egalitarianism implies the reinterpretation of the future-research variable, 'level of crowding,' so that *general* mammalian crowding and loss of life-equality is taken seriously, not only human crowding. (Research on the high requirements of free space of certain mammals has, incidentally, suggested that theorists of human urbanism have largely underestimated human life-space requirements. Behavioural crowding symptoms [neuroses, aggressiveness, loss of traditions . . .] are largely the same among mammals.)

c. *Principles of diversity and of symbiosis.* Diversity enhances the potentialities of survival, the chances of new modes of life, the richness of forms. And the so-called struggle of life, and survival of the fittest, should be interpreted in the sense of ability to coexist and cooperate in complex relationships, rather than ability to kill, exploit, and suppress. "Live and let live" is a more powerful ecological principle than "Either you or me."

The latter tends to reduce the multiplicity of kinds of forms of life, and also to create destruction within the communities of the same species. Ecologically inspired attitudes therefore favour diversity of human ways of life, of cultures, of occupations, of economies. They support the fiight against economic and cultural, as much as military, invasion and domination, and they are opposed to the annihilation of seals and whales as much as to that of human tribes or cultures.

d. *Anti-class posture.* Diversity of human ways of life is in part due to (intended or unintended) exploitation and suppression on the part of certain groups. The exploiter lives differently from the exploited, but both are adversely affected in their potentialities of self-realization. The principle of diversity does not cover differences due merely to certain attitudes or behaviours forcibly blocked or restrained. The principles of ecological egalitarianism and of symbiosis support the same anti-class posture. The ecological attitude favours the extension of all three principles to any group conflicts, including those of today between developing and developed nations. The three principles also favour extreme caution towards any over-all plans for the future, except those consistent with wide and widening classless diversity.

e. Fight against *pollution and resource depletion.* In this fight ecologists have found powerful supporters, but sometimes to the detriment of their total stand. This happens when attention is focused on pollution and resource depletion rather than on the other points, or when projects are implemented which reduce pollution but increase evils of the other kinds. Thus, if prices of life necessities increase because of the installation of anti-pollution devices, class differences increase too. An ethics of responsibility implies that ecologists do not serve the shallow, but the deep ecological movement. That is, not only point (e), but all seven points must be considered together.

Ecologists are irreplaceable informants in any society, whatever their political colour. If well organized, they have the power to reject jobs in which they submit themselves to institutions or to planners with limited ecological perspectives. As it is now, ecologists sometimes serve masters who deliberately ignore the wider perspectives.

f. *Complexity, not complication.* The theory of ecosystems contains an important distinction between what is complicated without any Gestalt or unifying principles—we may think of finding our way through a chaotic city—and what is complex. A multiplicity of more or less lawful, interacting factors may operate together to form a unity, a system. We make a shoe or use a map or integrate a variety of activities into a workaday pattern. Organisms, ways of life, and interactions in the biosphere in general, exhibit complexity of such an astoundingly high level as to colour the general outlook of ecologists. Such complexity makes thinking in terms of vast systems inevitable. It also makes for a keen, steady perception of the profound *human ignorance* of biospherical relationships and therefore of the effect of disturbances.

Applied to humans, the complexity-not-complication principle favours division of labour, *not fragmentation of labour.* It favours integrated actions in which the whole person is active, not mere reactions. It favours complex economies, an integrated variety of means of living. (Combinations of industrial and agricultural activity, of intellectual and manual work, of specialized and non-specialized occupations, of urban and non-urban activity, of work in city and recreation in nature with recreation in city and work in nature. . . .)

It favours soft technique and "soft future-research," less prognosis, more clarification of possibilities. More sensitivity towards continuity and live traditions, and—most importantly—towards our state of ignorance.

The implementation of ecologically responsible policies requires in this century an exponential growth of technical skill and invention—but in new directions, directions which today are not consistently and liberally supported by the research policy organs of our nation-states.

g. *Local autonomy and decentralization.* The vulnerability of a form of life is roughly proportional to the weight of influences from afar, from outside the local region in which that form has obtained an ecological equilibrium. This lends support to our efforts to strengthen local self-government and material and mental self-sufficiency. But these efforts presuppose an impetus towards decentralization. Pollution problems, including those of thermal pollution and recirculation of materials, also lead us in this direction, because increased local autonomy, if we are able to keep other factors constant, reduces energy consumption. (Compare an approximately self-sufficient locality with one requiring the importation of foodstuff, materials for house construction, fuel and skilled labour from other continents. The former may use only five per cent of the energy used by the latter.) Local autonomy is strengthened by a reduction in the number of links in the hierarchical chains of decision. (For example a chain consisting of local board, municipal council, highest sub-national decision-maker, a state-wide institution in a state federation, a federal national government institution, a coalition of nations, and of institutions, e.g. E.E.C. top levels, and a global institution, can be reduced to one made up of local board, nation-wide institution, and global institution.) Even if a decision follows majority rules at each step, many local interests may be dropped along the line, if it is too long.

Summing up, then, it should, first of all, be borne in mind that the norms and tendencies of the Deep Ecology movement are not derived from ecology by logic or induction. Ecological knowledge and the life-style of the ecological field-worker have *suggested, inspired, and fortified* the perspectives of the Deep Ecology movement. Many of the formulations in the above seven-point survey are rather vague generalizations, only tenable if made more precise in certain directions. But all over the world the inspiration from ecology has shown remarkable convergencies. The survey does not pretend to be more than one of the possible condensed codifications of these convergencies.

Secondly, it should be fully appreciated that the significant tenets of the Deep Ecology movement are clearly and forcefully *normative*. They express a value priority system only in part based on results (or lack of results, cf. point [f]) of scientific research. Today, ecologists try to influence policy-making bodies largely through threats, through predictions concerning pollutants and resource depletion, knowing that policy-makers accept at least certain minimum *norms* concerning health and just distribution. But it is clear that there is a vast number of people in all countries, and even a considerable number of people in power, who accept as valid the wider norms and values characteristic of the Deep Ecology movement. There are political potentials in this movement which should not be overlooked and which have little to do with pollution and resource depletion. In plotting possible futures, the norms should be freely used and elaborated.

Thirdly, in so far as ecology movements deserve our attention, they are *ecophilosophical* rather than ecological. Ecology is a *limited* science which makes *use* of scientific methods. Philosophy is the most general forum of debate on fundamentals, descriptive as well as prescriptive, and political philosophy is one of its subsections. By an *ecosophy* I mean a philosophy of ecological harmony or equilibrium. A philosophy as a kind of *sofia* wisdom, is openly normative, it contains *both* norms, rules, postulates, value priority announcements *and* hypotheses concerning the state of affairs in our universe. Wisdom is policy wisdom, prescription, not only scientific description and prediction.

The details of an ecosophy will show many variations due to significant differences concerning not only "facts" of pollution, resources, population, etc., but also value priorities. Today, however, the seven points listed provide one unified framework for ecosophical systems.

In general system theory, systems are mostly conceived in terms of causally or functionally interacting or interrelated items. An ecosophy, however, is more like a system of the kind constructed by Aristotle or Spinoza. It is expressed verbally as a set of sentences with a variety of functions, descriptive and prescriptive. The basic relation is that between subsets of premises and subsets of conclusions, that is, the relation of derivability. The relevant notions of derivability may be classed according to rigour, with logical and mathematical deductions topping the list, but also according to how much is implicitly taken for granted. An exposition of an ecosophy must necessarily be only moderately precise considering the vast scope of relevant ecological and normative (social, polticial, ethical) material. At the moment, ecosophy might profitably use models of systems, rough approximations of global systematizations. It is the global character, not preciseness in detail, which distinguishes an ecosophy. It articulates and integrates the efforts of an ideal ecological team, a team comprising not only scientists from an extreme variety of disciplines, but also students of politics and active policy-makers.

Under the name of *ecologism*, various deviations from the deep movement have been championed—primarily with a one-sided stress on pollution and resource depletion, but also with a neglect of the great differences between under- and over-developed countries in favour of a vague global approach. The global approach is essential, but regional differences must largely determine policies in the coming years.

Ecology and Ethics

THOMAS MCGINN

Thomas McGinn (1941–   ) writes on problems of ecology and teaches at Nakerere University, Uganda.

Philosophy of Value in the Ecological Context

There are at least five traditional areas of philosophy of value which must be explored in the light of the questions which ecology poses for man. They are: (1) the relation of instinct and reason in value judgements; (2) the objectivity of value; (3) the relation of ends and means in value systems; (4) the relation of part and whole in value systems; (5) technological development and moral responsibility.

At present it is possible to outline these problem areas and state directions for further inquiry into them. There is a sixth central area which goes beyond ethics into the metaphysics of immanence and transcendence. As noted, Levi-Strauss has affirmed against Sartre that any humanistic ethics assumes a philosophy of the transcendence of man and human consciousness. We question whether Levi-Strauss is consistently immanentist in all his writings. But it is still possible to agree with him that thinkers such as Sartre are still "tortured by transcendence" although they have no *rational* basis for their affirmation of man as supreme value. Levi-Strauss holds a non-humanist ethic because it seems more rational given the ecological realities. This requires at least an initial inquiry into reason and instinct in value judgements.

Source: Thomas McGinn, "Ecology and Ethics," *International Philosophical Quarterly* (June 1974), pp. 153–160. Reprinted by permission of the Quarterly and the author.

1. THE RELATION OF INSTINCT AND REASON IN VALUE JUDGEMENTS

A reason-based value philosophy will invariably find that the basic reason for a human activity is the survival of the individual or the group. An instinct-based value philosophy will admit rational factors based on self-preservation, but recognize further value-motives in human action.

An interesting case is the view of some popular ecology that primitive man considers himself to be part of nature, an integral part of the ecological process. But if human beings were strictly part of the natural ecological system and accepted as such, then their dead bodies should serve as compost for the next phase of the life cycle. The vast majority of the human race instinctively resists this rational move. Our ancestors' bodies could help our agriculture perform better, and this would be particularly true in the subsistence agricultures of simple societies. But we do not find that this is done. Instinct regards the human body as something special which is not to be treated as a purely functional natural object.

In an earlier work Levi-Strauss states that specifically human phenomena constitute a discontinuity with those of the non-human biological world. The system of family relationships among human beings does not emerge as a development of biological relationships among other animals. A human family system exists in human consciousness alone, and like language, constitutes a new set of phenomena which can only be studied by social science and not by natural science. This is an affirmation of transcendence in the same sense that a phenomenologist like Sartre uses the term. Once specifically human phenomena are admitted to exist in family relationships, they can readily be admitted in the realm of values. Biologically-based ethics will use self-preservation as the only motive for human action. But recognition of the human family as a new set of phenomena leads to an ethics in which respect or reverence for the human transcends utility. Care for the dead and repugnance for cannibalism illustrate this as does the incest prohibition itself, in which not every human being is an object of biological use.

There is certainly no rational justification for the practice of setting the dead apart. Hence this value-illustrating practice is founded on non-rational criteria. Caring for the dead does not prove a belief in immortality, but it does establish humanism as an instinctive *a priori* of mankind, although men are also quite conscious of belonging to the life-death ecological system.

The point here is that there is a reliance on instinct or non-rationally justifiable intuition in distinguishing the value of various beings. Any humanism rests on the possibility of such intuitions. Levi-Strauss neglects this real aspect of human ethical activity. He makes primitive societies into rationally schematized systems reflecting a corporate human rationality which precedes action. The importance of this corrective to previous anthropological theories, which reserved rationality to technically advanced societies, overlooks the equal non-rationality of basic value judgments which men make.

Nature is not a uniform indistinct matter for the instinctive judgment. It is at least seen as living and non-living. It is the function of the rationalist scientist to try to overcome this common-sense distinction through attention to the mathematical patterns which run through all beings. But the instinctive value judgment will always accord more value to living beings than to non-living ones.

The importance of this is that there is already a value-transcendence operating here. By a kind of animal faith the instinctive judgment holds life to be more important than non-life. When we look at the consequences of the Cartesian expulsion of life values from the world of objective nature in the name of reason, we may well accept that reason cannot properly grasp nature in a central aspect. The instinctive way of responding to nature is to see it as a mother and nourisher, not as a subject of exploitation. Primitive man is capable of apologizing to mother earth when he digs her up to plant crops. Contemporary man has indeed lost this sense of respect through his philosophy of exploitation.

The value of the life-sphere is intuited in its creative power. Man feels a greater affinity for what is living, for it does what he does and independently of him. He does not immediately observe any creative power in the mineral. Respect for the living being is based on admiration, not on utility. As Heidegger says, we do not ask the flower for what purpose it is beautiful, or what use its beauty is. Of course the scientist knows that the flower's beauty is functional and rational; it gets itself pollinated that way. But this is the flower of the botanist, not that of the man who simply looks at it. Further, the flower gives us something through an activity which is independent of our action. It is not an inert mass which is simply subject to human ordering for its qualitative value.

2. The Objectivity of Value

What has been stated is little different from traditional Romanticist objections to philosophies which mechanize nature. However, Romanticism seems inadequate for a value theory since it is generally subjectivist. One area in which the legacy of Idealism is almost totally dominant is in the widely-held theory of the subjectivity of value-constitution. Yet there is a problem about the perception of values which runs similar to the old idealist problem of whether there is sound when a tree falls in the forest and no one is there to hear it. While most contemporary thinkers will reject a completely subjectivist account of sense perception, they will hold, in somewhat the same proportion, to a subjectivist theory of the perception of values.

Yet the analogy between the two cases is perfect. There is a basis in the object for the perception of sound, although sound does not exist unless there is a hearer. And there is a basis in the object of value perception which founds the value judgment just as surely. The difference in the value of two objects, let us say one inanimate and the other animate, is not constituted by my expression of preference for one over the other. The human world is not the *human* world if man is the only being in an otherwise rock-filled desert. Neil Armstrong expressed this on coming back from the moon. It may become possible to survive on the moon, but the moon cannot be a human habitat unless a life world can be established there. The fight of the urban dweller to have a small yard with some grass is not just a bourgeois foible. It reflects an instinctive valuing of the life-world over the inanimate world. Any urban dweller senses some deprivation of contact with the life-world. It is not simply an *esthetic* preference for grass over concrete. Concrete can be made very beautiful but it can never function for man as does the world of vegetation. Is grass more valuable than gold for instance? Instinct says yes. *Homo economicus,* who might say no, has a long rationalist analytic utilitarian education. The old fable of King Midas establishes the instinctive judgment on the question. No one could stand to be completely surrounded by gold, whereas we do not make this objection to trees and flowers. What we think of gold in immediate intuitive evaluation is not much different from what we think of rocks. They leave us cold. We use gold, but we do not love it. But in the case of flowers, we can say that we love them but do not use them. If we do say that we love gold, this refers to use and not to intrinsic value. Other rocks are as beautiful. But there is almost an *amor amicitiae* between man and the life world. The love of flowers does not pertain to any use of them but is simply more like delight in the presence of a friend. The value of gold is therefore a more purely artificial value—a subjectively constituted value. We could use cowrie shells or brass given different historical circumstances. The value of flowers or even of grass is less determined by such subjective value constitution. These have a power to evoke value judgments, a power which is different from that of the mineral world. And so does the ecological system which is the process of the life world. Hence ecology stresses the objectivity of value structure.

3. The Relationship of Whole and Part in the Ecological System

Considered from a purely ecological point of view, man is part of a whole. Levi-Strauss judges him this way, as does Buddhism. The whole has value, and man has value insofar as he shares a place within the whole. If, however, he disturbs the whole, he acts immorally, for he attacks a value which is greater than his own.

The problem of organic unity emerges here. The analogy by which the universe is compared to an organic unity is an old one which today is applied appropriately to the ecological balance. In the human body, for example, we have instances of two things, e.g. the heart and the lungs, which endure for some time, and which have a mutual causal dependence. The notion of mutual causal dependence is characteristic not only of the human body, but also of the ecological life system, and the planetary system. So if we say that the human body has a value greater than the sum of its parts, can we not extend the analogy as value criterion to the life world as it includes man, and to the planetary system? Hence a part such as man is capable of becoming a cancer in the life system as it grows out of proportion to the whole.

But several problems arise when the organic unity notion is used within a philosophy of value. First, there is a causal dependence of man on nature, and conversely *no* causal dependence of nature on man for its existence. The ecological system could easily omit man, since other animals could fulfill his ecological functions. And given his present threat to the balance, a value system centered on nature could even require the elimination of man, the ethical position here moving from a non-humanist to an anti-humanist one. A non-humanist and an anti-humanist ethic are different only circumstantially.

But unlike dependence for existence, there is a dependence of nature on man for value and meaning. Levi-Strauss in fact denies that value and meaning are ultimately important in the scheme of things. Our quoted text at the beginning states this quite clearly. But a philosophy of value disappears in a system which makes man's value inferior to the value of the universe as a whole. Or otherwise put, the affirmation of value, though dependent in a real way on value structures which are objective, is formally and fully found only in human consciousness. Thus value really disappears as we apply the organic unity principle to man's role in the universe. For no one holds any longer that man represents an eternal intelligence in an eternal world. The universe may be eternal, but man clearly is not. Hence Levi-Strauss concludes that intelligence, purposiveness, and meaning are not the measure of anything, and that there is no basis for affirming them as values.

But here Levi-Strauss runs into a paradox, a practical one if not a theoretical one. He assumes a meaning to value in order to deny it. There is a close parallel with the *Cogito*. It is impossible to deny meaning without admitting meaning. What we have here is the negative dogmatism of Buddhism. But it is still a dogmatism and hence a truth. Or it is a denial of value which is held itself as a value. And this is contradictory. Of course the Buddhist has no theoretical problem with contradiction. He uses it to destroy reason and value. But Levi-Strauss has spent his life writing very meaningful theories about social structures which are closely linked with a theory about the nature of man. We cannot have here a theory that there is no theory, nor a value position that there are no values.

Denial of values is simply impossible in the man who denies them. For negation of value implies consciousness of value, just as doubt affirms consciousness of truth. Nor will a Buddhist suppression of consciousness do at all, for such an ascesis is a choice which has sought a good, and thus a value, no matter how negative. There is no way of holding an ethics without holding to human valuation as centered in human consciousness. Thus ecological realities can force a revision of certain ethical theories. But if the ecological metaphor of man as part of a natural whole is held too rigidly, we lose any ethics at all.

4. THE RELATION OF ENDS AND MEANS IN ECOLOGICAL SYSTEMS

The paradox of treating man as part of a value system centered outside himself throws us back to some sort of humanism as the basis of the reality of values. Yet man need not be the totality of value. The discussion must be removed definitively from the dialectical opposition between man and nature.

Is the biosphere a means to the end—man? If so, humanism is achieved. But cannot the question be analyzed without entering into this metaphysical thicket? If the biosphere is judged simply from the point of view of human action, it is clearly not just a means to serve man's conscious purposes. It is an essential part of the human environment and is a value co-extensive with the value of the human body. To conceive of it otherwise is to conceive of the human body as an instrument serving the goals of mind. But the human world *as a whole* has value. And thus the biosphere as the nourisher of the specifically human has a *human* value. This is not to separate the two and say that the natural world has a value equal to that of man. It has a value which participates in human value. Of course, in the evolutionary process, had the biosphere emerged without producing man, we can, in imagining this situation from our present standpoint, see that it would have a different value from that of the inanimate world without consciousness of this value. But being objectively closer to man the biosphere is more valuable than other parts of nature.

Could we not say that we are equally dependent on the sun? This in instinctive value judgments would be expressed in sun worship, with reverence for the source of life that it is. The sun and the planetary system definitely do share in human value as sources of human life. But the sun and the planetary balance are not as yet objects of human action since we do not at present seem liable to threaten the planetary balance. Hence they need not perhaps for some time be the object of ethical concern.

What has been discussed up to this point might indicate that a self-interest ethics could best deal with the problems posed by ecology. Man should preserve the balance of nature in his own interest. However it is difficult to see how a self-interest ethics can be extended beyond the interests of a particular generation which is acting and planning. If the future of the race is to be included in our planning, we would seem to have gone beyond self-interest in its usual sense to a real altruism.

A strict self-interest ethics must consider freedom from disease, economic well-being, and the overcoming of death as goods which man seeks out of his desire to preserve himself. But within an ethics conscious of ecology, affirmation of such self-interest as an ultimate good reaches a limit. Self-interest as it becomes enlightened by ecology goes against the self, even the collective group now living, as the sole criterion determining ethical judgments. For ecological considerations force us to look at the good of the race in the future, and not simply the maximum happiness of the individuals living at present. Indeed some things which are in the *ultimate interest* of individuals living at present must be given up for the sake of the race in the future. We can perhaps control population expansion or even economic growth as these become threats to the total environment. But we still have the ultimate self-interest expressed in the attempt to overcome death with heart transplants, etc., and the proposals to freeze the dead to preserve them indefinitely until a way is found to preserve individual life indefinitely. The ultimate goal of a self-interest ethics would logically be the overcoming of death for the present generation. But this would mean the end of birth and new personalities. It is in the interest of the race that its individuals die according to a certain rhythm. But it is never in the interest of individuals to die. Yet human ecology as we know it requires novelty in the race, and this presents self-interest ethics with the paradox that death is an ecological necessity for men just as much as for the rest of nature. But to admit death as a necessity within human ecology and will it as such, leads to an altruism in which we give up our lives to make place for others who can create for the race what we could not.

The foregoing retains man as the only complete end in the value system. But it does not make him the total one. Totality of end is different from completion of end, since man exists in a totality (the environment, the ecological system) by his body. Man is an end coextensive with the life world and the planetary order. These find complete value in producing him, but serve as complementary value with him in the total picture, *and must be willed as ends along with man*. Perhaps we could say not only "Love thy neighbor as thyself" but also "Love the world which nourishes thee as thyself." Cases could conceivably arise in which a man or men could sacrifice a major interest of their own for preserving and developing nature for future men. Hence we can love nature for the sake of another man, just as we love nature for our own sake. This combines the two precepts.

5. TECHNOLOGICAL DEVELOPMENT AND MORAL RESPONSIBILITY

If the positions outlined here are correct, developed countries have an obligation to restore a disturbed balance of nature. If man must respect nature as he respects his own body, a new emphasis on cooperation with natural processes must replace disruptive exploitation.

But economic and technological development looked at on a world scale raises the different problem of distributive justice. Western philosophy has considered nature to be exploitable without limit, but the facts have reversed this assumption. The immense exploitation which has occurred has, however, benefited only a part of the human race. The third world wants nothing more than development. Will it risk the problems which the West and Japan have created in order to attain it? The African student merely shakes his head when the Westerner speaks of ecological unbalance. It is of course against distributive justice for the West to try to halt economic development when the exploitation of nature has benefited the West almost exclusively. The main responsibility of the developed countries is in reference to themselves. They must avoid contaminating the biosphere any longer. If this requires an absolute stop to growth of gross national products, then a new non-Keynesian economics will have to be worked out. But perhaps economic growth need not automatically include an attack on the balance of nature. As usually happens, particular ethical responsibilities can be better determined by economists, sociologists, and government planners. But the ethics of ecology joined to the ethics of distributive justice furnish the necessary guidelines for this planning. Any further destruction of the balance of nature is an attack on man and as such can be condemned on humanistic moral grounds.

Removing the Rubbish: Reflections on the Ecological Craze

JOHN PASSMORE

John Passmore (1914–   ), professor of philosophy at Australian National University, has written a well-known book, *A Hundred Years of Philosophy* (1957). He has taught extensively in the United States as well as in England, and this article exemplifies his very wide intellectual interests.

I would not want to claim that I can solve any of the world's ecological problems. It would be inconsistent with one of my central theses. For ecological problems, or so I believe, can be solved only by the joint efforts of scientists, technologists, economists, statesmen, administrators. And a philosopher is none of these, let alone all of them conjointly. Then what can one do? To compare small things with great, I should seek, like John Locke, "to be employed as an under-labourer in clearing ground a little and removing some of the rubbish that lies in the way to knowledge"—and, by way of knowledge, to effective action. Let me now look more consecutively at what one must try to clear away.

First, mystical "rubbish," the view that mysticism can save us, where technology cannot.

Science and technology, democracy and free enterprise have always had their enemies; mysticism, primitivism, authoritarianism have always had their adherents. The ecologically-based protest—not only against shortsightedness and greed but, more fundamentally, against those attitudes to nature and society which are used to justify shortsightedness and greed—is, I freely admit, fully justified in itself. But it is being deployed as a new and powerful weapon in the old battle between rationality and mysticism, as when Fraser Darling tries to persuade us that the West can solve its ecological problems only by adopting "the philosophy of wholeness," or "the truth of Zoroastrianism . . . that we are all of one stuff, difference is only in degree, and God can be conceived as being in all and of all, the sublime and divine immanence." (In the currently fashionable manner Darling turns to Zoroaster for what he could easily have found further West.) A moment later we find him urging us to "exercise the ideal of our aristocratic nature, to be the servant of the planet to which we

Source: John Passmore, *Man's Responsibility for Nature* (New York, 1974), pp. 11–24. Copyright © 1974 by John Passmore. Reprinted by permission of Charles Scribner's Sons and Gerald Duckworth & Co. Ltd.

were born and to which we are still bound."[1] His simultaneous appeal to immanence and aristocracy—his simultaneous assertion and denial, that is, of fundamental differences—is only too typical, in its intellectual incoherence, of the Western mystical tradition. And the ideal of the aristocrat who is also a servant—whether of God, of the people, or of the planet—is just as characteristic of authoritarianism.

The "philosophy of wholeness," as in classical German Idealism, serves to link the two. The "total whole" is at once a social and a metaphysical absolute, in which the individual is totally submerged. Fraser Darling is not introducing a new element into Western civilisation; rather, he is trying to make dominant one of the most dangerous illusions to which it has been subject, the mystical, totalistic illusion. Against this attempt, I feel one must particularly protest.

There are, of course, special reasons why ecology should so often have been thought of as being in essence mystical, as anti-scientific, or as entailing "a philosophy of wholeness." The general tendency of Western science has been analytic, atomistic. It has explained large-scale behaviour in terms of the behaviour of particles. So classical soil-science analyses a clod of earth into a collection of molecules held together by physical forces. This way of looking at such a clod is of great importance in explaining, let us say, the behaviour of an area of land under the impact of heavy rain or of deep ploughing. The ecologist thinks of the land not as a set of clods but rather as an ingredient in an energy system, a larger whole.

> Land [writes Aldo Leopold] is not merely soil; it is a fountain of energy flowing through a circuit of soils, plants, and animals. Food chains are the living channels which conduct energy upward; death and decay return it to the soil.[2]

Changes in the soil's fertility he explains by pointing to break-downs in such chains, such cycles. Similarly, whereas the atomistic biologist studies an organism as a system of cells—and, beyond that, of molecules—the ecologist looks at its place in a broader system, its habitat, and at the relationship between that organism-in-its-habitat and still wider systems.

That does not mean, however, that the ecologist can eschew laboratory studies. If he hopes to understand, let us say, the way in which mercuric salts are built up in the human organism, he needs to investigate *both* the nature of the food chain which enables mercuric salts deposited in an estuary to find their way into the brains of human beings *and* what happens in the tissues of each of the members of that food chain. Nor does the mere fact that the ecologist makes use of such concepts as energy cycles or food chains in any way suggest that ecology is supra-scientific.

This is a crucial point. Science is not *intrinsically* atomistic. It explains the

---

[1] F. Fraser Darling, "Man's responsibility for the environment," in F. J. Ebling (ed.), *Biology and Ethics,* Symposium of the Institute of Biology, no. 18 (London, 1969), p. 119. On this general theme, see also George Seddon, "The rhetoric and ethics of the environmental protest movement," *Meanjin,* 31, 4 (December 1972), pp. 427–437.

[2] Aldo Leopold, *A Sand County Almanac,* p. 253.

behaviour of the tides, for example, by referring them to forces operating in the solar system. Sometimes, in order to explain a thing's behaviour, one needs only to look at the forms of activity which go on within it—or, as it would more commonly be put, at the particles which make it up. Sometimes one needs to look, rather, at the wider forms of activity within which its own forms of activity go on. But, more often than not, one needs to look at both—explaining a person's behaviour, for example, partly in terms of his "genetic constitution," the forms of activity he has inherited, partly in terms of the culture within which he was educated. He stammers, let us say, because he was born left-handed into a culture which demands right-handedness from its members.

No doubt, the ecologist's talk of chains and cycles may ring ancient bells by associative resonance. We think, perhaps, of the classical "great chain of being" or of those cycles beloved by mystics—"a perpetual circle for the Good, from the Good, in the Good, and to the Good."[3] But such associations are not justified by the actual procedures of ecologists. The "wholes" in which ecology is interested are not mystical unities—my back garden could constitute an ecosystem —nor are they (although Fraser Darling suggests otherwise) the kind of metaphysical whole within which all differences are converted into differences in degree. Indeed, although ecology can be studied at a high level of abstraction in terms of energy transfers, one of its main contributions to human understanding lies in its emphasis on the importance of individual differences, the far-reaching consequences which can result from what at first sight appears to be a very slight change in the membership of a system. Only in so far as it has wrongly been supposed that science must be atomistic does the Western scientific tradition have any quarrel with the rise of ecology.

This is not the sort of quarrel which can be resolved only by abandoning science in favour of mysticism.

Sacred Nature?

Nor, to solve our ecological problems, are we forced once more to think of nature as sacred. That doctrine, too, "lies in the way to knowledge." So to revert, I suggest, is to go back on the whole tradition of Western science, perhaps the greatest of man's achievements. For to regard nature as sacred is to think of it in the manner the Jews and the Greeks deliberately rejected, as having a "mysterious life" which it is improper, sacrilegious, to try to understand or control, a life we should submit to and worship.[4] Science, in contrast, converts mysteries into problems, to which it can hope to find solutions.

Such a reversion, furthermore, is neither necessary nor sufficient to save the biosphere. It is certainly not sufficient. Societies for whom nature is sacred

---

[3] C. E. Rolt (ed.), *Dionysius the Areopagite on the Divine Names and the Mystical Theology* (London, 1920), p. 107. Compare the diagram from the 14th century mystic Henry Suso in A. Nygren, *Agape and Eros* (tr. Watson, 1953), facing p. 616, with the diagram in 'Ecology: the new great chain of being," *Natural History*, 77, 10 (December 1968), p. 9.

[4] On this theme, see Henri Frankfort, *Kingship and the Gods*, pp. 342, 344.

have nonetheless destroyed their natural habitation. A passage from Plato's *Critias* will illustrate this point. He is describing Attica:

There are remaining only the bones of the wasted body, as they may be called . . . all the richer and softer parts of the soil having fallen away, and the mere skeleton of the land being left. But in the primitive state of the country, its mountains were high hills covered with soil, and the plains . . . were full of rich earth, and there was abundance of wood in the mountains.[5]

This decline, Plato tells us, is testified to by the fact that "sacred memorials" remain at points, by his time dry, where once flowed rivers and streams. Man does not necessarily preserve, that is, the stream he has dedicated to a god. Simple ignorance or greed can be as damaging as technological know-how. Nowhere, as we can see, is ecological destruction more apparent than in today's Japan, for all its tradition of nature-worship.

Indeed, to carry this argument further, the belief that nature is sacred can tell against attempts to preserve it. Just in virtue of its divinity, it may be argued, nature can be trusted to look after itself. Consider the case of Emerson. "In the woods," he tells us, "we return to reason and faith."

"There [he continues] I feel that nothing can befall me in life,—no disgrace, no calamity . . . which nature cannot repair; . . . the currents of the Universal Being circulate through me; I am part or parcel of God."[6]

Yet Emerson was indulgent towards the plunderers of the American countryside then making their way to the American West. "The recuperative powers of Nature" were, in his eyes, a sufficient guarantee that the self-reliance he admired would not issue in final devastation.[7] A nature which can heal men can surely heal itself, a nature that is divine men cannot destroy. To take our ecological crises seriously is to recognise, first, man's utter dependence on nature, but secondly, nature's vulnerability to human depredations: the *fragility,* that is, of both man and nature, for all their notable powers of recuperation. And this means that neither man nor nature is sacred or quasi-divine.[8]

There is more than a little paradox in the view, when it comes from ecologically-minded preservationists, that we need to revert to older, mystical attitudes to nature. For ecology, however much some of those who praise ecology would like to persuade us otherwise, is a serious scientific attempt, dependent on the aid of such technological innovations as the computer, to understand

---

[5] Plato's *Critias* (tr. B. Jowett, 1892), 111*b, c.*

[6] R. W. Emerson, *Nature: Addresses and Lectures* (Boston, 1876), p. 10.

[7] Compare S. L. Udall, *The Quiet Crisis* (1963), pp. 48–55.

[8] It may be true that in hunting societies—the example most often cited—the belief that nature is sacred and animals are capable of understanding served in some measure as a protection against the destruction of species. (Although man the hunter, it would now seem, was largely responsible for the disappearance of a great many of the large animals—the giant kangaroo in Australia, the moa in New Zealand, the woolly mammoth in North America.) But as matters stand, such beliefs are not merely so out of harmony with our traditions that to attempt to revive them would be to attempt the impossible. They simply would not serve.

what scientists still find mysterious—the ways in which populations respond to environmental fluctuations. This manner of looking at ecology is unpopular with those, like Theodore Roszak, who hoped that ecology would replace scientific analysis by

> a new science in which the object of knowledge will be rather like the poet's beloved: something to be contemplated but not analysed, something that is permitted to retain its mysteries.[9]

But if Roszak and his counter-cultural followers are disappointed to discover that ecology is after all another branch of science, that it *dispels* mysteries, many of us see in that fact, rather, a demonstration that Western science is still fecund, still capable of contributing to the solution of the problems which beset human beings, even when they are problems of the scientist's own making.

That science is still so fecund is just as well, seeing that ignorance is one of the most potent obstacles to our solving our ecological problems, an ignorance which only science can dispel. No doubt, the modern West has more knowledge at its disposal than has had any previous society. But it has neither the kind nor the degree of knowledge which it now needs. Our knowledge of the ways in which societies work is not at all comparable in extent with our knowledge of the workings, let us say, of the planetary system. We know little about the atmosphere, the seas, the life cycles of the scarcely numerable varieties of plant and animal life. While absolutely speaking we know a great deal, we are proportionally ignorant, proportionally in relation to what we need to know. The farmer tilling his fields by conventional methods and living in a traditional society did not need to know a great deal. But the task we have now to undertake, in attempting to estimate the long-term effects of our actions both on the biosphere and on human societies, is so immense that in relation to it our ignorance is almost total.

To correct this situation may well require, I am fully prepared to admit, a minor revolution within science. The scientist will be forced, in the unenthusiastic words of one of my scientific colleagues, "to slosh about in that primordial ooze known as inter-disciplinary studies." He will need to pay more respect to such scientists as work outside laboratories. There is a pecking-order in science; almost everybody pecks the "natural historian." The field naturalist is unlikely to find himself awarded a Nobel Prize or even a Fellowship of the Royal Society. But there are already signs that such a revolution is under way, if still very tentatively.[10] Field studies are beginning to regain something of their previous

---

[9] Theodore Roszak, "Ecology and mysticism," *Humanist* 86: 5 (May 1971), p. 136. See also Norman Brown, *Life Against Death* (1959), pt. 5, ch. 15, p. 236, and my summary in *The Perfectibility of Man,* pp. 306. See also Passmore, "The revolt against science," *Search* 3, 11–12 (November–December 1972), pp. 415–22.

[10] One of the most significant examples that has come my way is A. B. Pippard's Inaugural Lecture as Cavendish Professor of Physics in the University of Cambridge. It is time, he there suggests, for scientists to turn their attention "towards the difficult and less elegant phenomena of the real physical world" in contrast with their past concentration on simpler and more elegant natural laws. Coming from a Cavendish Professor, that is really something. See A. B. Pippard, *Reconciling Physics with Reality* (Cambridge, 1972).

status—Darwin did not, after all, work in a laboratory—and more and more distinguished scientists are at least dipping their fingers into the "primordial ooze." To say that science has need of new directions, however, is one thing; to say that the West ought to abandon its hard-won tradition of critical investigation is quite another. That tradition it needs more than ever before.

Man the Master?

What about the view, so often associated with science and technology, that man is master of the world? Must not that at least, if not science itself, be abandoned?

. . .

An intermediate interpretation, however, can be framed thus: men, uniquely, are capable of transforming the world into a civilised state; that is their major responsibility to their fellow-men.

The virtues of civilisation, no doubt, are now sometimes questioned. Once more the "noble savage" hunts his ecological way through intellectual drawing-rooms. Hsün Tzu's advice to his Chinese contemporaries:

> You glorify nature and meditate on her:
> Why not domesticate her and regulate her?
> You depend on things and marvel at them:
> Why not unfold your own ability and transform them?

finds itself reversed, as advice to the West:

> You have domesticated nature and regulated her:
> Why not glorify her and meditate on her?
> You have unfolded your own ability and transformed things:
> Why not depend on them and marvel at them?

This would, indeed, be the "great refusal," the rejection of all that man has discovered he can achieve. No doubt the West needs more fully to realise that it "depends on things" and so far to "meditate on" and even to "glorify" nature. But it cannot now turn back, so my argument runs, even if it were desirable that it should do so. Only by transforming nature can it continue to survive. There is no good ground, either, for objecting to transformation as such; it can make the world more fruitful, more diversified, and more beautiful.

Living Dangerously

If we ask, indeed, what human beings add to the world by their presence in it, there is, I should say, only one possible reply: civilisation. Were it not for his ability to civilise, man would be no more than a predator among the rest, more powerful, more aggressive, more violent, more skilful in capturing his prey but in no other respects superior, and in many respects inferior, to the prey he hunts. And man's great memorials—his science, his philosophy, his technology, his architecture, his countryside—are all of them founded upon his attempt to understand and subdue nature. Through their struggles with nature men have discovered their potentialities and developed those forms of enterprise which constitute their civilisation.

I have included the countryside in the list of man's memorials, because even the landscapes we now so greatly admire—the landscapes of Tuscany or of England or of Kyushu—are largely the creation of human enterprise, of human struggles. When Cowper wrote "God made the country; man made the town," he was simply mistaken. The 18th-century English countryside Cowper knew and loved was largely of human creation. (What god, for that matter, would not be proud of having created 18th-century Bath?) That is what, however obscurely, Hegel and his followers saw, and passed on to the Marxists. It is not merely out of arrogance that men think of themselves as having a "duty to subdue nature"; it is only they who can create. So far, and only so far, they can rightfully claim "dominion over nature."

Nor, however implausible the doctrine that nature exists only to serve man, is there any objection to the weaker view (to which Descartes subscribes) that whatever exists in nature is of some use to us. This is not, as it might at first seem to be, an empirical hypothesis, for there is no way of falsifying it. It always remains possible that something will turn out to be useful which we have cast aside as useless. But it can act as a guiding principle, encouraging men to look for uses in unexpected places, discouraging the destruction of what might eventually turn out to be of vital importance to them. In that form, it should certainly not be cast aside as "rubbish."

The danger in destroying is, of course, a point on which the eçological critics have particularly insisted. And quite clearly one has to concede, as Ehrlich puts it, that "any tinkering with an ecosystem may result in unforeseen and deleterious consequences."[11]

But man has had no option but to live dangerously. If he had let himself be too alarmed by the fact that, in a certain sense, he does not know what he is doing, he would never have ventured beyond his immediate environment. Nor would be, certainly, ever have embarked on the domestication of animals, let alone agriculture or industry. Indeed, if we follow to its logical conclusion Ehrlich's description of man as a dangerous tinkerer, we can scarcely stop short of that picture of man's relationships with nature at the very end of the 19th century by W. S. Blunt, the ecologist's poet-laureate.[12] Here is "unspoiled Nature" as Blunt sees it:

> Thou dost remember, Lord, the glorious World it was,
> The beauty, the abundance, the unbroken face
> Of undulant forest spread without or rent or seam,
> Thy lakes, Thy floods, Thy marshes, tameless, unbetrayed,
>
> All virgin of the spoiler, all inviolate,
> In beauty undeflowered, where fear was not nor hate.

[11] P. R. and A. H. Ehrlich, *Population Resources Environment*, p. 182.

[12] This poem, Blunt tell us, was "written to some extent in collaboration with the late Herbert Spencer." It sounds like it.

And here is man, that "lewd bare-buttocked ape":

> Man the senseless knave
> Who struck fire from his flint to burn Thy gorses brave,
> Thy heaths for his lean kine, who, being the one unclean,
> Defiled Thy flower-sweet Earth with ordure heaps obscene,
> To plant his rice, his rye.[13]

But the virtues of civilisation, many of us would wish to argue, are not to be so lightly set aside. It is one thing to recognise that human action has unintended consequences; quite another to suggest that man is nothing but the defiler of nature. Lewd he often is, no doubt, but the bareness of his buttocks is not the only thing which distinguishes him from the ape. If the "glorious world" of Blunt's imagination was a world without hate—although scarcely, as he suggests, without fear—it was also a world without love, without art, without science, without philosophy, with no Venice, no Nara, no Salzburg.[14] These are as much consequences of his "tinkering" as are "ordure heaps obscene." That we ought to attempt to try to preserve the spirit that creates them, I shall not even bother to argue.

Liberal Cant?

It is a much more particular assumption, however, that the democratic institutions, the spirit of enterprise, the liberal attitude characteristic of the modern West are worth preserving and maintaining. That requires separate argument.

No one with any knowledge of history could have any illusions about Western civilisation, modern or ancient, with its record of violence, cruelty, fanaticism, puritanism and avarice. What is particularly tragic is the way in which the best and the worst have so often gone together as the history of Florence from the 13th to the 15th century vividly exemplifies. Everything was there, genius in literature, painting, sculpture, science; cruelty and violence of the lowest, least forgivable, kind; even the egalitarian terrorism of Giano della

[13] Wilfred Scawen Blunt, "Satan Absolved: a Victorian mystery" (1899), in *The Poetical Works of W. S. Blunt* (1914), vol. 2, pp. 266, 275.

[14] Ian McHarg, in a much-reprinted paper rhetorically entitled "Is man a planetary disease?", is prepared to lay it down that "Algae know about creativity but man does not." There is no depth of masochistic nonsense to which in their moods of self-denigration men will not descend.

In Roeg's 1970 film *Walk-about* not man in general but only civilised man is diagnosed as a disease. The gentle self-reliant aborigine is contrasted with civilised men and women who are cruel, cold, mean-spirited, sexually repressed, devoted only to their possessions, utterly ruthless. Western art is depicted as childish play, its science as trivialities in a desert, its literature as a rambling story at once pointless and cruel, its education system as a training in futile snobberies, its industry as rusted debris, its technology as an instrument of slaughter, its mathematics as empty formulae.

If this indictment—or the picture of civilisation in Godard's *Weekend*—is at all points justified then, certainly, I should have no policy to advocate except mass suicide. The alternative—the hunting savage—arouses in my heart no enthusiasm whatsoever.

Bella. But it remains true, I believe, that outside Western civilisation men have nowhere so often risen to such great heights. This by no means implies, I should freely grant, that cultures which are not Western in type are valueless. No one who has even the slightest acquaintance with their cultural achievements or their social structures could possibly take that view. In its dealings with other cultures, the West has often shown itself at its arrogant, bigoted, greedy worst. But neither the simple sensualities of Tahiti nor the complex ritual of ancient Japan enabled the human spirit to expand to its fullest extent. A craftsman, a certain type of artist, might have found in such a society all that he needed; but a philosopher, a scientist, a dramatist, would not. The West has not conquered the world solely by the force of its arms or the flashier attractions of its consumer goods. Even a country like Japan has found the richness and diversity of Western culture profoundly stimulating, for all the importance of its own achievements.

One of the more fashionable forms of contemporary cant condemns as "racialist"—now an all-encompassing form of abuse—the description of any form of society as "higher" or "more advanced" or "better" than any other.

No doubt, as I grant, a less "advanced" society can possess virtues which a more "advanced" society lacks. The fact remains that there are familiar and quite proper ways of grading societies: in terms of the diversity of their culture, their humanitarianism, the degree of liberty they offer their citizens. By any of these criteria the liberal democratic West stands high. (Nor will it do to reply that this is not surprising, since the West invented these criteria. What other criteria are we offered?) Its range of cultural achievements in science, in philosophy, in art, is unequalled; few of its citizens starve in the streets or live by exhibiting their deformities; never before has personal liberty been so widely diffused.

If we judge modern Western democracies imperfect this is only by applying to them those absolute standards which the West has taught us. We take it for granted that they contain no Untouchables, no Etas. We condemn them, quite rightly, because they still discriminate against certain of their members, still confine personal liberty by absurd and pointless laws, still do not adequately educate their citizens, still do not do all that they might to help those—inside or outside their territories—whose life is nasty, brutish and short. If the liberal democracies collapse, this will be because they have aroused in their citizens aspirations which no society will ever completely satisfy, not because those aspirations are worthless.[15] To *seek* their destruction, with whatever noble

[15] It is very misleading, of course, to speak of the "West" in a monolithic way. I have often been told, if I wrote in modified praise of Western civilisation, that I had forgotten Newark and New York. The tragedy of New York no one could forget; that city and its inhabitants should be preserved for eternity in plasticised aspic as a memorial to the grandeur and the misery of the human condition. Newark, I confess, but seldom crosses my mind, less often than, let us say, Aarhus. Why should it? But Newark is no more typical of the West than is Calcutta of India or Osaka of Japan. I see no reason for believing, either, that it shows the West, as in a science-fiction mirror, what it is certain to become. Indeed, it is reminiscent of the 18th century rather than prophetic of the twenty-first. In many fundamental respects, America is a very old-fashioned country.

aims in mind, is to attempt to destroy the only sort of society which has ever come near to fulfilling those aspirations.

The view that ecological problems are more likely to be solved in an authoritarian than in any such liberal democratic society rests on the implausible assumption that the authoritarian state would be ruled by ecologist-kings. In practice, there is more hope of action in democratic societies. In the United States, particularly, the habit of local action, the capacity of individuals to initiate legal proceedings, the tradition of public disclosure are powerful weapons in the fight against ecological destruction. The democratic states should rather be condemned, I suggest, when they are tempted into exactly the same vices as the totalitarian states: spying, soothing utterances from central authorities, face-saving, bureaucratic inertia, censorship, concealment.[16]

Who Knows Best?

What about the metaphysical outlook characteristic of the West? That is exceptionally complex and diversified, by no means to be summed up as the view that nature is wax in man's hands.

Nor is the West, I should add, irrevocably commited to that Aristotelian-type metaphysics for which nature consists of substances with distinct properties, each of which can be separately modified without altering anything else. One of the most important alternative suggestions, dating back in essence to Heraclitus, is that the world consists of complex systems of interacting processes varying in their stability. Each such system—of which a human being is one—can survive, like a flame, only so long as it can interact with surrounding systems in certain particular ways, drawing upon and giving out to the systems around it. It can die by choking on its own wastes or because it has exhausted its resources. That way of looking at the world, which ecological investigations help to substantiate, makes it perfectly plain why "You can't do one thing at a time." It destroys, too, the belief that human beings are somehow different, outside the ecosystem, whether as villainous intruders or heroic manipulators. But it does so in a manner not in the least mystical, not in the least anti-scientific in spirit, not in the least implying that there is something intrinsically wrong with any attempt to make the world a better place.

.   .   .

Two traditional attitudes are, I suggest, promising—the first, that man should think of himself as a steward; the second, that in his attempts to transform nature he should cooperate with it. The "stewardship" attitude is often said to be peculiarly Christian; this I would deny. It is linked rather with the idea that man forms part of a chain of improvement, that he has responsibilities to those who come after him, responsibilities arising out of his attempt to preserve

[16] In so far as the ecological movement necessarily involves a critique of the creeping bureaucratisation so characteristic of our society, it has a social and political importance extending well beyond its immediate ecological ends. In so far as its practical policies would tend to encourage that bureaucratisation, it represents a social danger. For not only are man and nature fragile, so too is liberal civilisation, as the tragic history of inter-War Germany so vividly reminds us.

and develop what he loves. In its fullest implications this is a peculiarly Western and modern concept, dating back to Kant. Its ecological importance is manifest.

As for the view that man should cooperate with nature, this cannot, of course, be taken literally. Nature is not a semi-divine entity with aims which human beings can share. Against any such interpretation, Robert Boyle rightly protested. Interpreted less literally, however, it suggests a policy of ecological wisdom: to try to control pests by diversifying crops rather than by insecticides, to construct tourist hotels so that they make use of, rather than cut across, existing drainage contours, to grow what can be grown with least damage to the countryside. And so on, modestly but effectively. Read thus, it is by no means rubbish.

To accept it does not commit us, however, to Barry Commoner's "third law of ecology"—"nature knows best."[17]

It is true enough—as, like Ehrlich, Commoner argues—that every human intervention in an ecosystem is likely to disturb the workings of that system in a way that is detrimental to some member of it. So much is true of every change, man-induced or nature-induced. But it by no means follows, as his "law" might seem to suggest, that every such change, or even most such changes, will be detrimental to *human beings*. Unlike the watches to which he compares them, ecological systems were not designed for man's use. When men picked seeds off plants and sowed them on cleared ground, they acted in a way that was detrimental to the organic life which was accustomed to feed on the fallen seeds. But only the most unreconstructed primitivist would suggest that the actions of our agricultural forefathers were destructive of human interests. A nature left entirely alone as "knowing best" would support only the dreariest and most monotonous of lives. Even the primitive hunter found it necessary to burn; the fires he lit have transformed the face of the earth.[18]

It is, indeed, absurd to suggest that man can find in nature, at hand for his taking, all that he needs to live a good life. So much, in principle, the authors of Genesis saw: nature has its "thorns and thistles" which man has no option but to root out.

In his essay on "Nature," J. S. Mill mounts a general attack on the injunction that men ought to "cooperate with nature."

Her powers [as Mill puts it] are often towards man in the position of enemies, from whom he must wrest, by force and ingenuity, what little he can for his own use.[19]

One may well warm to the enthusiasm with which Mill attacks the more sentimental nature-lovers. Anyone who lives on the inhospitable shores of Australia will certainly appreciate his feelings. To think of nature as an

[17] Barry Commoner, *The Closing Circle* (1972) p. 41.

[18] O. C. Stewart: "Fire as the first great force employed by man," in W. L. Thomas, Jr. (ed.), *Man's Role in Changing the Face of the Earth* (1956), pp. 115–133.

[19] J. S. Mill, *Three Essays on Religion*, p. 15.

"enemy," however, is not the alternative to thinking of it as a "friend." Natural processes, and this must be constantly emphasised, go on in their own way indifferent to human interests. But we shall do best to learn how they operate, not supposing that they will immediately respond to our whims or miraculously suspend their modes of operation so as to permit us harmlessly to convert rain-forests into agricultural lands or rivers into sewers.

A New Morality?

What of the view that the West now needs not only a new concept of nature but a new set of moral principles to act as a guide in its relationships with nature? That, I think, is not entirely wrong-headed. During most of the West's history, its moral philosophers, Stoic or Christian, denied that man's relationship with nature is governed by any moral considerations whatsoever. From Montaigne onwards, however, to say nothing of his neo-Platonic predecessors, sceptics and humanists took a different view. And by the end of the 18th century even Christians began to argue, although often against fierce opposition from their co-religionists, that callousness towards animal suffering was morally wrong.

. . .

The traditional moral teaching of the West, Christian or utilitarian, has always taught men, however, that they ought not so to act as to injure their neighbours. And we have now discovered that the disposal of wastes into sea or air, the destruction of ecosystems, the procreation of large families, the depletion of resources constitute injury to our fellow-men, present and future. To that extent, conventional morality, without any supplementation whatsoever, suffices to justify our ecological concern, our demand for action against the polluter, the depleter of natural resources, the destroyer of species and wildernesses.

One of my colleagues, an ardent preservationist, condemns me as a "human chauvinist." What he means is that in my ethical arguments, I treat human interests as paramount. I do not apologise for that. An "ethic dealing with man's relation to land and to the plants and animals growing on it" would not only be about the behaviour of human beings, as is sufficiently obvious, but would have to be justified by reference to human interests. The land which a bad farmer allows to slip into a river did not have a "right" to stay where it was. The supposition that anything but a human being has "rights" is, or so I have suggested, quite untenable.

This insistence on the primacy of human interest does not imply, however, that the only question at issue is whether someone's *income* will decline as a result of the silting of the river. The silting of a sparkling river, the replacement of a forested slope by an eroded hillside, is a loss to mankind even if it does not lessen anyone's income. To cause it to happen constitutes an act of vandalism, the destruction of something worth enjoying for its own sake. Only in so far as Western moralists have suggested otherwise, have suggested that no form of human activity has any value unless it involves a direct relationship with God or (for moralists of a more secular cast of mind) a relationship to a narrowly conceived economic prosperity, can the West plausibly be said to need a "new ethic." What it needs, for the most part, is not so much a "new ethic" as a more general adherence to a perfectly familiar ethic.

. . .

The End of Growth?

The traditions I have so far explored, whether with sympathy or antipathy, have a long history. I have said almost nothing so far about a factor which many would regard as far more ecologically significant than metaphysical principles and moral ideas—industrial growth. I cannot conclude without considering, however inadequately, the problems it raises.

Industrial growth is a new phenomenon and the attitudes of mind it has generated, however powerfully, are still so new that it is somewhat odd to call them traditions. It is only very recently that nations have boasted of their Gross National Product, that a society has condemned itself, or been condemned, because its *per capita* growth rate is low, that consumers have come to expect an endless flow of new types of product, that industry has been geared to meet the needs of an affluent society. Here, many would say, lies the real crux of our problem. The changes of heart to which I have drawn attention—the intimations of a new, more considerate attitude to nature—are, on this view, of no fundamental importance. It is the crudest sort of sentimentalism—rubbish, my critics would say—to see in the spectacle of Boy Scouts collecting bottles or "conservation" groups preventing the construction of this or that freeway anything more than a middle-class game. At best the participants in such enterprises are like children constructing a sand barrier to protect their castle from the tide-turned sea. At most they distract attention from the fundamental issues. For what is at fault, so it is said, is the total system, the scientific-technological-industrial complex on which the middle-class reformers depend for their livelihood and its social position.

This is one of the points where I find myself least certain of my ground. The issues involved are so large, so complex, so difficult that I can do little more than raise them. To what degree is the further emancipation of the human spirit, in the East as well as in the West, inevitably tied up with the advance of industry? Can resources safely be diverted from industrial development to less-despoiling tertiary activities? Can industries be cabined and confined without undermining the spirit of enterprise which has brought them to birth? On the face of it, one can no doubt reply that the historical connections between industry and freedom are not inevitable. There can be heavy industry, as in Russia, where there is little or no freedom. Neither Greek democracy nor the Enlightenment came into being within a highly industralised society. There are good reasons for believing, furthermore, that the emergence of large industrial complexes represents a threat to (rather than a necessary condition of) the further emancipation of mankind. Yet one is still left uneasy about our capacity, without destroying liberty, effectively to redeploy our forces.

Not uncommonly, we are told that what has to be abandoned is the ideal, much loved by politicians, of economic growth. This concept, however, is far from being a perspicuous one, and its ambiguities are of first importance. If economic growth is defined as the more effective utilisation of scarce resources, better economising, then what is commonly described as economic growth may in fact be economic recession.

Let us take a simple case. A park is built over to provide new office space. The park had made available such scarce commodities in an urban context as space, light, quiet, air, the sight and smell of flowers and trees and shrubs. Should not the construction of such buildings count as economic recession and the reverse process, the destruction of buildings to construct parks, as economic growth?

. . .

This is a point in respect to which some conservationists are remarkably insouciant.

> By the use of such specious arguments as the loss of jobs, the lowering of living standards, and the raising of prices [one of them has written of the anti-ecologists], they are endeavouring to turn the citizen away from those who are striving to save a viable environment for future generations.[20]

But the spectacle of an unemployed man or an old-age pensioner, faced by rising prices, is at least as pitiable as the spectacle of an oil-soaked mutton bird. Arguments which direct attention to economic costs are not necessarily "specious."

On the other side, the question now is whether the liberal-democratic West can afford *not* to cut down its industrial activity or, at the very least, to alter its direction. We can perhaps speak of an "ecological transition," a point at which a country's industrial activity reduces rather than enhances the quality of life of its citizens, at which increased industrial activity, at least in its conventional forms, is profitable only when its costs are estimated by grossly inadequate methods of accounting, accounting which entirely ignores the public squalor it creates.

. . .

One difficulty is to avoid the costs of industrial slow-downs, or re-deployment, from falling very unevenly. It is not the reformers who would lose their jobs if, to take a very minor proposal, regulations were introduced which made it illegal for automobile companies to change their models except in so far as by so doing they saved resources or diminished pollution. No doubt, every citizen might have to meet increased taxation. But that is nothing compared with seeing one's entire mode of life vanish overnight. It is cruel foolishness to suggest that people would be perfectly content to turn their lathes into pitchforks.

Ecological Innocence?

So far we have looked at changes in the rate of industrial growth only from the point of view of developed countries. But it could also greatly affect the

[20] Denis Puleston, "Protecting the environment," *New Scientist* (28 September 1972), p. 558.

developing countries, whose conviction that they would bear the brunt of any attempt on the part of Western nations to solve the world's ecological problems is clearly reflected in a number of the consensus resolutions put forward by the 1972 Stockholm Conference.

Consider, for example, the eleventh "principle":

> The environmental policies of all States *should enhance and not adversely affect the present or future development potential of developing countries.*

Or even more strikingly, the twenty-third principle, not in the original proposals but introduced in the course of discussion:

> Without prejudice to such criteria as may be agreed upon by the international community . . . it will be essential in all cases to consider the system of values prevailing in each country, and the extent of the applicability of standards which are valid for the most advanced countries but which may be *inappropriate and of unwarranted social cost for the developing countries.*

In other words, do not expect the developing countries to proceed as if *they* had reached the point of "ecological transition"!

. . .

They fear, too, that if they attempt to limit industrial growth, the industrial countries will reduce their imports from the developing countries. If in he course of writing this, I have ever felt cheerfulness breaking in, a moment's reflection on the plight of the developing countries has been sufficient to dispel it.

. . .

To sum up: I find it impossible to sum up, to arrive at any neat, tidy, quotable conclusions. As I have written, I have become more and more conscious of the complexity of every problem I have touched upon. I have tried to clear some intellectual ground, so that the alternatives before us are a little less obscured by undergrowth, but the problems remain. Yet nothing could be worse than to allow ourselves to slip into the doomsday mood of paranoic melancholia. The elderly, especially, are only too liable to this mood, whether taking pleasure in the reflection that by dying they will miss nothing but calamities or seeking an illusory grandeur as prophets of death and destruction. But in the young, too, apocalyptic prophecy can serve as a substitute for the overwhelming responsibility of action.

There is certainly a risk that we shall be utterly discouraged by the implications of Barry Commoner's "first ecological law"—"everything is connected to everything else"—for this makes it appear that to act at all is the height of imprudence. But fortunately I do not, before I swat a mosquito, have to calculate the consequences of my act on the sun's output of cosmic rays or the eutrophication of Lake Erie. It is just not true that everything I do has effects on *everything* else. What we do need always to remember, however—and this is sufficiently alarming—is that the unintended consequences of our actions are often surprisingly remote in time and place from those actions. (Skin cancer forty years after exposure to the sun; the excess fertiliser from my garden feeding algae in a remote stream.) Commoner's "law" somewhat resembles the old Heraclitean dictum "expect the unexpected." Valuable as a warning, it is useless as a guide to action.

Natural World, or Social Traditions?

What in general I want to emphasise is that, if the world's ecological problems are to be solved at all, it can only be by that old-fashioned procedure, thoughtful action. We may, of course, think to no purpose; by acting thoughtfully we may make matters worse. As we know quite well in our personal lives, we are sometimes saved by rashness, destroyed by prudence. Looking before we leap may make cowards of us. But there is no alternative policy. Mystical contemplation will not clean our streams or feed our peoples. No invisible guiding hand, whether Providence or History, guarantees our salvation. In the biosphere man has no tenure; his own folly may, at any time, lose him his precarious occupancy.

Spying, Liberalism, and Privacy

A. K. BIERMAN

A. K. Bierman (1923–   ) is professor of philosophy at San Francisco State University. He has worked with unions, civil liberties groups, and community arts projects.

> Necessity is the plea of every infringement of human freedom. It is the argument of tyrants; it is the creed of slaves.
> —William Pitt (as quoted by George Meany)

Tom Charles Huston, the author of the "Huston Plan" for increased intelligence gathering, a plan developed jointly by the FBI, CIA, DIA, NSA, and each of the military services, wrote in his memorandum to H. R. Haldeman a passage that would not have surprised William Pitt: "The first 23 pages of the report constitute an assessment of the existing internal security threat, our current intelligence coverage of this threat, and areas where our coverage is inadequate" (*New York Times,* June 7, 1973).

The Huston Plan was adopted by President Nixon in July of 1970, and supposedly rescinded five days after its adoption. Haldeman directed Huston to request that the various intelligence agencies involved in the Plan return their copies of President Nixon's "Decision Memorandum." It is difficult to determine if this "request" was construed as rescission. The "surreptitious entries" of Daniel Ellsberg's psychiatrist's office (1971) and the Watergate Democratic headquarters (1972) are among the kinds of acts the Plan recommended.

The Huston Plan provided for: A. Monitoring U.S. citizens' communications sent via international facilities; this was to be done by the NSA (National

Source: Journal of Social Philosophy, vol. 5, no. 2 (April 1974), pp. 15–21.

Security Agency); B. Electronic surveillance and penetrations of persons and groups who "pose a major threat to the internal security," which includes the Communist Party, diplomatic establishments, organized crime, and New Left groups; C. Removal of legal restraints on mail inspection and relaxation of restraints on covert coverage of the mails; D. Modify present restrictions on surreptitious entry ("Use of this technique is clearly illegal: it amounts to burglary." It "would be particularly helpful if used against the Weathermen and Black Panthers."); E. Develop campus information sources because "the campus is the battleground of the revolutionary protest movement;" ". . . where exposure occurs the adverse publicity is moderate and short-lived. It is a price we must be willing to pay for effective coverage of the campus scene;" F. Retain the restrictions on the use of military undercover agents.

The flavor of Huston's Plan is reflected in his "Rationale" 's, for example, "There is no valid argument against use of legal mail covers except Mr. Hoover's concern that the civil liberties people may become upset. This risk is surely an acceptable one and hardly serious enough to justify denying ourselves a valuable and legal intelligence tool."

In another "Rationale," he points out that surreptitious entry is better than using expensive machine time to break codes. "One successful surreptitious entry can do the job successfully at no dollar cost."

Not only "civil liberties people," but liberals as well "may become upset" by the Huston Plan's recommendations, which I will refer to hereinafter as spying. This includes not only a conservative liberal such as Milton Friedman, who, in his *Capitalism and Freedom*, argues that the ultimate value for the classical liberal is individual freedom, but also a 'critical' liberal such as Michael Weinstein (this *Journal*, April, 1972), who defines liberalism "as that political philosophy which holds that the public situation should be continually transformed in the direction of enhancing human freedom."

Governmental spying on citizens would normally be interpreted as a diminution of their freedom. One freedom particularly diminished by spying is privacy; other freedoms might also be affected. Governmental spying is *prima facie* grounds, then, for liberals' "upset" with and protest of a policy that sanctions spying.

Liberals would receive scant comfort from Huston's plaint: "In the Nixon White House it was damn tough for a man of ideas to survive; for a man of conservative ideas and a modest dose of self-respect, it was virtually impossible." ("The Nixon Monument," *The Alternative*, June–September, 1973) The article by Huston shows that he is a man of ideas, that he is concerned with freedom, and that he very likely was convinced that the policies on spying he was advocating were intellectually defensible.

Were Huston to defend his recommendations, liberals would be forced dialectically to advance past the *prima facie* grounds that spying diminishes the freedom of privacy; Huston knows that some persons' privacy would be reduced as well as liberals do; he also knows that such an advance would require recourse to theory. It raises an interesting question of what tack a liberal should take were Huston to use the same theory that liberals use and were he able to make out as good a case for his recommendations as liberals could make out against them. If Huston would and could, should liberals give up their theory or is the "right" to privacy and the inviolability of the individual a breachable barrier?

I am bothered by this choice because I write this in the spirit of "we liberals" rather than "them liberals."

The choice raises a methodological issue. On one hand, the rational man expects to resort to theory to help him make decisions. On the other hand, he knows that his theory has to be justified if his resort to it is to be justified. But how is one to justify a moral and/or political theory? John Rawls (*A Theory of Justice;* all page references to Rawls are to this volume.), whom we have to consider a liberal because of the priority he gives, and believes rational men would give, to liberty (p. 43 and p. 243), says of his own theory of justice as fairness (p. 111) that if it "fits our considered judgments in reflective equilibrium, and if it enables us to say all that on due examination we want to say, then it provides a way of eliminating customary phrases in favor of other expressions." The theory, in short, makes an advance over "customary" modes of conceptualizing moral and political decisions.

Rawls recognizes that at bottom we need to test a theory against the standard of "our considered judgments." In the present instance, suppose that Huston can use liberals' own theory to justify the diminishment of privacy. Is the liberal to conclude that the theory is not justified because it does not measure up to "our considered judgment" that personal privacy is inviolable?

If the liberal were to abandon his theory because it didn't square with the inviolability of privacy, he would have given priority to privacy over his theory, a not unreasonable position given the traditional concept of liberalism. This, however, would put the utility and contract liberal on unwanted, deontological grounds: The deontologist holds that there is a plurality of irreducible, basic principles ("considered judgments" such as "Privacy is inviolable"). Two liberal theories, utilitarianism and Rawls' contract theory (p. 34), have found a plurality of "basic" principles unsatisfactory; inevitably, in their view, this plurality leads to a conflict of principles which can be resolved only with a "higher" theory such as theirs. Both theories claim to supply the "higher" principles needed for conflict resolution.

Of course, if privacy were admittedly violable, then it would no longer serve as a standard against which a liberal could measure his theory; that is, a theory that sanctioned the violation of privacy would not be discredited if the liberal admitted that privacy is violable.

But, reality forces us to acknowledge that we liberals have a "gut reaction" against a Huston Plan that advocates violating our privacy. Are we to smother this by sober theoretical reflection? Is our "upset" and outrage an anti-theoretical, irrational, emotional response? Yes, if privacy is violable and if the Huston Plan is defensible on liberal theoretical principles. There can be no "liberal crisis" if the Huston Plan is not a Liberal Plan. Unfortunately, I think, it is a Liberal Plan.

We can dispose rather quickly of the civil libertarians' argument against the Huston Plan. This would be based on the U.S. Constitution's Fourth Amendment: The right of the people to be secure in their persons, houses, papers, and effects, against unreasonable searches and seizures, shall not be violated, and no warrants shall issue, but upon probable cause. . . .

Because the Huston Plan called for violation of persons' privacy without first seeking judicial warrants, it violated the Constitution, and, therefore, is to be condemned. While this is a good legal argument, it does not probe deeply enough to shed any light on more fundamental issues. Suppose that the Plan did call for warrants, and suppose that judges did grant them because they were not considered "unreasonable searches," then the legality would be satisfied. Still, we would want to know when it would be "unreasonable" to insist on preserving privacy.

Huston could move to utilitarian theory after patching up the illegalities in the Huston Plan. Since the right of privacy is not an absolute right in the Constitution, a legitimate question arises about the occasions on which we are justified in breaching citizens' privacy.

Pitt suggests that necessity is the argument used by tyrants to infringe freedom. One would hope that they would use at least this strong an argument. Further, given that for a utilitarian there is no rule (nor act) which is absolute, always being subject to the test of utility, it is logically possible that on some occasion there could be sufficient utility in diminishing privacy.

An argument could go like this. The United States is a relatively free country. There are persons who threaten the security of our government, persons whose avowed policy would provide less freedom than we have now were they to seize control of our government. If invasion of their privacy were done to secure our government, then the utility of that act is greater than not invading their privacy; therefore, we are justified in diminishing the privacy of some persons, including those that surveillance might show are not security threats.

The soundness of this argument depends upon the facts about the degree of actual threat. Huston could claim greater knowledge about it than we persons who are not privy to FBI, CIA, *etc,* information as Huston was. Any outrage we feel, as any "thinking liberal" knows, would be premature if we did not know the facts—unless we are deontological about liberty. Further, there could be an occasion when liberals, too, might agree that there is a genuine threat. This means that utilitarian theory is consistent with diminution of privacy and that utilitarian liberals may have to suppress their "deontological" outrage at such diminution.

Huston would have no difficulty in handling a liberal theory such as Rawls. Rawls' First Principle is about liberty, calling for its equal distribution in the most extensive way possible. It has priority over his Second, the social and economic welfare, Principle. This means that liberty can be less extensive or unequally distributed only for the sake of liberty.

Huston could argue that although the invasion of privacy proposed in his Plan would mean that some would have less liberty than others, this is justified because it is for the sake of preserving the most extensive liberty possible, using the facts outlined in the utilitarian argument above.

The contract theorist might reply that enactment of the Plan would have a "chilling effect" on every one, thus bringing about a less extensive liberty as well.

Huston could reply that this would happen only if the Plan were publicly known; therefore, the contract liberal has an obligation to keep silent about it. This seems to conform with the conditions Rawls stipulates for limiting liberty (p. 213). Once again, the facts about the security threat would be highly relevant to the soundness of Huston's conclusion. However, a liberal contract theorist has to allow that on some occasion the facts and his theory could justify a Huston Plan. No casuistical elaboration can dodge this factual possibility.

Because neither the utilitarian nor the contract liberal theory distinguishes between moral and political systems, neither can appeal to a higher moral principle to save privacy from political incursion. (See my article in this *Journal*, "On the Relation Between Politics and Morals," April, 1972; and Rawls, pp. 17, 51, and 110.)

Diminution of privacy presents a hard test case for a liberal. He is committed to maximum freedom or liberty. At the same time, he wants a rational theory. Presumably, if any "considered judgment" is to be a test of a liberal theory, privacy should be it; that is, methodologically, theory must take second place to some practice; consequently, given a primary commitment to privacy, a theory that allows Huston the latitude he wants is unsatisfactory to the liberal, no matter what its historical track record nor how hardly it has been won. Theory has to be tested against *something*.

Perhaps the contempt the New Left has shown for "liberals" is justified by liberals' willingness to damp their outrage at governmental excesses; perhaps their theory is too soft to stiffen their resistance against attacks on their "ultimate value," freedom. The elasticity of liberal casuistry has been demonstrated over and over again, not only to justify imperialist wars but to dispatch police against students and to deplore the "excesses" of affirmative action, any one of which has either diminished the extensity or sanctioned the unequal distribution of liberty.

Perhaps we liberals should entertain the possibility of becoming crusty, uncompromising deontologists and giving our utility and contract theories the sack. Or, perhaps, those theories are pointing in the right direction, privacy being a virtue that thrives only in a mistrustful, mercantile, alienating, utility-prone capitalist structure; perhaps it is privacy that should be sacked, along with the context that makes it a political virtue rather than a vice. Is it possible to conceive a radically different structure in which there is government by people rather than by government? One in which political (as opposed to personal) privacy would nullify one's effectiveness rather than enhancing it?

Something is to be done and thought.

The New Biology: Engineered Human Beings

LEON R. KASS

Leon R. Kass (1925–) teaches at St. John's College, Annapolis, Maryland. He was Secretary of the Committee on Life Sciences and Social Policy, National Academy of Sciences.

Recent advances in biology and medicine suggest that we may be rapidly acquiring the power to modify and control the capacities and activities of men by direct intervention and manipulation of their bodies and minds. Certain means are already in use or at hand, others await the solution of relatively minor technical problems, while yet others, those offering perhaps the most precise kind of control, depend upon further basic research. Biologists who have considered these matters disagree on the question of how much how soon, but all agree that the power for "human engineering," to borrow from the jargon, is coming and that it will probably have profound social consequences.

These developments have been viewed both with enthusiasm and with alarm; they are only just beginning to receive serious attention. Several biologists have undertaken to inform the public about the technical possibilities, present and future. Practitioners of social science "futurology" are attempting to predict and describe the likely social consequences of and public responses to the new technologies. Lawyers and legislators are exploring institutional innovations for assessing new technologies. All of these activities are based upon the hope that we can harness the new technology of man for the betterment of mankind.

Yet this commendable aspiration points to another set of questions, which are, in my view, sorely neglected—questions that inquire into the meaning of phrases such as the "betterment of mankind." A *full* understanding of the new technology of man requires an exploration of ends, values, standards. What ends will or should the new techniques serve? What values should guide society's adjustments? By what standards should the assessment agencies access? Behind these questions lie others: what is a good man, what is a good life for man, what is a good community? This article is an attempt to provoke discussion of these neglected and important questions.

While these questions about ends and ultimate ends are never unimportant or irrelevant, they have rarely been more important or more relevant. That this is so can be seen once we recognize that we are dealing here with a group of technologies that are in a decisive respect unique: the object upon which they operate is man himself. The technologies of energy or food production, of com-

Source: Leon R. Kass, "The New Biology: What Price Relieving Man's Estate?" *Science,* Vol. 174 (November 19, 1971), pp. 779–788. Copyright © 1971 by the American Association for the Advancement of Science. Reprinted by permission of *Science* and the author.

munication, of manufacture, and of motion greatly alter the implements available to man and the conditions in which he uses them. In contrast, the biomedical technology works to change the user himself. To be sure, the printing press, the automobile, the television, and the jet airplane have greatly altered the conditions under which and the way in which men live; but men as biological beings have remained largely unchanged. They have been, and remain, able to accept or reject, to use and abuse these technologies; they choose, whether wisely or foolishly, the ends to which these technologies are means. Biomedical technology may make it possible to change the inherent capacity for choice itself. Indeed, both those who welcome and those who fear the advent of "human engineering" ground their hopes and fears in the same prospect: *that man can for the first time recreate himself.*

Engineering the engineer seems to differ in kind from engineering his engine. Some have argued, however, that biomedical engineering does not differ qualitatively from toilet training, education, and moral teachings—all of which are forms of so-called "social engineering," which has man as its object, and is used by one generation to mold the next. In reply, it must at least be said that the techniques which have hitherto been employed are feeble and inefficient when compared to those on the horizon. This quantitative difference rests in part on a qualitative difference in the means of intervention. The traditional influences operate by speech or by symbolic deeds. They pay tribute to man as the animal who lives by speech and who understands the meanings of actions. Also, their effects are, in general, reversible, or at least subject to attempts at reversal. Each person has greater or lesser power to accept or reject or abandon them. In contrast, biomedical engineering circumvents the human context of speech and meaning, bypasses choice, and goes directly to work to modify the human material itself. Moreover, the changes wrought may be irreversible.

In addition, there is an important practical reason for considering the biomedical technology apart from other technologies. The advances we shall examine are fruits of a large, humane project dedicated to the conquest of disease and the relief of human suffering. The biologist and physician, regardless of their private motives, are seen, with justification, to be the well-wishers and benefactors of mankind. Thus, in a time in which technological advance is more carefully scrutinized and increasingly criticized, biomedical developments are still viewed by most people as benefits largely without qualification. The price we pay for these developments is thus more likely to go unrecognized. For this reason, I shall consider only the dangers and costs of biomedical advance. As the benefits are well known, there is no need to dwell upon them here. My discussion is deliberately partial.

I begin with a survey of the pertinent technologies. Next, I will consider some of the basic ethical and social problems in the use of these technologies. Then, I will briefly raise some fundamental questions to which these problems point. Finally, I shall offer some very general reflections on what is to be done.

The Biomedical Technologies

The biomedical technologies can be usefully organized into three groups, according to their major purpose: (1) control of death and life, (2) control of human potentialities, and (3) control of human achievement. The corresponding technologies are (1) medicine, especially the arts of prolonging life and of controlling reproduction, (2) genetic engineering, and (3) neurological and psychological manipulation. I shall briefly summarize each group of techniques.

1. *Control of death and life.* Previous medical triumphs have greatly increased average life expectancy. Yet other developments, such as organ transplantation or replacement and research into aging, hold forth the promise of increasing not just the average, but also the maximum life expectancy. Indeed, medicine seems to be sharpening its tools to do battle with death itself, as if death were just one more disease.

More immediately and concretely, available techniques of prolonging life—respirators, cardiac pacemakers, artificial kidneys—are already in the lists against death. Ironically, the success of these devices in forestalling death has introduced confusion in determining that death has, in fact, occurred. The traditional signs of life—heartbeat and respiration—can now be maintained entirely by machines. Some physicians are now busily trying to devise so-called "new definitions of death," while others maintain that the technical advances show that death is not a concrete event at all, but rather a gradual process, like twilight, incapable of precise temporal localization.

The real challenge to death will come from research into aging and senescence, a field just entering puberty. Recent studies suggest that aging is a genetically controlled process, distinct from disease, but one that can be manipulated and altered by diet or drugs. Extrapolating from animal studies, some scientists have suggested that a decrease in the rate of aging might also be achieved simply by effecting a very small decrease in human body temperature. According to some estimates, by the year 2000 it may be technically possible to add from 20 to 40 useful years to the period of middle life.

Medicine's success in extending life is already a major cause of excessive population growth: death control points to birth control. Although we are already technically competent, new techniques for lowering fertility and chemical agents for inducing abortion will greatly enhance our powers over conception and gestation. Problems of definition have been raised here as well. The need to determine when individuals acquire enforceable legal rights gives society an interest in the definition of human life and of the time when it begins. These matters are too familiar to need elaboration.

Technologies to conquer infertility proceed alongside those to promote it. The first successful laboratory fertilization of human egg by human sperm was reported in 1969.[1] In 1970, British scientists learned how to grow human embryos in the laboratory up to at least the blastocyst stage [that is, to the age

---

[1] R. G. Edwards, B. D. Bavister, P. C. Steptoe, *Nature,* vol. 221, 632 (1969).

of 1 week].[2] We may soon hear about the next stage, the successful reimplantation of such an embryo into a woman previously infertile because of oviduct disease. The development of an artificial placenta, now under investigation, will make possible full laboratory control of fertilization and gestation. In addition, sophisticated biochemical and cytological techniques of monitoring the "quality" of the fetus have been and are being developed and used. These developments not only give us more power over the generation of human life, but make it possible to manipulate and to modify the quality of the human material.

2. *Control of human potentialities.* Genetic engineering, when fully developed, will wield two powers not shared by ordinary medical practice. Medicine treats existing individuals and seeks to correct deviations from a norm of health. Genetic engineering, in contrast, will be able to make changes that can be transmitted to succeeding generations and will be able to create new capacities, and hence to establish new norms of health and fitness.

Nevertheless, one of the major interests in genetic manipulation is strictly medical: to develop treatments for individuals with inherited diseases. Genetic disease is prevalent and increasing, thanks partly to medical advances that enable those affected to survive and perpetuate their mutant genes. The hope is that normal copies of the appropriate gene, obtained biologically or synthesized chemically, can be introduced into defective individuals to correct their deficiencies. This *therapeutic* use of genetic technology appears to be far in the future. Moreover, there is some doubt that it will ever be practical, since the same end could be more easily achieved by transplanting cells or organs that could compensate for the missing or defective gene product.

Far less remote are technologies that could serve *eugenic* ends. Their development has been endorsed by those concerned about a general deterioration of the human gene pool and by others who believe that even an undeteriorated human gene pool needs upgrading. Artificial insemination with selected donors, the eugenic proposal of Herman Muller,[3] has been possible for several years because of the perfection of methods for long-term storage of human spermatozoa. The successful maturation of human oocytes in the laboratory and their subsequent fertilization now make it possible to select donors of ova as well. But a far more suitable technique for eugenic purposes will soon be upon us—namely, nuclear transplantation, or cloning. Bypassing the lottery of sexual recombination, nuclear transplantation permits the asexual reproduction or copying of an already developed individual. The nucleus of a mature but unfertilized egg is replaced by a nucleus obtained from a specialized cell of an adult organism or embryo (for example, a cell from the intestines or the skin). The egg with its transplanted nucleus develops as if it had been fertilized and, barring complications, will give rise to a normal adult organism. Since almost all the hereditary material (DNA) of a cell is contained within its nucleus, the renucleated egg and the individual into which it develops are genetically identical to the adult organism that was the source of the donor nucleus. Cloning could be used to

[2] R. G. Edwards, P. C. Steptoe, J. M. Purdy, *Nature,* vol. 227, 1307 (1970).

[3] H. J. Muller, *Science,* vol. 134, 643 (1961).

produce sets of unlimited numbers of genetically identical individuals, each set derived from a single parent. Cloning has been successful in amphibians and is now being tried in mice; its extension to man merely requires the solution of certain technical problems.

Production of man–animal chimeras by the introduction of selected nonhuman material into developing human embryos is also expected. Fusion of human and nonhuman cells in tissue culture has already been achieved.

Other, less direct means for influencing the gene pool are already available, thanks to our increasing ability to identify and diagnose genetic diseases. Genetic counselors can now detect biochemically and cytologically a variety of severe genetic defects (for example, Mongolism, Tay-Sachs disease) while the fetus is still in utero. Since treatments are at present largely unavailable, diagnosis is often followed by abortion of the affected fetus. In the future, more sensitive tests will also permit the detection of heterozygote carriers, the unaffected individuals who carry but a single dose of a given deleterious gene. The eradication of a given genetic disease might then be attempted by aborting all such carriers. In fact, it was recently suggested that the fairly common disease cystic fibrosis could be completely eliminated over the next 40 years by screening all pregnancies and aborting the 17,000,000 unaffected fetuses that will carry a single gene for this disease. Such zealots need to be reminded of the consequences should each geneticist be allowed an equal assault on his favorite genetic disorder, given that each human being is a carrier for some four to eight such recessive, lethal genetic diseases.

3. *Control of human achievement.* Although human achievement depends at least in part upon genetic endowment, heredity determines only the material upon which experience and education impose the form. The limits of many capacities and powers of an individual are indeed genetically determined, but the nurturing and perfection of these capacities depend upon other influences. Neurological and psychological manipulation hold forth the promise of controlling the development of human capacities, particularly those long considered most distinctively human: speech, thought, choice, emotion, memory, and imagination.

These techniques are now in a rather primitive state because we understand so little about the brain and mind. Nevertheless, we have already seen the use of electrical stimulation of the human brain to produce sensations of intense pleasure and to control rage, the use of brain surgery (for example, frontal lobotomy) for the relief of severe anxiety, and the use of aversive conditioning with electric shock to treat sexual perversion. Operant-conditioning techniques are widely used, apparently with success, in schools and mental hospitals. The use of so-called consciousness-expanding and hallucinogenic drugs is widespread, to say nothing of tranquilizers and stimulants. We are promised drugs to modify memory, intelligence, libido, and aggressiveness.

The following passages from a recent book by Yale neurophysiologist José Delgado—a book instructively entitled *Physical Control of the Mind: Toward a Psychocivilized Society*—should serve to make this discussion more concrete. In the early 1950's, it was discovered that, with electrodes placed in certain discrete regions of their brains, animals would repeatedly and indefatigably press levers to stimulate their own brains, with obvious resultant enjoyment. Even starving animals preferred stimulating these so-called pleasure centers to eating. Delgado comments on the electrical stimulation of a similar center in a human subject.[4]

> The patient reported a pleasant tingling sensation in the left side of her body "from my face down to the bottom of my legs." She started giggling and making funny comments, stating that she enjoyed the sensation "very much." Repetition of these stimulations made the patient more communicative and flirtatious, and she ended by openly expressing her desire to marry the therapist.

And one further quotation from Delgado.[5]

> Leaving wires inside of a thinking brain may appear unpleasant or dangerous, but actually the many patients who have undergone this experience have not been concerned about the fact of being wired, nor have they felt any discomfort due to the presence of conductors in their heads. Some women have shown their feminine adaptability to circumstances by wearing attractive hats or wigs to conceal their electrical headgear, and many people have been able to enjoy a normal life as outpatients, returning to the clinic periodically for examination and stimulation. In a few cases in which contacts were located in pleasurable areas, patients have had the opportunity to stimulate their own brains by pressing the button of a portable instrument, and this procedure is reported to have therapeutic benefits.

It bears repeating that the sciences of neurophysiology and psychopharmacology are in their infancy. The techniques that are now available are crude, imprecise, weak, and unpredictable, compared to those that may flow from a more mature neurobiology.

Basic Ethical and Social Problems in the Use of Biochemical Technology

After this cursory review of the powers now and soon to be at our disposal, I turn to the questions concerning the use of these powers. First, we must recognize that questions of use of science and technology are always moral and political questions, never simply technical ones. All private or public decisions to develop or to use biomedical technology—and decisions *not* to do so—inevitably contain judgments about value. This is true even if the values guiding those decisions are not articulated or made clear, as indeed they often are not. Secondly, the value judgments cannot be derived from biomedical science. This is true even if scientists themselves make the decisions.

These important points are often overlooked for at least three reasons.

1. They are obscured by those who like to speak of "the control of nature by science." It is men who control, not that abstraction "science." Science may provide the means, but men choose the ends; the choice of ends comes from beyond science.

[4] J. M. R. Delgado, *Physical Control of the Mind: Toward a Psychocivilized Society* (New York: Harper & Row, 1969). p. 185–88.
[5] Ibid.

2. Introduction of new technologies often appears to be the result of no decision whatsoever, or of the culmination of decisions too small or unconscious to be recognized as such. What can be done is done. However, someone is deciding on the basis of some notions of desirability, no matter how selfserving or altruistic.

3. Desires to gain or keep money and power no doubt influence much of what happens, but these desires can also be formulated as reasons and then discussed and debated.

Insofar as our society has tried to deliberate about questions of use, how has it done so? Pragmatists that we are, we prefer a utilitarian calculus: we weigh "benefits" against "risks," and we weigh them for both the individual and "society." We often ignore the fact that the very definitions of "a benefit" and "a risk" are themselves based upon judgments about value. In the biomedical areas just reviewed, the benefits are considered to be self-evident: prolongation of life, control of fertility and of population size, treatment and prevention of genetic disease, the reduction of anxiety and aggressiveness, and the enhancement of memory, intelligence, and pleasure. The assessment of risk is, in general, simply pragmatic—will the technique work effectively and reliably, how much will it cost, will it do detectable bodily harm, and who will complain if we proceed with development? As these questions are familiar and congenial, there is no need to belabor them.

The very pragmatism that makes us sensitive to considerations of economic cost often blinds us to the larger social costs exacted by biomedical advances. For one thing, we seem to be unaware that we may not be able to maximize all the benefits, that several of the goals we are promoting conflict with each other. On the one hand, we seek to control population growth by lowering fertility; on the other hand, we develop techniques to enable every infertile woman to bear a child. On the one hand, we try to extend the lives of individuals with genetic disease; on the other, we wish to eliminate deleterious genes from the human population. I am not urging that we resolve these conflicts in favor of one side or the other, but simply that we recognize that such conflicts exist. Once we do, we are more likely to appreciate that most "progress" is heavily paid for in terms not generally included in the simple utilitarian calculus.

To become sensitive to the larger costs of biomedical progress, we must attend to several serious ethical and social questions. I will briefly discuss three of them: (1) questions of distributive justice, (2) questions of the use and abuse of power, and (3) questions of self-degradation and dehumanization.

Distributive Justice

The introduction of any biomedical technology presents a new instance of an old problem—how to distribute scarce resources justly. We should assume that demand will usually exceed supply. Which people should receive a kidney transplant or an artificial heart? Who should get the benefits of genetic therapy or of brain stimulation? Is "first-come, first-served" the fairest principle? Or are certain people "more worthy," and if so, on what grounds?

It is unlikely that we will arrive at answers to these question in the form of deliberate decisions. More likely, the problem of distribution will continue to be decided ad hoc and locally. If so, the consequence will probably be a sharp increase in the already far too great inequality of medical care. The extreme case will be longevity, which will probably be, at first, obtainable only at great expense. Who is likely to be able to buy it? Do conscience and prudence permit us to enlarge the gap between rich and poor, especially with respect to something as fundamental as life itself?

Questions of distributive justice also arise in the earlier decisions to acquire new knowledge and to develop new techniques. Personnel and facilities for medical research and treatment are scarce resources. Is the development of a new technology the best use of the limited resources, given current circumstances? How should we balance efforts aimed at prevention against those aimed at cure, or either of these against efforts to redesign the species? How should we balance the delivery of available levels of care against further basic research? More fundamentally, how should we balance efforts in biology and medicine against efforts to eliminate poverty, pollution, urban decay, discrimination, and poor education? This last question about distribution is perhaps the most profound. We should reflect upon the social consequences of seducing many of our brightest young people to spend their lives locating the biochemical defects in rare genetic diseases, while our more serious problems go begging. The current squeeze on money for research provides us with an opportunity to rethink and reorder our priorities.

Problems of distributive justice are frequently mentioned and discussed, but they are hard to resolve in a rational manner. We find them especially difficult because of the enormous range of conflicting values and interests that characterizes our pluralistic society. We cannot agree—unfortunately, we often do not even try to agree—on standards for just distribution. Rather, decisions tend to be made largely out of a clash of competing interests. Thus, regrettably, the question of how to distribute justly often gets reduced to who shall decide how to distribute. The question about justice has led us to the question about power.

Use and Abuse of Power

We have difficulty recognizing the problems of the exercise of power in the biomedical enterprise because of our delight with the wondrous fruits it has yielded. This is ironic because the notion of power is absolutely central to the modern conception of science. The ancients conceived of science as the *understanding* of nature, pursued for its own sake. We moderns view science as power, as *control* over nature; the conquest of nature "for the relief of man's estate" was the charge issued by Francis Bacon, one of the leading architects of the modern scientific project.[6]

Another source of difficulty is our fondness for speaking of the abstraction "Man." I suspect that we prefer to speak figuratively about "Man's power over Nature" because it obscures an unpleasant reality about human affairs. It is in

---

[6] F. Bacon, *The Advancement of Learning, Book I,* H. G. Dick, ed. (New York: Random House, 1955), p. 193.

fact particular men who wield power, not Man. What we really mean by "Man's power over Nature" is a power exercised by some men over other men, with a knowledge of nature as their instrument.

While applicable to technology in general, these reflections are especially pertinent to the technologies of human engineering, with which men deliberately exercise power over future generations. An excellent discussion of this question is found in *The Abolition of Man,* by C. S. Lewis.[7]

> It is, of course, a commonplace to complain that men have hitherto used badly, and against their fellows, the powers that science has given them. But that is not the point I am trying to make. I am not speaking of particular corruptions and abuses which an increase of moral virtue would cure: I am considering what the thing called "Man's power over Nature" must always and essentially be. . . .
>
> In reality, of course, if any one age really attains, by eugenics and scientific education, the power to make its descendants what it pleases, all men who live after it are the patients of that power. They are weaker, not stronger: for though we may have put wonderful machines in their hands, we have preordained how they are to use them. . . . The real picture is that of one dominant age . . . which resists all previous ages most successfully and dominates all subsequent ages most irresistibly, and thus is the real master of the human species. But even within this master generation (itself an infinitesimal minority of the species) the power will be exercised by a minority smaller still. Man's conquest of Nature, if the dreams of some scientific planners are realized, means the rule of a few hundreds of men over billions upon billions of men. There neither is nor can be any simple increase of power on Man's side. Each new power won *by* man is a power *over* man as well. Each advance leaves him weaker as well as stronger. In every victory, besides being the general who triumphs, he is also the prisoner who follows the triumphal car.

Please note that I am not yet speaking about the problem of the misuse or abuse of power. The point is rather that the power which grows is unavoidably the power of only some men, and that the number of powerful men decreases as power increases.

Specific problems of abuse and misuse of specific powers must not, however, be overlooked. Some have voiced the fear that the technologies of genetic engineering and behavior control, though developed for good purposes, will be put to evil uses. These fears are perhaps somewhat exaggerated, if only because biomedical technologies would add very little to our highly developed arsenal for mischief, destruction, and stultification. Nevertheless, any proposal for large-scale human engineering should make us wary. Consider a program of positive eugenics based upon the widespread practice of asexual reproduction. Who shall decide what constitutes a superior individual worthy of replication? Who shall decide which individuals may or must reproduce, and by which method? These are questions easily answered only for a tyrannical regime.

Concern about the use of power is equally necessary in the selection of means for desirable or agreed-upon ends. Consider the desired end of limiting population growth. An effective program of fertility control is likely to be coercive.

[7] C. S. Lewis, *The Abolition of Man* (New York: Macmillan, 1965), pp. 69–71.

Who should decide the choice of means? Will the program penalize "conscientious objectors"?

Serious problems arise simply from obtaining and disseminating information, as in the mass screening programs now being proposed for detection of genetic disease. For what kinds of disorders is compulsory screening justified? Who shall have access to the data obtained, and for what purposes? To whom does information about a person's genotype belong? In ordinary medical practice, the patient's privacy is protected by the doctor's adherence to the principle of confidentiality. What will protect his privacy under conditions of mass screening?

More than privacy is at stake if screening is undertaken to detect psychological or behavioral abnormalities. A recent proposal, tendered and supported high in government, called for the psychological testing of all 6-year-olds to detect future criminals and misfits. The proposal was rejected; current tests lack the requisite predictive powers. But will such a proposal be rejected if reliable tests become available? What if certain genetic disorders, diagnosable in childhood, can be shown to correlate with subsequent antisocial behavior? For what degree of correlation and for what kinds of behavior can mandatory screening be justified? What use should be made of the data? Might not the dissemination of the information itself undermine the individual's chance for a worthy life and contribute to his so-called antisocial tendencies?

Consider the seemingly harmless effort to redefine clinical death. If the need for organs for transplantation is the stimulus for redefining death, might not this concern influence the definition at the expense of the dying? One physician, in fact, refers in writing to the revised criteria for declaring a patient dead as a "new definition of heart donor eligibility".[8]

Problems of abuse of power arise even in the acquisition of basic knowledge. The securing of a voluntary and informed consent is an abiding problem in the use of human subjects in experimentation. Gross coercion and deception are now rarely a problem; the pressures are generally subtle, often related to an intrinsic power imbalance in favor of the experimentalist.

A special problem arises in experiments on or manipulations of the unborn. Here it is impossible to obtain the consent of the human subject. If the purpose of the intervention is therapeutic—to correct a known genetic abnormality, for example—consent can reasonably be implied. But can anyone ethically consent to nontherapeutic interventions in which parents or scientists work their wills or their eugenic visions on the child-to-be? Would not such manipulation represent in itself an abuse of power, independent of consequences?

There are many clinical situations which already permit, if not invite, the manipulative or arbitrary use of powers provided by biomedical technology: obtaining organs for transplantation, refusing to let a person die with dignity, giving genetic counselling to a frightened couple, recommending eugenic sterilization for a mental retardate, ordering electric shock for a homosexual. In each situation, there is an opportunity to violate the will of the patient or subject. Such opportunities have generally existed in medical practice, but the dangers

[8] D. D. Rutstein, *Daedalus* (Spring 1969), p. 526.

are becoming increasingly serious. With the growing complexity of the technologies, the technician gains in authority, since he alone can understand what he is doing. The patient's lack of knowledge makes him deferential and often inhibits him from speaking up when he feels threatened. Physicians *are* sometimes troubled by their increasing power, yet they feel they cannot avoid its exercise. "Reluctantly," one commented to me, "we shall have to play God." With what guidance and to what ends I shall consider later. For the moment, I merely ask: "By whose authority?"

While these questions about power are pertinent and important, they are in one sense misleading. They imply an inherent conflict of purpose between physician and patient, between scientist and citizen. The discussion conjures up images of master and slave, of oppressor and oppressed. Yet it must be remembered that conflict of purpose is largely absent, especially with regard to general goals. To be sure, the purposes of medical scientists are not always the same as those of the subjects experimented on. Nevertheless, basic sponsors and partisans of biomedical technology are precisely those upon whom the technology will operate. The will of the scientist and physician is happily married to (rather, is the offspring of) the desire of all of us for better health, longer life, and peace of mind.

Most future biomedical technologies will probably be welcomed, as have those of the past. Their use will require little or no coercion. Some developments, such as pills to improve memory, control mood, or induce pleasure, are likely to need no promotion. Thus, even if we should escape from the dangers of coercive manipulation, we shall still face large problems posed by the voluntary use of biomedical technology, problems to which I now turn.

Voluntary Self-Degradation and Dehumanization

Modern opinion is sensitive to problems of restriction of freedom and abuse of power. Indeed, many hold that a man can be injured only by violating his will. But this view is much too narrow. It fails to recognize the great dangers we shall face in the use of biomedical technology, dangers that stem from an excess of freedom, from the uninhibited exercises of will. In my view, our greatest problem will increasingly be one of voluntary self-degradation, or willing dehumanization.

Certain desired and perfected medical technologies have already had some dehumanizing consequences. Improved methods of resuscitation have made possible heroic efforts to "save" the severely ill and injured. Yet these efforts are sometimes only partly successful; they may succeed in salvaging individuals with severe brain damage, capable of only a less-than-human, vegetating existence. Such patients, increasingly found in the intensive care units of university hospitals, have been denied a death with dignity. Families are forced to suffer seeing their loved ones so reduced, and are made to bear the burdens of a protracted death watch.

Even the ordinary methods of treating disease and prolonging life have impoverished the context in which men die. Fewer and fewer people die in the familiar surroundings of home or in the company of family and friends. At that time of life when there is perhaps the greatest need for human warmth and comfort, the dying patient is kept company by cardiac pacemakers and defibrillators, respirators, aspirators, oxygenators, catheters, and his intravenous drip.

But the loneliness is not confined to the dying patient in the hospital bed. Consider the increasing number of old people who are still alive, thanks to medical progress. As a group, the elderly are the most alienated members of our society. Not yet ready for the world of the dead, not deemed fit for the world of the living, they are shunted aside. More and more of them spend the extra years medicine has given them in "homes for senior citizens," in chronic hospitals, in nursing homes—waiting for the end. We have learned how to increase their years, but we have not learned how to help them enjoy their days. And yet, we bravely and relentlessly push back the frontiers against death.

Paradoxically, even the young and vigorous may be suffering because of medicine's success in removing death from their personal experience. Those born since penicillin represent the first generation ever to grow up without the experience or fear of probable unexpected death at an early age. They look around and see that virtually all of their friends are alive. A thoughtful physician, Eric Cassell, has remarked on this in "Death and the Physician."[9]

> While the gift of time must surely be marked as a great blessing, the *perception* of time, as stretching out endlessly before us, is somewhat threatening. Many of us function best under deadlines, and tend to procrastinate when time limits are not set. . . . Thus, this unquestioned boon, the extension of life, and the removal of the threat of premature death, carries with it an unexpected anxiety: the anxiety of an unlimited future.
>
> In the young, the sense of limitless time has apparently imparted not a feeling of limitless opportunity, but increased stress and anxiety, in addition to the anxiety which results from other modern freedoms: personal mobility, a wide range of occupational choice, and independence from the limitations of class and familial patterns of work. . . . A certain aimlessness (often ringed around with great social consciousness) characterizes discussions about their own aspirations. The future is endless, and their inner demands seem minimal. Although it may appear uncharitable to say so, they seem to be acting in a way best described as "childish"— particularly in their lack of a time sense. They behave as though there were no tomorrow, or as though the time limits imposed by the biological facts of life had become so vague for them as to be nonexistent.

the project that will enable us to control numbers and to treat individuals with genetic desease. But our desires outrun these defensible goals. Many would welcome the chance to become parents without the inconvenience of pregnancy; others would wish to know in advance the characteristics of their offspring (sex, height, eye color, intelligence); still others would wish to design these characteristics to suit their tastes. Some scientists have called for the use of the new technologies to assure the "quality" of all new babies.[10] As one obstetrician put it: "The business of obstetrics is to produce *optimum* babies." But the price to be paid for the "optimum baby" is the transfer of procreation from the home to

[9] E. J. Cassell, *Commentary* (June 1969), p. 76.
[10] B. Glass, *Science,* vol. 171, 23 (1971).

the laboratory and its coincident transformation into manufacture. Increasing control over the product is purchased by the increasing depersonalization of the process. The complete depersonalization of procreation (possible with the development of an artificial placenta) shall be, in itself, seriously dehumanizing, no matter how optimum the product. It should not be forgotten that human procreation not only issues new human beings, but is itself a human activity.

Procreation is not simply an activity of the rational will. It is a more complete human activity precisely because it engages us bodily and spiritually, as well as rationally. Is there perhaps some wisdom in that mystery of nature which joins the pleasure of sex, the communication of love, and the desire for children in the very activity by which we continue the chain of human existence? Is not biological parenthood a built-in "mechanism," selected because it fosters and supports in parents an adequate concern for and commitment to their children? Would not the laboratory production of human beings no longer be *human* procreation? Could it keep human parenthood human?

The dehumanizing consequences of programmed reproduction extend beyond the mere acts and processes of life-giving. Transfer of procreation to the laboratory will no doubt weaken what is presently for many people the best remaining justification and support for the existence of marriage and the family. Sex is now comfortably at home outside of marriage; child-rearing is progressively being given over to the state, the schools, the mass media, and the child-care centers. Some have argued that the family, long the nursery of humanity, has outlived its usefulness. To be sure, laboratory and governmental alternatives might be designed for procreation and child-rearing, but at what cost?

This is not the place to conduct a full evaluation of the biological family. Nevertheless, some of its important virtues are, nowadays, too often overlooked. The family is rapidly becoming the only institution in an increasingly impersonal world where each person is loved not for what he does or makes, but simply because he is. The family is also the institution where most of us, both as children and as parents, acquire a sense of continuity with the past and a sense of commitment to the future. Without the family, we would have little incentive to take an interest in anything after our own deaths. These observations suggest that the elimination of the family would weaken ties to past and future, and would throw us, even more than we are now, to the mercy of an impersonal, lonely present.

Neurobiology and psychobiology probe most directly into the distinctively human. The technological fruit of these sciences is likely to be both more tempting than Eve's apple and more "catastrophic" in its result.[11] One need only

[11] It is, of course, a long-debated question as to whether the fall of Adam and Eve ought to be considered "catastrophic," or more precisely, whether the Hebrew tradition considered it so. I do not mean here to be taking sides in this quarrel by my use of the term "catastrophic," and, in fact, tend to line up on the negative side of the questions, as put above. Curiously, as Aldous Huxley's *Brave New World* [(New York: Harper & Row, 1969)] suggests, the implicit goal of the biomedical technology could well be said to be the reversal of the Fall and a return of man to the hedonic and immortal existence of the Garden of Eden. Yet I can point to at least two problems. First, the new Garden of Eden will probably have no gardens; the received, splendid world of nature will be buried beneath asphalt, con-

consider contemporary drug use to see what people are willing to risk or sacrifice for novel experiences, heightened perceptions, or just "kicks." The possibility of drug-induced, instant, and effortless gratification will be welcomed. Recall the possibilities of voluntary self-stimulation of the brain to reduce anxiety, to heighten pleasure, or to create visual and auditory sensations unavailable through the peripheral sense organs. Once these techniques are perfected and safe, is there much doubt that they will be desired, demanded, and used?

What ends will these techniques serve? Most likely, only the most elemental, those most tied to the bodily pleasures. What will happen to thought, to love, to friendship, to art, to judgment, to public-spiritedness in a society with a perfected technology of pleasure? What kinds of creatures will we become if we obtain our pleasure by drug or electrical stimulation without the usual kind of human efforts and frustrations? What kind of society will we have?

We need only consult Aldous Huxley's prophetic novel *Brave New World* for a likely answer to these questions. There we encounter a society dedicated to homogeneity and stability, administered by means of instant gratifications and peopled by creatures of human shape but of stunted humanity. They consume, fornicate, take "soma," and operate the machinery that makes it all possible. They do not read, write, think, love, or govern themselves. Creativity and curiosity, reason and passion, exist only in a rudimentary and mutilated form. In short, they are not men at all.

True, our techniques, like theirs, may in fact enable us to treat schizophrenia, to alleviate anxiety, to curb aggressiveness. We, like they, may indeed be able to save mankind from itself, but probably only at the cost of its humanness. In the end, the price of relieving man's estate might well be the abolition of man.[12]

There are, of course, many other routes leading to the abolition of man. There are many other and better known causes of dehumanization. Disease, starvation, mental retardation, slavery, and brutality—to name just a few—have long prevented many, if not most, people from living a fully human life. We should work to reduce and eventually to eliminate these evils. But the existence of these evils should not prevent us from appreciating that the use of the

---

crete, and other human fabrications, a transformation that is already far along. (Recall that in *Brave New World* elaborate consumption-oriented, mechanical amusement parks—featuring, for example, centrifugal bumble-puppy—had supplanted wilderness and even ordinary gardens.) Second, the new inhabitant of the new "Garden" will have to be a creature for whom we have no precedent, a creature as difficult to imagine as to bring into existence. He will have to be simultaneously an innocent like Adam and a technological wizard who keeps the "Garden" running. (I am indebted to Dean Robert Goldwin, St. John's College, for this last insight.)

[12] Some scientists naively believe that an engineered increase in human intelligence will steer us in the right direction. Surely we have learned by now that intelligence, whatever it is and however measured, is not synonymous with wisdom and that, if harnessed to the wrong ends, it can cleverly perpetrate great folly and evil. Given the activities in which many, if not most, of our best minds are now engaged, we should not simply rejoice in the prospect of enhancing IQ. On what would this increased intelligence operate? At best, the programming of further increases in IQ. It would design and operate techniques for prolonging life, for engineering reproduction, for delivering gratifications. With no gain in wisdom, our gain in intelligence can only enhance the rate of our dehumanization.

technology of man, uninformed by wisdom concerning proper human ends, and untempered by an appropriate humility and awe, can unwittingly render us all irreversibly less than human. For, unlike the man reduced by disease or slavery, the people dehumanized à la *Brave New World* are not miserable, do not know that they are dehumanized, and, what is worse, would not care if they knew. They are, indeed, happy slaves, with a slavish happiness.

Some Fundamental Questions

The practical problems of distributing scarce resources, of curbing the abuses of power, and of preventing voluntary dehumanization point beyond themselves to some large, enduring, and most difficult questions: the nature of justice and the good community, the nature of man and the good for man. My appreciation of the profundity of these questions and my own ignorance before them makes me hesitant to say any more about them. Nevertheless, previous failures to find a shortcut around them have led me to believe that these questions must be faced if we are to have any hope of understanding where biology is taking us. Therefore, I shall try to show in outline how I think some of the larger questions arise from my discussion of dehumanization and self-degradation.

My remarks on dehumanization can hardly fail to arouse argument. It might be said, correctly, that to speak about dehumanization presupposes a concept of "the distinctively human." It might also be said, correctly, that to speak about wisdom concerning proper human ends presupposes that such ends do in fact exist and that they may be more or less accessible to human understanding, or at least to rational inquiry. It is true that neither presupposition is at home in modern thought.

The notion of the "distinctively human" has been seriously challenged by modern scientists. Darwinists hold that man is, at least in origin, tied to the subhuman; his seeming distinctiveness is an illusion or, at most, not very important. Biochemists and molecular biologists extend the challenge by blurring the distinction between the living and the nonliving. The laws of physics and chemistry are found to be valid and are held to be sufficient for explaining biological systems. Man is a collection of molecules, an accident on the stage of evolution, endowed by chance with the power to change himself, but only along determined lines.

Psychoanalysts have also debunked the "distinctly human." The essence of man is seen to be located in those drives he shares with other animals—pursuit of pleasure and avoidance of pain. The so-called "higher functions" are understood to be servants of the more elementary, the more base. Any distinctiveness or "dignity" that man has consists of his superior capacity for gratifying his animal needs.

The idea of "human good" fares no better. In the social sciences, historicists and existentialists have helped drive this question underground. The former hold all notions of human good to be culturally and historically bound, and hence mutable. The latter hold that values are subjective: each man makes his own, and ethics becomes simply the cataloging of personal tastes.

Such appear to be the prevailing opinions. Yet there is nothing novel about reductionism, hedonism, and relativism; there are doctrines with which Socrates contended. What is new is that these doctrines seem to be vindicated by scientific advance. Not only do the scientific notions of nature and of man flower into verifiable predictions, but they yield marvelous fruit. The technological triumphs are held to validate their scientific foundations. Here, perhaps, is the most pernicious result of technological progress—more dehumanizing than any actual manipulation or technique, present or future. We are witnessing the erosion, perhaps the final erosion, of the idea of man as something splendid or divine, and its replacement with a view that sees man, no less than nature, as simply more raw material for manipulation and homogenization. Hence, our peculiar moral crisis. We are in turbulent seas without a landmark precisely because we adhere more and more to a view of nature and of man which both gives us enormous power and, at the same time, denies all possibility of standards to guide its use. Though well-equipped, we know not who we are nor where we are going. We are left to the accidents of our hasty, biased, and ephemeral judgments.

Let us not fail to note a painful irony: our conquest of nature has made us the slaves of blind chance. We triumph over nature's unpredictabilities only to subject ourselves to the still greater unpredictability of our capricious wills and our fickle opinions. That we have a method is no proof against our madness. Thus, engineering the engineer as well as the engine, we race our train we know not where.[13]

While the disastrous consequences of ethical nihilism are insufficient to refute it, they invite and make urgent a reinvestigation of the ancient and enduring questions of what is a proper life for a human being, what is a good community, and how are they achieved.[14] We must not be deterred from these questions simply because the best minds in human history have failed to settle them.

---

[13] The philosopher Hans Jonas has made the identical point: "Thus the slow-working accidents of nature, which by the very patience of their small increments, large numbers, and gradual decisions, may well cease to be 'accident' in outcome, are to be replaced by the fast-working accidents of man's hasty and biased decisions, not exposed to the long test of the ages. His uncertain ideas are to set the goals of generations, with a certainty borrowed from the presumptive certainty of the means. The latter presumption is doubtful enough, but this doubtfulness becomes secondary to the prime question that arises when man indeed undertakes to 'make himself': in what image of his own devising shall he do so, even granted that he can be sure of the means? In fact, of course, he can be sure of neither, not of the end, nor of the means, once he enters the realm where he plays with the roots of life. Of one thing only can he be sure: of his power to move the foundations and to cause incalculable and irreversible consequences. Never was so much power coupled with so little guidance for its use." [*J. Cent. Cong. Amer. Rabbis* (January 1968), p. 27.] These remarks demonstrate that, contrary to popular belief, we are not even on the right road toward a rational understanding of and rational control over human nature and human life. It is indeed the height of irrationality triumphantly to pursue rationalized technique, while at the same time insisting that questions of ends, values, and purposes lie beyond rational discourse.

[14] It is encouraging to note that these questions are seriously being raised in other quarters —for example, by persons concerned with the decay of cities or the pollution of nature. There is a growing dissatisfaction with ethical nihilism. In fact, its tenets are unwittingly abandoned, by even its staunchest adherents, in any discussion of "what to do." For ex-

(Continued)

Should we not rather be encouraged by the fact that they considered them to be the most important questions?

As I have hinted before, our ethical dilemma is caused by the victory of modern natural science with its nonteleological view of man. We ought therefore to reexamine with great care the modern notions of nature and of man, which undermine those earlier notions that provide a basis for ethics. If we consult our common experience, we are likely to discover some grounds for believing that the questions about man and human good are far from closed. Our common experience suggests many difficulties for the modern "scientific view of man." For example, this view fails to account for the concern for justice and freedom that appears to be characteristic of all human societies.[15] It also fails to account for or to explain the fact that men have speech and not merely voice, that men can choose and act and not merely move or react. It fails to explain why men engage in moral discourse, or, for that matter, why they speak at all. Finally, the "scientific view of man" cannot account for specific inquiry itself, for why men seek to know. Might there not be something the matter with a knowledge of man that does not explain or take account of his most distinctive activities, aspirations, and concerns.[16]

Having gone this far, let me offer one suggestion as to where the difficulty might lie: in the modern understanding of knowledge. Since Bacon, as I have mentioned earlier, technology has increasingly come to be the basic justification for scientific inquiry. The end is power, not knowledge for its own sake. But power is not only the end. It is also an important *validation* of knowledge. One definitely knows that one knows only if one can make. Synthesis is held to be the ultimate proof of understanding.[17] A more radical formulation holds that one knows only what one makes: knowing *equals* making.

---

ample, in the biomedical area, everyone, including the most unreconstructed and technocratic reductionist, finds himself speaking about the use of powers for "human betterment." He has wandered unawares onto ethical ground. One cannot speak of "human betterment" without considering what is meant by *the human* and by the related notion of *the good for man*. These questions can be avoided only be asserting that practical matters reduce to tastes and power, and by confessing that the use of the phrase "human betterment" is a deception to cloak one's own will to power. In other words, these questions can be avoided only by ceasing to discuss.

[15] Consider, for example, the widespread acceptance, in the legal systems of very different societies and cultures, of the principle and the practice of third-party adjudication of disputes. And consider why, although many societies have practiced slavery, no slave-holder has preferred his own enslavement to his own freedom. It would seem that some notions of justice and freedom, as well as right and truthfulness, are constitutive for any society, and that a concern for these values may be a fundamental characteristic of "human nature."

[16] Scientists may, of course, continue to believe in righteousness or justice or truth, but these beliefs are not grounded in their "scientific knowledge" of man. They rest instead upon the receding wisdom of an earlier age.

[17] This belief, silently shared by many contemporary biologists, has recently been given the following clear expression: "One of the acid tests of understanding an object is the ability to put it together from its component parts. Ultimately, molecular biologists will attempt to subject their understanding of all structure and function to this sort of test by trying to synthesize a cell. It is of some interest to see how close we are to this goal." [P. Handler, ed. *Biology and the Future of Man* (New York: Oxford Univ. Press, 1970), p. 55.]

Yet therein lies a difficulty. If truth be the power to change or to make the object studied, then of what do we have knowledge? If there are no fixed realities, but only material upon which we may work our wills, will not "science" be merely the "knowledge" of the transient and the manipulatable? We might indeed have knowledge of the laws by which things change and the rules for their manipulation, but no knowledge of the things themselves. Can such a view of "science" yield any knowledge about the nature of man, or indeed, about the nature of anything? Our questions appear to lead back to the most basic of questions: What does it mean to know? What is it that is knowable?[18]

We have seen that the practical problems point toward and make urgent certain enduring, fundamental questions. Yet while pursuing these questions, we cannot afford to neglect the practical problems as such. Let us not forget Delgado and the "psychocivilized society." The philosophical inquiry could be rendered moot by our blind, confident efforts to dissect and redesign ourselves. While awaiting a reconstruction of theory, we must act as best we can.

What Is To Be Done?

First, we sorely need to recover some humility in the face of our awesome powers. The arguments I have presented should make apparent the folly of arrogance, of the presumption that we are wise enough to remake ourselves. Because we lack wisdom, caution is our urgent need. Or to put it another way, in the absence of that "ultimate wisdom," we can be wise enough to know that we are not wise enough. When we lack sufficient wisdom to do, wisdom consists in not doing. Caution, restraint, delay, abstention are what this second-best

[18] When an earlier version of this article was presented publicly, it was criticized by one questioner as being "antiscientific." He suggested that my remarks "were the kind that gave science a bad name." He went on to argue that, far from being the enemy of morality, the pursuit of truth was itself a highly moral activity, perhaps the highest. The relation of science and morals is a long and difficult question with an illustrious history, and it deserves a more extensive discussion than space permits. However, because some readers may share the questioner's response, I offer a brief reply. First, on the matter of reputation, we should recall that the pursuit of truth may be in tension with keeping a good name (witness Oedipus, Socrates, Galileo, Spinoza, Solzhenitsyn). For most of human history, the pursuit of truth (including "science") was not a reputable activity among the many, and was, in fact, highly suspect. Even today, it is doubtful whether more than a few appreciate knowledge as an end in itself. Science has acquired a "good name" in recent times largely because of its technological fruit; it is therefore to be expected that a disenchantment with technology will reflect badly upon science. Second, my own attack has not been directed against science, but against the use of *some* technologies and, even more, against the unexamined belief—indeed, I would say, superstition—that all biomedical technology is an unmixed blessing. I share the questioner's belief that the pursuit of truth is a highly moral activity. In fact, I am inviting him and others to join in a pursuit of the truth about whether all these new technologies are really good for us. This is a question that merits and is susceptible of serious intellectual inquiry. Finally, we must ask whether what we call "science" has a monopoly on the pursuit of truth. What is "truth"? What is knowable, and what does it mean to know? Surely, these are also questions that can be examined. Unless we do so, we shall remain ignorant about what "science" is and about what it discovers. Yet "science"—that is, modern natural science—cannot begin to answer them; they are philosophical questions, the very ones I am trying to raise at this point in the text.

(and, perhaps, only) wisdom dictates with respect to the technology for human engineering.

If we can recognize that biomedical advances carry significant social costs, we may be willing to adopt a less permissive, more critical stance toward new developments. We need to reexamine our prejudice not only that all biomedical innovation is progress, but also that it is inevitable. Precedent certainly favors the view that what can be done will be done, but is this necessarily so? Ought we not to be suspicious when technologists speak of coming developments as automatic, not subject to human control? Is there not something contradictory in the notion that we have the power to control all the untoward consequences of a technology, but lack the power to determine whether it should be developed in the first place?

What will be the likely consequences of the perpetuation of our permissive and fatalistic attitude toward human engineering? How will the large decisions be made? Technocratically and self-servingly, if our experience with previous technologies is any guide. Under conditions of laissez-faire, most technologists will pursue techniques, and most private industries will pursue profits. We are fortunate that, apart from the drug manufacturers, there are at present in the biomedical area few large industries that influence public policy. Once these appear, the voice of "the public interest" will have to shout very loudly to be heard above their whisperings in the halls of Congress. These reflections point to the need for institutional controls.

Scientists understandably balk at the notion of the regulation of science and technology. Censorship is ugly and often based upon ignorant fear; bureaucratic regulation is often stupid and inefficient. Yet there is something disingenuous about a scientist who professes concern about the social consequences of science, but who responds to every suggestion of regulation with one or both of the following: "No restrictions on scientific research," and "Technological progress should not be curtailed." Surely, to suggest that *certain* technologies ought to be regulated or forestalled is not to call for the halt of *all* technological progress (and says nothing at all about basic research). Each development should be considered on its own merits. Although the dangers of regulation cannot be dismissed, who, for example, would still object to efforts to obtain an effective, complete, global prohibition on the development, testing, and use of biological and nuclear weapons?

The proponents of laissez-faire ignore two fundamental points. They ignore the fact that not to regulate is as much a policy decision as the opposite, and that it merely postpones the time of regulation. Controls will eventually be called for—as they are now being demanded to end environmental pollution. If attempts are not made early to detect and diminish the social costs of biomedical advances by intelligent institutional regulation, the society is likely to react later with more sweeping, immoderate, and throttling controls.

The proponents of laissez-faire also ignore the fact that much of technology is already regulated. The federal government is already deep in research and development (for example, space, electronics, and weapons) and is the principal sponsor of biomedical research. One may well question the wisdom of the direction given, but one would be wrong in arguing that technology cannot survive social control. Clearly, the question is not control versus no control, but rather what kind of control, when, by whom, and for what purpose.

Means for achieving international regulation and control need to be devised. Biomedical technology can be no nation's monopoly. The need for international agreements and supervision can readily be understood if we consider the likely American response to the successful asexual reproduction of 10,000 Mao Tse-tungs.

To repeat, the basic short-term need is caution. Practically, this means that we should shift the burden of proof to the *proponents* of a new biomedical technology. Concepts of "risk" and "cost" need to be broadened to include some of the social and ethical consequences discussed earlier. The probable or possible harmful effects of the widespread use of a new technique should be anticipated and introduced as "costs" to be weighed in deciding about the *first* use. The regulatory institutions should be encouraged to exercise restraint and to formulate the grounds for saying "no." We must all get used to the idea that biomedical technology makes possible many things we should never do.

But caution is not enough. Nor are clever institutional arrangements. Institutions can be little better than the people who make them work. However worthy our intentions, we are deficient in understanding. In the *long* run, our hope can only lie in education: in a public educated about the meanings and limits of science and enlightened in its use of technology; in scientists better educated to understand the relationships between science and technology on the one hand, and ethics and politics on the other; in human beings who are as wise in the latter as they are clever in the former.

Alienated Man

KARL MARX

Karl Marx (1818–1883), together with Friedrich Engels, collaborated on *The Communist Manifesto* (1848) and wrote *Das Kapital* (1867–1888). Marx is the most important single figure in the development of the modern communist philosophy. Marx rebelled against the Hegelian philosophy and said "the most important task of the philosopher is not to know the world but to change it."

We have proceeded from the premises of political economy. We have accepted its language and its laws. We presupposed private property, the separation of labor, capital and land, and of wages, profit of capital and rent of land—likewise division of labor, competition, the concept of exchange-value, etc. On the basis of political economy itself, in its own words, we have shown that the worker sinks to the level of a commodity and becomes indeed the most wretched of commodities; that the wretchedness of the worker is in inverse proportion to the

Source: Karl Marx, *Economic and Philosophic Manuscripts of 1844,* trans. by Martin Milligan (Moscow: Progress Publishers, 1959).

power and magnitude of his production; that the necessary result of competition is the accumulation of capital in a few hands, and thus the restoration of monopoly in a more terrible form; and that finally the distinction between capitalist and land rentier, like that between the tiller of the soil and the factory worker, disappears and that the whole of society must fall apart into the two classes—the property *owners* and the propertyless *workers*.

Political economy starts with the fact of private property, but it does not explain it to us. It expresses in general, abstract formulas the *material* process through which private property actually passes, and these formulas it then takes for *laws*. It does not *comprehend* these laws, i.e., it does not demonstrate how they arise from the very nature of private property. Political economy does not disclose the source of the division between labor and capital, and between capital and land. When, for example, it defines the relationship of wages to profit, it takes the interest of the capitalists to be the ultimate cause, i.e., it takes for granted what it is supposed to explain. Similarly, competition comes in everywhere. It is explained from external circumstances. As to how far these external and apparently accidental circumstances are but the expression of a necessary course of development, political economy teaches us nothing. We have seen how exchange itself appears to it as an accidental fact. The only wheels which political economy sets in motion are *greed* and the war *amongst the greedy—competition*.

Precisely because political economy does not grasp the way the movement is connected, it was possible to oppose, for instance, the doctrine of competition to the doctrine of monopoly, the doctrine of the freedom of the crafts to the doctrine of the guild, the doctrine of the division of landed property to the doctrine of the big estate—for competition, freedom of the crafts and the division of landed property were explained and comprehended only as accidental, premeditated and violent consequences of monopoly, of the guild system, and of feudal property, not as their necessary, inevitable and natural consequences.

Now, therefore, we have to grasp the essential connection between private property, greed, and the separation of labor, capital and landed property; between exchange and competition, value and the devaluation of men, monopoly and competition, etc.—the connection between this whole estrangement and the *money* system.

Do not let us go back to a fictitious primordial condition as the political economist does, when he tries to explain. Such a primordial condition explains nothing; it merely pushes the question away into a gray nebulous distance. It assumes in the form of a fact, of an event, what the economist is supposed to deduce—namely, the necessary relationship between two things—between, for example, division of labor and exchange. Theology in the same way explains the origin of evil by the fall of man; that is, it assumes as a fact, in historical form, what has to be explained.

We proceed from an economic fact *of the present*.

The worker becomes all the poorer the more wealth he produces, the more his production increases in power and size. The worker becomes an ever cheaper commodity the more commodities he creates. With the *increasing value* of the world of things proceeds in direct proportion the *devaluation* of the world of men. Labor produces not only commodities: it produces itself and the worker as a *commodity*—and this in the same general proportion in which it produces commodities.

This fact expresses merely that the object which labor produces—labor's product—confronts it as *something alien*, as a *power independent* of the producer. The product of labor is labor which has been embodied in an object, which has become material: it is the *objectifications* of labor. Labor's realization is its objectification. In the sphere of political economy this realization of labor appears as *loss of realization* for the workers; objectification as *loss of the object* and *bondage to it;* appropriation as *estrangement,* as *alienation.*

So much does labor's realization appear as loss of realization that the worker loses realization to the point of starving to death. So much does objectification appear as loss of the object that the worker is robbed of the objects most necessary not only for his life but for his work. Indeed, labor itself becomes an object which he can obtain only with the greatest effort and with the most irregular interruptions. So much does the appropriation of the object appear as estrangement that the more objects the worker produces the less he can possess and the more he falls under the sway of his product, capital.

All these consequences result from the fact that the worker is related to the *product of his labor* as to an *alien* object. For on this premise it is clear that the more the worker spends himself, the more powerful becomes the alien world of objects which he creates over and against himself, the poorer he himself—his inner world—becomes, the less belongs to him as his own. It is the same in religion. The more man puts into God, the less he retains in himself. The worker puts his life into the object; but now his life no longer belongs to him but to the object. Hence, the greater this activity, the greater is the worker's lack of objects. Whatever the product of his labor is, he is not. Therefore the greater this product, the less is he himself. The *alienation* of the worker in his product means not only that this labor becomes an object, an *external existence,* but that it exists *outside him,* independently, as something alien to him, and that it becomes a power on its own confronting him. It means that the life which he has conferred on the object confronts him as something hostile and alien.

Let us now look more closely at the *objectification,* at the production of the worker; and in it at the *estrangement,* the *loss* of the object, of his product.

The worker can create nothing without *nature,* without the *sensuous external world*. It is the material on which his labor is realized, in which it is active, from which and by means of which it produces.

But just as nature provides labor with the *means of life* in the sense that labor cannot *live* without objects on which to operate, on the other hand, it also provides the *means of life* in the more restricted sense, i.e., the means for the physical subsistence of the *worker* himself.

Thus the more the worker by his labor *appropriates* the external world, hence sensuous nature, the more he deprives himself of *means of life* in a double manner: first, in that the sensuous external world more and more ceases to be an object belonging to his labor—to be his labor's *means of life;* and secondly, in that it more and more ceases to be *means of life* in the immediate sense, means for the physical subsistence of the worker.

In both respects, therefore, the worker becomes a slave of his object, first, in that he receives an *object of labor,* i.e., in that he receives *work;* and secondly, in that he receives *means of subsistence.* Therefore, it enables him to exist, first, as a *worker;* and, second as a *physical subject.* The height of this bondage is that it is only as a *worker* that he continues to maintain himself as a *physical subject,* and that it is only as a *physical subject* that he is a *worker.*

(The laws of political economy express the estrangement of the worker in his object thus: the more the worker produces, the less he has to consume; the more values he creates, the more valueless, the more unworthy he becomes; the better formed his product, the more deformed becomes the worker; the more civilized his object, the more barbarous becomes the worker; the more powerful labor becomes, the more powerless becomes the worker; the more ingenious labor becomes, the less ingenious becomes the worker and the more he becomes nature's bondsman.)

Political economy conceals the estrangement inherent in the nature of labor by not considering the direct relationship between the worker (labor) *and production.* It is true that labor produces for the rich wonderful things—but for the worker it produces privation. It produces palaces—but for the worker, hovels. It produces beauty—but for the worker, deformity. It replaces labor by machines, but it throws a section of the workers back to a barbarous type of labor, and it turns the other workers into machines. It produces intelligence—but for the worker stupidity, cretinism.

The direct relationship of labor to its products is the relationship of the worker to the objects of his production. The relationship of the man of means to the objects of production and to production itself is only a *consequence* of this first relationship—and confirms it. We shall consider this other aspect later.

When we ask, then, what is the essential relationship of labor we are asking about the relationship of the *worker* to production.

Till now we have been considering the estrangement, the alienation of the worker only in one of its aspects, i.e., the worker's *relationship to the products of his labor.* But the estrangement is manifested not only in the result but in the *act of production,* within the *producing activity,* itself. How could the worker come to face the product of his activity as a stranger, were it not that in the very act of production he was estranging himself from himself? The product is after all but the summary of the activity, of production. If then the product of labor is alienation, production itself must be active alienation, the alienation of activity, the activity of alienation. In the estrangement of the object of labor is merely summarized the estrangement, the alienation, in the activity of labor itself.

What, then, constitutes the alienation of labor?

First, the fact that labor is *external* to the worker, i.e., it does not belong to his essential being; that in his work, therefore, he does not affirm himself but denies himself, does not feel content but unhappy, does not develop freely his physical and mental energy but mortifies his body and ruins his mind. The worker therefore only feels himself outside his work, and in his work feels outside himself. He is at home when he is not working, and when he is working he is not at home. His labor is therefore not voluntary, but coerced; it is *forced labor*. It is therefore not the satisfaction of a need; it is merely a *means* to satisfy needs external to it. Its alien character emerges clearly in the fact that as soon as no physical or other compulsion exists, labor is shunned like the plague. External labor, labor in which man alienates himself, is a labor of self-sacrifice, of mortification. Lastly, the external character of labor for the worker appears in the fact that it is not his own, but someone else's, that it does not belong to him, that in it he belongs, not to himself, but to another. Just as in religion the spontaneous activity of the human imagination, of the human brain and the human heart, operates independently of the individual—that is, operates on him as an alien, divine or diabolical activity—so is the worker's activity not his spontaneous activity. It belongs to another; it is the loss of his self.

As a result, therefore, man (the worker) only feels himself freely active in his animal functions—eating, drinking, procreating, or at most in his dwelling and in dressing-up, etc.; and in his human functions he no longer feels himself to be anything but an animal. What is animal becomes human and what is human becomes animal.

Certainly eating, drinking, procreating, etc., are also genuinely human functions. But abstractly taken, separated from the sphere of all other human activity and turned into sole and ultimate ends, they are animal functions.

We have considered the act of estranging practical human activity, labor, in two of its aspects. (1) The relation of the worker to the *product of labor* as an alien object exercising power over him. This relation is at the same time the relation to the sensuous external world, to the objects of nature, as an alien world inimically opposed to him. (2) The relation of labor to the *act of production* within the *labor* process. This relation is the relation of the worker to his own activity as an alien activity not belonging to him; it is activity as suffering, strength as weakness, begetting as emasculating, the worker's *own* physical and mental energy, his personal life indeed, what is life but activity?—as an activity which is turned against him, independent of him and not belonging to him. Here we have *self-estrangement*, as previously we had estrangement of the *thing*.

We have still a third aspect of *estranged labor* to deduce from the two already considered.

Man is a species being, not only because in practice and in theory he adopts the species as his object (his own as well as those of other things), but—and this is only another way of expressing it—also because he treats himself as the actual, living species; because he treats himself as a *universal* and therefore a free being.

The life of the species, both in man and in animals, consists physically in the fact that man (like the animal) lives on inorganic nature; and the more universal man is compared with an animal, the more universal is the sphere of inorganic nature on which he lives. Just as plants, animals, stones, air, light, etc., constitute theoretically a part of human consciousness, partly as objects of natural science, partly as objects of art—his spiritual inorganic nature, spiritual nourishment which he must first prepare to make palatable and digestible—so also in the realm of practice they constitute a part of human life and human activity. Physically man lives only on these products of nature, whether they appear in the form of food, heating, clothes, a dwelling, etc. The universality of man appears in practice precisely in the universality which makes all nature his *inorganic* body—both inasmuch as nature is (1) his direct means of life, and (2) the material, the object, and the instrument of his life activity. Nature is man's *inorganic body*—nature, that is, in so far as it is not itself the human body. Man *lives* on nature—means that nature is his *body*, with which he must remain in continuous interchange if he is not to die. That man's physical and spiritual life is linked to nature means simply that nature is linked to itself, for man is a part of nature.

In estranging from man (1) nature, and (2) himself, his own active functions, his life activity, estranged labor estranges the *species* from man. It changes for him the *life of the species* into a means of individual life. First it estranges the life of the species and individual life, and secondly it makes individual life in its abstract form the purpose of the life of the species, likewise in its abstract and estranged form.

Indeed, labor, *life-activity, productive life* itself, appears in the first place merely as a *means* of satisfying a need—the need to maintain physical existence. Yet the productive life is the life of the species. It is life-engendering life. The whole character of a species—its species character—is contained in the character of its life activity; and free, conscious activity is man's species character. Life itself appears only as a *means to life*.

The animal is immediately one with its life activity. It does not distinguish itself from it. It is *its life activity*. Man makes his life activity itself the object of his will and of his consciousness. He has conscious life activity. It is not a determination with which he directly merges. Conscious life activity distinguishes man immediately from animal life activity. It is just because of this that he is a species being. Or rather, it is only because he is a species being that he is a conscious being, i.e., that his own life is an object for him. Only because of that is his activity free activity. Estranged labor reverses this relationship, so that it is just because man is a conscious being that he makes his life activity, his *essential* being, a mere means to his *existence*.

In creating a *world of objects* by his practical activity, in *his work upon* inorganic nature, man proves himself a conscious species being, i.e., as a being that treats the species as its own essential being, or that treats itself as a species being. Admittedly animals also produce. They build themselves nests, dwellings, like the bees, beavers, ants, etc. But an animal only produces what it immediately needs for itself or its young. It produces one-sidedly, whilst man produces universally. It produces only under the dominion of immediate physical need, whilst man produces even when he is free from physical need and only truly produces in freedom therefrom. An animal produces only itself, whilst man reproduces the whole of nature. An animal's product belongs immediately to its physical body, whilst man freely confronts his product. An animal forms things in accordance with the standard and the need of the species to which it belongs, whilst man knows how to produce in accordance with the standard of every species, and knows how to apply everywhere the inherent standard to the object. Man therefore also forms things in accordance with the laws of beauty.

It is just in his work upon the objective world, therefore, that man first really proves himself to be a *species being*. This production is his active species life.

Through and because of this production, nature appears as *his* work and his reality. The object of labor is, therefore, the *objectification of man's species life:* for he duplicates himself not only, as in consciousness, intellectually, but also actively, in reality, and therefore he contemplates himself in a world that he has created. In tearing away from man the object of his production, therefore, estranged labor tears from him his *species life,* his real objectivity as a member of the species and transforms his advantage over animals into the disadvantage that his inorganic body, nature, is taken away from him.

Similarly, in degrading spontaneous, free, activity, to a means, estranged labor makes man's species life a means to his physical existence.

The consciousness which man has of his species is thus transformed by estrangement in such a way that species life becomes for him a means.

Estranged labor turns thus:

(3) *Man's species being,* both nature and his spiritual species property, into a being *alien* to him, into a *means* to his *individual existence.* It estranges from man his own body, as well as external nature and his spiritual essence, his *human being.*

(4) *An* immediate consequence of the fact that man is estranged from the product of his labor, from his life activity, from his species being is the *estrangement of man* from *man.* When man confronts himself, he confronts the *other* man. What applies to a man's relation to his work, to the product of his labor and to himself, also holds of a man's relation to the other man, and to the other man's labor and object of labor.

In fact, the proposition that man's species nature is estranged from him means that one man is estranged from the other, as each of them is from man's essential nature.

The estrangement of man, and in fact every relationship in which man stands to himself, is first realized and expressed in the relationship in which a man stands to other men.

Hence within the relationship of estranged labor each man views the other in accordance with the standard and the relationship in which he finds himself as a worker.

We took our departure from a fact of political economy—the estrangement of the worker and his production. We have formulated this fact in conceptual terms as *estranged, alienated* labor. We have analyzed this concept—hence analyzing merely a fact of political economy.

Let us now see, further, how the concept of estranged, alienated labor must express and present itself in real life.

If the product of labor is alien to me, if it confronts me as an alien power, to whom, then, does it belong?

If my own activity does not belong to me, if it is an alien, a coerced activity, to whom, then, does it belong?

To a being *other* than myself.

Who is this being?

The *gods?* To be sure, in the earliest times the principal production (for example, the building of temples, etc., in Egypt, India and Mexico) appears to be in the service of the gods, and the product belongs to the gods. However, the gods on their own were never the lords of labor. No more was *nature*. And what a contradiction it would be if, the more man subjugated nature by his labor and the more the miracles of the gods were rendered superfluous by the miracles of industry, the more man were to renounce the joy of production and the enjoyment of the product in favor of these powers.

The *alien* being, to whom labor and the product of labor belongs, in whose service labor is done and for whose benefit the product of labor is provided, can only be *man* himself.

If the product of labor does not belong to the worker, if it confronts him as an alien power, then this can only be because it belongs to some *other man than the worker*. If the worker's activity is a torment to him, to another it must be *delight* and his life's joy. Not the gods, not nature, but only man himself can be this alien power over man.

We must bear in mind the previous proposition that man's relation to himself only becomes for him *objective* and *actual* through his relation to the other man. Thus, if the product of his labor, his labor *objectified,* is for him an *alien,* hostile, powerful object independent of him, then his position towards it is such that someone else is master of this object, someone who is alien, hostile, powerful, and independent of him. If his own activity is to him related as an unfree activity, then he is related to it as an activity performed in the service, under the dominion, the coercion, and the yoke of another man.

Every self-estrangement of man, from himself and from nature, appears in the relation in which he places himself and nature to men other than and differentiated from himself. For this reason religious self-estrangement necessarily appears in the relationship of the layman to the priest, or again to a mediator, etc., since we are here dealing with the intellectual world. In the real practical world self-estrangement can only become manifest through the real practical relationship to other men. The medium through which estrangement takes place is itself *practical*. Thus through estranged labor man not only creates his relationship to the object and to the act of production as to men that are alien and hostile to him; he also creates the relationship in which other men stand to his production and to his product, and the relationship in which he stands to these other men. Just as he creates his own production as the loss of his reality, as his punishment; his own product as a loss, as a product not belonging to him; so he creates the domination of the person who does not produce over production and over the product. Just as he estranges his own activity from himself, so he confers to the stranger an activity which is not his own.

We have until now only considered this relationship from the standpoint of the worker and later we shall be considering it also from the standpoint of the non-worker.

Through *estranged, alienated labor,* then, the worker produces the relationship to this labor of a man alien to labor and standing outside it. The relationship of the worker to labor creates the relation to it of the capitalist (or whatever one chooses to call the master of labor). *Private property* is thus the product, the result, the necessary consequence, of *alienated labor,* of the external relation of the worker to nature and to himself.

Private property thus results by analysis from the concept of *alienated labor,* i.e., of *alienated man,* of estranged labor, of estranged life, of *estranged* man.

True, it is as a result of the *movement of private property* that we have obtained the concept of *alienated labor (of alienated life)* from political economy. But on analysis of this concept it becomes clear that though private property appears to be the source, the cause of alienated labor, it is rather its consequence, just as the gods are *originally* not the cause but the effect of man's intellectual confusion. Later this relationship becomes reciprocal.

Only at the last culmination of the development of private property does this, its secret, appear again, namely, that on the one hand it is the *product* of alienated labor, and that on the other it is the *means* by which labor alienates itself, the *realization of this alienation.*

This exposition immediately sheds light on various hitherto unsolved conflicts.

1. Political economy starts from labor as the real soul of production; yet to labor it gives nothing, and to private property everything. Confronting this contradiction, Proudhon has decided in favor of labor against private property. We understand, however, that this apparent contradiction is the contradiction of *estranged labor* with itself, and that political economy has merely formulated the laws of estranged labor.

We also understand, therefore, that *wages* and *private property* are identical: since the product, as the object of labor, pays for labor itself, therefore the wage is but a necessary consequence of labor's estrangement. After all, in the wage of labor, labor does not appear as an end in itself but as the servant of the wage. We shall develop this point later, and meanwhile will only derive some conclusions.

An enforced increase of wages (disregarding all other difficulties, including the fact that it would only be by force, too, that higher wages, being an anomaly, could be maintained) would therefore be nothing but *better payment for the slave,* and would not win either for the worker or for labor their human status and dignity.

Indeed, even the *equality of wages* demanded by Proudhon only transforms the relationship of the present-day worker to his labor into the relationship of all men to labor. Society is then conceived as an abstract capitalist.

Wages are a direct consequence of estranged labor, and estranged labor is the direct cause of private property. The downfall of the one must involve the downfall of the other.

2. From the relationship of estranged labor to private property it follows further that the emancipation of society from private property, etc., from servitude, is expressed in the *political* form of the *emancipation of the workers;* not that *their* emancipation alone is at stake, but because the emancipation of the workers contains universal human emancipation—and it contains this, because the whole of human servitude is involved in the relation of the worker to production, and every relation of servitude is but a modification and consequence of this relation.

Just as we have derived the concept of *private property* from the concept of *estranged, alienated labor* by *analysis,* so we can develop every *category* of political economy with the help of these two factors; and we shall find again in each category, e.g., trade, competition, capital, money, only a *definite* and *developed expression* of these first elements.

Before considering this aspect, however, let us try to solve two problems.

1. To define the general *nature of private property,* as it has arisen as a result of estranged labor, in its relation to *truly human* and *social property.*

2. We have accepted the *estrangement of labor,* its *alienation,* as a fact, and we have analyzed this fact. How, we now ask, does *man* come to *alienate,* to estrange, *his labor?* How is this estrangement rooted in the nature of human development? We have already gone a long way to the solution of this problem by *transforming* the question of the *origin of private property* into the question of the relation of *alienated labor* to the course of humanity's development. For when one speaks of *private property,* one thinks of dealing with something external to man. When one speaks of labor, one is directly dealing with man himself. This new formulation of the question already contains its solution.

As to (1): The general nature of private property and its relation to truly human property.

Alienated labor has resolved itself for us into two elements which mutually condition one another, or which are but different expressions of one and the same relationship. *Appropriation* appears as *estrangement,* as *alienation;* and *alienation* appears as *appropriation, estrangement* as true introduction into society.

We have considered the one side—*alienated* labor in relation to the *worker* himself, i.e., the *relation of alienated labor to itself.* The *property relation of the non-worker to the worker and to labor* we have found as the product, the necessary outcome of this relationship. *Private property,* as the material, summary expression of alienated labor, embraces both relations—the *relation of the worker to work and to the produce of his labor and to the non-worker,* and the relation of the *non-worker to the worker and to the product of his labor.*

Having seen that in relation to the worker who *appropriates* nature by means of his labor, this appropriation appears as estrangement, his own spontaneous activity as activity for another and as activity of another, vitality as a sacrifice of life, production of the object as loss of the object to an alien power, to an *alien* person—we shall now consider the relation to the worker, to labor and its object of this person who is *alien,* to labor and the worker.

First it has to be noted that everything which appears in the worker as an *activity of alienation, of estrangement,* appears in the non-worker as a *state of alienation, of estrangement.*

Secondly, that the worker's *real, practical attitude* in production and to the product (as a state of mind) appears in the non-worker confronting him as a *theoretical* attitude.

Thirdly, the non-worker does everything against the worker which the worker does against himself; but he does not do against himself what he does against the worker.

Let us look more closely at these three relations.

[At this point the first manuscript breaks off unfinished.]

Three

The Arts and Mass Culture: Shaping Consciousness

> A society consists in the common way of life which its members practise; if
> they become so bored with this way of life that they begin to practise a different
> one, the old society is dead even if no one noticed its death.
>   —R. G. Collingwood

Introduction

"Aesthetics" is the name of that branch of philosophy that studies the concepts with which we try to comprehend the fine arts and natural beauty and
sublimity. It may also go under the name "philosophy of art."

An aesthetician asks such questions as what is art and what is not art? Is
Bach's music art and Frank Zappa's not art? Is a Rolls Royce art and a Ford
Pinto not art? Marcel Duchamp once entered a urinal in an art show and
entitled it "Fountain." If you were a museum director, would you consider it
art and put it on display as such? Aestheticians ask about the evaluation of
art objects: Are there criteria that we can agree on and mutually apply in
order to pronounce one object more beautiful than another? Is the beauty of
nature judged by the same criteria as the beauty of art? Each of us has
written poems, or drawn pictures, or composed a tune, or done a dance, or
acted in a play, and so forth. Some poems, or perhaps all, you threw away,
ashamed to have anyone else see them or read them aloud. You must have
some idea of what makes a poem a "good" one or you wouldn't have done
that. Perhaps you gave up "acting" after your first play, judging yourself less
talented than others. Trying to make our criteria for comparative judgments
of value explicit is one of the tasks to which aestheticians apply themselves.

Another aesthetical question is: what are the functions of art? These may
be multiple, although some of them may not be thought to be the function
of them as art per se. Art may instruct us; from *Moby Dick* we learn a
great deal about whales and whaling. However, someone might argue
that we are also instructed by a book on accounting, which can in no
way be considered a work of fine art; therefore, the function of instruction is
not per se a function of art. This kind of argument supposes that *the* function
of art objects is one that is not shared by other objects, that it has to be a
function peculiar to art.

Art may function to entertain us; it may refresh our perceptions by a novel arrangement of material, such as paint, words, and movement; it may function as a mode of expression; it may uplift us, as religious music does; it may arouse our moral indignation, as *Catch-22* does; it may provide an incentive to action, as a war dance or a stirring military march does; it may serve us as historical data about the manners and morals of another time, as Homer's *Iliad* does; it may rationalize a political point of view, as some of Shakespeare's plays did; it may serve as an ideological tool for shaping our consciousness by those who control the arts.

In this chapter our essays concentrate on the ideological function of art, or so-called art, as in Collingwood's case. Collingwood points out that "a society consists in the common way of life which its members practise." Humans are subjects, not objects; as such, they behave in learned ways. In the main, a society consists of persons who act in coordinated ways; they learned common ways to behave; they also mutually recognize that each has learned these common ways. The boss knows that the employee knows that he or she is expected to be at work at eight o'clock and the employee knows that the boss expects him or her to be at work at eight o'clock; and, further, each knows that the other knows that each of them knows the above. These mutually known knowings about common behavior patterns collectively may be called a culture.

Shakespeare suggests that all the world is a stage on which we act our parts. Being born into and learning a culture means that a great part of our life has been written out for us; we are truly actors going through an assigned part; our stage parts are not, of course, written down to the last detail but that they are sketched out in considerable detail is evident when you think of the altered way of life you would have had were you born in another country, such as China or India or Indonesia. Had you been born there, you would not be acting as you do now; and the fact that most Chinese act in their cultural ways and that most of us in the United States act in our cultural ways shows that we did not freely choose our parts to play; we simply inherited them as laid out.

What accounts for this remarkable adherence to an inherited culture? How does a culture manage to maintain itself when obviously it could be different than it is? Members of a culture may have a certain degree of conviction about their way of life and may strive to continue to act in their usual behavior patterns, particularly if they are challenged by persons of another culture. A culture may be maintained despite persons' desire for change by making them feel helpless to change the culture; they may have been isolated from each other in such a way that the new mutual knowings required for a new culture never get articulated or learned sufficiently to replace the established mutual knowings. Or it may be maintained because people never consciously think about their mutual knowings, acting out of habit only; like the actor in the 200th performance of a part, we may simply somnambulate through our lines.

Culture, in our use, is a name for a group of persons' mutually recognized behavior patterns. As suggested above, we may be relatively unconscious and relatively conscious about our culture or parts of it. Our consciousness of it increases as the sharpness of a challenge to it increases. Let's call an articulated consciousness of a culture an *ideology;* it is a formulation of the ideas that persons have to have in mind in order to have the mutual knowings that they have as persons of a culture. Once we become conscious of our culture, we are in a position to look on it as a subject matter of which we may approve or disapprove, evaluate it as something good or as something bad and in need of change. Becoming conscious of our cultural patterns is a first step to rethinking them; once we are in the position of rethinking, we are in a position to ask each other whether or not our established mutual knowings should be altered, whether our actor's parts should be rewritten.

The essays in this chapter are conscious attempts to think about the role the arts, particularly the popular arts of radio, television, and film, play in maintaining our culture and its ideological support. Before turning to the essays on art, we should appreciate the enormous complexity of our mutual knowings that undergird our culture, and grasp, at least in outline, what we have to know to take a critical stance toward it, and realize what must be done to alter a culture significantly. This background will give a better setting in which to place these essays on the ideological role of the arts.

An interesting monograph, *Outline of Cultural Materials* (published by Human Relations Area Files, Inc.), provides an outline of the mutual knowings that need to be described by anyone interested in grasping the ideology of a culture. It has eighty-eight categories; we list a few to give you an idea of what they are: "geography, language, records, agriculture, clothing, adornment, exploitative activities, structures, energy and power, machines, finance, labor, living standards and routines, fine arts, individuation and mobility, social stratification, interpersonal relations, family, kinship, community, political behavior, justice, armed forces, sickness, death, religious beliefs, numbers and measures, sex, ideas about nature and man, socialization, education."

Under the category of interpersonal relations, for example, we find several subcategories. We list the subcategories to give you an idea of the kind of breakdown each category receives: "Social relationships and groups; Friendships; Cliques; Visiting and hospitality; Sodalities [fellowships]; Etiquette; Ethics; Ingroup antagonisms; Brawls, riots and banditry."

Digging deeper into the detail, we find under the subcategory of Ingroup antagonisms: "prevalence and importance of antagonisms within the society; sources (e.g., economic deprivation, sexual rivalry, political repression, ethnic and religious cleavages, rigor of socialization or social control); expression in individual behavior (e.g., snobbishness, intentional impoliteness ridicule, insults, vituperation); prevalence, causes and forms of quarrels; participants (e.g., husband and wife, business competitors, rival claimants to property); manifestations (e.g., verbal exchanges, fist fights, duels); reaction of onlookers; repression and control of aggression; etc."

Becoming conscious of your culture requires a great deal of sophistication; the descriptive task is quite enormous. It also requires assuming a certain detachment. A culture or a portion of it may become outmoded because the established behavior patterns are inadequate responses to changed conditions of life. Notice that more TV programs are presenting divorced adults; the increase in divorces is a changed situation that calls for different modes of behavior with children and other adults than is familiar to persons accustomed to live their whole lives with a single mate. The TV programs provide new behavior models that divorced people may emulate. Here are some other cultural changes listed by a philosophy student, in the order of importance given by him: (1) greater sexual freedom, (2) the use of drugs, (3) the decrease of power and influence of organized religion, (4) a greater number of educated people, (5) a movement away from accumulation of material goods and toward a reevaluation of the values of a materialistic society, (6) the politicalization of Third World people, (7) rapid technological advance, (8) an increased tendency to reexamine the value of established moral codes, and (9) a widening distrust in the credibility of government and authority.

Besides having a self-conscious description of a culture and a list of changed conditions of life with its concomitant cultural changes, we have to take an evaluative attitude toward them. Are these cultural changes desirable? Are they the best responses to the changed conditions? To know this you have to know what they are responses to. Is greater sexual freedom a behavioral response to a changed medical technology of birth control and abortion? It may not be a "liberating" response to birth control technology. Instead, it may be a desperate search for loving ties with others because the larger extended family has shrunk to the nuclear family of parents and children; the more extended family of grandparents, aunts, uncles, cousins flourishes only with stable geographical proximity; with increased mobility, the only family that stays together is the one that moves together. Displacement from the farm to the city brought about by industrialization, and/or search for better jobs and transfers to another branch of the business has led people to move. Perhaps the behavior pattern of sexual "freedom" is mislabeled; maybe it is a response to familial isolation. Seen as a response to alienation, changes in sexual patterns may be evaluated differently. Or we may be bored with our culture and seek excitement in sex. Cultural changes may not be what they seem; we have to dig beneath the journalistic labels to see what is really happening.

Supposing that it is worth our trouble to evaluate our established culture and its changes because we do not want our actor's parts to be written for us or we do not want them to just "happen" to us, a critical evaluation has to be supplemented with the projection of an ideal culture. We do not want to spend our life just running from our actor's parts; we want other, new, better, more fulfilling roles to play. Since these roles are not played out in isolation but in the company of others, we have to mutually establish new behavior patterns in order to establish a new culture because a culture, as we saw, exists by virtue of mutual knowings. These new mutual knowings must be articulated, disseminated, and learned in the company of others. Art can play a positive role here; it need not be used merely to reinforce a given culture, it may be an instrument in the projection and creation of a new one.

The articulated ideology of a new culture will remain a dream, a Utopian scheme, however, unless effective action is taken to bring it about. This may involve displacing people who presently wield the most power; that is, it may require a political revolution. But that is only part of the story; how does one use political revolution to make cultural changes? Do you use it to establish a return to the "old-time religion" or to advance to some new (to us) Eastern religion? Do we try to strengthen the family? Decentralize our government? Do away with private property? To say that any of these is the way to proceed is to suppose that they are the central dynamic factors in a culture; changing religious, or familial, or governmental, or economic behavior patterns has to be shown to have an effect on other cultural behavior patterns. To establish such cause–effect relations in culture requires an elaborate theory of society. Perhaps the best-worked-out one is provided by Marxism; it digs deep into the complex of capitalist relations and its effects on human beings; it criticizes the behavior patterns of capitalism and maintains that these affect all other cultural relations; it projects an ideal that has proved attractive to a large portion of the human race. From the Marxist perspective, art in the capitalist cultures serves the purpose of maintaining a capitalist ideology in the minds of its members; likewise, from the capitalist perspective, socialist art purveys a socialist ideology and shapes the consciousness of its culture's members into commitment to socialism. As Meredith Tax concludes in one of this chapter's essays, art is not neutral.

In summary, someone who wanted to write his or her own part for life would have to formulate an ideology. This would involve (1) a description of the present culture's behavior patterns and the mutual knowings under-girding it; (2) a list of the changed or changing or expected changes in the conditions of life; (3) an evaluation of the prevailing and changing behavioral responses to the conditions of life; (4) a projection of an ideal culture that will replace the present one, the ideal culture being better suited to the changed and changing conditions of life; (5) and the formulation of a theory of the dynamics of culture.

R. G. Collingwood tries to show that much of what passes for art is falsely called art; amusement art is one such false art. For Collingwood, "Art has something to do with emotion." True art is an expression of emotion; expression is something under our control; an emotion that gets expressed, then, too, is under our control and becomes something of which we are conscious and which we consciously form. Collingwood thinks of an emotion as a charge; it is first excited and then discharged. A child gets excited because a cap is on its head that wants removing; initially, "he is conscious of having an emotion, but not conscious of what this emotion is. All he is consicous of is a perturbation or excitement, which he feels going on within him, but of whose nature he is ignorant." At this point, the child "betrays" emotion by kicking, crying, screaming. It is only later when the child learns to express himself that he identifies what he feels; "I am hot and I want my cap off" expresses specifically what he feels and wants. Expression brings control over his emotion; it no longer controls him; his expression leads to discharge of his emotion in appropriate action (getting someone to remove the cap). Art has a civilizing function, according to Collingwood. Of course, not every expression is as banal as the one about caps. We live in complex situations, none of them exactly like any other; our emotional responses cannot be catalogued in a standard list; in fact, the most creative art contributes to the formation of new emotions; words like "anger," "love," and "hope" *name* emotions but do not *express* them; "Othello" expresses jealousy and anger; Othello's is a specific emotion; the whole play, not the words "jealousy" and "anger," expresses Othello's emotions. The "business of an artist" who is creating "art proper" is not to express just his or her own emotions; the artist should be the spokesperson for the community. Thus, the artist's task and art's function is to civilize all of us; the artist helps us to identify, make us conscious of, and helps us to control the charged excitations induced by our complex cultural situations.

Amusement art is not "art proper." It is not the expression of emotion; instead, it is the *evocation* of emotion. The true artist does not know before the expression of an emotion what emotion he or she has; true art is a voyage of discovery. Expression of art has a cognitive function; we teach ourselves about ourselves. Amusement artists, on the other hand, like engineers, design the amusement art with an emotive end already in mind; amusement art has a manipulative, not a cognitive, function.

Most so-called art in our time is amusement art. It performs the ideological function in our time that *panem et circenses* (bread and circuses) did in Roman times; it relieves our boredom. "The kinds of work on which the existence of a civilization like ours most obviously depends is an intolerable drudgery; . . . [amusement arts constitute] the feverish attempts to dispel this boredom by more amusement or by dangerous or criminal occupations. . . ."

Amusement art is able to keep a civilization's discontents in thrall because it evokes the charge of emotion in its consumers and, by the device of make-believe, discharges those emotions within the context of the art itself; the emotions excited are not used to accomplish anything useful in society; they do not lead to action.

We said that aestheticians ask what art is and what art is not. Collingwood's ideological analysis helps us to see why this is an important question. We have to learn to look around and ask what is art proper, what is amusement art (not art proper) in order to escape the manipulation of amusement artists.

Meredith Tax challenges the art-for-art's-sake orientation toward art. This orientation looks on art as something good for its own sake, as something that has its own distinctive value. We saw this orientation emerge in the argument that *Moby Dick's* instructiveness about whales and whaling was not an artistic function per se because accounting books also instruct and they are not really art. Tax does not accept this kind of argument. The fact that art works and nonart works might share functions does not lead her to conclude that such functions are not the functions of art per se. The advocates of art-for-art's-sake try to seal art off from other parts of life; the distinction between art and nonart, for them, requires a peculiar and isolated function for art. But Tax, in recalling her literary training, found that the "meaning" of the literary monuments she studied—"just their barefaced everyday philistine literal meaning"—was ignored. "And so we went through all the great works of literature, works which were often, at least until the modern period, passionately ideological, as if we had blinkers on."

In "the modern period," artists' productions have been ruled by what Marx called "commodity fetishism." She goes on to claim that "Most critical theory as currently practised is an extension of this commodity fetishism into the realm of culture." Tax is saying that modern art and critical discussions of it are not what they seem. We are cowed into thinking of art as something wondrous, strange, disconnected, peculiar, and with its own value. But it is not that at all. Attend to her explanation of "commodity fetishism" and how it is a feature of a bourgeois culture. If you have been feeling a bit disconnected with modern plays, poetry, music, dance, and so forth, it may be that, as Tax argues, it is the product of a "high-brow" culture that serves the bourgeois political interests. It is not art-for-art's-sake at all, but the instrument of a particular political orientation with which you are not connected or with which you wish to be disconnected. Earlier in this introduction, we talked about mislabeling a response; we said that easier and more sexual alliances may not be a liberation because of birth control technology but may be a search for affective relations with more people in an alienated racial environment. Here Tax tries to make us look at modern art as a product of commodity fetishism; she gives it a label that may be new to you; you may then come to reevaluate modern art now that it is seen as a response to a bourgeois political orientation. Trying to rethink our culture requires trying to redescribe it, to make it look unfamiliar and strange again; redescription gives us a detachment attitude because it breaks our habitual attachments.

We can introduce some corroborating testimony for Tax's thesis by noting some remarks of Robert Scheer's in his article, "Nelson Rockefeller Takes Care of Everybody" (*Playboy,* October 1975). Rockefeller's interest in the arts is discussed by Scheer. Rockefeller gave a speech at the Museum of Modern Art; "His great observation, then as so often, was that ideas and art need not be threatening to the rich of this country if only the rich will learn to manage these properly." Scheer then reports on Nancy Hank's service to Rockefeller; she was a long-time employee of Rockefeller's; now she chairs the federal government's National Endowment for the Arts. Scheer reports, "Art has its place, all right, and Nancy has worked out a scheme to make sure it doesn't become a public issue. For those interested in the subject, I would recommend a reading of *The Performing Arts*—the Rockefeller-panel reports on the future of theater, dance and music in America, which Nancy told me contain ten-year plans already implemented to prevent the socialization of American art."

With **Gunther Anders's** essay we get to television, the most dominant, omnipresent, mass culture device of our society. If there is anything to which we need a detached attitude, it is TV. How are we to redescribe our TV-watching behavior? What's really going on as we sit before the "boob tube"?

Anders claims that we aren't TV watchers, we're "consumers." Further, we're mass consumers of a mass product. What does this mass consumption do to us? It makes us into the "mass man." Further, we are not paid for this job of working at converting ourselves; "the homeworker, instead of receiving wages for his work, must pay for it by buying the means of production (the receiving sets and, in many countries, also the broadcasts) by the use of which he becomes transformed into mass man. In other words, he pays for selling himself: he must purchase the very unfreedom he himself helps to produce."

Anders points out, pertinent to our job of redescribing our culture, "Needless to say, this mass consumption is not usually called by its true name. On the contrary, it is represented as favoring the rebirth of the family and of privacy—an understandable hypocrisy." Note particularly how he redescribes "news broadcasts." On this topic he comes "to the heart of our subject." He lists nine "truly philosophic implications" of the world's events visiting *us at home.*

Parker Tyler writes about the movies in a way that helps us dig beneath the "amusement" label that Collingwood puts on them. Movies aren't just amusements; they purvey myths. These myths are ideologically important because they structure and/or reinforce the mutual knowings that sustain our culture. These myths are not lying on the surface where we recognize them, and recognizing them can assess, evaluate, stand off from them, and withhold their control over our mind if we wish; "the superstitious stratum of the human psyche lies below the surface, below the verbal and conscious fields of expression. . . ."

Tyler writes so clearly and straightforwardly that he needs no "explanation." We content ourselves here with noting that he, too, reveals the ideological function of the arts when he discusses movie comedians; they are a particular instance of Collingwood's point about amusement art but with the added punch that comedians' effects stem from our mutual mythic knowings about the "low" estate of the king's jester. "And they [the movie comedians] repeated the ancient pattern of distracting the mind from the serious and troublous matters on which it was engaged. . . . The modern clown is the inheritor of part of the medicine man's rôle as public benefactor, and in societies of high cultural development in the nearer centuries he has continued to relieve tension. . . . His ability to do this according to his own tradition is an idiosyncratic immunity to normal human feelings, the clown being, generally speaking, too ugly, deformed, or foolish to have serious sentiments." And because we sometimes laugh *with* the clown, not necessarily *at* him, we pronounce ourselves low, ugly, deformed, foolish?

Lee Nichols, a structuralist analyst of TV series, agrees with Tyler: The mass arts communicate myths. The search for mythic themes requires digging beneath the surface; its structure is what gives it away as a myth. Mannix, for example, is an instance of the salvation myth, a familiar aspect of the Christian religion, as well as many others. Nichols points out that "No one ever goes directly to Mannix for help. They go to the secretary. She intercedes with her boss, who then sacrifices himself, ritually, to save them:

Mannix is either beaten badly or drives down that Malibu mountain while somebody tries to force him off the road. He goes through it on show after show. But notice: Simply by having submitted himself to the danger, the threat is removed from the supplicants to Mannix, and by that they are saved. It is not a very new story. We hear it every Easter" (*Sacramento Bee,* January 24, 1976).

While Mannix is the salvation hero, how are we to redescribe his opposite, the gangster? The Christian story is a comedy; everything ends well and happily; Christ has arisen and believers are saved. But what about the gangster? Is he the tragic figure left out of the comedy? Yes, and necessarily so. He (or she?) is caught in the inevitable bind of fate reserved for tragic figures. But, of course, "our" gangster is a modern figure. His fate is a modern fate. Furthermore, he symbolizes the fate of us modern city dwellers, according to **Robert Warshow.** "The gangster is the man of the city," not the real but the imaginary city, which is the modern world; this "imaginary city produces the gangster: he is what we want to be and what we are afraid we may become." We do not want to be unlawful as the gangster is; what we want is his success. "This principle, too, belongs to the city; one must emerge from the crowd or else one is nothing. On that basis the necessity of the action is established, and it progresses by inalterable paths to the point where the gangster lies dead and the principle has been modified: there is really only one possibility—failure. The final meaning of the city is anonymity and death." It is not death which is the tragic feature, of course, for we must all come to that; rather, anonymity is our tragedy— being nothing; to die as if we were not. And the gangster is the new myth whose career expresses in structure our own; we are not amused by gangster movies; they dip us in our own brine. Beneath the surface of all these crime movies and TV series lies the truth of our own existence; does not Mannix as our salvation hero look good, though, now that we know we need saving from a fate which only the superhuman can defy?

Warshow asks us to redescribe ourselves; our cultural patterns in an industrial, metropolitanized society have made anonymity an inescapable fate. Not all the granite cemetery monuments will rescue us from this fate; dust unto dust. The redescription is: We are not something; we are nothing! We learn this from the gangster film when it is analyzed as a revelation of our mutual knowings, usually pathetically hidden and unspoken. "Thus the importance of the gangster film, and the nature and intensity of its emotional and aesthetic impact, cannot be measured in terms of the place of the gangster himself." Hello, midnight gangster. Gangster films have apparently slipped past the ideological censor; according to Warshow, mass culture's normal function is "to maintain public morale." Being faced with ultimate nothingness is not a morale "high." Evidently, the people who control arts for ideological purposes are not omniscient enough to keep gangster movies from us. There is some hope for you.

Art as Amusement

R. G. COLLINGWOOD

R. G. Collingwood (1889–1943), philosopher and historian, was Waynflete Professor of Metaphysical Philosophy, Oxford University. One of the most learned men of his generation, he had a remarkable breadth of interest and knowledge and originality of mind. He is the author of many notable books, including *The Idea of History, An Autobiography, Essay on Metaphysics, Essay on Philosophical Method, The Idea of Nature, The New Leviathan,* and, with J. N. L. Myres, *Roman Britain and the English Settlements.*

1. Amusement Art

If an artifact is designed to stimulate a certain emotion, and if this emotion is intended not for discharge into the occupations of ordinary life, but for enjoyment as something of value in itself, the function of the artifact is to amuse or entertain. Magic is useful, in the sense that the emotions it excites have a practical function in the affairs of every day; amusement is not useful but only enjoyable, because there is a watertight bulkhead between its world and the world of common affairs. The emotions generated by amusement run their course within this watertight compartment.

Every emotion, dynamically considered, has two phases in its existence: charge or excitation, and discharge. The discharge of an emotion is some act done at the prompting of that emotion, by doing which we work the emotion off and relieve ourselves of the tension which, until thus discharged, it imposes upon us. The emotions generated by an amusement must be discharged, like any others; but they are discharged within the amusement itself. This is in fact the peculiarity of amusement. An amusement is a device for the discharge of emotions in such a way that they shall not interfere with the concerns of practical life. But since practical life is only definable as that part of life which is not amusement, this statement, if meant for a definition, would be circular. We must therefore say: to establish a distinction between amusement and practical life[1] is to divide experience into two parts, so related that the emotions generated in the one are not allowed to discharge themselves in the other. In the one, emotions are treated as ends in themselves; in the other, as forces whose operation achieves certain ends beyond them. The first part is now called amusement, the second part practical life.

In order that emotion may be discharged without affecting practical life, a make-believe situation must be created in which to discharge it. This situation

[1] Aestheticians who discuss the relation between two mutually exclusive things called "Art" and "Life" are really discussing this distinction.

Source: R. G. Collingwood, *The Principles of Art* (Oxford, 1938), pp. 78–104. Reprinted by permission of Oxford University Press.

will of course be one which "represents" (cf. Chapter III, § 4) the real situation in which the emotion would discharge itself practically. The difference between the two, which has been indicated by calling them respectively real and make-believe, is simply this: the so-called make-believe situation is one in which it is understood that the emotion discharged shall be "earthed," that is, shall not involve the consequences which it would involve under the conditions of practical life. Thus, if one man expresses hatred for another by shaking his first at him, threatening him, and so forth, he will ordinarily be regarded as a dangerous character, dangerous in particular to the man he has threatened, who will therefore take steps of one kind or another to protect himself: perhaps by appeasing the first, perhaps by attacking him and overpowering him, perhaps by obtaining police protection. If it is understood that nothing of this sort is to be done, that life is to go on exactly as if nothing had happened, then the situation in which the anger was expressed is called a make-believe situation.

Situations of this kind resemble those created by magic in being representative, that is, in evoking emotions like those evoked by the situations they are said to represent. They differ in being "unreal" or "make-believe"; that is, in that the emotions they evoke are intended to be earthed instead of overflowing into the situations represented. This element of make-believe is what is known as (theatrical) "illusion," an element peculiar to amusement art, and never found either in magic or in art proper. If in a magical ritual one says of a painting "this is a bison," or of a wax figure "this is my enemy," there is no illusion. One knows perfectly well the difference between the two things. The make-believe of amusement art differs radically, again, from the so-called make-believe of childish games, which is not amusement but a very serious kind of work, which we call make-believe by way of assimilating it to something that occurs in our adult experience. Calling it by that misdescriptive name, we patronizingly license the child to go on with it; so that the child can work at the really urgent problems of its own life unhampered by the interference which would certainly be forthcoming if adults knew what it was doing.

Comparisons have often been made, sometimes amounting to identification, between art and play. They have never thrown much light on the nature of art, because those who have made them have not troubled to think what they meant by play. If playing means amusing onself, as it often does, there is no important resemblance between play and art proper; and none between play and representative art in its magical form; but there is more than a mere resemblance between play and amusement art. The two things are the same. If playing means taking part in ritual games, art proper bears little resemblance to that, and amusement art even less; but such games, as we have already seen, not only resemble magic, they are magic. But there is another thing we call play: that mysterious activity which occupies the waking and working lives of children. It is not amusement, though we adults may amuse ourselves by imitating it, and even on privileged occasions taking part in it. It is not magic, though in some ways rather like it. Perhaps it is a good deal like art proper. Giambattista Vico, who knew a lot both about poetry and about children, said that children were "sublime poets," and he may have been right. But no one knows what children are doing when they play; it is far easier to find out what poets are doing when they write, difficult though that is; and even if art proper and children's play are the same thing, no light is thrown for most of us on art proper by saying so.[2]

There is a hedonistic theory of art: open, like all forms of hedonism, to the objection that even if the function of art is to give "delight" (as many good artists have said), still this delight is not pleasure in general but pleasure of a particular kind. When this objection has been met, the theory is a fair enough account of amusement art. The artist as purveyor of amusement makes it his business to please his audience by arousing certain emotions in them and providing them with a make-believe situation in which these emotions can be harmlessly discharged.

The experience of being amused is sought not for the sake of anything to which it stands as means, but for its own sake. Hence, while magic is utilitarian, amusement is not utilitarian but hedonistic. The work of art, so called, which provides the amusement, is, on the contrary, strictly utilitarian. Unlike a work of art proper, it has no value in itself; it is simply means to an end. It is as skilfully constructed as a work of engineering, as skilfully compounded as a bottle of medicine, to produce a determinate and preconceived effect, the evocation of a certain kind of emotion in a certain kind of audience; and to discharge this emotion within the limits of a make-believe situation. When the arts are described in terms implying that they are essentially forms of skill, the reference, as the terms are ordinarily used nowadays, is to this utilitarian character of amusement art. When the spectator's reception of them is described in psychological terms as a reaction to stimulus, the reference is the same. Theoretically, in both cases, the reference might be to the magical type of representation; but in the modern world that is generally ignored. For the student of modern aesthetic, it is a good rule, whenever he hears or reads statements about art which seem odd or perverse or untrue, to ask whether their oddity (or apparent oddity) may not be due to a confusion between art proper and amusement; a confusion either in the mind of their authors, or in his own.

2. Profit and Delight[3]

Magical function and amusement function in a work of art are of course mutually exclusive, so far as a given emotion in a given audience at a given moment is concerned. You cannot arouse in your audience a certain emotion (say, hatred of the Persians) and arrange at one and the same moment for its discharge in an amusement form, by raising a laugh at their expense, and in a

[2] Dr. Margaret Lowenfeld (*Play in Childhood*, 1935) has devised a method for exploring the unknown world of children's play, and has made strange discoveries about the relation of this play to the child's health. My own interpretation of her discoveries may be expressed by saying that they suggest an identity between "play" in children and art proper. On the relation between art and health of mind (involving health of body so far as psychological causes may impair or improve bodily health), I shall have something to say later on (Chapter X, § 7; Chapter XII, § 3).

[3] The ends of all, who for the *Scene* doe write
Are, or should be, to profit, and delight.

B. Jonson, *Epicœne, or the Silent Woman*

practical form, by burning down their houses. But the emotion aroused by any given representation is never simple; it is always a more or less complicated stream or pattern of different emotions; and it is not necessary that all these should be provided with the same kind of discharge. In a general way, some are discharged practically, others earthed; the artist, if he knows his job, arranging which shall be discharged in this way, which in that. So Horace: *omne tulit punctum qui miscuit utile dulci;* where the *utile* is the discharge of an emotion into practice, the *dulce* its discharge in the make-believe of amusement. "We do not write these novels merely to amuse," says Captain Marryat in *Midshipman Easy;* and goes on to boast that he has used his novels not unsuccessfully in the past to advocate reforms in naval administration. Mr. Bernard Shaw is another devout follower of Horace. There has never been any damned nonsense about art with him; he has careered through life most successfully as an entertainer, careful always to keep a few ball cartridges among his blank, and send his audience home indignant about the way people treat their wives, or something like that. But although he follows the same tradition as Marryat, it is doubtful whether he could claim an equal record of success as a pamphleteer. The difference is not so much between one writer and another as between one age and another. In the hundred years that have elapsed since *Midshipman Easy* was published, the ability of both artists and public to mix a dose of magic with their amusement has sensibly declined. Mr. Galsworthy began his career by putting so much *utile* and so little *dulce* into his stage-puddings that only very determined stomachs could digest them at all. So he gave up playing with magic, and specialized in entertaining a rather grim class of readers with the doings of the Forsyte family.

People who are not really competent in magic, as the fairytales wisely tell us, should be careful to leave it alone. One of the typical features of late nineteenth- and early twentieth-century literature is the way in which sound knockabout entertainers like Jerome K. Jerome or successful ginger-beer merchants like Mr. A. A. Milne suddenly come over all solemn, pull themselves together, and decide to become good influences in the lives of their audience. Nothing quite like it had ever happened before. It is a curious and unpleasant instance of the decline in taste which the nineteenth century brought in its train.

In general, the representational artist urgently needs to be a man of taste, in the sense that he must, on pain of professional disaster, know what emotions to excite. Unless he means to act as a magician, like Timotheus in Dryden's ode, and excite passions which those who feel them cannot discharge in anything short of practical acts, he must choose passions which, in the case of this particular audience, will submit to make-believe gratification. There is always a danger that, when once an emotion has been aroused, it may break down the watertight bulkhead and overflow into practical life; but it is the aim of both the amuser and the amused that this disaster shall not happen, and that by a loyal co-operation the bulkhead shall remain intact. The artist must steer a middle course. He must excite emotions which are closely enough connected with his audience's practical life for their excitation to cause lively pleasure; but not so closely connected that a breach of the bulkhead is a serious danger. Thus, a play in which a foreign nation is held up to ridicule will not amuse an audience in whom there is no sense of hostility towards that nation; but neither will it amuse one in whom this hostility has come near to boiling-point. A smoking-room story which amuses middle-aged clubmen would not amuse an old man who had out-grown sexual desire, nor a young man in whom it was agonizingly strong.

3. Examples of Amusement Art

The emotions which admit of being thus played upon for purposes of amusement are infinitely various; we shall take a few examples only. Sexual desire is highly adaptable to these purposes; easily titillated, and easily put off with make-believe objects. Hence the kind of amusement art which at its crudest and most brutal is called pornography is very common and very popular. Not only the representation of nudity which reappeared in European painting and sculpture at the Renaissance, when art as magic was replaced by art as amusement, but the novel, or story based on a sexual motive, which dates from the same period, is essentially an appeal to the sexual emotions of the audience, not in order to stimulate these emotions for actual commerce between the sexes, but in order to provide them with make-believe objects and thus divert them from their practical goal in the interests of amusement. The extent to which this make-believe sexuality has affected modern life can hardly be believed until the fact has been tested by appeal to the circulating libraries, with their flood of love-stories; the cinema, where it is said to be a principle accepted by almost every manager that no film can succeed without a love-interest; and above all the magazine and newspaper, where cover-designs, news-items, fiction, and advertisement are steeped in materials of the same kind: erotic stories, pictures of pretty girls variously dressed and undressed, or (for the female reader) of attractive young men: pornography homoeopathically administered in doses too small to shock the desire for respectability, but quite large enough to produce the intended effect. Small wonder that Monsieur Bergson has called ours an "aphrodisiac civilization." But the epithet is not quite just. It is not that we worship Aphrodite. If we did, we should fear these make-believes as a too probable cause of her wrath. An aphrodisiac is taken with a view to action: photographs of bathing girls are taken as a substitute for it. The truth may rather be that these things reveal a society in which sexual passion has so far decayed as to have become no longer a god, as for the Greeks, or a devil, as for the early Christians, but a toy: a society where the instinctive desire to propagate has been weakened by a sense that life, as we have made it, is not worth living, and where our deepest wish is to have no posterity.

The case of sexual fantasy is peculiar, because it seems in this way to have got out of hand, and thus to betray something amiss with our civilization as a whole. There are plenty of other cases where this complication is absent. For example, much pleasure may be derived from the emotion of fear; and to-day this is provided by a galaxy of talent devoted to writing stories of terrible adventure. The "thriller," to give the thing its current name, is not new. We find it on the Elizabethan stage, in the charnel-house sculpture of seventeenth-century tombs (the Last Judgements of medieval art were aimed not at making flesh creep but at reforming sinful lives), in the novels of Mrs. Radcliffe and "Monk" Lewis, in the engravings of Doré, and, raised to the level of art proper, in the first movement of Beethoven's Fifth Symphony and the Finale of Mozart's *Don Giovanni*. Among ourselves, the spread of literacy has begotten upon the old penny dreadful a monstrous progeny of hair-raising fiction concerned with arch-criminals, gunmen, and sinister foreigners. Why the ghost story, once so valuable for this purpose, has lost its efficacy, although heathenish rites, with much explicit bloodshed and even more hinted obscenity, are still in lively demand, is a curious problem for the historian of ideas.

The detective story, the most popular form of amusement offered by the profession of letters to the modern public, is based partly on appeal to the reader's fear, but partly on a rich medley of other emotions. In Poe the element of fear was exceedingly strong, and either because of his influence, or because of something ingrained in the civilization of the United States, the present-day American detective story shows a stronger inclination towards that type than those of any other nation. American corpses are the bloodiest and most horribly mangled; American police the most savage in their treatment of suspects.[4] Another emotion of great importance in such stories is the delight in power. In what may be called the Raffles period, this was gratified by inviting the reader to identify himself with a gallant and successful criminal; nowadays the identification is with the detective. A third is the intellectual excitement of solving a puzzle; a fourth, the desire for adventure, that is to say, the desire to take part in events as unlike as possible to the dreary business of actual everyday life. Members of the scholastic and clerical professions from time to time express a belief that young people who read these stories, and see films resembling them, are thereby incited to a career of crime. This is bad psychology. There is no evidence that stories of crime are the favourite reading of habitual criminals. In point of fact, those who constantly read them are on the whole thoroughly law-abiding folk; and this is only natural, for the constant earthing of certain emotions, by arousing and discharging them in make-believe situations, makes it less likely that they will discharge themselves in practical life.

No one has yet taken up the detective story and raised it to the level of genuine art. Miss Sayers, indeed, has given reasons why this cannot be done. Perhaps one reason is the mixture of motives which this *genre* has traditionally accepted as inevitable. A mixture of motives is, on the whole, favourable to good amusement, but it can never produce art proper.

Malice, the desire that others, especially those better than ourselves, should suffer, is a perpetual source of pleasure to man; but it takes different shapes. In Shakespeare and his contemporaries, bullying in its most violent form is so common that we can only suppose the average playgoer to have conceived it as the salt of life. There are extreme cases like *Titus Andronicus* and *The Duchess*

---

[4] Cf. Superintendent Kirk: ". . . I couldn't rightly call them a mellering influence to a man in my line. I read an American story once, and the way the police carried on—well, it didn't seem right to me." Dorothy L. Sayers, *Busman's Honeymoon*, p. 161.

of Malfi, where torture and insult form the chief subject-matter; cases like *Volpone* or *The Merchant of Venice,* where the same motive is veiled by a decent pretence that the suffering is deserved; and cases like *The Taming of the Shrew,* where it is rationalized as a necessary step to domestic happiness. The same motive crops out so repeatedly in passages like the baiting of Malvolio or the beating of Pistol, passages wholly unconnected with the plot of the play, so far as these plays have a plot, that it has obviously been dragged in to meet a constant popular demand. The theme is raised to the level of art proper here and there in Webster, in a few of Shakespeare's tragedies, and above all in Cervantes.

In a society which has lost the habit of overt bullying, the literature of violence is replaced by the literature of cattishness. Our own circulating libraries are full of what is grandiloquently called satire on the social life of our time; books whose popularity rests on the fact that they give the reader an excuse for ridiculing the folly of youth and the futility of age, despising the frivolity of the educated and the grossness of the uneducated, gloating over the unhappiness of an ill-assorted couple, or triumphing over the feebleness of a henpecked merchant prince. To the same class of pseudo-art (they are certainly not history) belong the biographies of cattishness, whose aim is to release the reader from the irksome reverence he has been brought up to feel for persons who were important in their day.

If the Elizabethan was by temperament a bully, the Victorian was by temperament a snob. Literature dealing with high life at once excites and in fancy gratifies the social ambition of readers who feel themselves excluded from it; and a great part of the Victorian novelist's work was devoted to making the middle classes feel as if they were sharing in the life of the upper. Nowadays, when "society" has lost its glamour, a similar place is taken by novels and films dealing with millionaires, criminals, film-stars, and other envied persons. There is even a literature catering for the snobbery of culture: books and films about Beethoven, Shelley, or, combining two forms of snobbery in one, a lady in high station who wins fame as a painter.

There are cases in which we find, not a mixture of amusement and magic, but a wavering between the two. A considerable literature exists devoted to sentimental topography: books about the charm of Sussex, the magic of Oxford, picturesque Tyrol, or the glamour of old Spain. Are these intended merely to recall the emotions of returned travellers and to make others feel as if they had travelled, or are they meant as an invocation—I had almost said, to call fools into a circle? Partly the one and partly the other; if the choice had been decisively made, literature of this kind would be better than it is. Similar cases are the sentimental literature of the sea, addressed to landsmen, and of the country, addressed to town-dwellers; folk-songs as sung not in pubs and cottages but in drawing-rooms; pictures of horses and dogs, deer and pheasants, hung in billiard-rooms partly as charms to excite the sportsman, partly as substitutes for sport. There is no reason why works of this kind should not be raised to the level of art, though cases in which that has happened are exceedingly rare. If it is to happen, there is one indispensable condition: the ambiguity of motive must first be cleared up.

4. Representation and the Critic

The question may here be raised, how the practice of art-criticism is affected by identifying art with representation in either of its two forms. The critic's business, as we have already seen, is to establish a consistent usage of terms: to settle the nomenclature of the various things which come before him competing for a given name, saying, "this is art, that is not art," and, being an expert in this business, performing it with authority. A person qualified so to perform it is called a judge; and judgements means verdict, the authoritative announcement that, for example, a man is innocent or guilty. Now, the business of art-criticism has been going on ever since at least the seventeenth century; but it has always been beset with difficulties. The critic knows, and always has known, that in theory he is concerned with something objective. In principle, the question whether this piece of verse is a poem or a sham poem is a question of fact, on which every one who is properly qualified to judge ought to agree. But what he finds, and always has found, is that in the first place the critics as a rule do not agree; in the second place, their verdict is as a rule reversed by posterity; and in the third place it is hardly ever welcomed and accepted as useful either by the artists or by the general public.

When the disagreements of critics are closely studied, it becomes evident that there is much more behind them than mere human liability to form different opinions about the same thing. The verdict of a jury in court, as judges are never tired of telling them, is a matter of opinion; and hence they sometimes disagree. But if they disagreed in the kind of way in which art-critics disagree, trial by jury would have been experimented with only once, if that, before being abolished for ever. The two kinds of disagreement differ in that the juror, if the case is being handled by a competent judge, has only one point at which he can go wrong. He has to give a verdict, and the judge tells him what the principles are upon which he must give it. The art-critic also has to give a verdict; but there is no agreement between him and his colleagues as to the principles on which it must be given.

This divergence of principle is not due to unsolved philosophical problems. It does not arise from divergences between rival theories of art. It arises at a point in thought which is prior to the formation of any aesthetic theory whatever. The critic is working in a world where most people, when they speak of a good painting or a good piece of writing, mean simply that it pleases them, and pleases specifically in the way of amusement. The simpler and more vulgar make no bones about this; I don't know what's good, they say, but I know what I like. The more refined and artistic reject this idea with horror. It makes no difference whether you like it or not, they retort; the question is whether it is good. The protest is in principle perfectly right; but in practice it is humbug. It implies that whereas the so-called art of the vulgar is not art but only amusement, about which there is of course no objective goodness or badness but only the fact that a given thing amuses or does not amuse a given audience, the art of more refined persons is not amusement but art proper. This is simply snobbery. There is no difference in attitude between the people who go to see Gracie

Fields and the people who go to see Ruth Draper except that, having been differently brought up, they are amused by different things. The cliques of artists and writers consist for the most part of a racket selling amusement to people who at all costs must be prevented from thinking themselves vulgar, and a conspiracy to call it not amusement but art.

The people who fancy themselves altogether above the vulgar level of amusement art, but are actually disporting themselves in that level and nowhere else, call their own amusements good art in so far as they find them amusing. The critic is therefore in a false position. He is committed, in so far as he himself belongs to these people and shares their shibboleths, to treating what is in fact a question of their likes and dislikes, their taste in amusements, as if it were that totally different thing, a question of merits and demerits in a given artist's work. And even that way of putting it makes his task seem easier than it really is. If these refined persons formed a perfectly compact psychological mob, what amused one would amuse all, as the same joke may please all members of a mess or a common-room. But in so far as their only bond is the negative one of refinement, which only means being unlike the people they regard as vulgar, they cannot as a whole exhibit a compact mob-psychology, and different fractions will be amused by different things. The critic's task is now hopeless, because the reasons why some people belonging to these circles call a book or a picture good will be the very same reasons why others, equally entitled to life, liberty, and the pursuit of amusement, will call it bad. And even if a certain kind of taste may for a time dominate the whole, or a large part of it, this is sure to be succeeded by another, from whose point of view the things that amused the earlier will be said to "date"; a very curious word, which nicely blows the gaff of all this sham criticism; for if it had been a question of genuine art—"voyons, Monsieur, le temps ne fait rien à l'affaire."

The critic is generally despised, but he ought rather to be pitied. The villains of the piece are the self-styled artists. They have assured him that they are doing something which it will be worth his while to study, and have then done something else, on which no critic would waste an hour's thought. If the gigantic ramp by which the trade in genteel amusements passes itself off as art were once for all exposed, the critics could either come out frankly as the advertisement writers which many of them are, or stop bothering about sham art and concentrate, as some of them already do, on the real thing.

So long as art is identified with amusement, criticism is impossible; and the fact of its having been so long and so valiantly attempted is a remarkable proof of the tenacity with which the modern European consciousness sticks to its point that there is such a thing as art, and that some day we shall learn how to distinguish it from the amusement trade.[5] If art is identified with magic, the

---

[5] It is hardly necessary to remark that the amusement racket has succeeded in corrupting quite a number of academic and other theoretical writers who base their aesthetic, or rather anti-aesthetic, on the identification of art with that which evokes a certain kind of emotion; with the consequence that "beauty" is "subjective," Man (and what a man!) is the measure of all things, and the critics, not (presumably) being Men but only heroes who have held a key-position of the civilized world for two centuries and a half against overwhelming odds, find that the pass has been sold behind their backs.

same conclusion follows; but this conclusion, in a society where magic is at all vigorous, may easily be masked by the substitution of a false objectivity for a true objectivity, an empirical generality for a strict universality. A matter of fact, as that this person did this act, or that this thing is a poem, is valid for everybody at every time and place. The "goodness" or "beauty" of a "work of art," if goodness or beauty means power of exciting certain emotions in the person using the word, has no such validity; it exists only in relation to the person in whom these emotions are aroused. It may happen that the same work will arouse the same emotions in others; but this will happen on a considerable scale only when the society in which it occurs thinks it necessary to its welfare.

That phrase is susceptible, we may note in passing, of two interpretations. (1) On a biological view of society, a society will consist of animals of a certain kind which through the action of such causes are heredity all possess a certain type of psychological organization. Owing to the uniformity of this organization, a stimulus of a specific kind will produce in all members of the society a specific type of emotion. The emotion will be necessary to the welfare of the society, because it is part and parcel of the psychological organization whose identity in all members of the society constitutes its principle of unity; and in so far as its members are conscious of this principle they will see that this emotional unanimity is necessary to their corporate existence, as a biological fact on which that existence depends. (2) On an historical view of society, a society will consist of persons who through communication by language have worked out a certain way of living together. So far as each one of them feels his own interests as bound up with those of the society, everything which forms part of this common way of living will have to him an emotional value, the strength of this emotion being the force that binds the society together. In that case, anything intimately connected with their common way of living will arouse in all members of the society the same type of emotional response.

On either view, therefore, wherever there is a society of any kind, there will be certain established forms of corporate magic, whereby certain standard stimuli evoke certain standard emotional responses from all its members. If these stimuli are called "works of art," they are conceived as possessing a "goodness" or "beauty" which in fact is merely their power to evoke these responses. In so far as the society is really a society, the appropriate response is really evoked in all its members, and if they misuse words in this way, they will all agree that the "work of art" is "good" or "beautiful." But this agreement is only an empirical generality, holding good within the society because the society just consists of those persons who share it. Enemies without, or even mere foreigners, and traitors within, will just as necessarily disagree. So long as magic is taken for art, these agreements and disagreements will be taken for criticism; and in any given society it will be thought the mark of a good critic to insist that the common magic of the society is good art.

Reduced to these terms, criticism becomes nugatory. In this country and at the present time there is not much danger of the reduction. There are not many people, or if there are they are not influential, who think we ought to support home industries by taking pains to bestow special admiration on English poetry or English music or English painting because it is English; or even that a decent patriotism should prevent us from criticizing the words or music of *God Save the King* or the annual Academy portraits of the Royal Family. But mistakes are often made by inverting the same misconception. As we saw at the end of the preceding chapter, many things which are or might be called art, even among ourselves and to-day, are in fact a combination of art and magic in which the predominant motive is magical. What is demanded of them is that they should discharge a magical function, not an artistic one. If a musical critic tells us that *God Save the King* is a bad tune, well and good; it is a matter on which he has a right to speak. Perhaps after all the Elizabethans were wrong to think John Bull a competent musician. But if he goes on to tell us that we ought on that account to replace it with a new national anthem by a better composer, he is confusing an artistic question with a magical one. To condemn magic for being bad art is just as foolish as to praise art for being good magic. And when we find an artist trying to convince us that our public statues, for example, are artistically bad and ought on that account to be demolished, we cannot help wondering whether he is a fool or a knave: a fool for not knowing these things to be primarily magic, valuable for their magical qualities and not at all for their artistic, or a knave for knowing this perfectly well, but concealing it in order to use his own artistic prestige as a stalking-horse behind which he can make a treacherous attack on the emotions which bind our society together.

5. Amusement in the Modern World

We have already seen that amusement implies a bifurcation of experience into a "real" part and a "make-believe" part, and that the make-believe part is called amusement in so far as the emotions aroused in it are also discharged in it and are not allowed to overflow into the affairs of "real" life.

This bifurcation is no doubt as ancient as man himself; but in a healthy society it is so slight as to be negligible. Danger sets in when by discharging their emotions upon make-believe situations people come to think of emotion as something that can be excited and enjoyed for its own sake, without any necessity to pay for it in practical consequences. Amusement is not the same thing as enjoyment; it is enjoyment which is had without paying for it. Or rather, without paying for it in cash. It is put down in the bill and has to be paid for later on. For example, I get a certain amount of fun out of writing this book. But I pay for it as I get it, in wretched drudgery when the book goes badly, in seeing the long summer days vanish one by one past my window un-used, in knowing that there will be proofs to correct and index to make, and at the end black looks from the people whose toes I am treading on. If I knock off and lie in the garden for a day and read Dorothy Sayers, I get fun out of that too; but there is nothing to pay. There is only a bill run up, which is handed in next day when I get back to my book with that Monday-morning feeling. Of course, there may be no Monday-morning feeling: I may get back to the book feeling fresh and energetic, with my staleness gone. In that case my day off turned out to be not amusement but recreation. The difference between them consists in the debit or credit effect they produce on the emotional energy available for practical life.

Amusement becomes a danger to practical life when the debt it imposes on these stores of energy is too great to be paid off in the ordinary course of living. When this reaches a point of crisis, practical life, or "real" life, becomes emotionally bankrupt; a state of things which we describe by speaking of its intolerable dullness or calling it a drudgery. A moral disease has set in, whose symptoms are a constant craving for amusement and an inability to take any interest in the affairs of ordinary life, the necessary work of livelihood and social routine. A person in whom the disease has become chronic is a person with a more or less settled conviction that amusement is the only thing that makes life worth living. A society in which the disease is endemic is one in which most people feel some such conviction most of the time.

A moral (or in modern jargon a psychological) disease may or may not be fatal to the person suffering from it; he may be driven to suicide, as the only release from *taedium vitae,* or he may try to escape it by going in for crime or revolution or some other exciting business, or he may take to drink or drugs, or simply allow himself to be engulfed in a slough of dullness, a dumbly accepted life in which nothing interesting ever happens, tolerable only when he does not think how intolerable it is. But moral diseases have this peculiarity, that they may be fatal to a society in which they are endemic without being fatal to any of its members. A society consists in the common way of life which its members practise; if they become so bored with this way of life that they begin to practise a different one, the old society is dead even if no one noticed its death.

This is perhaps not the only disease from which societies may die, but it is certainly one of them. It is certainly, for example, the disease from which Greco-Roman society died. Societies may die a violent death, like the Inca and Aztec societies which the Spaniards destroyed with gunpowder in the sixteenth century; and it is sometimes thought by people who have been reading historical thrillers that the Roman Empire died in the same way, at the hands of barbarian invaders. That theory is amusing but untrue. It died of disease, not of violence, and the disease was a long-growing and deep-seated conviction that its own way of life was not worth preserving.

The same disease is notoriously endemic among ourselves. Among its symptoms are the unprecedented growth of the amusement trade, to meet what has become an insatiable craving; an almost universal agreement that the kinds of work on which the existence of civilization like ours most obviously depends (notably the work of industrial operatives and the clerical staff in business of every kind, and even that of the agricultural labourers and other food-winners who are the prime agents in the maintenance of every civilization hitherto existing) is an intolerable drudgery; the discovery that what makes this intolerable is not the pinch of poverty or bad housing or disease but the nature of the work itself in the conditions our civilization has created; the demand arising out of this discovery, and universally accepted as reasonable, for an increased provision of leisure, which means opportunity for amusement, and of amusements to fill it; the use of alcohol, tobacco, and many other drugs, not for ritual purposes, but to deaden the nerves and distract the mind from the tedious and irritating concerns of ordinary life; the almost universal confession that boredom, or lack of interest in life, is felt as a constant or constantly recurring state of mind; the feverish attempts to dispel this boredom either by more amusement or by dangerous or criminal occupations; and finally (to cut the catalogue short) the discovery, familiar *mutatis mutandis* to every bankrupt in the last stages of his progress, that customary remedies have lost their bite and that the dose must be increased.

These symptoms are enough to alarm any one who thinks about the future of the world in which he is living; enough to alarm even those whose thought for the future goes no farther than their own lifetime. They suggest that our civilization has been caught in a vortex, somehow connected with its attitude towards amusement, and that some disaster is impending which, unless we prefer to shut our eyes to it and perish, if we are to perish, in the dark, it concerns us to understand.

A history of amusement in Europe would fall into two chapters. The first, entitled *panem et circenses,* would deal with amusement in the decadent world of antiquity, the shows of the Roman theatre and amphitheatre, taking over their material from the religious drama and games of the archaic Greek period; the second, called *le monde où l'on s'amuse,* would describe amusement in the Renaissance and modern ages, at first aristocratic, furnished by princely artists to princely patrons, then transformed by degrees through the democratization of society into the journalism and cinema of to-day, and always visibly drawing its material from the religious painting and sculpture and music, architecture and pageantry and oratory, of the Middle Ages.

The first chapter would begin with Plato. Plato's observations about poetry and the other arts are difficult for us to understand, not, as historians of thought generally assume, because 'aesthetic was in its infancy' and Plato's thoughts about it inchoate and confused; still less, as others fancy, because Plato was a philistine with no interest in art; but because the issues with which he was dealing were not the familiar problems of academic art-philosophy which we expect them to be, but issues of a quite different kind, highly relevant to our own practical situation. Plato lived at a time when the religious art of the earlier Greeks, such as the Olympian sculptures and the Aeschylean drama, had decisively given way to the new amusement art of the Hellenistic age. He saw in this change not only the loss of a great artistic tradition and the coming of an artistic decadence, but also a danger to civilization as a whole. He grasped the distinction between magical art and amusement art, and attacked amusement art with all the power of his logic and eloquence.

Modern readers, prejudiced by the current nineteenth-century identification of art with amusement, have commonly misinterpreted Plato's attack on amusement as an attack on art, have taken upon themselves to resent it in the name of sound aesthetic theory, and have praised Aristotle for a juster appreciation of the value of art. In fact, however, Plato and Aristotle do not differ so very much in their views on poetry, except at one point. Plato saw that amusement art arouses emotions which it does not direct to any outlet in practical life; and wrongly inferred that its excessive development would breed a society overcharged with purposeless emotions. Aristotle saw that this did not follow, because the emotions generated by amusement art are discharged by the amusement itself. Plato's error on this point led him to think that the evils of a world given over to amusement could be cured by controlling or abolishing amusements. But when the vortex has once established itself, that cannot be done; cause and effect are now interlocked in a vicious circle, which will mend itself wherever you break it; what began as the cause of the disease is now only a symptom, which it is useless to treat.[6]

The dangers to civilization foreseen by Plato's prophetic thought were a long time maturing. Greco-Roman society was vigorous enough to go on paying the interest on the accumulating debt out of the energies of its everyday life for six or seven centuries. But from Plato onwards its life was a rearguard action against emotional bankruptcy. The critical moment was reached when Rome created an urban proletariat whose only function was to eat free bread and watch free shows. This meant the segregation of an entire class which had no work to do whatever; no positive function in society, whether economic or military or administrative or intellectual or religious; only the business of being supported and being amused. When that had been done, it was only a question of time until Plato's nightmare[7] of a consumer's society came true: the drones set up their own king, and the story of the hive came to an end.

Once a class had been created whose only interest lay in amusement, it acted as an abscess which by degrees drew away all emotional energies from the affairs of real life. Nothing could arrest the spread of amusement; no one, though many tried, could regenerate it by infusing into it a new spirit of religious purpose or artistic austerity. The vortex revolved, through manifestations now wholly forgotten except by a few curious scholars, until a new consciousness grew up for which practical life was so interesting that organized amusement was no longer needed. The consciousness of the old civilization, now bifurcated down to its very foundations, fell to pieces before the onslaught of this new unified consciousness, and theatre and amphitheatre were deserted by a world that had become Christian. The Middle Ages had begun, and a new magico-religious art was born: this time, an art serving those emotions which went to the invigorating and perpetuating of Christian society.

The second chapter would begin with the fourteenth century, when merchants and princes began to change the whole character of artistic work by diverting it from the Church's use to their own personal service. It would show how, from a quite early stage, this new movement provoked violent hostility, such as that which drove Savonarola to burn Michelangelo's picture; and how this hostility was drawn into the service of the Reformation until it became, unlike the so-called "puritanism" of Plato, even more bitter against magical art than against amusement art. It would show how the tradition of this hostility entered into the main stream of modern civilization through its inheritance by nonconformist bankers and manufacturers, the class which became dominant in the modern

[6] It should be added that in both Plato and Aristotle, and especially in Plato, the genuine problems of aesthetic are not wholly absent from the discussion; they lurk in the background, and from time to time loom up and overshadow those of amusement art.

[7] *Republic*, 573 A–B. Cf. Rostovtzeff, *Social and Economic History of the Roman Empire*, ch. ix–xi. I have worked out the consequences for one province of the Roman Empire in *Oxford History of England*, i (1937), ch. xii–xiii; cf. especially p. 207.

world; and how that event drove the artistic consciousness of the modern world, at the very moment when it was liberating itself from the shackles of amusement, into the position of something outcast and persecuted.

It would show how the new plutocracy, entrenched in their hereditary anti-artistic point of view, came with their new social and political domination to ape the ways of the gentry they had displaced; how in the course of this process they made a truce with the arts on condition that the arts should accept once more the status of amusements; and how the new dominant classes persuaded themselves to reconcile their enjoyment of these amusements with a religious principle according to which there was no room in life for anything but work. The effect on both parties was disastrous. The artists, who had struggled from the seventeenth to the early nineteenth century to work out a new conception of art, detaching it from the ideas of amusement and magic alike, and thus liberating themselves from all service, whether of church or of patron, stifled these thoughts, spared themselves the labour of developing their new conception to the height of its potentialities, and put on again the servant's liveries they had thrown aside. But they had changed for the worse, as always happens when revolted slaves go back to slavery. Their old masters had been, according to their lights, liberal and encouraging patrons, anxious for the best their servants could give them. The new masters wanted something far short of that. There was to be no danger of a new Restoration comedy or a Chaucerian or Shakespearian freedom of speech. Bowdler was king. And so the nineteenth century went on its way, with a constant decline in artistic standards as compared with those of its early years, until by degrees (since slaves come to learn the desires their lords disown) respectable people began to think of art as not only an amusement but a shady one.

The masters, too, were the worse for it. Conscience allowed no place in their lives for amusement; and by accepting the arts as amusements they were touching the forbidden thing. The gospel of work ceased to hold them. They got into the habit of deserting their business on making a fortune, and "retiring" into a state of pseudo-gentility, distinguished from real gentility not by their pronunciation or their table-manners, which were no odder than those of many a squire, but by the fact that they had no duties to the community, whether military or administrative or magical, such as occupied the real gentry. They had nothing to do but amuse themselves, and many of them did so by collecting pictures and so forth as the eighteenth-century nobility had set them example. The art-galleries of northern towns are there in evidence. But the poor, who are always the last guardians of a tradition, knew that the curse of God rested on idleness, and spoke of three generations from clogs to clogs.

That was the first stage in the formation of the vortex. The second, far graver, was the corruption of the poor themselves. Until close on the end of the nineteenth century, the rustic population of England had an art of its own, rooted in the distant past but still alive with creative vigour: songs and dances, seasonal feasts and dramas and pageantry, all of magical significance and all organically connected with agricultural work. In a single generation this was wiped out of existence by the operation of two causes: the Education Act of 1870, which, as imposing on the countryman an education modelled on town-dwellers' standards, was one stage in the slow destruction of English rural life by the dominant industrial and commercial class; and the "agricultural depression," to give that vague and non-committal name to the long series of events, partly accidental and partly deliberate, which between 1870 and 1900 wrecked the prosperity of the English agricultural population.[8]

A similar process was going on among the poor of the towns. They too had a vital and flourishing folk-art of the same magical type; they too were deprived of it by the organized forces of the law acting as the secular arm of the ruling industrialists' puritanism. This is not the place for a narrative of the long persecution; it is enough to say that by about 1900 town and country alike had been properly purged of the magical art that had come to be known as folklore, except for a few harmless and pitiful survivals. The attack on magical art was over. The mind of the poor was a house empty, swept, and garnished.

Then came amusement art. Football—mushroom amusement growth of what had, till lately, been a ritual practised on religious feast-days in north-country towns—came first; then came the cinema and the wireless; and the poor, throughout the country, went amusement mad. But another event was happening at the same time. Increased production combined with the break-down of economic organization led to the appearance of an unemployed class, forced unwillingly into a parasitic condition, deprived of the magical arts in which their grandfathers took their pleasure fifty years ago, left functionless and aimless in the community, living only to accept *panem et circenses,* the dole and the films.

Historical parallels are blind guides. There is no certainty that our civilization is tracing a path like that of the later Roman Empire. But the parallel, so far as it has yet developed, is alarmingly close. The disaster may be preventible, but the danger is real. Is there anything we can do?

There are certain things we need not try to do. Plato's remedy is no use. A dictator might try to close the cinemas, shut down the wireless except for the transmission of his own voice, confiscate the newspapers and magazines, and in every possible way block the supplies of amusement. But no such attempts would succeed, and no one clever enough to become dictator would be fool enough to make them.

The highbrow remedy is no use. The masses of cinema goers and magazine readers cannot be elevated by offering them, instead of these democratic amusements, the aristocratic amusements of a past age. This is called bringing art to the people, but that is clap-trap; what is brought is still amusement, very cleverly designed by a Shakespeare or a Purcell to please an Elizabethan or Restoration audience, but now, for all its genius, far less amusing than Mickey Mouse or jazz except to people laboriously trained to enjoy it.

The folk-song remedy is no use. English folk-art was a magical art, whose value to its possessors lay not in its aesthetic merits (critics who quarrel about these merits need not offer us their views) but in its traditional connexion with the works and days of their calendar. Its possessors have been robbed of it. The tradition has been broken. You cannot mend a tradition, and you would be

[8] Cf. R. C. K. Ensor, *Oxford History of England,* vol. xiv (1936), ch. iv, ix.

foolish to give it back broken. Remorse is useless. There is nothing to be done except face the fact.

The gunman's remedy is no use. We need not buy revolvers and rush off to do something drastic. What we are concerned with is the threatened death of a civilization. That has nothing to do with my death or yours, or the deaths of any people we can shoot before they shoot us. It can be neither arrested nor hastened by violence. Civilizations die and are born not with waving of flags or the noise of machine-guns in the streets, but in the dark, in a stillness, when no one is aware of it. It never gets into the papers. Long afterwards a few people, looking back, begin to see that it has happened.

Then let us get back to our business. We who write and read this book are persons interested in art. We live in a world where most of what goes by that name is amusement. Here is our garden. It seems to need cultivating.

Culture Is Not Neutral

MEREDITH TAX

Meredith Tax (1940–   ) taught literary criticism at Brandeis University. She now lives in Chicago and is active in writing on the women's movement.

The thesis I wish to present here is that culture is not neutral politically, and that it is as impossible for it to be so as it is impossible for any other product of human labour to be detached from its conditions of production and reception. All culture serves someone's interest. Cultural products which present foreign wars as the heroic effort of a master race to ennoble mankind are, to the degree that they are successful as art, objectively in the interests of imperialists, who are people who make foreign wars against other races for profit. Cultural products that present people who have no money or power as innately stupid or depraved, and thus unworthy of money or power, are in the interests of the ruling class and the power structure as it stands. Cultural products which present women who do not want to be household slaves or universal mothers or sex objects as bitches or sexual failures objectively aid male supremacy.

Some writers are overtly political—though to be so in America has taken more courage or vision than most writers since the Second World War have had. Most writers avoid mentioning overtly political issues. But this does not mean they are disengaged from them. In our times, to refrain from mentioning genocide, racism, cultural schizophrenia, sexual exploitation, and the systematic starvation of entire populations is itself a political act. For no one in our time

From Meredith Tax, "Introductory: Culture Is Not Neutral, Whom Does It Serve," in *Radical Perspectives in the Arts,* ed. by Lee Baxandall (New York and London: Penguin Books, 1972), pp. 15–29. Reprinted by permission of the author.

can be awake enough to write and have avoided noticing these phenomena—though he may not recognize them for what they are. As our bankrupt civilization draws to its close, and as the violence of the powerful against the weak, of the rich against the poor, of the few against the many, becomes more and more apparent, until it becomes impossible to watch a news broadcast and remain unaware of it for a second—as this situation becomes exacerbated, to refrain from mentioning it becomes more and more clearly a political act, an act of censorship or cowardice.

Yet very few of our establishment writers and artists, let alone of our literary critics, think these things are important enough to mention in their work. They may bear witness as private individuals, but they do not allow their private concern to interfere with business as usual. Let us paraphrase any well-adjusted academic critic's attitude toward the poet's method of dealing with this problem.

"A poet's job is to do his thing," he will say. "Naturally he will write about what is important or central to him personally, and who am I to interfere with another man's system of values? If Wallace Stevens chooses to write about arpeggios and pineapples rather than about racial tensions in Hartford or the practices of the insurance company he was vice-president of in regard to people on welfare, this was his decision; what's it to me? And as for the implication that his position as a member of the ruling class may have governed his perception of the importance of such problems, or led him to fear dignifying them by the poetic process, why, I think that's extremely unfair and full of all kinds of critical fallacies."

And, perhaps, considered from the strictly *professional* point of view of keeping up standards within the criticism business, and not rocking the boat, this may be so. But let us, for the moment, consider the problem from a *human* rather than a *professional* point of view.

Bertolt Brecht, a German Communist poet, wrote an essay in 1935 entitled: "Writing the Truth: Five Difficulties." In it he states:

> Nowadays, anyone who wishes to combat lies and ignorance and to write the truth must overcome at least five difficulties. He must have the *courage* to write the truth when truth is everywhere opposed; the *keenness* to recognize it, although it is everywhere concealed; the *skill* to manipulate it as a weapon; *the judgement* to select those in whose hands it will be effective; and the *cunning* to spread the truth among such persons. These are formidable problems for a writer living under Fascism, but they exist also for those writers who have fled or been exiled; they exist even for writers working in countries where civil liberty prevails.

Brecht goes on to discuss the problem of *what* truths are worth telling, a problem of peculiar relevance to us.

> First of all we strike trouble in determining *what* truth is worth the telling. For example, before the eyes of the whole world one great civilized nation after the other falls into barbarism. Moreover, everyone knows that the domestic war which is being waged by the most ghastly methods can at any moment be converted into a foreign war which may well leave our continent a heap of ruins. This, undoubtedly, is one truth, but there are others. Thus, for example, it is not untrue that chairs have seats and that rain falls downward. Many poets write truths of this sort. They are like a painter adorning the walls of a sinking ship with a still life. . . . Those

in power cannot corrupt them, but neither are they disturbed by the cries of the oppressed. . . . At the same time, it is not easy to realize that their truths are truths about chairs or rain; they usually sound like truths about important things. For it is the nature of artistic creation to confer importance. But upon closer examination it is possible to see that they say merely: a chair is a chair; and: no one can prevent the rain from falling down.

I went through a respectable liberal education, one purpose of which was to outfit me as a literary critic and teacher of literature. We studied a great many monuments of culture in my classes. We discussed the form of these works, either in itself, or in relation to other things written at the time; we occasionally speculated as to whether there were any eternal truths concealed in these works; or whether they had any relation to works of art in other genres; but mostly we just discussed the form of these works in exhaustive detail—the words, how they operated in tension with each other, the length of the poetic line, the use of symbols, etcetera.

The one thing we never discussed about any cultural monuments was their *meaning*—just their barefaced everyday philistine literal meaning. I think that if any of us had thought to bring this problem up we would have been laughed at. Of course, none of us ever did bring it up, because we wanted the approval of our teachers, and because we had never heard that one should take literature seriously enough to worry about what it meant in terms of one's own life. At most, we had heard that form and content were the same in great works, so that there was clearly no importance to discussing anything but form.

And so we went through all the great works of literature, works which were often, at least until the modern period, passionately ideological, as if we had blinkers on. It is indeed a characteristic of the modern period that reality in it is so intolerable that most artists and critics cannot bear to deal with it directly. But some of them, at least, allude to it if not confront it. Take, for instance, the poem "Easter 1916" by Yeats, a poem frequently studied in school.

> We know their dream; enough
> To know they dreamed and are dead;
> And what if excess of love
> Bewildered them till they died?
> I write it out in a verse—
> MacDonagh and MacBride
> And Connolly and Pearse
> Now and in time to be,
> Wherever green is worn,
> Are changed, changed utterly:
> A terrible beauty is born.

What are the political implications of this verse? What does it mean? What is he trying to get us to think or to do? And how is it that such questions so seldom arise in the consideration of a poem?

What Yeats is getting at becomes clearer when his poem is put next to Brecht's "To Posterity," another great poem, which is however never taught in literature classes. Brecht's poem ends:

You, who shall emerge from the flood
In which we are sinking,
Think—
When you speak of our weaknesses,
Also of the dark time
That brought them forth.
For we went, changing our country more often than our shoes,
In the class war, despairing
When there was only injustice and no resistance.
For we knew only too well:
Even hatred of squalor
Makes the brow grow stern.
Even anger against injustice
Makes the voice grow harsh. Alas, we
Who wished to lay the foundations of kindness
Could not ourselves be kind.
But you, when at last it comes to pass
That man can help his fellow man,
Do not judge us
Too harshly.

Brecht and Yeats are talking of the same phenomena, of what happens to people who commit themselves to revolutionary politics. Their ordinary life is transformed; and personal values, as trivially defined, become less important to them than the good of all people. This involves certain kinds of sacrifice that often seem bizarre or incomprehensible to people who do not get the point. Brecht speaks of this, and of what he has missed out on in his personal life, in an earlier stanza of the same poem:

I ate my food between massacres.
The shadow of murder lay upon my sleep.
And when I loved, I loved with indifference.
I looked upon nature with impatience.
So the time passes away
Which on earth was given me.

Yeats is talking about the same withdrawals and austerities in his central metaphor of the stone in the midst of the living stream:

Hearts with one purpose alone
Through summer and winter seem
Enchanted to a stone
To trouble the living stream.
The horse that comes from the road,
The rider, the birds that range
From cloud to trembling cloud,
Minute by minute they change;
A shadow of cloud on the stream
Changes minute by minute;
A horse-hoof slides on the brim,
And a horse plashes within it;

The long-legged moor-hens dive,
And hens to moor-cocks call;
Minute by minute they live;
The stone's in the midst of all.

Too long a sacrifice
Can make a stone of the heart.

Brecht devoted his life and his work to making sure, to the best of his ability, that certain things happened in the world. He ends his poem by looking ahead with absolute confidence to a time after the revolution, when people will have changed, when circumstances will have ceased to require that they be as hard and purposeful as he needed to be. This is what is important to him, that the quality of life will change, and that people will cease to have to be deformed by their environment as he was.

In Yeats' poem, what is important is not whether the revolutionaries he writes about win or lose, not whether their political ideas are right or wrong, but whether individual heroism and aesthetic beauty are the products of their struggle. "O when may it suffice?" he asks of their sacrifice, and answers, leave it to heaven, we can't know; our job is to make verses which tell how they have been personally ennobled.

We know their dream; enough
To know they dreamed and are dead . . .
Are changed, changed utterly:
A terrible beauty is born.

What does this mean but that, in the end, aesthetic values are the most important; and beauty of a certain noble kind is more important than success? And what is this but to focus on a few heroes, as if the whole meaning of the struggle dwelt in their features, and forget the thousands that followed behind them, peasants, workers, not aristocrats, and less beautiful than themselves, but to whom an end of colonialism was literally a matter of life or death. Their lives do not come into the poem; and this fact determines its political meaning— it is a beautiful expression of a certain kind of romantic élitism, and a betrayal of the Irish Revolution.

The ideas that aesthetic values are primary, and that personal heroism is the kind to focus on, are typical of late bourgeois poetry, in that they express the privatization of bourgeois life, and the divorcement of modern art from the base of society.

Let us take a longer look at the philosophy of art-for-art's-sake: that is, at the ideology that art is justified by its existence, that it does not and should not serve any social purpose, that it frequently has no reference to anything outside itself, and that it is expressive of the vision of the individual poet, if of anything. The accompanying critical doctrine is that any criticism of a poem in terms other than these is an importation of irrelevant values: "A poem should not mean but be."

The thing we tend to forget is that this aesthetic philosophy developed at a certain historical moment—it didn't always exist, and is in fact fairly recent.

"Art-for-art's-sake" was the response of the producers of art to a market which was as mysterious and alienating to them as it was to the producers of other commodities. In most cultures prior to that of industrial capitalism, artists have had a well-defined and clearly understood relation to some part of their society, some group of consumers. In a primitive tribe or collective, art is the expression of the whole tribe—later, some people may be specially good at it, or hereditarily trained to it, and take on the production of artifacts as their work, but they work surrounded by the community, and work for the community's immediate and obvious benefit. In other periods of history, the artist has produced for a court, for a personal patron, for a religious sect, or for a political party. It is only with the dominance of the capitalist system that the artist has been put in the position of producing for a *market,* for strangers far away, whose life styles and beliefs and needs are completely unknown to him, and who will either buy his works or ignore them for reasons that are equally inscrutable and out of his control.

In the sphere of production, Marxists call the attitude that results from this process "commodity fetishism." The processes of production and distribution— that is: the gathering of raw materials, the inventing of machines and processes, the organization of labour into successive stages of work on the different stages of manufacture, distribution, marketing, advertising, and all the rest—all make up a process so infinitely complex that neither the consumer who buys the finished product nor the producer of any one stage of it, has any clear idea what is going on. You buy a chair. You have no idea who made it, what the materials in it are and where they came from and what they originally cost, how much the labour in it cost, and how much the price of the chair has been jacked up by profit and by waste like advertising. All of this is no more mysterious to you than it is to the factory worker who made one ingredient of the plastic that the seat of the chair is made of. In this kind of economy, objects are regarded as though they had originated by magic and appeared in the shops, not as if they were made by people for other people to use.

Most critical theory as currently practised is an extension of this commodity fetishism into the realm of culture. A poem is not thought of as something made by a man for other men to use—it is thought of as having come about by some incomprehensible process, and for no clear end but its own existence. It is thought of in this way even by its producer, the poet. Like the factory worker he sends his product out into an unfriendly void. The use of his product, if any, is conjectural; he probably thinks it has none to anyone but himself. How can he be other than alienated from his work? How can he justify its existence, when he cannot *see* or *know* the people who use it, except by making its clear lack of relation to his society into an artistic creed, which becomes in its turn a critical dogma?

Art has not always been isolated in this way. An Italian fresco painter knew exactly who he was decorating a church for—who would pay him and what families would worship in that church. Voltaire knew who he wanted to reach with *Candide,* and what he wanted them to think. Even Samuel Richardson managed to get in touch with a circle of correspondents, whose reaction to his books he could judge as he went along and thus determine whether he was achieving the desired moral effects. And contemporary Soviet poets are in touch with mass audiences who will flock to hear them read their latest. Writers in conditions like these are not alienated from their own work to the extent that they think it isn't good for anything, and isn't meant to reach anyone but a few friends.

In the period of bourgeois culture that is drawing to a close, two kinds of art have been produced: "high-brow" and "low-brow" as they are often called. Both have served the political end of pacifying or immobilizing parts of the population potentially hostile to the system as it stands.

"High-brow" culture is directed at the upper middle class, students, and intellectuals, who tend to take jobs such as teachers, health workers, social workers, etc., whose social function in our society is to control the lives and minds of others. This form of culture militates against the perception of the political solutions of political problems by purveying ideas which are in their implications and social use, if not in the motives of the people who produced them, reactionary. These are the central ideas of the art of the modern period, expressed in its form as well as its content. Some of them are:

1. That life is absurd, meaningless.

2. That we are all victims, and to be conscious is to despair.

3. That any communication or understanding between human beings is *a priori* impossible because the human condition is one of quintessential isolation.

4. That one's perception of reality is both subjective and uncontrollably fragmented; that there is no way of integrating the different parts of one's experience and the external world.

5. That most of life and most people are disgusting, vulgar and stupid. The class bias inherent in the word "vulgar" is quite conscious in this formulation.

6. That there are no real objective truths, including the above.

This is what most serious modern literature teaches us. It's no accident. The extreme inhumanity of our civilization—its class system, its racism, its gross commercialism, its male chauvinism, its institutionalized violence, its imperialist wars—all these factors make consciousness almost unbearable to people who have not looked behind these symptoms to their causes and cure, who do not see that they make up the fabric of a particular social and economic system which is different from those of the past and can be superseded in the future. What has been made by people can, in the long run, be understood and changed by them.

The other kind of culture purveyed in our society is "low-brow" or mass culture—a kind we are taught to despise as we are taught to despise those who consume it. This art, in fact, expresses nothing about the people who consume it but their deprivation. It is a mass-produced means of social control by manipulation of the national fantasy life. It is no more a product of any working-class culture than are the can-openers and Fords produced in our factories. I'm talking about TV, Westerns, Mickey Spillane and Erle Stanley Gardner, drugstore romances, sexy novels, Mantovani and Muzak, Norman Rockwell and the Keuhns. This is proletarianized art: it implicitly expresses its consumers' consciousness of their oppression, while at the same time preventing them from changing it. Christopher Caudwell described it thirty years ago in his book *Illusion and Reality:*

> Because art's role is now that of adapting the multitude to the dead mechanical existence of capitalist production, in which work sucks them of their vital energies without awakening their instincts, where leisure becomes a time to deaden the mind with the easy fantasy of films, simple wish-fulfilment writing, or music that is mere emotional massage—because of this the paid craft of writing becomes as tedious and wearisome as that of machine-minder . . . [this art] is at once an expression of real misery and a protest against the real misery. This art, universal, constant, fabulous, full of the easy gratifications of instincts starved by modern capitalism, peopled by passionate lovers and heroic cowboys and amazing detectives, is the religion of today, as characteristic an expression of proletarian exploitation as Catholicism is of feudal exploitation. It is the opium of the people; it pictures an inverted world because the world of society *is* inverted.

But times are changing. And in certain small ways, art is beginning to reflect these changes. For the first time since the Industrial Revolution it has become possible for artists to define themselves against the values of capitalist society and at the same time have an audience, a definite and large subgroup of the population, that they are producing for, an audience that also defines itself in opposition to the dominant culture. We have the makings of a revolutionary culture, that tells the truth about our society, demonstrates opposition to what is going on, and sometimes even poses alternatives. I'm not saying this *is* a revolutionary culture yet—you don't get a revolutionary culture until you get a revolution. But something is happening here.

There are three things about this new counter-culture that I find especially interesting and positive in terms of the social values they imply.

The first is that this culture is in many cases the product of collective effort rather than of bourgeois individualism. Rock groups, street theatre groups, poster workshops, art crews for demonstrations—all of these are forms of creativity that are social and shared.

The second thing is that many of these cultural forms are conceived of as participatory; these would include a lot of theatre which demands audience participation and response; poetry which demands being read out loud; and music that needs dance to fulfil it, and which is participated in by people who dance.

The third thing is that many of these new art expressions mix media and genres to a new extent. The rock groups that combine posters, slides, light shows, music, poetry, dance and special effects are one example. Such art breaks down very old divisions of labour; and any breakdown of the division of labour in the arts seems a hopeful sign of our growing ability to integrate different kinds of experience.

This new art is often explicitly political, political in a sense that embraces all of experience, not just the narrow realm defined by poli. sci. Take for instance The Cream's song called "Politician," which begins, "Come on, baby, get into my big black car, I'm going to show you just what my politics are."

The conditions of production and even more of distribution of this poetry are a long way from being ideal. Rock performers are exploited by their merchandisers and preyed upon by their public to a degree unusual even in the mass performing arts. There is much that is religious about mass art, and some rock performers have become to some degree human sacrifices; the confusion between the demands of their art, of their public, and of the business, and the confusion between their public-performing and private selves is alienating in the extreme. But this very alienation, in artists that can hold out (and most groups are short-lived) produces a degree of political consciousness and explicitness that is incredible when you realize that it is marketed by the very forces it is battling against, and that it is accepted wholeheartedly by millions of people. Bob Dylan is the most striking example of this consciousness. He writes for kids in a language they can understand, that is hip and full of symbols of the things that oppress all of us. As in "Subterranean Homesick Blues":

> Johnny's in the basement
> Mixing up the medicine
> I'm on the pavement
> Thinking about the government
> The man in the trenchcoat
> Badge out, laid off
> Says he's got a bad cough
> Wants to get paid off
> Look out kid
> It's something you did
> God knows when
> But you're doin' it again . . .
>
> Ah, get born, keep warm
> Short pants, romance, learn to dance
> Get dressed, get blessed
> Try to be a success
> Please her, please him, buy gifts
> Don't steal, don't lift
> Twenty years of schoolin'
> And they put you on the day shift
> Look out kid they keep it all hid
> Better jump down a manhole
> Buy yourself a candle, don't wear sandals
> Try to avoid the scandals
> Don't wanna be a bum
> You better chew gum
> The pump don't work
> Cause the vandals took the handles.

Dylan is a mass poet. People follow his work and wait for his latest releases with an eagerness that no poet has received in this country since at least the Industrial Revolution. People talk about his work and his changes as if they had participated in them. They see his poetry as a *process*—a living, growing thing—not as a mysterious product in an aesthetic universe apart from life.

time was to find the truth, what
do you think?

I feel that TV could be very
good if it is used not abused. (TV
can be just a psychologically damaging
as drugs or alcohol) I think it
is good for entertainment — in moderation —
and it can bring many things closer.
So that you'll investigate further.
I watched, but I could not be an
inventor one source of entertainment.

This sense of art as process is crucial to the revitalization of it. As politics must teach people the ways and give them the means to take control over their own lives, art must teach people, in the most vivid and imaginative ways possible, how to take control over their own experience and observations, how to link these things with theory, and how to connect both with the experience of others.

The Phantom World of TV

GUNTHER ANDERS

Gunther Anders (1908–   ) has lived all his life in Germany, where he is a prize-winning cameraman and mass media critic.

I

Modern mass consumption is a sum of solo performances; each consumer, an unpaid homeworker employed in the production of the mass man.

In the days before the cultural faucets of radio and television had become standard equipment in each home, the Smiths and Millers used to throng the motion picture theaters where they collectively consumed the stereotyped mass products manufactured for them. One might be tempted to regard it as peculiarly appropriate that the mass product should be thus consumed by a compact mass. Such a view, however, would be mistaken. Nothing contradicts the essential purpose of mass production more completely than a situation in which a single specimen of a commodity is simultaneously enjoyed by several, let alone by numerous, consumers. Whether this consumption is a "genuine communal experience" or merely the sum of many individual experiences, is a matter of indifference to the mass producer. What he needs is not the compact mass as such, but a mass broken up or atomized into the largest possible number of customers; he does not want all of his customers to consume one and the same product, he wants all of his customers to buy identical products on the basis of an identical demand which has also to be produced.

In countless industries this ideal has more or less been achieved. Whether the motion picture industry can ever achieve it seems doubtful, because this industry continues the tradition of the theater: the commodity it produces is a spectacle designed for simultaneous consumption by a large number of spectators. Such a situation is obsolete. No wonder that the radio and television industries could enter into competition with the motion picture despite the latter's tremendous development: for the two newer industries benefited from the possibility of marketing, in addition to the commodity to be consumed, the devices required

Source: Gunther Anders, "The Phantom World of TV," trans. by Norbert Guterman, *Dissent,* Vol. 3 (1956), pp. 14–24. Copyright © 1956 by Dissent Publishing Association. Reprinted by permission.

for its consumption, devices that, unlike the motion pictures, could be sold to almost everyone. And so it came about that many of the evenings the Smith and Millers had formerly spent together in motion picture theaters, they began to spend at home. The situation that is taken for granted in the motion picture theater—the consumption of the mass product by a mass of people—was thus done away with. Needless to say, this did not mean a slowing-up of mass production; rather, mass production for the mass men, indeed mass production of the mass man himself, was speeded up daily. Millions of listeners were served the identical product; each of these was treated as a mass man, "an indefinite article"; each was confirmed in his character—or absence of character—as a mass man. But with this difference, that collective consumption became superfluous through the mass production of receiving sets. The Smiths consumed the mass products *en famille* or even singly; the more isolated they became, the more profits they yielded. The mass-produced hermit came into being as a new human type, and now millions of them, cut off from each other, yet identical with each other, remain in the seclusion of their homes. Their purpose, however, is not to renounce the world, but to be sure they won't miss the slightest crumb of the world as image on a screen.

It is well known that the principle of industrial centralization, which ruled unchallenged only a generation ago, has now been dropped, mainly for strategic reasons, in favor of the principle of dispersal. It is less known that this principle of dispersal is also applied in the production of the mass man. Although we have so far spoken only of dispersed consumption, we are justified in speaking of production because in this case both coincide in a peculiar way. As the German proverb has it, *Mensch ist was er isst,* "man is what he eats" (in a nonmaterialistic sense): it is through the consumption of mass commodities that mass men are produced. This implies that the consumer of the mass commodity becomes, through his consumption, one of the workers contributing to his own transformation into a mass man. In other words, consumption and production coincide. If consumption is "dispersed," so is the production of the mass man. And this production takes place wherever consumption takes place— in front of each radio, in front of each television set.

Everyone is, so to speak, employed as a homeworker—a homeworker of a most unusual kind: for he performs his work—which consists in transforming himself into a mass man—through his consumption of the mass product offered him, i.e., through leisure. Whereas the classical homeworker manufactured his wares in order to secure a minimum of consumer goods and leisure, the modern homeworker consumes a maximum of leisure products in order to help produce the mass man. To complete the paradox, the homeworker, instead of receiving wages for his work, must pay for it by buying the means of production (the receiving sets and, in many countries, also the broadcasts) by the use of which he becomes transformed into mass man. In other words, he pays for selling himself: he must purchase the very unfreedom he himself helps to produce.

This conclusion may seem far-fetched. But no one will deny that for the production of the kind of mass man that is desired today, the formation of actual mass gatherings is no longer required. Le Bon's observations on the psychology of crowds have become obsolete, for each person's individuality can be erased and his rationality leveled down in his own home. The stage-managing of masses in the Hitler style has become superfluous: to transform a man into a nobody (and one who is proud of being a nobody) it is no longer necessary to drown him in the mass or to enlist him as an actual member of a mass organization. No method of depersonalizing man, of depriving him of his human powers, is more effective than one which seems to preserve the freedom of the person and the rights of individuality. And when the conditioning is carried out separately for each individual, in the solitude of his home, in millions of secluded homes, it is incomparably more successful. For this conditioning is disguised as "fun"; the victim is not told that he is asked to sacrifice anything; and since the procedure leaves him with the delusion of his privacy or at least of his private home, it remains perfectly discreet. The old saying "a man's own home is as precious as gold" has again become true, though in an entirely new sense. For today, the home is valuable not only to its owner, but also to the owners of the home-owners—the caterers of radio and television who serve the home-owner his daily fare.

II

Radio set and telescreen become transformed into a negative family table; the family into a miniature audience.

Needless to say, this mass consumption is not usually called by its true name. On the contrary, it is represented as favoring the rebirth of the family and of privacy—an understandable hypocrisy.

In actual fact, the type of mass consumption discussed here threatens to dissolve the family under the guise of fostering the intimacy of family life. For what now dominates in the home, thanks to television, is the outside world—real or fictional; and this outside world is so unrestrictedly dominant that the reality of the home—not only the four walls and furniture, but precisely the shared family life—becomes inoperative and phantom-like. When that which is remote becomes familiar, that which is familiar becomes remote. When the phantom becomes real, reality becomes a phantom. The home tends to become a container, its function to be reduced to containing a video screen for the outside world. The realm of the phantoms is victorious over the realm of the home without even the chance of a contest between the two; it triumphs the moment the television set enters the home: it comes, it is seen, it conquers. At once the ceiling is full of leaks, the walls become transparent, the cement uniting the members of the family crumbles away, the shared privacy disintegrates.

Decades ago it was possible to observe that the social hallmark of the family —the massive table in the center of the living room, which served as the gathering point of the family—had begun to lose its force of attraction, had become obsolete. Eventually the living room table was eliminated from the modern home. Now it has found its authentic successor, the television set, a piece of furniture whose social symbolism and persuasive power can measure against those of the former table. This does not mean, however, that the television set has become the family center; on the contrary, what the set embodies is rather the decentralization of the family, its ex-centricity: it is, so to speak, the *negative* family table. It does not provide a common *center,* but rather a common avenue of escape. Whereas the table was a centripetal force; its existence encouraged the members of the family seated around it to continue weaving the cloth of family life as the shuttles of interest, glances and conversations ran back and forth. The influence exerted by the television screen is centrifugal. The seats in front of the screen are so arranged that the members of the family no longer face each other; they can see or look at each other only at the price of missing something on the screen; they converse (if they still can or want to talk with each other) only by accident. They are no longer together, they are merely placed one beside the other, as mere spectators. There can no longer be any question of a world formed or shared by them. The only thing the members of the family do together—though never as an integrated family group—is to take excursions into a realm of unreality, a world they actually share with no one (for they themselves do not really share in it); or if they do share it, it is only with all those millions of "soloists" of mass consumption who, like them and simultaneously with them, stare at their television screens. The family has been re-structured into a miniature audience, and the home into a miniature theater modeled on the movie house.

III

Because the receiving sets speak in our place, they gradually deprive us of the power of speech, thus transforming us into passive dependents.

Television viewers, we have said, converse with each other only by accident—in so far as they still retain the will or the ability to speak.

This is true even of radio listeners. They too speak only by mistake. Their will and ability to speak decrease from day to day—and this does not mean that they become silent in the literal sense, but that their garrulousness has assumed a purely passive form. Since the receiving sets speak in our place, they progressively rob us of our ability to speak, of our opportunities for speaking, and finally even of our pleasure in expressing ourselves, just as the phonograph and radio have robbed us of live music performed in our homes.

The pairs of lovers sauntering along the shores of the Hudson, the Thames or the Danube with a portable radio do not talk to each other but listen to a third person—the public, usually anonymous, voice of the program which they walk like a dog, or, more accurately, which walks them like a pair of dogs. Since they are an audience in miniature which follows the voice of the broadcast, they take their walk not alone, but in company of a third person. Intimate conversation is eliminated in advance; and whatever intimate contacts take place between the lovers are introduced and even stimulated not by them, but by that third party—the husky or crowing voice of the program which (for is that not the very meaning of "program"?) tells both lovers what and how to feel or do. Since they do what they are told to do in the presence of a third party, they do it in an acoustically indiscreet situation. However entertaining their obedience may seem to the lovers, it is certain that they do not entertain *each other;* rather both are entertained by that third party which alone has a voice; and this voice does not entertain them only in the sense of keeping them occupied and diverting them, but also in the sense of providing them with support: as the third party in the alliance, this voice gives them that support which they, in their ignorance of what they can do with themselves, cannot give each other. Indeed, there is reason to throw the cloak of silence over the fact that today even love-making often takes place to the accompaniment of the radio. The radio set that is admitted or desired in every possible situation is reminiscent of the torch-bearing female guide whom the ancients tolerated or invited as witness to their amorous pleasures; the difference between the two consists in this, that the modern guide is a mechanized public utility, that her torch serves to provide not only illumination but also warmth, and that under no circumstances must she keep her mouth shut, but on the contrary, is expected to talk her head off; she has to supply a background of noise in the form of songs or words and to silence that *horror vacui* which does not loosen its grip on the pair of lovers even *in actu.*

But the situation of love-making is only an example, the most blatant. People keep themselves similarly "entertained" in every situation, even while they work; and if by some mistake they talk to each other, the radio voice speaks in the background as the main protagonist, giving them the comforting and reassuring feeling that it will continue to speak even after they themselves have had their say—even after they are dead.

For them words are no longer something one speaks, but something one merely hears; speaking is no longer something that one does, but something that one receives. No matter in what cultural or political milieu this development toward an existence without speech takes place, its end result must be everywhere the same—a type of man who, because he no longer speaks himself, has nothing more to say; and who, because he only listens, will do no more than listen. The initial effects of this development are manifest even today: the languages of all advanced countries have become cruder, poorer; and there is a growing disinclination to use langauge. But that is not all: human experience, and hence man himself, also becomes progressively cruder and poorer. For man's inward life, its richness and subtlety, cannot endure without the richness and subtlety of language; man not only expresses himself through his speech, he is also the product of his language.

IV

We see the world only when we are inside our homes. The events come to us, not we to them.

The consumer goods by means of which such a transformation of human nature is achieved are brought into our homes, just as is gas or electricity. The deliveries are not confined to artistic products, such as music or radio dramas; they also include actual events, at least those events which are selected and processed to represent "reality" or to serve as substitutes for it. A man who wants to be "in the swim," to know what is going on outside, must go to his home, where the events are waiting for him, like water ready to flow from the faucet. For if he stayed outside, in the chaos of reality, how could he pick out anything "real" of more than local significance? Only after he has closed the door behind him, does the outside world become visible to him; only after we have been transformed into windowless monads, does the universe reflect itself in us.

This brings us to the heart of our subject. For the fact that the events of the day—the events themselves, not reports of events—that football matches, church services, atomic explosions, *visit us at home;* that the mountain comes to the prophet, the world to man, that fact, next to the mass production of hermits and the transformation of the family into a miniature audience, is the revolutionary change brought about by radio and television.

The truly philosophic implications of this change will become apparent from the following tentative list of some of its consequences:

1. When the world comes to us, instead of our going to it, we are no longer "in the world," but only listless, passive consumers of the world.

2. Since the world comes to us only as an image, it is half-present and half-absent, in other words, phantom-like; and we too are like phantoms.

3. When the world speaks to us, without our being able to speak to it, we are deprived of speech, and hence condemned to be unfree.

4. When the world is perceivable, but no more than that, i.e., not subject to our action, we are transformed into eavesdroppers and Peeping Toms.

5. When an event that occurs at a definite place is broadcast, and when it can be made to appear at any other place as a "broadcast," it becomes a movable, indeed, almost ubiquitous object, and has forfeited its spatial location, its *principium individuationis.*

6. When the event is no longer attached to a specific location and can be reproduced virtually any number of times, it acquires the characteristics of an assembly-line product; and when we pay for having it delivered to our homes, it is a commodity.

7. When the actual event is socially important only in its reproduced form, i.e., as a spectacle, the difference between being and appearance, between reality and image of reality, is abolished.

8. When the event in its reproduced form is socially more important than the original event, this original must be shaped with a view to being reproduced: in other words, the event becomes merely a master matrix, or a mold for casting its own reproductions.

9. When the dominant experience of the world thrives on such assembly-line products, the concept "the world" is abolished in so far as it denotes that *in which* we live. The real world is forfeited; the broadcasts, in other words, further an idealistic orientation.

V

Because the world is brought into our homes, we do not have to explore it; as a result, we do not acquire experience. Modern man travels only as a last resort.

In a world that comes to man, man has no need to go to the world in order to explore or experience it; that which was once called "experience" has become superfluous.

Up until recently, expressions such "to go into the world," or "to experience" have denoted important anthropological concepts. Since man is being relatively little endowed with instincts, he has been compelled to experience and know the world *a posteriori* in order to find his place in it; only in this way could he reach his goal and become "experienced." Life used to consist in a voyage of exploration; that is why the great *Erziehungs romane* ("educational novels") dealt with the ways man—although always in the world—had to travel in order to get to know the world. Today, because the world comes to him—as an image —he need not bother to explore it; such explorations and experiences are superfluous, and since all superfluous functions become atrophied, he can no longer engage in explorations and become experienced. It is indeed evident that the type of "experienced man" is becoming increasingly rare, and that age and experience tend to be regarded as less and less valuable. Like pedestrians who have taken to flying we no longer need roads; in consequence, our knowledge of the ways of the world, which we formerly used to explore, and which made us experienced, is declining. Simultaneously with this, the world itself becomes a pathless wilderness. Whereas formerly we stored up experience by means of traveling, today the world is "stored up" for us like a commodity put aside for future use; we do not have to go to the events, the events are paraded before us.

Such a portrait of our contemporaries may at first sight appear distorted. For it has become customary to look upon the automobile and the airplane as symbols of modern man, a being whose essence is travel. What is in question is precisely the correctness of this definition. For modern man does not attach value to his traveling because of any interest in the regions he visits, actually or vicariously; he does not travel to become experienced but to still his hunger for omnipresence and for rapid change as such. Moreover, the speed of his movement deprives him of the opportunity for experience (to the extent that speed itself has now become his sole and ultimate experience)—not to mention the fact that the number of objects worthy of being experienced and capable of adding to his experience is continually decreased by his successful efforts to make the world uniform, and that even today he feels at home, in need of no experience, wherever he may land. A publicity poster of a well-known airline, utterly confusing provincialism and globalism, appeals to its customers with these words: "When you use our services, you are everywhere at home." Everywhere at home: there is indeed good reason to assume that today any trip (even though the man who takes it may sleep comfortably in his electrically heated cabin while flying over the North Pole) is felt to be an antiquated, uncomfortable and inadequate method of achieving omnipresence. Modern man still resorts to this method precisely because, despite all his efforts, he has not yet succeeded in having everything delivered to his home—something he has come to regard as his inherent right.

Such a situation points to a mode of existence, a relation to the world so extraordinarily preverse that even Descartes' malicious demon would be incapable of devising a comparable deception. Such a mode of existence may be described as "idealistic" in two ways:

1. Although we actually live in an alienated world, this world is presented to us in such a manner that it seems to exist for us, as though it were our own and like ourselves.

2. We "take" (i.e., regard and accept) it as such, although we stay at home in our chairs. We do not actually "take" it, in the manner of a devouring beast or a conqueror, and we do not actually make it our own; but the average radio listener or television viewer looks upon the world that is served him in the form of reproduced sounds and pictures as his own. As a result he develops into a kind of Peeping Tom ruling over a phantom world.

VI

The world brought into our homes by radio and television is a debased, philistinized world; pseudo-familiarity is an aspect of alienation.

This is not the place to discuss the origin and symptomatology of alienation. The literature of the subject is enormous, and we must take this phenomenon for granted. The particular deception in question here consists in this, that the radio listener or television viewer, although living in an alienated world, is made to believe that he is on a footing of the greatest intimacy with everything and everybody. He is not invited to become acquainted with an unfamiliar world; instead, people, countries, situations, events, particularly the least familiar of them, are presented to him as though he had always known them; they are thoroughly philistinized in advance.

Whereas our next-door neighbors usually do not know us, and the distance between them and us remains unbridged for years on end, film stars, girls whom we never meet personally but whom we have seen countless times and whose spiritual and physical characteristics are known to us more completely than those of our co-workers, appear to us in the guise of old friends, of "chums." We are automatically on a footing of intimacy, we refer to them by their first names.

To bring about such a state of affairs, to enable the program consumer to treat the world as something familiar, the televised image must address him as an old chum. In fact, every broadcast has this chummy quality. When I tune in on the President, he suddenly sits next to me at the fireplace, chatting with me, although he may be thousands of miles away. (I am only marginally aware of the fact that this intimacy exists in millions of copies). When the girl announcer appears on the screen, she speaks to me in a tone of complete frankness, as though I were her bosom friend. (That she is also the bosom friend of all men is again only a marginal realization.)

All of them come to me as intimate or indiscreet visitors, all of them find me ready to be chummy with them. Not one of these people who are transported into my house retains even an atom of unfamiliarity. And this is true not only of persons, but of everything else, of the world as a whole. Things, places, events, situations—everything reaches us with a chummy smile on its lips.

We have now achieved a footing of intimacy not only with film stars but also with the stars of the firmament; we speak of "good old Cassiopeia" just as readily as of Marilyn or Rita. And this is not meant as a joke. The fact that laymen and scientists regard it as possible and even probable that the inhabitants of other planets who allegedly operate the flying saucers have, like us and precisely in our time, no other worry but to undertake interplanetary voyages, proves that we look upon everything in the universe as "one of our sort." This is a sign of an anthropomorphism against which the anthropomorphism of so-called primitive civilizations strikes one as timid. The purveyors of the vulgarized universe realize that unless they bring nature down to our level they will not sell it—which would be to miss a profitable opportunity. But we, the consumers, are systematically transformed into boon companions of everything on our planet and in the universe—no more than boon companions, for of course there can be no question of genuine fraternization or identification.

What we have said of things and persons distant in space, also applies to things and persons distant in time. The past too is philistinized. I shall not speak of the historical motion pictures in which such a treatment is the rule. But even in a serious, vividly written American academic book, Socrates is described as "quite a guy"—in other words he is put in a category that brings the distant great man seemingly close to the reader; for, needless to say, the reader too is "quite a guy." This label gives the reader the unconsciously gratifying feeling that Socrates, if he had not happened to live in that remote past, would be essentially like us, would not have anything to say that is essentially different from what we have to say, and in no case could claim greater authority than we do.

Others perceive historical figures as comical by definition (e.g., their reactions to historical films); this is so because such figures strike them as provincials in the realm of time, as creatures that have not grown up in the capital—the Now—and for that reason behave like village idiots of history or superstitious backwoodsmen; every electrical invention made since their time is looked upon as an eloquent proof of their inferiority. Finally, to many of our contemporaries historical figures appear as nonconformists, as suspiciously queer fellows, for it is obvious that they regard themselves as something quite special —namely, unlike every decent man who chooses to live in the present, they prefer to take up residence in a cavern of the past. (This is the source of comic effects in several pieces by Mark Twain.) But whether a great man of the past is regarded as "quite a guy," a queer fellow, or a provincial, these categories denote proximity, and hence are variations of the chum.

As for the typical case of "Socrates, the guy," the epithet here is obviously based on the great political principle formulated in the Declaration of the Rights of Man, "All men are born equal," which has now been extended into the assertion of the equality of all citizens of the commonwealth of times past and present. Needless to say, such an extension of the principle of equality suggests not only a false historical proximity, but also a misconception of the common denominator of all mankind—for after all the essence of Socrates consists in the very thing that "our sort" is lacking. The method allegedly intended to bring the object close to us, actually serves to veil the object, to alienate it, or simply to do away with it altogether. For once you project history on a single plane of boon companionship, it has actually ceased to exist *qua* history—and this is perhaps even more plausible than our general thesis, that when all the various and variously distant regions of the world are brought equally close to us, the world as such vanishes.

Magic, Myth, and Comedy in the Movies

PARKER TYLER

Parker Tyler (1919–1961) was a poet and movie critic who wrote many well-known books, including *Magic and Myth in the Movies* (1955) and *Underground Film* (1960).

That the movies offer nothing but entertainment is a myth in a sense never used or implied in the following pages. I am not denying that millions of America's movie fans succeed in finding only entertainment in the nation's theaters. Aside from the newsreels and the documentaries given impetus by the war, entertainment remains all that is consciously demanded by those paying rising prices at movie box offices. Yet as a fact there *is* more, and that margin, which I regard as the essence of the matter, is the subject of this as of my previous book on American cinema. Patrons of all art media may get more than they demand as well as less, and since the surplus is not precisely expected, it may register vaguely, obliquely, unconsciously. Especially is this true of the movie audience, if only because as a large mass it is critically inarticulate. . . . Hollywood is a vital, interesting phenomenon, at least as important to the spiritual climate as daily weather to the physical climate. A myth foisted specifically on the movies proper rather than on the reaction of audiences is furnished, as I explain later on, by devotees of both stage and novel who scorn movies as below the serious level—as standing in relation to true art somewhat as the circus does to the legitimate stage. But unfortunately these judges, unaware of the ritual importance of the screen, its baroque energy and protean symbolism, are unwarrantably summary, basically uneducated in the movie medium.

. . .

The proposition I have to offer now is: the true field of the movies is not *art* but *myth*, between which—in the sense "myth" is invariably used here—there is a perhaps unsuspectedly wide difference. Assuredly a myth is a fiction, and this is its bare link with art, but a myth is specifically a free, unharnessed

Source: Parker Tyler, *Magic and Myth in the Movies* (New York, 1947, 1970), pp. viii–xviii, 31–52. Copyright © 1947 by Parker Tyler. Introduction copyright © 1970 by Simon & Schuster, Inc. Reprinted by permission of Simon & Schuster, Inc.

fiction, a basic, prototypic pattern capable of many variations and distortions, many betrayals and disguises, even though it remains *imaginative* truth.

. . .

Essentially the *scene* of imaginative truth, or art, is the mind itself, but in some manner this truth must be objective, capable of projection onto the screen of the world. In a sense man *is* his past, the past of his race, and all the beliefs he ever held. Reality cannot be made up from the material facts of his existence, his immediate sensory reactions; nor can it be fundamentally a world that never was. Certainly man has ceased to believe much he used to believe. "Oh, that is a myth," we say, meaning that even if significant, it is an ideal or an illusion, a thing that has no substance. But psychology has taught us the strange reality of chimeras, their symbolic validity; and comparative mythology has revealed the great persistence of psychic patterns, with special reference to the supernatural, whose continuity in human belief is sometimes surprisingly self-evident. At one time men believed the earth was flat. Today this is a purely ornamental myth; it has died because imagining the earth is flat has no relation to our desires or employments. At one time the pagans believed in Diana as goddess of the moon and the hunt. Today this also might be considered a decorative myth, something in the fairytale class. Yet like so many legends it holds a mesmeric appeal for the mind; Diana represents, as a matter of fact, a certain sexual type—the vigorous virgin, the woman resistant to love; and yet according to the legend Endymion made her lose her heart; that is, the man lived who could break down her defenses merely through his physical image. Obviously this sexual pattern is repeated today. The modern belief that the earth is round corresponds to the conditions of our planetary existence insofar as, proceeding on this premise, our astronomical calculations work out. The belief is consistent with *all the facts*. Today the fact that Diana once had for the pagans a reality she does not have for us means merely that the myth lives in another form. It is an ideal archetype, a past of human experience that has its home in the imagination. And yet . . . that which was true once may become true again. What was symbolized by the Diana myth in actual human experience is a permanent legacy of the race. So the essence of myth also has the status of permanent possibility . . . in short, *desires* may have the same power over the mind and behavior, indeed a much greater power, than *facts*.

In the following pages I have occasion to refer specifically to the great researches made in ancient magic by Sir James Frazer. That there are anthropological assumptions contradictory to various of Frazer's own premises is of no importance to the point I am making. In order to explain a single phenomenon, the priest cult of the King of the Wood at Nemi, Frazer accumulated into one work a prodigious array of ancient primitive beliefs and customs suggesting the limitless lineage of the relatively recent cult at Nemi. At this moment, as when his book was written, nobody is a devotee of this cult; nobody believes in the magic of the golden bough that had to be plucked by the aspirant to Diana's priesthood before he was empowered to kill in single combat the incumbent priest. And yet those who do not profoundly know anthropology might be astonished to learn how much of our personal lives is influenced by all the ancient magical and religious beliefs connected with this one cult. The whole history of the decay and fall of gods, the extermination of divine hierarchies, could be told with just the Nemian cult as basis. In discussing in later pages the male comics of the screen who entertained troops all over the world during the war, I show how they may be considered modern medicine men or primitive priests, scapegoats who transferred to themselves the inner fears of the soldier striving to be brave and made cowardice and bravery alike into a kind of joke. Consequently in relation to my argument the myth is not, as a psychological or historical nucleus of fact, necessarily to be judged as true or false, illusory or real, according to its specific labels, its historic status, its literal beliefs. Essentially myths are not factual but symbolic. I assume that movies are essentially likewise.

Into the present book I have put a number of analyses I term "magic-lantern metamorphoses." Not only do these sometimes show how significantly a movie differs from the literary original from which it was made, but also I have tried to reveal that the conscious purpose of the screen story is by no means the true substance of its message. Briefly movies, similar to much else in life, are seldom what they seem. In this sense—being, to begin with, fiction—movies are dreamlike and fantastic, their fantasy and dreamfulness having actually come to the fore at the moment of writing as consciously embodying certain assumptions of my previous book. These assumptions are simple: (*a*) the existence of the unconscious mind as a dynamic factor in human action and (*b*) the tendency of screen stories to emphasize—unintentionally—neuroses and psychopathic traits discovered and formulated by psychoanalysis. Unaware of the precise function of the unconscious mind, Hollywood movie-makers are used to combining their own automatism of mental and physical behavior with that of the characters in their products.

. . .

It is not news that what is known as superstition has a powerful hold on the popular mind. What is not so generally realized is the extent to which the superstitious stratum of the human psyche lies below the surface, below the verbal and conscious fields of expression, and how great is the symbolic potential of the material there. It is perfectly logical that Hollywood's lust to display the *obvious,* the *sure-fire,* the *sensational,* guarantees for its products the latent presence of the most venerable stereotypes of emotion. Sometimes it is not a case of the survival of ancient patterns per se but of their strictly modern form and the place of that form in movie plot or character pattern; examples of this are the folk myths of the absent-minded professor, of the efficiency expert, and of the eccentricity of genius—all considered in the chapter on schizophrenic motifs.

. . .

The fundamental eye trickery that is a genius of the camera—you see the object, yet it isn't there—came to the fore in the movies and ever since then has mocked with its dynamic plasticity the very form from which it developed, the still camera. Today the movie has all the flexibility of the novel as well as the vision and speech of the stage. In striving through imaginative works to create the illusion of reality the movie screen must constantly transcend its own mirror nature of literal reflection. Camera trickery is really camera magic, for illusion can be freely created by the movie camera with more mathematical accuracy and stock value than by sleight-of-hand magic or stage illusion. The very homogeneity of cinema illusion—the images of the actors themselves are illusive, their corporal bodies absent—creates a throwback in the mood of the spectator to the vestiges of those ancient beliefs that I discuss in detail later in the chapter on supernaturalism, such as beliefs in ghosts, secret forces, telepathy, etc.

Moreover, the movie-theater rite corresponds directly to the profoundly primitive responses of the audience; the auditorium is dark, the spectator is relaxed, the movie in front of him requires less sheer mental attention than would a novel or stage play—less attention because all movement seems to exist on the screen; even the background changes easily, quickly; the whole world moves around the spectator, who is a still point. From the capacity of the screen for trick illusion, plus the dark-enshrouded passivity of the spectator, issues a state of daydream, which I termed in my previous book "the daylight dream" because it occurs in the dark: the screen is the focus of light, while the spectator is conscious in a darkness of the bedroom. It is in daydreams that magic seems to operate, in daydreams that things begin to seem rather than to be. "The movie theater," to quote directly from my previous book, "is the psychoanalytic clinic of the average worker's daylight dream." It is likewise in the process of psychoanalysis, where the *part*, truly recognized as symbol, transforms the meaning of the whole. The movie process is a complex myth of sheer synecdoche. People go to the movies merely to see a favorite player, or for the locale or period, or for the genre, or because they are bored almost to death. How, under these conditions, can anyone hope to appreciate the *whole* movie, especially since, to begin with, the movie can hardly be considered a whole?

No longer does man believe in myth or magic. No! For magic has been sifted and reorganized into science and governs only his material world, not the realm of his spirit, while comparative mythology and anthropology merely comprise school subjects. The sects of Christian religion have organized Western man's spiritual beliefs under one heading: the myth of Christ. Yet Christ's myth too can be related to pagan myths. The very fact that for children the Bible itself is but another series of fairy tales, weighted but little by a sense of historical fact, alone demonstrates my point as to the basic importance of myth with regard to popular or folk art. Our imaginary lives as children survive in us as adults and enrich our subsequent natures. So the fairy-tale lives of primitive races, our ancient antecedents, survive in the religions we formally believe in today as well as among those tribes still unassimilated to modern civilization. I do not claim my absolute value for the myth and magic of Hollywood or for those modern vestiges of the old Greek divinities I have dubbed "the gods and goddesses of Hollywood." On the contrary the principle I mean is one of relativity and metamorphosis rather than absolutism and changelessness: just as a word has synonyms—and antonyms—so has a myth. In psychoanalytical symbolism, the deepest symbolism of the mind, the identity of objects is established by a complex frame of reference in which an image may represent one of three objects or all three objects at once. If, then, I say that the actors of Hollywood are an enlarged personnel of the realistically anthropomorphic deities of ancient Greece, I do not indulge in a mere bit of verbal humor, satiric or otherwise; on the other hand neither am I proposing or assuming the existence of an unconscious cult of supernatural worship. I feel I am but calling attention to the fact that the glamour actors and actresses of the movie realm are fulfilling an ancient need, unsatisfied by popular religions of contemporary times. Those men and women who perform for us are human, as we are; they have homes, children, love affairs; they suffer and die. And yet a magic barrier cuts across the texture of our mutual humanity; somehow their wealth, fame, and beauty, their apparently unlimited field of worldly pleasure—these conditions tinge them with the supernatural, render them immune to the bitterness of ordinary frustrations. It does not matter if this thought is a mythological exaggeration. It is a *tendency* of the popular imagination. The secret of the power of Hollywood gods and goddesses is that they seem to do everything anyone else does except that when they die—in movies—they die over and over; when they love, they love over and over. Even as the gods do, they undergo continual metamorphoses, never losing their identities, being Rita Hayworth or Glenn Ford no matter what their movie aliases. . . .

High, Low, Comedy Jack, and the Game

The most traditional conception of the comedian is that he is low. He was the king's shadow and parody, the unserious essence of the king that by some dialectic law of nature came to his rescue in his darkest moments and by pointing out the ultimate absurdity and vanity of life afforded him a salutary detachment, a respite that psychologically caused him to bear misfortune or anxiety with more grace. Therefore the most beautiful clown I can think of is the Fool, companion of Lear; for seeing the mad old king, the Fool knows his liege is beyond the medicinal aid of comic philosophy, and so is humbled—having been robbed of his own meaning, comedy, in the presence of a victim deprived by insanity of the noble significance of tragedy. Lear is a poor, bereft person in great trouble, a man fallen lower even than the Fool, not only because he actually has fallen from a great height but because, being completely irrational, he does not know he is being a fool. Here the Fool, like the king, is thrown out of his job.

In modern civilization and especially in the movies the low estate of clowns is a lucrative profession and therefore raised to such a lofty commercial level that it is quite natural to call Chaplin, for instance, the King of Comedy. If the clown has any socio-psychological function, it is no longer to console kings, for clowns are not privately maintained even by industrialists or financiers, whereas public careers are automatically open to them. But naturally a still deeper reason exists for their absence from the ranks of domestic retainers. Their lowness would provide no really dramatic contrast with the natures of their masters. All that personal power in society today can command in the way of the clown is the stooge, often on the surface a quite serious character whose status is not actually that of an employee. But a stooge essentially is only a clown's servant—the butt, the foil, of the master comedian. Through his mask of the perennial underdog the truly great clown achieves a subjective independence of style in his profession of art.

I recall a French movie, whose title I forget, in which one can see the origin of all modern clowns and the prototype indeed of all movie comedians of today. He was a Frenchman of the sixteenth century whose rhymes used to delight the Parisian populace and help them to forget they were hungry. The plot of this film was concerned with how this idol of his people, a tailor by vocation, a poet and singer by avocation, mediates between the rebellious anger of the populace and the haughty indifference of the nobles until his tricks actually avert a revolution. The point was that he loved fun and had a sincere, albeit realistic, admiration for the aristocracy. In the end he proves entertaining not only to *hoi polloi* but to the palace gentry. But he is paid, you may be certain, by the queen's lover, the cardinal. Here the clown was servant to the noble class as in olden times, but in this case he was an economic stooge. Diplomats and other strategists, we may note, employ less obviously comic stooges.

It seems not farfetched to draw a general parallel and say that Chaplin and the numerous latter-day galaxy of funny men, in making millions laugh, help them to bear their troubles, especially their economic troubles. After all, this is a function which is not exactly news. Movie comedians such as Bob Hope and Joe E. Brown were among the most active and indefatigable of entertainers at army camps. And they repeated the ancient pattern of distracting the mind from the serious and troublous matters on which it was engaged. Comedians, along with singers, were most frequently called upon to entertain soldiers and sailors, not only because one-man shows such as Hope are much more portable than whole casts and orchestras but because Hope and others like him are spontaneous, funny, ad lib, and become pals across the footlights with their hordes of listeners. They knew what made the common man laugh and momentarily forget the seriousness of the fighting job he had to do.

. . .

The modern clown is the inheritor of part of the medicine man's rôle as public benefactor, and in societies of high cultural development in the nearer centuries he has continued to relieve tension, caused by high matters and the tragic aspect of destiny, through mimicking them as though they were shallow affairs. His ability to do this according to his own tradition is an idiosyncratic immunity to normal human feelings, the clown being, generally speaking, too ugly, deformed, or foolish to have serious sentiments.

. . .

Today the generic clown as public entertainer is the circus clown, whose fantastically painted face and professional costume separate him from the civilized human being and render him a sort of savage mask and fabulous apparition. It is quite logical, therefore, that Chaplin himself, the great wistful clown of the movies, should have added to his repertory a film called *The Circus*.

Chaplin has been greater than any of the others, not only because he is a greater pantomimist than any comedian I know of but because he is the strict humanization, in mythical terms, of the traditional clown. His history as a movie mime bears increasing witness to an accent on a serious or relatively realistic treatment of pathos and the emotion of love, with its concomitant of chivalric courage. But as a matter of fact I feel that the more serious treatment, parallel with a certain modernizing, proved a loss to Chaplin's art, because his best pictures in my opinion are *The Gold Rush* and *City Lights,* which come at the beginning and end of his middle period, before he began to invest his work with what might be called conscious social content.

In *City Lights* there was a most revealing master-slave, knight-clown relationship brought down to the present and showing the split that may occur in aggressive ruling-class personalities as the result of ambiguously acquired temporal power, a split that accounts in our society for the more usual symptoms of megalomania. In this movie Charlie was a tramp who ran into a rich man in his cups and who became the recipient of his kindness to such an extent that he found himself established in the man's home, but finally emerging from his alcoholic bout, Charlie's patron sees him with detestation as great as his former love for him and drives him out. The comedy of alternating drunken affection and sober aversion continues to the bewilderment of Charlie, with many hilarious chases and embraces. The analysis is fairly simple: the gross culture of the class of rich men in our time, with its necessary concessions to money standards and materialistic thinking, engenders an inner spite toward easy-going, humorous fellows who take life lightly—that is, fellows epitomized by Charlie's tramp, who can't seem to earn a decent living; when in their cups, however, these hard-boiled, well-upholstered gentlemen relax and think up dreams of a truer grandeur wherein they can regard poor fools as symptoms of cosmic irony and as delightfully amusing, because by them they measure their own high estate. However, in the arid chambers of complete sobriety or modern common sense, Charlie becomes a moral allergy, there being no room for him in a society which binds wealth to poverty in so mechanical, direct, and compromising a manner. The point is that there is actually not complete forgetfulness of his drunkenness in the turncoat behavior of the rich man toward Charlie, although the simple convention of the comedy would make it seem complete, but rather a fatal memory by whose dim dream he accurately measures his present state; for he sees Charlie as two people, and both are himself: one is himself before he made or inherited all his money, and the other is the part of himself that, languid, human, smiling, and ironic—like Charlie—had told him unavailingly that material success was all too much trouble, all too ephemeral. That easygoing self he all too coldly destroyed, but he hankers for it whenever he gets drunk, which indeed may be why he does get drunk; and lo! —it happens to appear incarnate in the little tramp, Charlie! Yet Charlie seems to him, after he has sobered up, the self he relentlessly drove out, and, some compulsion arising, he must do so again, especially as the tramp is a phantom of the class created and maintained by inordinate wealth. Here the rich man, thrown out of his job of magician-king, a supernatural being, is forced to drive the true clown out of his life, for he evokes only memories of his former forgotten glory, when he hallucinated his grandeur so successfully that he could laugh at it with his fool.

In considering Chaplin we must not overlook the basic things about so universal a comedian. First, he is short—and in the literal sense of stature therefore is *low.* One cannot conceive a tall comedian very well, unless a comic butler, and I note that of tall comedians only one stands out in my mind, and that is a woman: Charlotte Greenwood, of stage and screen; but after all, excessive height in a woman is correspondingly as absurd as excessive diminutiveness in a man. Moreover, Mr. Chaplin is no Adonis even out of his comic mask. Yet his private life tells us bountifully that he has always been filled with the tender emotion and that his filmic amours are no mere professional charade. As Charlie, the early screen figure, he is a homely, quaint little man, very shy of women, to whom, however, he is very sentimentally attracted. He is as chivalrous as Don Quixote—and indeed is a curious compound of Don Quixote and his servant, Sancho Panza.

. . .

One of the great characteristics of the fool, a part of his natural unfitness, was that, unlike his masters, the king and the knight, his blood was presumably mixed with water. He had the opposite of a warrior's courage: he was a coward. As we know, the classic comic heroes of the slapstick screen—Chaplin, Lloyd, Keaton—all had innate courage if also physical and temperamental drawbacks. Chaplin especially tried to crossbreed the knight and the fool, unite chivalry with the craven and eccentric. We realize that traditionally the underdog rises up, the worm turns. But this is not the professional essence of the matter. The rôle of the clown, mythologically speaking, is still to provide a contrast to the knight, to illustrate by a kind of magic that the knight may project on the fool—who accepts it—every base qualm or cowardly quaver and thus purify his knighthood. So what did we have in the army camps where performed movie comedians like Hope and Skelton, whose dominant make-believe characteristic is identically a jittery sort of cowardice? We had the fool, as of old, continuing his inheritance from the medicine man and purifying the knight, reassuring him that he is bold and brave and nothing else, that only fools—the mentally or physically deficient—are cowards.

It is curious and instructive to note the extent to which the effeminate is also identified with the traits of the fool. For women and fools are traditionally— even if, today of all days, anachronistically—often lumped together: "only a fool or a woman," etc. Part of the routines of Hope, Skelton, and Kaye is female impersonation, merely a logical extension of their character idiosyncrasy of cowardice. I recall that in one movie the talented Skelton gave, without benefit of costume, a pantomimic imitation of a young woman arising from bed in the morning and performing her entire elaborate toilet: it was extremely funny and authentic; and in the same movie he joined a ballet class of young women and vied with them in pirouettes, leaps and *entrechats*. He was far more graceful than some of the young ladies, although presumed, considering his football player's physique, to be excruciatingly inept. In fact the hard-boiled quality of all this, the palatable flavoring, is that gents such as Hope and Skelton are huskies, their physiques thus belying their unstable guts. Oddly enough, concomitant with the gelatinous state of their courage—incidentally, I think that Hope wins the chocolate cake for sustained trembling—is an almost pathological susceptibility to the ladies; this trait stresses the little-recognized tradition that the tender emotion is incompatible with the warrior's character. At any rate, so far as the blood of comedy jacks is concerned, Sparta may be considered as perpetually at war with Athens: the virus of war and abstinence versus the virus of art and love.

. . .

Comedy itself is a game, the traditional game of life played on the level of philosophic cheer, with the emotions as strictly ambivalent counters, its tears being those of joy, chagrin, or a transient grief. Perhaps laughter is less close to life as it is lived in the heart than are secret, terrible tears and the solemn trying to do things and get places. Assuredly, however, screen comedy has a much higher esthetic rating than screen drama, whose sentimentality and dishonest mummery are so often ruinous. Especially in the figure of the solo comedian, the pure entertainer, rather than the comic hero with his Chaplinesque ambiguity, screen low jinks deserve royal-flush prestige and the best prizes of Hollywood. Yet comedians in Hollywood are almost completely ignored for the regular acting awards. Perhaps comedy seems not arty enough, seems too closely wedded to the everyday chore, even to that of the comedian himself, to be hailed as exceptional or superlative. In a sense this is quite true. A great comedian of Hollywood always does his act, goes through his business, everything being entirely expected and perennial—that the most popular dramatic actors, willy nilly, do the same, is less widely recognized and assumed.

Chaplin's full-length mask is but one of a familiar repertory of screen motleys, current or historic, that outlast 95 per cent of movieland's seriously composed faces. The idea of the mask, the unchanged and unchanging dominant expression, calls to mind the classic device of actually using a mask, a false face that obliterates the clown's own features. In respect to comedy it provides the *Pagliacci* pattern implying that two realities exist in the representation: art and life, or specifically laughter and tears. In classical Greece the tragic mask existed too, since at that time visual artifice in connection with the actor was valued on a higher level than on the popular stage developed later.

If we think of the masks of tragedy and comedy that were familiar decorative motifs of the Greeks, we think of two fixed expressions, one an inversion of the other, the tragic mask having the corners of its mouth turned down, whereas the comic has the corners turned up. A modern theory of laughter has it that the historic root of its physiology—the opened jaws, the sudden inhalation and exhalation of breath, the upturned corners of the mouth, and the jerky palpitation of the diaphragm—originated from the hunger cry of the jungle breast and implied the presage of food in the flesh of its victim and the licking of the chops that would follow the meal; that is, the anticipated sensation of well-being, whose dynamism caused the animal's mouth to curl up in a smile of contentment. We all have a vivid memory of the image of the animated-cartoon tiger smiling like the cat that has eaten the canary. This image is assuredly as much a comic mask as the most conventional ever designed.

The Gangster as Tragic Hero

ROBERT WARSHOW

Robert Warshow (1917–1955) wrote *The Immediate Experience* and was an editor of *Commentary* for many years.

America, as a social and political organization, is committed to a cheerful view of life. It could not be otherwise. The sense of tragedy is a luxury of aristocratic societies, where the fate of the individual is not conceived of as having a direct and legitimate political importance, being determined by a fixed and supra-political—that is, non-controversial—moral order or fate. Modern equalitarian societies, however, whether democratic or authoritarian in their political forms, always base themselves on the claim that they are making life happier; the avowed function of the modern state, at least in its ultimate terms, is not only to regulate social relations, but also to determine the quality and the possibilities of human life in general. Happiness thus becomes the chief political issue—in a sense, the only political issue—and for that reason it can never be treated as an issue at all. If an American or a Russian is unhappy, it implies a certain reprobation of his society, and therefore, by a logic of which we can all recognize the necessity, it becomes an obligation of citizenship to be cheerful; if the authorities find it necessary, the citizen may even be compelled to make a public display of his cheerfulness on important occasions, just as he may be conscripted into the army in time of war.

Naturally, this civic responsibility rests most strongly upon the organs of mass culture. The individual citizen may still be permitted his private unhappiness so long as it does not take on political significance, the extent of his tolerance being determined by how large an area of private life the society can accommodate. But every production of mass culture is a public act and must conform with accepted notions of the public good. Nobody seriously questions the principle that it is the function of mass culture to maintain public morale, and certainly nobody in the mass audience objects to having his morale maintained.[1] At a time when the normal condition of the citizen is a state of anxiety, euphoria spreads over our culture like the broad smile of an idiot. In terms of attitudes towards life, there is very little difference between a "happy" movie like *Good News,* which ignores death and suffering, and a "sad" movie like *A Tree Grows*

---

[1] In her testimony before the House Committee on Un-American Activities, Mrs. Leila Rogers said that the movie *None But the Lonely Heart* was un-American because it was gloomy. Like so much else that was said during the unhappy investigation of Hollywood, this statement was at once stupid and illuminating. One knew immediately what Mrs. Rogers was talking about; she had simply been insensitive enough to carry her philistinism to its conclusion.

Source: Robert Warshow, *The Immediate Experience* (New York: Doubleday & Company, 1962), pp. 127–133. Reprinted by permission of Paul Warshow.

in Brooklyn, which uses death and suffering as incidents in the service of a higher optimism.

But, whatever its effectiveness as a source of consolation and a means of pressure for maintaining "positive" social attitudes, this optimism is fundamentally satisfying to no one, not even to those who would be most disoriented without its support. Even within the area of mass culture, there always exists a current of opposition, seeking to express by whatever means are available to it that sense of desperation and inevitable failure which optimism itself helps to create. Most often, this opposition is confined to rudimentary or semi-literate forms: in mob politics and journalism, for example, or in certain kinds of religious enthusiasm. When it does enter the field of art, it is likely to be disguised or attenuated: in an unspecific form of expression like jazz, in the basically harmless nihilism of the Marx Brothers, in the continually reasserted strain of hopelessness that often seems to be the real meaning of the soap opera. The gangster film is remarkable in that it fills the need for disguise (though not sufficiently to avoid arousing uneasiness) without requiring any serious distortion. From its beginnings, it has been a consistent and astonishingly complete presentation of the modern sense of tragedy.[2]

In its initial character, the gangster film is simply one example of the movies' constant tendency to create fixed dramatic pattern that can be repeated indefinitely with a reasonable expectation of profit. One gangster film follows another as one musical or one Western follows another. But this rigidity is not necessarily opposed to the requirements of art. There have been very successful types of art in the past which developed such specific and detailed conventions as almost to make individual examples of the type interchangeable. This is true, for example, of Elizabethan revenge tragedy and Restoration comedy.

For such a type to be successful means that its conventions have imposed themselves upon the general consciousness and become the accepted vehicles of a particular set of attitudes and a particular aesthetic effect. One goes to any individual example of the type with very definite expectations, and originality is to be welcomed only in the degree that it intensifies the expected experience without fundamentally altering it. Moreover, the relationship between the conventions which go to make up such a type and the real experience of its audience or the real facts of whatever situation it pretends to describe is of only secondary importance and does not determine its aesthetic force. It is only in an ultimate sense that the type appeals to its audience's experience of reality: much more immediately, it appeals to previous experience of the type itself: it creates its own field of reference.

Thus the importance of the gangster film, and the nature and intensity of its emotional and aesthetic impact, cannot be measured in terms of the place of the gangster himself or the importance of the problem of crime in American life. Those European movie-goers who think there is a gangster on every corner

---

[2] Efforts have been made from time to time to bring the gangster film into line with the prevailing optimism and social constructiveness of our culture; *Kiss of Death* is a recent example. These efforts are usually unsuccessful; the reasons for their lack of success are interesting in themselves, but I shall not be able to discuss them here.

in New York are certainly deceived, but defenders of the "positive" side of American culture are equally deceived if they think it relevant to point out that most Americans have never seen a gangster. What matters is that the experience of the gangster *as an experience of art* is universal to Americans. There is almost nothing we understand better or react to more readily or with quicker intelligence. The Western film, though it seems never to diminish in popularity, is for most of us no more than the folklore of the past, familiar and understandable only because it has been repeated so often. The gangster film comes much closer. In ways that we do not easily or willingly define, the gangster speaks for us, expressing that part of the American psyche which rejects the qualities and the demands of modern life, which rejects "Americanism" itself.

The gangster is the man of the city, with the city's language and knowledge, with its queer and dishonest skills and its terrible daring, carrying his life in his hands like a placard, like a club. For everyone else, there is at least the theoretical possibility of another world—in that happier American culture which the gangster denies, the city does not really exist; it is only a more crowded and more brightly lit country—but for the gangster there is only the city; he must inhabit it in order to personify it: not the real city, but that dangerous and sad city of the imagination which is so much more important, which is the modern world. And the gangster—though there are real gangsters—is also, and primarily, a creature of the imagination. The real city, one might say, produces only criminals; the imaginary city produces the gangster: he is what we want to be and what we are afraid we may become.

Thrown into the crowd without background or advantages, with only those ambiguous skills which the rest of us—the real people of the real city—can only pretend to have, the gangster is required to make his way, to make his life and impose it on others. Usually, when we come upon him, he has already made his choice or the choice has already been made for him, it doesn't matter which: we are not permitted to ask whether at some point he could have chosen to be something else than what he is.

The gangster's activity is actually a form of rational enterprise, involving fairly definite goals and various techniques for achieving them. But this rationality is usually no more than a vague background; we know, perhaps, that the gangster sells liquor or that he operates a numbers racket; often we are not given even that much information. So his activity becomes a kind of sure criminality: he hurts people. Certainly our response to the gangster film is most consistently and most universally a response to sadism; we gain the double satisfaction of participating vicariously in the gangster's sadism and then seeing it turned against the gangster himself.

But on another level the quality of irrational brutality and the quality of rational enterprise become one. Since we do not see the rational and routine aspects of the gangster's behavior, the practice of brutality—the quality of unmixed criminality becomes the totality of his career. At the same time, we are always conscious that the whole meaning of his career is a drive for success: the typical gangster film presents a steady upward progress followed by a very precipitate fall. Thus brutality itself becomes at once the means to success and the content of success—a success that is defined in its most general terms, not as accomplishment or specific gain, but simply as the unlimited possibility of aggression. (In the same way, film presentations of businesses tend to make it appear that they achieve their success by talking on the telephone and holding conferences and that success in talking on the telephone and holding conferences.)

From this point of view, the initial contact between the film and its audience is an agreed conception of human life: that man is a being with the possibilities of success or failure. This principle too, belongs to the city; one must emerge from the crowd or else one is nothing. On that basis the necessity of the action is established, and it progresses by inalterable paths to the point where the gangster lies dead and the principle has been modified: there is really only one possibility—failure. The final meaning of the city is anonymity and death.

In the opening scene of *Scarface,* we are shown a successful man; we know he is successful because he has just given a party of opulent proportions and because he is called Big Louis. Through some monstrous lack of caution, he permits himself to be alone for a few moments. We understand from this immediately that he was about to be killed. No convention of the gangster film is more strongly established than this: it is dangerous to be alone. And yet the very conditions of success make it impossible not to be alone, for success is always the establishment of an *individual* preeminence, that must be imposed on others, in whom it automatically arouses hatred; the successful man is an outlaw. The gangster's whole life is an effort to assert himself as an individual, to draw himself out of the crowd, and he always dies *because* he is an individual; the final bullet thrusts him back, makes him, after all a failure. "Mother of God," says the dying Little Caesar, "is this the end of Rico?"— speaking of himself thus in the third person because what has been brought low is not the undifferentiated man, but the individual with a name, the gangster, the success; even to himself he is a creature of the imagination. (T. S. Eliot has pointed out that a number of Shakespeare's tragic heroes have this trick of looking at themselves dramatically; their true identity, the thing that is destroyed when they die, is something outside themselves—not a man, but a style of life, a kind of meaning.)

At bottom, the gangster is doomed because he is under the obligation to succeed, not because the means he employs are unlawful. In the deeper layers of the modern consciousness, *all* means are unlawful, every attempt to succeed is an act of aggression, leaving one alone and guilty and defenseless among enemies: he is *punished* for success. This is our intolerable dilemma: that failure is a kind of death and success is evil and dangerous, is—ultimately—impossible. The effect of the gangster film is to embody his dilemma in the person of the gangster and resolve it by his death. The dilemma is resolved because it is *his* death, not ours. We are safe; for the moment, we can acquiesce in our failure, we can choose to fail.

Four

Reflections on Human Knowledge

The intellectual life of man consists almost wholly in his substitution of a conceptual order for the perceptual order in which his experience originally comes.
—William James

Introduction

The central concept of this chapter is knowledge; the philosophical branch that concentrates on knowledge is called by two names, "theory of knowledge" or "epistemology;" "episteme" is the Greek word for knowledge and "ology" signifies "theory."

Seeking knowledge is one of the central activities of humans; think of how many years you've spent in school acquiring knowledge and skills; and when you go to work, you have to acquire new skills and learn new knowledge in order to make and keep yourself a valued employee or an effective manager of your own affairs. C. I. Lewis opens his book *Knowledge and Valuation* with these remarks, "Knowledge, action, and evaluation are essentially connected. The primary and pervasive significance of knowledge lies in its guidance of action: knowing is for the sake of doing. And action, obviously, is rooted in evaluation. For a being which did not assign comparative values, deliberate action would be pointless; and for one which did not know, it would be impossible."

Knowledge, Lewis points out, is essentially connected to human action and human valuing. In reflecting on knowledge, it is important to keep this larger human picture in mind. The essays in this chapter were chosen in part because we hold this picture before us in their discussion of knowledge and its allied concepts.

In another remark, Lewis tells us what the connections between knowledge, action, and evaluation are: "The utility of knowledge lies in the control it gives us, through appropriate action, over the quality of our future experience. And such control will be exercised in the interest of realizing that which we value, and of obviating or avoiding what is undesirable" (p. 4). We can illustrate these connections by reflecting on the action of crossing a city street. Your eyes and ears are distance receptors; a quickly growing roaring sound and a quickly growing shape are sensory data that enable you to take account of distant objects approaching you; your previous acquaintance with these objects enables you to identify the approaching object as a truck; knowing that a truck is fast approaching enables you to take "appropriate action"; you run out of the truck's path; this knowledge enables us to control "the quality of our future experience"; we want that quality to be the sensations of an unhurt body; with such control over our future experience we can realize the value of being unhurt and avoid the undesirable sensation of being hurt; our knowledge, that is, our ability to connect the sounds and sights with possible future events, is something dearly prized because it enables us to control the quality of our lives, the rest of which is in the future. Just as our eyes and ears are distance receptors, so is our mind a "future receptor."

Because knowledge is so valuable to us, it is important to distinguish between those of our thoughts that are knowledge from those that are not. Are thoughts based on numerology knowledge? It is reported that Hitler based many of his military decisions on numerological ideas; he scheduled many of his largest attacks on the seventh of the month. Does the fact that Hitler's Germany lost World War II prove that numerological claims are not knowledge?

Many people go to palm readers. They want to know what the future holds for them. With trepidation, palpitations, and anxiety, they offer their perspiring palms to the palmist fully believing that knowledge of their future fate will be told them. Do you think that a palmist's readings are knowledge? Could they be known to be knowledge if we cannot trace a connection between the lines on a person's palms and the causes of future events? Why should the lines in their palms be a better basis for divining persons' fates than the lines on their feet? Or than the lines on another person's palms?

Many newspapers carry horoscopes. Here are a couple of entries from Carroll Righter's column. "Scorpio (Oct. 23 to Nov. 21) Reach a better meeting of minds with partners so work can be done more intelligently. A civic matter requires fast action." How can the date of a person's birth and the planetary arrangements be connected to a "civic action." And if it is a civic action, wouldn't it apply equally to every person's horoscope resident in the civic area regardless of their birthdate? Here's another: "Capricorn (Dec. 22 to Jan. 20) Do not be overly sensitive with partners due to the planetary positions or you alienate them." Why should our moral conduct toward others be guided by planetary positions? (Or is Righter telling horoscope readers not to take horoscopes too seriously?) The claimed connection between planetary positions and human character and the morality of actions seems as unexplained as does the claimed connection between palm lines and future events.

Then, too, there are tea-leaf readers. The reliability of tea leaves' arrangement seems as uncertain a source of knowledge as chickens' entrails. Ancient Romans used to rely on what seers saw in a chicken's entrails. You may dismiss the Romans as superstitious primitives. Aren't believers in palmistry, horoscopes, and tealeaf arrangements also to be dismissed as superstitious primitive holdovers? If you suspect so, you think we can distinguish between superstitions and knowledge. If we can distinguish, there must be a way of doing it. What is that way? To answer this question requires some idea of what knowledge is; it requires us to make an analysis of the concept of knowledge, one of the tasks of epistemology.

Ever since Plato wrote the *Theatetus,* the first systematic tract on epistemology, thinkers have distinguished between knowledge "that" and knowledge "how." Knowledge-that is knowledge expressible by a sentence with which we make a statement or judgment; we predicate something of a subject. Knowledge-how is a skill or an ability to perform or do something, such as make shoes or throw basketballs through hoops or ride bicycles.

To make an analysis of a concept is to determine with which other concepts it is necessarily related. A standard analysis of knowledge, again first clearly expressed by Plato in the *Theatetus,* connects the concept of knowledge to three other concepts: truth-value, belief, and evidence. Of any statement that expresses a person's knowledge, we should be able to say also: (1) that it is believed by the person making the statement, (2) that the statement is true, and (3) that the person making the statement has evidence for its truth.

How does this analysis help us to distinguish superstition from knowledge? We can ask, first, does the palmist, for example, believe what he or she says? A palmist could merely be trying to make a living off other people's fears, knowing that the fearful person is anxious to believe almost anything; the palmist may not believe what he or she is saying. In that case the palmist does not provide a person with knowledge.

We can ask, second, whether what the horoscope writer says, for example, is true. Such writers usually try to meet this test of truth, but they may do it in such a way that they can hardly miss the truth; the statement is almost vacuously true. Consider Righter's "A civic matter requires fast action." This is almost as bad as the familiar crystal-ball joke about "having a tall, dark man in your life," who, it turns out, is your Uncle Charlie, or the neighbor who borrows a cup of sugar. *"A civic matter"* could be almost anything; in which city is left unsaid; what is meant by "fast action" is unclear; and "requires" is quite vague as a measure of urgency. You would hardly consider yourself as prescient, whether with the aid of a crystal ball, the planetary positions, or tea-leaf arrangements, if you claimed that "Someone somewhere is in trouble."

We can ask, third, whether the person making a statement has evidence for it at the time the statement is made. I might say "The butler killed the duchess." This might turn out to be true, and I might believe the butler did it; but if I do not have the kind of evidence that would be needed in court to convict the butler, I could not be said "to know" that the butler was the culprit. Without the evidence, I do not know; I can only guess. The question we want to put to the horoscope writer is: Why do the positions of the planets constitute evidence for a civic matter requiring fast action? We can ask the palmist why palm lines are evidence for future events in a person's life. We can ask the tea-leaf seer why tea leaves are evidence for our fate. When the detective comes into court, he might cite the fact that there were powder burns on the butler's hands, blood on the butler's clothes matching the victim's blood type, and so forth. These are evidence because there are well-known causal laws connecting powder burns, gunshots, bullets, blood, and death. There are no such well-known laws connecting tea-leaf arrangements, palm lines, or planetary positions with events in our lives. In the absence of such laws, the evidence that is needed to assure us that palmists', seers', and horoscopists' claims are knowledge is missing; no evidence, no knowledge.

How do we proceed to gather evidence? What methods should we use? Because the concept of evidence is essentially connected to the concept of knowledge, and because knowledge is of utility in leading a good life, these questions about method are important.

It would be unwise to oversimplify; there may be more than a single method for gathering evidence and knowledge. There are different objects of knowledge; each or some of them may require a different method. Our knowledge of animate and inanimate objects is not always gathered in the same way. If I want to know the length of a rope, I use some standard unit of measurement and am then able to predicate of the rope that it is five feet six inches long. But this would be a wholly inappropriate way of determining the "social" order of army ants. And finding the social order of a group of human beings would engage other methods—spoken and written testimony, for example—than it would in the case of army ants. Further, finding out about other persons is different from finding out things about ourselves; we can be introspective about ourselves but not about others.

The methods for gathering evidence and knowledge about events are unlike those for animate or inanimate objects, although they may encompass the method for gaining knowledge about objects. Think of an explosion; coming upon a scene where you notice a depression in the earth, a scattering of objects in a circular area, masses of broken objects, dead animals in the vicinity, and so forth, would lead you to conclude that an explosion had taken place; this is a complex of effects on the properties of objects all of which are traced to the "event" of an explosion. This tracing requires knowledge of laws, as in the earlier example of gathering evidence for the event of the butler killing the duchess.

Knowledge and evidence about past events depends rather more on memory than knowledge about future events, where future events may require prediction; memory and prediction are different methods of gathering evidence and knowledge.

We have seen that knowledge of events is essentially connected with knowledge of laws. Laws enable us to make connections between past events or possible future events and present events. One of the persistent differences in philosophy of knowledge is that some thinkers believe that the method by which we gain knowledge of the connections between social events has to be different from the method by which we gain knowledge about natural events; others think there is no difference, all laws being "natural" laws. Those who think that social laws are not eliminable in favor of natural laws might cite an event such as a male and female passing through a doorway in a culture where the male regularly opens the door and allows the female to pass through first. In such a case, there is no "natural" law that explains this as there is when we explain why water runs downhill; in social events, the regularity is explained by citing courtesy rules mutually acknowledged by males and females. Further, as a result of moral changes brought about by a women's liberation movement, for example, such a courtesy rule might be changed; no such changes occur in natural laws. Thus, the methods for learning about natural laws and social laws appear to be different.

A familiar distinction is the one drawn between "concrete" and "abstract" objects. This distinction is not an easy one to draw or apply and, for this reason, may not be as useful as it seems initially. But we can give extremes of them; a rock is a concrete, physical object that has effects on our senses; a number—not a printed or written or spoken numeral—is often cited as an example of an abstract object; a number is not something physical that has effects on our senses; it is something that is thought or conceived by the mind. Mathematics deals with numbers and relations between numbers; our mathematical knowledge and evidence does not come to us by the method of observation through our senses; in mathematics our method is by reasoning through proofs. This distinction between concrete and abstract objects is matched by an appropriate distinction between two kinds of knowledge, *a posteriori* and *a priori* knowledge. *A posteriori* signifies knowledge acquired after (post) an experience or observation; I know the color of your eyes after I observe them. *A priori* knowledge does not require this sense experience; by our thought alone, we supposedly come to have knowledge that, for example, four is a larger number than three.

This brief background in epistemology will help to understand the main points in this chapter's essays.

Plato was as good a writer as he was a philosopher. In our selection from his *The Republic,* we have two of his most famous images, the Divided Line and the Allegory of the Cave. The Divided Line image contains his classification of the objects of knowledge and of the methods appropriate to each, a topic which we discussed above. The main division in the Divided Line separates perceptible objects from intelligible objects; about the former, we gain only "opinion," a lower form of knowledge; about the latter, we can gain higher degrees of knowledge; the degree of knowledge increases as we ascend the divided line going from perceptible shadows to physical objects to intelligible mathematical objects to the Forms or Ideas. The highest kind of knowledge is of the Forms; in *The Republic,* Plato sets out a course of education for philosophers designed to enable them to gain knowledge of the Forms. The Forms are named by concept words such as justice, truth, good, one, unity, identity, and so forth. Plato and Socrates, as represented in Plato's dialogue, search for definitions; good definitions will express knowledge about the Forms. A Platonic dialogue represents a dialectical question-and-answer method of reasoning oneself toward a correct definition. The Form whose definition Socrates is seeking in *The Republic* is justice; in the *Theaetetus* it is knowledge; Socrates asks "What is justice?" and "What is knowledge?" and expects a definition from the person questioned; he then examines it to see if it is a "wind egg" or a defensible definition. The arguments and reasoning used in the dialogue exhibit the dialectical method of gaining knowledge about the intelligible Forms.

Plato did not think that we could gain knowledge about justice by sensory observation. Justice is a concept and is not perceptible. I can watch someone do something to someone else; or I can hear a judge pronounce sentence on a convicted prisoner; but I cannot see or hear the justice. I cannot tell what is an instance of justice unless I know what to look for. And I do not know what to look for unless I have a concept of "justice." Unless I knew what justice was before I heard the judge pronounce sentence, I would not be able to decide that what I heard was an instance of justice or not. For Plato, the world given to our senses is not knowable without having prior knowledge of the Forms; it is the Forms that enable us to sort out perceptible physical and human objects and events seen, heard, tasted, or touched. The intelligible world makes knowledge of the perceptible world possible; this means that in comprehending the world, we should give first priority to philosophical knowledge of the Forms.

This priority is illustrated by Plato in his Allegory of the Cave. Persons who do not know the Forms, who are ignorant of the intelligible world, are like prisoners in the Cave, condemned to live among dim shadows. Philosophy is liberation represented by the escaped prisoner who emerges into the sunlight and sees the world as it is for the first time.

In the Cave allegory, the sun makes objects visible to the former prisoner; object and sight need the sun if the object is to be seen and if sight is to be fulfilled. Plato remarks that the Form of the Good is to intelligible objects and the mind as the sun is to perceptible objects and our eyes. He never fully explains this analogy and it is a difficult notion to interpret. One thing, at least, that we can say of it is that knowledge is not something sought for its own sake; it is sought for its revelation of the good life, the same idea that was expressed in the quotations from C. I. Lewis cited at the beginning of this chapter's introduction. One way to understand Plato's analogy is to interpret him as saying that each concept Form is an "ideal" Form; without knowing the Form of the Good, we have no way of picking which of competing definitions of a Form expresses true knowledge of the Form. Take justice as an example. Upon being asked what justice is, the first answer might be a "vulgar" one, simply reflecting the most common, ordinary notion of what people in a society think justice is, such as doing good for your friends and harming your enemies. A majority of persons in a society may subscribe to this notion of justice, but should they? In asking if they "should," we are asking if this is a "good" notion of justice. We might want to reject this vulgar conception of justice because it does not have the Form of Good in it; it is not what it should be. How can harming someone be "just?" The "ideal" Form of Justice cannot be something that is not good; but to decide it is not good requires that you know the Form of the Good; without it, you will not be able to determine if you have the right notion of ideal justice. And that is precisely why Plato thinks that the Good is the first among the Forms and is like the sun; without knowing it, you will not be able to reach knowledge of "good" justice.

One of the perennial issues in epistemology is scepticism. Is it possible to have any knowledge at all? We are often deceived by our senses; we do not know it at the time; we might be deceived on every preceptual occasion without our being aware of it. We often incorrectly reason; think of how many times you have misadded your bank account. How do you know that your last addition is any more accurate than your first one?

David Hume raises a sceptical doubt about one of the most important propositions we human beings have ever entertained. He doubts that there is any rational basis for believing that the future will be like the past. "These two propositions are far from being the same, *I have found that such an object has always been attended with such an effect,* and *I forsee, that other objects, which are, in appearance, similar, will be attended with similar effects.*" For example, eating food has always been followed by a full feeling in the past; that eating food tomorrow will likewise be so followed is not something that we can count on, claims Hume.

That this is an important proposition can readily be discerned by reminding ourselves of Lewis's point: Knowledge is for the sake of action; we want to so act now that we favorably affect the quality of our future experience. To apprehend future events is to predict what will occur; in predicting what will occur, we need to have laws of relations between events. Such laws to be useful must be general, covering instances in the past as well as instances in the future; from past instances, we wish *to infer,* as Hume says, to future events.These laws may state a relation between an event-cause and an event-effect, a relation on which, according to Hume, "All reasonings concerning matter of fact seem to be founded. . . ."

Another way of putting this is to say that our laws will not enable us to predict events in the future unless nature is uniform, unless the future is like the past. Hume denies that the uniformity of nature is known *a priori;* neither can it be demonstrated by reasonings because it "implies no contradiction that the course of nature may change. . . ."

Might we not show that nature is uniform, then, by recourse to experience, by recourse to our *a posteriori* knowledge? No, because that would be arguing in a circle, assuming the very proposition we wish to establish. Consider the following argument:

1. Effect *E* has always followed cause *C*.
2. The future will be like the past (uniformity of nature).
3. Therefore, the next *C* will be followed by *E*.

Now, the proposition we want to establish is (2), the one about which Hume is sceptical. But to try to establish it *a posteriori* by appeal to past experience, "Nature has always been uniform," would be useless because the very thing we want to know is whether this past experience will be duplicated in the future, whether nature will continue to be uniform. We cannot say it will be unless we assume the uniformity of nature, which is circularly assuming the very proposition that we were supposed to establish by reasoning from experience.

Given that we cannot intuit *a priori* the truth of the proposition about the uniformity of nature, or demonstrate it by reasoning, or establish it by appeal to experience; and given that there are no other methods of knowing available to us, we have to remain sceptical about the proposition.

Yet, we do believe it rather strongly. Why? Just because our mind is of such a nature that the repetition of *E* following *C* sets up the habit of expecting the same to occur in the future. This habit is without rational basis. It just occurs. There are some things we just cannot explain. And remarks Hume, "Thus the observation of human blindness and weakness is the result of all philosophy, and meets us at every turn, in spite of our endeavours to elude or avoid it."

Hume, like other writers of this chapter's essays, is interested in epistemology for the light it sheds on human action and valuation. His epistemology is a preparation for his moral theory. Farther on in his *Enquiries* (Section VIII, Part I) he remarks about the habit of cause-and-effect association in human action. "Thus it appears, not only that the conjunction between motives and voluntary actions is as regular and uniform as that between the cause and effect in any part of nature; but also that this regular conjunction has been universally acknowledged among mankind. . . . And indeed, when we consider how aptly *natural* and *moral* evidence link together, and form only one chain of argument, we shall make no scruple to allow that they are of the same nature, and derived from the same principles." Hume's ultimate philosophic aim is to show that moral and natural knowledge are of the same kind; this is an anticipation of a point of view prevalent today among those who believe that we may have a "science" of psychology and sociology, a science of humans taken individually and collectively.

William James writes so well, vividly, graciously, and with such a leisurely amplitude, that his essay needs little explanation. We simply call to your attention that here he tries to acknowledge the plausibility but inadequacy of each of two extreme views about the nature of thought. Plato, a rationalist, placed an emphasis on conceptual thought about intelligibles; while Hume, the classical empiricist, places an emphasis on the perceptual flux. James tries to steer a course away from these extreme directions; recognizing the role that concepts play in organizing the flux but also recognizing that the rationalistic mind with its analytic approach cuts up this flux and, if relied on exclusively, makes some things we know, such as our own identity, motion, and change, incapable of being understood. Extreme rationalism also blinds us to novelty; "Philosophy, like life, must keep the doors and windows open."

In order to keep intellectual conceptualization in its proper place, James advocates applying the Pragmatic Rule. "Test every concept by the question: What sensible difference to anybody will its truth make?"

Mao Tse-tung is the closest that a contemporary person has come to Plato's ideal of a philosopher-king. Plato thought that the best ruler is one who knows, and one who knows is the one who has knowledge of the Forms (justice, good, honor, temperance, wisdom, and so forth), and the one who has knowledge of the Forms is the philosopher.

Mao's writings here show that he is a philosopher, but he does not think that a ruler should make all the decisions for others. His writings form the basis in China of giving philosophic guidelines for solving national and local problems; his writings stress a method rather than a conclusion. This is a reasonable position to take given that the natural and social world is continually changing; a solution to today's problem may not be appropriate for tomorrow's problem. Mao's writings serve as a philosophic handbook; he recognizes that human problems are many, detailed, particular, and must be solved by people on the spot rather than by rulers in some remote capital.

The problems to be addressed are not abstract philosophic ones; they are day-to-day, practical problems. You'll note that Mao ties theoretical knowledge and practical action together; theory and practice go hand in hand. Mao says, "Marxist philosophy holds that the most important problem does not lie in understanding the laws of the objective world and thus being able to explain it, but in applying the knowledge of these laws actively to change the world."

Mao's writings on theory of knowledge serve as a theoretical orientation to the solution of practical problems. Practical problems arise because contradictions exist in the natural and social world. Mao's philosophic works are used to try to understand and solve the contradictions that exist in China's social and political life; they are epistemological chapbooks for the most populous country on earth. An interesting little book, *Philosophy Is No Mystery* (Peking, 1972), gives examples of the use to which Mao's works are put. At the opening of it we read: "This collection of accounts from Chinchien Production Brigade of Kiangshan County, Chekiang Province, tells something of the commune members' study and application of Chairman Mao's philosophic work 'On Contradiction.' As for contradictions, they do exist objectively, always and everywhere, and everyone has to deal with them every day. But to correctly understand the nature of contradictions, and solve them, is quite another thing."

Here is an example from the book.

A complicated problem arose: How to handle the contradiction between stronger and weaker labor power in Chinchien Brigade?

One day when Secretary Chiang Ju-wang went to the 5th team, he overheard an argument between two men and two women who had been assigned to work the waterwheel that day.

The two men complained: "Just our bad luck to be assigned to work with two women; we have to do most of the work."

The women commune members protested: "You may be stronger and get higher wages, but in pedalling the wheel you exploit us."

"How do we exploit you?"

"All of us pedal the wheel with our feet, there's no difference. But your wages are higher than ours. Is this not exploitation?"

The two men were stumped and said: "Let's drop it. Anyhow a hen can't crow like a cock, and a woman is a woman."

Chiang was listening and thinking: "It sounds like a major contradiction. What's the nature of it? Which is the principal aspect? [See Section

IV of "On Contradiction."] I must investigate and think it over to find the principal aspect." Chiang decided to call a meeting and let the masses air their views.

That evening when the commune members gathered for the meeting, Chiang started off: "Today strong workers had an argument with weaker ones. Let's talk about this problem tonight. There's a contradiction which should be exposed and analyzed. The two aspects of the contradiction should present their views clearly. Both strong workers and the weaker ones should speak. Now, who will speak first?"

No sooner had he finished than a strong man jumped up and said, "The weaker ones pull us back. Women are not only weaker, they don't know how to work either. They're just a drag on us. If the whole team were strong workers, we could guarantee harvest increasing twenty or thirty per cent every year."

The team leader followed up: "That's right. The weaker ones are always dragged along by the stronger. Without strong workers for the ploughing and threshing there would be no crops."

The women members retorted angrily: "That's enough! You're strong, so of course everything you say about work goes. We of course have no right at all to speak."

This retort struck Chiang, and he felt that the principal aspect of the contradiction was the stronger labor power. . . . He should also listen to those with weaker labor power so as to get a full picture of the problem. Then he raised the question: "Do strong workers remain strong workers under all circumstances? Is it not possible for them to become the weaker ones?"

The commune members were puzzled by this question. Chiang went on: "We must always remember this teaching of Chairman Mao: 'We must learn to look at problems all-sidedly, seeing the reverse as well as the obverse side of things.' So we must listen not only to the strong workers but also to the weaker ones' opinions."

After a silence a young man spoke up. "I think the status of strong or weak is not absolute, but relative. Take me for example, this year I'm only seventeen so I'm not a strong worker. But in ten years I'll be twenty-seven and I will be one, won't I?"

An old man added: "When I was young I was a strong worker, but now I'm sixty so I've become a weak one, haven't I?"

Everyone chuckled. A woman spoke next. "The team leader has said ploughing and threshing depend on strong workers. That's a one-sided way of looking at things. Without the buffalo boys to tend the buffalos, how would we plough? Without the women to dry the rice, how could we eat it?"

A man answered. "That's right. If we tended the buffalos or sunned the rice, we wouldn't be making full use of our strength, would we. . . ?"

"It's like that in other work too," a woman rose and said. Pointing to a strapping young man of about twenty, she said: "Last time we went to dig peanuts, you went for only two days and each day you only dug twenty *jin*. I went for five days and dug forty *jin* every day. And at the end of the second day you were standing up to stretch yourself and complain how tired you were. 'I see stars when I stand up.' you said, and you didn't show up any more."

Everybody laughed.

Secretary Chiang Ju-wang felt he could now sum up the discussion and said: "We cannot look at things absolutely. Strong and weak are the two aspects of a contradiction, but each exists in the other and is related to the other."

"That's right. Without pebbles large stones cannot make a wall," an old poor peasant said. . . .

Through the argument over weak and strong workers the commune members came to understand the law of the unity of opposites. The strong and weak workers have become more united and worked harder shoulder to shoulder to build the socialist countryside (pp. 64–68).

Near the beginning of Section V of "On Contradiction," Mao gives a list of "contradictory aspects," a list of "opposites." One of the more difficult concepts in Mao, and other Marxists, is this notion of contradiction. Aristotle is helpful here; he distinguishes four different kinds of "opposites" in his *Categories* (11b16–23). "We must next explain the various senses in which the term 'opposite' is used. Things are said to be opposed in four senses: (i) as correlatives to one another, (ii) as contraries to one another, (iii) as privatives to positives, (iv) as affirmatives to negatives. Let me sketch my meaning in outline. An instance of the use of the word 'opposite' with reference to correlatives is afforded by the expressions 'double' and 'half'; with reference to contraries by 'bad' and 'good.' Opposites in the sense of 'privatives' and 'positives' are 'blindness' and 'sight'; in the sense of affirmatives and negatives, the propositions 'he sits', 'he does not sit'."

Because knowledge and action are tied to evaluation for Mao, each of the three other kinds of opposites must be tied to the contrary evaluative opposites of "good" and "bad"; social and political contradictions are in need of solution because, since each of them is tied to the good and bad, each contradiction necessarily brings some bad with it; this bad is eliminated only if the contradiction is solved; and this solution is not something achieved in thought only but requires action; thought or theory is needed as a guide to practical action to know how to solve the contradiction.

Karl Mannheim, too, reminds us of the connection between thought and action; he looks at action from the perspective of a sociologist; that is, he stresses that human action is "collective," not individual. This is important for epistemology, he insists, because in trying to understand human knowledge we have to grasp it in its actual social and historical setting; "Strictly speaking it is incorrect to say that the single individual thinks. Rather it is more correct to insist that he participates in thinking further what other men have thought before him."

After making this point, Mannheim goes on to consider some sociological factors that have to be considered in trying to grasp the central features of thought in our own time. He discusses the influence of social stability on the unity of a social group's world view; the sceptical effect of horizontal and vertical mobility; and the disappearance in our time, so Mannheim claims, of an intelligentsia with "monopolistic control over the moulding of that society's world-view."

Some thinkers have vigorously opposed a "sociology of knowledge." One claim is that it denies the existence of a trans-social standpoint for assessing knowledge claims. If the thought of a person is dominated by the thought patterns of his social group or class, and another is dominated by the different thought patterns of another social group or class, there is no way for either to transcend those social limitations to determine which of their contrary or contradictory beliefs is knowledge. We have a social relativity of knowledge, which is a kind of scepticism about rationality. Without having truth criteria that transcend social factors, there is no way rationally to find the truth; disagreement between persons is resolvable only by resort to force then.

Karl Popper, a critic of the sociology of knowledge, approvingly quotes Bertrand Russell, who writes, "Rationality, in the sense of an appeal to a universal and impersonal standard of truth, is of supreme importance . . . not only in ages in which it easily prevails, but also, and even more, in those less fortunate times in which it is despised and rejected as the vain dream of men who lack the virility to kill where they cannot agree."

The advocate of the sociology of knowledge might well concede that the possession of a "universal and impersonal standard of truth" would indeed be desirable but might go on to point out that it is a vain wish; the conditions for knowing are so thoroughly socialized that to suppose we can transcend them would be wholly to abandon any reality orientation toward thought; the dream of nonsocial thought is an impossible one.

John Rex's essay affords us a concrete example of an epistemological issue that he claims cannot be properly understood except from the viewpoint of a sociology of knowledge. Arthur Jensen, H. J. Eysenck, and William Shockley purport to find evidence that links IQ with genetic factors. Blacks have, according to them, a lower average IQ, and they claim that this is due to their genetic structure; nurture cannot overcome this nature factor; blacks are thus consigned to a lower intelligence status than whites in perpetuity without hope of escape. The determination of IQ is one of the subjects of psychometry—psychological measurement.

Proponents of psychometry claim that their methods are scientifically objective and value-neutral; they are just stating the facts, such as IQ level, as revealed by reliable measurement techniques. Rex doubts this. His first point is that studies of humans differ from studies of inanimate objects; "while natural science is an activity in which scientists have concepts about things, in the human sciences the scientist has concepts about things which themselves have concepts." Ignoring this difference leads psychometrists to form "a simple mechanistic model" of human actions. Once this model is known to be inadequate, that psychometry is "objective" is not as obvious as it seemed originally.

Rex's second point is that psychometrists cannot be value-free any more than they can be objective. The sociology of knowledge becomes important to an understanding of the IQ controversy because it reminds us that psychometrists live and think in a social context. This context is a racist one in a racist society; thus, the claims of Jensen et al. have to be judged with this sociological context in mind; without intending to be racist, a psychometrist might so design his or her investigations that they bear out racist and other attitudes endemic to the society. Rex concludes his essay with: "What is argued here is that the misrepresentations of the psychometricians is not simply a matter of a random 'mistake' but is directly related to the beliefs of the society in which they operate."

Rex points out that racism surfaces during times of economic competition; whites become hostile to blacks when jobs are scarce. The forms that expressions of racism take are several; racial jokes are the lowest level of expression; they may grow more systematic as racism becomes more "scientific." Psychometry is potentially very dangerous just because its supposed "scientific objectivity" gives greater credence and justification to racist beliefs; it helps make racism "respectable." Thus, the epistemological attempt to establish an "objective" method for studying humans is not a purely philosophic problem; according to Rex and other sociologists of knowledge, it is a social and political problem as well. Epistemology is not value-neutral.

The Cave of Ignorance and the Divided Line

PLATO

Plato (427/8-347/8 B.C.), one of the great Greek philosophers, has exerted more influence upon the development of Western philosophy than any other writer with
the possible exception of his student, Aristotle. He established the Academy in
Athens, the first of the major schools of ancient Greece. His works, written in
dialogue form and featuring his teacher Socrates as the principal figure, have
continued to be widely read, not only for their intellectual content but also for their
literary merit. Among his writings of interest to the student of ethics are
Euthyphro, Apology, Crito, Phaedo, The Republic, Protagoras, Gorgias, and *Philebus.*

Necessarily, he said, but you also, Socrates, must tell us whether you consider
the good to be knowledge, or pleasure, or something else.

What a man! I said. It has been clear for some time that the opinion of others
on this subject would not satisfy you.

Well, Socrates, he said, it does not seem right to me to be able to tell the
opinions of others and not one's own, especially for a man who has spent so
much time as you have occupying himself with this subject.

Why? said I. Do you think it right to talk about things one does not know
as if one knew them?

Not as if one knew them, he said, but for a man who has an opinion to say
what that opinion is.

And have you not noticed that opinions not based on knowledge are ugly
things? The best of them are blind; or do you think that those who express a
true opinion without knowledge are any different from blind people who yet follow the right road?—They are no different.

Do you want to contemplate ugly, blind, and crooked things when you can
hear bright and beautiful things from others?

By Zeus, Socrates, said Glaucon, do not stand off as if you had come to the
end. We shall be satisfied if you discuss the Good in the same fashion as you
did justice, moderation, and the other things.

That, my friend, I said, would also quite satisfy me, but I fear I shall not be
able to do so, and that in my eagerness I shall disgrace myself and make myself
ridiculous. But, my excellent friends, let us for the moment abandon the quest
for the nature of the Good itself, for that I think is a larger question than what
we started on, which was to ascertain my present opinion about it. I am willing

Source: Plato, *The Republic,* trans. by George M. A. Grube (Indianapolis, Ind., 1975), pp.
161–166, 168–173. Copyright © 1974. Reprinted by permission of George M. A. Grube and
Hackett Publishing Company, Inc.

to tell you what appears to be the offspring of the Good and most like it, if that is agreeable to you. If not, we must let the question drop.

Well, he said, tell us. The story of the parent remains a debt which you will pay us some other time.

I wish, I said, that I could pay it in full now, and you could exact it in full and not, as now, only receive the interest.[1] However, accept then this offspring and child of the Good. Only be careful that I do not somehow deceive you unwillingly by giving a counterfeit account of this offspring.—We shall be as careful as we can. Only tell us.

I will, I said, after coming to an agreement with you and reminding you of the things we said before, and also many times elsewhere.—What are these things?

We speak of many beautiful things and many good things, and we say that they are so and so define them in speech.—We do.

And Beauty itself and Goodness itself, and so with all the things which we then classed as many; we now class them again according to one Form of each, which is one and which we in each case call that which is.—That is so.

And we say that the many things are the objects of sight but not of thought, while the Forms are the objects of thought but not of sight.—Altogether true.

With what part of ourselves do we see the objects that are seen?—With our sight.

And so things heard are heard by our hearing, and all that is perceived is perceived by our other senses?—Quite so.

Have you considered how very lavishly the maker of our senses made the faculty of seeing and being seen?—I cannot say I have.

Look at it this way: do hearing and sound need another kind of thing for the former to hear and the latter to be heard, and in the absence of this third element the one will not hear and the other not be heard.—No, they need nothing else.

Neither do many other senses, if indeed any, need any such other thing, or can you mention one?—Not I.

But do you not realize that the sense of sight and that which is seen do have such a need?—How so?

Sight may be in the eyes, and the man who has it may try to use it, and colours may be present in the objects, but unless a third kind of thing is present, which is by nature designed for this very purpose, you know that sight will see nothing and the colours remain unseen.—What is this third kind of thing?

What you call light, I said.—Right.

So to no small extent the sense of sight and the power of being seen are yoked together by a more honourable yoke than other things which are yoked together, unless light is held in no honour.—That is far from being the case.

Which of the gods in the heavens can you hold responsible for this, whose light causes our sight to see as beautifully as possible, and the objects of sight to be

---

[1] Plato is punning on the Greek word *tokos* which means a child, and in the plural was used also of the interest on capital, a pleasant and common metaphor.

seen?—The same as you would, he said, and as others would; obviously the answer to your question is the sun.

And is not sight naturally related to the sun in this way?—Which way?

Sight is not the sun, neither itself nor that in which it occurs which we call the eye.—No indeed.

But I think it is the most sunlike of the organs of sense.—Very much so.

And it receives from the sun the capacity to see as a kind of outflow.—Quite so.

The sun is not sight, but is it not the cause of it, and is also seen by it?—Yes.

Say then, I said, that it is the sun which I called the offspring of the Good, which the Good begot as analogous to itself. What the Good itself is in the world of thought in relation to the intelligence and things known, the sun is in the visible world, in relation to sight and things seen.—How? Explain further.

You know, I said, that when one turns one's eyes to those objects of which the colours are no longer in the light of day but in the dimness of the night, the eyes are dimmed and seem nearly blind, as if clear vision was no longer in them.— Quite so.

Yet whenever one's eyes are turned upon objects brightened by sunshine, they see clearly, and clear vision appears in those very same eyes?—Yes indeed.

So too understand the eye of the soul: whenever it is fixed upon that upon which truth and reality shine, it understands and knows and seems to have intelligence, but whenever it is fixed upon what is mixed with darkness—that which is subject to birth and destruction—it opines and is dimmed, changes its opinions this way and that, and seems to have no intelligence.—That is so.

Say that what gives truth to the objects of knowledge, and to the knowing mind the power to know, is the Form of Good. As it is the cause of knowledge and truth, think of it also as being the object of knowledge. Both knowledge and truth are beautiful, but you will be right to think of the Good as other and more beautiful than they. As in the visible world light and sight are rightly considered sun-like, but it is wrong to think of them as the sun, so here it is right to think of knowledge and truth as Good-like, but wrong to think of either as the Good, for the Good must be honoured even more than they.

This is an extraordinary beauty you mention, he said, if it provides knowledge and truth and is itself superior to them in beauty. You surely do not mean this to be pleasure!

Hush! said I, rather examine the image of it in this way.—How?

You will say, I think, that the sun not only gives to the objects of sight the capacity to be seen, but also that it provides for their generation, increase, and nurture, though it is not itself the process of generation.—How could it be?

And say that as for the objects of knowledge, not only is their being known due to the Good, but also their being, though the Good is not being but superior to and beyond being in dignity and power.

Glaucon was quite amused and said: By Apollo, a miraculous superiority!

It is your own fault, I said, you forced me to say what I thought about it.

Don't you stop, he said, except for a moment, but continue to explain the similarity to the sun in case you are leaving something out.

I am certainly leaving out a good deal, I said.—Don't omit the smallest point.

Much is omitted, I said. However, as far as the explanation can go at present, I will not omit anything.—Don't you!

Understand then, I said, that, as we say, there are those two, one reigning over the intelligible kind and realm, the other over the visible (not to say heaven, that I may not appear to play the sophist about the name[2]). So you have two kinds, the visible and the intelligible.—Right.

It is like a line divided[3] into two unequal parts, and then divide each section in the same ratio, that is, the section of the visible and that of the intelligible. You will then have sections related to each other in proportion to their clarity and obscurity. The first section of the visible consists of images—and by images I mean shadows in the first instance, then the reflections in water and all those on close-packed, smooth, and bright materials, and all that sort of thing, if you understand me.—I understand.

In the other section of the visible, place the models of the images, the living creatures around us, all plants, and the whole class of manufactured things.—I so place them.

Would you be willing to say that, as regards truth and untruth, the division is made in this proportion: as the opinable is to the knowable so the image is to the model it is made like?—Certainly.

Consider now how the section of the intelligible is to be divided.—How?

In such a way that in one section the soul, using as images what before were models, is compelled to investigate from hypotheses, proceeding from these not

[2] He means play on the similarity of sound between *ouranos*, the sky, and *horaton*, visible.

[3] It is clear that Plato visualizes a vertical line (511d and throughout) with *B* as the highest point in the scale of reality and *A* as the lowest form of existence. The main division is at *C*. *AC* is the visible and being in the intelligible world, *AD* is the world of images (and perhaps, though Plato does not say so, works of art), mathematical realities are contained in *CE*, the Platonic Forms in *EB*, with the Good presumably at *B*.

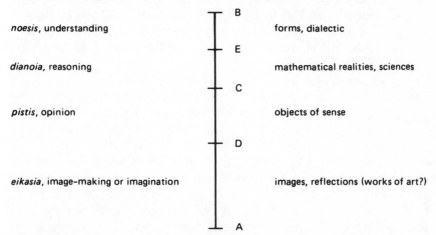

noesis, understanding	B	forms, dialectic
dianoia, reasoning	E	mathematical realities, sciences
pistis, opinion	C	objects of sense
eikasia, image-making or imagination	D	images, reflections (works of art?)
	A	

The names of the four mental processes—*noesis, dianoia, pistis,* and *eikasia*—are more or less arbitrary, and Plato does not use them regularly in these precise senses in the rest of the *Republic*.

to a first principle but to a conclusion. The other section which leads to a first principle that is not hypothetical, proceeding from a hypothesis without using the images of the other section, by means of the Forms themselves and proceeding through these.—I do not, he said, quite understand what you mean.

Let us try again, I said, for you will understand more easily because of what has been said. I think you know that students of geometry, calculation, and the like assume the existence of the odd and the even, of figures, of three kinds of angles, and of kindred things in each of their studies, as if they were known to them. These they make their hypotheses and do not deem it necessary to give any account of them either to themselves or to others as if they were clear to all; these are their starting points, and going through the remaining steps they reach an agreed conclusion on what they started out to investigate.—Quite so, I understand that.

You know also that they use visible figures and talk about them, but they are not thinking about them but about the models of which these are likenesses; they are making their points about the square itself, the diameter itself, not about the diameter which they draw, and similarly with the others. These figures which they fashion and draw, of which shadows and reflections in the water are images, they now in turn use as images, in seeking to understand those others in themselves, which one cannot see except in thought.—That is true.

This is what I called the intelligible class, and said that the soul is forced to use hypotheses in its search for it, not travelling up to a first principle, since it cannot reach beyond its hypotheses, but it uses as images those very things which at a lower level were models and which, in comparison with their images, were thought to be clear and honoured as such.—I understand, he said, that you mean what happens in geometry and kindred sciences.

Understand also that by the other section of the intelligible I mean that which reason itself grasps by the power of dialectic. It does not consider its hypotheses as first principles, but as hypotheses in the true sense of stepping stones and starting points, in order to reach that which is beyond hypothesis, the first principle of all that exists. Having reached this and keeping hold of what follows from it, it does come down to a conclusion without making use of anything visible at all, but proceeding by means of Forms and through Forms to its conclusions which are Forms.

I understand, he said, but not completely, for you seem to be speaking of a mighty task—that you wish to distinguish the intelligible reality contemplated by the science of dialectic as clearer than that viewed by the so-called sciences, for which their hypotheses are first principles. The students of these so-called sciences are, it is true, compelled to study them by thought and not by sense perception, yet because they do not go back to a first principle but proceed from hypotheses, you do not think that they have any clear understanding of their subjects, although these can be so understood if approached from a first principle. You seem to me to call the attitude of mind of geometers and such reasoning but not understanding, reasoning being midway between opinion and understanding.

You have grasped this very satisfactorily, I said. There are four such processes in the soul, corresponding to the four sections of our line: understanding for the highest, reasoning for the second; give the name of opinion to the third, and imagination to the last. Place these in the due terms of a proportion and consider that each has as much clarity as the content of its particular section shares in truth.—I understand, and I agree and arrange them as you say.

Next, I said, compare the effect of education and the lack of it upon our human nature to a situation like this: imagine men to be living in an underground cave-like dwelling place, which has a way up to the light along its whole width, but the entrance is a long way up. The men have been there from childhood, with their neck and legs in fetters, so that they remain in the same place and can only see ahead of them, as their bonds prevent them turning their heads. Light is provided by a fire burning some way behind and above them. Between the fire and the prisoners, some way behind them and on a higher ground, there is a path across the cave and along this a low wall has been built, like the screen at a puppet show in front of the performers who show their puppets above it.—I see it.

See then also men carrying along that wall, so that they overtop it, all kinds of artifacts, statues of men, reproductions of other animals in stone or wood fashioned in all sorts of ways, and, as is likely, some of the carriers are talking while others are silent.—This is a strange picture, and strange prisoners.

They are like us, I said. Do you think, in the first place, that such men could see anything of themselves and each other[4] except the shadows which the fire casts upon the wall of the cave in front of them?—How could they, if they have to keep their heads still throughout life?

And is not the same true of the objects carried along the wall?—Quite.

If they could converse with one another, do you not think that they would consider these shadows to be the real things?—Necessarily.

What if their prison had an echo which reached them from in front of them? Whenever one of the carriers passing behind the wall spoke, would they not think that it was the shadow passing in front of them which was talking? Do you agree?—By Zeus I do.

Altogether then, I said, such men would believe the truth to be nothing else than the shadows of the artifacts?—They must believe that.

Consider then what deliverance from their bonds and the curing of their ignorance would be if something like this naturally happened to them. Whenever one of them was freed, had to stand up suddenly, turn his head, walk, and look up toward the light, doing all that would give him pain, the flash of the fire would make it impossible for him to see the objects of which he had earlier seen the shadows. What do you think he would say if he was told that what he saw then was foolishness, that he was now somewhat closer to reality and turned to things that existed more fully, that he saw more correctly? If one then pointed

---

[4] These shadows of themselves and each other are never mentioned again. A Platonic myth or parable, like a Homeric simile, is often elaborated in considerable detail. These contribute to the vividness of the picture but often have no other function, and it is a mistake to look for any symbolic meaning in them. It is the general picture that matters.

to each of the objects passing by, asked him what each was, and forced him to answer, do you not think he would be at a loss and believe that the things which he saw earlier were truer than the things now pointed out to him?—Much truer.

If one then compelled him to look at the fire itself, his eyes would hurt, he would turn round and flee toward those things which he could see, and think that they were in fact clearer than those now shown to him.—Quite so.

And if one were to drag him thence by force up the rough and steep path, and did not let him go before he was dragged into the sunlight. Would he not be in physical pain and angry as he was dragged along? When he came into the light, with the sunlight filling his eyes, he would not be able to see a single one of the things which are now said to be true.—Not at once, certainly.

I think he would need time to get adjusted before he could see things in the world above; at first he would see shadows most easily, then reflections of men and other things in water, then the things themselves. After this he would see objects in the sky and the sky itself more easily at night, the light of the stars and the moon more easily than the sun and the light of the sun during the day. —Of course.

Then, at last, he would be able to see the sun, not images of it in water or in some alien place, but the sun itself in its own place, and be able to contemplate it.—That must be so.

After this he would reflect that it is the sun which provides the seasons and the years, which governs everything in the visible world, and is also in some way the cause of those other things which he used to see.—Clearly that would be the next stage.

What then? As he reminds himself of his first dwelling place, of the wisdom there and of his fellow prisoners, would he not reckon himself happy for the change, and pity them?—Surely.

And if the men below had praise and honours from each other, and prizes for the man who saw most clearly the shadows that passed before them, and who could best remember which usually came earlier and which later, and which came together and thus could most ably prophesy the future, do you think our man would desire those rewards and envy those who were honoured and held power among the prisoners, or would he feel, as Homer put it, that he certainly wished to be "serf to another man without possessions upon the earth"[5] and go through any suffering, rather than share their opinions and live as they do?— Quite so, he said, I think he would rather suffer anything.

Reflect on this too, I said. If this man went down into the cave again and sat down in the same seat, would his eyes not be filled with darkness, coming suddenly out of the sunlight?—They certainly would.

And if he had to contend again with those who had remained prisoners in recognizing those shadows while his sight was affected and his eyes had not settled down—and the time for this adjustment would not be short—would he not be ridiculed? Would it not be said that he had returned from his upward journey with his eyesight spoiled, and that it was not worthwhile even to attempt

[5] *Odyssey* 11, 489–490, where Achilles says to Odysseus, on the latter's visit to the underworld, that he would rather be a servant to a poor man on earth than king among the dead.

to travel upward? As for the man who tried to free them and lead them upward, if they could somehow lay their hands on him and kill him, they would do so.—They certainly would.

This whole image, my dear Glaucon, I said, must be related to what we said before. The realm of the visible should be compared to the prison dwelling, and the fire inside it to the power of the sun. If you interpret the upward journey and the contemplation of things above as the upward journey of the soul to the intelligible realm, you will grasp what I surmise since you were keen to hear it. Whether it is true or not only the god knows, but this is how I see it, namely that in the intelligible world the Form of the Good is the last to be seen, and with difficulty; when seen it must be reckoned to be for all the cause of all that is right and beautiful, to have produced in the visible world both light and the fount of light; while in the intelligible world it is itself that which produces and controls truth and intelligence, and he who is to act intelligently in public or in private must see it.—I share your thought as far as I am able.

Come then, share with me this thought also: do not be surprised that those who have reached this point are unwilling to occupy themselves with human affairs, and that their souls are always pressing upward to spend their time there, for this is natural if things are as our parable indicates.—That is very likely.

Further, I said, do you think it at all surprising that anyone coming to the evils of human life from the contemplation of the divine behaves awkwardly and appears very ridiculous while his eyes are still dazzled and before he is sufficiently adjusted to the darkness around him, if he is compelled to contend in court or some other place about the shadows of justice or the objects of which they are shadows, and to carry through the contest about these in the way these things are understood by those who have never seen Justice itself?—That is not surprising at all.

Anyone with intelligence, I said, would remember that the eyes may be confused in two ways and from two causes, coming from light into darkness as well as from darkness into light. Realizing that the same applies to the soul, whenever he sees a soul disturbed and unable to see something, he will not laugh mindlessly but will consider whether it has come from a brighter life and is dimmed because unadjusted, or has come from greater ignorance into greater light and is filled with a brighter dazzlement. The former he would declare happy in its life and experience, the latter he would pity, and if he should wish to laugh at it, his laughter would be less ridiculous than if he laughed at a soul that has come from the light above.—What you say is very reasonable.

We must then, I said, if these things are true, think something like this about them, namely that education is not what some declare it to be; they say that knowledge is not present in the soul and that they put it in, like putting sight into blind eyes.—They surely say that.

Our present argument shows, I said, that the capacity to learn and the organ with which to do so are present in every person's soul. It is as if it were not possible to turn the eye from darkness to light without turning the whole body; so one must turn one's whole soul from the world of becoming until it can endure to contemplate reality, and the brightest of realities, which we say is the Good.—Yes.

Education then is the art of doing this very thing, this turning around, the knowledge of how the soul can most easily and most effectively be turned around; it is not the art of putting the capacity of sight into the soul; the soul possesses that already but it is not turned the right way or looking where it should. This is what education has to deal with.—That seems likely.

Now the other so-called virtues of the soul seem to be very close to those of the body—they really do not exist before and are added later by habit and practice—but the virtue of intelligence belongs above all to something more divine, it seems, which never loses its capacity but, according to which way it is turned, becomes useful and beneficial or useless and harmful. Have you never noticed in men who are said to be wicked but clever, how sharply their little soul looks into things to which it turns its attention? Its capacity for sight is not inferior, but it is compelled to serve evil ends, so that the more sharply it looks the more evils it works.—Quite so.

Yet if a soul of this kind had been hammered at from childhood and those excrescences had been knocked off it which belong to the world of becoming and have been fastened upon it by feasting, gluttony, and similar pleasures, and which like leaden weights draw the soul to look downward—if, being rid of these, it turned to look at things that are true, then the same soul of the same man would see these just as sharply as it now sees the things towards which it is directed.—That seems likely.

Further, is it not likely, I said, indeed it follows inevitably from what was said before, that the uneducated who have no experience of truth would never govern a city satisfactorily, nor would those who are allowed to spend their whole life in the process of educating themselves; the former would fail because they do not have a single goal at which all their actions, public and private, must aim; the latter because they would refuse to act, thinking that they have settled, while still alive, in the faraway islands of the blessed.—True.

It is then our task as founders, I said, to compel the best natures to reach the study which we have previously said to be the most important, to see the Good and to follow that upward journey. When they have accomplished their journey and seen it sufficiently, we must not allow them to do what they are allowed to do today.—What is that?

To stay there, I said, and to refuse to go down again to the prisoners in the cave, there to share both their labours and their honours, whether these be of little or of greater worth.[6]

Are we then, he said, to do them an injustice by making them live a worse life when they could live a better one?

You are again forgetting, my friend, I said, that it is not the law's concern to make some one group in the city outstandingly happy but to contrive to spread happiness throughout the city, by bringing the citizens into harmony with each other by persuasion or compulsion, and to make them share with each other the benefits which each group can confer upon the community. The law has not made

---

[6] Plato does indeed require his philosopher to go back into the cave to help those less fortunate than himself, but only as a duty, not because he loves his neighbour or gets any emotional satisfaction from helping him.

men of this kind in the city in order to allow each to turn in any direction they wish but to make use of them to bind the city together.—You are right, I had forgotten.

Consider then, Glaucon, I said, that we shall not be doing an injustice to those who have become philosophers in our city, and that what we shall say to them, when we compel them to care for and to guard the others, is just. For we shall say: "Those who become philosophers in other cities are justified in not sharing the city's labours, for they have grown into philosophy of their own accord, against the will of the government in each of those cities, and it is right that what grows of its own accord, as it owes no debt to anyone for its upbringing, should not be keen to pay it to anyone. But we have made you in our city kings and leaders of the swarm, as it were, both to your own advantage and to that of the rest of the city; you are better and more completely educated than those others, and you are better able to share in both kinds of life. Therefore you must each in turn go down to live with other men and grow accustomed to seeing in the dark. When you are used to it you will see infinitely better than the dwellers below; you will know what each kind of image is and of what it is an image, because you have seen the truth of things beautiful and just and good, and so, for you as for us, the city will be governed as a waking reality and not as in a dream, as the majority of cities are now governed by men who are fighting shadows and striving against each other in order to rule as if this were a great good." For this is the truth: a city in which the prospective rulers are least keen to rule must of necessity be governed best and be most free from civil strife, whereas a city with the opposite kind of rulers is governed in the opposite way.—Quite so.

Do you think that those we have nurtured will disobey us and refuse to share the labours of the city, each group in turn, though they may spend the greater part of their time dwelling with each other in a pure atmosphere?

They cannot, he said, for we shall be giving just orders to just men, but each of them will certainly go to rule as to something that must be done, the opposite attitude from that of the present rulers in every city.

That is how it is, my friend, I said. If you can find a way of life which is better than governing for the prospective governors, then a well-governed city can exist for you. Only in that city will the truly rich rule, not rich in gold but in the wealth which the happy man must have, a life with goodness and intelligence. If beggars hungry for private goods go into public life, thinking that they must snatch their good from it, the well-governed city cannot exist, for then office is fought for, and such a war at home inside the city destroys them and the city as well.—Very true.

Can you name, I said, any other life than that of true philosophy which disdains political office?—No, by Zeus.

And surely it is those who are no lovers of governing who must govern. Otherwise, rival lovers of it will fight them.—Of course.

What other men will you compel to become guardians of the city rather than those who have the best knowledge of the principles that make for the best government of a city and who also know honours of a different kind, and a better life than the political?—No one else.

Do you want us to examine how such men will come to be in our city, and how one will lead them to the light, as some are said to have gone up from the underworld to join the gods?—Of course I want it.

This is not a matter of spinning a coin[7] but of turning a soul from a kind of day that is night to the true day, being the upward way to reality which we say is true philosophy.—Quite so.

[7] A proverbial saying, referring to a children's game in which the players were divided into two groups. A shell or potsherd, white on one side and black on the other, was then thrown in the space between them to the cry of "night or day" (note the reference to night and day which immediately follows) and, according as the white or black fell uppermost, one group ran away pursued by the other. The meaning here is much the same as in our expression "spinning a coin," namely that this was not a matter to be settled in a moment or by chance.

Sceptical Doubts Concerning the Operations of the Human Understanding

DAVID HUME

David Hume (1711–1776), an outstanding British empiricist, not only wrote upon philosophical subjects but also became famous as a historian. Among his major works are *A Treatise of Human Nature* (1739–1740), *Essays, Moral and Political* (1741–1742), and *The History of England* (1754–1762).

Part I

All the objects of human reason or enquiry may naturally be divided into two kinds, to wit, *Relations of Ideas,* and *Matters of Fact.* Of the first kind are the sciences of Geometry, Algebra, and Arithmetic; and in short, every affirmation which is either intuitively or demonstratively certain. *That the square of the hypothenuse is equal to the square of the two sides,* is a proposition which expresses a relation between these figures. *That three times five is equal to the half of thirty,* expresses a relation between these numbers. Propositions of this kind are discoverable by the mere operation of thought, without dependence on what is anywhere existent in the universe. Though there never were a circle or triangle in nature, the truths demonstrated by Euclid would for ever retain their certainty and evidence.

Matters of fact, which are the second objects of human reason, are not ascertained in the same manner; nor is our evidence of their truth, however great, of a like nature with the foregoing. The contrary of every matter of fact

Source: David Hume, *Enquiry Concerning Human Understanding* (1748).

is still possible; because it can never imply a contradiction, and is conceived by the mind with the same facility and distinctness, as if ever so conformable to reality. *That the sun will not rise to-morrow* is no less intelligible a proposition, and implies no more contradiction than the affirmation, *that it will rise*. We should in vain, therefore, attempt to demonstrate its falsehood. Were it demonstratively false, it would imply a contradiction, and could never be distinctly conceived by the mind.

It may, therefore, be a subject worthy of curiosity, to enquire what is the nature of that evidence which assures us of any real existence and matter of fact, beyond the present testimony of our senses, or the records of our memory. This part of philosophy, it is observable, has been little cultivated, either by the ancients or moderns; and therefore our doubts and errors, in the prosecution of so important an enquiry, may be the more excusable; while we march through such difficult paths without any guide or direction. They may even prove useful, by exciting curiosity, and destroying that implicit faith and security, which is the bane of all reasoning and free enquiry. The discovery of defects in the common philosophy, if any such there be, will not, I presume, be a discouragement, but rather an incitement, as is usual, to attempt something more full and satisfactory than has yet been proposed to the public.

All reasonings concerning matter of fact seem to be founded on the relation of *Cause and Effect*. By means of that relation alone we can go beyond the evidence of our memory and senses. If you were to ask a man, why he believes any matter of fact, which is absent; for instance, that his friend is in the country, or in France; he would give you a reason; and this reason would be some other fact; as a letter received from him, or the knowledge of his former resolutions and promises. A man finding a watch or any other machine in a desert island, would conclude that there had once been men in that island. All our reasonings concerning fact are of the same nature. And here it is constantly supposed that there is a connexion between the present fact and that which is inferred from it. Were there nothing to bind them together, the inference would be entirely precarious. The hearing of an articulate voice and rational discourse in the dark assures us of the presence of some person: Why? because these are the effects of the human make and fabric, and closely connected with it. If we anatomize all the other reasonings of this nature, we shall find that they are founded on the relation of cause and effect, and that this relation is either near or remote, direct or collateral. Heat and light are collateral effects of fire, and the one effect may justly be inferred from the other.

If we would satisfy ourselves, therefore, concerning the nature of that evidence, which assures us of matters of fact, we must enquire how we arrive at the knowledge of cause and effect.

I shall venture to affirm, as a general proposition, which admits of no exception, that the knowledge of this relation is not, in any instance, attained by reasonings *a priori;* but arises entirely from experience, when we find that any particular objects are constantly conjoined with each other. Let an object be presented to a man of ever so strong natural reason and abilities; if that object be entirely new to him, he will not be able, by the most accurate examination of its sensible qualities, to discover any of its causes or effects. Adam, though his rational faculties be supposed, at the very first, entirely perfect, could not have inferred from the fluidity and transparency of water that it would suffocate him, or from the light and warmth of fire that it would consume him. No object ever discovers, by the qualities which appear to the senses, either the causes which produced it, or the effects which will arise from it; nor can our reason, unassisted by experience, ever draw any inference concerning real existence and matter of fact.

This proposition, *that causes and effects are discoverable, not by reason but by experience,* will readily be admitted with regard to such objects, as we remember to have once been altogether unknown to us; since we must be conscious of the utter inability, which we then lay under, of foretelling what would arise from them. Present two smooth pieces of marble to a man who has no tincture of natural philosophy; he will never discover that they will adhere together in such a manner as to require great force to separate them in a direct line, while they make so small a resistance to a lateral pressure. Such events, as bear little analogy to the common course of nature, are also readily confessed to be known only by experience; nor does any man imagine that the explosion of gunpowder, or the attraction of a loadstone, could ever be discovered by arguments *a priori.* In like manner, when an effect is supposed to depend upon an intricate machinery or secret structure of parts, we make no difficulty in attributing all our knowledge of it to experience. Who will assert that he can give the ultimate reason, why milk or bread is proper nourishment for a man, not for a lion or a tiger?

But the same truth may not appear, at first sight, to have the same evidence with regard to events, which have become familiar to us from our first appearance in the world, which bear a close analogy to the whole course of nature, and which are supposed to depend on the simple qualities of objects, without any secret structure of parts. We are apt to imagine that we could discover these effects by the mere operation of our reason, without experience. We fancy, that were we brought on a sudden into this world, we could at first have inferred that one Billiard-ball would communicate motion to another upon impulse; and that we needed not to have waited for the event, in order to pronounce with certainty concerning it. Such is the influence of custom, that, where it is strongest, it not only covers our natural ignorance, but even conceals itself, and seems not to take place, merely because it is found in the highest degree.

But to convince us that all the laws of nature, and all the operations of bodies without exception, are known only by experience, the following reflections may, perhaps, suffice. Were any object presented to us, and were we required to pronounce concerning the effect, which will result from it, without consulting past observation; after what manner, I beseech you, must the mind proceed in this operation? It must invent or imagine some event, which it ascribes to the object as its effect; and it is plain that this invention must be entirely arbitrary. The mind can never possibly find the effect in the supposed cause, by the most accurate scrutiny and examination. For the effect is totally different from the cause, and consequently can never be discovered in it. Motion in the second Billiard-ball is a quite distinct event from motion in the first; nor is there anything in the one to suggest the smallest hint of the other. A stone or piece of metal raised into the air, and left without any support, immediately falls: but to consider the matter *a priori,* is there anything we discover in this situation which can beget the idea of a downward, rather than an upward, or any other motion, in the stone or metal?

And as the first imagination or invention of a particular effect, in all natural operations, is arbitrary, where we consult not experience; so must we also esteem the supposed tie or connexion between the cause and effect, which binds them together, and renders it impossible that any other effect could result from the operation of that cause. When I see, for instance, a Billiard-ball moving in a straight line towards another; even suppose motion in the second ball should by accident be suggested to me, as the result of their contact or impulse; may I not conceive, that a hundred different events might as well follow from that cause? May not both these balls remain at absolute rest? May not the first ball return in a straight line, or leap off from the second in any line or direction? All these suppositions are consistent and conceivable. Why then should we give the preference to one, which is no more consistent or conceivable than the rest? All our reasonings *a priori* will never be able to show us any foundation for this preference.

In a word, then, every effect is a distinct event from its cause. It could not, therefore, be discovered in the cause, and the first invention or conception of it, *a priori,* must be entirely arbitrary. And even after it is suggested, the conjunction of it with the cause must appear equally arbitrary; since there are always many other effects, which, to reason, must seem fully as consistent and natural. In vain, therefore, should we pretend to determine any single event, or infer any cause or effect, without the assistance of observation and experience.

Hence we may discover the reason why no philosopher, who is rational and modest, has ever pretended to assign the ultimate cause of any natural operation, or to show distinctly the action of that power, which produces any single effect in the universe. It is confessed, that the utmost effort of human reason is to reduce the principles, productive of natural phenomena, to a greater simplicity, and to resolve the many particular effects into a few general causes, by means by reasonings from analogy, experience, and observation. But as to the causes of these general causes, we should in vain attempt their discovery; nor shall we ever be able to satisfy ourselves, by any particular explication of them. These ultimate springs and principles are totally shut up from human curiosity and enquiry. Elasticity, gravity, cohesion of parts, communication of motion by impulse; these are probably the ultimate causes and principles which we shall ever discover in nature; and we may esteem ourselves sufficiently happy, if, by accurate enquiry and reasoning, we can trace up the particular phenomena to, or near to, these general principles. The most perfect philosophy of the natural kind only staves off our ignorance a little longer: as perhaps the most perfect philosophy of the moral or metaphysical kind serves only to discover larger portions of it. Thus the observation of human blindness and weakness is the result of all philosophy, and meets us at every turn, in spite of our endeavours to elude or avoid it.

Nor is geometry, when taken into the assistance of natural philosophy, ever able to remedy this defect, or lead us into the knowledge of ultimate causes, by all that accuracy of reasoning for which it is so justly celebrated. Every part of mixed mathematics proceeds upon the supposition that certain laws are established by nature in her operations; and abstract reasonings are employed, either to assist experience in the discovery of these laws, or to determine their influence in particular instances, where it depends upon any precise degree of distance and quantity. Thus, it is a law of motion, discovered by experience, that the moment or force of any body in motion is in the compound ratio or proportion of its solid contents and its velocity; and consequently, that a small force may remove the greatest obstacle or raise the greatest weight, if, by any contrivance or machinery, we can increase the velocity of that force, so as to make it an overmatch for its antagonist. Geometry assists us in the application of this law, by giving us the just dimensions of all the parts and figures which can enter into any species of machine; but still the discovery of the law itself is owing merely to experience, and all the abstract reasonings in the world could never lead us one step towards the knowledge of it. When we reason *a priori*, and consider merely any object or cause, as it appears to the mind, independent of all observation, it never could suggest to us the notion of any distinct object, such as its effect; much less, show us the inseparable and inviolable connexion between them. A man must be very sagacious who could discover by reasoning that crystal is the effect of heat, and ice of cold, without being previously acquainted with the operation of these qualities.

Part II

But we have not yet attained any tolerable satisfaction with regard to the question first proposed. Each solution still gives rise to a new question as difficult as the foregoing, and leads us on to farther enquiries. When it is asked, *What is the nature of all our reasonings concerning matter of fact?* the proper answer seems to be, that they are founded on the relation of cause and effect. When again it is asked, *What is the foundation of all our reasonings and conclusions concerning that relation?* it may be replied in one word, Experience. But if we still carry on our sifting humour, and ask, *What is the foundation of all conclusions from experience?* this implies a new question, which may be of more difficult solution and explication. Philosophers, that give themselves airs of superior wisdom and sufficiency, have a hard task when they encounter persons of inquisitive dispositions, who push them from every corner to which they retreat, and who are sure at last to bring them to some dangerous dilemma. The best expedient to prevent this confusion, is to be modest in our pretensions; and even to discover the difficulty ourselves before it is objected to us. By this means, we may make a kind of merit of our very ignorance.

I shall contend myself, in this section, with an easy task, and shall pretend only to give a negative answer to the question here proposed. I say then, that, even after we have experience of the operations of cause and effect, our conclusions from that experience are *not* founded on reasoning, or any process of the understanding. This answer we must endeavour both to explain and to defend.

It must certainly be allowed, that nature has kept us at a great distance from all her secrets, and has afforded us only the knowledge of a few superficial qualities of objects; while she conceals from us those powers and principles on which the influence of those objects entirely depends. Our senses inform us of the colour, weight, and consistence of bread; but neither sense nor reason can ever inform us of those qualities which fit it for the nourishment and support of a human body. Sight or feeling conveys an idea of the actual motion of bodies; but as to that wonderful force or power, which would carry on a moving body for ever in a continued change of place, and which bodies never lose but by communicating it to others; of this we cannot form the most distant conception. But notwithstanding this ignorance of natural powers[1] and principles, we always presume, when we see like sensible qualities, that they have like secret powers, and expect that effects, similar to those which we have experienced, will follow from them. If a body of like colour and consistence with that bread, which we have formerly eat, be presented to us, we make no scruple of repeating the experiment, and foresee, with certainty, like nourishment and support. Now this is a process of the mind or thought, of which I would willingly know the foundation. It is allowed on all hands that there is no known connexion between the sensible qualities and the secret powers; and consequently, that the mind is not led to form such a conclusion concerning their constant and regular conjunction, by anything which it knows of their nature. As to past *Experience*, it can be allowed to give *direct* and *certain* information of those precise objects only, and that precise period of time, which fell under its cognizance: but why this experience should be extended to future times, and to other objects, which for aught we know, may be only in appearance similar; this is the main question on which I would insist. The bread, which I formerly eat, nourished me; that is, a body of such sensible qualities was, at that time, endued with such secret powers: but does it follow, that other bread must also nourish me at another time, and that like sensible qualities must always be attended with like secret powers? The consequence seems nowise necessary. At least, it must be acknowledged that there is here a consequence drawn by the mind; that there is a certain step taken; a process of thought, and an inference, which wants to be explained. These two propositions are far from being the same, *I have found that such an object has always been attended with such an effect*, and *I foresee, that other objects, which are, in appearance, similar, will be attended with similar effects*. I shall allow, if you please, that the one proposition may justly be inferred from the other: I know, in fact, that it always is inferred. But if you insist that the inference is made by a chain of reasoning, I desire you to produce that reasoning. The connexion between these propositions is not intuitive. There is required a medium, which may enable the mind to draw such an inference, if indeed it be drawn by reasoning and argument. What that medium is, I must confess, passes my comprehension; and it is incumbent on those to produce it, who assert that it really exists, and is the origin of all our conclusions concerning matter of fact.

This negative argument must certainly, in process of time, become altogether

---

[1] The word, Power, is here used in a loose and popular sense. The more accurate explication of it would give additional evidence to this argument. See Sect. 7.

convincing, if many penetrating and able philosophers shall turn their enquiries this way and no one be ever able to discover any connecting proposition or intermediate step, which supports the understanding in this conclusion. But as the question is yet new, every reader may not trust so far to his own penetration, as to conclude, because an argument escapes his enquiry, that therefore it does not really exist. For this reason it may be requisite to venture upon a more difficult task; and enumerating all the branches of human knowledge, endeavour to show that none of them can afford such an argument.

All reasonings may be divided into two kinds, namely, demonstrative reasoning, or that concerning relations of ideas, and moral reasoning, or that concerning matter of fact and existence. That there are no demonstrative arguments in the case seems evident; since it implies no contradiction that the course of nature may change, and that an object, seemingly like those which we have experienced, may be attended with different or contrary effects. May I not clearly and distinctly conceive that a body, falling from the clouds, and which, in all other respects, resembles snow, has yet the taste of salt or feeling of fire? Is there any more intelligible proposition than to affirm, that all the trees will flourish in December and January, and decay in May and June? Now whatever is intelligible, and can be distinctly conceived, implies no contradiction, and can never be proved false by any demonstrative argument or abstract reasoning *à priori*.

If we be, therefore, engaged by arguments to put trust in past experience, and make it the standard of our future judgement, these arguments must be probable only, or such as regard matter of fact and real existence, according to the division above mentioned. But that there is no argument of this kind, must appear, if our explication of that species of reasoning be admitted as solid and satisfactory. We have said that all arguments concerning existence are founded on the relation of cause and effect; that our knowledge of that relation is derived entirely from experience; and that all our experimental conclusions proceed upon the supposition that the future will be conformable to the past. To endeavour, therefore, the proof of this last supposition by probable arguments, or arguments regarding existence, must be evidently going in a circle, and taking that for granted, which is the very point in question.

In reality, all arguments from experience are founded on the similarity which we discover among natural objects, and by which we are induced to expect effects similar to those which we have found to follow from such objects. And though none but a fool or madman will ever pretend to dispute the authority of experience, or to reject that great guide of human life, it may surely be allowed a philosopher to have so much curiosity at least as to examine the principle of human nature, which gives this mighty authority to experience, and makes us draw advantage from that similarity which nature has placed among different objects. From causes which appear *similar* we expect similar effects. This is the sum of all our experimental conclusions. Now it seems evident that, if this conclusion were formed by reason, it would be as perfect at first, and upon one instance, as after ever so long a course of experience. But the case is far otherwise. Nothing so like as eggs; yet no one, on account of this appearing similarity, expects the same taste and relish in all of them. It is only after a long course of uniform experiments in any kind, that we attain a firm reliance and security with regard to a particular event. Now where is that process of reasoning which, from one instance, draws a conclusion, so different from that which it infers from a hundred instances that are nowise different from that single one? This question I propose as much for the sake of information, as with an intention of raising difficulties. I cannot find, I cannot imagine any such reasoning. But I keep my mind still open to instruction, if any one will vouchsafe to bestow it on me.

Should it be said that, from a number of uniform experiments, we *infer* a connexion between the sensible qualities and the secret powers; this, I must confess, seems the same difficulty, couched in different terms. The question still recurs, on what process of argument this *inference* is founded? Where is the medium, the interposing ideas, which join propositions so very wide of each other? It is confessed that the colour, consistence, and other sensible qualities of bread appear not, of themselves, to have any connexion with the secret powers of nourishment and support. For otherwise we could infer these secret powers from the first appearance of these sensible qualities, without the aid of experience; contrary to the sentiment of all philosophers, and contrary to plain matter of fact. Here, then, is our natural state of ignorance with regard to the powers and influence of all objects. How is this remedied by experience? It only shows us a number of uniform effects, resulting from certain objects, and teaches us that those particular objects, at that particular time, were endowed with such powers and forces. When a new object, endowed with similar sensible qualities, is produced, we expect similar powers and forces, and look for a like effect. From a body of like colour and consistence with bread we expect like nourishment and support. But this surely is a step or progress of the mind, which wants to be explained. When a man says, *I have found, in all past instances, such sensible qualities conjoined with such secret powers:* And when he says, *Similar sensible qualities will always be conjoined with similar secret powers,* he is not guilty of a tautology, nor are these propositions in any respect the same. You say that the one proposition is an inference from the other. But you must confess that the inference is not intuitive; neither is it demonstrative: Of what nature is it, then? To say it is experimental, is begging the question. For all inferences from experience suppose, as their foundation, that the future will resemble the past, and that similar powers will be conjoined with similar sensible qualities. If there be any suspicion that the course of nature may change, and that the past may be no rule for the future, all experience becomes useless, and can give rise to no inference or conclusion. It is impossible, therefore, that any arguments from experience can prove this resemblance of the past to the future; since all these arguments are founded on the supposition of that resemblance. Let the course of things be allowed hitherto ever so regular; that alone, without some new argument or inference, proves not that, for the future, it will continue so. In vain do you pretend to have learned the nature of bodies from your past experience. Their secret nature, and consequently all their effects and influence, may change, without any change in their sensible qualities. This happens sometimes, and with regard to some objects: Why may it not happen always, and with regard to all objects? What logic, what process of argument secures you against this supposition? My practice, you say, refutes my doubts. But you mistake the purport of my question. As an agent, I am quite satisfied in the point; but as a philosopher, who has some share of curiosity, I will not say scepticism, I want to learn the foundation of this inference. No reading, no enquiry has yet been able to remove my difficulty, or give me satisfaction in a matter of such importance. Can I do better than propose the difficulty to the public, even though, perhaps, I have small hopes of obtaining a solution? We shall at least, by this means, be sensible of our ignorance, if we do not augment our knowledge.

I must confess that a man is guilty of unpardonable arrogance who concludes, because an argument has escaped his own investigation, that therefore it does not really exist. I must also confess that, though all the learned, for several ages, should have employed themselves in fruitless search upon any subject, it may still, perhaps, be rash to conclude positively that the subject must, therefore, pass all human comprehension. Even though we examine all the sources of our knowledge, and conclude them unfit for such a subject, there may still remain a suspicion, that the enumeration is not complete, or the examination not accurate. But with regard to the present subject, there are some considerations which seem to remove all this accusation of arrogance or suspicion of mistake.

It is certain that the most ignorant and stupid peasants—nay infants, nay even brute beasts—improve by experience, and learn the qualities of natural objects, by observing the effects which result from them. When a child has felt the sensation of pain from touching the flame of a candle, he will be careful not to put his hand near any candle; but will expect a similar effect from a cause which is similar in its sensible qualities and appearance. If you assert, therefore, that the understanding of the child is led into this conclusion by any process of argument or ratiocination, I may justly require you to produce that argument; nor have you any pretence to refuse so equitable a demand. You cannot say that the argument is abstruse, and may possibly escape your enquiry; since you confess that it is obvious to the capacity of a mere infant. If you hesitate, therefore, a moment, or if, after reflection, you produce any intricate or profound argument, you, in a manner, give up the question, and confess that it is not reasoning which engages us to suppose the past resembling the future, and to expect similar effects from causes which are, to appearance, similar. This is the proposition which I intended to enforce in the present section. If I be right, I pretend not to have made any mighty discovery. And if I be wrong, I must acknowledge myself to be indeed a very backward scholar; since I cannot now discover an argument which, it seems, was perfectly familiar to me long before I was out of my cradle.

Percept and Concept and Their Practical Uses

WILLIAM JAMES

William James (1842–1910) was professor of philosophy at Harvard University. He is the author of several important books, including *The Principles of Psychology* (1890), *The Will To Believe* (1897), *The Varieties of Religious Experience* (1902), *Pragmatism* (1907), *A Pluralistic Universe* (1909), *The Meaning of Truth* (1909), and *Some Problems of Philosophy* (1911).

. . .

Sensation and thought in man are mingled, but they vary independently. In our quadrupedal relatives thought proper is at a minimum, but we have no reason to suppose that their immediate life of feeling is either less or more copious than ours. Feeling must have been originally self-sufficing; and thought appears as a superadded function, adapting us to a wider environment than that of which brutes take account. Some parts of the stream of feeling must be more intense, emphatic, and exciting than others in animals as well as in ourselves; but whereas lower animals simply react upon these more salient sensations by appropriate movements, higher animals remember them, and men react on them intellectually, by using nouns, adjectives, and verbs to identify them when they meet them elsewhere.

The great difference between percepts and concepts[1] is that percepts are continuous and concepts are discrete. Not discrete in their *being,* for conception as an *act* is part of the flux of feeling, but discrete from each other in their several *meanings*. Each concept means just what it singly means, and nothing else; and if the conceiver does not know whether he means this or means that, it shows that his concept is imperfectly formed. The perceptual flux as such, on the contrary, *means* nothing, and is but what it immediately is. No matter how small a tract of it be taken, it is always a much-at-once, and contains innumerable aspects and characters which conception can pick out, isolate, and thereafter always intend. It shows duration, intensity, complexity or simplicity, interestingness, excitingness, pleasantness or their opposites. Data from all our senses enter into it, merged in a general extensiveness of which each occupies a big or little share. Yet all these parts leave its unity unbroken. Its boundaries are no more distinct than are those of the field of vision. Boundaries are things

---

[1] In what follows I shall freely use synonyms for these two terms. "Idea," "thought," and "intellection" are synonymous with "concept." Instead of "percept" I shall often speak of "sensation," "feeling," "intuition," and sometimes of "sensible experience" or of the "immediate flow" of conscious life. Since Hegel's time, what is simply perceived has been called the "immediate," while the "mediated" is synonymous with what is conceived.

Source: William James, *Some Problems in Philosophy* (1911).

that intervene; but here nothing intervenes save parts of the perceptual flux itself, and these are overflowed by what they separate, so that whatever we distinguish and isolate conceptually is found perceptually to telescope and compenetrate and diffuse into its neighbors. The cuts we make are purely ideal. If my reader can succeed in abstracting from all conceptual interpretation and lapse back into his immediate sensible life at this very moment, he will find it to be what someone has called a big blooming buzzing confusion, as free from contradiction in its "much-at-onceness" as it is all alive and evidently there.[2]

Out of this aboriginal sensible muchness attention carves out objects, which conception then names and identifies forever—in the sky "constellations," on the earth "beach," "sea," "cliff," "bushes," "grass." Out of time we cut "days" and "nights," "summers" and "winters." We say *what* each part of the sensible continuum is, and all these abstracted *whats* are concepts.[3]

The intellectual life of man consists almost wholly in his substitution of a conceptual order for the perceptual order in which his experience originally comes.

. . .

From Aristotle downwards, philosophers have frankly admitted the indispensability, for complete knowledge of fact, of both the sensational and the intellectual contribution.[4] For complete knowledge of fact, I say; but facts are particulars and connect themselves with practical necessities and the arts; and Greek philosophers soon formed the notion that a knowledge of so-called "universals," consisting of concepts of abstract forms, qualities, numbers, and relations was the only knowledge worthy of the truly philosophic mind. Particular facts decay and our perceptions of them vary. A concept never varies; and between such unvarying terms the relations must be constant and express eternal verities. Hence there arose a tendency, which has lasted all through philosophy, to contrast the knowledge of universals and intelligibles, as godlike, dignified,

---

[2] Compare W. James: *A Pluralistic Universe,* pp. 282–288. Also *Psychology, Briefer Course,* pp. 157–166.

[3] On the function of conception consult: Sir William Hamilton's *Lectures on Logic,* 9, 10; H. L. Mansel, *Prolegomena Logica,* chap. i; A. Schopenhauer, *The World as Will,* etc., Supplements 6, 7 to book ii; W. James, *Principles of Psychology,* chap. xii; *Briefer Course,* chap. xiv. Also J. G. Romanes: *Mental Evolution in Man,* chaps. iii, iv; Th. Ribot: *l'Evolution des Idées Générales,* chap. vi; Th. Ruyssen, *Essai sur l'Evolution psychologique du Jugement,* chap. vii; Laromiguière, *Leçons de Philosophie,* part 2, lesson 12. The account I give directly contradicts that which Kant gave which has prevailed since Kant's time. Kant always speaks of the aboriginal sensible flux as a "manifold" of which he considers the essential character to be its disconnectedness. To get any togetherness at all into it requires, he thinks, the agency of the "transcendental ego of apperception," and to get any definite connections requires the agency of the understanding, with its synthetizing concepts or "categories." "Die Verbindung (conjunctio) eines Mannigfaltigen kann überhaupt niemals durch Sinne in uns kommen, und kann also auch nicht in der reinen Form der sinnlichen Anschauung zugleich mit enthalten sein; denn sie ist ein Actus der Spontaneität der Einbildungskraft, und, da man diese, zum Unterschiede von der Sinnlichkeit, Verstand nennen muss, so ist alle Verbindung . . . eine Verstandeshandlung." K. d. r. V., 2te, Aufg., pp. 129–130. The reader must decide which account agrees best with his own actual experience.

[4] See, for example, book i, chap. ii, of Aristotle's *Metaphysics.*

and honorable to the knower, with that of particulars and sensibles as something relatively base which more allies us with the beasts.[5]

For rationalistic writers conceptual knowledge was not only the more noble knowledge, but it originated independently of all perceptual particulars. Such concepts as God, perfection, eternity, infinity, immutability, identity, absolute beauty, truth, justice, necessity, freedom, duty, worth, etc., and the part they play in our mind, are, it was supposed, impossible to explain as results of practical experience. The empiricist view, and probably the true view, is that they do result from practical experience.[6] But a more important question than that as to the origin of our concepts is that as to their functional use and value; —is *that* tied down to perceptual experience, or out of all relation to it? Is conceptual knowledge self-sufficing and a revelation all by itself, quite apart from its uses in helping to a better understanding of the world of sense?

Rationalists say, Yes. For, as we shall see in later places, the various conceptual universes referred to can be considered in complete abstraction from perceptual reality, and when they are so considered, all sorts of fixed relations can be discovered among their parts. From these the *a priori* sciences of logic,

[5] Plato in numerous places, but chiefly in books 6 and 7 of the *Republic,* contrasts perceptual knowledge as "opinion" with real knowledge, to the latter's glory. For an excellent historic sketch of this platonistic view see the first part of E. Laas's *Idealismus und Positivismus,* 1879. For expressions of the ultra-intellectualistic view, read the passage from "Plotinus on the Intellect" in C. M. Bakewell's *Source-book in Ancient Philosophy,* N.Y., 1907, pp. 353f.; Bossuet, *Traité de la Connaissance de Dieu,* chap. iv, §§ v, vi; R. Cudworth, *A Treatise concerning eternal and immutable Morality,* books iii, iv.—"Plato," writes Prof. Santayana, "thought that all the truth and meaning of earthly things was the reference they contained to a heavenly original. This heavenly original we remember to recognize even among the distortions, disappearances, and multiplications of its ephemeral copies. . . . The impressions themselves have no permanence, no intelligible essence, but are always either arising or ceasing to be. There must be, he tells us, an eternal and clearly definable object of which the visible appearances to us are the multiform semblance; now by one trait, now by another, the phantom before us reminds us of that half-forgotten celestial reality and makes us utter its name. . . . We and the whole universe exist only in the attempt to return to our perfection, to lose ourselves again in God. That ineffable good is our natural possession; and all we honor in this life is but a partial recovery of our birthright; every delightful thing is like a rift in the clouds, through which we catch a glimpse of our native heaven. And if that heaven seems so far away, and the idea of it so dim and unreal, it is because we are so far from perfect, so immersed in what is alien and destructive to the soul." ("Platonic Love in some Italian Poets," in *Interpretations of Poetry and Religion,* 1896.) This is the interpretation of Plato which has been current since Aristotle. It should be said that its profundity has been challenged by Prof. A. J. Stewart. (*Plato's Doctrine of Ideas,* Oxford, 1909.)

Aristotle found great fault with Plato's treatment of ideas as heavenly originals, but he agreed with him fully as to the superior excellence of the conceptual or theoretic life. In chapters vii and viii of book x of the *Nicomachean Ethics* he extols contemplation of universal relations as alone yielding pure happiness. "The life of God, in all its exceeding blessedness, will consist in the exercise of philosophic thought; and of all human activities, that will be the happiest which is most akin to the divine."

[6] John Locke, in his *Essay concerning Human Understanding,* books i, ii, was the great popularizer of this doctrine. Condillac's *Traité des Sensations,* Helvetius's work, *De l'Homme,* and James Mill's *Analysis of the Human Mind* were more radical successors of Locke's great book.

mathematics, ethics, and æsthetics (so far as the last two can be called sciences at all) result. Conceptual knowledge must thus be called a self-sufficing revelation; and by rationalistic writers it has always been treated as admitting us to a diviner world, the world of universal rather than that of perishing facts, of essential qualities, immutable relations, eternal principles of truth and right. Emerson writes: "Generalization is always a new influx of divinity into the mind: hence the thrill that attends it." And a disciple of Hegel, after exalting the knowledge of "the General, Unchangeable, and alone Valuable" above that of "the Particular, Sensible and Transient," adds that if you reproach philosophy with being unable to make a single grass-blade grow, or even to know how it does grow, the reply is that since such a particular "how" stands not above but below knowledge, strictly so-called, such an ignorance argues no defect.[7]

To this ultra-rationalistic opinion the empiricist contention that *the significance of concepts consists always in their relation to perceptual particulars* has been opposed. Made of percepts, or distilled from parts of percepts, their essential office, it has been said, is to coalesce with percepts again, bringing the mind back into the perceptual world with a better command of the situation there. Certainly whenever we *can* do this with our concepts, we do *more* with them than when we leave them flocking with their abstract and motionless companions. It is possible therefore, to join the rationalists in allowing conceptual knowledge to be self-sufficing, while at the same time one joins the empiricists in maintaining that the full *value* of such knowledge is got only by combining it with perceptual reality again. This mediating attitude is that which this book must adopt. But to understand the nature of concepts better we must now go on to distinguish their *function* from their *content*.

The concept "man," to take an example, is three things: 1, the word itself; 2, a vague picture of the human form which has its own value in the way of beauty or not; and 3, an instrument for symbolizing certain objects from which we may expect human treatment when occasion arrives. Similarly of "triangle," "cosine,"—they have their substantive value both as words and as images suggested, but they also have a functional value whenever they lead us elsewhere in discourse.

There are concepts, however, the image-part of which is so faint that their whole value seems to be functional. "God," "cause," "number," "substance," "soul," for example, suggest no definite picture; and their significance seems to consist entirely in their *tendency,* in the further turn which they may give to our action or our thought.[8] We cannot rest in the contemplation of their form, as we can in that of a "circle" or a "man"; we must pass beyond.

Now however beautiful or otherwise worthy of stationary contemplation the substantive part of a concept may be, the more important part of its significance may naturally be held to be the consequences to which it leads. These may lie

---

[7] Michelet, *Hegel's Werke,* vii, 15, quoted by A. Gratry, *De la Connaissance de l'Âme,* i, 231. Compare the similar claim for philosophy in W. Wallace's *Prolegomena to Hegel,* 2d ed., 1894, pp. 28–29, and the long and radical statement of the same view in book iv of Ralph Cudworth's *Treatise on Eternal and Immutable Morality.*

[8] On this functional tendency compare H. Taine, *On Intelligence,* book i, chap. ii (1870).

either in the way of making us think, or in the way of making us act. Whoever has a clear idea of these knows effectively what the concept practically signifies, whether its substantive content be interesting in its own right or not.

This consideration has led to a method of interpreting concepts to which I shall give the name of *the Pragmatic Rule.*[9]

The pragmatic rule is that the meaning of a concept may always be found, if not in some sensible particular which it directly designates, then in some particular difference in the course of human experience which its being true will make. Test every concept by the question "What sensible difference to anybody will its truth make?" and you are in the best possible position for understanding what it means and for discussing its importance. If, questioning whether a certain concept be true or false, you can think of absolutely nothing that would practically differ in the two cases, you may assume that the alternative is meaningless and that your concept is no distinct idea. If two concepts lead you to infer the same particular consequence, then you may assume that they embody the same meaning under different names.

This rule applies to concepts of every order of complexity, from simple terms to propositions uniting many terms.

. . .

Does our conceptual translation of the perceptual flux enable us also to understand the latter better? What do we mean by making us "understand"? Applying our pragmatic rule to the interpretation of the word, we see that the better we understand anything the more we are able to *tell about it.* Judged by this test, concepts do make us understand our percepts better: knowing *what* these are, we can tell all sorts of farther truths about them, based on the relation of those whats to other whats. The whole system of relations, spatial, temporal, and logical, of our fact, gets plotted out. An ancient philosophical opinion, inherited from Aristotle, is that we do not understand a thing until we know it by its causes. When the maid-servant says that "the cat" broke the tea-cup, she would have us conceive the fracture in a causally explanatory way. No otherwise when Clerk-Maxwell asks us to conceive of gas-electricity as due to molecular bombardment. An imaginary agent out of sight becomes in each case a part of the cosmic context in which we now place the percept to be explained; and the explanation is valid in so far as the new causal *that* is itself conceived in a context that makes its existence probable, and with a nature agreeable to the effects it is imagined to produce. All our scientific explanations would seem to conform to this simple type of the "necessary cat." The conceived order of nature built round the perceived order and explaining it theoretically, as we say, is only a system of hypothetically imagined *thats,* the *whats* of which harmoniously connect themselves with the *what* of any *that* which we immediately perceive.

The system is essentially a typographic system, a system of the distribution of things. It tells us what's what, and where's where. In so far forth it merely prolongs that opening up of the perspective of practical consequences which we

[9] Compare, W. James, *Pragmatism,* chap. ii and *passim;* also Baldwin's *Dictionary of Philosophy,* article "Pragmatism," by C. S. Peirce.

found to be the primordial utility of the conceiving faculty: it adapts us to an immense environment. Working by the causes of things we gain advantages which we never should have compassed had we worked by the things alone.

. . .

The "rationalization" of any mass of perceptual fact consists in assimilating its concrete terms, one by one, to so many terms of the conceptual series, and then in assuming that the relations intuitively found among the latter are what connect the former too. Thus we rationalize gas-pressure by identifying it with the blows of hypothetic molecules; then we see that the more closely the molecules are crowded the more frequent the blows upon the containing walls will become; then we discern the exact proportionality of the crowding with the number of blows; so that finally Mariotte's empirical law gets rationally explained. All our transformations of the sense-order into a more rational equivalent are similar to this one. We interrogate the beautiful apparition, as Emerson calls it, which our senses ceaselessly raise upon our path, and the items there refer us to their interpretants in the shape of ideal constructions in some static arrangement which our mind has already made out of its concepts alone. The interpretants are then substituted for the sensations, which thus get rationally conceived. To "explain" means to coördinate, one to one, the *thises* of the perceptual flow with the *whats* of the ideal manifold, whichever it be.[10]

We may well call this a theoretic conquest over the order in which nature originally comes. The conceptual order into which we translate our experience seems not only a means of practical adaptation, but the revelation of a deeper level of reality in things. Being more constant, it is *truer*, less illusory than the perceptual order, and ought to command our attention more.

There is still another reason why conception appears such an exalted function. Concepts not only guide us over the map of life, but we *revalue* life by their use. Their relation to percepts is like that of sight to touch. Sight indeed helps us by preparing us for contacts while they are yet far off, but it endows us, in addition, with a new world of optical splendor, interesting enough all by itself to occupy a busy life. Just so do concepts bring their proper splendor. The mere possession of such vast and simple pictures is an inspiring good: they arouse new feelings of sublimity, power, and admiration, new interests and motivations.

Ideality often clings to things only when they are taken thus abstractly. "Causes, as anti-slavery, democracy, etc., dwindle when realized in their sordid particulars. Abstractions will touch us when we are callous to the concrete instances in which they lie embodied. Loyal in our measure to particular ideals, we soon set up abstract loyalty as something of a superior order, to be infinitely loyal to; and truth at large becomes a 'momentous issue' compared with which truths in detail are 'poor scraps, mere crumbling successes.' "[11] So strongly do

---

[10] Compare W. Ostwald: *Vorlesungen über Naturphilosophie, Sechste Vorlesung*.

[11] J. Royce: *The Philosophy of Loyalty,* 1908, particularly Lecture vii, § 5.

Emerson writes: "Each man sees over his own experience a certain stain of error, whilst that of other men looks fair and ideal. Let any man go back to those delicious relations which make the beauty of his life, which have given him sincerest instruction and nourish-

objects that come as universal and eternal arouse our sensibilities, so greatly do life's values deepen when we translate percepts into ideals! The translation appears as far more than the original's equivalent.

Concepts thus play three distinct parts in human life.

1. They steer us practically every day, and provide an immense map of relations among the elements of things, which, though not now, yet on some possible future occasion, may help to steer us practically;

2. They bring new values into our perceptual life, they reanimate our wills, and make our action turn upon new points of emphasis;

3. The map which the mind frames out of them is an object which possesses, when once it has been framed, an independent existence. It suffices all by itself for purposes of study. The "eternal" truths it contains would have to be acknowledged even were the world of sense annihilated.

We thus see clearly what is gained and what is lost when percepts are translated into concepts. Perception is solely of the here and now; conception is of the like and unlike, of the future, of the past, and of the far away. But this map of what surrounds the present, like all maps, is only a surface; its features are but abstract signs and symbols of things that in themselves are concrete bits of sensible experience. We have but to weigh extent against content, thickness against spread, and we see that for some purposes the one, for other purposes the other, has the higher value. Who can decide off-hand which is absolutely better to live or to understand life? We must do both alternately, and a man can no more limit himself to either than a pair of scissors can cut with a single one of its blades.

Percept and Concept—The Abuse of Concepts

. . .

Having now set forth the merits of the conceptual translation, I must proceed to show its shortcomings. We extend our view when we insert our percepts into our conceptual map. We learn *about* them, and of some of them we transfigure the value; but the map remains superficial through the abstractness, and false through the discreteness of its elements; and the whole operation, so far from making things appear more rational, becomes the source of quite gratuitous unintelligibilities. Conceptual knowledge is forever inadequate to the fulness of the reality to be known. Reality consists of existential particulars as well as of essences and universals and class-names, and of existential particulars we become aware only in the perceptual flux. The flux can never be superseded. We must carry it with us to the bitter end of our cognitive business, keeping it

---

ment, he will shrink and moan. Alas! I know not why, but infinite compunctions embitter in mature life the remembrances of budding joy, and cover every beloved name. Everything is beautiful seen from the point of view of the intellect, or as truth, but all is sour, if seen as experience. Details are melancholy; the plan is seemly and noble. In the actual world— the painful kingdom of time and place—dwell care, and canker, and fear. With thought, with the ideal, is immortal hilarity, the rose of Joy. Round it all the muses sing. But grief clings to names and persons, and the partial interests of to-day and yesterday." (Essay on "Love.")

in the midst of the translation even when the latter proves illuminating, and falling back on it alone when the translation gives out. "The insuperability of sensation" would be a short expression of my thesis.

To prove it, I must show: 1. That concepts are secondary formations, in-adequate, and only ministerial; and 2. That they falsify as well as omit, and make the flux impossible to understand.

1. Conception is a secondary process, not indispensable to life. It presup-poses perception, which is self-sufficing, as all lower creatures, in whom conscious life goes on by reflex adaptations, show.

To understand a concept you must know what it *means*. It means always some *this*, or some abstract portion of a *this*, with which we first made ac-quaintance in the perceptual world, or else some grouping of such abstract portions. All conceptual content is borrowed: to know what the concept "color" means, you must have *seen* red or blue, or green. To know what "resistance" means, you must have made some effort; to know what "motion" means, you must have had some experience, active or passive, thereof. This applies as much to concepts of the most rarified order as to qualities like "bright" and "loud." To know what the word "illation" means one must once have sweated through some particular argument. To know what a "proportion" means one must have compared ratios in some sensible case. You can create new concepts out of old elements, but the elements must have been perceptually given; and the famous world of universals would disappear like a soap-bubble if the definite contents of feeling, the *thises* and *thats*, which its terms severally de-note, could be at once withdrawn. Whether our concepts live by returning to the perceptual world or not, they live by having come from it. It is the nourish-ing ground from which their sap is drawn.

2. Conceptual treatment of perceptual reality makes it seem paradoxical and incomprehensible; and when radically and consistently carried out, it leads to the opinion that perceptual experience is not reality at all, but an appearance or illusion.

Briefly, this is a consequence of two facts: First, that when we substitute concepts for percepts, we substitute their relations also. But since the relations of concepts are of static comparison only, it is impossible to substitute them for the dynamic relations with which the perceptual flux is filled. Secondly, the conceptual scheme, consisting as it does of discontinuous terms, can only cover the perceptual flux in spots and incompletely. The one is no full measure of the other, essential features of the flux escaping whenever we put concepts in its place.

This needs considerable explanation, for we have concepts not only of qual-ities and relations, but of happenings and actions; and it might seem as if these could make the conceptual order active.[12]

---

[12] Prof. Hibben, in an article in the *Philosophic Review*, vol. xix, pp. 125ff. (1910), seeks to defend the conceptual order against attacks similar to those in the text, which, he thinks, come from misapprehensions of the true function of logic. "The peculiar function of thought is to represent the continuous," he says, and he proves it by the example of the calculus. I reply that the calculus, in substituting for certain perceptual continuities its peculiar sym-

Whenever we conceive a thing we *define* it; and if we still don't understand, we define our definition. Thus I define a certain percept by saying "this is motion," or "I am moving"; and then I define motion by calling it the "being in new positions at new moments of time." This habit of telling what everything is becomes inveterate. The farther we push it, the more we learn *about* our subject of discourse, and we end by thinking that knowing the latter always consists in getting farther and farther away from the perceptual type of experience. This uncriticized habit, added to the intrinsic charm of the conceptual form, is the source of "intellectualism" in philosophy.

But intellectualism quickly breaks down. When we try to exhaust motion by conceiving it as a summation of parts, *ad infinitum,* we find only insufficiency. Although, when you have a continuum given, you can make cuts and dots in it, *ad libitum,* enumerating the dots and cuts will not give you your continuum back. The rationalist mind admits this; but instead of seeing that the fault is with the concepts, it blames the perceptual flux.

. . .

If we take a few examples, we can see how many of the troubles of philosophy come from assuming that to be understood (or "known" in the only worthy sense of the word) our flowing life must be cut into discrete bits and pinned upon a fixed relational scheme.

. . .

Example. *Knowledge Is Impossible;* for knower is one concept, and known is another. Discrete, separated by a chasm, they are mutually "transcendent" things, so that how an object can ever get into a subject, or a subject ever get at an object, has become the most unanswerable of philosophic riddles. An insincere riddle, too, for the most hardened "epistemologist" never really doubts that knowledge somehow does come off.

Example. *Personal Identity Is Conceptually Impossible.* "Ideas" and "states of mind" are discrete concepts, and a series of them in time means a plurality of disconnected terms. To such an atomistic plurality the associationists reduce our mental life. Shocked at the discontinuous character of their scheme, the spiritualists assume a "soul" or "ego" to melt the separate ideas into one collective consciousness. But this ego itself is but another discrete concept; and the only way not to pile up more puzzles is to endow it with an in-

---

bols, lets us follow changes point by point, and is thus their *practical,* but not their *sensible* equivalent. It cannot *reveal* any change to one who never felt it, but it can lead him to where the change would lead him. It may practically replace the change, but it cannot *reproduce* it. What I am contending for is that the non-reproducible part of reality is an essential part of the content of philosophy, whilst Hibben and the logicists seem to believe that conception, if only adequately attained to, might be all-sufficient. "It is the peculiar duty and privilege of philosophy," Mr. Hibben writes, "to exalt the prerogatives of intellect." He claims that universals are able to deal adequately with particulars, and that concepts do not so exclude each other, as my text has accused them of doing. Of course "synthetic" concepts abound, with subconcepts included in them, and the *a priori* world is full of them. But they are all designative; and I think that no careful reader of my text will accuse me of identifying "knowledge" with either perception or conception absolutely or exclusively. Perception gives "intension," conception gives "extension" to our knowledge.

comprehensible power of producing that very character of manyness-in-oneness of which rationalists refuse the gift when offered in its immediate perceptual form.

Example. *Motion and Change Are Impossible.* Perception changes pulse-wise, but the pulses continue each other and melt their bounds. In conceptual translation, however, a continuum can only stand for elements with other elements between them *ad infinitum,* all separately conceived; and such an infinite series can never be exhausted by successive addition. From the time of Zeno the Eleatic, this intrinsic contradictoriness of continuous change has been one of the worst skulls at intellectualism's banquet.

Practice and Contradiction

MAO TSE-TUNG

Mao Tse-tung (1893–1976) was Chairman of the Communist Party of the Peoples' Republic of China and the leader of some 800 million Chinese. His numerous writings include *New Democracy* (1944), *The Fight for a New China* (1945), and *Quotations from Chairman Mao Tse-tung* (1966).

On Practice[1]

ON THE RELATION BETWEEN KNOWLEDGE AND PRACTICE, BETWEEN KNOWING AND DOING

Before Marx, materialism examined the problem of knowledge apart from the social nature of man and apart from his historical development, and was therefore incapable of understanding the dependence of knowledge on social practice, that is, the dependence of knowledge on production and the class struggle.

Above all, Marxists regard man's activity in production as the most fundamental practical activity, the determinant of all his other activities. Man's

[1] There used to be a number of comrades in our Party who were dogmatists and who for a long period rejected the experience of the Chinese revolution, denying the truth that "Marxism is not a dogma but a guide to action" and overawing people with words and phrases from Marxist works, torn out of context. There were also a number of comrades who were empiricists and who for a long period restricted themselves to their own fragmentary experience and did not understand the importance of theory for revolutionary practice or see the revolution as a whole, but worked blindly though industriously. The erroneous ideas of these two types of comrades, and particularly of the dogmatists, caused enormous losses to the Chinese revolution during 1931–34, and yet the dogmatists, cloaking themselves as Marxists, confused a great many comrades. "On Practice" was written in order to expose the subjectivist errors of dogmatism and empiricism in the Party, and especially the error of dogmatism, from the standpoint of the Marxist theory of knowledge. It was entitled "On Practice" because its stress was on exposing the dogmatist kind of subjectivism, which belittles practice. The ideas contained in this essay were presented by Comrade Mao Tse-tung in a lecture at the Anti-Japanese Military and Political College in Yenan.

knowledge depends mainly on his activity in material production, through which he comes gradually to understand the phenomena, the properties and the laws of nature, and the relations between himself and nature; and through his activity in production he also gradually comes to understand, in varying degrees, certain relations that exist between man and man. None of this knowledge can be acquired apart from activity in production. In a classless society every person, as a member of society, joins in common effort with the other members, enters into definite relations of production with them and engages in production to meet man's material needs. In all class societies, the members of the different social classes also enter, in different ways, into definite relations of production and engage in production to meet their material needs. This is the primary source from which human knowledge develops.

Man's social practice is not confined to activity in production, but takes many other forms—class struggle, political life, scientific and artistic pursuits; in short, as a social being, man participates in all spheres of the practical life of society. Thus man, in varying degrees, comes to know the different relations between man and man, not only through his material life but also through his political and cultural life (both of which are intimately bound up with material life.) Of these other types of social practice, class struggle in particular, in all its various forms, exerts a profound influence on the development of man's knowledge. In class society everyone lives as a member of a particular class, and every kind of thinking, without exception, is stamped with the brand of a class.

. . .

Marxists hold that man's social practice alone is the criterion of the truth of his knowledge of the external world. What actually happens is that man's knowledge is verified only when he achieves the anticipated results in the process of social practice (material production, class struggle or scientific experiment). If a man wants to succeed in his work, that is, to achieve the anticipated results, he must bring his ideas into correspondence with the laws of the objective external world; if they do not correspond, he will fail in his practice. After he fails, he draws his lessons, corrects his ideas to make them correspond to the laws of the external world, and can thus turn failure into success; this is what is meant by "failure is the mother of success" and "a fall into the pit, a gain in your wit." The dialectical-materialist theory of knowledge places practice in the primary position, holding that human knowledge can in no way be separated from practice and repudiating all the erroneous theories which deny the importance of practice or separate knowledge from practice. Thus Lenin said, *"Practice is higher than (theoretical) knowledge, for it has not only the dignity of universality, but also of immediate actuality."* The Marxist philosophy of dialectical materialism has two outstanding characteristics. One is its class nature: it openly avows that dialectical materialism is in the service of the proletariat. The other is its practicality: it emphasizes the dependence of theory on practice, emphasizes that theory is based on practice and in turn serves practice. The truth of any knowledge or theory is determined not by subjective feelings, but by objective results in social practice. Only social practice can be the criterion of truth. The standpoint of practice is the primary and basic standpoint in the dialectical-materialist theory of knowledge.

But how then does human knowledge arise from practice and in turn serve practice? This will become clear if we look at the process of development of knowledge.

In the process of practice, man at first sees only the phenomenal side, the separate aspects, the external relations of things. For instance, some people from outside come to Yenan on a tour of observation. In the first day or two, they see its topography, streets and houses; they meet many people, attend banquets, evening parties and mass meetings, hear talk of various kinds and read various documents, all these being the phenomena, the separate aspects and the external relations of things. This is called the perceptual stage of cognition, namely, the stage of sense perceptions and impressions. That is, these particular things in Yenan act on the sense organs of the members of the observation group, evoke sense perceptions and give rise in their brains to many impressions together with a rough sketch of the external relations among these impressions: this is the first stage of cognition. At this stage, man cannot as yet form concepts, which are deeper, or draw logical conclusions.

As social practice continues, things that give rise to man's sense perceptions and impressions in the course of his practice are repeated many times; then a sudden change (leap) takes place in the brain in the process of cognition, and concepts are formed. Concepts are no longer the phenomena, the separate aspects and the external relations of things; they grasp the essence, the totality and the internal relations of things. Between concepts and sense perceptions there is not only a quantitative but also a qualitative difference. Proceeding further, by means of judgement and inference one is able to draw logical conclusions. The expression in *San Kuo Yen Yi*, "knit the brows and a stratagem comes to mind," or in everyday language, "let me think it over," refers to man's use of concepts in the brain to form judgements and inferences. This is the second stage of cognition. This stage of conception, judgement and inference is the more important stage in the entire process of knowing a thing; it is the stage of rational knowledge. The real task of knowing is, through perception, to arrive at thought, to arrive step by step at the comprehension of the internal contradictions of objective things, of their laws and of the internal relations between one process and another, that is, to arrive at logical knowledge. To repeat, logical knowledge differs from perceptual knowledge in that perceptual knowledge pertains to the separate aspects, the phenomena and the external relations of things, whereas logical knowledge takes a big stride forward to reach the totality, the essence and the internal relations of things and discloses the inner contradictions in the surrounding world. Therefore, logical knowledge is capable of grasping the development of the surrounding world in its totality, in the internal relations of all its aspects.

. . .

If you want to know a certain thing or a certain class of things directly, you must personally participate in the practical struggle to change reality, to change that thing or class of things, for only thus can you come into contact with them as phenomena; only through personal participation in the practical struggle to change reality can you uncover the essence of that thing or class of things and comprehend them. This is the path to knowledge which every man actually travels, though some people, deliberately distorting matters, argue to the contrary. The most ridiculous person in the world is the "know-all" who picks up a smattering of hearsay knowledge and proclaims himself "the world's Number One authority"; this merely shows that he has not taken a proper measure of himself. Knowledge is a matter of science, and no dishonesty or conceit whatsoever is permissible. What is required is definitely the reverse—honesty and modesty. If you want knowledge, you must take part in the practice of changing reality. If you want to know the taste of a pear, you must change the pear by eating it yourself. If you want to know the structure and properties of the atom, you must make physical and chemical experiments to change the state of the atom. If you want to know the theory and methods of revolution, you must take part in revolution. All genuine knowledge originates in direct experience. But one cannot have direct experience of everything; as a matter of fact, most of our knowledge comes from indirect experience, for example, all knowledge from past times and foreign lands. To our ancestors and to foreigners, such knowledge was—or is—a matter of direct experience, and this knowledge is reliable if in the course of their direct experience the requirement of "scientific abstraction," spoken of by Lenin, was—or is—fulfilled and objective reality scientifically reflected; otherwise it is not reliable. Hence a man's knowledge consists only of two parts, that which comes from direct experience and that which comes from indirect experience. Moreover, what is indirect experience for me is direct experience for other people. Consequently, considered as a whole, knowledge of any kind is inseparable from direct experience. All knowledge originates in perception of the objective external world through man's physical sense organs. Anyone who denies such perception, denies direct experience, or denies personal participation in the practice that changes reality, is not a materialist. That is why the "know-all" is ridiculous. There is an old Chinese saying, "How can you catch tiger cubs without entering the tiger's lair?" This saying holds true for man's practice and it also holds true for the theory of knowledge. There can be no knowledge apart from practice.

. . .

From the Marxist viewpoint, theory is important, and its importance is fully expressed in Lenin's statement, "Without revolutionary theory there can be no revolutionary movement." But Marxism emphasizes the importance of theory precisely and only because it can guide action. If we have a correct theory but merely prate about it, pigeonhole it and do not put it into practice, then that theory, however good, is of no significance. Knowledge begins with practice, and theoretical knowledge is acquired through practice, and must then return to practice. The active function of knowledge manifests itself not only in the active leap from perceptual to rational knowledge, but—and this is more important—it must manifest itself in the leap from rational knowledge to revolutionary practice. The knowledge which grasps the laws of the world, must be redirected to the practice of changing the world, must be applied anew in the practice of production, in the practice of revolutionary class struggle and revolutionary national struggle and in the practice of scientific experiment. This is the process of testing and developing theory, the continuation of the whole process of cognition. The problem of whether theory corresponds to objective reality is not, and cannot be, completely solved in the movement of knowledge from the perceptual to the rational, mentioned above. The only way to solve this problem completely is to redirect rational knowledge to social practice, apply theory to practice and see whether it can achieve the objectives one has in mind.

. . .

In the present epoch of the development of society, the responsibility of correctly knowing and changing the world has been placed by history upon the shoulders of the proletariat and its party. The struggle of the proletariat and the revolutionary people to change the world comprises the fulfilment of the following tasks: to change the objective world and, at the same time, their own subjective world—to change their cognitive ability and change the relations between the subjective and the objective world.

On Contradiction[2]

The law of contradiction in things, that is, the law of the unity of opposites, is the basic law of materialist dialectics. Lenin said, "Dialectics in the proper sense is the study of contradiction *in the very essence of objects*." Lenin often called this law the essence of dialectics; he also called it the kernel of dialectics. In studying this law, therefore, we cannot but touch upon a variety of questions, upon a number of philosophical problems. If we can become clear on all these problems, we shall arrive at a fundamental understanding of materialist dialectics. The problems are: the two world outlooks, the universality of contradiction, the particularity of contradiction, the principal contradiction and the principal aspect of a contradiction, the identity and struggle of the aspects of a contradiction, and the place of antagonism in contradiction.

. . .

THE TWO WORLD OUTLOOKS

Throughout the history of human knowledge, there have been two conceptions concerning the law of development of the universe, the metaphysical conception and the dialectical conception, which form two opposing world outlooks.

. . .

In China another name for metaphysics is *hsuan-hsueh*. For a long period in history whether in China or in Europe, this way of thinking, which is part and parcel of the idealist world outlook, occupied a dominant position in human thought. In Europe, the materialism of the bourgeoisie in its early days was also metaphysical.

. . .

The metaphysical or vulgar evolutionist world outlook sees things as isolated, static and one-sided. It regards all things in the universe, their forms and their

---

[2] This essay on philosophy was written by Comrade Mao Tse-tung after his essay "On Practice" and with the same object of overcoming the serious error of dogmatist thinking to be found in the Party at the time. Originally delivered at lectures at the Anti-Japanese Military and Political College in Yenan, it was revised by the author on its inclusion in his *Selected Works*.

species, as eternally isolated from one another and immutable. Such change as there is can only be an increase or decrease in quantity or a change of place. Moreover, the cause of such an increase or decrease or change of place is not inside things but outside them, that is, the motive force is external.

. . .

As opposed to the metaphysical world outlook, the world outlook of materialist dialectics holds that in order to understand the development of a thing we should study it internally and in its relations with other things; in other words, the development of things should be seen as their internal and necessary self-movement, while each thing in its movement is interrelated with and interacts on the things around it. The fundamental cause of the development of a thing is not external but internal; it lies in the contradictoriness within the thing. There is internal contradiction in every single thing, hence its motion and development. Contradictoriness within a thing is the fundamental cause of its development, while its interrelations and interactions with other things are secondary causes. Thus materialist dialectics effectively combats the theory of external causes, or of an external motive force, advanced by metaphysical mechanical materialism and vulgar evolutionism. It is evident that purely external causes can only give rise to mechanical motion, that is, to changes in scale or quantity, but cannot explain why things differ qualitatively in thousands of ways and why one thing changes into another.

. . .

In order to reveal the particularity of the contradictions in any process in the development of a thing, in their totality or interconnections, that is, in order to reveal the essence of the process, it is necessary to reveal the particularity of the two aspects of each of the contradictions in that process; otherwise it will be impossible to discover the essence of the process. This likewise requires the utmost attention in our study.

There are many contradictions in the course of development of any major thing. For instance, in the course of China's bourgeois-democratic revolution, where the conditions are exceedingly complex, there exist the contradiction between all the oppressed classes in Chinese society and imperialism, the contradiction between the great masses of the people and feudalism, the contradiction between the proletariat and the bourgeoisie, the contradiction between the peasantry and the urban petty bourgeoisie on the one hand and the bourgeoisie on the other, the contradiction between the various reactionary ruling groups, and so on. These contradictions cannot be treated in the same way since each has its own particularity; moreover, the two aspects of each contradiction cannot be treated in the same way since each aspect has its own characteristics. We who are engaged in the Chinese revolution should not only understand the particularity of these contradictions in their totality, that is, in their interconnections, but should also study the two aspects of each contradiction as the only means of understanding the totality. When we speak of understanding each aspect of a contradiction, we mean understanding what specific position each aspect occupies, what concrete forms it assumes in its interdependence and in its contradiction with its opposite, and what concrete methods are employed in the struggle with its opposite, when the two are both interdependent and in contradiction, and also after the interdependence breaks down. Lenin said:

. . .

> . . . in order really to know an object we must embrace, study, all its sides, all connections and "mediations". We shall never achieve this completely, but the demand for all-sidedness is a safeguard against mistakes and rigidity.

We should remember his words. To be superficial means to consider neither the characteristics of a contradiction in its totality nor the characteristics of each of its aspects; it means to deny the necessity for probing deeply into a thing and minutely studying the characteristics of its contradiction, but instead merely to look from afar and, after glimpsing the rough outline, immediately to try to resolve the contradiction (to answer a question, settle a dispute, handle work, or direct a military operation). This way of doing things is bound to lead to trouble.

. . .

Without concrete analysis there can be no knowledge of the particularity of any contradiction. We must always remember Lenin's words, the concrete analysis of concrete conditions.

Marx and Engels were the first to provide us with excellent models of such concrete analysis. .

. . .

When Marx applied this law to the study of the economic structure of capitalist society, he discovered that the basic contradiction of this society is the contradiction between the social character of production and the private character of ownership. This contradiction manifests itself in the contradiction between the organized character of production in individual enterprises and the anarchic character of production in society as a whole. In terms of class relations, it manifests itself in the contradiction between the bourgeoisie and the proletariat.

THE PRINCIPAL CONTRADICTION AND THE PRINCIPAL ASPECT OF A CONTRADICTION

. . .

There are still two points in the problem of the particularity of contradiction which must be singled out for analysis, namely, the principal contradiction and the principal aspect of a contradiction.

There are many contradictions in the process of development of a complex thing, and one of them is necessarily the principal contradiction whose existence and development determine or influence the existence and development of the other contradictions.

For instance, in capitalist society the two forces in contradiction, the proletariat and the bourgeoisie, form the principal contradiction. The other contradictions, such as those between the non-monopoly capitalists and the monopoly capitalists, between bourgeois democracy and bourgeois fascism, among the capitalist countries and between imperialism and the colonies, are all determined or influenced by this principal contradiction.

.   .   .

But whatever happens, there is no doubt at all that at every stage in the development of a process, there is only one principal contradiction which plays the leading role.

Hence, if in any process there are a number of contradictions, one of them must be the principal contradiction playing the leading and decisive role, while the rest occupy a secondary and subordinate position. Therefore, in studying any complex process in which there are two or more contradictions, we must devote every effort to finding its principal contradiction. Once this principal contradiction is grasped, all problems can be readily solved.

.   .   .

But, in any given contradiction, whether principal or secondary, should the two contradictory aspects be treated as equal? Again, no. In any contradiction the development of the contradictory aspects is uneven. Sometimes they seem to be in equilibrium, which is however only temporary and relative, while unevenness is basic. Of the two contradictory aspects, one must be principal and the other secondary. The principal aspect is the one playing the leading role in the contradiction. The nature of a thing is determined mainly by the principal aspect of a contradiction, the aspect which has gained the dominant position.

.   .   .

We often speak of "the new superseding the old." The supersession of the old by the new is a general, eternal and inviolable law of the universe. The transformation of one thing into another, through leaps of different forms in accordance with its essence and external conditions—this is the process of the new superseding the old. In each thing there is contradiction between its new and its old aspects, and this gives rise to a series of struggles with many twists and turns.

.   .   .

In capitalist society, capitalism has changed its position from being a subordinate force in the old feudal era to being the dominant force, and the nature of society has accordingly changed from feudal to capitalist. In the new, capitalist era, the feudal forces changed from their former dominant position to a subordinate one, gradually dying out. Such was the case, for example, in Britain and France. With the development of the productive forces, the bourgeoisie changes from being a new class playing a progressive role to being an old class playing a reactionary role, until it is finally overthrown by the proletariat and becomes a class deprived of privately owned means of production and stripped of power, when it, too, gradually dies out.

.   .   .

The Identity and Struggle of the Aspects of a Contradiction

When we understand the universality and the particularity of contradiction, we must proceed to study the problem of the identity and struggle of the aspects of a contradiction.

Identity, unity, coincidence, interpenetration, interpermeation, interdependence (or mutual dependence for existence), interconnection or mutual cooperation—all these different terms mean the same thing and refer to the following two points: first, the existence of each of the two aspects of a contradiction in the process of the development of a thing presupposes the existence of the other aspect, and both aspects coexist in a single entity; second, in given conditions, each of the two contradictory aspects transforms itself into its opposite. This is the meaning of identity.

. . .

The fact is that no contradictory aspect can exist in isolation. Without its opposite aspect, each loses the condition for its existence. Just think, can any one contradictory aspect of a thing or of a concept in the human mind exist independently? Without life, there would be no death; without death, there would be no life. Without "above," there would be no "below"; without "below," there would be no "above." Without misfortune, there would be no good fortune; without good fortune, there would be no misfortune. Without facility, there would be no difficulty; without difficulty, there would be no facility. Without landlords, there would be no tenant-peasants; without tenant-peasants, there would be no landlords. Without the bourgeoisie, there would be no proletariat; without the proletariat, there would be no bourgeoisie. Without imperialist oppression of nations, there would be no colonies or semi-colonies; without colonies or semi-colonies, there would be no imperialist oppression of nations. It is so with all opposites; in given conditions, on the one hand they are opposed to each other, and on the other they are interconnected, interpenetrating, interpermeating and interdependent, and this character is described as identity. In given conditions, all contradictory aspects possess the character of non-identity and hence are described as being in contradiction. But they also possess the character of identity and hence are interconnected. This is what Lenin means when he says that dialectics studies "how *opposites* can be . . . *identical*." How then can they be identical? Because each is the condition for the other's existence. This is the first meaning of identity.

But is it enough to say merely that each of the contradictory aspects is the condition for the other's existence, that there is identity between them and that consequently they can coexist in a single entity? No, it is not. The matter does not end with their dependence on each other for their existence; what is more important in their transformation into each other. That is to say, in given conditions, each of the contradictory aspects within a thing transforms itself into its opposite, changes its position to that of its opposite. This is the second meaning of the identity of contradiction.

The Sociology of Knowledge

KARL MANNHEIM

Karl Mannheim (1893–1947) was a renowned professor of sociology at the University of Frankfurt until 1933, when he fled to London, where he taught until his death. Among his books are *Ideology and Utopia* (1936) and *Diagnosis of Our Time* (1943).

Preliminary Approach to the Problem

1. THE SOCIOLOGICAL CONCEPT OF THOUGHT

This book is concerned with the problem of how men actually think. The aim of these studies is to investigate not how thinking appears in textbooks on logic, but how it really functions in public life and in politics as an instrument of collective action.

Philosophers have too long concerned themselves with their own thinking. When they wrote of thought, they had in mind primarily their own history, the history of philosophy, or quite special fields of knowledge such as mathematics or physics. This type of thinking is applicable only under quite special circumstances, and what can be learned by analysing it is not directly transferable to other spheres of life. Even when it is applicable, it refers only to a specific dimension of existence which does not suffice for living human beings who are seeking to comprehend and to mould their world.

Meanwhile, acting men have, for better or for worse, proceeded to develop a variety of methods for the experiential and intellectual penetration of the world in which they live, which have never been analysed with the same precision as the so-called exact modes of knowing. When, however, any human activity continues over a long period without being subjected to intellectual control or criticism, it tends to get out of hand.

Hence it is to be regarded as one of the anomalies of our time that those methods of thought by means of which we arrive at our most crucial decisions, and through which we seek to diagnose and guide our political and social destiny, have remained unrecognized and therefore inaccessible to intellectual control and self-criticism. This anomaly becomes all the more monstrous when we call to mind that in modern times much more depends on the correct thinking through of a situation than was the case in earlier societies. The significance of social knowledge grows proportionately with the increasing necessity of regulatory intervention in the social process. This so-called pre-scientific inexact mode of thought, however (which, paradoxically, the logicians and philosophers also use when they have to make practical decisions), is not to be understood solely by the use of logical analysis. It constitutes a complex which can-

Source: Karl Mannheim, *Ideology and Utopia: An Introduction to the Sociology of Knowledge,* trans. by Louis Wirth and Edward Shils (New York, 1936), pp. 1–11. Reprinted by permission of Harcourt Brace Jovanovich, Inc., and Routledge & Kegan Paul Ltd.

not be readily detached either from the psychological roots of the emotional and vital impulses which underlie it or from the situation in which it arises and which it seeks to solve.

It is the most essential task of this book to work out a suitable method for the description and analysis of this type of thought and its changes, and to formulate those problems connected with it which will both do justice to its unique character and prepare the way for its critical understanding. The method which we will seek to present is that of the sociology of knowledge.

The principal thesis of the sociology of knowledge is that these are modes of thought which cannot be adequately understood as long as their social origins are obscured. It is indeed true that only the individual is capable of thinking. There is no such metaphysical entity as a group mind which thinks over and above the head of individuals, or whose ideas the individual merely reproduces. Nevertheless it would be false to deduce from this that all the ideas and senti- ments which motivate an individual have their origin in him alone, and can be adequately explained solely on the basis of his own life-experience.

Just as it would be incorrect to attempt to derive a language merely from observing a single individual, who speaks not a language of his own but rather that of his contemporaries and predecessors who have prepared the path for him, so it is incorrect to explain the totality of an outlook only with reference to its genesis in the mind of the individual. Only in a quite limited sense does the single individual create out of himself the mode of speech and of thought we attribute to him. He speaks the language of his group; he thinks in the manner in which his group thinks. He finds at his disposal only certain words and their meanings. These not only determine to a large extent the avenues of approach to the surrounding world, but they also show at the same time from which angle and in which context of activity objects have hitherto been perceptible and accessible to the group or the individual.

The first point which we now have to emphasize is that the approach of sociology of knowledge intentionally does not start with the single individual and his thinking in order then to proceed directly in the manner of the philoso- pher to the abstract heights of "thought as such." Rather, the sociology of knowledge seeks to comprehend thought in the concrete setting of an historical- social situation out of which individually differentiated thought only very grad- ually emerges. Thus, it is not men in general who think, or even isolated individuals who do the thinking, but men in certain groups who have developed a particular style of thought in an endless series of responses to certain typical situations characterizing their common position.

Strictly speaking it is incorrect to say that the single individual thinks. Rather it is more correct to insist that he participates in thinking further what other men have thought before him. He finds himself in an inherited situation with patterns of thought which are appropriate to this situation and attempts to elaborate further the inherited modes of response or to substitute others from them in order to deal more adequately with the new challenges which have arisen out of the shifts and changes in his situation. Every individual is there- fore in a two-fold sense predetermined by the fact of growing up in a society:

on the one hand he finds a ready-made situation and on the other he finds in that situation performed patterns of thought and of conduct.

The second feature characterizing the method of the sociology of knowledge is that it does not sever the concretely existing modes of thought from the context of collective action through which we first discover the world in an intellectual sense. Men living in groups do not confront the objects of the world from the abstract levels of a contemplating mind as such, nor do they do so exclusively as solitary beings. On the contrary they act with and against one another in diversely organised groups, and while doing so they think with and against one another. These persons, bound together into groups, strive in accordance with the character and position of the groups to which they belong to change the surrounding world of nature and society or attempt to maintain it in a given condition. It is the direction of this will to change or to maintain, of this collective activity, which produces the guiding thread for the emergence of their problems, their concepts, and their forms of thought. In accord with the particular context of collective activity in which they participate, men always tend to see the world which surrounds them differently. Just as pure logical analysis has severed individual thought from its group situation, so it also separated thought from action. It did this on the tacit assumption that those inherent connections which always exist in reality between thought on the one hand, and group and activity on the other, are either significant for "correct" thinking or can be detached from these foundations without any resultant difficulties. But the fact that one ignores something by no means puts an end to its existence. Nor can anyone who has not first given himself wholeheartedly to the exact observation of the wealth of forms in which men really think decide a priori whether this serverance from the social situation and context of activity is always realizable. Nor indeed can it be determined offhand that such a complete dichotomy is fully desirable precisely in the interest of objective factual knowledge.

It may be that, in certain spheres of knowledge, it is the impulse to act which first makes the objects of the world accessible to the acting subject, and it may be further that it is this factor which determines the selection of those elements of reality which enter into thought. And it is not inconceivable that if this volitional factor were entirely excluded (in so far as such a thing is possible), the concrete content would disappear from the concepts, and the organizing principle which first makes possible an intelligent statement of the problem would be lost.

But this is not to say that in those domains where attachment to the groups and orientation towards action seem to be an essential element in the situation, every possibility of intellectual, critical self-control is futile. Perhaps it is precisely when the hitherto concealed dependence of thought on group existence and its rootedness in action becomes visible that it really becomes possible for the first time, through becoming aware of them, to attain a new mode of control over previously uncontrolled factors in thought.

This brings us to the central problem of the book. These remarks would make it clear that a preoccupation with these problems and their solution will furnish a foundation for the social sciences and answer the question as to the possibility of the scientific guidance of political life. It is, of course, true that in the social sciences, as elsewhere, the ultimate criterion of truth or falsity is to be found in the investigation of the object, and the sociology of knowledge is no substitute for this. But the examination of the object is not an isolated act; it takes place in a context which is coloured by values and collective-unconscious, volitional impulses. In the social sciences it is this intellectual interest, oriented in a matrix of collective activity, which provides not only the general questions, but the concrete hypotheses for research and the thought-models for the ordering of experience. Only as we succeed in bringing into the area of conscious and explicit observation the various points of departure and of approach to the facts which are current in scientific as well as popular discussion, can we hope, in the course of time, to control the unconscious motivations and presuppositions which, in the last analysis, have brought these modes of thought into existence. A new type of objectivity in the social sciences is attainable not through the exclusion of evaluations but through the critical awareness and control of them.

2. THE CONTEMPORARY PREDICAMENT OF THOUGHT

It is by no means an accident that the problem of the social and activistic roots of thinking has emerged in our generation. Nor is it accidental that the unconscious, which has hitherto motivated our thought and activity, has been gradually raised to the level of awareness and thereby made accessible to control. It would be a failure to recognize its relevance to our own plight if we did not see that it is a special social situation which has impelled us to reflect about the social roots of our knowledge. It is one of the fundamental insights of the sociology of knowledge that the process by which collective-unconscious motives become conscious cannot operate in every epoch, but only in a quite specific situation. This situation is sociologically determinable. One can point out with relative precision the factors which are inevitably forcing more and more persons to reflect not merely about the things of the world, but about thinking itself and even here not so much about truth in itself, as about the alarming fact that the same world can appear differently to different observers.

It is clear that such problems can become general only in an age in which disagreement is more conspicuous than agreement. One turns from the direct observation of things to the consideration of ways of thinking only when the possibility of direct and continuous elaboration of concepts concerning things and situations has collapsed in the face of a multiplicity of fundamentally divergent definitions. Now we are enabled to designate more precisely than a general and formal analysis makes possible, exactly in which social and intellectual situation such a shift of attention from things to divergent opinions and from there to the unconscious motives of thought must necessarily occur. In what follows we wish to point out only a few of the most significant social factors which are operating in this direction.

Above all, the multiplicity of ways of thinking cannot become a problem in periods when social stability underlies and guarantees the internal unity of a world-view. As long as the same meanings of words, the same ways of deducing ideas, are inculcated from childhood on into every member of the group, divergent thought-processes cannot exist in that society. Even a gradual modification in ways of thinking (where it should happen to arise), does not become perceptible to the members of a group who live in a stable situation as long as the tempo in the adaptations of ways of thinking to new problems is so slow that it extends over several generations. In such a case, one and the same generation in the course of its own life span can scarcely become aware that a change is taking place.

But in addition to the general dynamics of the historical process, factors of quite another sort must enter before the multiplicity of the ways of thinking will become noticeable and emerge as a theme for reflection. Thus it is primarily the intensification of social mobility which destroys the earlier illusion, prevalent in a static society, that all things can change, but thought remains eternally the same. And what is more, the two forms of social mobility, horizontal and vertical, operate in different ways to reveal this multiplicity of styles of thought. Horizontal mobility (movement from one position to another or from one country to another without changing social status) shows us that different peoples think differently. As long, however, as the traditions of one's national and local group remain unbroken, one remains so attached to its customary ways of thinking that the ways of thinking which are perceived in other groups are regarded as curiosities, errors, ambiguities, or heresies. All this stage one does not doubt either the correctness of one's own traditions of thought or the unity and uniformity of thought in general.

Only when horizontal mobility is accompanied by intensive vertical mobility, i.e., rapid movement between strata in the sense of social ascent and descent, is the belief in the general and eternal validity of one's own thought-forms shaken. Vertical mobility is the decisive factor in making persons uncertain and sceptical of their traditional view of the world. It is, of course, true that even in static societies with very slight vertical mobility, different strata within the same society have had different ways of experiencing the world. It is the merit of Max Weber to have clearly shown in his sociology of religion how often the same religion is variously experienced by peasants, artisans, merchants, nobles, and intellectuals. In a society organized along the lines of closed castes or ranks the comparative absense of vertical mobility served either to isolated from each other the divergent world-views or if, for example, they experienced a common religion, according to their different contexts of life, they interpreted it in a different way. This accounts for the fact that the diversity of modes of thought of different castes did not converge in one and the same mind and hence could not become a problem. From a sociological point of view, the decisive change takes place when that stage of historical development is reached in which the previously isolated strata begin to communicate with one another and a certain social circulation sets in. The most significant stage of this communication is reached when the forms of thought and experience, which had hitherto developed independently, enter into one and the same consciousness impelling the mind to discover the irreconcilability of the conflicting concepts of the world.

In a well stabilized society the mere infiltration of the modes of thought of the lower strata into the higher would not mean very much since the bare perception by the dominant group of possible variations in thinking would not result in their being intellectually shaken. As long as society is stabilized on the basis of authority, and social prestige is accorded only to the achievements of the upper stratum, this class has little cause to call into question its own social existence and the value of its achievements. Apart from a considerable social ascent, it is not until we have a general democratization that the rise of the lower strata allows their thinking to acquire public significance. This process of democratization first makes it possible for the ways of thinking of the lower strata, which formerly had no public validity, to acquire validity and prestige. When the stage of democratization has been reached, the techniques of thinking and the ideas of the lower strata are for the first time in a position to confront the ideas of the dominant strata on the same level of validity. And now, too, for the first time these ideas and modes of thought are capable of impelling the person who thinks within their framework to subject the objects of his world to a fundamental questioning. It is with this clashing of modes of thought, each of which has the same claims to representational validity, that for the first time there is rendered possible the emergence of the question which is so fateful, but also so fundamental in the history of thought, namely, how it is possible that identical human thought-processes concerned with the same world produce divergent conceptions of that world. And from this point it is only a step further to ask: Is it not possible that the thought-processes which are involved here are not at all identical? May it not be found, when one has examined all the possibilities of human thought, that there are numerous alternative paths which can be followed?

Was it not this process of social ascent which in the Athenian democracy called forth the first great surge of scepticism in the history of Occidental thought? Were not the Sophists of the Greek Enlightenment the expression of an attitude of doubt which arose essentially out of the fact that in their thinking about every object, two modes of explanation collided? On the one hand was the mythology which was the way of thinking of a dominant nobility already doomed to decline. On the other hand was the more analytical habit of thought of an urban artisan lower stratum, which was in the process of moving upwards. Inasmuch as these two forms of interpreting the world converged in the thought of the Sophists, and since for every moral decision there were available at least two standards, and for every cosmic and social happening at least two explanations, it is no wonder that they had a sceptical notion of the value of human thought. It is therefore pointless to censure them in schoolmaster fashion for having been sceptics in their epistemological efforts. They simply had the courage to express what every person who was really characteristic of the epoch felt, namely, that the previous unambiguity of norms and interpretations had been shattered, and that a satisfactory solution was to be found only in a thoroughgoing questioning and thinking through of the contradictions. This general uncertainty was by no means a symptom of a world doomed to general decay, but it was rather the beginning of a wholesome process which marked a crisis leading to recovery.

Was it not, furthermore, the great virtue of Socrates that he had the courage to descend into the abyss of this scepticism? Was he not originally also a

Sophist who took up the technique of raising questions and then raising further questions, and made it his own? And did he not overcome the crisis by questioning even more radically than the Sophists and thus arrive at an intellectual resting-point which, at least for the mentality of that epoch, showed itself to be a reliable foundation? It is interesting to observe that thereby the world of norms and of being came to occupy the central place in his inquiry. Furthermore, he was at least as intensively concerned with the question as to how individuals are able to think of and judge the same facts in different ways as he was with the facts themselves. Even at this stage in the history of thought it becomes apparent that in various periods the problems of thinking can be solved not solely by preoccupation with the object but rather only through discovering why opinions concerning them really differ.

In addition to those social factors which account for the early unity and subsequent multiplicity in the dominant forms of thought, another important factor should be mentioned. In every society there are social groups whose special task it is to provide an interpretation of the world for that society. We call these the "intelligentsia." The more static a society is, the more likely is it that this stratum will acquire a well-defined status or the position of a caste in that society. Thus the magicians, the Brahmins, the medieval clergy are to be regarded as intellectual strata, each of which in its society enjoyed a monopolistic control over the moulding of that society's world-view, and over either the reconstruction or the reconciliation of the differences in the naively formed world-views of the other strata. The sermon, the confession, the lesson, are in this sense, means by which reconciliation of the different conceptions of the world takes place at less sophisticated levels of social development.

This intellectual stratum, organized as a caste and monopolizing the right to preach, teach, and interpret the world is conditioned by the force of two social factors. The more it makes itself the exponent of a thoroughly organized collectivity (e.g., the Church), the more its thinking tends towards "scholasticism." It must give a dogmatically binding force to modes of thought which formerly were valid only for a sect and thereby sanction the ontology and epistemology implicit in this mode of thought. The necessity of having to present a unified front to outsiders compels this transition. The same result may also be brought about by the possibility that the concentration of power within the social structure will be so pronounced that uniformity of thought and experience can be imposed upon the members of at least one's own caste with greater success than heretofore.

The second characteristic of this monopolistic type of thought is its relative remoteness from the open conflicts of everyday life; hence it is also "scholastic" in this sense, i.e., academic and lifeless. This type of thought does not arise primarily from the struggle with concrete problems of life nor from trial and error, nor from experiences in mastering nature and society, but rather much more from its own need for systematization, which always refers the facts which emerge in the religious as well as in other spheres of life back to given traditional and intellectually uncontrolled premises. The antagonisms which emerge in these discussions do not embody the conflict of various modes of experience so much as various positions of power within the same social structure, which have at the time identified themselves with the different possible interpretations of the dogmatized traditional "truth." The dogmatic content of the premises with which these divergent groups start and which this thought then seeks in different ways to justify turns out for the most part to be a matter of accident, if judged by the criteria of factual evidence. It is completely arbitrary in so far as it depends upon which sect happens to be successful, in accordance with historical-political destiny, in making its own intellectual and experiential traditions of the entire clerical caste of the church.

From a sociological point of view the decisive fact of modern times, in contrast with the situation during the Middle Ages, is that this monopoly of the ecclesiastical interpretation of the world which was held by the priestly caste is broken, and in the place of a closed and thoroughly organized stratum of intellectuals, a free intelligentsia has arisen. Its chief characteristic is that it is increasingly recruited from constantly varying social strata and life-situations, and that its mode of thought is no longer subject to regulation by a caste-like organization. Due to the absence of a social organization of their own, the intellectuals have allowed those ways of thinking and experiencing to get a hearing which openly competed with one another in the larger world of the other strata. When one considers further that with the renunciation of the monopolistic privileges of a caste type of existence, free competition began to dominate the modes of intellectual production, one understands why, to the extent that they were in competition, the intellectuals adopted in an ever more pronounced fashion the most various modes of thought and experience available in society and played them off against one another. They did this inasmuch as they had to compete for the favour of a public which, unlike the public of the clergy, was no longer accessible to them without their own efforts. This competition for the favour of various public groups was accentuated because the distinctive modes of experiencing and thinking of each attained increasing public expression and validity.

In this process the intellectual's illusion that there is only one way of thinking disappears. The intellectual is now no longer, as formerly, a member of a caste or rank whose scholastic manner of thought represents for him thought as such. In this relatively simple process is to be sought the explanation for the fact that the fundamental questioning of thought in modern times does not begin until the collapse of the intellectual monopoly of the clergy. The almost unanimously accepted world-view which had been artificially maintained fell apart the moment the socially monopolistic position of its producers was destroyed. With the liberation of the intellectuals from the rigorous organization of the church, other ways of interpreting the world were increasingly recognized.

The disruption of the intellectual monopoly of the church brought about a sudden flowering of an unexampled intellectual richness. But at the same time we must attribute to the organizational disintegration of the unitary church the fact that the belief in the unity and eternal nature of thought, which had persisted since classical antiquity, was again shaken. The origins of the profound disquietude of the present day reach back to this period, even though in most recent times additional causes of a quite different nature have entered into the process. Out of this first upsurge of the profound disquietude of modern man there emerged those fundamentally new modes of thought and investigation, the epistemological, the psychological, and the sociological, without which to-day we could not even formulate our problem. . . .

Race and Intelligence

JOHN REX

John Rex (1925–   ) is a professor of sociology at the University of Warwick, England. Among his books are *Problems of Sociological Theory* (1961) and *Race, Community, and Conflict* (1967).

The Misuse of Quantitative Methods

Quantitative methods in the social sciences have much to commend them. If used sensitively and with understanding, they ensure that the observations of any one scientist or observer may be replicated by another. The great danger, however, is that if they are used insensitively the social scientist may seek to quantify for the sake of quantification, and, if the issue under discussion is not capable of easy quantification, it is likely to be put on one side and replaced by another. Too often, quantitative social scientists give us exact but irrelevant answers to the questions we are asking.

When we speak of "sensitivity" on the part of a social scientist we refer to his awareness of the relationship of that which he measures to a body of theory and, through this body of theory, to other measurable concepts. We also refer to the sensitivity of the social scientist to the meaning of human action for the participant actors whom he observes. In a word, it is a requirement of sensitive social science that the social scientist should be aware of the fundamental epistemological problem of the human studies, namely that, while natural science is an activity in which scientists have concepts about things, in the human sciences the scientist has concepts about things which themselves have concepts.

These observations have led in recent times to a revolution in the social sciences. It has been argued, for instance in relation to criminal statistics, that official statistics have not recorded the quantitative occurrence of an act of a certain kind, but rather the numbers of those acts which other people such as the officers of the law categorize in a certain way. Similarly, most demographic and ecological statistics, when they are probed, turn out to refer, not to simple attributes of persons and their behaviour but rather to the way in which people are classified in practical situations.

The ideology of empiricism and operationalism seeks to avoid these problems

Source: John Rex, "Nature Versus Nurture: The Significance of the Revived Debate," in *Race and Intelligence*, ed. by Richardson and Spears (Harmondsworth, England: Penguin Books Ltd., 1972), pp. 167–177. Reprinted by permission of John Wolfers.

by arguing that, since there are no "essences" in the world to be measured, the measurable variables are definable simply in terms of the tests which are to be used to make a measurement. Thus, for example, a foot is that which is measured by a foot rule, intelligence is that which is measured by intelligence tests, and so on.

What is called psychometrics is perhaps the least sensitive and the brashest of the empirical human studies, as may be seen from some of the preceding chapters. On the matters just discussed it seeks to get the best of both worlds. It claims, on the one hand, that it makes no assertions about essential intelligence and that what it refers to is simply measured intelligence. On the other hand, however, it pretends that this measured intelligence has no reference to practical, social and political contexts.

The first point which we need to make here in asserting the need for a genuine sociology and psychology which is theoretically founded and aware that it is dealing with meaningful action, is that the position of the psychometrist, who pretends that what he says about measurable difference has no practical significance, but simply refers to facts which may be classified as true or false, is untenable. The intelligence tests to which he refers are used in practical contexts, as a matter of empirical fact to assign children to different forms of education, to choose between one individual and another in job placement, and generally to set one man above another. It is therefore not possible for a psychometrician to say "I am merely facing up to a scientific truth, albeit an uncomfortable one." What he does when he rates individuals or groups of individuals on a scale of measured intelligence is to say and to predict that one group of individuals rather than another should have privileges. It is of little use, therefore, that a writer like Eysenck should protest that there is a total disjunction between his scientific observations and his moral views. Scientific observations have political implications and the scientist should beware that that which he reveals may contribute to, or ease, human suffering. This, of course, is not in itself an argument for not facing up to facts. It is, however, an argument for the human sciences to beware of jumping to rash conclusions on the basis of simplistic scales of measurement.

If we look at the popularizations of Jensen's ideas on racial differences, we find no such circumspection. The problem not merely of the nature of intelligence, but of its causes and correlates, is over-simplified to an almost incredible degree. According to Eysenck, for example, the issue is between "interactionists" like himself who believe that both nature and nurture contribute to test intelligence and those whom he calls environmentalists who are supposed to hold that intellectual capacity is solely the product of a few easily measurable environmental factors, such as amount of income, type of residential neighbourhood and years of schooling. All that is necessary to disprove the "environmental hypothesis" and thence by implication to prove its opposite is to show that when these few environmental factors are held constant, observed differences between individuals or between groups, are maintained.

The reply to this rests first of all upon the recognition that intellectual arguments which go on between social scientists on the matter of nature and nurture do not involve one side which is simply environmentalist in Eysenck's usage of that term. Those whom he specifically attacks, namely, UNESCO and a distinguished line of social scientists who have worked since 1945 to expose fallacies of racism, have always recognized that there is ground for supporting that there is a genetic component in measured intelligence. Moreover, they have also recognized that the processes of selection and isolation do lead to groups of men having different gene pools. What they have disputed is that these differences are so great that manipulation of the environment is not capable of fundamentally altering them.

More important than this, however, is the naive belief that environment can be reduced to an index based upon the few quantitive variables (some of the failures in this belief are explored in chapter 8). Such a view naturally commends itself to those taking a simple mechanistic model, who refuse to accept that the relationship between the performance of acts and the events which precede and follow them may be meaningful rather than simply casual. But even if we take the assertions of psychometric empiricism in their own terms, it seems clear that the argument that any measured differences not assignable to the size of income, type of residence or length of schooling, must, due to genetic factor, shows a remarkable overeagerness to jump to conclusions.

When such a method is applied to the comparison of Negro and white intelligence in the United States, there are obviously a great many other variables which should be controlled. They cannot all be summed up under something as simple as "motivation" (one of the factors discussed by Jensen and Eysenck). It matters as is shown in chapter 3, that the Negro group is continually exposed to a picture of American society, in which, if it is not subject to racial exploitation, is, at least the object of benevolent paternalism. Moreover, if one looks at the content of schooling, it is clear that Negroes studying American history in which the heroes are all white, are bound to respond differently to their education from their white school-fellows.

Curiously, Eysenck asks that those who oppose him should offer 'experimental' evidence. Fortunately, neither he nor his opponents are able to undertake such experiments. Since, however, the crucial variable is the difference between white and Negro history and the fact that Negro history involves the fact of slavery, experiment would mean subjecting the group of Negroes to white experience over several hundred years, or subjecting a group of whites to Negro experience. The empirical study which holds constant, size of income, type of neighbourhood and length of schooling in the United States of the present day, therefore, should in theory be supplemented for an experiment in which the peoples of Africa conquer, capture and enslave some millions of European and American whites under conditions in which a very large proportion of the white population dies and in which the white culture is systematically destroyed, and in which finally a group of emancipated whites living in "good neighbourhoods" are then compared to their Negro masters. It is not sufficient to brush aside this assertion, merely by saying that we should not draw conclusions from "hypothetical experiments." The fact is that the differences in the history of Negroes and whites are a factor of immense significance and that any statistical reasoning which leaves them out can reach no conclusions of any value whatever.

One of the difficulties which the empiricist has, of course, is that he deals only in the external attributes of individuals. He cannot concede that intelligence or any other attribute of the individual may be understandable in terms of the meaning of an individual's environment to him. What has happened to the Negro over several hundred years is a process of Sambofication, a process by which he is first stripped of all identity and then forced to become the happy, shambling and incompetent child of the slave owner. White society maintains this stereotype of the black, and the black behaves in accordance with its expectations. As Elkins, amongst others, has pointed out, the nearest comparable process, of which we had to have evidence, is what happened to the inmates of German concentration camps. Similarly, the environment of a young, educated American Negro today is apprehended as one in which he seeks politically for a new identity and in which white education and the white police are equally agencies which undermine that identity.

This is only one aspect of the meaningful environment of minority groups in the United States. What is necessary before we can draw conclusions about the performance of one group or another is that we should understand on a meaningful level, the type of relationship which a minority group has to American society. Thus, for example, one cannot regard the relationship of Negroes, the descendants of slaves, to that society as qualitatively the same as that of American Indians, sidetracked from absorption by their life on reservations, or Oriental immigrants, who might be descended from indentured labourers, and who are very often engaged in one or other minor commercial occupation. Any acquaintance at all with the literature on the sociology of plural societies makes it clear that, given the very different relationships to a social system which minorities might have, it is quite meaningless to compare them as though the only environmental differences between them are those of socio-economic status.

The insensitivity of the psychometricians fails to take any account of these complexities of the real world. Their blind use of IQ test data, which on the surface resembles a valid attempt at quantification, leads to conclusions which are not only erroneous but lack any kind of reality. Unfortunately these conclusions cannot be dismissed as irrelevant but, as we shall see below, they have profound social consequences.

The Rebirth of Racism

It should of course, be noticed that Jensen and his supporters do not claim that they have reached final conclusions. At best they say that it is important that certain hypotheses should still be regarded as open to test. But, the mere assertion that these hypotheses are important in a scientific sense is taken by many to mean that the notion that there are genetically based differences in intelligence between the races is no longer simply a notion of racists. A view of racial inequality is then revived which was common in the early 1930s, but which was discredited in democratic countries after the defeat of Hitler. The main problem which we have to face then is one in the sociology of knowledge as it effects race relations. What difference does it make to our total political situation that scientists appear to be unconvinced that racial differences in intelligence are not innate.

In one sense it may be argued that this fact is not particularly important. After all, there have been long periods of history in which nations and other groups have exploited each other without seeking any scientific validation for their views. Moreover, it is true, particularly since 1945, that very few politicians indeed have claimed that discrimination is justifiable because of inherited differences in intelligence. Nonetheless, what we shall argue here is that, given our culture and the set of beliefs in that culture about the nature of science, the basing of racial inequality on a scientific proof of differences in intelligence makes that inequality far more permanent and durable than it otherwise would be.

At the lowest level, individuals find themselves in competition or opposed to members of ethnic groups and come to express hostile sentiments towards other groups. Action in these matters usually precedes that of rationalization. It is only as the individual seeks validation and justification for his views amongst his fellows that the process of rationalization begins. Very often the highest level of rationalization which is reached is the sharing of an anecdote about an out-group amongst members of an in-group. Yet the process whereby such low-level rationalizations are achieved connects with rationalizations at a higher level which are provided by the definitions of social reality contained in media messages and in the statements of influential local leaders, such as ministers of religion and political leaders.

All individuals finding themselves in new situations seek to arrive at a shared definition of these situations with their fellows. Most of us do not really feel that we know what the world, and particularly the social world, is like until we have corroborated our views by checking them with those of our intimates, but more systematic rationalizations occur when individuals are affected in their definitions of reality by what the newspapers or television programmes have to say. In a quite different and more trivial field than that of race relations, for instance, it is interesting to notice how the judgement of the followers of the main spectator sports are limited and shaped by the picture of the sporting world which is provided by sports journalists.

The level at which the popular press, radio and television provide rationalizations for action is of course itself fairly unsystematic. In the field of race relations, one does not expect to find systematic argument about the nature versus nurture controversy in the columns of, say, the *News of the World*. What one does expect to find there are anecdotes; yet such anecdotes may be of great importance. To give an example, on the Sunday evening which followed the first of Mr Enoch Powell's speeches on the subject of race, BBC television presented a programme in a story series about a local councillor, in which an outbreak of stomach trouble was traced to an Indian restauranteur who offered his customers cat food instead of fresh meat. Such a programme may be expected to have had the effect of reinforcing one of the best known myths about Asian immigrant communities. The belief referred to here is widely held, but its inclusion in a serious BBC programme gives it a kind of legitimacy which it could not otherwise hope to have.

Those who control the popular mass media may or may not be aware of the extent to which they help to define social reality for their public. There may, on the one hand, be cases of sheer manipulation of public opinion, but on the other, there will be cases in which the media merely reflect what are known to be popularly held beliefs. In either case, however, popular mass media do have some sociological significance.

Just as the images of reality which result from face-to-face sharing of experiences are influenced and reinforced by the messages of the popular media, so these latter are affected by more systematic formulations to be found in other 'more serious' publications. What is said in a loose language of sentiment in the popular papers and programmes is said more systematically and intellectually at a higher level in the quality papers and quality television and radio programmes. Such programmes attempt to deal with problems of current affairs in terms of relatively consistent and coherent sets of beliefs, even though the set of positions which they occupy falls far short of a systematic scientific statement.

On the whole, the quality media have not been entirely useful in promoting racism. They represent the public face of a culture and society and must adhere to a minimal standard of political beliefs from which those which foster racialism tend to be excluded. Such a situation, however, might still change if those occupying positions of authority and moral respect by-pass the quality newspapers and other media and lend their support directly to reinforce the racist definitions of social reality which are to be found at the grass roots.

One of the features of most advanced industrial societies is the down-to-earth outspoken politician who is willing to say things which are believed, but which have become taboo in quality discussion. We sometimes say that such politicians produce a gut reaction, rather than an intellectual response, but for all that, their political speeches are of the greatest importance in that they raise the level of respect which is to be accorded to racist myths and anecdotes. Neither the quality papers nor the populist politicians' utterances however, have anything like the systematic deterministic nature of scientific statements. Indeed they do not form any kind of coherent theory at all. It is only when they in turn are subject to rationalization that the higher forms of systematic knowledge become related to political action. At this level we find political intellectuals who write books and argue in public places, defending their beliefs in a systematic way. They may argue from a cultural, historical, sociological or religious standpoint, or they may argue from the point of view of science.

While the big taboo on scientific theories of race was maintained 1945–67, individuals seeking to rationalize racial discrimination would refer to the differences in history and culture between groups or occasionally to religious belief systems. In most cases the picture of the world which they were able to draw was not a deterministic one. Man may after all change his culture or his religion even though there have been some cases, as in South Africa, where doctrines like that of predestination have been used to suggest that there are immutable differences between groups which are ordained by God. While, however, religious beliefs usually involve some possibility of the individual's transformation through a process of salvation, it is a feature of scientific theories about human nature that they tend to be deterministic. Increasingly, in our culture, we are encouraged to believe that what we can do depends upon scientific possibilities and those scientific possibilities are held to be determinate. Thus, when it is said Negroes are genetically inferior to whites, the differences which exist between them are thought to be entirely immutable. Undoubtedly it is the consciousness of many scientists that this would be the effect of their talking loosely about racial differences which has led them to be very careful and cautious in what they say.

If, then there is nothing like a conclusive case for the genetic determination of racial differences in intelligence, as shown in chapter 5, why is it that at this moment in our history, theories which have remained dormant for thirty years, are suddenly revived? The answer to this must surely be that the enuncia-tion of such theories fulfils a political and social need. It may be suggested that it is precisely when there is a gap between theory and practice in matters of race relations that the support of science is sought in order to bridge this gap. Thus, in the United States, the arguments of Jensen have been used against the acceptance of various poverty programmes. The popularization of his ideals by C. P. Snow and Eysenck may also serve to provide rationalizations for racial inequality in contemporary Britain.

Interestingly enough, these are not the only scientific theories which help to validate racialism and inequality. One significant phenomenon in our scientific history has been the revival of "biological" explanations of criminality (e.g. the 2y chromosome theory). Another is the body of ideas associated with the words, ecology, conservation, pollution, etc. In this latter case human political judge-ment is no longer considered, even as an intervening variable. The ills of the world are simply explained as being due to inexorable scientific laws.

The crux of the sociological argument about racist biological theories there-fore is this. On the political level societies may pass through periods in which there is no great need for any kind of theory which emphasizes the differences and incompatibilities between different ethnic or religious or "racial" groups. In such periods popular maxims and anecdotes will affirm the essential similari-ties between men, and informed opinion will deplore the political behaviour of the small minority of disturbed persons at home who are "prejudiced" and of governments abroad which work on a basis of racial supremacy. As strains in such a society develop however there is a ground-swell of opinion in which popular maxims and anecdotes guiltily and uneasily spotlight racial differences. Thus in Britain, for example, towards the end of the 1950s racist jokes began to be heard in working men's clubs.

This first guilty snigger of racism however gained a new significance when leading politicians of both parties began to include hostile references to im-migrant minorities in their speeches. Some like the late Lord Carron included ambiguous references to immigrants in the course of general attacks on govern-ment policy. Others like labour leader Robert Mellish found themselves drawing attention to the contrast between political ideals and the realities of the situation with which they were forced to deal at the level of local government.

In the next stage, however, the diagnosis of the problem became more systematic. Mr Enoch Powell, widely recognized as an intellectual in British politics, argued that basic issues were becoming suppressed and set out his own arguments as to the way in which the presence of a large proportion of immigrants in the population of British cities must undermine British culture.

Although Mr Powell's speeches produced widespread public support, they neither claimed that immigrants were in any sense inferior or that the differences between them and their British hosts were innate. The effect of world scientific opinion and the work of UNESCO since 1945 was such that responsible politicians were wary of committing themselves to such views. Mr Powell therefore based his case on the inadequacies of official statistics which, he argued, underestimated the number of immigrants, and the clear cultural differences between immigrants, particularly Asian immigrants, and a pseudo-sociological concept of territoriality.

The possibility always existed, however, that the immigrant population of Britain would become something of an underclass, deprived of housing and employment. Mr Powell's speeches gave only marginal help in fostering this situation. True, his insistence on the impossibility of assimilation gave some kind of basis to those who wished to discriminate. But the argument was never as water-tight as it could have been had it been based upon a theory of the biological basis of racial difference.

Whether they have intended it or not the popularizers of Jensen in Great Britain have now fundamentally altered the situation. The politicians who favour discrimination may in future argue not merely that Indians, Pakistanis and West Indians should not be assimilated and given equality of opportunity. They will now point to Eysenck's or Jensen's work and argue that assimilation is impossible and that equality of opportunity can only guarantee that Negroes at least will under such circumstances find their own level. There will of course be little hesitation about invalidly applying results from tests on American Negroes to all blacks in Britain. But in all likelihood it will not be long before American experiments are replicated with Indian, Pakistani and West Indian subjects in Britain.

Five

Crime and Punishment

If there is a state there is necessarily domination and consequently slavery. A state without slavery, open or disguised, is inconceivable—that is why we are enemies of the state.

—Michael Bakunin

Introduction

The legal philosopher Roscoe Pound, in *An Introduction to the Philosophy of Law,* surveyed various notions of what law is, starting with the first known written laws and continuing to the present day. He found that what thinkers believe law *is* is closely tied to what they think law is *for.* Abstracting from the various notions of what law is, he found that the abiding purposive factor is the search for security. However, the concept of security is not stable; it varies, depending upon the circumstances of life in which people find themselves.

Pound outlines four different notions of security, each one specifying differently what the law is for. Saying what the law "is for" is saying what end it is supposed to serve. Once we know the end, then any particular law being a means designed to secure that end, the end provides us with a basis for evaluating laws. We declare a law to be desirable or undesirable, depending on the law's suitability as a means of gaining the desired end; if undesirable, we know that we need to eliminate it and replace or reform it.

The four notions of security are: keeping the peace, maintaining the status quo, maximizing free self-assertion, and maximizing the satisfactions of wants.

The most primitive notion of security is keeping the peace. This was prominent, for example, in ancient Greece at the time that the system of kin organizations was breaking up. Political organization began replacing family governments; law was intended to secure the safety of individuals no longer protected by the family and for keeping the peace between drifters no longer controlled by the kin organizations.

The next notion of security Pound traces to the Greek philosophers, who construed law as an instrument for maintaining the status quo. Hybris was a Greek concept prominent in the Greek tragedies; it is the vice of overstepping one's proper bounds; even the gods had their bounds. The Greek philosophers saw law as a way of conserving their social institutions; persons governed by these institutions had their "appointed grooves" and by keeping to them avoided friction with others. This new concept of security was suitable for the city-state, which was the political successor to the systems of kin organizations. The status quo concept of security dominated, according to Pound, Roman jurisprudence, the Middle Ages, and feudal society.

The third notion of security emerged "with the gradual disintegration of this [feudal] order and the growing importance of the individual in a society engaged in discovery, colonization, and trade. . . ." Now the end of law "comes to be conceived as a making possible of the maximum of individual free self-assertion."

This free-assertion view of law's security function began to be replaced when the world became more crowded and resources less plentiful; in such a setting, free self-assertion began to create more friction than it relieved. Thus, at the end of the last century and continuing to the present, the end of law began to be reconceived; security came and is still coming to be conceived of as a maximizing of satisfaction of wants.

Each of these conceptions of what law is for is formulated with a threat in mind, a threat that needs to be dealt with. In each case, the threat is seen as an impending violation of the person which needs to be held in check; this impending violation motivates the formulation of a set of laws. But the bare existence of laws is insufficient to deter some one from committing a violation; the laws need to be backed by the counterthreat of punishment. This punishment threat won't be effective unless there is sufficient power to overcome those who defy the law. Thus, the criminal must be denied powers reserved to upholders of the law.

These points are obvious enough. We make them in order to remind ourselves that the concepts of law, violation of persons, crime, punishment, and power are interconnected. These concepts are discussed in the essays in this chapter.

Law and the State

In this section, the connection between law, state, and power is explored. We remarked that the security of persons through law requires law enforcement through punishment, which, in turn, will take place only if the upholders of law have more power than the law breakers. The classical solution to the power problem is the formation of the "state." The state makes laws, detects law breakers, enforces law, and punishes outlaws; once upon a time heads of families did all this; to a certain extent, the Mafia still does this, refusing to replace the kin form of human organization with the state-political form.

Is the state-law apparatus the best way to secure persons against violation?

One often hears it said that the best country is a nation of laws and not of men. That is, a country governed by men who are governed by law is more likely to have a just society than one governed by men who are not governed by law.

Monarchies and dictatorships are cited as examples of government by men who are not governed by law; monarchs and dictators have no legal limits on their power. Their sound judgments or absurd whims are equally sufficient bases for governmental decisions. In the United States, the Constitution was expressly framed to provide legal limits on the men who govern the country: the executives, the legislators, and the judges.

Although the long-range likelihood that there will be greater justice in a nation of laws than in a nation of men may be correct, the civil rights movement, the Vietnam war, and the Third World dissent against domestic colonialism have shown that to be a nation of laws may not be enough to guarantee a just society. The laws must also be just.

Of course, it is not enough to have just laws on the books. The people in a society must obey the just laws if the society is to be just. Although school desegregation is required by law, there are many communities and cities, north and south, that have not desegregated or that have given merely token obeisance to the law. Thus, even if a country's government is subject to law, and even if its laws are just, if a country's citizens do not obey the laws, it is a country of men and not of laws.

When people do not obey just laws, society is justified in taking appropriate legal steps to enforce the laws. But what if a person who fails to obey the law does so not out of malicious intent but because he honestly believes the law is unjust? Since any law that has been passed in accordance with authorized procedures is "legal," it is not possible to appeal to the law itself to challenge the law. It appears that one must appeal to extralegal concepts and principles in order to challenge, or justify, the justness of a disputed law. It is a well-known fact that people often believe they are morally justified in disobeying a law because by moral standards they judge the law to be unjust. If laws are to be evaluated by moral standards, moral standards must supersede legal standards as a basis for our actions; therefore, a person who believes that a law is unjust is morally obligated to disobey the law.

Plato's account of Socrates' trial, conviction, and death is very moving. Surely, if ever a person had morality on his side against the state, Socrates did, according to Plato's interpretation. By our argument above, we should conclude that Socrates should disobey the law by escaping from prison and his executioner. Here, it appears, the Athenian state-law apparatus is shown to be unsatisfactory, in this instance at least.

However, Plato has Socrates argue in the *Crito* that we should never disobey the law. Several considerations to support this claim are given, but the following is an important argument to be extracted from the *Crito:* No man may do wrong. To harm anyone is to do a wrong. Disobeying a law (just or unjust) is harming the state (and eventually other citizens). Even if the law is unjust, disobeying an unjust law harms someone, and, so, wrongs someone. Therefore, disobeying the law is to do a wrong; hence, no man may disobey the law.

A counterargument, using Socrates' first premise but turning on an act of omission rather than commission, can be fashioned as follows: No man may do wrong (Socrates' first premise). To allow someone to be harmed (omission) is to do a wrong. If obeying a law (just or unjust) deters one from preventing harm, then he has done a wrong. Therefore, obeying a law is to do a wrong; hence, no man may obey the law.

This last argument applies to Socrates in jail because the state is going to harm him unjustly; if he does not escape, he will be allowing the state to harm him, something that should never be done; therefore, by an error of omission, that is, by not escaping, he has not prevented a harm and so has done a wrong.

The idea that a law or some laws of a state may be unjust is easily thinkable and plausible. Given human fallibility, we are not surprised that the state-law apparatus makes mistakes. Further, we may agree with Pound that our ideas of the purpose of the law may shift over time. Obviously, there will be a lag in changing the laws to fit a changed conception of the purpose of law. In the nineteenth century in the United States, laws were designed for maximizing free self-assertion. Later, particularly around the time of President Franklin Roosevelt's first election in 1932, we saw an explicit shift to laws designed to satisfy more people's wants. More aid for the unemployed, social security, more regulatory agencies, and so forth were laws that were fitted to help fulfill human wants. But, there were and still are old laws of free self-assertion on the books. This lag will naturally yield laws that are no longer considered desirable; it takes time to shift the laws from one conception of law's purpose to another. Still, this lag deficiency does not lead most people to condemn the state-law apparatus because it is only a deficiency with some, not all, of the laws, and may eventually be overcome.

A more radical critique of the state-law answer to security against violation comes from the anarchists. For them, security by means of the state is wholly unsatisfactory. The state dominates and, so, enslaves citizens. It is always rule by a minority over a majority. Peter Kropotkin was a philosophical anarchist who pointed out a consequence of this minority–majority distinction: "Customs, absolutey essential to the very being of society, are, in the [legal] code intermingled with usages imposed by the ruling caste, and both claim equal respect from the crowd. . . . Such was law; and it has maintained its two-fold character to this day. Its origin is the desire of the ruling class to give permanence to customs imposed by themselves for their own advantage."

For Kropotkin and other anarchists, laws, instead of being a source of justice, are the chief source of injustice because they are promulgated by the people in power, who devise the laws in their own interest. Justice implies that no class or group of persons should use the state to serve their own interests at the expense of the rest of the citizens. But laws designed for special interests do not satisfy this minimum requirement of justice; therefore, laws are a source of injustice.

Michael Bakunin, in the essay selected here, agrees with Kropotkin. He says that anarchists "are indeed enemies of all power, knowing that power corrupts those in whom it is vested just as much as those who are forced to submit to it. Under its pernicious influence the former become ambitious and self-seeking despots, exploiting society for their own benefit or the benefit of their class, and the latter become slaves." You should note that anarchists should not be confused with a certain kind of Marxist, one who advocates the continuance of the state as a means of securing human rights and satisfactions. Bakunin is an avowed and passionate critic of such Marxists.

This antagonism between anarchists and state-Marxists was especially sharp in Spain before and during the Spanish civil war begun by Francisco Franco. That war, according to some historians, was not a two-way war of the Republicans against the Fascists but a three-way war among the anarchists, communists, and fascists. The Spanish history is interesting for another reason. The first doubt normally expressed about anarchism is not its ideal but its practicality. People doubt that anarchism can be realized, human nature being what it is. They are sceptical that the following vision of Bakunin is realizable. "We believe that the people will be happy and free only when they build their own life by organizing themselves from below upward, by means of autonomous and totally free associations, subject to no official tutelage but exposed to the influence of diverse individuals and parties enjoying mutual freedom."

Anarchism could not be so easily dismissed as unworkable if it had actually worked somewhere. That it did actually work, and on a large scale, not just in an isolated Utopian commune, is a fact according to Sam Dolgoff. In his *The Anarchist Collectives,* Dolgoff writes, "The Spanish Revolution is an example of a libertarian social revolution where genuine workers' self-management was successfully tried. . . . The Bolshevik Revolution, by contrast, was controlled by an elite party and was a political revolution." In his "Introduction" to Dolgoff's book, Murray Bookchin says, "It is essential to emphasize that Spanish anarchism was not merely a program embedded in a dense theoretical matrix. It was a way of life: partly, the life of the Spanish people as it was lived in the closely-knit villages of the countryside and the intense neighborhood life of the working class barrios; partly, too, the theoretical articulation of that life as projected by Bakunin's concepts of decentralization, mutual aid, and popular organs of self-management."

Entertaining the thought that anarchism might work should induce you to rethink your habitual linkage of law and the state.

The Citizen and the Law

PLATO

CRITO: . . . But, oh! my beloved Socrates, let me entreat you once more to take my advice and escape. For if you die I shall not only lose a friend who can never be replaced, but there is another evil: people who do not know you and me will believe that I might have saved you if I had been willing to give money, but that I did not care. Now, can there be a worse disgrace than this—that I should be thought to value money more than the life of a friend? For the many will not be persuaded that I wanted you to escape, and that you refused.

SOCRATES: But why, my dear Crito, should we care about the opinion of the many? Good men, and they are the only persons who are worth considering, will think of these things truly as they occurred.

CR.: But you see, Socrates, that the opinion of the many must be regarded, for what is happening shows that they can do the greatest evil to any one who has lost their good opinion.

SOC.: I only wish it were so, Crito; and that the many could do the greatest evil; for then they would also be able to do the greatest good—and what a fine thing this would be! But in reality they can do neither; for they cannot make a man either wise or foolish; and whatever they do is the result of chance.

CR.: Well, I will not dispute with you; but please tell me, Socrates, whether you are not acting out of regard to me and your other friends: are you not afraid that if you escape from prison we may get into trouble with the informers for having stolen you away, and lose either the whole or great part of our property; or that even a worse evil may happen to us? Now, if you fear on our account, be at ease; for in order to save you, we ought surely to run this, or even a greater risk; be persuaded, then, and do as I say.

SOC.: Yes, Crito, that is one fear which you mention, but by no means the only one.

CR.: Fear not—there are persons who are willing to get you out of prison at no great cost; and as for the informers, they are far from being exorbitant in their demands—a little money will satisfy them. My means,

Source: The Apology, in The Dialogues of Plato, Benjamin Jowett, trans. (3rd ed.; London: The Macmillan Company, Ltd., 1892).

which are certainly ample, are at your service, and if you have a scruple about spending all mine, here are strangers who will give you the use of theirs; and one of them, Simmias the Theban, has brought a large sum of money for this very purpose; and Cebes and many others are prepared to spend their money in helping you to escape. I say, therefore, do not hesitate on our account, and do not say, as you did in the court, that you will have a difficulty in knowing what to do with yourself anywhere else. For men will love you in other places to which you may go, and not in Athens only; there are friends of mine in Thessaly, if you like to go to them, who will value and protect you, and no Thessalian will give you any trouble. Nor can I think that you are at all justified, Socrates, in betraying your own life when you might be saved; in acting thus you are playing into the hands of your enemies, who are hurrying on your destruction. And further I should say that you are deserting your own children; for you might bring them up and educate them; instead of which you go away and leave them, and they will have to take their chance; and if they do not meet with the usual fate of orphans, there will be small thanks to you. No man should bring children into the world who is unwilling to persevere to the end in their nurture and education. But you appear to be choosing the easier part, not the better and manlier, which would have been more becoming in one who professes to care for virtue in all his actions, like yourself. And indeed, I am ashamed not only of you, but of us who are your friends, when I reflect that the whole business will be attributed entirely to our want of courage. The trial need never have come on, or might have been managed differently; and this last act, or crowning folly, will seem to have occurred through our negligence and cowardice, who might have saved you, if you had been good for anything; and you might have saved yourself, for there was no difficulty at all. See now, Socrates, how sad and discreditable are the consequences, both to us and you. Make up your mind then, or rather have your mind already made up, for the time of deliberation is over, and there is only one thing to be done, which must be done this very night, and if we delay at all will be no longer practicable or possible; I beseech you therefore, Socrates, be persuaded by me, and do as I say.

soc.: Dear Crito, your zeal is invaluable, if a right one; if wrong, the greater the zeal the greater the danger; and therefore we ought to consider whether I shall or shall not do as you say. For I am and always have been one of those natures who must be guided by reason, whatever the reason may be which upon reflection appears to me to be the best; and now that this chance has befallen me, I cannot repudiate my own words: the principles which I have hitherto honoured and revered I still honour, and unless we can at once find other and better principles, I am certain not to agree with you; no, not even if the power of the multitude could inflict many more imprisonments, confiscations, deaths, frightening us like children with hobgoblin terrors. What will be the fairest way of considering the question? Shall I return to your old argument about the opinions of men?—we are saying that some of them are to be regarded, and others not. Now were we right in maintaining this before I was condemned? And has the argument which was once good now proved to be talk for the sake of talking—mere childish nonsense? That is what I want to consider with your help, Crito: whether, under my present circumstances, the argument appears to be in any way different or not; and is to be allowed by me or disallowed. That argument, which, as I believe, is maintained by many persons of authority, was to the effect, as I was saying, that the opinions of some men are to be regarded, and of other men not to be regarded. Now you, Crito, are not going to die to-morrow—at least, there is no human probability of this—and therefore you are disinterested and not liable to be deceived by the circumstances in which you are placed. Tell me then, whether I am right in saying that some opinions, and the opinions of some men only, are to be valued, and that other opinions, and the opinions of other men, are not to be valuable. I ask you whether I was right in maintaining this?

CR.: Certainly.

SOC.: The good are to be regarded, and not the bad?

CR.: Yes.

SOC.: And the opinions of the wise are good, and the opinions of the unwise are evil?

CR.: Certainly.

SOC.: And what was said about another matter? Is the pupil who devotes himself to the practice of gymnastics supposed to attend to the praise and blame and opinion of every man, or of one man only—his physician or trainer, whoever he may be?

CR.: Of one man only.

SOC.: And he ought to fear the censure and welcome the praise of that one only, and not of the many?

CR.: Clearly so.

SOC.: And he ought to act and train, and eat and drink in the way which seems good to his single master who has understanding, rather than according to the opinion of all other men put together?

CR.: True.

SOC.: And if he disobeys and disregards the opinion and approval of the one, and regards the opinion of the many who have no understanding, will he not suffer evil?

CR.: Certainly he will.

SOC.: And what will the evil be, whither tending and what affecting, in the disobedient person?

CR.: Clearly, affecting the body; that is what is destroyed by the evil.

SOC.: Very good; and is not this true, Crito, of other things which we need not separately enumerate? In questions of just and unjust, fair and foul, good and evil, which are the subjects of our present consultation, ought we to follow the opinion of the many and to fear them; or the opinion of the one man who has understanding? ought we not to fear and reverence him more than all the rest of the world: and if we desert him shall we not destroy and injure that principle in us which may be assumed to be improved by justice and deteriorated by injustice;—there is such a principle?

CR.: Certainly there is, Socrates.

SOC.: Take a parallel instance:—if, acting under the advice of those who have no understanding, we destroy that which is improved by health and is deteriorated by disease, would life be worth having? And that which has been destroyed is—the body?

CR.: Yes.

SOC.: Could we live, having an evil and corrupted body?

CR.: Certainly not.

SOC.: And will life be worth having, if that higher part of man be destroyed, which is improved by justice and depraved by injustice? Do we suppose that principle, whatever it may be in man, which has to do with justice and injustice, to be inferior to the body?

CR.: Certainly not.

SOC.: More honourable than the body?

CR.: Far more.

SOC.: Then, my friend, we must not regard what the many say of us: but what he, the one man who has understanding of just and unjust, will say, and what the truth will say. And therefore you begin in error when you advise that we should regard the opinion of the many about just and unjust, good and evil, honourable and dishonourable,—"Well," some one will say, "but the many can kill us."

CR.: Yes, Socrates; that will clearly be the answer.

SOC.: And it is true: but still I find with surprise that the old argument is unshaken as ever. And I should like to know whether I may say the same of another proposition—that not life, but a good life, is to be chiefly valued?

CR.: Yes, that also remains unshaken.

SOC.: And a good life is equivalent to a just and honourable one—that holds also?

CR.: Yes, it does.

SOC.: From these premisses I proceed to argue the question whether I ought or ought not to try and escape without the consent of the Athenians: and if I am clearly right in escaping, then I will make the attempt; but if not, I will abstain. The other considerations which you mention, of money and loss of character and the duty of educating one's children are, I fear, only the doctrines of the multitude, who would be as ready to restore people to life, if they were able, as they are to put them to death —and with as little reason. But now, since the argument has thus far prevailed, the only question which remains to be considered is, whether we shall do rightly either in escaping or in suffering others to aid in our escape and paying them in money and thanks, or whether in reality we shall not do rightly; and if the latter, then death or any other calamity which man may ensue on my remaining here must not be allowed to enter into the calculation.

CR.: I think that you are right, Socrates; how then shall we proceed?

SOC.: Let us consider the matter together, and do you either refute me if you can, and I will be convinced; or else cease, my dear friend, from repeating to me that I ought to escape against the wishes of the Athenians: for I highly value your attempts to persuade me to do so, but I may not be persuaded against my own better judgment. And now please to consider my first position, and try how you can best answer me.

CR.: I will.

SOC.: Are we to say that we are never intentionally to do wrong, or that in one way we ought and in another we ought not to do wrong, or is doing wrong always evil and dishonourable, as I was just now saying, and as has been already acknowledged by us? Are all our former admissions which were made within a few days to be thrown away? And have we, at our age, been earnestly discoursing with one another all our life long only to discover that we are no better than children? Or, in spite of the opinion of the many, and in spite of consequences whether better or worse, shall we insist on the truth of what was then said, that injustice is always an evil and dishonour to him who acts unjustly? Shall we say so or not?

CR.: Yes.

SOC.: Then we must do no wrong?

CR.: Certainly not.

SOC.: Nor when injured injure in return, as the many imagine; for we must injure no one at all?

CR.: Clearly not.

SOC.: Again, Crito, may we do evil?

CR.: Surely not, Socrates.

SOC.: And what of doing evil in return for evil, which is the morality of the many—is that just or not?

CR.: Not just.

SOC.: For doing evil to another is the same as injuring him?

CR.: Very true.

SOC.: Then we ought not to retaliate or render evil for evil to any one, whatever evil we may have suffered from him. But I would have you consider, Crito, whether you really mean what you are saying. For this opinion has never been held, and never will be held, by any considerable number of persons; and those who are agreed and those who are not agreed upon this point have no common ground, and can only despise one another when they see how widely they differ. Tell me, then, whether you agree with and assent to my first principle, that neither injury nor retaliation nor warding off evil by evil is ever right. And shall that be the premiss of our argument? Or do you decline and dissent from this? For so I have ever thought, and continue to think; but, if you are of another opinion, let me hear what you have to say. If, however, you remain of the same mind as formerly, I will proceed to the next step.

CR.: You may proceed, for I have not changed my mind.

SOC.: Then I will go on to the next point, which may be put in the form of a question:—Ought a man to do what he admits to be right, or ought he to betray the right?

CR.: He ought to do what he thinks right.

SOC.: But if this is true, what is the application? In leaving the prison against the will of the Athenians, do I wrong any? or rather do I not wrong those whom I ought least to wrong? Do I not desert the principles which were acknowledged by us to be just—what do you say?

CR.: I cannot tell, Socrates; for I do not know.

SOC.: Then consider the matter in this way:—Imagine that I am about to play truant (you may call the proceeding by any name which you like), and the laws and the government come and interrogate me: "Tell us, Socrates," they say, "what are you about? are you not going by an act of yours to overturn us—the laws, and the whole state, as far as in you lies? Do you imagine that a state can subsist and not be overthrown, in which the decisions of law have no power, but are set aside and trampled upon by individuals?" What will be our answer, Crito, to these and the like words? Any one, and especially a rhetorician, will have a good deal to say on behalf of the law which requires a sentence to be carried out. He will argue that this law should not be set aside; and shall we reply, "Yes; but the state has injured us and given an unjust sentence." Suppose I say that?

CR.: Very good, Socrates.

SOC.: "And was that our agreement with you?" the law would answer; "or were you to abide by the sentence of the state?" And if I were to express my astonishment at their words, the law would probably add: "Answer, Socrates, instead of opening your eyes—you are in the habit of asking and answering questions. Tell us,—What complaint have you to make against us which justifies you in attempting to destroy us and the state? In the first place did we not bring you into existence? Your father married your mother by our aid and begat you. Say whether you have any objection to urge against those of us who regulate marriage?" None, I should reply. "Or against those of us who after birth regulate the nurture and education of children, in which you also were trained? Were not the laws, which have the charge of education, right in commanding your father to train you in music and gymnastic?" Right, I should reply. "Well then, since you were brought into the world and nurtured and educated by us, can you deny in the first place that you are our child and slave, as your fathers were before you? And if this is true you are not on equal terms with us; nor can you think that you have a right to do to us what we are doing to you. Would you have any right to strike or revile or do any other evil to your father or your master, if you had one, because you have been struck or reviled by him, or received some other evil at his hands?—you would not say this? And because we think right to destroy you, do you think that you have any right to destroy us in return, and your country as far as in you lies? Will you, O professor of true virtue, pretend that you are justified in this? Has a philosopher like you failed to discover that our country is more to be valued and higher and holier far than mother or father or any ancestor, and more to be regarded in the eyes of the gods and of men of understanding? Also to be soothed, and gently and reverently entreated when angry, even more than a father, and either to be persuaded, or if not persuaded, to be obeyed? And when we are punished by her, whether with imprisonment or stripes, the punishment is to be endured in silence; and if she leads us to wounds or death in battle, thither we follow as is right; neither may any one yield or retreat or leave his rank, but whether in battle or in a court of law, or in any other place, he must do what his city and his country order him; or he must change their view of what is just: and if he may do no violence to his father or mother, much less may he do violence to his country." What answer shall we make to this, Crito? Do the laws speak truly, or do they not?

CR.: I think that they do.

SOC.: Then the laws will say, "Consider, Socrates, if we are speaking truly that in your present attempt you are going to do us an injury. For, having brought you into the world, and nurtured and educated you, and given you and every other citizen a share in every good which we had to give, we further proclaim to any Athenian by the liberty which we allow him, that if he does not like us when he has become of age and has seen the ways of the city, and made our acquaintance, he may go where he pleases and take his goods with him. None of us laws will forbid him or interfere with him. Any one who does not like us and the city, and who wants to emigrate to a colony or to any other city, may go where he likes, retaining his property. But he who has experience of the manner in which we order justice and administer the state, and still remains, has entered into an implied contract that he will do as we command him. And he who disobeys us is, as we maintain, thrice wrong; first, because in disobeying us he is disobeying his parents; secondly, because we are the authors of his education; thirdly, because he has made an agreement with us that he will duly obey our commands; and he neither obeys them nor convinces us that our commands are unjust; and we do not rudely impose them, but give him the alternative of obeying or convincing us;—that is what we offer, and he does neither.

"These are the sort of accusations to which, as we were saying, you, Socrates will be exposed if you accomplish your intentions; you, above all other Athenians." Suppose now I ask, why I rather than anybody else? they will justly retort upon me that I above all other men have acknowledged the agreement. "There is clear proof," they will say, "Socrates, that we and the city were not displeasing to you. Of all Athenians you have been the most constant resident in the city, which, as you never leave, you may be supposed to love. For you never went out of the city either to see the games, except once when you went to the Isthmus, or to any other place unless when you were on military service; nor did you travel as other men do. Nor had you any curiosity to know other states or their laws: your affections did not go beyond us and our state; we were your special favourites, and you acquiesced in our government of you; and here in this city you begat your children, which is a proof of your satisfaction. Moreover, you might in the course of the trial, if you had liked, have fixed the penalty at banishment; the state which refuses to let you go now would have let you go then. But you pretended that you preferred death to exile, and that you were not unwilling to die. And now you have forgotten these fine sentiments, and pay no respect to us the laws, of whom you are the destroyer; and are doing what only a miserable slave would do, running away and turning your back upon the compacts and agreements which you made as a citizen. And first of all answer this very question: Are we right in saying that you agreed to be governed according to us in deed, and not in word only? Is that true or not?" How shall we answer, Crito? Must we not assent?

CR.: We cannot help it, Socrates.

SOC.: Then will they not say: "You, Socrates, are breaking the covenants and agreements which you made with us at your leisure, not in any haste or under any compulsion or deception, but after you have had seventy years to think of them, during which time you were at liberty to leave the city, if we were not to your mind, or if our covenants appeared to you to be unfair. You had your choice, and might have gone either to Lacedaemon or Crete, both which states are often praised by you for their good government, or to some other Hellenic or foreign state. Whereas you, above all other Athenians, seemed to be so fond of the state, or, in other words, of us her laws (and who would care about a state which has no laws?), that you never stirred out of her; the halt, the blind, the maimed were not more stationary in her than you were. And now you run away and forsake your agreements. Not so, Socrates, if you will take our advice; do not make yourself ridiculous by escaping out of the city.

"For just consider, if you trangress and err in this sort of way, what good will you do either to yourself or to your friends? That your friends will be driven into exile and deprived of citizenship, or will lose their property, is tolerably certain; and you yourself, if you fly to one of the neighboring cities, as, for example, Thebes or Megara, both of which are well governed, will come to them as an enemy, Socrates, and their government will be against you, and all patriotic citizens will cast an evil eye upon you as a subverter of the laws, and you will confirm in the minds of the judges the justice of their own condemnation of you. For he who is a corrupter of the laws is more than likely to be a corrupter of the young and foolish portion of mankind. Will you then flee from well-ordered cities and virtuous men? and is existence worth having on these terms? Or will you go to them without shame, and talk to them, Socrates? And what will you say to them? What you say here about virtue and justice and institutions and laws being the best things among men? Would that be decent of you? Surely not. But if you go away from well-governed states to Crito's friends in Thessaly, where there is great disorder and licence, they will be charmed to hear the tale of your escape from prison, set off with ludicrous particulars of the manner in which you were wrapped in a goatskin or some other disguise, and metamorphosed as the manner is of runaways; but will there be no one to remind you that in your old age you were not ashamed to violate the most sacred laws from a miserable desire of a little more life? Perhaps not, if you keep them in a good temper; but if they are out of temper you will hear many degrading things; you will live, but how?—as the flatterer of all men, and the servant of all men; and doing what?—eating and drinking in Thessaly, having gone abroad in order that you may get a dinner. And where will be your fine sentiments about justice and virtue? Say that you wish to live for the sake of your children—you want to bring them up and educate them—will you take them into Thessaly and deprive them of Athenian citizenship? Is this the benefit which you will confer upon them? Or are you under the impression that they will be better cared for and educated here if you are still alive, although absent from them; for your friends will take care of them? Do you fancy that if you are an inhabitant of Thessaly they will take care of them, and if you are an inhabitant of the other world that they will not take care of them? Nay; but if they who call themselves friends are good for anything, they will—to be sure they will.

"Listen, then, Socrates, to us who have brought you up. Think not of life and children first, and of justice afterwards, but of justice first, that you may be justified before the princes of the world below. For neither will you nor any that belong to you be happier or holier or juster in this life, or happier in another, if you do as Crito bids. Now you depart in innocence, a sufferer and not a doer of evil; a victim, not of the laws but of men. But if you go forth, returning evil for evil, and injury for injury, breaking the covenants and agreements which you have made with us, and wronging those whom you ought least of all to wrong, that is to say, yourself, your friends, your country, and us, we shall be angry with you while you live, and our brethren, the laws of the world below, will receive you as an enemy; for they will know that you have done your best to destroy us. Listen, then, to us and not to Crito."

This, dear Crito, is the voice which I seem to hear murmuring in my ears, like the sound of the flute in the ears of the mystic; that voice, I say, is humming in my ears and prevents me from hearing any other. And I know that anything more which you may say will be in vain. Yet speak, if you have anything to say.

CR.: I have nothing to say, Socrates.

SOC.: Leave me then, Crito, to fulfill the will of God, and to follow whither he leads.

State, Law, and Anarchy

MICHAEL BAKUNIN

Michael Bakunin (1814–1876) was a famous exiled Russian anarchist who organized social democratic parties throughout Europe and who strongly opposed the Marxists. Above all, he was anti-state. He wrote many pamphlets advocating autonomous associations in place of the state.

I

In science the living, concretely rational method of procedure is to go from the actual fact to the thought that embraces it, expresses it, and thereby explains it. In the practical world it is the movement from social life to the most rational possible organization of it in accordance with the indications, conditions, needs, and more or less passionate demands of life itself.

That is the broad popular way, the way of real and total liberation, open to anyone and therefore truly popular. It is the way of the *anarchistic* social revolution, which arises of itself among the people and destroys everything that obstructs the broad flow of popular life, in order then to create new forms of free social existence from the very depths of the people's being.

The way of the metaphysicians is quite different. The people we call metaphysicians are not just the followers of Hegel's doctrines, who are no longer very numerous, but also the positivists and all the contemporary devotees of

Source: Archives Bakounine, Vol. 3, ed. by Arthur Lehning, trans. by Marshall Shatz (Leiden, 1972). Reprinted by permission of E. J. Brill.

the goddess science; all those who, by one means or another, such as a meticulous but necessarily always imperfect study of the past and present, have devised an ideal of social organization to which, like a new Procrustes, they want to make the life of future generations conform whatever the cost; in a word, all those who, instead of regarding thought or science as one of the necessary manifestations of natural and social life, regard this poor life as a practical manifestation of their own thought and their own science, which, of course, is always imperfect.

Whether metaphysicians or positivists, all these knights of science and thought, in the name of which they believe themselves called to prescribe the laws of life, are conscious or unconscious reactionaries. This is exceedingly easy to prove.

Without speaking of metaphysics in general, which only a few individuals studied during the periods of its most brilliant flowering, science in the broader sense of the word, any serious science at all worthy of the name, is accessible even now only to an extremely insignificant minority. For example, in Russia, with its eighty million inhabitants, how many serious scholars can you count? The people who talk about science may perhaps number in the thousands, but you will find scarcely a few hundred who are at all closely acquainted with it. But if science is to prescribe the laws of life, then the vast majority of the population, millions of people, are to be governed by a hundred or two hundred scholars, or in substance even a much smaller number, since it is not just any science that makes a man capable of governing society but the science of sciences, the crown of all the sciences—sociology, which assumes in the fortunate scholar a prior knowledge of all the other sciences. And are there many such scholars, not just in Russia but in the whole of Europe? Maybe twenty or thirty! And these twenty or thirty scholars are to govern the whole world! Can you imagine a more absurd and repulsive depotism than that?

In the first place these twenty scholars will most likely quarrel among themselves, but if they do unite it will be to the detriment of all mankind. A scholar by his very nature is inclined to all sorts of intellectual and moral corruption, his main vice being the exaltation of his knowledge and his own intellect, and scorn for all the ignorant. Let him govern and he will become the most unbearable tyrant, for scholarly pride is repulsive, offensive, and more oppressive than any other kind. To be the slaves of pedants—what a fate for mankind! Give them free rein and they will start performing the same experiments on human society that they now perform for the benefit of science on rabbits, cats, and dogs.

We will respect scholars for their services, but for the salvation of their intellect and their morality we must not grant them any social privileges or accord them any right other than the general right of freedom to propagate their convictions, thoughts, and knowledge. We must not give power to them any more than to anyone else, for whoever is invested with power by an immutable socialist law[1] will without fail become the oppressor and exploiter of society.

[1] Bakunin perhaps meant "social law."

But it will be said that science will not always be the property of just a few people; the time will come when it will be accessible to everyone. Well, that time is still a long way off, and many social upheavals will have to take place before it comes. Until then, who will consent to put his fate in the hands of scholars, in the hands of the priests of science? Why bother wresting it from the hands of the Christian priests?

It seems to us that those who imagine that after the social revolution everyone will be equally learned are severely mistaken. Then as now, science as science will remain one of the numerous social specializations. The only difference is that this specialization, now accessible only to members of the privileged classes, will then, with class distinctions abolished once and for all, become accessible to anyone who has the vocation and inclination to study it—though not at the expense of general manual labor, which will be obligatory for everyone.

Only general scientific education will become common property, and particularly a familiarity with scientific method, the habit of thinking scientifically, i.e., of generalizing facts and drawing more or less correct conclusions for them. But encyclopedic minds, and therefore learned sociologists, will always be very few. Woe to mankind if thought should ever become the source and sole guide of life, if the sciences and learning should direct the government of society. Life would run dry and human society would turn into a dumb and servile herd. The government of life by science could have no other result than the stupefaction of the whole of humanity.

As revolutionary anarchists we advocate universal education, liberation, and the broad development of social life, and therefore we are enemies of the state and of any kind of state administration. In contrast to all metaphysicians, positivists, and learned or unlearned worshipers of the goddess science, we maintain that natural and social life always precedes thought (which is only one of its functions) but is never its result; that life develops from its own inexhaustible depths by means of a series of diverse facts, not a series of abstract reflections; and that the latter, always produced by life but never producing it, are like milestones, merely indicating its direction and the different phases of its autonomous and natural development.

In accordance with this conviction, not only do we have neither the intention nor the least desire to impose upon our own or any other nation any ideal of social organization that we have found in books or invented; but in the belief that the masses bear all the elements of their future pattern of organization in their own more or less historically developed instincts, in their own vital demands, and in their own conscious or unconscious aspirations, we seek this ideal in the people themselves. Since any state power, any government by its nature and position stands outside and above the people, and must necessarily try to subordinate them to alien regulations and purposes, we declare ourselves the enemies of all governmental or state power, the enemies of state organization altogether. We believe that the people will be happy and free only when they build their own life by organizing themselves from below upward, by means of autonomous and totally free associations, subject to no official tutelage but exposed to the influence of diverse individuals and parties enjoying mutual freedom.

These are the convictions of social revolutionaries, for which we are called anarchists. We do not object to the name because we are indeed enemies of all power, knowing that power corrupts those in whom it is vested just as much as those who are forced to submit to it. Under its pernicious influence the former become ambitious and self-seeking despots, exploiting society for their own benefit or the benefit of their class, and the latter become slaves.

Idealists of all sorts, metaphysicians, positivists, champions of the predominance of science over life, doctrinaire revolutionaries—with different arguments but identical fervor they all defend the idea of the state and of state power, which they see, *perfectly logically* from their point of view, as the sole salvation of society. *Perfectly logically* because they take as their foundation the principle, which we believe to be utterly false, that thought precedes life, that abstract theory precedes social practice, and that sociological science must therefore be the starting point for social revolution and reconstruction; and from this they necessarily draw the conclusion that since thought, theory, and science are at least for now the property of a very few people, those few ought to be the directors of social life—not just the agents but the managers of all popular movements. On the day after the revolution a new organization of society is to be created not by the free union of popular associations, communes, counties, and districts from below upward, in conformity with the people's needs and instincts, but solely by the dictatorial power of this learned minority which is *supposed* to express the will of the whole people.

The fiction of popular representation, and the actual fact of government of the masses by an insignificant handful of privileged individuals elected—or even not elected—by hordes of people driven to the polls without ever knowing what or whom they are voting for; the false and abstract expression of an imaginary popular thought and will of which the real and living people haven't the slightest idea—these are the foundations of both the theory of the state and the theory of the so-called revolutionary dictatorship.

The differences between a revolutionary dictatorship and a state are merely external. In essence they both represent government of the majority by a minority in the name of the alleged stupidity of the former and the alleged intelligence of the latter. Therefore they are equally reactionary, both of them having the direct and unavoidable result of consolidating the political and economic privileges of the ruling minority and the political and economic slavery of the masses.

Now it is clear why the *doctrinaire revolutionaries,* who have as their objective the overthrow of the existing governments and regimes in order to found their own dictatorship on the ruins, have never been and will never be enemies of the state. On the contrary, they have always been and will always be its most ardent defenders. They are enemies only of the existing authorities, because they want to take their place, enemies of the existing political institutions because these preclude the possibility of their own dictatorship. But at the same time they are the warmest friends of state power, for if it were not retained the revolution, once it had truly liberated the masses, would deprive this pseudo-revolutionary minority of all hope of putting them in a new harness and conferring on them the benefits of its own governmental decrees.

So true is this that now, when reaction is triumphing all over Europe, when all states are gripped by a malicious spirit of self-preservation and popular repression, clad from head to toe in the triple armor of military, political, and financial power, and, under the supreme command of Prince Bismarck, preparing for a desperate struggle against social revolution—now, when it would seem that all sincere revolutionaries ought to unite in order to repulse the desperate attack of international reaction, we see instead the doctrinaire revolutionaries under the leadership of Mr. Marx everywhere taking the side of the state and the statesmen against popular revolution.

. . .

Now it is clear why most of the doctors of philosophy of Hegel's school, for all their fiery revolutionism in the world of abstract ideas, in actuality in 1848 and 1849 proved to be not revolutionaries but reactionaries, and why the majority of them have now become confirmed partisans of Prince Bismarck.

II

We have several times voiced a deep aversion to the theory of Lassalle[2] and Marx, which recommends to the workers as their immediate main goal, if not their ultimate ideal, *the establishment of a people's state.* This, they explain, will be nothing other than "the proletariat raised to the position of ruling class."[3]

If the proletariat is to be the ruling class, one may ask whom will it govern? There must be yet another proletariat that will be subjected to this new domination, this new state. It might be the peasant rabble, for instance, which we know does not enjoy the favor of the Marxists and, with its lower level of culture, will probably be governed by the urban factory proletariat. Or, if we look at the question from a national point of view, then for identical reasons the Slavs will be reduced to the same servile position in relation to the victorious German proletariat that the latter now occupies under its own bourgeoisie.

If there is a state there is necessarily domination and consequently slavery. A state without slavery, open or disguised, is inconceivable—that is why we are enemies of the state.

What does it mean, the proletariat elevated to a ruling class? Is the whole proletariat going to direct the administration? There are about forty million Germans. Are all forty million going to be members of the government? The whole people will govern, and no one will be governed. Then there will be no government and no state; but if there is a state, people will be governed and there will be slaves.

---

[2] Ferdinand Lassalle, a highly flamboyant personality, was killed in a duel in 1864. He was the creator of the General German Workers' Association, which later became part of the German Social Democratic party. Lassalle's views were an amalgam of Marxism and Hegelianism, and Marx in fact disagreed with his conviction that socialism could be realized within the existing state system.

[3] See *The Communist Manifesto,* section II.

This dilemma in the Marxist's theory is resolved quite simply. By popular government they mean government of the people by a small number of representatives elected by the people. Election of so-called popular representatives and directors of the state by universal suffrage—the last word of the Marxists, as well as of the democratic school—is a lie which conceals the despotism of a ruling minority, a lie that is all the more dangerous because it is presented as the expression of the alleged will of the people.

And so, from whatever angle you look at this question you come to the same sad conclusion: government of the vast majority of the masses by a privileged minority. But this minority, the Marxists say, will consist of workers. Yes, of *former* workers, perhaps, who as soon as they become rulers or representatives of the people will cease to be workers and will start viewing the laborer's world from the heights of the state, they will no longer represent the people, only themselves and their pretensions to rule the people. Anyone who doubts this is just not familiar with the nature of man.

But these elected representatives will be passionately committed as well as learned socialists. The words "learned socialists" and "scientific socialism" which recur constantly in the writings and speeches of the Lassalleans and Marxists are themselves proof that the fictitious people's state will be nothing but a highly despotic rule of the masses by a new and highly restricted aristocracy of real or pretended scholars. The people are not learned, and therefore they will be liberated entirely from the cares of governing and cast into the governed herd. A fine liberation!

The Marxists sense this contradiction, and while admitting that a government of scholars—the most burdensome, offensive, and contemptible kind of government there is—will be a true dictatorship regardless of its democratic forms, they offer the consolation that this dictatorship will be provisional and brief. They say that its sole concern and purpose will be to educate the people and to raise them economically and politically to such a level that all government will soon become unnecessary. The state will then shed its political, or authoritarian, character and will of itself turn into a totally free organization of economic interests and communes.

There is a flagrant contradiction here. If their state is really a people's state, then why abolish it? And if it is necessary to abolish it in order to achieve true liberation of the people, then how do they dare to call it a people's state? By our polemics against them we have brought them to the recognition that freedom, or anarchy, i.e., the free organization of the working masses from below upward, is the ultimate goal of social development, and that any state, including even their people's state, is a yoke which engenders despotism on the one hand and slavery on the other.

They say that this yoke of theirs is a transitional device for the attainment of total popular liberation: anarchy, or freedom, is the end, and the state, or dictatorship, the means. Thus, to liberate the masses it is necessary to enslave them first.

For the moment our polemics have focused on this contradiction. They maintain that only a dictatorship—theirs, of course—can create popular liberty.

We reply that no dictatorship can have any goal but self-perpetuation, and that it is capable only of engendering and inculcating slavery in a nation that puts up with it. Freedom can be created only by freedom, that is, by a national uprising and the free organization of the working masses from below upward.

The political and social theory of the antistate socialists, or anarchists, leads them resolutely and directly to a complete break with all governments and all forms of bourgeois politics, leaving them no alternative but social revolution. Meanwhile the converse theory, the theory of the state communists and scientific authority, just as resolutely entangles its adherents, on the pretext of political tactics, in a constant succession of deals with governments and various bourgeois political parties. In other words, it pushes them straight into reaction.

Its main foundation was Lassalle's political and social program, the communist theory created by Mr. Marx.

The basic point of this program is the liberation (imaginary) of the proletariat *solely by means of the state.* But this requires that the state agree to be the liberator of the proletariat from the yoke of bourgeois capital. And how is the state to be instilled with such a desire? There can be only two ways. The proletariat must make a revolution for the purpose of seizing the state—this is the heroic way. In our opinion, once it is seized it must immediately be destroyed as the age-old prison of the masses; but according to Mr. Marx's theory the people not only must not destroy it but on the contrary must reinforce it and make it stronger and in this form put it at the full disposal of their benefactors, guardians, and teachers—the communist party chiefs, in a word, Mr. Marx and his friends, who will proceed to liberate the people in their own way. They will gather up the reins of government in a strong hand because the ignorant people need strong guardians; they will establish a single state bank, concentrating in their own hands all commercial and industrial, agricultural, and even scientific production; and they will divide the mass of the people into two armies, one industrial and one agrarian, under the direct command of state engineers, who will form a new privileged scientific-political caste.[4]

See what a splendid goal the school of German communists sets up for the people! But to attain all these blessings one innocent little step has to be taken first—a revolution! And just try waiting until the Germans make a revolution! They will endlessly discuss revolution, perhaps, but as for making one . . .

What prevents the people from carrying out a victorious revolution? Is it the lack of a common ideal capable of conceiving a popular revolution and giving it a definite goal? Without an ideal, as we have already said, a simultaneous and universal uprising of the entire nation, and hence the very success of the revolution, are impossible.

It is clear that if the people do not develop this ideal from within themselves, no one will be able to give it to them. In general it should be observed that no one, neither an individual, a society, nor a nation, can be given anything that does not already exist within him, not just in embryo but developed to some degree. Let us take the individual. Unless an idea already exists within him as a living instinct and as a more or less clear conception which serves as the

[4] See *The Communist Manifesto,* section II.

initial expression of that instinct, you cannot explain it to him, and more important, you cannot pound it into him. Look at a bourgeois, content with his lot. Can you ever hope to explain to him the proletarian's right to full human development and to an equal share in all the pleasures, gratifications, and blessings of social life, or prove to him the legitimacy and the salutary necessity of social revolution? No, and unless you had gone out of your mind you wouldn't even try. And why not? Because you would be certain that even if this bourgeois were by nature good, wise, noble, magnanimous, and inclined to justice—you see the concessions I am making, there being few such bourgeois in existence —even if he were highly educated and even erudite, he would still not understand you and would not become a social revolutionary. And why wouldn't he? For the simple reason that his life has not aroused in him the instinctive urges that would correspond to your social-revolutionary idea. If, however, he did have those urges, in embryo or even in the most absurd conceptual forms, then whatever pleasure and pride his social position brought him he could not be content with himself.

On the other hand, take the most uneducated, uncouth fellow. If truly you discover in him the instincts and the honest though obscure yearnings that correspond to the social-revolutionary idea, then don't be frightened no matter how primitive his actual notions may be, just apply yourself to him seriously, with love, and you will see how broadly and passionately he will embrace and assimilate your idea—or, more precisely, his own idea, because it is nothing but the clear, complete, and logical expression of his own instinct. In essence, then, you will not have given him anything, you will not have brought him anything new but will merely have clarified what lived within him long before he met you. That is why I say that no one can give anyone anything.

But if this is true in respect to an individual, it is all the more true in respect to an entire people. You have to be a total innocent or an incurable doctrinaire to imagine that you can give anything to the people, that you can make them a gift of material prosperity or a new mentality or morality, a new truth, and arbitrarily give their lives a new direction.

Among the greatest geniuses hitherto there have been few who have really done anything for the people. A nation's geniuses are highly aristocratic, and everything they have done until now has served only to educate, strengthen, and enrich the exploiting minority. The poor masses, forsaken and stifled by all, with great martyrdom have had to forge their own way toward freedom and light by an endless succession of obscure and fruitless efforts. The greatest geniuses did not bring society a new content, or could they. Created by society themselves, they have carried on and augmented the work of many centuries, bringing only new forms to the old content which is constantly being regenerated and expanded by the very movement of social life.

But, I repeat, the most celebrated geniuses have done nothing, or very little, specifically for the people, that is, for the many millions of laboring proletarians. The people's life, development, and progress belong exclusively to the people themselves. This progress is achieved, of course, not by book learning but by a natural accumulation of experience and thought, transmitted from generation to generation and necessarily broadened, deepened, perfected, and given form very slowly. It is achieved by an unending succession of painful and bitter experiences which have at last, in our own time, brought the masses of all countries, or at least of all the European countries, to the realization that they can expect nothing from the privileged classes and existing states, or from political revolutions in general, and that they can be liberated only by their own efforts, by means of social revolution.

Violence

Someone asks YOU: Do you believe in violence?

YOU reply: Let's put it this way: I don't like it when other people do violence to me.

SHE: I'm not asking whether you like violence, done either to yourself or others, I want to know whether you think the use of violence is ever right.

YOU: Why, no. It's never right.

SHE: Oh. Then you're a pacifist, right?

YOU: No, I'm not. In my view, a pacifist is a person who thinks it's never right to use force, who remains passive no matter what anyone is doing to someone else, including injuring them. I'm not a pacifist, because I think it's OK to use force sometimes.

SHE: But then you couldn't believe the use of violence is always wrong if you think it's OK to use force sometimes.

YOU: Sure, I can believe violence is always wrong. It's easy. It's as easy as believing being bad is always wrong. Violence is just another form of badness. To be violent is to be bad.

Using force isn't necessarily a form of badness. In fact, nothing can be done in the world without using force. Every human act is moving the body in some way, and that takes force.

SHE: So?

YOU: So, since some human acts are good, the use of force in those cases is good. That's why you can't equate force and violence.

SHE: Then sometimes the use of force is good and sometimes it's bad.

YOU: Right. When force is good, we call it benevolence; when force is bad, we call it violence.

SHE: How can you tell the difference between the two? How can you tell when there is violence? That seems pretty important to me.

YOU: I think it's important, too. And so do philosophers. **Newton Garver** [first essay in this section], for example, writes a whole essay just concentrating on what violence is, on trying to define violence.

SHE: How does he tell when the use of force is violence?

YOU: For him, you have to consider a person's rights. When his rights, such as the right to his body, or to make his own decisions, or to the product of his labor, are violated by the use of physical or psychological force, then force is violence.

SHE: I'm not sure I agree that violence is always bad. It seems to me that sometimes it's legitimate to use violence.

YOU: How can that be if violence is bad?

SHE: Because sometimes one bad thing isn't as bad as another bad thing, and because occasionally the situation in the world is such that a person is forced to choose doing either of two bad things. We don't always have the luxury of doing pure good. Sometimes doing good is doing what is least bad.

For example, a policeman may have to wound a person if he catches him trying to kill another person. Wounding him isn't a pure good, but it is better than letting him kill. And when a dictator has a powerful hold on a country and enslaves the people, and makes arbitrary, unjust decisions, and exploits them, then it seems legitimate for the people to violently overthrow him; at least it's legitimate if they really don't think he can be overthrown nonviolently.

YOU: Interesting that you should use that example. Here's another essay, this one by **Robert Audi** [second essay in this section] that tries to make a similar point. He thinks social violence can sometimes be justified if it is the only way to secure freedom, justice, and/or social welfare.

SHE: Do you agree with him and me?

YOU: No.

SHE: You're just being stubborn.

YOU: I don't think so. I said that force in itself may be good or bad, depending on whether it is benevolence or violence. If force is bad, then it's violence. But if your examples show anything, they simply show what I said earlier, namely, that in some circumstances force is good—even though, as you say, what you accomplish, as in social revolution, isn't always purely good. The word "violence" is often wrongly used in place of "force." Audi, I think, uses "violence" when he should be using "force" instead. When we try to make the use of unusual force legitimate, we are trying to show that it is benevolence; we are not trying to show that violence is legitimate and, consequently, good. Violence is always bad; I still say so.

SHE: Still—if benevolence, when it involves the use of force that injures someone, can't really be good, just a lesser bad than some other action, how can you say that violence, being the opposite of benevolence, is always bad?

YOU: I'm not sure I get your point.

SHE: Since benevolence isn't always good, and violence is the opposite of benevolence, then I don't see how violence is always bad.

YOU: Maybe you mean "isn't always *purely* good" or *"purely* bad."

SHE: Yes, I think so.

YOU: Since nothing in this world may be purely bad or purely good, maybe "better" is the key moral term rather than "good" and "bad." When we choose how to use our force, perhaps our standard should not be "Which act will result in good and which in bad?" but "Which act's results are better?" The better act is benevolence and the worse act is violence.

SHE: Maybe.

YOU: Look, this isn't just my opinion. I realize that because someone else may agree with me doesn't prove I'm right, but **Kai Nielsen** has a pretty good argument about balancing good and evil to decide when the use of force is violence, hence wrong, and when it is benevolence, hence good. He says, "And surely it is right to see violence as an evil; for a person even to be a moral agent, he needs to recognize that to do violence to someone is to harm him and that this *always* stands in need of a special justification. But, in addition, one should recognize (a) that violence is not the only great evil in the world and that in deciding what to do, that evil must be counterbalanced against other evils, and (b) that in a situation in which a revolution could be made or would be justified, there would already exist in the oppression and degradation of human beings a vast amount of violence, namely, a pervasive institutionally sanctioned violation of their persons." And then Nielsen quotes one of Garver's main points, "We must remember that 'violence in human affairs is more closely connected with the idea of violation than with the idea of force.' "

SHE: So, violence is always evil; but since it may not be the most evil, and since we may be forced sometimes to choose between evils, choosing violence may be choosing the least evil. Right?

YOU: Right.

SHE: Assassinating a cruel tyrant may be less evil than permitting him or her to live. Assassination is murder. I wouldn't call murder good or benevolent.

YOU: Neither would I. But I would call it better and that's why I said "better" may be the more basic moral term.

What Violence Is

NEWTON GARVER

Newton Garver (1928–   ) teaches philosophy at the State University of New York, Buffalo. He has written a number of journal articles.

I

Most people deplore violence, many people embrace violence (perhaps reluctantly), and a few people renounce violence. But through all these postures there runs a certain obscurity, and it is never entirely clear just what violence is.

Those who deplore violence loudest and most publicly are usually identified with the status quo—school principals, businessmen, politicians, ministers. What they deplore is generally overt attacks on property or against the "good order of society." They rarely see violence in defense of the status quo in the same light as violence directed against it. At the time of the Watts riots in 1965 President Johnson urged Negroes to realize that nothing of any value can be won through violent means—an idea which may be true but which Johnson himself seemed to ignore in connection with the escalation of the Vietnam war he was simultane-

Source: Newton Garver, "What Violence Is," The Nation (June 24, 1968), pp. 817–822. (Revised by author.) Reprinted by permission of the author.

ously embarking upon. But the President [Johnson] is not the only one of us who deplores violence while at the same time perpetrating it, and a little more clarity about what exactly we deplore might help all around.

Those who renounce violence are equally hard to follow. Tolstoy, Gandhi, and Muste stand out among the advocates of nonviolence of the past century, and as one reads them it becomes clear that they do not all renounce exactly the same thing. There is much that is concrete and detailed in the writings of these men, but nonetheless it is not easy to avoid the impression that "nonviolence" is really just morality itself rather than a specific commitment to eschew a certain well-defined sort of behavior.

Those who embrace violence are in a much better position, for they stand ready to embrace whatever is "inevitable" or "necessary" in the circumstances, and hence the question of just where violence begins or leaves off does not arise for them. But if we want to know about the nature and varieties of violence, it does not help to be told that violence is unavoidable or that it is a necessary means to some end. There is a question about understanding violence before we come to adopt a posture toward it, and it is to that question we now turn.

II

What I want to do is to present a kind of typology of violence. I want, that is, to try to make clear what some of the different types and kinds and forms of violence are, and thereby to give a perspective of the richness of this topic. Unfortunately, I can't begin saying what the types of violence are without saying first what it is I'm giving you a typology of. So let's begin with a definition of violence.

What is violence? That is a typical philosophical question. The psychiatrists and the sociologists are interested in the questions: why is there violence? what causes violence? That's not my concern—at least not my professional concern nor my concern here. What I'm interested in is the old-fashioned philosophical question: What is the nature or essence of violence? We can make a good start etymologically. The word "violence" comes, of course, from the French, prior to that from the Latin, and you can find Greek roots if you're up to it—which I'm not. The Latin root of the word "violence" is a combination of two Latin words —the word *"vis"* (force) and the past participle *"latus"* of the word *"fero"* (to carry). The Latin word *"violare"* is itself a combination of these two words, and its present participle *"violans"* is a plausible source for the word "violence"— so that the word "violence," in its etymological origin, has the sense of to carry force at or toward. An interesting feature of the etymology is that the word "violation" comes from this very same source as the word "violence," which suggests to us the interesting idea that violence is somehow a violation of something: that carrying force against something constitutes in one way or another a violation of it.

The idea of force being connected with violence is a very powerful one. There is no question at all that in many contexts the word "force" is a synonym for the word "violence." This is particularly true if you talk about, for example, a violent blizzard: a violent blizzard is nothing but a blizzard with very great force. The same is true of a violent sea and other bits of violence in nature. It is simply some aspect of nature manifested to us with especially great force. But I don't want to talk about natural phenomena—certainly not meteorological phenomena. I want to talk instead about human phenomena. In human affairs violence cannot be equated with force.

One of the very first things to understand about violence in human affairs is that it is not the same thing as force. It is clear that force is often used on another person's body and there is no violence done. For example, if a man is drowning—thrashing around and apparently unable to save himself—and you use the standard Red Cross life-saving techniques, you will use force against his body although certainly you won't be doing any violence to him. You will, in fact, be saving his life instead. To think so rigidly of force and violence being identical with one another that you call this sort of life-saving an act of violence is to have lost sight entirely of the significance of the concept. Similarly, surgeons and dentists use force on our bodies without doing violence to us.

The idea of violence in human affairs is much more closely connected with the idea of violation than it is with the idea of force. What is fundamental about violence in human affairs is that a person is violated. Now that is a tough notion to explain. It is easy enough to understand how you can violate a moral rule or a parking regulation, but what in the world does it mean to talk about "violating a person"? That, I think, is a very important question, and because it can give a fresh perspective on what it means to be human it deserves fuller consideration than I can give it in this context. If it makes sense to talk about violating a person, that just is because a person has certain rights which are undeniably, indissolubly, connected with his being a person. The very idea of natural rights is controversial since it is redolent of Scholasticism, but I find myself forced to accept natural rights in order to understand the moral dimension of violence. One of the most fundamental rights a person has is a right to his body—to determine what his body does and what is done to his body—because without his body he wouldn't be a person anymore. The most common way a person ceases to exist is that his body stops functioning—a point which appeals especially forcefully if you think of a person as a living, growing thing rather than as something static or as a substance in the traditional sense. Apart from a body what is essential to one's being a person is dignity in something like the existentialist sense. The dignity of a person does not consist in his remaining prim and proper or dignified and unruffled, but rather in his making his own decisions. In this respect what is fundamental about a person is radically different from what is fundamental, for example, about a dog. I have a dog. I don't expect him to make decisions: When I tell him to sit or to stay I expect him just to do it, not to decide. And, indeed, the way I have treated my dog, which seems to be a good way to treat a dog, is to train him to respond in a more or less mechanical way to certain commands. Now that, it seems to me, is to give a dog a very good place in life, at least as we have arranged it. However, to treat a human being that way is an affront to his dignity as a human being, just because it is essential to a human being that he have a kind of dignity or "autonomy," as Kant put it.

The right to one's body and the right to autonomy are undoubtedly the most fundamental natural rights of persons, but there are subsidiary ones that deserve mention as part of the background for our discussion of violence. One of these stems from the right to autonomy. It is characteristic of human action to be purposive and to have results and consequences, and freedom therefore is normally conceived as involving not only the right to decide what to do but also the right to dispose of or cope with the consequences of one's action. One aspect of this right is the right to the product of one's labor, which has played an important role in the theory of both capitalism and communism. Both Marx and Locke, in two entirely different traditions as we think of it nowadays, have a labor theory of economic value: that the inherent value of something is determined by the amount of labor that is required to produce it. It is one of the ironies of intellectual history that the right of persons to the product of their labor constitutes the basis for both Locke's defense of private property and Marx's attack on it. If we follow this line of thought to the extent that we consider one's property as an extension of his person, the scope of the concept of violence becomes greatly enlarged, perhaps in harmony with popular thought on the subject, at least on the part of propertied persons; but one should always bear in mind that a person can reconcile himself much more readily to loss of property than he can to loss of life.

If we say that the results of what a person does belongs to him, we should have in mind not only this kind of labor theory of value but also the more or less natural and expectable consequences of a person's action. One of Jean-Paul Sartre's most interesting plays, *Altona,* develops this theme. In this play Sartre depicts a young man who does things that would normally have very serious consequences, probably his death. At one time he defies the Nazis, at another time the American Military Government that is occupying the country. On both occasions his father intervenes and cuts him off from the normal, expected consequences of his actions, consequences which anybody else would have suffered. Sartre shows what an awful impact it has upon this man, as a person, to have the consequences of his actions cut off in this way. In the end this victim of paternalism is one of Sartre's rather hideous characters, sequestered in a room in the center of his father's grand mansion having hallucinations of crabs and visions of expiation.

Here then is an indication of what is involved in talking about the violation of a person, and it seems to me that violence in human affairs comes down to violating persons. With that in mind, let me turn now to discussion of the different types and forms of violence. Violence can be usefully classified into four different kinds based on two criteria, whether the violence is personal or institutionalized and whether the violence is overt or a kind of covert or quiet violence.

III

Overt physical assault of one person on the body of another is the most obvious form of violence. Mugging, rape, and murder are the flagrant "crimes of violence," and when people speak of the danger of violence in the streets it is usually visions of these flagrant cases that float before their minds. I share the general concern over the rising rate of these crimes, but at the same time I deplore the tendency to cast our image of violence just in the mold of these flagrant cases. These are cases where an attack on a human body is also clearly an attack on a person and clearly illegal. We must not tie these characteristics in too tight a package, for some acts of violence are intended as a defense of law or a benefit to the person whose body is beaten—e.g. ordinary police activity (not "police brutality")[1] and the corporal punishment of children by parents and teachers. The humbler cases are violence too, although the fact that policemen, teachers, and parents have socially defined roles which they invoke when they resort to violence indicates that these cases have institutional aspects that overshadow the purely personal ones. These institutional overtones make a great deal of difference but they cannot erase that there is violence done. Of course not all cases are so clear: I leave to the reader to ponder whether all sex acts are acts of violence, or just how to distinguish in practical terms those that are from those that are not. Whenever you do something to another person's body without his consent you are attacking not just a physical entity—you are attacking a person. You are doing something by force, so the violence in this case is something that is easily visible, has long been recognized as violence, and is a case of overt, personal violence.

In cases of war, what one group tries to do to another group is what happens to individuals in cases of mugging and murder. The soldiers involved in a war are responsible for acts of violence against "the enemy," at least in the sense that the violence would not have occurred if the soldiers had refused to act. (Of course some other violence might have occurred. But in any case I do not wish to try to assess blame or lesser evils.) The Nuremberg trials after World War II attempted to establish that individual soldiers are responsible morally and legally too, but this attempt overlooked the extent to which the institutionalization of violence changes its moral dimension. On the one hand an individual soldier is not acting on his own initiative and responsibility, and with the enormous difficulty in obtaining reliable information and making a timely confrontation of government claims, not even U.S. Senators, let alone soldiers and private citizens, are in a good position to make the necessary judgments about the justice of a military engagement. On the other hand a group does not have a soul and cannot act except through the agency of individual men. Thus there is a real difficulty in assigning responsibility for such institutional violence. The other side of the violence, its object, is equally ambiguous, for "the enemy" are being attacked as an organized political force rather than as individuals, and yet since a group does not have a body any more than it has a soul "the enemy" is attacked by attacking the bodies of individual men (and women and children). Warfare, therefore, because it is an institutionalized form of violence, differs from murder in certain fundamental respects.

Riots are another form of institutionalized violence, although their warlike character was not widely recognized until the publication of the report of the

[1] A persuasive account of the extent to which law itself can be a form of violence, rather than an alternative to it, is to be found in E. Z. Friedenberg's essay "A Violent Country" in the *New York Review*, October 20, 1966.

President's National Advisory Commission on Civil Disorders (the "Riot" Commission). In a riot, as in a war, there are many instances of personal violence, and some persons maintain that the civil disorders are basically massive crime waves. But on the other hand there is also much of a warlike character. One of the characteristics of the Watts riot, as any will know who have read Robert Conot's very interesting book, *The Rivers of Blood, Years of Darkness,* is that in that riot the people who were supposed to be controlling the situation, the Los Angeles police and their various reinforcements, simply did not know basic facts about the community. In particular they did not know who was the person who could exercise a sort of leadership if the group were left alone and that person's hand was strengthened. One incident illustrates the sort of thing that happened. A Negro policeman was sent in plain clothes into the riot area and told to call back into the precinct whenever there was anything to report. He was told, furthermore, not to identify himself as a policeman under any conditions for fear of jeopardizing himself. At one point, he tried to intervene when some cops were picking on just altogether the wrong person and he ended up getting cursed and having his head bashed in by one of his fellow members of the Los Angeles police force. The police were in such a state that they couldn't even refrain from hitting a Negro policeman who was sent on a plain-clothes assignment into that area. In effect, the Los Angeles police and their various allies conducted what amounted to a kind of war campaign. They acted like an army going out to occupy a foreign territory where they didn't know the people and didn't speak the language. The result was that their actions had the effect of breaking down whatever social structure there might have been. And the breakdown of the social structure then had the effect of releasing more and more overt violence. The military flavor of our urban disturbances has increased over the years, and 1967 saw the appearance not only of machine guns and automatic rifles but also of tanks and armored personnel carriers in Newark and Detroit, in what the Kerner Commission characterized as "indiscriminate and excessive use of force." For that reason the urban disorders that we've been having in recent summers are really a kind of institutionalized violence where there are two sides in combat with one another. It is quite different from a normal criminal situation where police act against individual miscreants.

Since these overt forms of violence are, on the whole, fairly easily recognized, let us go on to consider the other forms of violence, the quiet forms which do not necessarily involve any overt physical assault on anybody's person or property. There are both personal and institutional forms of quiet violence, and I would like to begin with a case of what we might call psychological violence, where individuals are involved as individuals and there are not social institutions responsible for the violation of persons that takes place. Consider the following news item.[2]

> PHOENIX, Ariz., Feb. 6 (AP)—Linda Marie Ault killed herself, policemen said today, rather than make her dog Beauty pay for her night with a married man.
> The police quoted her parents, Mr. and Mrs. Joseph Ault, as giving this account:

[2] *New York Times,* February 7, 1968.

Linda failed to return home from a dance in Tempe Friday night. On Saturday she admitted she had spent the night with an Air Force lieutenant.

The Aults decided on a punishment that would "wake Linda up." They ordered her to shoot the dog she had owned about two years.

On Sunday, the Aults and Linda took the dog into the desert near their home. They had the girl dig a shallow grave. Then Mrs. Ault grasped the dog between her hands, and Mr. Ault gave his daughter a .22-caliber pistol and told her to shoot the dog.

Instead, the girl put the pistol to her right temple and shot herself.

The police said there were no charges that could be filed against the parents except possibly cruelty to animals.

Obviously, the reason there can be no charges is that the parents did no physical damage to Linda. But I think your reaction might be the same as mine—that they really did terrible violence to the girl by the way they behaved in this situation. Of course one might agree that Linda did violence to herself, but that is not the whole account of the violence in this case. The parents did far more violence to the girl than the lieutenant, and the father recognized that when he said to a detective, "I killed her. I killed her. It's just like I killed her myself." If we fail to recognize that there is really a kind of psychological violence that can be perpetrated on people, a real violation of their autonomy, their dignity, their right to determine things for themselves, their right to be humans rather than dogs, then we fail to realize the full dimension of what it is to do violence to one another.

One of the most obvious transition cases between overt personal violence and quiet personal violence is the case of a threat. Suppose a robber comes into a bank with a pistol, threatens to shoot one of the tellers, and walks out with money or a hostage or both. This is a case of armed robbery, and we rightly lump it together with cases of mugging and assault, morally and legally speaking, even if everybody emerges from the situation without any bruises or wounds. The reason is that there is a clear threat to do overt physical violence. By means of such a threat a person very often accomplishes what he might otherwise accomplish by actual overt violence. In this case the robber not only gets as much loot but he also accomplishes pretty much the same thing with respect to degrading the persons he is dealing with. A person who is threatened with being shot and then does something which he certainly would never otherwise do is degraded by losing his own autonomy as a person. We recognize that in law and morals: If a person who is threatened with a revolver takes money out of a safe and hands it to the robber we don't say that the person who has taken the money out of the safe has stolen it. We say that the person acted under compulsion, and hence the responsibility for what is done does not lie with him but with the person who threatened him.

It is very clear, and very important, that in cases where there is a threat of overt physical violence that we acknowledge that a person acting under that sort of a threat loses his autonomy. Of course, he needn't surrender his autonomy: he could just refuse to hand over the loot. There can be a great deal of dignity in such a refusal, and one of the messages of Sartre's moral philosophy, his existentialism, is that whenever you act other than with full responsibility yourself for your own actions that you are acting in bad faith. Now that is a very demanding philosophy, but it is one which puts a great deal of emphasis upon autonomy and dignity in human action and is not to be lightly dismissed. Nevertheless we do not expect that people will act with such uncompromising strength and dignity. To recognize that people can be broken down by threats and other psychological pressures, as well as by physical attack, and that to have acted under threat or duress is as good an excuse before the law as physical restraints—these recognitions constitute acknowledgement of the pertinence of the concept of psychological violence.

Psychological violence often involves manipulating people. It often involves degrading people. It often involves a kind of terrorism one way or another. Perhaps these forms that involve manipulation, degradation and terror are best presented in George Orwell's book, *1984*. In that book the hero is deathly afraid of being bitten by a rat. He never is bitten by the rat, but he is threatened with the rat and the threat is such as to break down his character in an extraordinary way. Here what might be called the phenomenology of psychological violence is presented in as convincing a form as I know.

Apart from these cases of terror and manipulation and degradation there are certain other forms of psychological violence. One of the most insidious is what might be called the "Freudian rebuff."[3] The Freudian rebuff works something like this. A person makes a comment on the Vietnam war or on civil rights or on some other current topic. The person he is talking to then says, "Well, you're just saying that because of your Oedipal relations with your father." The original speaker naturally objects, "Don't be silly. Of course I had a father and all that. But look at the facts." And then he starts bringing out the journals and newspapers and presents facts and statistics from them. "You must have a terrible Oedipal complex; you're getting so excited about this." And the person then says, "Look, I've had some fights with my father, but I'm not hung-up on him, I just have normal spats and affection. I've read the paper and I have an independent interest in the civil rights question. It has nothing to do with my relations with my father." To which the response is, "Well, your denial just proves how deep your Oedipal complex is." This type of Freudian rebuff has the effect of what John Henry Newman[4] called "poisoning the wells." It gives its victim just no ground to stand on. If he tries to stand on facts and statistics, they are discounted and his involvement is attributed to Freudian factors. If he tries to prove that he doesn't have the kind of psychological aberration in question, his very attempt to prove that he doesn't have it is taken to be evidence that he does. He can't get out of the predicament. It is like a quagmire in which the victim sinks deeper no matter which way he moves. So long as the proffered definition of the situation is imposed on him, a person has no way to

---

[3] Of course this is an aspect of cocktail-party Freudianism rather than of psychoanalytic theory, and what Freud invented was not this little ploy but the concepts that were later distorted into it.

[4] In his famous debate with Charles Kingsley. See his *Apologia Pro Vita Sua*, conveniently available in a paperback edition, Garden City, N.Y., Doubleday, 1956.

turn: there is no possible sort of response that can extricate him from that charge laid upon him. To structure a situation against a person in such a manner does violence to him by depriving him of his dignity: no matter what he does there is no way at all, so long as he accepts the problem in the terms in which it is presented, for him to make a response that will allow him to emerge with honor.

Although this sort of cocktail-party Freudianism is not very serious in casual conversations where the definition of the situation can be challenged or the whole matter just shrugged off, it must be kept in mind that there are many forms of this ploy and that sometimes the whole life and character of a person may be involved. A classic literary and religious version is the dispute between Charles Kingsley and John Henry Newman in the 19th century, in which Kingsley challenged Newman's integrity and ended up losing his stature as a Protestant spokesman, and which is written up in fascinating detail in Newman's *Apologia*. A political variation is the Marxian rebuff where, of course, it is because of your class standing that you have such and such a view, and if you deny that the class standing is influencing you in that way your very denial shows how imbued you are with the class ideology. Between parent and child as well as between husband and wife there are variations of this ploy which turn around the identification (by one insistent party) of love with some particular action or other, so that the other party must either surrender his autonomy or acknowledge his faithlessness.

The cases where this sort of psychological violence are damaging are those where the person structuring the situation is in some position of special authority. Another form particularly virulent in urban schools—and probably suburban schools too—is the teacher's rebuff. An imaginative child does something out of the ordinary, and the teacher's response is that he is a discipline problem. It now becomes impossible for the child to get out of being a problem. If he tries to do something creative he will be getting out of line and thereby "confirm" that he is a discipline problem. If he stays in line he will be a scholastic problem, thereby "confirming" that he did not have potential for anything but mischief. The result is a kind of stunted person typical of schools in large urban areas, where it is common for a child to enter the public schools half a year behind according to standard tests. Such a child has undoubtedly been a discipline problem during this time and the teacher has spent her effort trying to solve the discipline problem and keep him from getting out of line— that is, from learning anything.[5]

This last variation of the psychological rebuff brings us to the fourth general category of violence, institutionalized quiet violence. The schools are an institution, and teachers are hired not so much to act on their own in the class-

---

[5] Among the many works commenting on this aspect of public education, I have found those of Edgar Friedenberg and Paul Goodman most instructive. See Paul Goodman, *Compulsory Miseducation*, New York, Horizon, 1964; Edgar Z. Friedenberg, *The Vanishing Adolescent*, Boston, Beacon Press, 1959, and *Coming of Age in America*, New York, Knopf, 1963.

room as to fulfill a predetermined role. Violence done by the teacher in the classroom may therefore not be personal but institutional, done while acting as a faithful agent of the educational system. The idea of such institutional violence is a very important one.

A clearer example of quiet institutional violence might be a well established system of slavery or colonial oppression, or the life of contemporary American ghettos. Once established such a system may require relatively little overt violence to maintain it. It is legendary that Southerners used to boast, "We understand our nigras. They are happy here and wouldn't want any other kind of life,"—and there is no reason to doubt that many a Southerner, raised in the system and sheltered from the recurrent lynchings, believed it quite sincerely. In that sort of situation it is possible for an institution to go along placidly, as we might say, with no overt disturbances and yet for that institution to be one that is terribly brutal and that does great harm to its victims and which, incidentally, at the same time brutalizes people who are on top, since they lose a certain measure of their human sensitivity.

There is more violence in the black ghettos than there is anywhere else in America—even when they are quiet. At the time of the Harlem riots in 1964 the Negro psychologist, Kenneth Clark, said that there was more ordinary, day-to-day violence in the life of the ghettos than there was in any day of those disturbances. I'm not sure exactly what he meant. The urban ghettos are places where there is a great deal of overt violence, much of it a kind of reaction to the frustrations of ghetto life. Fanon describes the similar phenomenon of the growth of violence within the oppressed community in the colonial situation in Algeria.[6] When people are suppressed by a colonial regime, when they lack the opportunities which they see other people, white people, around them enjoying, then they become frustrated and have great propensities to violence. The safest target for such angry, frustrated people are their own kind. The Algerians did their first violence to other Algerians, in part because it wasn't safe to do it to a Frenchman. And the same is largely true of the situation that has developed in our urban ghettos. It isn't safe for a person living in the ghettos, if he is feeling frustrated and at the point of explosion, to explode against somebody outside the ghetto; but he can do it to his kids, his wife, his brother and his neighbor, and society will tend to look the other way. So there is a good deal of overt violence in the black ghettos. Perhaps, that is what Clark meant.

But we also have to recognize that there is sometimes a kind of quiet violence in the very operation of the system. Bernard Lafayette, who has worked in urban areas for both the American Friends Service Committee and the Southern Christian Leadership Conference, speaks angrily of the violence of the status quo: "The real issue is that part of the 'good order of society' is the routine oppression and racism committed against millions of Americans every day. That is where the real violence is."[7] The fact is that there is a black ghetto in most American cities which operates very like any system of slavery. Relatively little

---

[6] Franz Fanon, *The Wretched of the Earth,* New York, Grove Press, 1966.

[7] In *Soul Force,* February 15, 1968.

violence is needed to keep the institution going and yet the institution entails a real violation of the human beings involved, because they are systematically denied the options which are obviously open to the vast majority of the members of the society in which they live. A systematic denial of options is one way to deprive men of autonomy. If I systematically deprive a person of the options that are normal in our society, then he is no longer in a position to decide for himself what to do. Any institution which systematically robs certain people of rightful options generally available to others does violence to those people.

Perhaps denying options would not do violence to people if each individual person was an island unto himself and individuality were the full truth about human life. But it is not. We are social beings. Our whole sense of what we are is dependent on the fact that we live in society and have open to us socially determined options. I am now writing. As I write I make many choices about what to say, some having to do with whole paragraphs, some with single words, and some with punctuation. These choices are dependent upon a social institution, language. Unless I knew the language, and unless there were a society of language speakers, I would have no options at all about what to say. The options opened to us by language are very important, but language is only one part of our society. There are many sorts of options which are open to us and important to us as individuals. It is how we act, how we choose with respect to socially defined options, that constitutes what we really are as human beings.

What we choose to do with respect to our socially defined options is much more important than which language or which system of property rights we inherit at birth—provided we have access to the options defined in the system. By suppressing options you deprive a person of the opportunity to be somebody because you deprive him of choices. The institutional form of quiet violence operates when people are deprived of choices in a systematic way by the very manner in which transactions normally take place, without any individual act being violent in itself or any individual decision being responsible for the system.

These, then, are the main types of violence that I see. By recognizing those types of violence we begin to get the whole question of violence into a much richer perspective than when we hear the Chief of Police deplore violence. Such a richer perspective is vitally necessary, because we cannot do anything about the violence in our society unless we can see it, and most of us do not see it very well. Conceptions and perceptions are closely dependent on one another, and perhaps having a better idea of what violence is will enable us to recognize more readily the many sorts of violence that surround our lives.

IV

In concluding I would like to call attention to two aspects of violence. The first is that the concept of violence is a moral concept, but not one of absolute condemnation. Very often psychologists and sociologists and other scientists and students of animal behavior avoid the word "violence" just because it does have a moral connotation. The word "aggression" is sometimes used instead in some of the literature in psychology, and it is prominent in the title of Konrad

Lorenz's recent book on animal behavior and aggression.[8] They choose this word "aggression" because it lacks the moral connotations of the term "violence." I think it is important to recognize that the concept of violence is a moral concept, and that the moral elements come in through the fact that an act of violence is a violation of a person. I think that it is also important to recognize that the normal pattern of moral discourse allows for excuses and rationalization. We don't expect people never to do anything which is at all wrong: we allow for excuses.[9] Sartre's very hard line, that excuses undermine the dignity and moral strength of the person being excused, has not really won the day in law courts or in the general moral view; or perhaps what Sartre meant is that we should never allow ourselves excuses rather than that we should never allow them to others. When a person commits an act of violence he is not necessarily to be condemned, though he does have some explaining to do. The fact that we would require an excuse from him, or some justification of his behavior, indicates that a person's doing an act of violence puts the burden of proof on him; but it doesn't suffice to show that the case has gone against him yet.

The second thing I want to say is that it is entirely clear to me that there are degrees of violence. All these various forms of violence are indeed violence, but if I simply say of an act or an institution that it is violent I have not yet said enough to give a clear evaluation of that act. I must also take account of how *much* violence it does to persons affected. Unfortunately this is easier said than done. It might at first be thought that overt violence is always worse than quiet violence, but that rule does not hold generally except in the case of murder; in fact, physical injury often heals more readily than psychological damage. It is more plausible to argue that institutional violence is always of greater harm than personal violence, but that obviously depends on the degree of violence on each side—which means that we must be able to judge the degree of violence in an act or an institution independent of the kind of violence involved. What we need is a scale for measuring degrees of violence, and we don't have one. Still there are degrees of violence, and it is possible to achieve considerable inter-subjective agreement about comparisons of pairs of cases.

[8] A classic study in psychology is John Dollard et al., *Frustration and Aggression,* New Haven, Yale, 1939. See also A. Buss, *The Psychology of Aggression,* New York, Wiley, 1961; K. Lorenz, *On Aggression,* New York, Harcourt Brace, 1966.

[9] The late Prof. John L. Austin called the attention of moral philosophers to the importance of excuses in moral discourse. See "A Plea for Excuses," *Philosophical Papers,* London, Oxford University Press, 1961.

The Justification of Violence

ROBERT AUDI

Robert Audi (1941–   ) teaches philosophy at the University of Texas. He was a Woodrow Wilson fellow and received an award for his article on violence from the Council for Philosophical Studies.

Violence is the physical attack upon, or the vigorous physical abuse of, or vigorous physical struggle against, a person or animal; or the highly vigorous psychological abuse of, or the sharp, caustic psychological attack upon, a person or animal; or the highly vigorous, or incendiary, or malicious and vigorous, destruction or damaging of property of potential property.

. . .

In discussing the justification of violence I shall be primarily concerned with the sorts of considerations relevant to deciding whether its use is morally justified. After outlining what some of these considerations are, I shall go on in the next section to show some of their implications for various important views, most of them well known, about the conditions under which violence is morally justified.

The moral position I shall propose will be quite general. This should not be surprising: if I have been correct about how many ways there are in which people can do violence, then we should not ask about the justification of violence in the abstract; we must consider what kind of violence is in question, and this forces us to examine a very wide range of actions and activities. I shall be primarily concerned, however, with violence contemplated as a strategy for achieving social reform, particularly where the reform envisaged is regarded as the rectification of grave moral wrongs, and even where revolution is considered necessary to achieve the reform. At the present time, violence of this sort is perhaps more controversial than any other sort, though the question of the conditions, if any, under which one nation is justified in making war on another is also important and difficult. The position I shall take on the justification of violence will, I hope, provide a way of dealing with this latter question; but I shall not have space to address it explicitly. The question of the justification of violence in purely personal affairs is also an important one; but I shall only outline how my position would lead us to deal with the question.

In discussing the justification of violence as a strategy for achieving social reform, we must first recognize considerations of justice: as virtually everyone would grant, to say that a strategy, policy, or course of action would be unjust is to produce a moral consideration against it, one which is normally—and perhaps always—morally conclusive. It is equally clear that to say that something would be just is to produce a moral consideration in favor of it. . . .

Source: Robert Audi, "On the Meaning and Justification of Violence," in *Violence,* ed. by Jerome Shaffer (New York: 1971), pp. 59–60, 74, 75, 76–77, 80, 83–97. Copyright © 1971 by Robert Audi. Reprinted by permission of David McKay Company, Inc.

In addition to considerations of justice we must also recognize, in discussing the justification of violence as a strategy for achieving social reform considerations of freedom: whether the use of violence would enhance or diminish human freedom. . . .

The third consideration relevant to the justification of violence as a strategy for achieving social reform, is what we may roughly call welfare: that some action or program of action increases human happiness, and especially that it reduces human suffering, is a consideration which is nearly always relevant to any moral assessment of it. . . .

. . .

. . . It is worth making at least a very rough distinction between personal and social violence: personal violence has nonpolitical motives and is perpetrated by a single person or small group of persons against another person or small group; social violence is violence by a group of people, almost always directed against the state or against another group of people, and usually perpetrated for political reasons. A person's shooting an acquaintance would usually be a paradigm of personal violence; a large riot resulting in extensive personal injury would be a paradigm of social violence. It seems somewhat unnatural to speak of violence done by one army to another as social violence, and it is probably better to call this simply military violence, though it is certainly social as opposed to personal. We also need to distinguish between violence to persons and violence to property or other inanimate things; and it is important to distinguish homicidal from nonhomicidal violence; and morally injurious violence—violence which violates someone's rights—from morally excusable violence, that is, violence which does not violate anyone's rights, as in the case of most violent athletic contests. Perhaps we should also distinguish hand-to-hand violence, as in the case of a fist fight, from violence "at a distance"—such as sniping, shelling, and bombing. There also seems to be an important difference between defensive and offensive violence, the former being violence undertaken on a reasonable belief that using it is necessary to protect one's moral rights, the latter being violence undertaken in order to subjugate someone or otherwise violate his moral rights. But this is a very difficult distinction to draw, nor do defensive and offensive violence seem to exhaust the possibilities of violence, since spontaneous violence might well be of neither kind.

What seems of greatest philosophical interest at present among the kinds of violence just mentioned is social violence, both to people and to property, homicidal and nonhomicidal, defensive and offensive, and whether hand-to-hand or done at a distance. In particular, I am concerned with the justifiability of such forms of violence in civil disobedience, in resistance, in revolution, and in attempts to achieve social progress that cannot be placed in any of these three categories. In discussing each case I shall appeal primarily to the three moral principles outlined above, and I shall proceed from arguing the inadequacy of various mistaken views about the justifiability of violence to some constructive suggestions about its use in civil disobedience, resistance, revolution, and social reform. Although the discussion will be focused on violence, what I have to say will have important application to questions concerning the justification of force as a strategy for achieving social reform and to various other moral questions concerning policies of social action.

This is not meant to suggest that the principles proposed have no application to the justification of personal violence; as moral principles of the most general sort, at least one of them should have an indirect bearing on any moral issue. But in a great many cases, particularly in deciding what moral obligations one individual has to another individual of his acquaintance, their bearing is very often only indirect: they may be appealed to in justifying the subsidiary moral principals which "govern" much of our conduct toward other individuals; but a great many of our typical obligations toward other individuals, for example, to do what we have promised to do, have their immediate basis in these more specific principles. To apply this to a case of personal violence, imagine a man who is contemplating beating his wife. My position does not imply that in deciding whether it would be right to do this he is free to appeal directly to the three general principles; as the wording of the principles suggests, they are intended to apply primarily to policies, strategies, practices, and other general prescriptions of conduct. Their rigorous application to the kind of case imagined would, I think, support the principle that (possibly with a few very special exceptions) we ought not to beat people. I would also hold, though I cannot argue for it here, that my principles would support both some form of the ordinary moral principles requiring truth-telling and promise-keeping, and the ordinary moral conviction that people in certain special relations to others, such as parents and children, acquire special obligations. None of this implies that it is never morally right to call ordinary moral principles into question; the point is simply that in deciding what is morally obligatory or permissible in our relations with other individuals, we cannot bypass moral principles ordinarily relevant to the kind of situation in question, though where two such principles conflict, we may in most cases appeal to one or more of the three general principles.

Let us take first the extreme view that no one is ever justified in using violence. The natural thing to say here is that if violence is necessary to stop a Hitler from carrying out his planned atrocities, then it should be used. Most people would find it hard to deny this, but advocates of nonviolence might well argue that in fact it is never necessary to use violence, even to stop a man like Hitler, particularly if nonviolent protests are used at the first signs of evil. Although I find this claim highly implausible, neither a philosopher nor anyone else can assess it, as applied to an actual case, without a thorough analysis of the facts regarding various societies. But what chiefly needs to be said here is that it is certainly conceivable that a man like Hitler might be stopped only through violence; and insofar as there is good reason to think that only violence can stop him, the use of at least some violence, especially non-homicidal violence aimed at bringing about a coup or forcing the needed change in social policy, might obviously be justified by the moral principles to which I am appealing.

Another extreme position would be that violence is always justified if it is the most efficient means of throwing off oppression or rectifying some other form of injustice. This position seems almost as implausible as the first: clearly injustice and suffering created by the violence might substantially outweigh the burden of using a less efficient means of reform. Suppose that nonviolent protest could bring down an oppressive but unstable regime in a somewhat longer time than would be required by the use of violence. If it were evident that the violence would probably involve suffering and deaths, the nonviolent protest would almost certainly be preferable. Here it is important to mention something which seems both obvious and important, but which is much too rarely taken into account in discussions of violence and revolution: that there is simply no way to compare with any precision the moral "cost" of taking a man's life, especially an innocent man's life, with the moral value of reducing suffering or eliminating oppression or some other form of injustice. No doubt there is a level of atrocity at which almost anyone would say—and could justifiably say—that there is so much oppression, injustice, or suffering that if, in order to improve the situation substantially, we have to do something that might well take an innocent man's life we ought still to do it. To be sure, if it is a certainty that some innocent person must die, particularly if his identity is known, the situation becomes even more problematic and violence would be much more difficult—perhaps impossible—to justify. It seems clear that in deciding whether to use violence that might result in death, especially the death of someone not guilty of whatever wrong must justify the use of violence in the first place, we have to make every possible effort to find a nondeadly alternative; and we should be extremely careful not to exaggerate the moral outrage that requires rectification, particularly if we regard ourselves as the victims. But there is no simple way, perhaps no way at all, to answer the question how to weigh the taking of lives, especially of people innocent or largely innocent of the moral wrongs we want to rectify, against the moral gains we might make through their rectification. The principles of justice, maximization of freedom, and maximization of welfare suggest why this should be so; for how can we say how much injustice we do to a man in taking his life, or how much freedom or happiness we deprive him of? Given that the preservation of human life is of very great moral value on almost any moral outlook, and certainly on the principles proposed above, this is surely one of the most powerful arguments that can be brought against most of the typical uses of violence.

Two other views that deserve mention are (a) that violence of the sort we are concerned with—social violence done out of a genuinely moral desire to achieve social change—cannot be justified unless all channels of nonviolent protest have been exhausted, and (b) that violence is never justified in a democratic society. Regarding (a), it is not clear that there usually *is* any definite number of channels of nonviolent protest, or what it takes to exhaust a channel of protest. Yet even assuming that there were a definite number and that we could exhaust them, this might take so long and allow so much moral wrong in the meantime that some degree of nonhomicidal violence, and especially violence to property, would be warranted if it could be reasonably argued to be necessary to rectifying the moral wrongs in question. If nonviolent means of eliminating oppressive curfews and arbitrary travel restrictions, or of providing a minority group with the rights of citizens, would take many years, whereas damaging a few non-residential buildings could achieve the needed changes in a few months or a year, the latter course could perhaps be justified by the principles of justice, maximization of freedom, and maximization of welfare. This point depends, of course, not only on the view that violence is not "by definition" unjustifiable, but also on the view that certain kinds of damage to property constitute violence; yet I believe I have argued adequately for these views in defending my analysis of the concept of violence. I would not claim, however, that a situation of the sort envisaged here is probable; more important, I am certainly not denying that there is a strong prima facie obligation to try a reasonable amount of nonviolent protest before using violence, nor would I claim that we can usually be at all sure that social violence can be prevented from becoming homicidal. But even the minimal claims I have made suggest that we cannot reasonably hold that violence is never justified unless all channels of nonviolent protest have been exhausted.

Regarding (b), the thesis that social violence of that sort that concerns us is never justified in a democratic society, I would first want to say that much depends on what we mean by "democratic." If it means something like "such that political power lies in the hands of the people," then the thesis is surely false. For the majority of people in a society could be, and indeed at times have been, deceived into accepting or voting for measures whose injustice might in some cases be eradicable only by violent, though not necessarily homicidal, protest. If, on the other hand, "democratic" is used, as it often is nowadays, in such a way that a society is not considered democratic unless certain moral rights are guaranteed and the government has a certain minimum concern for the welfare of the citizens, then there is no clear answer to the question whether violence is ever justified in a democratic society. For it is not clear that the term "democratic," used this way, would ever apply to a society in which the three principles I am appealing to are seriously violated. In any case, the general position I want now to propose should enable us to deal with the issues concerning the justification of violence regardless of the kind of political system with respect to which they arise.

What I propose is that in deciding whether violence would be justified in a given case in which it is being considered as a means of correcting certain grave moral wrongs, we should ascertain its probable consequences for justice, freedom, and human welfare, and compare these with the probable consequences of the most promising nonviolent alternative(s) we can think of on careful reflection, choosing the course of action which satisfies, or comes closest to satisfying, the requirements of the principles of justice, maximization of freedom, and maximization of welfare. The restriction to cases in which violence is being considered as a means of correcting certain grave moral wrongs is important: these would have to be cases in which a serious attempt has been made, or at least considered, to solve the problem through legal or other nonviolent procedures; and they would usually be cases of serious injustice, such as deprivations of freedom, though certain other serious moral wrongs—such as a government's neglecting the welfare of its people—might sometimes justify the consideration of some forms of violence. It would certainly not do to say that, regardless of the moral grievance and regardless of whether nonviolent means have been tried, it is morally legitimate to consider using violence; and while I believe this sort of restriction would follow from the principles I am using, it seems best to include it at the outset in the interest of explicitness and brevity.

It is important to reemphasize my position that considerations of justice and freedom have priority over considerations of welfare. In comparing violent and nonviolent strategies of reform, our first concern should be to determine what would establish, or come closest to establishing, justice and the maximum freedom possible within the limits of justice. Secondarily, we should consider the consequences for welfare of adopting a violent as opposed to a nonviolent strategy; but these considerations could be decisive only where the more fundamental considerations weighed equally in favor of some violent and some nonviolent strategy, or perhaps, with the qualifications suggested earlier, where a huge gain in welfare is balanced against a minor injustice. Suppose that a group of young men who have vigorously protested the Vietnam War have very good evidence that records of their public protests are being kept by their draft boards and will be used unfairly against them, say in drafting them as a punitive measure. They might face the alternatives of violently breaking into the office and burning all its records or, on the other hand, taking the case to the courts. My point here would be that the most important consideration should be what is required by the principles of justice and freedom; and as I see it they would here require, assuming there is legal recourse for the grievance, that efforts be made to take the case to the courts: for the men to violate laws which the great majority of others respect and obey, often with considerable sacrifice, would be a prima facie violation of the requirement that benefits and burdens be distributed equally, and hence a prima facie injustice; and breaking into the office would be, prima facie, an unjustified violation of others' rights and an interference with their freedom to carry out their regular jobs. Even if it could be shown that all concerned would be happier if the men simply broke into the office and burned the records, this would not be a substantial consideration in favor of the violent alternative, and it is worth pointing out that the publicity which injustice receives from court proceedings is often an important step toward reform, even if the case is initially lost and sometimes when it is lost in the highest courts.

Let us now complicate the example by supposing that the men go to the very highest court and lose. What now should they do? Much depends on whether they lost the principle that punitive use of the draft is unjust or simply failed to win the point that their draft board was planning it. Suppose they lose the latter point. What then? For one thing, this may indicate some weakness in their evidence against their draft board; secondly, in many societies, nonviolent resistance would in this case be both the morally courageous course of action and most likely to arouse the conscience of people who might help. If, on the other hand, we suppose that the men's evidence against their draft board is of the sort a reasonable man would consider conclusive, but that they lost because their witnesses were afraid to testify, then the case becomes even more problematic. One consideration not yet mentioned would be the kind and degree of immorality of the war for which they were to be drafted; another would be what they might be able to do by some new nonviolent attempt to expose those who have perpetrated the injustice against them and their witnesses. There are other considerations, and I cannot now go into sufficient detail to try to settle the question, though perhaps enough has been said to suggest that the kind of limited violence envisaged here is not obviously impossible to justify under any circumstances whatever, even if it does appear that in a country like America today nonviolent protest would be morally preferable. The case would have been equally complicated had we supposed that, in the highest court of the land, the men had lost the principle that punitive use of the draft, especially against political dissenters, is unjust. Here we would have an even larger issue which might well warrant the consideration, though not necessarily the adoption, of revolution.

There are, of course, a number of difficulties confronting the view I propose regarding the justification of violence. I have already mentioned the impossibility of weighing with any precision the moral cost of taking a human life, especially an innocent life, against moral gains in justice, freedom, and welfare. But this is likely to be a serious problem for any plausible position on the justification of violence, and we can at least say that there is one kind of case in which some weighing might be possible: when the risks to human life of undertaking violence can be compared with the risks to it of abstaining from violence. Thus, if violence that would probably cost about a hundred lives could be shown necessary to save thousands, it would presumably be justified if it did not have certain other morally undesirable consequences such as the brutalization of a large number of people.

Secondly, there are profound difficulties in measuring justice or injustice, freedom or its curtailment, and happiness or suffering. It would be wrong to conclude, however, that there are not even rough standards which are in practice very useful. While the notions of equality and of a justified exception to the principle that men should be treated equally are vague, it is nonetheless clear that denying various civil liberties on grounds of color is not a justified inequality, whereas denying voting privileges to children is; and a great many injustices, particularly those serious enough to warrant the consideration of violence, are equally obvious. Moreover, even if we grant that there is an area of reasonable disagreement concerning a large number of freedoms, there is wide agreement on such fundamental freedoms as freedom of speech, freedom of worship, and freedom of personal movement; and these are the sorts of freedoms whose curtailment would be appealed to in most cases in which considerations of freedom might warrant the use of violence.

Finally, it is clear that there are rough indices of suffering and happiness which make possible at least judgments about the suffering or happiness of one person or group as compared to that of another or to their own suffering or happiness at different times: we can consider disease as opposed to physical well-being; psychological well-being (insofar as this can be measured without indulging any moral prejudice); poverty as opposed to comfortable income; observations and subjective reports of pain, tension, and malaise, as opposed to observations and subjective reports of zest, comfort, and satisfaction; and proportion of things done or submitted to that are wanted as opposed to unwanted.

Let me now comment briefly on the implications of my position for the use of violence in civil disobedience, resistance, revolution, and social reform. To begin with civil disobedience, one may reasonably question whether there is any kind of violence with which it is logically compatible. Certainly in the clear cases of civil disobedience the protest is both nonviolent and orderly; and if we think of civil disobedience as undertaken in protest against some particular law(s), but out of respect for law as an institution, one may well question whether violence could be a part of it. Suppose, that a group of students decided to block the pathway of some unarmed fellow students engaging in military drill and soon to go to war; and suppose the protesters were unarmed and planned not to use violence. If violence broke out but remained on the level of mild fisticuffs, with the protesters fighting only defensively, and if the protesters were willing to accept punishment if the courts demanded it, would we have to say that they had not succeeded in practicing civil disobedience? The answer to this question does not seem to be simply that they did not succeed, though it perhaps would be if, even without having planned to use violence, the protesters did initiate it. Civil disobedience requires that those practicing it be making a reasoned attempt to appeal to the conscience of others; they must not be attempting to impose their will on others through the use of force, which they would certainly be doing if violence were a calculated part of civil disobedience. On the other hand, if violence "spontaneously" breaks out, particularly where the protesters fight only defensively, it is entirely possible that we could speak of their having succeeded in committing civil disobedience. Perhaps we could say that in certain cases civil disobedience may be accompanied by violence, even on the part of those committing the disobedience, but the violence must not have been calculated; nor can a protest count as civil disobedience if the protesters respond to violence with substantially greater violence than is required for self-defense. If violence has any place in civil disobedience, then, it seems to be a very minor and restricted one.

The case with resistance is different, and what chiefly needs to be said here is that there is no moral justification for the use of large-scale social violence except where injustice or some other form of moral wrong is very serious and where nonviolent means of rectification have been carefully considered and, if possible, attempted. It seems reasonable to maintain that justice, maximization of freedom, and maximization of welfare should be the guiding principles; and they should be applied in the light of questions like the following: What are the chances of death and in how many cases? How many are likely to suffer violence, and what sort of violence would it be—bodily violence or violence to property? To what extent are those who use violence likely to be brutalized by it or come to use it indiscriminately, either at the time in question or at a later time? How much violence is likely to be evoked as a *response* to the violence being considered? Of those who may suffer violence, how many are guilty of creating or perpetuating the moral wrongs which might justify the violence, and how many are innocent or largely innocent in this respect? How effective will the contemplated violence be in rectifying the wrongs it is meant to reduce or remove? Is the immorality which might warrant violence getting worse or better, and what is the likelihood of dealing with it nonviolently in a reasonable length of time? Is violence to be definitely planned, or is it simply to be approved should certain circumstances arise?

Questions like these seem to be equally relevant to the justifiability of attempting a revolution. But since revolution almost necessarily requires very extensive violence, even greater care must be taken in attempting to justify it. The questions I suggest we ask in considering whether to use violence are very difficult; and it is not surprising that many of them have not been faced, much less answered, by advocates of violence. Yet it is only through rigorously pursuing these and similar questions that we can weigh the consequences for justice, freedom, and welfare, of using a violent as opposed to a nonviolent method of moral rectification, and decide whether the best course of action would be nonviolent protest within the law, civil disobedience, resistance, or revolution, which is likely to require widespread and deadly violence.

Regarding the use of violence to achieve social reforms that do not qualify as the correction of injustice—such as certain improvements in state services or in the material well-being of large groups of people—it seems reasonable to say that particularly where material well-being is already at a level representing a secure and not uncomfortable life, any appreciable violence to persons could not be justified. For even assuming that there is no legal or other nonviolent way of achieving the goal, violence would probably require injustice to someone, and I am supposing that the gains in happiness that might result would not outweigh the injustice done. Suppose that a highway, which was a mere convenience to a large number of people, would have to go through a place where some American Indians who had been living there for generations were determined to stay unless bodily ejected. If we assume that neither they nor the larger community has a clear right in the dispute, probably the state would not be justified in using violence (or even force) to remove them, even if the convenience to the community could be reasonably claimed to outweigh substantially the inconvenience to them. Of course, if the disparity between what the community stands to gain and what a few stand to lose in being forced, violently if necessary, to comply with the community's wishes, becomes very great, the issue becomes more complex and we may being to ask how much convenience a small group has a *right* to deny to a much larger group, especially to the community as a whole. In this case the minority's insistence on what it wants could be unjust, since it could be an interference with the community's freedom to do what it has a right to do; but it still seems clear that, with perhaps very few exceptions, if gains in happiness which do not represent what anyone has a right to should require violence to persons, the violence should not be used. For surely it is reasonable to give considerations of justice very high priority over considerations of welfare, as I have already suggested in discussing possible conflicts among the three moral principles proposed; and doing violence to someone, at least violence of the sort relevant here, unless it can be shown to be required to rectify some serious injustice, is certainly doing him an injustice.

The Ethics of Revolution

KAI NIELSEN

Kai Nielsen (1928–   ), professor of philosophy at the University of Toronto, has written a great deal in the areas of religion and social-political philosophy. Among his books are *Reason and Practice* (1971) and *Scepticism* (1973).

> It was said long ago that politics is the art of the possible. That does not suppress our initiative: since we do not *know* the future, we have only, after carefully weighing everything, to push in our direction. But that reminds us of the gravity of politics; it obliges us, instead of simply forcing our will, to look hard among the facts for the shape they should take.
> —Merleau-Ponty
> When a great social revolution shall have mastered the results of the bourgeois epoch, the market of the world and the modern powers of production, and subjected them to the common control of the most advanced peoples, then only will human progress cease to resemble that hideous pagan idol, who would not drink the nectar but from the skulls of the slain.
> —Marx

I

What are the degrees of moral outrage by a government which justifies resistance by violent, and also by illegal, means? One would be where our basic liberties were being taken from us and where we had no effective legal or nonviolent means of redress. If we were deprived or were being deprived of such basic liberties as freedom of speech and assembly, the right to stand for public office, liberty of conscience and freedom of thought, including the right to print, circulate and promulgate our beliefs, and there was no effective legal or nonviolent, non-legal way, such as by civil disobedience, to correct this situation, then we would be justified in violent rebellion or revolution, if we could not be so acting bring on even a greater injustice and/or more suffering all around.

However, while this is one standard situation in which persons would be justified in resistance to a government—indeed here a tyranny—by violent means, this is not the only situation in which revolutionary activity would be justified. The other situation is where one class, a ruling, small elite, runs society (including, of course, the government) in its own interests and exploits another class or group making up the vast majority of the people. In short, in Marx's terms where we have a ruling class of capitalists exploiting and oppressing proletarians (who are the vast majority of the people), then, when they reasonably can without bringing about even greater all around misery and injustice, they should make a socialist revolution.

The qualification in both cases about "greater injustice and/or more suffering all around" and "even greater all around misery and injustice" is crucial and we

Source: Kai Neilsen, "On the Ethics of Revolution," *Radical Philosophy* 6 (1974), pp. 17–18. Reprinted by permission of *Radical Philosophy* and the author.

should be quite clear about what is intended here. I think, as Marcuse has recognized, that here we must make rough historical calculations about the consequences of revolution and about the consequences of continued acquiescence in an exploitative and repressive *status quo*.[1] My claim is that, where practically feasible, a socialist revolution would be justified where by making it less suffering for the mass of mankind would obtain and greater satisfaction of desire would occur and where this would obtain under the constraints of—be compatible with—a form of egalitarian justice, namely a system of justice committed to the following two Rawlsian principles: (1) that each person has an equal right to the most extensive equal liberties and opportunities compatible with similar liberties and opportunities for all and (2) that inequalities in liberty are justified, as hopefully temporary necessary evils, only when and to the extent that they are in everyone's advantage and most particularly they must be to the advantage of the least advantaged stratum of society.[2] The addition of such a principle of justice is necessary, for if the revolution were to lessen suffering (when everything was considered) only slightly over a previous state of affairs— but to do so at the expense of an enhanced suffering for a small oppressed but relatively powerless *Lumpenproletariat,* say Metis, Indians or Blacks, then that revolution would not be justified. When the general conditions I have characterized obtain, and it is practically feasible, then and only then is revolution justified.

II

What I would now like to do is to turn to an examination of criticisms of such a cryptically drawn view. There is first an objection which might come from a certain sort of revolutionary. We would say that all such calculations of consequences are far too unrealistic. When we look back, from our historical vantage point, on the French Revolution, we can indeed say that its long range effects were in sum beneficial to humankind: the sum total of human oppression and suffering was lightened. We can see that, the objector grants, but just before the revolution, during the revolution and during the early reactionary restorations the agents involved could not have known that. It is only from the long hindsight of a considerable historical distance that this could be known. What we can and must do, the objection would continue, if we are to be revolutionaries working for a socialist revolution and a truly humane socialist society, is to revolt when we can see around us intolerable conditions of repression and de-humanization. That is to say, in such circumstances we are to attempt to make a revolution against our oppressors. What we cannot and should not do in such a situation

[1] Herbert Marcuse, "Ethics and Revolution" in *Ethics and Society,* ed. by Richard T. De George (Garden City, New York: Anchor Books, 1966) Note, also in this connection, Eric Hobsbawm, "An Appraisal of Terrorism," *Canadian Dimension,* Vol. 9, No. 1 (October 1972), pp. 11–14.

[2] John Rawls, *A Theory of Justice* (Cambridge, Massachusetts: Harvard University Press, 1971), p. 60. I refer to them as "Rawlsian," for I have *slightly* altered their formulation from the formulation favoured by Rawls.

is to try to make calculations about the long term effects of our actions. It will only cripple our resolve to act.

I understand and indeed sympathize with the sentiment that goes into this. It is linked with a revulsion against injustice and inhumanity and tries to affirm one's sense of human dignity by refusing to acquiesce in one's own de-humanization or the de-humanization of those around one. And in such a situation, it stresses the necessity to act and to act with resolve. Yet there are many ways to resist tyranny and oppression and even personal rebellion is far short of the attempt at the mass overturn of the social order that goes with revolution.[3]

If people live in indignity and severe oppression and yet conditions are such that an attempt at revolution or revolt against their oppressors will only result in their increased oppression and indeed spread it, then it is irresponsible and, I believe, effectively counter-revolutionary to call at that time for the attempted seizure of power that goes with a revolution. Marx, correctly I believe, stressed the folly of trying to make a revolution before the socio-economic conditions were ripe and before the revolutionaries had a mass base. The Jacobins, he thought, made the crucial error of trying to impose by sheer force what was not yet inherent in their situation. It is true that a very cautious waiting for the time to be right may have the effect of endlessly putting off, through rationalization, revolutionary activity. It can, that is, be rationalized into a kind of waiting for Godot. And indeed that is a practical difficulty which needs to be faced squarely. But an awareness of this capacity for and indeed propensity towards rationalization can put one on guard against it. But it still remains the case, taking all accessible factors into consideration, that what we must do is to learn to make a realistic appraisal of the situation. While it is the case that we cannot know with any considerable exactitude the future consequences of such actions, it is also true that we are not entirely in the dark about them. If in the United States, ghetto Blacks were to attempt an armed uprising, we can rather safely predict the general consequences of such action. Any revolutionary programme which urged them at the present time to fight their oppression by an armed up-rising could only ensure that those Black revolutionaries would be crushed along with other progressive Blacks and that it would very likely be the case that even harsher oppressive measures would be directed against the Black population. Indeed it *might* have the spin off effect of raising the consciousness of Blacks, but this can be done by other means as well and it is also known that in parallel situations sometimes such harsh oppression, after an abortive uprising, only deepens despair and apathy and leads to an utter withdrawal from political struggle. The central point at issue here is that in some important circumstances at least, we can have some idea of the probable consequences of revolutionary activity. Certainty, or even anything like it, is not, of course, at issue, but this is generally true in the social arena. What we need to see is that while our under-standing is not of any high order here, it is often not the case that we simply

[3] I have tried exactly to characterize revolution in my "On the Choice Between Reform and Revolution," in *Philosophy and Political Action,* ed. by Virginia Held, Kai Nielsen and Charles Parsons (Toronto: Oxford University Press, 1972), pp. 21–28.

must take a kind of Kierkegaardian leap in the dark. That is, it need not be the case that we either have faith in the efficacy of revolution or we do not. It is indeed true that we should not let concern for certainty cripple practice but we need not and indeed should not view ourselves as simply responding to our heart-felt anguish at the spectacle of injustice and oppression and then rebelling quite independently of any calculations of our chances or of what our revolt would lead us into.

III

There is, ironically enough, a parallel objection to my account of justifying revolution which sometimes comes from conservatives but often comes from even left leaning people and indeed even extreme revisionists who have reluctantly come, after reflection on the costs of revolution and the horrors of war, to a principled commitment to always stick to reformism.[4] They renounce violence and revolutionary activity as an instrument of social change. They reject the idea that violence can be justified by beneficial results for the future; they reject the idea that violence is justified even if it does lead to the abolition of violence and to a more egalitarian and humane society.

One of the more interesting statements of this view comes from Leszek Kolakowski, a Polish "Marxist" revisionist.[5] (I do not use "revisionist" as a term of abuse.) Referring to a set of arguments by Merleau-Ponty, which bear some family resemblance to mine, Kolakowski argues that in deciding what is to be done "we would do well . . . to justify our decisions not by appeals to historical reason but only by the simplest moral considerations."[6] We should not think in terms of any philosophy of historical progress but we should reason in this domain with a scepticism about "grand schemes" concerning human liberation. Where such a revolutionary theory conflicts with our reflective, rock bottom moral responses, the theory, not our moral responses, should give way. Aguing in a way that resembles Prichard, Kolakowski contends that these simple moral considerations are more reliable than any ramified abstract moral arguments involving such historical moral calculations as the ones I have made above. We can be more confident, he tells us, that brotherhood and freedom will not emerge from mass terror, oppression and lies than we can be confident of any theory which makes predictions about the emergence of the second stage of communism from its first stage. We must, he argues, encourage scepticism about such claims of a necessary human development and above all we must undermine naive beliefs in the universal efficacy of violence to improve the human condition. We must rather take our stand as something which is morally speaking rock bottom in a commitment to the protection of the most basic human rights and decencies.

[4] J. M. Cameron, "The Ethics of Violence," in *The New York Review of Books,* Vol. XV, No. 1 (July 2, 1970), pp. 24–32.

[5] Leszak Kolakowski, "Merleau-Ponty and Communist Terror," in No. 4 (September 3, 1970), pp. 23–24.

[6] Ibid., p. 24.

We must remember that Kolakowski writes out of a deep first hand experience with Stalinism and we should also, I believe, acknowledge that he is most probably right in his belief that brotherhood and freedom will not emerge from mass terror, oppression and lies. But why assume that a commitment to a revolutionary strategy commits one to anything like that or even tolerates it? Marx repeatedly criticized terrorism. The use of terror, lies and propaganda are only desperate devices used in an attempt to impose a revolution from above when the conditions for its occurrence are not ripe. Moreover, we should remember that the terrible experiences of the Russian Revolution have not been the general run of socialist revolutions: contrast the Russian Revolution with the Chinese, Cuban and Yugoslavian Revolutions. The revolution in Indo-China is the hell and slaughterhouse it is, not because of socialist revolutionaries but because of the counter-revolutionary invasion first by the French and then by American imperialist forces. They are the ones who have devastated the country and murdered the population. We must not allow ourselves to be conned into an utter rejection of revolution as a possible humane alternative for social change and reconstruction by our awareness of the terrible toll of the Russian Revolution and its grotesque aftermath. There are not even nearly sufficient grounds for thinking that this is *the* model for revolution.

In arguing that a revolution is justified, if there are good reasons for believing that by making it less suffering and greater realization of human potential and happiness will be achievable in the long run, there is no commitment to or acquiescence in the methods of Stalinism that Kolakowski rightly decries. It is evident enough that lies only breed contempt and utter scepticism about human progress, that terror may push a population into line but that it will not produce co-operation and brotherhood, let alone socialist persons. But nothing of this Stalinism need be or should be part of a revolutionary programme for socialists.

What is more deeply involved in Kolakowski's argument is a steadfast and correct recognition of the evil of violence coupled with a scepticism concerning our knowledge of what will be the likely outcome of revolutionary actions. And surely it is right to see violence as an evil; for a person even to be a moral agent, he needs to recognize that to do violence to someone is to harm him and that this *always* stands in need of a special justification. But in addition one should recognize (a) that violence is not the only great evil in the world and that in deciding what to do, that evil must be counterbalanced against other evils, and (b) that in a situation in which a revolution could be made or would be justified, there would already exist in the oppression and degradation of human beings a vast amount of violence, namely a pervasive institutionally sanctioned violation of their persons.[7] We must remember that "violence in human affairs is more closely connected with the idea of violation than with the idea of force."[8] It is a situation in which our rights as persons are being violated —a situation where we do not have the right to decide our own futures or act

[7] Newton Garver, "What Violence Is," in *Moral Problems,* ed. by James Rachels (New York: Harper and Row, Publishers, 1971), pp. 242–43.

[8] Ibid., p. 242.

as self-directing human agents. In this connection, Merleau-Ponty has well said that "Communism does not invent violence but find it already institutionalized."

Kolakowski might respond that while this is indeed so, we are never justified in "fighting fire with fire" or "doing evil that good may come." But, if this is the way the argument goes, we have gone past anything which could reasonably be taken as a primitive moral certainty. Both the socialist revolutionary and Kolakowski agree that violence is an evil to be avoided wherever possible. But where they appear at least not to agree is about whether one may ever deliberately kill or resort to force to bring about socialism in a repressive society where repression and exploitation are rampant.[9] Kolakowski, like Popper, is willing to speak of a "justified and violent resistance to violence," which contrasts with "aggressive violence," which is not justified.[10] He suggests, though he does not actually assert, what Popper indeed claims, namely that the use of violence to bring about social change is never justified. Rather violence is only justified as a response to revolutionary violence.[11] What is crucial to see here is that this stance is a highly controversial moral stance. There could be no appeal here to a moral certainty which will be accepted by all reflective moral agents. (It is politically questionable as well for it has the effect of reinforcing the power of the *status quo*.)

In moral situations we are sometimes faced with an anguishing choice between evils, e.g. the mother or the child in a difficult birth, the terrible choices forced on the Jewish leaders in the Warsaw Ghetto, the choice between ten lives or a hundred. I suppose a Christian could, and some would, in some of these circumstances, say "It is all in God's hands" and forebear to do a lesser evil while knowingly allowing what they acknowledge is a greater evil. *Perhaps,* that is all right for a Christian or a man who believes in a God similar to the Christian God, but for one who does not, there is no other responsible act but to sometimes deliberately choose between evils, not wishing to "play God" or indeed even doing so, but acting as a morally responsible agent in a Godless world or at least in a world which seems to him or her on an honest appraisal to be Godless. And in choosing between evils what other alternative is there but to choose what seems, on a careful and non-evasive appraisal of things, to be the lesser evil? This is surely what I was doing in laying out what I take to be the logic of a justification for revolution. This could be upset, if it could be shown that we can never have a reasonable idea of the likelihood of the consequences in human harm or well being of making a revolution or failing to. But we do in some circumstances have some understanding of the likely consequences and under those conditions we can say when a revolution would or would not be justified. We surely, in most instances, anyway, cannot say this with certainty. But moral certainty is a rare bird in the moral life.

[9] Kolakowski, op. cit., p. 24. I may do Kolakowski an injustice here. His remarks are not very clear. He may still be more of a Marxist than the above reading would allow.

[10] Ibid.

[11] Karl Popper, *Conjectures and Refutations* (3rd ed. London: Routledge & Kegan Paul, 1969), pp. 355–63. I have criticized Popper's argument in my "On the Choice Between Reform and Revolution," op. cit. pp. 32–51. See also Roy Edgley's convincing criticism of Popper on this point in his "Reason and Violence," *Radical Philosophy* No. 4 (1973).

Crime

Humans violate one another's legally defined rights; sometimes these injure others; such illegal acts that injure others are called crimes; for these the state imposes punishments.

In this section the first two essays deal with the concept of crime and the difficulties in defining "crime" and so with the difficulty of determining which acts are crimes and which are not. The distinction is of crucial importance because crimes are punishable, and no one should be punished for an act that ought not to be considered a crime.

Blackstone defined a crime as "A crime or misdemeanour is an act committed or omitted, in violation of a public law either forbidding or commanding it." The emphasis here is on "act," which is criticized by Rollin Perkins in his book, *Criminal Law and Procedure.* Perkins argues (p. 1) that a person, D, may stab another, X. X might die from the stab wound six weeks later or might not because a surgeon happened along right after the stabbing and applied a suture. Now whichever resulted from the act of stabbing, death or continued life, the act of wielding the knife remains unchanged. But if X dies, the charge against D is murder; if X lives, the charge is unlawful wounding. Since the act is the same and the consequences tremendously different, according to Perkins, Blackstone's definition should be revised; instead of defining a crime in terms of the act, it should be defined in terms of the resultant harm. Perkins' definition of crime is: "A crime is any social harm defined and made punishable by law."

We normally make a distinction between an immoral act and a criminal act (identified as such by reference to the intention of the agent and to the consequences of the act), one difference being that criminal acts are defined and prohibited by laws; of course, a criminal act may also be immoral; but some acts are immoral that are not criminal. This leads us to ask: Given that the set of immoral acts is larger but includes the set of criminal acts, which immoral acts are to be designated criminal acts as well? This question shows that, although factual reference to laws may help us to decide which acts are considered criminal in a particular society, the laws do not help us to decide which *ought* to be considered criminal acts.

Let us remind ourselves of Garver's discussion of violence. The basic concept of violence is violation of a person; a person has rights to his or her body, decisions, and product of labor. We might define a criminal act as one that violates these. But, in fact, we know that some of the violations Garver discusses are not considered crimes. For example, he made some fairly extensive remarks about the institutional violence done to persons because they live in ghettos; however, there is no attempt to isolate those acts that violate people who live in ghettos; not having isolated them, we cannot specify which persons should be held responsible for those acts; hence, people who could be classified as criminals are not; they get off without being punished for their crimes.

Not only are some violations of persons not considered criminal, but even when they are, we find a disparity in punishment. *Forbes,* an investment magazine, pointed out this disparity when C. Arnhold Smith was given "the merest slap on the wrist" even though he is "one of the greatest swindlers of our time." Smith pleaded no contest to misdeeds leading to the loss of millions of dollars—a violation of persons' rights to the product of their labor—and was fined $30,000, to be paid at the rate of $100 a month, with no interest. A *Forbes* writer remarks: "If you rob a bank with a gun and take, say, $50,000, you go to jail. What happens if you rob it of say, a few million, but with a pen, not a gun? The apparent answer is: Next to nothing happens to you."

Why are some acts deserving to be classified as criminal not so classified, and why are criminals given such differential treatment? Because the law so defines and is so applied. But why? Here we are once again dealing with the state-law apparatus. Since laws are a product of a political state, law is a political product. The passage and application of laws are political acts. The answer to our question is to be found by inquiring about who wields dominant political power. If the power were possessed by ghetto residents, we might expect to have different laws from those we have now. Crime is a political concept. This is argued by **Stephen Schafer** in this section's first essay.

Schafer says, "When the political state power expresses its ideology, or value system, through the regulations of the criminal code, it determines the 'norms of action.' . . . The question of which specific values or interests are so protected is dependent upon the legislators, as the political agents of the state power who conceive and pass criminal laws. . . . Thus, all crimes may be qualified as political crimes." Schafer recognizes that by "political crime" people try to distinguish one kind from another "ordinary" kind of crime. He maintains that this is simply a matter of degree. He claims that "The stiff qualitative separation of ordinary and political crimes can be seen as diametrically opposed to the real purpose of criminal law. . . . As a matter of fact, all crimes are socially dangerous. . . . Indeed, criminal laws do not even distinguish between ordinary and political crimes, criminal codes just talk about crimes in general. . . . Shoplifting and robbery, for example, are criminal attacks against the value attached to private property. . . . The political nature of these crimes is only occasionally conspicuous; thus, these 'ordinary' crimes may be tentatively called 'relative political crimes.' . . . But where the unlawful battery of the criminal is aimed at the sum total of the lawfully prevailing ideology or value system or at least at one of its representative or critical institutions . . . the violation of the legal norm might be called an 'absolute political crime.' "

For Schafer, then, all crimes are political crimes; those with the greatest danger of subverting the value system are what are usually called "political crimes"; however, in fact, there is no qualitative difference between them. The absolute political criminal who commits treason, spies, rebels, foments revolution, sabotages, and so forth, can find little comfort from Schafer. Such a person tries to justify his or her acts to rally others to the cause or to arouse sympathy by claiming that the acts are attempts to bring about a juster state. (See the articles in the previous section justifying revolution.) Schafer denies that there is an absolute justice to which the absolute political criminal can appeal. "But the ruthless fact is that the social-political power has the monopolized authority to define justice. . . . The relativity of the concept of the political criminal rests with this relativity of justice." Until she or he has the power, the bank robber cannot claim to be a victimized "political prisoner."

Not only may a state err in its promulgation of laws because some acts that should be defined as crimes are not, but it may err also because some acts are defined as crimes that should not be. "Victimless crimes" is a phrase that is used to refer to acts that should not be considered crimes; thus the phrase is really a contradiction in terms; if an act is "victimless," it ought not be considered a "crime" because something is a crime only if it violates another person; but, since some acts are performed by two or more persons willingly, each giving their consent, no one has been violated; hence, the acts cannot be crimes. Of course, people who coined and use the phrase, such as **Edwin M. Schur,** the author of this section's second essay, understand this; "crime" refers to the fact that the acts they have in mind are defined as crimes by the law, even though they perhaps should not be.

Homosexual acts, prostitution, masturbation, underage sex, drug taking, incest, and so forth are examples often given of victimless crimes. Those who believe such acts should be considered crimes are often said to be trying to "legislate morals." This imposition is argued to be unfair as long as no one outside the transaction is harmed and as long as persons to the transaction consent; we have a right to choose our life-style without being dictated to by others who want to live differently; tolerance is a virtue that "blue noses" ought to take more seriously.

The line between victimless and victim crimes may not be easy to make because there are often difficult factual questions about the extent or existence of harm to others. We saw that Perkins' criticism of Blackstone's definition of crime turned on the notion of the consequence of an act. How far afield should our search for consequences go in determining if harm has been done by an act or if harm is being done to a person by branding his or her acts as crimes? Schur's discussion will be helpful to you in answering this question, a question you will want to answer because you may fairly regularly commit "victimless crimes."

You may have the opportunity of sitting on a jury sometime in your life, and may have to make a recommendation on the "fit" punishment for someone you have found guilty of a crime. How will you determine what a fit punishment is? Faced with this question, you would have to think about the concept of punishment, what its purpose is, and how its purpose is suited to the character of the person you have found guilty. "An eye for an eye" is one measure, but what if someone has robbed another at knife point of $25? You cannot have the victim rob the robber at knife point of $25. Returning the $25 does not seem equivalent. What is equivalent to the fear of being held at knife-point? Maybe that is not the important issue to think about, anyway. Maybe the aim of punishment is to prevent the robber and others from committing robbery. Which punishment will accomplish this, if any? Further, punishment is not the only preventive measure that might be taken. In fact, some other treatment than punishment might be a more effective prevention. Should you withhold punishment and administer the other treatment instead?

Lon Fuller's essay discusses and weighs four different theories of punishment and the difficulties with them. He quotes Norbert Wiener's expression of them: "Law seems to consider punishment, now as a threat to discourage other possible criminals, now as a ritual act of expiation on the part of the guilty man, now as a device for removing him from society and for protecting the latter from the danger of repeated misconduct, and now as an agency for the social and the moral reform of the individual."

Power and the Definition of "Crime"

STEPHEN SCHAFER

Stephen Schafer (1900–   ), an internationally known criminologist, is professor of law at Northwestern University. He is the author of many books, including *The Political Criminal* (1974).

Distinction Between Ordinary and Political Crimes

In the broadest sense, it may be argued that all crimes are political crimes inasmuch as all prohibitions with penal sanctions represent the defense of a given value system, or morality, in which the prevailing social power believes. Taking this to the very extreme, even a bank robbery, a shoplifting, or a rape is a political crime. After all, making such acts criminal offenses is a protection of the interests, values, and beliefs of the lawmaking power, actually the political-social system, which regards certain things as right and worthy of safeguarding with the threat of penal consequences.[1]

Whatever is called crime in law, by definition, constitutes a legal relationship between the official state and the members of the society. But this seemingly administrative and formalistic legal relationship is in its real essence a political relationship, since it pertains to the terms of existence between the state, as a political power, and the members of the society who live under this power, or rather, to the place and role of these men in their state. That is, it defines what is permitted and what is prohibited them in their political society. Thus, the legal relationship between the state and its members is an ideological-societal relationship where the stipulations of criminal law serve as safeguards of the various values of the ideology that the state power wants to see implemented. While it is not uncommon to meet arguments which strive admirably to propose that the political state power is for creating conditions to implement the values and goals of the society, the brutal reality suggests that the power creates the societal values and goals and enforces the conditions in which they are fulfilled.

Human behaviors that are qualified as crimes by the law, therefore, represent

[1] A somewhat similar stand was taken by Maurice Parmelee in *Criminology* (New York, 1918), p. 92. Thorsten Sellin's "culture conflict" theory in *Culture Conflict and Crime* (Social Science Research Council, New York, 1938) may also be far from supporting such a contention. The Soviet concept of "social danger" strongly leans toward such an understanding.

Source: Stephen Schafer, *The Political Criminal* (New York, 1974), pp. 19–39. Copyright © 1974 by The Free Press, a division of Macmillan Publishing Co., Inc. Reprinted with permission of Macmillan Publishing Co., Inc.

counterideological-societal conditions declared as nondesirable by the social-political state power. The interests, values, and beliefs of this power, whatever its operational structure may be, are expressed through legal norms. Among these norms are the rules and definitions of criminal law which, in order to enable the state to exercise control over accentuated ideological issues, declare certain acts to be crimes. In the definition of crimes, then, the state power's political ideology is translated into legal terms. Bank robbery, shoplifting, and rape, to mention examples, are crimes because the political state power ideologically believes in protecting other people's money, in allowing honest customers to browse through displayed goods in stores, and in protecting the bodily or sexual integrity of females. From this point of view, David Riesman's question, "Who has the power?"[2] and the contention of C. Wright Mills that the power is in the hands of an exploitative elite[3] are irrelevant, since all types of social powers are political powers and all have some kind of ideology mirrored by the criminal law.

When the political state power expresses its ideology, or value system, through the regulations of the criminal code, it determines the "norms of action" (*norma agendi*) and, at the same time, authorizes the executive organs of the state to apply penal sanctions in order to enforce the observance of these norms or, in other words, the acceptance of the value system. The question of which specific values or interests are so protected is dependent upon the legislators, as the political agents of the state power who conceive and pass criminal laws.

Since the analysis of what political crime is requires a conceptual rather than a definitional approach,[4] the general notion of political offenses might reasonably be equated with the concept of ordinary crimes. Whether it be treason, murder, drug use, embezzlement, homosexuality, arson, or whatever, ultimately and in the final examination, each is determined to be a crime by the legislators' philosophical, ideological, and political postures that construct in the form of law "the formal expression of the value system of the prevailing social power."[5] Assuming this is so, the distinction between ordinary and political crimes becomes difficult to determine since all crimes might be viewed from the concept of political orientation and as ideological in nature. Thus, all crimes may be qualified as political crimes.

As a matter of fact, the more pronounced the ideology of the political-social power, and the less possible the participation of ordinary men and social groups in the decision-making processes, then the easier it is to see that all crimes are of a political nature. In the heavily ideological political structure, the concept of criminal responsibility is spelled out more vividly, the ideological basis of all crime definitions is less concealed, and the suprauniversalistic inter-

---

[2] David Riesman, "Who Has the Power?" in Reinhard Bendix and Seymour M. Lipset (eds.), *Class, Status and Power* (New York, 1966).

[3] C. Wright Mills, *The Power Elite* (New York, 1956).

[4] William Thomas Mallison, "Political Crimes in International Law: Concepts and Consequences," *Newsletter* of the American Section of the Association Internationale de Droit Pénale, no. 9 (December 1971), Washington, D.C., p. 10.

[5] Stephen Schafer, *Theories in Criminology: Past and Present Philosophies of the Crime Problem* (New York, 1969), p. 17.

pretation of the crime problem is more openly admitted. In this suprauniversalistic understanding of crime, the political-social power emphasizes the political ideology so that it stands above not only individual interests, but also above the conventional group interests of the society (that is, the interests of the "universe").[6]

While in other types of political structures the ideological foundations of the so-called ordinary crimes are not so apparent, and these crimes are most often seen only as disturbances of legally protected individual interests, in the suprauniversalistically oriented societies criminal law offers direct protection and care not so much to individuals or groups, but outrightly to the ideas of the ideology itself.

The German *Täterstrafrecht* (criminal law as it involves the criminal) in the Third Reich, for example, tended to disregard the rigidly formalistic definition of crimes and to establish the degree of responsibility in accordance with the political personality of the criminal, even if he was the perpetrator of a traditionally "ordinary" crime. This proposition, to some extent, separated the criminal from his objective relation to his crime and victim and subjected his human conduct to a judgment directed by the supreme ideology. This approach attempted to find what was called the "normative type" of criminal, and the penal consequences of his responsibility would be decided by the deviation of his personality—and not his actions—from the ideologically saturated and politically interpreted norm. Capital punishment under this concept would not necessarily be inflicted on a person who actually committed a murder, but on any individual who, in view of his total personality, should be regarded as a "murderer type," regardless of whether he committed a homicide or not.

This concept ideologized the interpretation of all crimes so extensively that the criminal act and its legal definition were no more than aids to the political evaluation of crimes. It suggested that the *Volksanschauung* (public view) cannot be satisfied with a simple "symptom" (that is, the criminal offense), because the criminal is not always what one particular crime makes him appear to be. Eric Wolf claimed that "political liberalism and religious naturalism" are over, and therefore the "ethically indifferent positivistic individualism" should be replaced by "phenomenological personalism."[7] Wolf as well as George Dahm,[8] the pioneers of this normative typology, emphasized an ideological understanding of crime, in fact of all crimes, and proposed that the *Volksanschauung* should operate to control "disobedience and resistance" against the "national socialistic state."

In this kind of elastic concept, which so strongly disregards any distinction between ordinary and political crimes, not the personal drama of the criminal and his victim, but the drama of the offender and the ideology is of paramount

---

[6] Stephen Schafer, *The Victim and His Criminal: A Study in Functional Responsibility* (New York, 1968), pp. 33–36.

[7] Eric Wolf, *Vom Wesen des Täters* (Berlin, 1932); "Richtiges Recht im nationalsozialistischen Staat," *Freiburger Universitätsreden*, vol. 13 (1934).

[8] Georg Dahm, "Die Erneuerung der Ehrenstrafrecht," *Deutsche Juristenzeitung*, 1934, *Der Tätertyp im Strafrecht* (Leipzig, 1940).

importance, and all crimes are actually confused with political sins. In this supra universalistic concept of crime, the virtual absence of ordinary offenses has substituted for the personal victim the idea of a victimized ideology. The net result of this exaggeration by which all crimes are seen as having political origins is, necessarily, the suppression of legal arguments, and it may ultimately make the judicial agents of the political-social power the definers of what a crime actually is.

In a less overtaxed exposition, the Soviet Union may be seen as another example where all crimes are soaked in the substance of ideology, and unreservedly political motives are injected even into what are conventionally called ordinary criminal offenses. In social structures like that of the Soviet Union and other socialist countries, where the political and economic system holds a crucially significant position and where a determined move toward an ideological goal represents the social dynamics, the traditional understanding of crime could not provide satisfactory protection of the system and its future development. In a socialist-type social structure that is projected toward future goals and developments, law has little to do with the protection of what is usually called civil rights. That is, law sets few limitations on the state power's freedom to intrude on the individual man.

Consequently, a broader and stronger concept of criminal responsibility has to be created, based on an ideological and political interpretation of all criminal offenses. "A program of action" in the Soviet Union is "expected to improve the economic and political status of both peasants and workmen";[9] therefore the question of criminal responsibility and the evaluation of crime factors have to yield to the supremacy of the governing political philosophy. "Not merely the act," writes Harold J. Berman, "but the 'whole man' is tried; at the same time, his crime is considered in the context of the 'whole community.' "[10]

Since the social control exercised by the political power is based on ideology-directed social defense, the interpretation of crime, whatever the criminal offense may be, and the criminal's responsibility are necessarily politically subjective. All crimes are viewed from the angle of the ruling doctrines as designed by those in power, and all criminals are evaluated and judged according to the political-ideological value of their crime target. Therefore, as John N. Hazard put it, even the "court is an instrument of state policy and by no means impartial."[11]

In view of the utmost importance of defending the ruling ideology and so protecting the political system, the central issue of the conception of all crimes in the Soviet Union and other socialist countries is the idea of "social danger." Although this term has been widely used since the time of the pioneering Enrico Ferri, socialist criminology has changed its original meaning to serve ideological purposes. Since crimes are "actions of the people's enemies, foreign agents, and their accomplices, wreckers and saboteurs, spies and traitors, and manifest forms of the open battle waged by the capitalistic world" against the

[9] John N. Hazard, *The Soviet System of Government* (Chicago, 1964), p. 2.
[10] Harold J. Berman, *Justice in the U.S.S.R.* (rev. ed., New York, 1963), p. 257.
[11] Hazard, op. cit., p. 168.

socialist societies,[12] "the consequence of a human action, and especially the socially dangerous consequence, occupies a central place in the system of Soviet criminal law."[13] Any crime is a "social danger," meaning that it exposes the political and economic institutions, as the representations of the ideology, to harm, risk, or peril. Logically enough, the criminal is viewed in the same context; according to M. D. Shargorodskii and N. A. Beliaev, guilt means a person's *otnoshenie:* his mental attitude toward his socially dangerous conduct.[14]

The notion of social danger is not only "the pivot around which the whole system of Soviet criminal law is constructed,"[15] but also a flexible idea that makes it possible to establish the social dangerousness even *ex nunc,* rather than *ex tunc,* that is, at the time the act is being judged, rather than at the time it took place. This is all the less surprising since the Soviet criminal law, as one of the state superstructures by which power is imposed on the members of the society and one of the crucial protectors of the ruling power's ideology, has to approximate the political developments in the Soviet society, and the Soviet outlook on crime at any given moment has to reflect the changes, goals, and political decisions set by the authorities of the power.

The creators of the Napoleonic Code thought that they had prepared a legal system that would last for centuries, and they were not wholly wrong. Socialist lawmakers can have no similar long-range goals; inevitable developmental forces of the socialist system prevent making laws for generations or even for a decade or a year. This in itself explains why in the Soviet-type systems political thought dominates the concept of all crimes and makes the distinction between ordinary and political crimes obscure, if not in fact, absent. Or, viewed from the angle of the demands of the political ideological structure of this kind of society, it explains why traditional "guilt" has given way to the idea of social danger—danger to the political power's value system.

Nevertheless, even in those social systems where the political ideology of the ruling power is not so visibly involved in the understanding of crime and where the values of the political power do not strike the eye in reading the definitions of criminal offenses, the commonly believed distinction between ordinary and political crimes seems to come from a failure to consider the true profile of lawmaking.

The stiff qualitative separation of ordinary and political crimes can be seen as diametrically opposed to the real purpose of criminal law, actually the most important instrument of social control, which cannot tolerate ontological arguments in distinguishing between one crime and another by sorting them out into different classes. As a matter of fact, all crimes are socially dangerous, and all crime definitions reflect the value system of the social controllers. All social systems design one or another kind of social order, and all construct norms and

[12] V. D. Menshagin, A. A. Gertsenzon, M. M. Ishaiev, A. A. Piontovskii, and B. S. Utevskii, *Szovjet Büntetöjog,* Egyetemi Tankönyv, official edition of the university textbook of the Soviet criminal law, in Hungarian (Budapest, 1951), p. 247.

[13] F. J. Feldbrugge, *Soviet Criminal Law: General Part* (Leyden, 1964), p. 101.

[14] M. D. Shargorodskii and N. A. Beliaev (eds.), *Sovetskoe Ugolovnoe Pravo, Obshchaia Chast* (Moscow, 1960), p. 313.

[15] Feldbrugge, op. cit., p. 169.

rules to ensure the effective operation of the particular society. The violation of any of these norms and rules, to one degree or another, endangers the smooth operation of the particular political order. When Martitz claimed that the term "political crime" is an expression of the political language, and not the language of the law,[16] he did not pay attention to the real world's cruel fact that the language of the law in truth is the political language.

Indeed, criminal laws do not even distinguish between ordinary and political crimes, criminal codes just talk about crimes in general, even if the definition of one or another crime indicates the element of "political" motives, and only a few codes, if any, qualify certain criminal offenses explicitly as political crimes. The term "political crime," as commonly used, is not the offspring of criminal law. It is in fact a somewhat artificial and arbitrary product of international law which facilitates the processes of extradition and the possibility of offering asylum for certain fugitive criminals. How much of these crimes, then, demonstrates political motivation, and how much displays the components of a so-called ordinary crime, is a question that does not clearly lead to a general classification that would distinctly differentiate between the ordinary and political violations of law. The catalog of political crimes only shows that hardly any of them lack at least a portion of the act that would be judged as an ordinary criminal offense if they were not committed from political motives. This dioecious nature of political crimes prompted Heinrich Lammasch to call them relative offenses.[17]

However, in view of the political-ideological cradle of all crimes, it might be more appropriate to see the common or ordinary offenses as relative political crimes, as opposed to the absolute political crimes where the target of the lawbreaking is the ruling power's value system as a whole, rather than a part or an issue of it. Shoplifting and robbery, for example, are criminal attacks against the value attached to private property, and even abortion and homosexuality are assaults only against single issues of the political power's ideology. The political nature of these kinds of crimes is only occasionally conspicuous; thus, these "ordinary" crimes may be tentatively called "relative political crimes." But where the unlawful battery of the criminal is aimed at the sum total of the lawfully prevailing ideology or value system, or at least at one of its representative or critical institutions, for the sake of approaching the concept of the political criminal, and through that the problem of morality and crime, the violation of the legal norm might be called an "absolute political crime."

Lawmaking and Justice

The absolute political criminals, that is, those who inflict a criminal blow upon the ideology as a whole or who at least attempt to assault it, almost always act in the name of what they think is justice. They believe in an ideal

---

[16] Fr. Martitz, *Internationale Rechtschilfe in Strafsachen* (Leipzig, 1888/1897), vol. 1, p. 139.

[17] Heinrich Lammasch, *Das Recht der Auslieferung wegen politscher Verbrechen* (Vienna, 1884) ; *Auslieferungspflicht und Asylrecht* (Leipzig, 1887).

universal concept of justice, often confused with morality, that would symbolize an unqualified, unconditional, and self-existent fairness, as they conceive it, and they usually refuse to accept the thesis which suggests that justice means only what those who are in power agree to make it mean.[18] They believe in the unjust nature of the prevailing value system and the law that reflects it, and they tend to reject hearing Northrop's question: Is there any objectively determinable standard, in other words an "is" other than the living law against which the goodness or badness of the living law can be measured?[19]

The political criminal is both appalled and perturbed by the a priorism, subjectivism, and complacency of the lawmakers, with their enthusiasm for sitting in armchairs and laying down the social-political power's law about the functioning of the human mind, the human predicament, and so forth, and their rationales for doing so. However, hardly any political criminal can be persuaded to assume that he himself would not act otherwise, should he be the one who is sitting in this armchair in the event that his crime, aimed at replacing other people's justice with his own, is successful.

The discrepancy between the ruling power and the political criminal on the nature of lawmaking and justice is a disconcerting theme common to all ages. The quest for an answer (incidentally, often neglected by sociological criminology in the search for social crime factors) has failed to achieve a comforting resolution. It offers only a frustrating and depressing experience to both parties as well as to those students of sociology and criminology who are interested in the puzzle of lawmaking and justice, or better, in the justice of lawmaking.

Law, in view of its representing the governing value system, is a political phenomenon. And, perhaps, the depth of this petulant disagreement on the meaning of the battered idea of justice between the ruling power and the absolute political criminal calls for the challenge of the tempering assumption that the two positions are logically not incompatible, appearance notwithstanding, since no lawmaking is really conceivable without manipulated justice. It is a familiar ground to students of the sociology of law that although the procedure of a trial, so the myth runs, is designed by neutral rules to find the truth, the judges are likely to confuse the combat against crime, which is their business, and the fight against broader social menace, which is not. The courtroom is almost always stuffed with the ruling power's value system, and the outcome of a case is dependent on the judges' perception of these values.

The painful pivot of the question to keep in mind is that both the bearer of the social-political power and the political criminal are men. Therefore, the man-committed crimes in general, and naturally among them the so-called political crimes, are dependent upon the man-made law, and, thus, as long as the existing power prevails, its understanding of justice, as ritually declared, is "right" and consequently must not be attacked beyond certain limits.[20] Since

[18] Schafer, *Theories*, p. xi.

[19] Filmer Stuart Cuckow Northrop, "Ethical Relativism in the Light of Recent Legal Science," *Journal of Philosophy,* vol. 51 (Nov. 10, 1955), pp. 649–662.

[20] Schafer, *Theories*, op. cit., p. 14.

by definition the "conservatives" tend to conserve this justice, the "radicals" are those who attempt to change it, and thus are usually, or rather necessarily, the political criminals.

This idea probably motivated Havelock Ellis to suggest that the word criminal in the expression "political criminal" is a euphemism to spell out the suppression of a small minority by the majority.[21] And while Hugo Grotius, from the opposite point of view, cited Tertullian, who proposed that every man is by birth a soldier with a mission to combat criminals guilty of treason, Louis Proal, a judge of the Court of Appeal at Aix, cited the anarchist Valliant, who proposed that the citizen has the same rights whether acting in self-defense against the tyrant or against an enemy.[22]

The question, of course, is who are the "radicals" and "anarchists" and who are the "conservatives," and which of them, and in what circumstances, are really the political criminals. The question inevitably leads to the problem of the relativity of law and justice, and, consequently, to the riddle of relativity in the concept of "absolute political crime," a characteristic that is only rarely obvious in the changing nature of "relative political crimes," or, as they are commonly called, "ordinary crimes." Ultimately it is a question that guides us to the understanding of man, should he be the powerful or the powerless—a multi-dimensional being whose consciousness, morality, justice, and freedom can be approached from different points of view, none of which can claim to be the only legitimate one.[23]

Perhaps this consideration led Havelock Ellis to contend that the word criminal in the term "political criminal" is "an abuse of language," and to suggest that such a concept may be necessary only to ensure the supremacy of a government, just as the concept of heresy is necessary to ensure the supremacy of the Church. The political criminal of our time or place, he argued, may be the hero, martyr, or saint of another age or land.[24] A monarch, for example, is the incarnate personification of conservation, and yet, as Maurice Parmelee contrasted, Charles I in England and Louis XVI in France were beheaded as political criminals. And, as he continued, although "there is perhaps nothing in human culture more archaic than religion," under the French Revolution the clergy were proscribed as criminals.[25] To mention a more modern example, the abrupt and rapid changes in the lawmaking power structure at the time of the Hungarian revolution in 1956 resulted in criminals becoming

<hr />

[21] Havelock Ellis, The Criminal (5th ed., New York, n.d., preface to 4th ed., dated 1910), p. 2.

[22] Louis Proal, Political Crime, trans. unknown (New York, 1898), pp. 50–51, first published under the title La criminalité politique (Paris, 1895). To regard the state as criminal and the members of the society as victims is the crux of the problem and philosophically a highly controversial contention that leads to the problems of the natural law and to the assumption that there exists only a single justice.

[23] See Schafer, Theories, op. cit., p. 11; also the general tone in Pratima Bowers, Consciousness and Freedom (London, 1971).

[24] Ellis, op. cit., pp. 1–2.

[25] Parmelee, op. cit., p. 461.

heroes and then again criminals, and law-abiding citizens turning into criminals and then again into conformists—all within eight days.[26]

These few examples may sufficiently demonstrate that there is great complexity in the structure of the idea of justice and that the assessor of the battle between the lawmaking ruling power and the political criminal cannot safely determine which of them is supported by justice. The history of the philosophy of law, from the earliest beliefs in divine or superhuman commands to contemporary models of social engineering, could not reflect an agreement in a universally valid formulation of what justice should really mean.

From the time of primitive societies, credulity regarding the supernatural has been present in one form or another, and much of the profound reverence for the gods is due to the deities having been garbed in the same sanctity as the human sovereign; the authority to decide the meaning of justice is also attributed to them. The great Christian philosophers of the Middle Ages turned away from the world around them to dream of a heavenly kingdom. The *City of God* of St. Augustine, the *Summa theologica* of Thomas Aquinas, and the works of others contended that justice is part of the law in the divine world, and man-made laws can reflect justice only if completely subordinated to God's order. Similarly, the idea of "earthly" justice, which emerged early in Greek philosophy, has also become a central target of speculative efforts. From the harsh and retributive Draconians through the Socratic-Platonic and Aristotelian views of natural law, the Epicureans' approach to justice oriented to human happiness, the Spinozian and Pufendorfian justice based on man's natural reason, to Kant's "categorical imperative," and many other thinkers' desperate and gloriously noble endeavors, an endless series of dignified mental struggles prove that the definition of an absolute justice or an unalterable and uniform law has not been found.

Even if the law could determine (as it cannot) "what resemblances and differences among individuals" are, to use H. L. A. Hart's words, and could recognize "if its rules are to treat like cases alike" in order to be regarded as "just," even if so, fundamental differences in political and moral views "may lead to irreconcilable differences and disagreement as to what characteristics of human beings are to be taken as relevant for the criticism of law as unjust."[27] Not even Hart's "minimum content of natural law," a strong hint that survival is a universal human goal[28] and an admirable struggle to save at least something for the "absolute" in lawmaking, seems to be able to avoid the emergence of what some people may regard as "injustice," since throughout the social history of man a great number of legal actions or laws have proved that the "justice of survival" has been justified with injustices.

This is not to eliminate the recognition of man's natural needs, a basic claim of the adherents of natural law who demand the consideration of some kind of

---

[26] Stephen Schafer, "The Concept of the Political Criminal," *The Journal of Criminal Law, Criminology and Police Science,* vol. 62, no. 3 (1971), p. 381. Adapted by special permission.

[27] Herbert Lionel Adolphus Hart, *The Concept of Law* (Oxford, 1961), p. 157.

[28] Ibid., pp. 189–195.

inherent human rights in their attempt to construct the absolute justice. Neither Jeremy Bentham nor John Austin, to mention only two outstanding positivists, missed this consideration, although surely not to the satisfaction of our contemporary sociologists. Dennis Lloyd defends this stance by stating that it is not inconsistent with a positivist outlook to acknowledge the essential role of human values in law and society. "What the positivist rejects," he continues, "is neither valuations nor their effect on human institutions, but only the logical or practical possibility of establishing a scale of absolute values which govern mankind universally without distinction of time or place."[29]

When the political criminal assaults the ruling power's justice by claiming that it is unjust and by contending that his own justice *is* just, he might be right, but only in a relative sense. All laws are formulated on the unspoken assumption that they are just and represent the right justice, even though they may not appear so to all members of the society and especially not to the political criminal. The laws are just and they reflect justice: This has to be learned by all aspirants of political crimes, at least insofar as they are defined by the ruling social-political power and so long as the existing power prevails. "For . . . what is Justice," suggested Thomas Hobbes in *Leviathan,* "there is need of the Ordinances of Sovereign Power."[30] This power, and not the political criminal, knows what is just or unjust, and in the form of commands or "ordinances" raises the law to the level of "justice." Cicero told the story of a captured pirate who defended himself before Alexander the Great by saying that he did exactly what the great conqueror did but that he was to be punished as a pirate rather than a conqueror just because he operated with a small boat rather than a large armada.[31]

Of course, the case of the pirate is not as simple as that. The question of who or what has the right to declare what right is, or who can claim his justice as just, is a centuries-old problem that has been studied by jurists as well as by sociologists. Perhaps one of the reasons for their long-standing disagreement in finding an answer is that lawyers are too close to the problem and sociologists are too distant from it, and both seem to be reluctant to meet in the domain of legal philosophy or in what is called the sociology of law. By the way, at this point it is difficult not to let slip the suggestion that one of the decisive factors in the impasse on the general crime problem is our contemporary sociological criminologists' hesitancy to relate their etiological research to the speculations and findings of the philosophy of law and the norm system. Of course, much more is involved in the idea of law than sheer obedience and blind acceptance of the power-conceived justice, and usually a rich and complex interplay among individuals, groups, and conflicting values takes place before a law is created. Yet, in the ultimate analysis, the definition and interpretation of justice, and lawmaking accordingly, are always monopolies in the exclusive possession and under the exclusive control of the social-political power.

[29] Dennis Lloyd, *Introduction to Jurisprudence,* with selected texts (2d ed., London, 1969), p. xvii.

[30] Thomas Hobbes, *Leviathan* (first publ. 1651), Part II, "Of Commonwealth," ch. XXVI, "Of Civill Lawes," p. 4.

[31] Cicero, *De republica,* III. 12.

The greatest obstacle to understanding this tenet is our reluctance to accept that what we think of as right and just does not necessarily represent the only correct view. We tend to think in terms of a single immutable truth and conclude that therefore there is only one possible system of justice. The claim that the social system and its law are just and fair rests upon the dubious hypothesis that there is only one just and fair code of values.

The political criminal gets involved in law violation by professing that his code is the only just and fair set of values, which represents the only justice. But the ruthless fact is that the social-political power has the monopolized authority to define justice. Exclusively this power defines the rightness or wrongness of the modes of human conduct. And whatever is defined by the ruling power as right or wrong, whatever is qualified as justice or injustice, must be accepted by those who are required to obey so long as the power is a "power." The relativity of the concept of the political criminal rests with this relativity of justice. In harmony with this precept one may argue for the assumption that all components of the problem of political criminality—law, justice, crime, power, and others—are relative and changing phenomena, and the ruling power is the central element that breeds this overall relativity.

The story of the "Lords Appellant," the plotters of the "loyal conspiracy" under Richard II in England, at the end of 1387, may serve as a historical example for demonstrating the crucial role of the political power's relative nature in generating the relativity of political crimes, and perhaps all crimes. The five magnates, Thomas of Woodstock the Duke of Gloucester, Richard the Earl of Arundel, Thomas the Earl of Warwick, Henry Bolingbroke the Earl of Derby, and Thomas Mowbray the Earl of Nottingham, revolted against Richard II. They wanted to make him their tool, and they named and "appealed" several of the King's close associates as traitors in the Parliament. However, a decade later Richard, having regained full power, took revenge by executing Arundel, murdering Gloucester, confiscating the lands of Warwick, and exiling Bolingbroke and Mowbray. Richard, who was only ten when he became king, after the reign of Edward III, inherited renewed outbreaks of political disorder, and he allegedly suffered a progressive mental disease that apparently helped to reduce his political commonsense and increase his somewhat fanatic and tyrannical manner of ruling. Yet he was the king: He made the law, distributed justice, and created the values, which had to be vacillating and changing. Anthony Goodman, who injected flesh and blood into theoretical analyses of examining this part of English history, contends that Richard II's reign was the crisis in a system of political conversions.[32] Indeed, the sovereign power shapes and molds the concept of justice in any given society, and it is this justice, changing even under the same reign, that may make the discontented man a political criminal and may lead him to act criminally for the sake of another justice he conceives.

[32] Anthony Goodman, *The Loyal Conspiracy: The Lords Appellant under Richard II* (London, 1972).

Victimless Crimes

EDWIN M. SCHUR

Edwin M. Schur (1900–   ) is a sociologist and teaches at New York University. Dr. Schur is Associate Editor of the journal *Social Problems* and has written *Narcotic Addiction in Britain and America: The Impact of Public Policy* (1962), and *Radical Nonintervention: Rethinking the Delinquency Problem* (1973).

The "Creation" of Deviance

In the study of deviant behavior and crime, much more attention has been focused on the deviating individuals than on the social "definitions" of the deviance. Yet, as Howard S. Becker has pointed out:

> Deviance is *not* a quality of the act the person commits, but rather a consequence of the application by others of rules and sanctions to an "offender." The deviant is one to whom that label has successfully been applied; deviant behavior is behavior that people so label.[1]

When definitions of deviance take the specific form of criminal laws, the sociologist may be particularly likely to neglect their bearing on the behavior in question. Understandably, sociologists are somewhat less interested in law than lawyers are. Furthermore, there has been a general tendency for sociologists to focus greater attention on informal mechanisms of social control. In many instances, however, no real sociological understanding of the deviance problem being considered is possible unless the role of legal norms is examined. This is not to suggest that the sociologist need engage himself in detailed or technical legal analysis; rather, he must consider the important ways in which specific legal definitions and law enforcement policies influence the development of such problems.

. . .

Now that several crimes without victims have been examined in some detail, it may be useful to consider more generally the meaning and significance of that phrase. It refers essentially to the willing exchange, among adults, of strongly demanded but legally proscribed goods or services. Do prohibitions of this sort, and the social problems to which they are directed (and of which they are a part), constitute a sociologically meaningful category? H. L. A. Hart has asked: "Ought immorality as such to be a crime?"[2] Crimes without victims

---

[1] H. L. A. Hart, *Law, Liberty and Morality* (Stanford: Stanford University Press, 1963), p. 4.

[2] I am grateful to David Matza for suggesting this point and the general relevance of the black market example.

Source: Edwin M. Schur, *Crimes Without Victims: Deviant Behavior and Public Policy,* © 1965, pp. 169–173. Reprinted by permission of Prentice-Hall, Inc., Englewood Cliffs, New Jersey.

involve attempts to legislate morality for its own sake; the two conceptions very largely relate to the same thing. From the sociological standpoint, however, reference to the victimless nature of the offense may have certain advantages. It reveals the basis for saying that certain laws are indeed designed merely to legislate morality. It also highlights an important criterion for determining which laws fall into this category—the question: "Is there, in this particular situation, any real victimization?"

Another concept closely related to the analysis in this book is *dissensus*. With respect to each of the cases examined here, there is a lack of public consensus about the law. However, consensus is similarly lacking in the enactment and execution of other criminal laws, yet not all those instances involve the peculiar characteristics of the deviance situations described here. For instance, not only is there extensive violation of existing income tax laws, but there also appears to be considerable ambivalence in public attitudes toward these statutes (at least toward their specific provisions if not their very existence). But although these laws are not easily or completely enforceable, they do not give rise to the secondary elaboration of deviance and the related problems evident in the examples discussed above. A main point of differentiation seems to be *the element of transaction, or exchange*. Crimes without victims may be limited to those situations in which one person obtains from another, in a fairly direct exchange, a commodity or personal service which is socially disapproved and legally proscribed.

This limitation is admittedly somewhat arbitrary. It can be seen that there are other offenses in which there really is no victim. And if one were solely concerned with straight description, the phrase *exchange crimes* or even *business crimes* (i.e., offenses giving rise to illegal businesses) might be almost as appropriate a label for the subject matter of this book. But, as already mentioned, the concept of victimless crime helps to pinpoint a major criterion for evaluating policies, and this, too, is of concern in this discussion. The limitation of the concept to the exchange situations keeps it from getting out of hand. In a sense, every criminal law represents a societal judgment establishing both an offender and an individual or collective victim. Where there is direct offense by one person against another person or his property, the victim and victimizer are easily identified. On the other hand, in a crime against the state or a crime against morals, the victim becomes more elusive. And when the law specifically insists that a person is a victim even if the facts contradict that contention— for instance, sexual intercourse with a girl "under the age of consent" is statutory rape, even though she consents—the victim element is blurred still further.

In the examples considered here, the "harm" seen in the proscribed transaction seems primarily to be *harm to the participating individuals themselves* (apart from any alleged harm to general morals). Does the term *self-harm*, then, adequately describe the situations being considered? Not quite. In the first place, there is much dispute as to the extent of self-harm actually involved in the various proscribed behaviors. But, beyond that, not all proscriptions of self-harm produce situations of the sort analyzed here. Thus legal attempts to ban suicide or masturbation might seem to establish victimless crime situations in the sense of prohibiting self-harm, but precisely because the offense involves only the lone individual there is little or no basis for any elaboration of the deviance. Perhaps it is *the combination of an exchange transaction and lack of apparent harm* to others that constitutes the core of the victimless crime situation as here defined. Not all "exchange crimes" would qualify, because in some there may be evident harm to others. This is seen in the case of wartime black-market operations, in which the exchange of proscribed but strongly demanded goods between willing sellers and buyers does work patently to the disadvantage of many other individuals. Perhaps it is because the buyer of such goods is attempting to get more than his fair share of commodities desired by a large proportion of the general citizenry that dispassionate observers can easily view his behavior as harmful to society.[3] Of course it must be kept in mind that even dispassionate analysts will differ in their assessments of the harm involved in particular situations, and indeed there will be some individuals who see distinct harm to others even in the nonvictim situations described in this book.

One feature which seems to characterize all crimes without victims is the unenforceability of the laws surrounding them. Such *unenforceability stems directly from the lack of a complainant* and the consequent difficulty in obtaining evidence. Also significant is the low visibility of these offenses. If for some reason the proscribed exchanges had to occur always in public, enforcement would be far more efficient. Obviously the willing nature of the interpersonal exchange and the privacy in which it can take place are related. Another apparent consequence of privacy and lack of a complainant (combined with public ambivalence about the law) is the invitation to police corruption. Outside of these points, however, there is considerable variation within the category of crimes without victims. A comparison of the three situations analyzed in this book may provide some hints as to the factors determining the expansion of deviance in the victimless crime sphere.

The Self-Image

In all three cases, the individuals involved tend to develop, in some degree, a deviant self-image. This is largely the result of the dominant social definition of their behavior as being outside the pale of respectability, and the more specific labeling of the behavior as "criminal" reinforces and heightens this process. It is, of course, very difficult if not impossible to draw a clear-cut distinction between a deviant self-image and a criminal one. In a sense perhaps only differences of degree exist. Yet the criminalization of deviance may have an especially crucial influence on the individual's view of himself. Thus, the realization that they are considered criminals and—even more significantly—the need to act like criminals causes most drug addicts in this country to develop—at the very least—a pronouncedly antisocial outlook. The doctor-

---

[3] See Edwin Lemert, *Social Pathology* (New York: McGraw-Hill Book Company, Inc., 1951), especially Chap. 4, pp. 82–83.

addict, though also clearly a deviant, is unlikely to consider himself a criminal because he can maintain his habit with relative ease and through quasilegal means. The extent of deviant self-image seems, then, to be directly related to the degree of primacy[4] taken on by the deviant role, or the extent to which the deviant behavior comes to be elaborated into a role at all. And primacy relates closely to the *extent to which the deviant must, in order to satisfy the proscribed demand, engage himself in various instrumental and supportive activities.*

The Subculture

This raises the matter of subculture, the development of which is similarly dependent on the nature and extent of the engagement or involvement required of the particular type of deviant. There is pronounced subcultural development in the cases of homosexuality and drug addiction but none in the case of abortion. (Quite simply, in getting what she is looking for, the woman who has had an abortion has no need for frequent or continuing contact with other abortion-seekers.) Partly, it would seem, the development of a subculture has something to do with the continuing nature of the deviant behavior. Generally speaking, abortion is a discrete act, which one can easily bracket in time and space. This explanation is too simple, however, for the physician-addict is indeed continuously addicted yet he does not display subcultural involvement. It is not then merely the continuing nature of the basic deviant act that establishes the basis for a subculture but, again, the *need for continuous contact with other like individuals in order for the basic deviant acts to be carried out.* (There are, of course, psychological considerations which—as noted in the specific studies—may well exert some pressure on deviants to come together, even in the absence of practical need.) This assertion still leaves open the question of how and to what extent legal repression affects such need. Earlier chapters have suggested some instances of fairly specific and direct influence. Perhaps the best example is drug addiction, where it seems clear that the curbing of legitimate supplies tremendously increases the addict's practical need for involvement with other addicts. The role of law in stimulating the development of deviant subculture is less clear in the case of homosexuality. It is interesting to speculate, for example, that the homosexual subculture would be appreciably weaker if all confirmed homosexuals were free to embark on homosexual marriages without fear of legal interference. As noted in the introduction, it is extremely difficult, in trying to answer such questions, to analyze the effects of legal sanctions apart from the influence of the concurrently existing general social disapproval.

It should be clear from this discussion that deviant self-images and involvement in deviant subcultures are interrelated phenomena. Involvement in such a subculture, however, is not an absolute prerequisite to the development of a deviant self-concept. The physician-addict, for example, may well have a consciousness of his continuing deviance and experience great uneasiness about it, even if he has not become generally alienated and totally self-condemning. Like-

[4] Paul Reiwald, *Society and Its Criminals,* trans. by T. E. James (London: William Heinemann, Ltd., 1949), p. 173.

wise, engagement in deviant or criminal behavior may have a pronounced impact on one's self-concept even when the individual is not involved in continuous behavior patterns that imply taking on a set and deviant role. The guilt feelings of the aborted woman serve to illustrate such possibilities.

Punishment and the Purpose of Law

LON FULLER

Lon Fuller (1902–   ), Carter Professor of Jurisprudence at Harvard University and a leading American legal realist, is the author of many books, including *The Morality of Law* (1964).

One who has followed up to this point the account here given of "pervasive problems of the law" may be inclined to say of these problems something like this: The ills and disorders of a legal system—at least those that come about despite reasonably good intentions—can all be attributed to the fact that those concerned with the law are not clear as to what it is they are trying to do. If the law as a whole could be assigned some understandable general purpose, and if each separate law carried its own distinct purpose, plainly stated, then all these difficulties would disappear. Judges would then know how to interpret the law, the agencies of enforcement would know what their task was, and the general public would understand what was going on and would be able to pass an intelligent judgment on it. Finally, if the legislator were compelled to clarify his aims and to set them forth plainly, he would not be able to visit his obfuscations on the work of others. Everyone's task would then receive new meaning and direction. In other words, what we need, it may be said, is a good dose of the simple wisdom Hobbes expressed when he wrote:

> . . . in all your actions, look often upon what you would have, as the thing that directs all your thoughts in the way to attain it. (*Leviathan*, part I, ch. 3.)

The need for this simple cure may seem peculiarly acute in the branch of the law with which we have so far been chiefly concerned, the criminal law. This branch of the law is notoriously afflicted by disputes as to what it is for. There are commonly said to be four "theories" of the criminal law, that is, four distinct notions about what it should be trying to do. Let us at this point allow the famous mathematician, Norbert Wiener, the father of cybernetics, to

Source: Lon Fuller, *Anatomy of the Law* (New York, 1968), pp. 45–60. Reprinted by permission of Praeger Publishers, Inc.

state what these theories are and to express some of his distress that the law of crimes cannot make up its mind among discrepant ideas about what it is for:

> Where the law of Western countries is at present least satisfactory is on the criminal side. Law seems to consider punishment, now as a threat to discourage other possible criminals, now as a ritual act of expiation on the part of the guilty man, now as a device for removing him from society and for protecting the latter from the danger of repeated misconduct, and now as an agent for the social and the moral reform of the individual. These are four different tasks, to be accomplished by four different methods; and unless we know an accurate way of proportioning them, our whole attitude to the criminal will be at cross-purposes. At present, the criminal law speaks now in one language, and now in another. Until we in the community have made up our minds that what we really want is expiation, or removal, or reform, or the discouragement of potential criminals, we shall get none of these, but only a confusion in which crime breeds more crime. Any code which is made, one-fourth on the eighteenth-century British prejudice in favor of hanging, one-fourth on the removal of the criminal from society, one-fourth on a halfhearted policy of reform, and one-fourth on the policy of hanging up a dead crow to scare away the rest, is going to get us precisely nowhere.
>
> Let us put it this way: the first duty of the law, whatever the second and third ones are, is to know what it wants.[1]

These are strong words. Let us take them seriously and see what can be done to carry out the program they propose.

First, it may be said—and it *has* been said many times—that we should start by purging the law entirely of the notion that its function is to make the guilty man "pay" for his crime. This justification for the criminal law has been castigated as brutal and primitive, as an anachronistic survival, in Wiener's words, of "the eighteenth-century British prejudice in favor of hanging." It should be eliminated entirely, so it is said, from a civilized system of justice.

But the first question that must be faced is, *Can* it be eliminated? If there were no punishment of criminals it is reasonable to suppose that many acts now penalized by the state would become objects of private revenge. An unregulated private vengeance would inevitably degenerate into a war of reprisals and counter-reprisals. Such a condition is by no means unknown in primitive societies. One of the ancient roots of the modern criminal law can be discerned when social control was first asserted over acts of private vengeance and they were made subject to a kind of tariff of permitted, but limited, retributions.

There is a famous remark by Sir James Fitzjames Stephen to the effect that the criminal law bears to the instinct of revenge the same relation that the institution of marriage bears to the sexual instinct. Both regularize and control a deep impulse of human nature that if not given legitimate expression is bound to find disruptive outlets. Now it is apparent that this explanation or justification for punishment cannot be extended to the whole spectrum of crimes as they appear in a modern criminal code. It presupposes some person deeply injured by a crime committed against himself or someone close to him. It has no

---

[1] Norbert Wiener, *The Human Use of Human Beings,* Houghton Mifflin Co., Boston, 1950, pp. 116–117.

application to what have been called "crimes without victims." It has only an attenuated relevance to crimes where the "victim" is the public interest, as, for example, where the criminal act consists in an embezzlement of public funds. While such an act may arouse a general indignation, it seems unlikely that even the most public-spirited citizen would feel any impulse to work physical violence on the embezzler.

At this point, however, there enters another possible justification for the penal or retributive theory of criminal law. It will be recalled that, in one of his descriptions of this theory, Wiener spoke of it as calling for "a ritual act of expiation on the part of the guilty man." Now it is by no means clear that it is only in primitive societies that ritualistic or symbolic acts can serve a useful social purpose. There is a fairly respectable view, especially espoused by certain psychoanalysts, that the public trial and condemnation of the criminal serves the symbolic function of reinforcing the public sense that there are certain acts that are fundamentally wrong, that must not be done. This view is perhaps most persuasive precisely in those cases where the crime in question does not stir instincts of personal revenge, for the reason that the harm done is to a general, rather than to an individual, interest. Here we may mention particularly "white collar crimes" such as embezzlement, the sale of influence, and bribery. Under certain social conditions a general deterioration in the moral sense may occur which makes these crimes seem almost innocent.

There are many situations in society where a man—a public official, say, or a corporate executive—must choose among competitors for the same advantage. The corporate purchasing agent, for example, must decide whether to place a profitable supply contract with Acme Manufacturing or Exatronics, Inc.; the public official must choose one among many contenders for appointment to office. In such situations—pervasive in a complex society—there is a natural tendency toward the development of a certain sense of reciprocity between those who seek advantages and those who control access to them. This reciprocity may start on a comparatively innocent level as a mere exchange of social amenities. But it has a strong tendency to creep toward more tangible forms of expression. What starts as an exchange of reciprocal esteem may gradually become an explicit trade of material advantages; what began as an expression of gratitude for past favours may shift its position in time by anticipating favours to come. When this anticipation reaches the explicitness of a bargain we are, of course, confronted with unambiguous bribery.

The usual pleas of the bribe-giver or taker is that he only followed the example he saw everywhere about him, that he only did directly and candidly what others were doing indirectly and hypocritically. In such a moral atmosphere, it may be argued, men need to have their sense of guilt restored; they must be brought to see that certain things are fundamentally wrong and that it makes no difference how much company the criminal has in his wrongdoing. For this purpose "a ritual act of expiation" may not be an inappropriate measure.

Before surrendering ourselves to an uncritical enthusiasm for this function of the criminal law we must recall that the ritual of expiation loses its whole point if those who perform it do so with unclean hands. If the agencies of enforcement are themselves corrupt, if their administration of the law is lax and favouritistic, then any attempt by them to reanimate the public sense of sin will serve no purpose but to compound confusion. Furthermore, the law which furnishes the occasion for expiation must itself be free from moral taint. It would be grotesque indeed to select for purposes of moral pedagogy many statues in the books today. Take, for example, a price-fixing law obtained by the retail liquor trade to increase its profits, but justified on the ground that higher liquor prices will produce a more sober citizenry, an argument rendered doubly suspect when it is coupled with a contention that high prices are necessary to keep the small neighbourhood liquor store in business so that every citizen may have a source of supply at his elbow. When our statute books are filled with laws like this, it might be well, before any decision is made to erect a sacrificial altar for the immolation of the lawbreaker, to subject the House of Law itself to a thorough cleansing and fumigation.

Let us recall at this point that we are not directing our attention toward possible justifications for a view that attributes to the criminal law the simple and familiar purpose of punishment, of publicly visiting on the lawbreaker some penalty or disadvantage. We have considered two such justifications. The first sees the criminal law as acting in the place of those injured by the crime and as putting under public control the vengeance they might otherwise seek outside the forms of law. The other attributes to the criminal law the task of keeping alive a sense of guilt, in the words of one psychoanalyst, of providing "nutriment for the super-ego." Now neither of these arguments is likely to have much appeal to those of a strongly rationalistic and utilitarian bend of mind. Nor is the appeal for those of such a temperament likely to be enhanced by the fact that the one argument rests in part on primitive practices, and the other counts among its staunchest supporters certain disciples of Freud who give a strongly moralistic flavour to the teaching, of their master.

There is, however, another argument for the retributive theory, an argument that addresses its appeal to minds of the most sober and calculative disposition. It consists in shifting attention from the criminal to the honest man. It may seem inhumane and brutal to inflict a deliberate hurt on the guilty man simply because he has hurt another. But what of the law-abiding man? Is our compassion for the criminal to leave the honest citizen with no comparative advantage? Is he to gain nothing by being willing to accept the restraints of law? In gauging the force of this argument it should be recalled that in many contexts punishment and reward will appear as opposite sides of the same coin. Suppose, for example, that a statute provides that any motorist found guilty of a traffic violation shall incur a disadvantage by having to pay an increased premium for his automobile insurance. If an offensive penal implication is read into this statute, all we have to do to remove it is to view the statute, not as punishing bad driving, but as rewarding good driving. So, over the whole spectrum of the law of crimes, it may be said that it is necessary to maintain a proper balance of advantage between the criminal and the honest man, whether this is done by conferring a reward for law observance or by imposing a penalty for violation of the law. In most contexts it would obviously be impracticable (not to say ludicrous) to confer something like a prize for obeying the law. Hence we are compelled to accomplish this indirectly by imposing a disadvantage on the man found guilty of breaking the law. Unless this is done the scales of justice will weigh out short measure to the man willing to abide by the rules.

So much for the arguments in favour of retaining, as at least *one* of the purposes of the criminal law, the familiar object of punishment. Let us turn now to a purpose that stands at the other extreme from punishment, that of rehabilitation or reform. For just as punishment is often regarded as the most brutal purpose that can be assigned to the criminal law, rehabilitation has generally been considered the most humane.

Now it may seem at first glance as if there were no incompatibility between these two purposes, that they may well supplement each other. It may be said, for example, that there is no reason why the man who is punished by being sent to prison may not, while there, be taught a trade, be given psychiatric help, and generally be put in a condition to meet more adequately the demands of life after his release.

This is not the view generally taken, however, by those who would like to see rehabilitation made the dominant and central concern of the criminal law. They are likely to regard—with some reason—the degradation of punishment as an obstacle to the realization of their ideal. Indeed—and with much less reason— the more radical adherents of the rehabilitative ideal would like to initiate their whole program by completely purging the administration of the criminal law of any trace of the concept of punishment.

There are good grounds for believing that this cannot be done and should not be attempted. In the first place, there exists nothing at present that can be called a science of rehabilitation. The place such a science would occupy is today a battlefield for contending schools of thought. On this field meet protagonists of behaviouristic, psychoanalytic, mechanistic, and moralistic theories, as well as those who humbly ask only a chance to apply intuitive kindliness. That this conflict of method exists does not mean that nothing has been accomplished. On the contrary, the devotion, skill, and insight of individuals dedicated to the rehabilitative ideal have at times accomplished miracles. But there is as yet no communicable science of rehabilitation, no certain way of measuring the prospects of success in individual cases, and no procedures yielding a confident measure of success.

In this state of the art it is dangerous, indeed, to attempt to eliminate from the law an objective, that of punishment, which at least is familiar and not wholly lacking in rational justification. We should also remember that this objective has built-in limits. While there are no principles by which the appropriate punishments for particular crimes can be exactly set, there are common-sense considerations which suggest, for example, that a life sentence is an inappropriate penalty for a first offense in petty shoplifting. The rehabilitative principle contains no similar intrinsic limitation. From time to time shocking stories come to light of some harmless lunatic originally committed to an asylum for treatment and then kept confined for decades. An uncritical extension of the curative concept over the whole criminal law could easily lead to a multiplication of such incidents many times over.

Such incidents have indeed become much more common than is generally realized. In many states where the question of the sanity of a person accused of crime is raised, there is a procedure for referring to a state psychiatrist or a board of experts the decision whether the accused is "capable of standing trial." The assumption here is the wholly reasonable one that a man so deranged that he cannot properly cooperate with his attorney in his own defense is not in fit condition to be tried. If the decision is that he is not capable of standing trial then he may be committed to an insane asylum, where his stay may become indefinite. Furthermore, under the law of many states, if an insane patient presents serious problems of containment and discipline to the asylum, he may be transferred to a regular prison or penitentiary. The ironic result is that a man who if tried and convicted might have had to serve a five-year sentence in prison, ends by spending his entire life in the same prison—waiting until his condition improves sufficiently so that he may be deemed ready for trial.

When we bear in mind that these grotesque happenings are associated with the notion of rehabilitation and cure, we can sense some of the danger that would attend any attempt to supplant, wholesale and overnight, as it were, the objective of punishment with that of cure. A different facet of the problem is revealed when we ask whether this switch in the declared aim of the criminal law would in fact remove the stigma of conviction which adherents of the rehabilitative ideal find so objectionable. Do men in fact feel less shame in being formally declared to be functioning badly than they do in being found to have broken the rules? One perceptive observer has remarked that it is more of an affront to human dignity to subject a man to compulsory improvement than it is to punish him. The truth of this remark may be judged by any parent who will ask himself candidly whether he would rather have his child kept after school for misbehaving or because the child was stupid and needed special after-hours instruction lowered to the level of his capacities.

The most fundamental cleavage between the penal and rehabilitative theories comes to the surface when we ask, "What circumstances justify a forcible social intervention in the life of the individual?" The answer of the penal theory is fairly clear: "When the individual has been found to have committed an act defined by the law as a crime. The determination whether he has in fact committed such an act shall be made in a public trial, conducted according to the forms of law."

Now there are a number of reasons why this mode of determining the need for social intervention should be unsatisfactory to adherents of the rehabilitative ideal. In the first place, a public trial with its dramatic confrontation—sometimes, regrettably, with prosecutor and defense attorney competing for newspaper attention—is scarcely an auspicious beginning for a program of helping the criminal to adjust to the demands of everyday life. Furthermore, the emphasis placed by the law on the commission of some single act of criminality is itself uncongenial to the rehabilitative theory. From a therapeutic standpoint the commission of a criminal act is only one index among many of the need for curative measures. Even if it could by itself serve as a reliable indication of the need for such measures, those who drafted the statutory table of crimes certainly did not have that purpose in mind. When they decided to attach the brand of criminality to particular acts they may have weighed the damage done to others by the act in question, its propensity to stir imitation, and many other considerations. It is unlikely that they asked themselves whether the act was one which would reliably indicate that curative measures were needed and had some prospect of success. Even if all these difficulties could be resolved, the rehabilitative ideal would still remain unfulfilled as long as the application of curative measures has to await some manifestation of unsocial propensities in outward acts. For the logic of the rehabilitative ideal drives it toward prevention. If crime is the product of certain correctable impulses, it is reasonable to suppose that these impulses must exist in many persons who have as yet had no occasion to express them in overt acts. Why then not take corrective measures before the harm is done? Why not subject the population as a whole to a kind of prophylactic screening to discover who needs to be purged of latent tendencies toward crime?

Surely it requires no argument to demonstrate that any such inquisitorial paternalism could never be tolerated in a free society. Many measures short of so pervasive a surveillance would be equally unacceptable. For example, it is difficult to imagine acceptance of a system under which, instead of trial in open court, a quiet and secluded inquiry by a committee of social scientists would determine whether an individual should be subjected to compulsory detention.

As matters now stand, then, the rehabilitative effort receives into its hands human material that has been (1) branded with the stigma of crime and (2) selected by standards that do not reliably reflect either the need for curative measures or their prospective success. This is a situation with which the more ardent supporters of the rehabilitative ideal can hardly be expected to be happy. Yet what is involved is not a repudiation of the rehabilitative ideal, but a compromise to which that ideal must submit in the interest of freedom, human dignity, and due process. At present this compromise costs more than it should. In particular the criminal trial as it is now often conducted is unworthy of any ideal that could be ascribed to the criminal law. But with all allowance for improvement here and elsewhere in the administration of the law, some element of compromise between divergent goals must remain.

In other words, for the foreseeable future the rehabilitative and penal theories are condemned to live in an uneasy alliance from which neither can fully escape. As with an unhappy marriage where effective action has been excluded, the resulting frustration has tended to take itself out in words.

So we find adherents of the rehabilitative ideal attempting to rewrite the whole vocabulary of the criminal law in terms more congenial to its objectives. A draft code recently prepared for one of the new nations undertook a complete revision of the terminology of crime. The code itself was designed not as a Penal or Criminal Code, but as a Code of Correction. Arrest became a "taking into temporary custody." Crime itself was defined not as an offense against the law, but as "a condition subject to correction." How little is likely to be accomplished by such changes in nomenclature can be seen if we weigh the present connotations of expressions like "reformatory" and "house of correction" against the hopes that must have accompanied the original coinage of those terms.

The attempt to rewrite the criminal law in softer words may be attributed to laudable motives and may seem, in any event, relatively harmless. This impulse is far from harmless, however, when it extends to the definition of crime itself. When that definition is softened up beyond a certain degree, then the meaning of due process of law has been destroyed. One of the guiding principles of the rehabilitative ideal is that of "flexibility." Its object is to treat not the act, but the man, and every man is to some extent a special case. This view, with proper qualifications, has much to recommend it when it relates to the policy to be pursued *after conviction*. Matters stand quite otherwise, however, when the policy of flexibility is extended to the definition of crime itself. If the words used to state when a man is guilty of a criminal act, and when he is not, are loosely put together, then guarantees of fair trial become meaningless. One cannot measure out just treatment with a yardstick made of rubber.

Nor is the renaming of things always wholly innocent when it relates to matters other than the definition of crime. Imprisonment, by whatever name it is called, is a harsh thing, and the discipline that must be exercised over human beings in close confinement can never be wholly agreeable to those subject to it. When an attempt is made to hide the harsh realities of criminal justice behind euphemistic descriptions, a corrupting irony may be introduced into ordinary speech that is fully as frightening as Orwell's "Newspeak." A perceptive observer, reporting on a visit to an institution for boys with behaviour difficulties, recounts the following incident: one of the boys who had broken some disciplinary rule was "required to stand before a wall while a seventy-pound fire hose was played on his back. This procedure went under the name of 'hydrotherapy.' " That this ironic renaming is not entirely a modern invention is shown by an expression of long standing, "the water cure." This expression in turn has its ugly cousin in the familiar, "That'll teach you!" which so often accompanies acts of sheer retaliation.

In seeking the proper place for the rehabilitative ideal in the total administration of criminal justice, we must not imagine that the realization of this ideal will in practice be entrusted to a few perceptive and kindly social scientists. The person subjected to curative measures will inevitably have his chief and most intimate contact with attendants and caretakers, who will be ordinary human beings, subject to ordinary human frailties. If these persons are assigned a function they do not understand and are forced to employ a vocabulary foreign to their actual motives, then hypocrisy, ineptitude, and some measure of cruelty are inevitable. For it seems almost a law of human nature that when a man is compelled to act out a role in which he has no real belief, the result will be to bring out his worst qualities.

Before quitting the subject of rehabilitation, it might be well to remind the reader once again that there are many different kinds of crimes to be found listed in the statutes. There is a tendency in discussions about the theory or purpose of the criminal law to speak in terms of "crime" in general, and what lies in the back of the mind are the most obvious acts of violence, like murder and rape. But it is not crimes like these that form the longest chapters of the criminal code. As for rehabilitation, there would, for example, be a considerable incongruity, to say the least, if the convicted president of a huge corporation were turned over to a board of psychiatrists to be cured of the bad habit of violating the antitrust laws. When we speak of curing a man of a tendency toward crime, we must not forget what diverse activities make up the catalog of modern crimes.

There remain for brief treatment the two remaining functions or "theories" of the criminal law: deterrence and prevention.

Plainly there is no fundamental incompatibility between the penal theory and the objective of deterrence. Scholars debate the question whether the threat of punishment actually does deter. Stories are told of the days of public hangings in England when a man might be hanged for a great variety of minor offenses, including theft. It is said that pickpockets found in such occasions an excellent opportunity for plying their trade, especially during the time when the actual hanging was taking place and all eyes were on the dangling figure at the end of the rope. Ironically, that figure was himself not uncommonly a convicted pick-pocket.

Whatever moral may be derived from such stories, common sense tells us that the fear of punishment must in some measure, and for some persons, act as a deterrent to crime. A system of criminal law based on punishment will as a matter of course furnish this deterrence as a kind of by-product. There is, therefore, no fundamental incompatibility between the penal and deterrent theories.

One thing is perfectly clear, and that is that no civilized system of criminal law could take as its *exclusive* aim that of deterrence. This would mean that when an individual was found to have committed a criminal act, what would happen to him would have no relation to his deserts, but would be judged solely by its effect on others. It is, of course, quite true that during a real or supposed "crime wave" the sentences meted out will tend to be somewhat more severe than under ordinary conditions. In this way the objective of deterrence may enter into and give a special direction to the administration of the law. But this is a very different matter from making deterrence the chief or sole objective of the criminal law. No one could seriously recommend that when something goes wrong, and we cannot identify the culprit, we revert to the old practice of executing every tenth man.

With respect to the theory of *prevention* there is, again, ordinarily no fundamental incompatibility between it and the familiar objective of punishment. Most modern forms of punishment (in contrast with the ducking stool and the whipping post) serve to take the criminal out of society for a period and during that time preclude him from a repetition of his offense.

This does not mean that the administration of the law can disregard prevention as a separate objective and simply assume that it will be achieved through a system oriented toward the objectives of a penal theory. For one thing there is the well-known fact that during his imprisonment a criminal often picks up from his more experienced fellow prisoners skills that will serve his criminal career when he is released. Though this possibility raises some difficult questions of prison administration, it suggests no fundamental tension between the objectives of punishment and prevention.

As with the objective of deterrence, it is difficult to imagine a system of criminal law *exclusively* devoted to prevention. There is, however, one branch of the criminal law that approaches that orientation. This is found in laws having to do with what are called sexual psychopaths. If it were possible to cure such persons of their dangerous tendencies, their situation would present a powerful argument for supplanting punishment with a system exclusively devoted to curative measures. Unfortunately it is by no means clear that their condition can be cured. If it cannot, then, when we remember, for example, the psychic scars little children can receive from their advances or attacks, a good case can be made for removing psychopaths to a safe distance from society—indefinitely. But, here again, problems of fairness and due process arise to complicate the problem. Must such a person, before being put away, be convicted of crime, or is it enough that psychiatrists regard him as a potential danger? A clear-cut answer to questions of this sort is precluded by the fact that our knowledge of such conditions is still imperfect and what purports to be an answer given in the name of science is often no more than a reasonably informed guess. With matters in this state we are not yet ready to effect a final resolution among conflicting theories of the criminal law and here, as elsewhere, must be content with a kind of uneasy compromise.

Six

Freedom and Liberation

> Historically the best way of regarding the substance of liberty in the modern period as well as in the mediaeval is to realize that the new elements which enter into its composition at any given time have almost invariably been rationalizations of particular demands from some class or race or creed which have sought a place in the sun denied them.
>
> —Harold J. Laski

Introduction

Liberation movements are the most visible, organized feature of our present political and moral lives. They challenge long-established arrangements and conventions; the status quo is shaking and in many cases toppling. Passions run high and persistently.

What accounts for these strong and lasting passions for liberation and freedom? Why is such a high value placed upon them? Freedom has such a high value because it has been connected with our very essence as human beings. To be fully human requires being free. Immanuel Kant's third formulation of his categorical imperative draws a connection between essential human nature and freedom. The imperative reads: So act as to treat humanity, whether in thine own person or in that of any other, in every case as an end withal, never as a means only.

In explaining what he means by the imperative, Kant distinguishes between *things* and *persons.* We are perfectly free to do with objects as we wish in order to use them as a means to accomplish our chosen ends. A rock may be used for a foundation for a wall in your garden: or it may be broken for aggregate; or skipped over the water. A rock is not an "object of respect" as a human being is; it has no rights. Human beings, according to Kant, are due respect "because their very nature points them out as ends in themselves, that is, as something which must not be used merely as means." We should not do away with human beings as we do with rocks simply because we want human skin for a lampshade or to use their bodies as fertilizer for our pansies. Human beings are each an end to themselves, not a means to someone else's end; we are not free to use others because their being ends in themselves "restricts [our] freedom of action."

To bring out fully the concept of freedom, we should state it in both its negative and positive, reciprocal sense, and in such a way that its connection to human essence is brought out.

The reciprocal negative and positive sense is brought out by utilizing the prepositions "from" and "to." "X is free (or should be free) *from* Y" is another way of stating "X is free (or should be free) *to* do Z," where Y and Z are opposites or converses. For example, "X should be free *from* censorship (Y)" is the reciprocal of "X should be free *to* speak (Z)," where the act of speaking (Z) and the act of censoring (Y) are opposites.

To be negatively free is to be free *from* the interference of others; you have rights that others ought not to violate; you are an object of respect; you have a right to exist as an end for yourself and not as a means for the accomplishment of other persons' ends. This "other" includes such "legitimate" authority as governments. Isaiah Berlin points out that the main argument for negative liberty has recourse to human nature. "We must preserve a minimum area of personal freedom if we are not to "degrade or deny our nature. . . . What then must the minimum be? That which a man cannot give up without offending against the essence of his human nature." Freedom in the positive sense signifies persons' opportunity to perform self-chosen acts and to shape their own character and being. To understand the appeal of freedom in the positive sense requires connecting positive freedom with self-realization. When we are born, we are not yet what we will become; as infants we are not as fully human as we will become; further, at any stage of our life, we may not yet be as fully human as we wish to become. Becoming human is a process. This process can be seen as either a self-making, a molding by others, or a combination of them. To be free fully in the positive sense is to be wholly in charge of making yourself into the human being you wish to be; domestic animals and human slaves are examples of creatures maximally molded by others. Adolescence in our society is that interesting, traumatic period when we shift from being mainly molded by others to being mainly made by ourselves. Adolescence can be looked at more revealingly as a moral shift than as a psychological "stage."

Berlin catches the flavor and appeal of the positive sense of freedom (both Berlin quotes are from *Four Essays on Liberty,* partially reprinted in *Philosophy for a New Generation,* second edition). "The 'positive' sense of the word 'liberty' derives from the wish on the part of the individual to be his own master. I wish my life and decisions to depend on myself, not on external forces of whatever kind. I wish to be the instrument of my own, not of other men's, acts of will. I wish to be a subject, not an object; to be moved by reasons, by conscious purposes, which are my own, not by causes which affect me, as it were, from outside. I wish to be somebody, not a nobody; a doer-deciding, not being decided for, self directed and not acted upon by external nature or by other men as if I were a thing, or an animal, or a slave incapable of playing a human role, that is, of conceiving goals and policies of my own and realizing them."

In short, we prize positive freedom because we wish to make ourselves human; this ability to make our own essence is what distinguishes us as persons from other animals and from objects; it is the very essence of being human. Human survival has two dimensions: One is to survive as a living creature, the other is to survive as a human being rather than being reduced to living as a "lower" animal. None of us wants to live "a dog's life."

Harold J. Laski points out the positive–negative aspect of the meaning of "liberty" in the first essay in this chapter. "Liberty may be defined as the affirmation by an individual or group of his or its essences. It seems to require the presence of three factors. It seeks in the first place a certain harmonious balance of personality; it requires on the negative side the absence of restraint upon the exercise of that affirmation; and it demands on the positive the organization of opportunities for the exercise of a continuous initiative."

You should note two other important points of Laski's article. First, he reviews some history of liberty. He emphasizes that the content of liberty or freedom is always changing with conditions of time and place, a fact that reminds us that "liberty is always inherent in the social processes and is unintelligible apart from it." The idea of liberty was born in Athens as expressed by Pericles, given a religious sanction by Christianity, was oriented toward individuals in the Reformation, was at the core of the American Revolution against monarchy, blossomed into representative democracy, has been the rallying cry of colonial people trying to free themselves from imperialism, is central to the women's movement, and perhaps will emerge next in childrens', animals', and plants' liberation.

The second point to note in Laski's article is the connections, disconnections, and reconnections between liberty and the concepts of equality and justice that occurred in various historical periods. Freedom is not the only social value; it has to be fitted into place with other social values. Freedom and equality, for example, may not be compatible in their pure state. Pure, unfettered freedom in the economic sphere, for example, may lead to unequal distribution of material goods; employers may have to be restrained from firing workers for union activity in order that workers may collectively gain the power they need to force the employer to pay them an equitable wage and salary.

A liberal thinker such as **John Stuart Mill** is deeply concerned that other values people hold dear may be placed higher than liberty. He fears not only for excessive authority placed in the hands of govermental officials but also for social tyranny: "there needs protection also against the tyranny of the prevailing opinion and feeling; against the tendency of society to impose, by other means than civil penalties, its own ideas and practices as rules of conduct on those who dissent from them . . . and compels all characters to fashion themselves upon the model of its own." Mill believes that persons have a right to be unique, different, nonconformist, even deviant in whatever way they choose as long as it does not harm others.

The tyranny of the majority is very real and powerful, although we are not often conscious of it; our lives are mainly conformist because we are subject to the tyranny of the majority. To appreciate the extent and the hiddenness of this tyranny, you have only to read **Kate Millett**'s essay. She points out that there is sexual politics; that it is proper to use the term "politics" because we are dealing with the distribution of ruling power among the sexes, males dominating subordinate females; that the power is exercised by the extensive socialization women undergo, a socialization that "interiorizes" the subordinate role in women. This socialization also makes women's status and temperament seem "natural." To make us conscious of this interior colonization, Millett uncovers how ideological, biological, sociological, economic, educational, physical force, mythical and religious, and psychological factors are used to achieve this socialization.

Most of you can get an immediate appreciation of the power of the tyranny of the majority by approaching a person of the same sex as you who is attractive to you with the end in mind of having sexual relations. The "gay alternative" is something most people reject with strong feelings; it is not a cool, rational decision generally. Such a response would reveal that the power of the tyrannical majority has been interiorized in you unless you can show that by rational considerations you have concluded that homosexuality is immoral, or "unnatural," or an unsatisfactory relation to another human. **Ronald Atkinson** gives arguments against beliefs that homosexuality can be characterized in any of those ways. He examines the restraints placed on homosexuals; these restraints do inhibit the freedom of persons; they make it impossible or difficult or costly *to be* a certain kind of person, to choose an "essence" for oneself. (The relation of freedom to law is examined in Schur's article on victimless crime in Chapter Five.)

Linda Phelps addresses herself to the effects that women's subordination causes in sexual life; "most women, I suspect, have given up on sex, whether or not they have informed their husbands or lovers." In explaining why this is so, she finds that women are alienated from men because women are powerless; they are unequals in a male–female situation; being powerless and unequal, they are restrained and unfree. Alienation from men had made women unhealthy, schizophrenic, alienated from themselves; to be a healthy, self-actualizing human being one must move "through the world as an autonomous source of action." Once again, we find the concept of freedom being conceived as part of the essence of being human. Women, not being free, being subordinate to men, are treated as means, as objects, rather than as ends; men violate Kant's categorical imperative by the way they usually deal with women. Women are treated as sex-objects, rather than sex-persons, or as Phelps puts it, as "symbol-objects rather than person-objects." "Like the schizophrenic, we are alienated from our own experience and from our own self-powers of initiation. This form of alienation has to do with sex in a very direct way because women do not often take the initiative in relation to men. . . . We are also alienated because we are separated from our own experience by the prevailing male cultural definition of sex— the male fantasy of active man and passive woman."

Women, then, are kept from being human because they are alienated from sex; and they are alienated from sex because they are not free, autonomous human beings; they need liberation from male dominance.

Robert Solomon's essay has some interesting relations to Phelps'. His article is a response to Thomas Nagel's essay on sexual perversion. Nagel's discussion is partly based on Jean-Paul Sartre's "Of Self, the Other, and

Sex." Sartre believes that anyone who tries to incorporate another into his or her own world as a subject is doomed to fail. The reason is, on the one hand, that I reduce him or her to an object, and, on the other hand, he or she reduces me to an object for him or her. Solomon's summary of Sartre's position is that "sexual desire is the desire to possess, to gain recognition of one's own freedom at the expense of the other. By 'incarnating' and degrading him/her in flesh, one reduces him/her to an object." There can be no satisfactory, humanly fulfilling sexual relationships because part of the essence of being human is being free while, according to Sartre, the end of the sexual act is to degrade and dehumanize the other. This is a rather more pessimistic view of the outcome of sexual relations than Phelps offers; she at least allows that were women not in a subordinate status, they would cease being sex-objects and could become sex-persons.

According to Solomon, Nagel holds the "liberal" view about the end of the sexual relationship: The end is to obtain enjoyment. But, Nagel holds, it has to be enjoyment of the human kind. Borrowing from Sartre, Nagel thinks that human enjoyment requires mutual, reciprocal consciousness of the other; this occurs when each is conscious of the other; each is conscious of the other's consciousness; and each is conscious that the other is conscious of her or his consciousness. If we let the arrow, $\rightarrow$, stand for "being conscious of" or "being aware of," we can symbolize this mutual, reciprocal consciousness as follows; R symbolizes Romeo and J symbolizes Juliet:

1. $R \rightarrow J$ 2. $R \rightarrow (J \rightarrow R)$ 3. $R \rightarrow (J \rightarrow (R \rightarrow J))$
   $J \rightarrow R$ $J \rightarrow (R \rightarrow J)$ $J \rightarrow (R \rightarrow (J \rightarrow R))$

Nagel illustrates this mutual, reciprocal consciousness by placing Romeo and Juliet in a cocktail lounge. A humanly fulfilling sexual encounter will occur when the object of consciousness for Romeo and Juliet is the other person's sexual pleasure; Romeo is aware of Juliet's pleasure and she of his; Romeo is aware that Juliet is conscious of Romeo's pleasure and Juliet is aware that Romeo is conscious of Juliet's pleasure; and each is aware that the other is conscious of the other's consciousness of each's pleasure. Perverse sex is any sex that does not satisfy this consciousness complex; intercourse with animals would be an example of perversion, the animal being incapable of participating in this complex structure.

Solomon challenges Nagel's view that the "end" or purpose of sexual intercourse is pleasure. Orgasm is not its end but its "resolution." Instead, "Sexual activity consists in speaking what we might call 'body language.'" "Body language is essentially expressive, and its content is limited to interpersonal attitudes and feelings. . . ." This model of sex provides Solomon with a different theory of perversion. The interesting philosophic exercise to give yourself is to fit Solomon's "expressive" model of sexual intercourse and its perversion criterion to Phelps' account of sexual alienation. Is women's sexual alienation as construed by Phelps an instance of sexual perversion as construed by Solomon? Sexual perversion so construed might be a result of women's unfreedom. If it is, women's liberation will reduce sexual perversion.

Our society is not only sexist, it is also racist. **Lerone Bennett, Jr.,** maintains that racism, not to be identified solely with personal racial prejudice, is of no advantage to white people. He says, "My argument here is the very simple one that the depth of racism is a measure of the unfreedom in the white community." Thus, white people should be as interested in nonwhite liberation from whites' racism as nonwhite people are because the unfreedom of nonwhites is also the unfreedom of whites. His argument for the liberation of nonwhites is important for all of us, then.

A second feature of Bennett's article that is of special interest, and it is important to his "unfreedom" argument referred to above, deals with positive and negative freedom. He attempts to distinguish a kind of positive freedom that is not merely the reciprocal of negative freedom, unlike the positive freedom we discussed at the beginning of this introduction. Let's call the sense of positive freedom we discussed before the "liberal" sense and let's call Bennett's sense of positive freedom the "UN" (United Nations) sense.

Many have-nots are in agreement with the United Nations' statement of human rights; they think that liberalism's traditional political rights are only a partial list. They believe that people also have rights to such things as food, shelter, education, and work. The have-nots are pressing for new human rights to be added to those that Anglo-American liberalism has advocated. In their view, a society that is satisfied with maintaining the rights of free speech, assembly, and due process to the neglect of maintaining the rights to food and shelter is in need of reform or revolution.

Let us try to state the difference between "liberal rights and freedom" and "UN rights and freedom." For this we use the interlocked concepts of liberty, rights, and obligations.

Liberal Freedom. If some person, Black, has negative freedom, then Black has a negative right. There are *no* moral or legal restrictions on Black's acting in some specified way. He has, for instance, a legal right to free speech.

If Black has a right, it is a right against some other person, White, and White has a negative obligation to Black.

Suppose that Black's right is free speech; then White has an obligation not to interfere with Black's act of speaking.

UN Freedom. If Black has positive freedom, he has some socially approved need, goal, or ideal.

If Black has such a goal, he has a positive right to demand White's cooperation. That is, White has a positive obligation to Black.

Suppose that Black's goal is equal education. Then White has an obligation to act in cooperation with Black.

In more schematic form:

Black's negative freedom leads to Black's right leads to White's obligation *not to act.*

Black's positive freedom leads to Black's right leads to White's obligation *to act* cooperatively.

Liberal freedom obliges the other person's not acting and UN freedom obliges the other person's acting.

Liberal freedoms, such as the freedom of speech, assembly, and the vote, are negative freedoms; they imply rights that prohibit acts of interference. UN freedoms, such as freedom from starvation or freedom to obtain a fair portion of the world's food, freedom from exposure or freedom to take possession of shelter, and freedom from ignorance or freedom to participate in educational activities, are positive freedoms; they imply rights that place an obligation to cooperate in obtaining, taking, and participating.

Bennett remarks, "I believe America's trouble is at a deeper level. The problem, in my opinion, is structural, that is, institutional. We have not created a single community here." This emphasis on complex, structured factors as a cause of unfreedom is important because it keeps us from glibly thinking that a changed attitude toward nonwhites will "solve everything." A responsible attempt to provide for the liberation of a class of persons requires making an analysis of a complex of factors complexly interrelated.

The same point is the burden of **Juliet Mitchell**'s essay. **William T. Blackstone** usefully gives us a typology with which we may approach the immense amount of material on women's liberation. Mitchell occupies the "radical Marxist" place in his typology. In his footnote 9, Blackstone says, "I would not write off entirely the Marxist analysis of the oppression of women, but I am not all convinced that private property is the root of all social evils." It is important to note that this single-factor characterization of the Marxist analysis does not apply to Mitchell's analysis. Her basic point is that a Marxist analysis of women's position must deal with several factors complexity interrelated, namely, production, reproduction, sex, and the socialization of children. Any change in women's status must deal with the whole structure that contains these four factors, each of them being structurally complex, too. Women's liberation will not come from merely a heightened consciousness in women and a changed attitude in men: the whole society has to be restructured if women and nonwhites are to be liberated. We have much philosophizing to do if we are to liberate ourselves.

The last essay, by **William E. May,** deals with abortion. This issue presents us with a conflict between two freedoms: the freedom of a woman to control her own body and the freedom of a fetus to be born. Since freedom and rights are interconnected, we can also state the issue as a conflict between rights: the right of a woman to her body and the right of a fetus to be born. This conflict, as May points out, is often resolved by arguing that a fetus is not a person and, so does not have rights. This essay, not surprisingly in view of our claim in this introduction that freedom and human essence are intertwined concepts, attempts to give an account of human essence. May's account leads him to the conclusion that a fetus is a human and does have rights.

Freedom and Its Limits

The Tyranny of the Majority

JOHN STUART MILL

John Stuart Mill (1806–1873) was a very influential British philosopher in the nine-teenth century. His major works include *On Liberty* (1859), *Considerations on Repre-sentative Government* (1861), *Utilitarianism* (1863), and *The Subjection of Women* (1869).

The subject of this essay is not the so-called liberty of the will, so unfortunately opposed to the misnamed doctrine of philosophical necessity; but civil, or social liberty: the nature and limits of the power which can be legitimately exercised by society over the individual. A question seldom stated and hardly ever dis-cussed in general terms, but which profoundly influences the practical con-troversies of the age by its latent presence, and is likely soon to make itself recognized as the vital question of the future. It is so far from being new, that, in a certain sense, it has divided mankind almost from the remotest ages; but in the stage of progress into which the more civilized portions of the species have now entered, it presents itself under new conditions, and requires a different and more fundamental treatment.

The struggle between liberty and authority is the most conspicuous feature in the portions of history with which we are earliest familiar, particularly in that of Greece, Rome, and England. But in old times this contest was between subjects, or some classes of subjects, and the government. By liberty, was meant protec-tion against the tyranny of the political rulers. The rulers were conceived (except in some of the popular governments of Greece) as in a necessarily antagonistic position to the people whom they ruled. They consisted of a governing One, or a governing tribe or caste, who derived their authority from inheritance or con-quest, who, at all events, did not hold it at the pleasure of the governed, and whose supremacy men did not venture, perhaps did not desire, to contest, what-ever precautions might be taken against its oppressive exercise. Their power was regarded as necessary, but also as highly dangerous; as a weapon which they would attempt to use against their subjects, no less than against external enemies. To prevent the weaker members of the community from being preyed upon by innumerable vultures, it was needful that there should be an animal of prey stronger than the rest, commissioned to keep them down. But as the king of the vultures would be no less bent upon preying on the flock than any of the minor harpies, it was indispensable to be in a perpetual attitude of defense against his beak and claws. The aim, therefore, of patriots was to set limits to the power which the ruler should be suffered to exercise over the community; and this

Source: John Stuart Mill, *On Liberty* (1859).

limitation was what they meant by liberty. It was attempted in two ways. First, by obtaining a recognition of certain immunities, called political liberties or rights, which it was to be regarded as a breach of duty in the ruler to infringe, and which if he did infringe, specific resistance, or general rebellion, was held to be justifiable. A second, and generally a later expedient, was the establishment of constitutional checks, by which the consent of the community, or of a body of some sort, supposed to represent its interests, was made a necessary condition to some of the more important acts of the governing power. To the first of these modes of limitation, the ruling power, in most European countries, was compelled, more or less, to submit. It was not so with the second; and, to attain this, or when already in some degree possessed, to attain it more completely, became everywhere the principal object of the lovers of liberty. And so long as mankind were content to combat one enemy by another, and to be ruled by a master, on condition of being guaranteed more or less efficaciously against his tyranny, they did not carry their aspirations beyond this point.

A time, however, came, in the progress of human affairs, when men ceased to think it a necessity of nature that their governors should be an independent power, opposed in interest to themselves. It appeared to them much better that the various magistrates of the State should be their tenants or delegates, revocable at their pleasure. In that way alone, it seemed, could they have complete security that the powers of government would never be abused to their disadvantage. By degrees this new demand for elective and temporary rulers became the prominent object of the exertions of the popular party, wherever any such party existed; and superseded, to a considerable extent, the previous efforts to limit the power of rulers. As the struggle proceeded for making the ruling power emanate from the periodical choice of the ruled, some persons began to think that too much importance had been attached to the limitation of the power itself. *That* (it might seem) was a resource against rulers whose interests were habitually opposed to those of the people. What was now wanted was, that the rulers should be identified with the people; that their interest and will should be the interest and will of the nation. The nation did not need to be protected against its own will. There was no fear of its tyrannizing over itself. Let the rulers be effectually responsible to it, promptly removable by it, and it could afford to trust them with power of which it could itself dictate the use to be made. Their power was but the nation's own power, concentrated, and in a form convenient for exercise. This mode of thought, or rather perhaps of feeling, was common among the last generation of European liberalism, in the Continental section of which it still apparently predominates. Those who admit any limit to what a government may do, except in the case of such governments as they think ought not to exist, stand out as brilliant exceptions among the political thinkers of the Continent. A similar tone of sentiment might by this time have been prevalent in our own country, if the circumstances which for a time encouraged it had continued unaltered.

But in political and philosophical theories, as well as in persons, success discloses faults and infirmities which failure might have concealed from observation. The notions that the people have no need to limit their power over themselves might seem axiomatic when popular government was a thing only dreamed about, or read of as having existed at some distant period of the past. Neither was that notion necessarily disturbed by such temporary aberrations as those of the French Revolution, the worst of which were the work of a usurping few, and which, in any case, belonged not to the permanent working of popular institutions, but to a sudden and convulsive outbreak against monarchical and aristocratic despotism. In time, however, a democratic republic came to occupy a large portion of the earth's surface, and made itself felt as one of the most powerful members of the community of nations; and elective and responsible government became subject to the observations and criticisms which wait upon a great existing fact. It was now perceived that such phrases as "self-government," and the "power of the people over themselves," do not express the true state of the case. The "people" who exercise the power are not always the same people with those over whom it is exercised; and the "self-government" spoken of is not the government of each by himself, but of each by all the rest. The will of the people, moreover, practically means the will of the most numerous or the most active *part* of the people; the majority, of those who succeed in making themselves accepted as the majority: the people, consequently *may* desire to oppress a part of their number, and precautions are as much needed against this as against any other abuse of power. The limitation, therefore, of the power of government over individuals loses none of its importance when the holders of power are regularly accountable to the community, that is, to the strongest party therein. This view of things, recommending itself equally to the intelligence of thinkers and to the inclination of those important classes in European society to whose real or supported interests democracy is adverse, has had no difficulty in establishing itself; and in political speculations "the tyranny of the majority" is now generally included among the evils against which society requires to be on its guard.

Like other tyrannies, the tyranny of the majority was at first, and is still vulgarly, held in dread chiefly as operating through the acts of the public authorities. But reflecting persons perceived that when society is itself the tyrant— society collectively over the separate individuals who compose it—its means of tyrannizing are not restricted to the acts which it may do by the hands of its political functionaries. Society can and does execute its own mandates; and if it issues wrong mandates instead of right, or any mandates at all in things with which it ought not to meddle, it practices a social tyranny more formidable than many kinds of political oppression, since, though not usually upheld by such extreme penalties, it leaves fewer means of escape, penetrating much more deeply into the details of life, and enslaving the soul itself. Protection, therefore, against the tyranny of the magistrate is not enough: there needs protection also against the tyranny of the prevailing opinion and feeling; against the tendency of society to impose, by other means than civil penalties, its own ideas and practices as rules of conduct on those who dissent from them; to fetter the development, and if possible, prevent the formation, of any individuality not in harmony with its ways, and compels all characters to fashion themselves upon the model of its own. There is a limit to the legitimate interference of collective opinion with individual independence; and to find that limit, and maintain it against encroachment, is as indispensable to a good condition of human affairs, as protection against political despotism.

But though this proposition is not likely to be contested in general terms, the practical question, where to place the limit—how to make the fitting adjustment between individual independence and social control—is a subject on which nearly everything remains to be done. All that makes existence valuable to anyone depends on the enforcement of restraints upon the actions of other people. Some rules of conduct, therefore, must be imposed, by law in the first place, and by opinion on many things which are not fit subjects for the operation of law. What these rules should be is the principal question in human affairs; but if we except a few of the most obvious cases, it is one of those which least progress has been made in resolving. No two ages, and scarcely any two countries, have decided it alike; and the decision of one age or country is a wonder to another. Yet the people of any given age and country no more suspect any difficulty in it, than if it were a subject on which mankind had always been agreed. The rules which obtain among themselves appear to them self-evident and self-justifying. This all but universal illusion is one of the examples of the magical influence of custom, which is not only, as the proverb says, a second nature, but is continually mistaken of the first. The effect of custom, in preventing any misgiving respecting the rules of conduct which mankind impose on one another, is all the more complete because the subject is one on which it is not generally considered necessary that reasons should be given, either by one person to others or by each to himself. People are accustomed to believe, and have been encouraged in the belief by some who aspire to the character of philosophers, that their feelings, on subjects of this nature, are better than reasons, and render reasons unnecessary. The practical principle which guides them to their opinions on the regulation of human conduct, is the feeling in each person's mind that everybody should be required to act as he, and those with whom he sympathizes, would like them to act. No one, indeed, acknowledges to himself that his standard of judgment is his own liking; but an opinion on a point of conduct, not supported by reasons, can only count as one person's preference; and if the reasons, when give, are a mere appeal to a similar preference felt by other people, it is still only many people's liking instead of one. To an ordinary man, however, his own preference, thus supported, is not only a perfectly satisfactory reason, but the only one he generally has for any of his notions of morality, taste, of propriety, which are not expressly written in his religious creed; and his chief guide in the interpretation even of that. Men's opinions, accordingly, on what is laudable or blamable, are affected by all the multifarious causes which influence their wishes in regard to the conduct of others, and which are as numerous as those which determine their wishes on any other subject. Sometimes their reason, at other times their prejudices or superstitions; often their social affections, not seldom their antisocial ones, their envy or jealousy, their arrogance or contemptuousness: but most commonly their desires or fears for themselves—their legitimate or illegitimate self-interest. Wherever there is an ascendant class, a large portion of the morality of the country emanates from its class interests, and its feelings of class superiority. The morality between Spartans and Helots, between planters and Negroes, between princes and subjects, between nobles and roturiers, between men and women, has been for the most part the creation of these class interests and feelings; and the sentiments thus generated react in turn upon the moral feelings of the members of the ascendant class, in their relations among themselves. Where, on the other hand, a class, formerly ascendant, has lost its ascendancy, or where its ascendancy is unpopular, the prevailing moral sentiments frequently bear the impress of an impatient dislike of superiority. Another grand determining principle of the rules of conduct, both in act and forbearance, which have been enforced by law or opinion, has been the servility of mankind towards the supposed preferences or aversions of their temporal masters or of their gods. This servility, through essentially selfish, is not hypocrisy; it gives rise to perfectly genuine sentiments of abhorrence; it made men burn magicians and heretics. Among so many baser influences, the general and obvious interests of society have of course had a share, and a large one, in the direction of the moral sentiments; less, however, as a matter of reason, and on their own account, than as a consequence of the sympathies and antipathies which grew out of them; and sympathies and antipathies which had little or nothing to do with the interests of society, have made themselves felt in the establishment of moralities with quite as great force.

The likings and dislikings of society, or of some powerful portion of it, are thus the main thing which has practically determined the rules laid down for general observance, under the penalties of law or opinion. And in general, those who have been in advance of society in thought and feeling, have left this condition of things unassailed in principle, however they may have come into conflict with it in some of its details. They have occupied themselves rather in inquiring what things society ought to like or dislike, than in questioning whether its likings or dislikings should be a law to individuals. They preferred endeavoring to alter the feelings of mankind on the particular points on which they were themselves heretical, rather than make common cause in defense of freedom, with heretics generally. . . . The great writers to whom the world owes what religious liberty it possesses, have mostly asserted freedom of conscience as an indefeasible right, and denied absolutely that a human being is accountable to others for his religious belief. Yet so natural to mankind is intolerance in whatever they really care about, that religious freedom has hardly anywhere been practically realized, except where religious indifference, which dislikes to have its peace disturbed by theological quarrels, has added its weight to the scale. In the minds of almost all religious persons, even in the most tolerant countries, the duty of toleration is admitted with tacit reserves. One person will bear with dissent in matters of church government, but not of dogma; another can tolerate everybody, short of a Papist or a Unitarian; another everyone who believes in revealed religion; a few extend their charity a little further, but stop at the belief in a God and in a future state. Wherever the sentiment of the majority is still genuine and intense, it is found to have abated little of its claim to be obeyed.

In England, from the peculiar circumstances of our political history, though the yoke of opinion is perhaps heavier, that of law is lighter, than in most other countries of Europe; and there is considerable jealousy of direct interference, by the legislative or the executive power, with private conduct; not so much from any just regard for the independence of the individual, as from the still subsisting habit of looking on the government as representing an opposite interest to the public. The majority have not yet learnt to feel the power of the government their power, or its opinions their opinions. When they do so, individual liberty will probably be as much exposed to invasion from the government, as it already is from public opinion. But, as yet, there is a considerable amount of feeling ready to be called forth against any attempt of the law to control individuals in things in which they have not hitherto been accustomed to be controlled by it; and this with very little discrimination as to whether the matter is, or is not, within the legitimate sphere of legal control; insomuch that the feeling, highly salutary on the whole, is perhaps quite as often misplaced as well grounded in the particular instances of its application. There is, in fact, no recognized principle by which the propriety or impropriety of government interference is customarily tested. People decide according to their personal preferences. Some, whenever they see any good to be done, or evil to be remedied, would willingly instigate the government to undertake the business; while others prefer to bear almost any amount of social evil, rather than add one to the departments of human interests amenable to governmental control. And men range themselves on one or the other side in any particular case, according to this general direction of their sentiments; or according to the degree of interests which they feel in the particular thing which it is proposed that the government should do, or according to the belief they entertain that the government would, or would not, do it in the manner they prefer; but very rarely on account of any opinion to which they consistently adhere, as to what things are fit to be done by a government. . . .

The object of this essay is to assert one very simple principle, as entitled to govern absolutely the dealings of society with the individual in the way of compulsion and control, whether the means used be physical force in the form of legal penalties, or the moral coercion of public opinion. That principle is, that the sole end for which mankind are warranted, individually or collectively, in interfering with the liberty of action of any of their number, is self-protection. That the only purpose for which power can be rightfully exercised over any member of a civilized community, against his will, is to prevent harm to others. His own good, either physical or moral, is not a sufficient warrant. He cannot rightfully be compelled to do or forbear because it will be better for him to do so, because it will make him happier, because, in the opinions of others, to do so would be wise, or even right. These are good reasons for remonstrating with him, or reasoning with him, or persuading him, or entreating him, but not for compelling him, or visiting him with any evil in case he do otherwise. To justify that, the conduct from which it is desired to deter him must be calculated to produce evil to someone else. The only part of the conduct of anyone, for which he is amenable to society, is that which concerns others. In the part which merely concerns himself, his independence is, of right, absolute. Over himself, over his own body and mind, the individual is sovereign.

It is perhaps hardly necessary to say that this doctrine is meant to apply only to human beings in the maturity of their faculties. . . . Those who are still in a state to require being taken care of by others, must be protected against their own actions as well as against external injury. . . . Liberty, as a principle, has no application to any state of things anterior to the time when mankind have become capable of being improved by free and equal discussion. Until then, there is nothing for them but implicit obedience to an Akbar or a Charlemagne, if they are so fortunate as to find one. But as soon as mankind have attained the capacity of being guided to their own improvement by conviction or persuasion . . . , compulsion, either in the direct form or in that of pains and penalties for non-compliance, is no longer admissible as a means to their own good, and justifiable only for the security of others.

It is proper to state that I forego any advantage which could be derived to my argument from the idea of abstract right, as a thing independent of utility. I regard utility as the ultimate appeal on all ethical questions; but it must be utility in the largest sense, grounded on the permanent interests of a man as a progressive being. Those interests, I contend, authorized the subjection of individual spontaneity to external control, only in respect to those actions of each which concern the interest of other people. If anyone does an act hurtful to others, there is a *prima facie* case for punishing him, by law, or, where legal penalties are not safely applicable, by general disapprobation. There are also many positive acts for the benefit of others, which he may rightfully be compelled to perform: such as to give evidence in a court of justice; to bear his fair share in the common defense, or in any other joint work necessary to the interest of the society of which he enjoys the protection; and to perform certain acts of individual beneficience, such as saving a fellow-creature's life, or interposing to protect the defenseless against ill-usage, things which whenever it is obviously a man's duty to do, he may rightfully be made responsible to society for not doing. A person may cause evil to others not only by his actions but by his inaction, and in either case he is justly accountable to them for the injury. The latter case, it is true, requires a much more cautious exercise of compulsion than the former. To make anyone answerable for doing evil to others is the rule; to make him answerable for not preventing evil is, comparatively speaking, the exception. Yet there are many cases clear enough and grave enough to justify that exception. In all things which regard the external relations of the individual, he is *de jure* amenable to those whose interests are concerned, and, if need be, to society as their protector. There are often good reasons for not holding him to the responsibility; but these reasons must arise from the special expediencies of the case: either because it is a kind of case in which he is on the whole likely to act better, when left to his own discretion, than when controlled in any way in which society have it in their power to control him; or because the attempt to exercise control would produce other evils, greater than those which it would prevent. When such reasons as these preclude the enforcement of responsibility, the conscience of the agent himself should step into the vacant judgment seat, and protect those interests of others which have no external protection; judging himself all the more rigidly, because the case does not admit of his being made accountable to the judgment of his fellow-creatures.

But there is a sphere of action in which society, as distinguished from the individual, has, if any, only an indirect interest; comprehending all that portion of a person's life and conduct which affects only himself, or if it also affects others, only with their free, voluntary, and undeceived consent and participation. When I say only himself, I mean directly, and in the first instance; for whatever affects himself, may affect others through himself; and the objection which may be grounded on this contingency, will receive consideration in the sequel. This, then, is the appropriate region of human liberty. It comprises, *first,* the inward domain of consciousness; demanding liberty of conscience in the most comprehensive sense; liberty of thought and feeling; absolute freedom of opinion and sentiment on all subjects, practical or speculative, scientific, moral, or theological. The liberty of expressing and publishing opinions may seem to fall under a different principle, since it belongs to that part of the conduct of an individual which concerns other people; but, being almost of as much importance as the liberty of thought itself, and resting in great part on the same reasons, is practically inseparable from it. *Secondly,* the principle requires liberty of tastes and pursuits; of framing the plan of our life to suit our own character; of doing as we like, subject to such consequences as may follow: without impediment from our fellow-creatures, so long as what we do does not harm them, even though they should think our conduct foolish, perverse, or wrong. *Thirdly,* from this liberty of each individual, follows the liberty, within the same limits, of combination among individuals; freedom to unite, for any purpose not involving harm to others: the persons combining being supposed to be of full age, and not forced or deceived.

No society in which these liberties are not, on the whole, respected, is free, whatever may be its form of government; and none is completely free in which they do not exist absolute and unqualified. The only freedom which deserves the name, is that of pursuing our own good in our own way, so long as we do not attempt to deprive others of theirs, or impede their efforts to obtain it. Each is the proper guardian of his own health, whether bodily, or mental and spiritual. Mankind are greater gainers by suffering each other to live as seems good to themselves, than by compelling each to live as seems good to the rest.

Of the Liberty of Thought and Discussion

The time, it is to be hoped, is gone by, when any defence would be necessary of the "liberty of the press" as one of the securities against corrupt or tyrannical government. No argument, we may suppose, can now be needed, against permitting a legislature or an executive, not identified in interest with the people, to prescribe opinions to them, and determine what doctrines or what arguments they shall be allowed to hear. This aspect of the question, besides, has been so often and so triumphantly enforced by preceding writers, that it need not be specially insisted on in this place. Though the law of England, on the subject of the press, is as servile to this day as it was in the time of the Tudors, there is little danger of its being actually put in force against political discussion, except during some temporary panic, when fear of insurrection drives ministers and judges from their propriety; and, speaking generally, it is not, in constitutional countries, to be apprehended, that the government, whether completely responsible to the people or not, will often attempt to control the expression of opinion, except when in doing so it makes itself the organ of the general intolerance of the public. Let us suppose, therefore, that the government is entirely at one with the people, and never thinks of exerting any power of coercion unless in agreement with what it conceives to be their voice. But I deny the right of the people to exercise such coercion, either by themselves or by their government. The power itself is illegitimate. The best government has no more title to it than the worst. It is as noxious, or more noxious, when exerted in accordance with public opinion, than when in opposition to it. If all mankind minus one, were of one opinion, and only one person were of the contrary opinion, mankind would be no more justified in silencing that one person, than he, if he had the power, would be justified in silencing mankind. Were an opinion a personal possession of no value except to the owner; if to be obstructed in the enjoyment of it were simply a private injury, it would make some difference whether the injury was inflicted only on a few persons or on many. But the peculiar evil of silencing the expression of an opinion is, that it is robbing the human race; posterity as well as the existing generation; those who dissent from the opinion, still more than those who hold it. If the opinion is right, they are deprived of the opportunity of exchanging error for truth: if wrong, they lose, what is almost as great a benefit, the clearer perception and livelier impression of truth, produced by its collision with error.

The Changing Meaning of "Freedom"

HAROLD J. LASKI

Harold J. Laski (1893–1950) was professor of political science at the University of London and a leader of the British Labor Party. Among his books are *A Grammar of Politics* (1925), *Liberty in the Modern State* (1930), and *The Rise of European Liberalism* (1936).

The basic idea of liberty as a part of the armory of human ideals goes back to the Greeks and is born, as the funeral oration of Pericles makes abundantly clear, of two notions: the first is the protection of the group from attack, the second is the ambition of the group to realize itself as fully as possible. In such an organic society the concept of individual liberty was virtually unknown. But when the city-state was absorbed by the idea of empire, new elements came into play. Stoicism especially gave birth to the idea of the individual and made his self-realization the main objective of human endeavor. Christianity added little to this notion by way of substantial content; but it added to its force the

Source: From "Liberty," *Encyclopedia of the Social Sciences,* Seligman and Johnson, eds., vol. 9, pp. 442–446, © 1933 Macmillan Publishing Co., Inc.

impetus of a religious sanction, not improbably the more powerful because Christianity was in its original phase essentially a society of the disinherited, to whom the idea of the eminent dignity of human personality as such would necessarily make an urgent appeal. In this stage it is difficult to dissociate the idea of liberty from that of equality, with which it is frequently intertwined. But as Christianity became the triumphant religion of the western world, the idea of equality became largely relegated to the theoretical sphere; and the liberty in which the church became interested was that of ecclesiastical groups seeking immunity from invasion at the hands of the secular power. In this aspect the liberty it sought was in essence indistinct from the liberty claimed by other groups in the mediaeval community. For until the end of the fifteenth century, roughly, the defense of particular liberties against invasion by external authority was the work of a functional group, such as the barons of Runnymede or the merchants of London. In this period liberty may be said to have resolved itself into a system of liberties or customary negative rights which were bought and sold between the parties for hard cash. Custom became codified into law, and the invasion of custom came to be taken as a denial of liberty. There is little that is universal about such a conception of liberty; the group is largely defending itself from attack without undue regard to the interest of other groups. Thus in mediaeval England liberty had no meaning for the villein; and it is hardly illegitimate to argue that those who fought for liberty when they wrung Magna Carta from King John were good syndicalists whose minds were largely bounded by the narrow demands of a small group within the realm. Liberty has been as often the rallying cry of a selfish interest intent upon privilege for itself as it has been the basis for a demand which sought the realization of a good wider than that by which it was itself affected. It is therefore not unfair to describe the mediaeval idea of liberty as a system of corporate privileges wrung or purchased from the dominant power and affecting the individual less as himself than as a member of some group in whom those privileges cohere.

Philosophically no doubt restraint upon freedom of behavior has always been resented as an invasion of individual personality. But historically the best way of regarding the substance of liberty in the modern period as well as in the mediaeval is to realize that the new elements which enter into its composition at any given time have almost invariably been rationalizations of particular demands from some class or race of creed which have sought a place in the sun denied to them. Thus the history of religious liberty has been the demand for toleration by group after group of dissidents from recognized creeds, few of which have been willing to admit the claims of their rivals to toleration. So again the history of the franchise has been the demand of men for the right to share in political power, while many of those to whom the right has been granted have had no difficulty in urging that it was unwise or unjust to admit the next claimants to their place; Macaulay, who urged with passion the enfranchisement of the middle class, opposed not less urgently the grant of universal suffrage on the ground that it would necessarily dissolve the fabric of society.

The Reformation may be said to have been the most important factor in revitalizing the stoic doctrine of the primacy of the individual and in giving a new emphasis to individual rights as a separate and distinct subject of liberty. The breakdown of the *republica christiana* gave birth to new religions; these by demanding toleration gave birth, even if painfully and in doubt, to the idea of liberty of conscience. The centralization of monarchical power consequent upon the breakdown of feudalism made political liberty more abstract and general than it had previously been; and the discovery of the printing press gave to the idea of freedom of expression within the general concept of political liberty a valuable concreteness which it had never before possessed. Nor is this all. The voyages of discovery synchronized with the emergence of a capitalist economy, and the importance given by the character of this economy to the individual entrepreneur made the problems of civil and economic liberty take on a new sharpness of form. By the time of Locke the idea of the individual as the embodiment of certain natural and imprescriptible rights which authority is not entitled to invade had become a commonplace of political speculation.

In a sense the emergence of the Reformation state on the ruins of the mediaeval commonwealth meant the substitution of the idea of the nation for the idea of the group; and it would not be illegitimate to argue that until the maturity of capitalism in the nineteenth century the struggle for national liberty proceeds along parallel lines with that of individual liberty. The two become until the threshold of our own day the two supreme embodiments of that passion for self-realization which has always lain at the root of the idea of liberty. The nation rejects the subordination of itself to an external authority just as the individual seeks to define for himself spheres of conduct into which external authority is not entitled to enter. Each seeks to make its claims as absolute as possible. The one for that end assumes the panoply of a sovereign state, thereby recognizing no superior; the other attempts to define the limits of governmental interference in terms of wants he discovers as brooking no denial. The history of the search for national liberty resulted in a chaos of sovereignties which stood in sharp contrast to that unified economic life made possible by scientific discovery; and it was clear that the history of the twentieth century would be largely occupied in bringing order into the anarchy to which the struggle for national liberty had given birth.

Something not dissimilar occurred in the history of individual liberty. So long as it was conceived as a body of absolute rights inherent in the individual and entitled to be exerted without regard to their social consequences, liberty was divorced from the ideas of both equality and justice. The individual became the antithesis of the state; and liberty itself became, as with Herbert Spencer, a principle of anarchy rather than a body of claims to be read in the context of the social process. The reason for this evolution is clear. The body of ideas we call liberalism emphasized the undesirability of restraint, because those who gave it birth had mainly experienced the state as an organization interfering with the behavior they regarded as necessary to self-realization. Because of this they sought to reduce the state to the role of a mere guardian of order, keeping the ring in a vast competition of individual strivings of men who received in the social process the reward to which their effort and ability entitled them. Laissez faire was assumed at once to maximize self-realization on the one hand and on the other to serve the state by selecting the fittest for survival. Historic experience and biological principle seemed to the Victorian age to canonize the classic antithesis of individual and state.

The conception of an individual whose liberty was a function—the maintenance of order apart—of the weakness of the state was intelligible enough in its period. It failed to take account of the fact that the differences between men are too great under such conditions to make self-realization possible for more than a few. Liberty in a laissez faire society is attainable only by those who have the wealth or opportunity to purchase it; and these are always a negligible minority. Experience accordingly drove the state to interfere; and the liberal state of the nineteenth century was gradually replaced by the social service state of the twentieth. This may be described by saying that it again joins the ideal of liberty to that of equality, and this in the name of social justice. As the claims of liberty broke down the privileges of birth and creed, so with obvious logic they began an assault upon the claims of wealth also. The state was increasingly driven to widen its functions to mitigate the consequences of that social inequality to which the system of absolute liberty gave rise. Education, public health, provision against unemployment, housing, public parks and libraries are only a few of the outstanding services it was driven to organize in the interest of those who could not be expected to help themselves. Democratic agitation, which from 1600 to about 1870 had been occupied with the removal of barriers upon individual action, after 1870 began to press for the deliberate creation of equalitarian conditions. It has become clear, in a word, that the idea of liberty depends upon the results of the social process at any given time; and it is against that background that its essential elements require analysis.

Liberty may be defined as the affirmation by an individual or group of his or its own essence. It seems to require the presence of three factors. It seeks in the first place a certain harmonious balance of personality; it requires on the negative side the absence of restraint upon the exercise of that affirmation; and it demands on the positive the organization of opportunities for the exercise of a continuous initiative. The problem of liberty has always been the prevention of those restraints, upon the one hand, that men at any given period are not prepared to tolerate and, upon the other, the organization of those opportunities the denial of which results in that sense of frustration which when widely felt leads to imminent or actual disorder.

So regarded, two things are clear about liberty. While its large outlines may have a fairly permanent character, its particular content is always changing with the conditions of time and place. To one age the demand for liberty may express itself in an insistence upon religious toleration; to another political enfranchisement may be its essential expression. This serves to remind us that liberty is always inherent in a social process and is unintelligible apart from it. Liberty therefore must always be conceived, if its philosophy is to be an adequate one, as related to law. It can never be absolute; some restraints are inevitable, some opportunities must be denied, simply because men have to live with one another and move differently to the attainment of antithetic desires. So closely moreover is this network interwoven that we cannot ever seek permanently to define a sphere of conduct within which freedom of action may be defined as liberty. For while we may claim, to take an obvious example, that there is unlikely to be liberty in any community in which there is no legal right to freedom of speech, we cannot maintain that an absolute right to say what he pleases is or should be inherent in any person; it is not, as Mr. Justice Holmes has said, a denial of freedom of speech when a man is prohibited from crying "Fire!" in a crowded theater.

Liberty, in a word, has to be reconciled with the necessities of the social process; it has to find terms upon which to live with authority. Those terms have never been absolute or unchanging; they have always been a function of the historic environment in some given time and place. And that environment has always given birth to its own system of ideas, to which it has contributed some special emphasis in the notion of liberty, born of its peculiar conditions. That emphasis is always seeking its translation into an idea of law, whether by way of negation or affirmation; and the relation of authority to the substance of this idea is usually dependent upon what those who exercise authority consider will be the effect of the translation upon the order they seek to maintain. Trade unions demand the right to combine; authority admits that right or stigmatizes it as conspiracy, according to whether it considers the admission compatible with the way of life it seeks to uphold. A religious group demands the removal of the barriers upon the admission of its members to citizenship; the action of authority will turn upon its judgment of the consequences of the demand. Usually it will be found that the action of authority turns upon its estimate of the power possessed by those who make the demand and the way in which they will use their power; that is the truth embodied in Royer-Collard's great aphorism that liberty is the courage to resist.

The history of liberty since the Reformation has largely passed through two great periods. In the one the essence of the struggle for its realization has been to free the individual from subordination to a position, religious, political or economic, in which he has been placed by an authority external to himself. The effort has been the conferment upon him of rights—that is, of claims recognized by the law—which he is to enjoy without regard to the groups to which he may belong. This may be called the period of personal emancipation, and its classic expression is in the program of the French Revolution. The conception of society involved in it is that of an aggregate of persons; and it is argued that the fewer the restraints upon the free play of personality, the greater will be the liberty attained. Social effort is devoted to the destruction of privileges which inhere in some specially favored groups. It is generally conceived that the more men are let alone, the less positive the action of the state, the more likely is the individual to be free. In this period liberty is related to justice and equality in a negative way. My relation to my neighbor is deemed socially adequate if the state does not positively intervene to confer benefits upon him which I do not enjoy. Religious privilege, political privilege, privileges of birth or sex or race, little by little go by the board.

But in the period which roughly synchronizes with the growth of the modern proletariat it is rapidly discovered that the merely negative liberty to do what one can does not give freedom to the masses. We then enter upon the period of social emancipation. Government becomes increasingly paternalistic. It regulates the behavior of individuals and groups in the interest of an increasing complexion of equality in their lives. The size of the community tends to make the individual less and less significant. He has to obtain his liberty in concert with others similarly placed in the society to which he belongs. In this period the emphasis of liberty is predominantly in the economic sphere. Men become increasingly aware that grave inequalities in property mean grave differences in access to liberty. The struggle for freedom is largely transferred from the plane of political to that of economic rights. Men become less interested in the abstract fragment of political power an individual can secure than in the use of massed pressure of the groups to which they belong to secure an increasing share of the social product. Individualism gives way before socialism. The roots of liberty are held to be in the ownership and control of the instruments of production by the state, the latter using its power to distribute the results of its regulation with increasing approximation to equality. So long as there is inequality, it is argued, there cannot be liberty.

The historic inevitability of this evolution was seen a century ago by de Tocqueville. It is interesting to compare his insistence that the democratization of political power meant equality and that its absence would be regarded by the masses as oppression with the argument of Lord Acton that liberty and equality are antitheses. To the latter liberty was essentially an autocratic ideal; democracy destroyed individuality, which was the very pith of liberty, by seeking identity of conditions. The modern emphasis is rather toward the principle that material equality is growing inescapable and that the affirmation of personality must be effective upon an immaterial plane. It is found that doing as one likes, subject only to the demands of peace, is incompatible with either international or municipal necessities. We pass from contract to relation, as we have passed from status to contract. Men are so involved in intricate networks of relations that the place for their liberty is in a sphere where their behavior does not impinge upon that self-affirmation of others which is liberty.

In short, the problems of liberty in a pluralistic world are extraordinarily complex. The individual who seeks self-realization finds himself confronted by a network of protective relationships which restrain him at every turn. Trade unions, professional and employers' associations, statutory controls of every kind, limit his power of choice by standardizing the manner of his effort. He has to adjust himself to an atmosphere in which there is hardly an aspect of his life not suffused at least partially with social regulation. To do anything he must be one with other men; for it is only by union with his fellows that he can hope to make an impact upon his environment. And even outside the realm in which the state defines the contours of his effort he finds himself surrounded by a complex of social customs and habits which force him despite himself into conventional modes of behavior. The scale of the great society is definitely unfavorable to the individuality of an earlier period.

One other aspect of this position is notable. The history of liberty has been the growth of a tendency to take for granted certain constituent elements in its substance. There is certainly greater religious freedom, for example, than at any previous time. But when the causes of this change are analyzed, it will be found that the growth of religious freedom is a function of the growth of religious indifference. The battle of liberty is not won but merely transferred to another portion of the field. As the contest over the place of individual property in the state becomes more sharp, the state limits freedom of expression and association in those matters which seem to it dangerous to the principles it seeks to impose. Social instability and liberty are antithetic terms. A society is tolerant when men do not challenge the foundations upon which it rests. Wherever these are in question, it moves rapidly to the conditions of dictatorship; and the elements of liberty are unattainable until a new and acceptable equilibrium has been reached.

It is therefore relatively easy to say what things go to make up liberty; it is extraordinarily difficult to say how its atmosphere can be guaranteed. Liberty can be resolved into a system of liberties: of speech, of association, of the right to share fully in political power, of religious belief, of full and undifferentiated protection by the law. But the question of giving to these separate liberties factual realization turns upon the objects to which they are devoted in any particular society at a given time. No doubt in Soviet Russia a Communist has a full sense of liberty; no doubt also he has a keen sense that liberty is denied him in Fascist Italy. Liberty in fact always means in practise liberty within law, and law is the body of regulations enacted in a particular society for its protection. Their color for the most part depends upon its economic character. The main object of law is not the fulfillment of abstract justice but the conference of security upon a way of life which is deemed satisfactory by those who dominate the machinery of the state. Wherever my exercise of my liberty threatens this security, I shall always find that it is denied; and in an economically unequal society an effort on the part of the poor to alter in a radical way the property rights of the rich at once throws the whole scheme of liberties into jeopardy. In the last resort liberty is always a function of power.

It is no doubt true that men have endeavored to set the conditions upon which liberty depends beyond the reach of peradventure. Locke sought to do so by his conception of a limited liability state; but experience has grimly shown that in times of crisis the limits of the liability cannot be maintained. Montesquieu argued that liberty is born of the separation of powers in a state; but the truth of his argument is at bottom the very partial one that men are unlikely to be free unless the judicial authority is largely independent of executive and legislature. The constitutions of many modern states have sought to make the alterations of certain fundamentals a matter of special difficulty in order to protect the liberty of their subjects from invasion. Experience suggests that the technique is not without its value; but, as war and dictatorship have shown, it is an expedient for fair weather, always liable to fundamental neglect in times of crisis. It seemed to de Tocqueville that large local liberties were the secret of a general free atmosphere; liberty, he thought, is born of the wide distribution of power. But this appears to be true only when an equal society can take such advantage of the distribution as to make its benefits unbiased in their incidence; and in the struggle for such a society not the most unlikely thing is the rapid disappearance of this characteristic. The great idealist school of political philosophy has found the essence of freedom in obedience to the general will of the state; but it cannot be said that it has made clear, save to its own votaries, either the nature of a general will or the conditions under which a general will, if it exists, may be said to be in effective operation. An important school of modern publicists has sought to find the essential condition of liberty in a supply of truthful news, since in its absence no rational judgment is possible. But it is clear that the supply of truthful news depends upon men being equally interested in the results which the impact of news may make upon opinion; and no such equal interest exists, above all in an economically unequal society.

Generally it may be argued that the existence of liberty depends upon our willingness to build the foundations of society upon the basis of rational justice and to adjust them to changing conditions in terms of reasoned discussion and not of violence. But if that be the case, the existence of liberty depends upon the attainment of a society in which men are recognized to have an equal claim upon the results of social effort and the general admission that if differences are to obtain these must be proved desirable in terms of rational justice also. In this background, as Aristotle saw at the very dawn of political science, liberty is unattainable until the passion for equality has been satisfied. For the failure to satisfy that passion in an adequate way prevents the emergence of equilibrium in the state. Its foundations are then in jeopardy because men are disputing about fundamentals. In such circumstances proscription and persecution are inevitable, since the community will back that unified outlook upon the principles of its life of which liberty is the consequence. Men who differ upon ultimate matters, particularly in the realm of economic affairs, are rarely prepared to risk the prospect of defeat by submitting their disagreement to the arbitrament of reason. And when reason is at a discount, liberty has never had a serious prospect of survival.

Minority Needs and Positive Freedom

LERONE BENNETT, JR.

Lerone Bennett, Jr. (1928–   ) is senior editor of *Ebony* magazine. His numerous works on the Negro in America include *Before the Mayflower: A History of the Negro in America, 1619–1966* (3d ed., 1966), *The Negro Mood* (1964), and *Confrontation: Black and White* (1965).

If white men come forward now to claim their own freedom and individuality, America will become the America that was dreamed.

There has never been a free people, a free country, a real democracy on the face of this earth. In a city of some 300,000 slaves and 90,000 so-called free men, Plato sat down and praised freedom in exquisitely elegant phrases.

Source: Lerone Bennett, Jr., "What Do You Say?" *Negro Digest* (March 1967), pp. 4–8, 75–78. Copyright © March 1967 by *Negro Digest*. Reprinted by permission of *Black World*.

In a colony of 500,000 slaves and thousands of white indentured servants, Thomas Jefferson, a wealthy slaveowner, sat down and wrote the memorable words of the Declaration of Independence.

In a country with 10 million second-class citizens and millions on millions of poverty-stricken whites, Woodrow Wilson segregated the toilets in Washington, D.C., and went forth to make the world safe for democracy.

There has never been a free people, a free country, a real democracy in the recorded history of man.

The great masses of men have always lived in suburbs of hell.

The great masses of men and almost all women have always been anvils for the hammers of the few.

We have gathered therefore to talk about a subject which has no past, insofar as mankind is concerned, and which can have no future, unless it is visualized and made concrete in the body of mankind. And it seems to me that one forfeits the right to talk about freedom unless one is prepared to face that fact and to do something about it.

Almost 200 years ago at a time of revolutionary turbulence not unlike the present, Tom Paine held that unpalatable truth up to the unseeing eyes of his contemporaries. "Freedom," he said, "hath been hunted around the Globe . . . O! receive the fugitive, and prepare in time an asylum for mankind." Today, after a thousand evasions, after a thousand proclamations and manifestoes, freedom is still a fugitive—in America as well as in Russia, in Portugal as well as in Angola, in England as well as in Rhodesia, in Boston as well as in Mississippi.

We live in a world where two-thirds of the people are hungry.

We live in a world where most of the people are diseased and illiterate.

In such a world, who has the effrontery—who has the gall—to praise the state of freedom?

The whole problem of freedom in the white and nonwhite worlds must be placed first in this larger context, for henceforth it will be impossible to speak of freedom in terms of the concerns of the tiny minority of men who live in Europe and North America. We must note, moreover, that freedom in Western Europe and North America is abstract, negative and largely illusory. And even in these areas, millions live on the edge of despair, and millions more are slaves to their skin or to their omnivorous machines.

It will be my argument here that the truth of freedom in the world is the truth of the truly disinherited. And by that I mean that the state of freedom is most accurately reflected in the lives of the men on the bottom. The men on the top and the men in the middle can remain ignorant of what they do and of what they are. But the men on the bottom experience the truth of society irremediably. They are the truth of every society. In them, we can see what we are, and what we have become. In the mirror of their eyes, we can measure the depth of our alienation from freedom and from man.

To be even more explicit and to bring the matter closer to home, I intend to maintain here that racism is the best index of the failure of American society to create a human and equitable society *for white people.* My argument here is the very simple one that the depth of fascism is a measure of the unfreedom in the white community. And from that premise, we can conclude that black men are not free because white men are not free. And by all this we must understand that when the Emancipation Proclamation finally comes it will be most of all an emancipation of white people from the fears and frailties that cruelly twist and goad their lives.

Before pursuing that argument, let us pause for a moment and examine the meaning and implications of the word that everybody praises and few people live. As we all know, freedom lends itself to numerous interpretations. In the white Western world, it is usually defined negatively as "freedom from." This definition finds its truth in certain abstract liberties: freedom of speech, freedom of association, *et cetera*. To define freedom thusly, and to stop there, is, in my opinion, a perversion of freedom, for freedom also means "freedom to." And this positive definition finds its truth in concrete possibilities created in the social field in the right to work, in the right to eat, in the right to shelter, in the right to be.

There is still another definition of freedom, a psychological one, which stresses the act of willing or choosing. And this definition, in turn, is linked to a fourth one which contends that man—by his ability to rise above or transcend a situation, any situation, by his ability to say No—is the measure and the meaning of freedom in the world.

In my opinion, no definition of freedom is adequate in today's world which does not embrace all these meanings—freedom from, freedom to transcendence—in a concrete context linked to conditions that open or close real possibilities to concrete men in their social and historical situation. Such a definition would recognize the existentialist truth that man *is* freedom and would recognize that the alienation of the world from freedom is a measure of its alienation from man and the possibilities of man. It would also recognize the truth that man has not yet been created and that the creation of man—black man as well as white man—awaits the winning of real, concrete freedom for all men.

Here and there, across the great wastelands of time, little knots of men have glimpsed the terrifying possibilities of that paradox. I think particularly of African village democracy and other free forms developed by American Indians and other communal groups. But these groups were hemmed in by material limitations and it was left to Western Europe to free man from feudal restrictions and to hoist high the standards of individuality and personal autonomy. But Europe, in its lunge toward freedom, made three fatal errors. First of all, and most important of all, Europe experienced its newfound freedom as the untrammelled exercise of the ego. And in pursuit of the goal of possessive individualism it drew a circle around itself, excluding and enslaving three-fourths of mankind.

Second, out of sheer terror, Europe cut freedom into two parts, separating man into positive and negative poles, the mind and the body, reason and emotion, sex and the soul. Refusing to recognize the full force of freedom, which manifests itself in sex as well as in prayer, Europe facilitated that manic process by which men project their rejected freedom onto the scapegoats and outcasts of society.

In the third place, Europe refused to admit the full logic of its own idea.

Minority Needs and Positive Freedom   439

With few exceptions, Europeans and the sons of Europeans found it difficult to extend the idea of freedom to poor whites and impossible to extend it to non-whites. In Europe and in the extensions of Europe, freedom became a function of the skin and of property.

Despite the huge achievements of European technology and science, European freedom, beautiful as it was, was not freedom. Or better still: it was not yet freedom. Having freed man from arbitrary restraints, Europe stopped halfway, leaving man tied to the chains of caste, class and passion. Having expelled man from his tribal and feudal Eden, Europe retreated, in terror, from Nietzsche's lucid question:

"Not free from what, but free for what?"

America inherited Europe's immense achievements and its immense failures—and extended both. The history of America, like the history of Europe, has been a history of a magnificent evasion of the multiple meanings of freedom. The most obvious example of that failure is the black American. But the failure to integrate black people into the American community is only a part of our culture's general inability to create a just and human environment.

Despite our alleged affluence, 30 to 40 million Americans, many of them white, live in abject poverty, and millions more live lives of harrowing economic insecurity.

Despite our extraordinary mechanical ability, which cannot be praised so highly, we have failed to create a truly human community. Machines are more real here than human beings—and vastly more important. In a society of machines, by machines and for machines, we are increasingly powerless, and a nihilistic individualism has made conformists—and cowards—of us all. Dehumanized, depersonalized, distracted by bread and television, we have almost lost sight of man. Mystified by an ethic which confuses the verb to be with the verb to have, we try to staunch the running wound of our lives by adding layers and layers of mechanical band-aids. We lack passion, we lack purpose, and we decide nothing. The great alternatives are formulated by others, and in our name and without our assent men, women, and little children are killed in poverty-stricken countries. Increasingly irresponsible as our choices become fewer, and as the world becomes more threatening, we whirl around and in a materialistic inferno between collective madness and collective self-destruction.

And we are afraid.

We are afraid of our neighbors, of Negroes, of Chinese, of Communists, of four-letter words, sex . . . —we are afraid, in a word, of ourselves.

Because we fear ourselves and others, because we are dominated by machines and things, because we are not in control of our destiny, we are neither happy nor free.

"If one probes beneath the chrome-plated surface," Senator J. W. Fulbright says, "he comes inescapably to the conclusion that the American people by and large are not happy. . . . I believe . . . that America's trouble is basically one of aimlessness at home and frustration abroad."

As you have probably guessed by now, I believe America's trouble is at a deeper level. The problem, in my opinion, is structural, that is, institutional. We have not created a single community here. We have not even created a single community for white people. Men tell me that white people ought to love black people. But it is clear to me that white people don't love each other, not to speak of the fact that an incredibly large number of white Americans don't love themselves.

Racism in America is a reflection of this structural problem. As I have said elsewhere, we misunderstand racism completely if we do not see it as a confused and alienated protest against a suffocating reality. On the level of power, racism is used by men to effect magical solutions of the unresolved social problems in the white community. On a personal level, particularly among lower-income and middle-income whites, racism is an avenue of flight, a cry for help from desperate men stifling in the prisons of their skins. Viewed in this perspective, racism is a flight from freedom, a flight from the self, a flight from the intolerable burdens of being a man in a mechanized world.

There is considerable evidence that America's stress on possessive individualism induces exaggerated anxieties which are displaced onto the area of race relations. The fear of failure, the fear of competitors, the fear of losing status, of not living in the right neighborhood, of not having the right friends or the right gadgets: these fears weigh heavily on the minds of millions of Americans and lead to a search for avenues of escape. And so the factory worker or the poor farmer who finds himself at a dead end with a nagging wife, a problem child and past-due bill uses the black man as a screen to hide himself from himself and from an intolerable reality.

To adapt the perceptive words of Richard Wright, social discontent assumes many guises, and the social commentator who focuses on the police blotter misses the real clues to contemporary reality. By this I mean that it is possible to know, *before it happens,* that certain forms of violence will occur. It can be known, *before it happens,* that a native-born American, educated, healthy, with a pretty wife, a split-level house and two cars, with all the abstract liberties *but devoid of basic human satisfactions,* will seize upon a powerless black man and derive deep feelings of pleasure from hacking him to death with a chain. "But," as Wright said, "To know that a seemingly normal, ordinary American is capable of such brutality implies making a judgment about the nature and quality of our everyday American experiences which most Americans simply cannot do, FOR, TO ADMIT THAT OUR INDIVIDUAL EXPERIENCES ARE OF SO LOW A QUALITY . . . AS TO PRECLUDE THE DEEP, ORGANIC SATISFACTIONS NECESSARY FOR CIVILIZED, PEACEFUL LIVING, IS TO CONDEMN THE SYSTEM THAT PROVIDES THOSE EXPERIENCES."

The real question in America is how we build a society in which apparently normal people do not need scapegoats or whipping boys to build their egos and to maintain their dignity?

How can we build a society that will enhance freedom and integrity and obviate the need for racism?

First of all, we have to condemn the system.

And we have to condemn the system in the name of that America, of that Commonwealth of Silence, which was written, which was promised, and which has never existed. I am suggesting here that we must initiate a sustained dialogue on the foundations of our society. And we must demand the right to subject every institution to the claims of freedom.

Let me say immediately that I don't have all the answers. The only thing I know is that everything must be rethought again. We need a new definition of work embracing any act of value that a man brings to society and a new definition of politics embracing the full and effective participation of all men in formulating the alternatives and choosing between the alternatives of the political, economic and social decisions that affect their lives. We also need a new definition of sex which would free women for equal roles in the church, in labor unions, in the professions and every other institution of our society. I often say to my wife that women, not Negroes, are the most brainwashed people in the Western world. Of course, in this regard, I am very much like Thomas Jefferson. I want women to have absolute freedom everywhere right now—but I hope that the revolution starts with somebody else's wife.

But wherever the revolution starts, I am prepared to welcome it, for I believe that the future of freedom in America is dependent upon the formulation of a broader definition of freedom and of man and of woman than our society is based upon. And it seems to me that it is necessary to set liberty in the context of equality with the understanding that every individual is entitled to the space and the chance to fulfill himself, which is only another way of saying that every individual is entitled to the instruments that will permit him to go to the boundaries of himself.

This, I believe, is a precondition for black and white freedom in America. For if we want black men and white men to cooperate, we must create conditions that will make it possible for them to cooperate. In other words, we must change the conditions that lead white men to see black men as threats to their homes, to their jobs, to their masculinity. And to do this we must modify the situation of the white man from top to bottom. For to demand that white men give up their irrational responses to black reality is to demand that a situation which requires irrational responses be abolished.

We must conceive and organize in this country programs that will make it impossible for one man to profit by another man's falls.

We must conceive and organize in this community, and in every other community, programs that will relieve the economic pressures on all men so that some men will not find it to their short-term economic interest to keep other men down.

In other words, we must take the profit out of bigotry.

The first steps in this direction would be a guaranteed annual income, the extension of Medicare to all citizens, the elimination of regressive taxes, and housing and educational subsidies to lower- and middle-income groups.

Ultimately, however, such an effort would require a reevaluation of our dominant myths, including the myth of possessive individuality, which is the greatest single obstacle to individuality, and the myth of property, which is the greatest single obstacle to the free enjoyment of property by all men.

Let there be no misunderstanding here: I am not saying that property in itself is evil—what I'm saying is that property masquerading as God is the major roadblock to freedom in the world today. Men need a certain amount of property to validate themselves and their freedom, but freedom becomes unfreedom and life loses its meaning when property becomes an inhuman idol, when anything and everything is sacrificed to an abstract Thing.

There was an interesting article on this subject in the *New York Post* which I would like to quote at some length. The article referred to the summer marches by Dr. Martin Luther King, Jr., and his supporters through the Gage Park area of Chicago. Pete Hamill visited the neighborhood and wrote the following words:

"This was the way the Hollywood hustlers used to put their cardboard America together, in a time more innocent than ours.

"Children played in the streets, or burbled from baby carriages. Young boys mowed lawns which still smelled sweetly from the morning rains. Housewives pushed strollers to the grocery stores, or drove the family cars to the supermarkets. A man on vacation nailed a brass numeral to his front door. A lot of people seemed to be polishing automobiles with an almost reverent devotion. Gage Park on Monday afternoon seemed as innocuous as anyplace where Doris Day had ever lived on film.

"But underneath, past the front doors of those two-story houses, in the secret places behind those lawns and those automobiles and those smiling children, Gage Park was like a tray of summer worms. By the time the thing that is crawling through Gage Park has hooked its last inhabitant, that neighborhood is almost certainly going to murder someone. It is going to murder someone because of the accident of color. It is going to murder someone over the combination of wood, metal and concrete which the inhabitants fondly describe as their property."

The same animal is crawling through the Gage Parks of Boston and New York and California. And if we don't confront it soon, an unspeakably horrible disaster is going to happen here. It's going to happen because our churches and schools have not taught people that no thing is higher than man. It's going to happen because our civilization has not yet learned that men are important, whether they own property or not.

To a great extent, racism in America is grounded on the whole sick syndrome surrounding real estate, status, greed, and human pettiness. If we are serious about freedom, we are going to have to come to grips with that syndrome.

We hear a great deal about freedom and property, but we must have the courage to say that words cannot be prostituted with impunity. Freedom is a fine word, but it has its boundaries. Men who say the community is free when it is enslaved, men who say the sky is black when it is blue, are debasing reality and preparing the way for tyranny.

We can respect freedom only when it is intended for freedom. A freedom that denies freedom must be denied in the name of freedom. For to be free is not to have the power to do anything you want to do. I am oppressed if I am denied the right of free movement, but I am not oppressed if I am denied the right to deny my neighbor freedom of movement.

Beyond all that, we must note that the idea of one-class, one-kind neighborhoods is in and of itself a clear and present danger to American democracy. The standardized neighborhoods, the standardized house, the standardized minds and the standardized fears which stretch from one end of America to another are a denial of the movement of life which advances by integrating differences. As Chardin has said: "Joy lies not in exclusiveness and isolation, but in variety, which is the reservoir of experience and emotion." On the other hand, uniformity, sameness, standardization make for cultural stagnation and, as sure as night follows day, regimentation and eventually neo-Fascism.

In order to deal with the anti-democratic ideas, which have made deep inroads in American life, we must make revolutionary changes at every level of our lives. We confront, in a word, the need for not a law here or a law there but for a vital change in the whole spirit of our civilization.

.   .   .

This is an important moment in the history of the Commonwealth. There stretch out before us now two roads and two roads only. America must now become America or something else, a Fourth Reich perhaps or a Fourth Reich of the spirit. To put the matter bluntly—we must become what we say we are or give in to the secret dream that blights our hearts.

Let us rejoice that it has come to this.

Now that freedom is dangerous, perhaps men will stop prostituting it. Now that freedom is exploding in broad open daylight in the streets of America and Vietnam perhaps we will be able to recognize her true friends.

As individuals, we are called upon to make a creative response to this challenge by assuming our own freedom and validating it in social acts designed to create spaces in which the seeds of freedom can grow.

In a very real sense, the struggle in America is a struggle to free white Americans or, to be quite precise, it is a struggle to put them in the presence of their freedom. And it seems to me that it is the duty of this convocation to send abroad the good news that one can be free, even in Boston or Chicago or New York.

Freedom isn't something you can buy on the installment plan. It is not a gift, from anybody—it is a priceless possession that must be reclaimed and rewon every day. As Silone has said: "One can be free, even under a dictatorship. All you have to do is to struggle against it." He who thinks with his own head and acts with his own heart is free. He who is not afraid of his neighbors is free. He who struggles for what he believes in is a free man. On the other hand: If you live in the richest Boston suburb and if you are lazy, timid, conformist, you are not free, but a slave.

Because men deny the tiny bit of psychological freedom at their disposal, it is necessary to awaken them by social movements in which wills confront each other. This is the meaning of the Black Revolution, which is inviting us to become ourselves by going to the limits of ourselves. This revolution defines the state of freedom in America today, and it tells us that freedom has no future in America if the black man does not have a future in freedom.

More than 100 years ago, Walt Whitman told Ralph Waldo Emerson: "Master, I am a man who has perfect faith. But Master, we have not come through centuries, caste, heroism, fables, to halt in this land today."

The spirit of Walt Whitman is marching today in the Harlems of our mind. Men and women made in Whitman's image are saying to us: "Fellow Americans, we have perfect faith. But Fellow Americans, we have not come through slavery, segregation, degradation, blood, cotton, roaches, rats, to halt in this land today."

Black Americans, by daring to claim their freedom, are daring us to claim our own.

And the movement which expresses that thrust will continue despite the recent revelations of the depth and extent of racism in America. Whatever the problems, whatever the setbacks, whatever the dangers, oppression must be rejected at any cost. For, as [W. E. B.] Du Bois said, the price of freedom is always less than the cost of oppression.

In the Black Revolution, America comes hard up against a new fact: *the color of the world has changed*. And with that change, a terrifying freedom has become the burden of all men, especially those men who were tyrannized for so long by the arbitrary limitations of their skin. If white men come forward now to claim their own freedom and individuality, if they abandon their trenches and come out into the open, America will become the America that was dreamed.

This is the real meaning of the Black Revolution, which is a desperate attempt to place before our freedom the burning alternatives history is offering us.

Walt Whitman said:

"We have not come through centuries, caste, heroism, fables, to halt in this land today."

Black Americans are saying:

"We have not come through slavery, segregation, degradation to halt in this land today."

And the question now is:

What do you say?

Women's Liberation

Sexual Politics

KATE MILLETT

Kate Millett (1934–   ) is a professor, author, and feminist leader and is generally
known as the "principal theoretician" of the women's liberation movement. She
wrote *Sexual Politics* (1970).

In introducing the term "sexual politics," one must first answer the inevitable
question "Can the relationship between the sexes be viewed in a political light
at all?" The answer depends on how one defines politics.[1] This essay does not
define the political as that relatively narrow and exclusive world of meetings,
chairmen, and parties. The term "politics" shall refer to power-structured relationships, arrangements whereby one group of persons is controlled by another.
By way of parenthesis one might add that although an ideal politics might simply be conceived of as the arrangement of human life on agreeable and rational
principles from whence the entire notion of power *over* others should be ban-
ished, one must confess that this is not what constitutes the political as we
know it, and it is to this that we must address ourselves.

The following sketch, which might be described as "notes toward a theory of
patriarchy," will attempt to prove that sex is a status category with political
implications. Something of a pioneering effort, it must perforce be both tentative and imperfect. Because the intention is to provide an overall description,
statements must be generalized, exceptions neglected, and subheadings overlapping and, to some degree, arbitrary as well.

The word "politics" is enlisted here when speaking of the sexes primarily
because such a word is eminently useful in outlining the real nature of their
relative status, historically and at the present. It is opportune, perhaps today
even mandatory, that we develop a more relevant psychology and philosophy
of power relationships beyond the simple conceptual framework provided by our
traditional formal politics. Indeed, it may be imperative that we give some
attention to defining a theory of politics which treats of power relationships on

[1] The American Heritage Dictionary's fourth definition is fairly approximate: "methods or
tactics involved in managing a state or government." *American Heritage Dictionary* (New
York: American Heritage and Houghton Mifflin, 1969). One might expand this to a set of
stratagems designed to maintain a system. If one understands patriarchy to be an institution
perpetuated by such techniques of control, one has a working definition of how politics is
conceived in this essay.

Source: Kate Millett, *Sexual Politics* (New York, 1970), Chap. 2. Copyright © 1969, 1970
by Kate Millett. Reprinted by permission of Doubleday & Company, Inc.

grounds less conventional than those to which we are accustomed.[2] I have therefore found it pertinent to define them on grounds of personal contact and interaction between members of well-defined and coherent groups: races, castes, classes, and sexes. For it is precisely because certain groups have no representation in a number of recognized political structures that their position tends to be so stable, their oppression so continuous.

In America, recent events have forced us to acknowledge at last that the relationship between the races is indeed a political one which involves the general control of one collectivity, defined by birth, over another collectivity, also defined by birth. Groups who rule by birthright are fast disappearing, yet there remains one ancient and universal scheme for the domination of one birth group by another—the scheme that prevails in the area of sex. The study of racism has convinced us that a truly political state of affairs operates between the races to perpetuate a series of oppressive circumstances. The subordinated group has inadequate redress through existing political institutions, and is deterred thereby from organizing into conventional political struggle and opposition.

Quite in the same manner, a disinterested examination of our system of sexual relationship must point out that the situation between the sexes now, and throughout history, is a case of that phenomenon Max Weber defined as *herrschaft*, a relationship of dominance and subordinance.[3] What goes largely unexamined, often even unacknowledged (yet is institutionalized nonetheless) in our social order, is the birthright priority whereby males rule females. Through this system a most ingenious form of "interior colonization" has been achieved. It is one which tends moreover to be sturdier than any form of segregation, and more rigorous than class stratification, more uniform, certainly more enduring. However muted its present appearance may be, sexual dominion obtains nevertheless as perhaps the most pervasive ideology of our culture and provides its most fundamental concept of power.

This is so because our society, like all other historical civilizations, is a patriarchy.[4] The fact is evident at once if one recalls that the military, industry, technology, universities, science, political office, and finance—in short, every

[2] I am indebted here to Ronald V. Samson's *The Psychology of Power* (New York: Random House, 1968) for his intelligent investigation of the connection between formal power structures and the family and for his analysis of how power corrupts basic human relationships.

[3] "Domination in the quite general sense of power, i.e., the possibility of imposing one's will upon the behavior of other persons, can emerge in the most diverse forms." In this central passage of *Wirtschaft und Gesellschaft* Weber is particularly interested in two such forms: control through social authority ("patriarchal, magisterial, or princely") and control through economic force. In patriarchy as in other forms of domination "that control over economic goods, i.e. economic power, is a frequent, often purposively willed, consequence of domination as well as one of its most important instruments." Quoted from Max Rheinstein's and Edward Shil's translation of portions of *Wirtschaft und Gesellschaft* entitled *Max Weber on Law in Economy and Society* (New York: Simon and Schuster, 1967), pp. 323–324.

[4] No matriarchal societies are known to exist at present. Matrilineality, which may be, as some anthropologists have held, a residue or a transitional stage of matriarchy, does not constitute an exception to patriarchal rule, it simply channels the power held by males through female descent—, e.g., the Avunculate.

avenue of power within the society, including the coercive force of the police, is entirely in male hands. As the essence of politics is power, such realization cannot fail to carry impact. What lingers of supernatural authority, the Deity, "His" ministry, together with the ethics and values, the philosophy and art of our culture—its very civilization—as T. S. Eliot once observed, is of male manufacture.

If one takes patriarchal government to be the institution whereby that half of the populace which is female is controlled by that half which is male, the principles of patriarchy appear to be two fold: male shall dominate female, elder male shall dominate younger. However, just as with any human institution, there is frequently a distance between the real and the ideal; contradictions and exceptions do exist within the system. While patriarchy as an institution is a social constant so deeply entrenched as to run through all other political, social, or economic forms, whether of caste or class, feudality or bureaucracy, just as it pervades all major religions, it also exhibits great variety in history and locale. In democracies,[5] for example, females have often held no office or do so (as now) in such minuscule numbers as to be below even token representation. Aristocracy, on the other hand, with its emphasis upon the magic and dynastic properties of blood, may at times permit women to hold power. The principle of rule by elder males is violated even more frequently. Bearing in mind the variation and degree in patriarchy—as say between Saudi Arabia and Sweden, Indonesia and Red China—we also recognize our own form in the U.S. and Europe to be much altered and attenuated by the reforms described in the next chapter.

I. Ideological

Hannah Arendt[6] has observed that government is upheld by power supported either through consent or imposed through violence. Conditioning to an ideology amounts to the former. Sexual politics obtains consent through the "socialization" of both sexes to basic patriarchal polities with regard to temperament, role, and status. As to status, a pervasive assent to the prejudice of male superiority guarantees superior status in the male, inferior in the female. The first item, temperament, involves the formation of human personality along stereotyped lines of sex category ("masculine" and "feminine"), based on the needs and values of the dominant group and dictated by what its members cherish in themselves and find convenient in subordinates; aggression, intelligence, force, and efficacy in the male; passivity, ignorance, docility, "virtue," and ineffectuality in the female. This is complemented by a second factor, sex role, which decrees a consonant and highly elaborate code of conduct, gesture and attitude for each sex. In terms of activity, sex role assigns domestic service and at-

---

[5] Radical democracy would, of course, preclude patriarchy. One might find evidence of a general satisfaction with a less than perfect democracy in the fact that women have so rarely held power within modern "democracies."

[6] Hannah Arendt, "Speculations on Violence," *The New York Review of Books,* Vol. XII No. 4, February 27, 1969, p. 24.

tendance upon infants to the female, the rest of human achievement, interest, and ambition to the male. The limited role allotted the female tends to arrest her at the level of biological experience. Therefore, nearly all that can be described as distinctly human rather than animal activity (in their own way animals also give birth and care for their young) is largely reserved for the male. Of course, status again follows from such an assignment. Were one to analyze the three categories one might designate status as the political component, role as the sociological, and temperament as the psychological—yet their interdependence is unquestionable and they form a chain. Those awarded higher status tend to adopt roles of mastery, largely because they are first encouraged to develop temperaments of dominance. That this is true of caste and class as well is self-evident.

II. Biological

Patriarchal religion, popular attitude, and to some degree, science as well[7] assumes these psycho-social distinctions to rest upon biological differences between the sexes, so that where culture is acknowledged as shaping behavior, it is said to do no more than cooperate with nature. Yet the temperamental distinctions created in patriarchy ("masculine" and "feminine" personality traits) do not appear to originate in human nature, those of role and status still less.

. . .

Not only is there insufficient evidence for the thesis that the present social distinctions of patriarchy (status, role, temperament) are physical in origin, but we are hardly in a position to assess the existing differentiations, since distinctions which we know to be culturally induced at present so outweigh them. Whatever the "real" differences between the sexes may be, we are not likely to know them until the sexes are treated differently, that is alike. And this is very far from being the case at present. Important new research not only suggests that the possibilities of innate temperamental differences seem more remote than ever, but even raises questions as to the validity and permanence of psychosexual identity. In doing so it gives fairly concrete positive evidence of the overwhelmingly *cultural* character of gender, i.e., personality structure in terms of sexual category.

What Stoller and other experts define as "core gender identity" is now thought to be established in the young by the age of eighteen months. This is how Stoller differentiates betweeen sex and gender:

Dictionaries stress that the major connotation of sex is a biological one, as for example, in the phrases sexual relations or the male sex. In agreement with this, the word sex, in this work will refer to the male or female sex and the component biological parts that determine whether one is a male or a female; the word sexual will have connotations of anatomy and physiology. This obviously leaves tremendous

[7] The social, rather than the physical sciences are referred to here. Traditionally, medical science had often subscribed to such beliefs. This is no longer the case today, when the best medical research points to the conclusion that sexual stereotypes have no bases in biology.

areas of behavior, feelings, thoughts and fantasies that are related to the sexes and yet do not have primarily biological connotations. It is for some of these psychological phenomena that the term gender will be used: one can speak of the male sex or the female sex, but one can also talk about masculinity and femininity and not necessarily be implying anything about anatomy or physiology. Thus, while sex and gender seem to common sense inextricably bound together, one purpose of this study will be to confirm the fact that the two realms (sex and gender) are not inevitably bound in anything like a one-to-one relationship, but each may go into quite independent ways.[8]

In cases of genital malformation and consequent erroneous gender assignment at birth, studied at the California Gender Identity Center, the discovery was made that it is easier to change the sex of an adolescent male, whose biological identity turns out to be contrary to his gender assignment and conditioning—through surgery—than to undo the educational consequences of years, which have succeeded in making the subject temperamentally feminine in gesture, sense of self, personality and interests. Studies done in California under Stoller's direction offer proof that gender identity (I am a girl, I am a boy) is the primary identity any human being holds—the first as well as the most permanent and far-reaching. Stoller later makes emphatic the distinction that sex is biological, gender psychological, and therefore cultural: *"Gender* is a term that has psychological or cultural rather than biological connotations. If the proper terms for sex are "male" and "female," the corresponding terms for gender are "masculine" and "feminine"; these latter may be quite independent of (biological) sex."[9] Indeed, so arbitrary is gender, that it may even be contrary to physiology: ". . . although the external genitalia (penis, testes, scrotum) contribute to the sense of maleness, no one of them is essential for it, not even all of them together. In the absence of complete evidence, I agree in general with Money, and the Hampsons who show in their large series of intersexed patients that gender role is determined by postnatal forces, regardless of the anatomy and physiology of the external genitalia."[10]

. . .

III. Sociological

Patriarchy's chief institution is the family. It is both a mirror of and a connection with the larger society; a patriarchal unit within a patriarchal whole. Mediating between the individual and the social structure, the family effects control and conformity where political and other authorities are insufficient.[11] As the fundamental instrument and the foundation unit of patriarchal society the family and its roles are prototypical. Serving as an agent of the larger society, the family not only encourages its own members to adjust and conform,

[8] Robert J. Stoller, *Sex and Gender* (New York: Science House, 1968), from the preface, pp. viii–ix.

[9] Ibid., p. 9.

[10] Ibid., p. 48.

[11] In some of my remarks on the family I am indebted to Goode's short and concise analysis. See William J. Goode, *The Family* (Englewood Cliffs, New Jersey: Prentice-Hall, 1964).

but acts as a unit in the government of the patriarchal state which rules its citizens through its family heads. Even in patriarchal societies where they are granted legal citizenship, women tend to be ruled through the family alone and have little or no formal relation to the state.[12]

As co-operation between the family and the larger society is essential, else both would fall apart, the fate of three patriarchal institutions, the family, society, and the state are interrelated. In most forms of patriarchy this has generally led to the granting of religious support in statements such as the Catholic precept that "the father is head of the family," or Judaism's delegation of quasi-priestly authority to the male parent. Secular governments today also confirm this, as in census practices of designating the male as head of household, taxation, passports, etc. Female heads of household tend to be regarded as undesirable; the phenomenon is a trait of poverty or misfortune. The Confucian prescription that the relationship between ruler and subject is parallel to that of father and children points to the essentially feudal character of the patriarchal family (and conversely, the familial character of feudalism) even in modern democracies.[13]

. . .

IV. Class

It is in the area of class that the castelike status of the female within patriarchy is most liable to confusion, for sexual status often operates in a superficially confusing way within the variable of class. In a society where status is dependent upon the economic, social, and educational circumstances of class, it is possible for certain females to appear to stand higher than some males. Yet not when one looks more closely at the subject. This is perhaps easier to see by means of analogy: a black doctor or lawyer has higher social status than a poor white sharecropper. But race, itself a caste system which subsumes class, persuades the latter citizen that he belongs to a higher order of life, just as it oppresses the black professional in spirit, whatever his material success may be. In much the same manner, a truck driver or butcher has always his "manhood" to fall back upon. Should this final vanity be offended, he may contemplate more violent methods. The literature of the past thirty years provides a staggering number of incidents in which the caste of virility triumphs over the social status of wealthy or even educated women. In literary contexts one has to deal here with wish-fulfillment. Incidents from life (bullying, obscene, or hostile remarks) are probably another sort of psychological gesture of ascendancy. Both convey more hope than reality, for class divisions are generally quite impervious to the hostility of individuals. And yet while the existence of class division is not seriously threatened by such expressions of enmity, the existence of sexual

[12] Family, society, and state are three separate but connected entities: women have a decreasing importance as one goes from the first to the third category. But as each of the three categories exists within or is influenced by the overall institution of patriarchy, I am concerned here less with differentiation than with pointing out a general similarity.

[13] J. K. Folsom makes a convincing argument as to the anomalous character of patriarchal family systems within democratic society. See Joseph K. Folsom, *The Family and Democratic Society* (New York: John Wiley, 1934, 1943).

hierarchy has been re-affirmed and mobilized to "punish" the female quite effectively.

The function of class or ethnic mores in patriarchy is largely a matter of how overtly displayed or how loudly enunciated the general ethic of masculine supremacy allows itself to become. Here one is confronted by what appears to be a paradox: while in the lower social strata, the male is more likely to claim authority on the strength of his sex rank alone, he is actually obliged more often to share power with the women of his class who are economically productive; whereas in the middle and upper classes, there is less tendency to assert a blunt patriarchal dominance, as men who enjoy such status have more power in any case.[14]

It is generally accepted that Western patriarchy has been much softened by the concepts of courtly and romantic love. While this is certainly true, such influence has also been vastly overestimated. In comparison with the candor of "machismo" or oriental behavior, one realizes how much of a concession traditional chivalrous behavior represents—a sporting kind of reparation to allow the subordinate female certain means of saving face. While a palliative to the injustice of woman's social position, chivalry is also a technique for disguising it. One must acknowledge that the chivalrous stance is a game the master group plays in elevating its subject to pedestal level. Historians of courtly love stress the fact that the raptures of the poets had no effect upon the legal or economic standing of women, and very little upon their social status.[15] As the sociologist Hugo Beigel has observed, both the courtly and the romantic versions of love are "grants" which the male concedes out of his total powers.[16] Both have had the effect of obscuring the patriarchal character of Western culture and in their general tendency to attribute impossible virtues to women, have ended by confining them in a narrow and often remarkably conscribing sphere of behavior. It was a Victorian habit, for example, to insist the female assume the function of serving as the male's conscience and living the life of goodness he found tedious but felt someone ought to do anyway.

The concept of romantic love affords a means of emotional manipulation which the male is free to exploit, since love is the only circumstance in which the female is (ideologically) pardoned for sexual activity. And convictions of romantic love are convenient to both parties since this is often the only condition in which the female can overcome the far more powerful conditioning she has received toward sexual inhibition. Romantic love also obscures the realities of female status and the burden of economic dependency. As to "chivalry," such gallant gesture as still resides in the middle classes has degenerated to a

[14] Goode, op. cit., p. 74.

[15] This is the gist of Valency's summary of the situation before the troubadours, acknowledging that courtly love is an utter anomaly: "With regard to the social background, all that can be stated with confidence is that we know nothing of the objective relationships of men and women in the Middle Ages which might conceivably motivate the strain of love-poetry which the troubadours developed." Maurice Valency, *In Praise of Love* (New York: Macmillan, 1958), p. 5.

[16] Hugo Beigel, "Romantic Love," *The American Sociological Review*, Vol. 16, 1951, p. 331.

tired ritualism, which scarcely serves to mask the status situation of the present.

Within patriarchy one must often deal with contradictions which are simply a matter of class style. David Riesman has noted that as the working class has been assimilated into the middle class, so have its sexual mores and attitudes. The fairly blatant male chauvinism which was once a province of the lower class or immigrant male has been absorbed and taken on a certain glamour through a number of contemporary figures, who have made it, and a certain number of other working-class male attitudes, part of a new, and at the moment, fashionable life style. So influential is this working-class ideal of brute virility (or more accurately, a literary and therefore middle-class version of it) become in our time that it may replace more discreet and "gentlemanly" attitudes of the past.[17]

One of the chief effects of class within patriarchy is to set one woman against another, in the past creating a lively antagonism between whore and matron, and in the present between career woman and housewife. One envies the other her "security" and prestige, while the envied yearns beyond the confines of respectability for what she takes to be the other's freedom, adventure, and contact with the great world. Through the multiple advantages of the double standard, the male participates in both worlds, empowered by his superior social and economic resources to play the estranged women against each other as rivals. One might also recognize subsidiary status categories among women: not only is virtue class, but beauty and age as well.

Perhaps, in the final analysis, it is possible to argue that women tend to transcend the usual class stratifications in patriarchy, for whatever the class of her birth and education, the female has fewer permanent class associations than does the male. Economic dependency renders her affiliations with any class a tangential, vicarious, and temporary matter. Aristotle observed that the only slave to whom a commoner might lay claim was his woman, and the service of an unpaid domestic still provides working-class males with a "cushion" against the buffets of the class system which incidentally provides them with some of the psychic luxuries of the leisure class.

· · ·

V. Economic and Educational

One of the most efficient branches of patriarchal government lies in the agency of its economic hold over its female subjects. In traditional patriarchy, women, as non-persons without legal standing, were permitted no actual economic existence as they could neither own nor earn in their own right. Since women have always worked in patriarchal societies, often at the most routine or strenu-

[17] Mailer and Miller occur to one in this connection, and Lawrence as well. One might trace Rojack's very existence as a fictional figure to the virility symbol of Jack London's Ernest Everhard and Tennessee Williams' Stanley Kowalski. That Rojack is also literate is nothing more than an elegant finish upon the furniture of his "manhood" solidly based in the hard oaken grain of his mastery over any and every "broad" he can better, bludgeon, or bugger.

ous tasks, what is at issue here is not labor but economic reward. In modern reformed patriarchal societies, women have certain economic rights, yet the "woman's work" in which some two thirds of the female population in most developed countries are engaged is work that is not paid for.[18] In a money economy where autonomy and prestige depend upon currency, this is a fact of great importance. In general, the position of women in patriarchy is a continuous function of their economic dependence. Just as their social position is vicarious and achieved (often on a temporary or marginal basis) though males, their relation to the economy is also typically vicarious or tangential.

· · ·

Since education and economy are so closely related in the advanced nations, it is significant that the general level and style of higher education for women, particularly in their many remaining segregated institutions, is closer to that of Renaissance humanism than to the skills of mid-twentieth-century scientific and technological society. Traditionally patriarchy permitted occasional minimal literacy to women while higher education was closed to them. While modern patriarchies have, fairly recently, opened all educational levels to women,[19] the kind and quality of education is not the same for each sex. This difference is of course apparent in early socialization, but it persists and enters into higher education as well. Universities, once places of scholarship and the training of a few professionals, now also produce the personnel of a technocracy. This is not the case with regard to women. Their own colleges typically produce neither scholars nor professionals nor technocrats. Nor are they funded by government and corporations as are male colleges and those co-educational colleges and universities whose primary function is the education of males.

· · ·

In keeping with the inferior sphere of culture to which women in patriarchy have always been restricted, the present encouragement of their "artistic" interests through study of the humanities is hardly more than an extension of the "accomplishments" they once cultivated in preparation for the marriage market. Achievement in the arts and humanities is reserved, now, as it has been historically, for males. Token representation, be it Susan Sontag's or Lady Murasaki's, does not vitiate this rule.

[18] Sweden is an exception in considering housework a material service rendered and calculable in divorce suits, etc. Thirty-three to forty per cent of the female population have market employment in Western countries: this leaves up to two thirds out of the market labor force. In Sweden and the Soviet Union that figure is lower.

[19] We often forget how recent an event is higher education for women. In the U.S. it is barely one hundred years old; in many Western countries barely fifty. Oxford did not grant degrees to women on the same terms as to men until 1920. In Japan and a number of other countries universities have been open to women only in the period after World War II. There are still areas where higher education for women scarcely exists. Women do not have the same access to education as do men. The Princeton Report stated that "although at the high school level more girls than boys receive grades of 'A,' roughly 50% more boys than girls go to college." *The Princeton Report to the Alumni on Co-Education* (pamphlet), Princeton, N.J. 1968, p. 10. Most other authorities give the national ratio of college students as two males to one female. In a great many countries it is far lower.

VI. Force

We are not accustomed to associate patriarchy with force. So perfect is its system of socialization, so complete the general assent to its values, so long and so universally has it prevailed in human society, that it scarcely seems to require violent implementation. Customarily, we view its brutalities in the past as exotic or "primitive" custom. Those of the present are regarded as the product of individual deviance, confined to pathological or exceptional behavior, and without general import. And yet, just as under other total ideologies (racism and colonialism are somewhat analogous in this respect) control in patriarchal society would be imperfect, even inoperable, unless it had the rule of force to rely upon, both in emergencies and as an ever-present instrument of intimidation.

Historically, most patriarchies have institutionalized force through their legal systems. For example, strict patriarchies such as that of Islam, have implemented the prohibition against illegitimacy or sexual autonomy with a death sentence. In Afghanistan and Saudi Arabia the adulteress is still stoned to death with a mullah presiding at the execution. Execution by stoning was once common practice through the Near East. It is still condoned in Sicily. Needless to say there was and is no penalty imposed upon the male correspondent. Save in recent times or exceptional cases, adultery was not generally recognized in males except as an offense one male might commit against another's property interest. . . .

. . .

Excepting a social license to physical abuse among certain class and ethnic groups, force is diffuse and generalized in most contemporary patriarchies. Significantly, force itself is restricted to the male who alone is psychologically and technically equipped to perpetrate physical violence.[20] Where differences in physical strength have become immaterial through the use of arms, the female is rendered innocuous by her socialization. Before assault she is almost universally defenseless both by her physical and emotional training. Needless to say, this has the most far-reaching effects on the social and psychological behavior of both sexes.

. . . In rape, the emotions of aggression, hatred, contempt, and the desire to break or violate personality, take a form consummately appropriate to sexual politics. . . .

. . .

VII. Anthropological: Myth and Religion

Evidence from anthropology, religious and literary myth all attests to the politically expedient character of patriarchal convictions about women. One

[20] Vivid exceptions come to mind in the wars of liberation conducted by Vietnam, China, etc. But through most of history, women have been unarmed and forbidden to exhibit any defense of their own.

anthropologist refers to a consistent patriarchal strain of assumption that "woman's biological differences set her apart . . . she is essentially inferior," and since "human institutions grow from deep and primal anxieties and are shaped by irrational psychological mechanisms . . . socially organized attitudes toward women arise from basic tensions expressed by the male."[21] Under patriarchy the female did not herself develop the symbols by which she is described. As both the primitive and the civilized worlds are male worlds, the ideas which shaped culture in regard to the female were also of male design. The image of women, as we know it is an image created by men and fashioned to suit their needs. These needs spring from a fear of the "otherness" of woman. Yet this notion itself presupposes that patriarchy has already been established and the male has already set himself as the human norm, the subject and referent to which the female is "other" or alien. Whatever its origin, the function of the male's sexual antipathy is to provide a means of control over a subordinate group and a rationale which justifies the inferior station of those in a lower order, "explaining" the oppression of their lives.

The feeling that woman's sexual functions are impure is both world-wide and persistent. One sees evidence of it everywhere in literature, in myth, in primitive and civilized life. It is striking how the notion persists today. The event of menstruation, for example, is a largely clandestine affair, and the psycho-social effect of the stigma attached must have great effect on the female ego. There is a large anthropological literature on menstrual taboo; the practice of isolating offenders in huts at the edge of the village occurs throughout the primitive world. . . .

Primitive peoples explain the phenomenon of the female's genitals in terms of a wound, sometimes reasoning that she was visited by a bird or snake and mutilated into her present condition. Once she was wounded, now she bleeds. Contemporary slang for the vagina is "gash." The Freudian description of the female genitals is in terms of a "castrated" condition. The uneasiness and disgust female genitals arouse in patriarchal societies is attested to through religious, cultural, and literary proscription. In preliterate groups fear is also a factor, as in the belief in a castrating vagina dentata. The penis, badge of the male's superior status in both preliterate and civilized patriarchies, is given the most crucial significance, the subject both of endless boasting and endless anxiety.

. . .

The Pandora myth is one of two important Western archetypes which condemn the female through her sexuality and explain her position as her well-deserved punishment for the primal sin under whose unfortunate consequences the race yet labors. Ethics have entered the scene, replacing the simplicities of ritual, taboo, and mana. The more sophisticated vehicle of myth also provides official explanations of sexual history. In Hesiod's tale, Zeus, a rancorous and arbitrary father figure, in sending Epimetheus evil in the form of female

---

[21] H. R. Hays, *The Dangerous Sex, the Myth of Feminine Evil* (New York: Putnam, 1964). Much of my summary in this section is indebted to Hays's useful assessment of cultural notions about the female.

genitalia, is actually chastising him for adult heterosexual knowledge and activity. In opening the vessel she brings (the vulva or hymen, Pandora's "box") the male satisfies his curiosity but sustains the discovery only by punishing himself at the hands of the father god with death and the assorted calamities of postlapsarian life. The patriarchal trait of male rivalry across age or status line, patricularly those of powerful father and rival son, is present as well as the ubiquitous maligning of the female.

The myth of the Fall is a highly finished version of the same themes. As the central myth of the Judeo-Christian imagination and therefore of our immediate cultural heritage, it is well that we appraise and acknowledge the enormous power it still holds over us even in a rationalist era which has long ago given up literal belief in it while maintaining its emotional assent intact.[22] This mythic version of the female as the cause of human suffering, knowledge, and sin is still the foundation of sexual attitudes, for it represents the most crucial argument of the patriarchal tradition in the West.

The Israelites lived in a continual state of war with the fertility cults of their neighbors; these latter afforded sufficient attraction to be the source of constant defection, and the figure of Eve, like that of Pandora, has vestigial traces of a fertility goddess overthrown. There is some, probably unconscious, evidence of this in the Biblical account which announces, even before the narration of the fall has begun—"Adam called his wife's name Eve; because she was the mother of all living things." Due to the fact that the tale represents a compilation of different oral traditions, it provides two contradictory schemes for Eve's creation, one in which both sexes are created at the same time, and one in which Eve is fashioned later than Adam, an afterthought born from his rib, peremptory instance of the man's expropriation of the life force through a god who created the world without benefit of female assistance.

The tale of Adam and Eve is, among other things, a narrative of how humanity invented sexual intercourse. Many such narratives exist in preliterate myth and folk tale. Most of them strike us now as delightfully funny stories of primal innocents who require a good deal of helpful instruction to figure it out. There are other major themes in the story: the loss of primeval simplicity, the arrival of death, and the first conscious experience of knowledge. All of them revolve about sex. Adam is forbidden to eat of the fruit of life or of the knowledge of good and evil, the warning states explicitly what should happen if he tastes of the latter: "in that day that thou eatest thereof thou shalt surely die." He eats but fails to die (at least in the story), from which one might infer that the serpent told the truth.

But at the moment when the pair eat of the forbidden tree they awake to their

[22] It is impossible to assess how deeply embedded in our consciousness is the Eden legend and how utterly its patterns are planted in our habits of thought. One comes across its tone and design in the most unlikely places, such as Antonioni's film *Blow-Up,* to name but one of many striking examples. The action of the film takes place in an idyllic garden, loaded with primal overtones largely sexual, where, prompted by a tempter with a phallic gun, the female again betrays the male to death. The photographer who witnesses the scene reacts as if he were being introduced both to the haggard knowledge of the primal scene and original sin at the same time.

nakedness and feel shame. Sexuality is clearly involved, though the fable insists it is only tangential to a higher prohibition against disobeying orders in the matter of another and less controversial appetite—one for food. Róheim points out that the Hebrew verb for "eat" can also mean coitus. Everywhere in the Bible "knowing" is synonymous with sexuality, and clearly a product of contact with the phallus, here in the fable objectified as a snake. To blame the evils and sorrows of life—loss of Eden and the rest—on sexuality, would all too logically implicate the male, and such implication is hardly the purpose of the story, designed as it is expressly in order to blame all this world's discomfort on the female. Therefore it is the female who is tempted first and "beguiled" by the penis, transformed into something else, a snake. Thus Adam has "beaten the rap" of sexual guilt, which appears to be why the sexual motive is so repressed in the Biblical account. Yet the very transparency of the serpent's universal phallic value shows how uneasy the mythic mind can be about its shifts. Accordingly, in her inferiority and vulnerability the woman takes and eats, simple carnal thing that she is, affected by flattery even in a reptile. Only after this does the male fall, and with him, humanity—for the fable has made him the racial type, whereas Eve is a mere sexual type and, according to tradition, either expendable or replaceable. And as the myth records the original sexual adventure, Adam was seduced by woman, who was seduced by a penis. "The woman whom thou gavest to be with me, she gave me of the fruit and I did eat" is the first man's defense. Seduced by the phallic snake, Eve is convicted for Adam's participation in sex.

Adam's curse is to toil in the "sweat of his brow," namely the labor the male associates with civilization. Eden was a fantasy world without either effort or activity, which the entrance of the female, and with her sexuality, has destroyed. Eve's sentence is far more political in nature and a brilliant "explanation" of her inferior status. "In sorrow thou shalt bring forth children. And thy desire shall be to thy husband. And he shall rule over thee." Again, as in the Pandora myth, a proprietary father figure is punishing his subjects for adult heterosexuality. It is easy to agree with Róheim's comment on the negative attitude the myth adopts toward sexuality: "Sexual maturity is regarded as a misfortune, something that has robbed mankind of happiness . . . the explanation of how death came into the world."

What requires further emphasis is the responsibility of the female, a marginal creature, in bringing on this plague, and the justice of her suborned condition as dependent on her primary role in this original sin. The connection of woman, sex, and sin constitutes the fundamental pattern of western patriarchal thought thereafter.

VIII. Psychological

The aspects of patriarchy already described have each an effect upon the psychology of both sexes. Their principal result is the interiorization of patriarchal ideology. Status, temperament, and role are all value systems with endless psychological ramifications for each sex. Patriarchal marriage and the family with its ranks and division of labor play a large part in enforcing them. The male's superior economic position, the female's inferior one have also grave implications. The large quantity of guilt attached to sexuality in patriarchy is overwhelmingly placed upon the female, who is, culturally speaking, held to be the culpable or the more culpable party in nearly any sexual liaison, whatever the extenuating circumstances. A tendency toward the reification of the female makes her more often a sexual object than a person. This is particularly so when she is denied human rights through chattel status. Even where this has been partly amended the cumulative effect of religion and custom is still very powerful and has enormous psychological consequences. Woman is still denied sexual freedom and the biological control over her body through the cult of virginity, the double standard, the prescription against abortion, and in many places because contraception is physically or psychically unavailable to her.

. . .

When in any group of persons, the ego is subjected to such invidious versions of itself through social beliefs, ideology, and tradition, the effect is bound to be pernicious. This coupled with the persistent though frequently subtle denigration women encounter daily through personal contacts, the impressions gathered from the images and media about them, and the discrimination in matters of behavior, employment, and education which they endure, should make it no very special cause for surprise that women develop group characteristics common to those who suffer minority status and a marginal existence. A witty experiment by Philip Goldberg proves what everyone knows, that having internalized the disesteem in which they are held, women despise both themselves and each other.[23] This simple test consisted of asking women undergraduates to respond to the scholarship in an essay signed alternately by one John McKay and one Joan McKay. In making their assessments the students generally agreed that John was a remarkable thinker, Joan an unimpressive mind. Yet the articles were identical: the reaction was dependent on the sex of the supposed author.

As women in patriarchy are for the most part marginal citizens when they are citizens at all, their situation is like that of other minorities, here defined not as dependent upon numerical size of the group, but on its status. "A minority group is any group of people who because of their physical or cultural characteristics, are singled out from others in the society in which they live for differential and unequal treatment." Only a handful of sociologists have ever addressed themselves in any meaningful way to the minority status of women. And psychology has yet to produce relevant studies on the subject of ego damage to the female which might bear comparison to the excellent work done on the effects of racism on the minds of blacks and colonials. The remarkably small amount of modern research devoted to the psychological and social effects of masculine supremacy on the female and on the culture in general attests to the widespread ignorance or unconcern of a conservative social science which takes patriarchy to be both the status quo and the state of nature.

What little literature the social sciences afford us in this context confirms the presence in women of the expected traits of minority status: group self-hatred

[23] Philip Goldberg, "Are Women Prejudiced Against Women?" *Transaction*, April 1968.

and self-rejection, a contempt both for herself and for her fellows—the result of that continual, however subtle, reiteration of her inferiority which she eventually accepts as a fact.[24] Another index of minority status is the fierceness with which all minority group members are judged. The double standard is applied not only in cases of sexual conduct but other contexts as well. In the relatively rare instances of female crime too: in many American states a woman convicted of crime is awarded a longer sentence.[25] Generally an accused woman acquires a notoriety out of proportion to her acts and due to sensational publicity she may be tried largely for her "sex life." But so effective is her conditioning toward passivity in patriarchy, woman is rarely extrovert enough in her maladjustment to enter upon criminality. Just as every minority member must either apologize for the excesses of a fellow or condemn him with a strident enthusiasm, women are characteristically harsh, ruthless and frightened in their censure of aberration among their numbers.

. . .

Perhaps patriarchy's greatest psychological weapon is simply its universality and longevity. A referent scarcely exists with which it might be contrasted or by which it might be confuted. While the same might be said of class, patriarchy has a still more tenacious or powerful hold through its successful habit of passing itself off as nature. Religion is also universal in human society and slavery was once nearly so; advocates of each were fond of arguing in terms of fatality, or irrevocable human "instinct"—even "biological origins." When a system of power is thoroughly in command, it has scarcely need to speak itself aloud; when its workings are exposed and questioned, it becomes not only subject to discussion, but even to change.

SUGGESTED READINGS

1. ADLER, MORTIMER J., *The Idea of Freedom*, 2 vols. (Garden City, N.Y.: Doubleday, 1958–1961).
2. CHAFEE, Z., *Free Speech in the United States* (Cambridge, Mass.: Harvard University Press, 1940).
3. FRIEDRICH, CARL J. (ed.), *Liberty; Nomos IV* (New York: Atherton, 1962). An anthology devoted to Mill's essay "On Liberty."
4. MACCALLUM, GERALD C., JR., "Negative and Positive Freedom," *Philosophical Review*, Vol. 76, No. 3 (July 1967), 312–333.
5. MULLER, HERBERT J., *Issues of Freedom: Paradoxes and Promises* (New York: Harper, 1960).

[24] My remarks on the minority status of women are summarized from all the articles listed, and I am particularly indebted to an accomplished critique of them in an unpublished draft by Professor Marlene Dixon, formerly of the University of Chicago's Department of Sociology and the Committee on Human Development, presently of McGill University.

[25] See The Commonwealth v. Daniels, 37 L.W. 2064, Pennsylvania Supreme Court, 7/1/68 (reversing 36 L.W. 2004).

Four Theories on Women's Liberation

WILLIAM BLACKSTONE

William T. Blackstone (1931–   ) is a professor of philosophy and chairman of the department of social sciences at the University of Georgia. Among his works are *The Problem of Religious Knowledge* (1963), *Meaning and Existence* (1971), and *Political Philosophy* (1973).

The women's liberation movement is a complex phenomenon. Within it there are widely different views of the causes of the oppression of women and, consequently, widely different views of what is required to overcome that oppression. Put in a different way, the movement includes widely different views of what constitutes a free person in the social and political sense and, hence, different views of the sort of society required to assure freedom. The full range of political philosophies are represented in this movement. In this paper I want to focus briefly on some of the more radical claims made in the feminist movement. In order to make my target clear, I will sketch in very general terms several positions within or on the feminist movement.[1]

1. The traditionalist stance can hardly be classified as being *within* the women's liberation movement, but it has many advocates and it constitutes one of the parameters on this issue. The traditionalist holds that everything is all right the way it is (or at least it was all right before the feminists came along). Women are different from men and, in many ways, inferior; they are passive, submissive, and are meant to perform different roles. Sex-differentiated labor, sex stereotyping, and the restriction of females in terms of opportunities and roles are not oppression but the fulfillment of women's nature and necessary for family and social cohesion. Women's real freedom and equality are found within these restrictions, and the state should in no way interfere with those social conventions and practices.

2. The liberal, on the other hand (and I have in mind those like Betty Friedan in *The Feminine Mystique* and John Stuart Mill in *The Subjection of Women*), argues that sex-role stereotyping results in great social injustice, that

---

[1] Detailed accounts of various positions within the feminist movements are found in Juliet Mitchell's *Woman's Estate* (Baltimore: Penguin Books, 1966); Leslie B. Tanner, ed., *Voices from Women's Liberation* (New York: Signet Books, New American Library, 1970); V. Gornick and B. Moran, *Women in Sexist Society* (New York: Signet Books, New American Library, 1971); and an excellent unpublished essay by Alison Jaggar, "Four Views of Women's Liberation," which was presented at the American Philosophical Association meeting, Western Division, May 4–6, 1972.

Source: William T. Blackstone, "Freedom and Women," *Ethics*, Vol. 85, No. 3 (April 1975), pp. 243–248. Reprinted by permission of The University of Chicago Press and the author.

if a woman wants to be a housewife and mother and perform these traditional roles it is perfectly all right, but she should not be systematically excluded from other alternatives or options on account of her sex. If there are relevant differences between men and women which prevent women from filling certain roles or from performing certain roles well, then discriminatory treatment may be justified, but if there are no relevant differences, then discrimination against women is unjust. Women should have equal rights with men—social, economic, political, and legal—the liberal holds, and equal responsibilities. They should be judged as individuals and on the basis of their ability and performance—just as men. To permit this freedom and equality, men must be prepared to assume more responsibility in child rearing; and the state, or private enterprise (some liberals are more laissez faire than others!), must assist in providing some of the conditions required for genuine freedom and equality for women—day-care centers, for example. The liberal does not require the abolition of all traditional sex roles, nor does he (she) challenge traditional family values, though he insists on other options as life-styles.

3. Whereas the liberal thinks freedom can be had by reforming the system, the radical argues that freedom is possible only with the overthrow of the political system, and the political system is seen in very broad terms.[2] Marriage and the family are political institutions which oppress women. They must go, as well as the more overt social and legal rules. Radical feminists cover a wide spectrum, but those with leftist leanings believe, with Marx, that the state must "wither away" before genuine freedom is possible and that the economic system of capitalism and the class system which it presupposes must be abolished, for that system is the fundamental cause of all oppression. The oppression of women, in other words, cannot be overcome independently of other oppressions. It is part of a package which must be disposed of altogether. As Margaret Bengsten, a radical leftist feminist, puts it, women in a capitalist system are defined "as that group of people who are responsible for the production of simple use-values in those activities associated with the home and family."[3] She continues: "The material basis for the inferior status of women is to be found in just this definition of women. In a society in which money determines value, women are a group who work outside the money economy. Their work is not worth money, is therefore valueless, is therefore not even real work. And women themselves, who do this valueless work, can hardly be expected to be worth as much as men, who work for money."[4] The means of production must be socialized; there must be "a reintroduction of the entire female sex into public industry," as Engels claims; goods and services must be distributed on the basis of needs; and society as a whole, *not* the family, must be made responsible for the welfare of children, as for everyone else. The radical feminist advocates total revolution, then, not mere reform within the system.

[2] Margaret Bengsten is an example of a radical leftist feminist; see her "Political Economy of Women's Liberation," *Monthly Review,* vol. 21 (September 1969), reprinted in *Voices from Women's Liberation* (see n. 1). Mitchell (n. 1) spells out in detail the leftist feminist position.

[3] Bengsten, p. 281.

[4] Ibid., p. 282.

4. Some radical feminists do not buy the entire Marxist line, and they should be accorded a category of their own. I have in mind Shulamith Firestone and her followers. I quote: "There is a level of reality that does not stem directly from economics. . . ."[5] Firestone attempts to develop "a materialist view of history based on sex itself," arguing that "for feminist revolution we shall need an analysis of the dynamics of sex war as comprehensive as the Marx-Engels analysis of class antagonism was for economic revolution. More comprehensive. For we are dealing with a larger problem, with an oppression that goes back beyond recorded history to the animal kingdom itself."[6] Firestone sees economic class analysis of social injustice as secondary to sex analysis. The biological differences between men and women—the general physical strength of men plus the weakness of women due to childbearing—made men dominant and women dependent. Oppression resulted. Liberation for females is possible only by overcoming these biological differences through technology. Contraception and "artificial reproduction" will free women from their biological inequalities and, subsequently, from social inequalities. Liberation requires the abolition of the whole sex-role system (including childbearing), marriage, and the family. It requires, to quote Firestone, "freedom from sexual classification altogether rather than merely an equalization of sex roles."[7] Freedom and equality, within this radical picture, preclude even the choice of a traditional female role.

Within these four inadequately sketched positions, there is wide disagreement on the meaning of freedom (and equality) for women and on what is required to attain it.

Feminist critics, it seems to me, are in general correct in their claim that women in our society (and others) are oppressed as a class. Many of our laws and our extralegal practices discriminate unfairly against women. I will not attempt to provide the data for that assessment here. The sex-based discrimination of many state laws is well known[8]—laws which permit women to be imprisoned for three years for habitual drunkenness while restricting the penalty for the same offense to thirty days for males; laws which "excuse" all women from jury duty; which permit the withholding of credit from married women on the assumption that they are all financially dependent on their husbands; which permit the plea of "passion" killing for wronged husbands but not wronged wives; which make the father, not the mother or the parents, the "natural guardian" of children; which give the husband right of action in divorce in cases of adultery but not the wife; and work practices in which women are paid less than men for the same work; and so on.

Rather than focus on those feminist evaluations which seem so obviously correct, I will examine some of the more philosophically controversial evaluations and theses in the feminist movement. I beg off on those expressed in (3) above. Any treatment of the Marxist feminist position would require an assessment of

---

[5] Shulamith Firestone, *The Dialectic of Sex* (New York: Jonathan Cape, 1971), p. 6.

[6] Ibid., p. 2.

[7] Shulamith Firestone, "On American Feminism," in *Woman in Sexist Society* (see n. 1), p. 686, n. 4.

[8] See, for example, Diane B. Schulder, "Does the Law Oppress Women?" in *Sisterhood Is Powerful,* ed. Robin Morgan (New York: Random House, 1970), pp. 139–157.

the cluster of factual and valuational assumptions of the political philosophy of communism.[9] I will focus briefly on only a few of the claims in (4) which can stand independently of these assumptions: the theses that childbearing is a restraint on the freedom of women, that it is an unjustified restraint, and that freedom (and equality or social justice) for women requires biological equality, the total abolition of sexual classification, and the abolition of the traditional institutions of marriage and the family. There are other factual and normative theses within (4) which I will not examine, including the claim that "pregnancy is barbaric";[10] the belief that technology not only will be developed to perform the childbearing function but will also free all humans from the necessity to work;[11] the thesis that all sexual repression ought to cease and will cease with the demise of the biological family (everyone, including children, will be permitted "to do whatever they want sexually. . . . humanity could finally revert to its natural 'polymorphously perverse' sexuality");[12] the claim that wealth should be distributed on the basis of need; and the belief that a communist anarchy is the proper form of government for liberated persons.

First, is childbearing or the capacity to bear children a restraint? The capacity to bear children is a natural capacity which females possess and males do not. We would not say that males are under a restraint because they cannot bear children. Would we say that females are because they can? In neither case is the capacity or incapacity something which is imposed by the social and legal structure. The decision to exercise that capacity for some women may be imposed via an inculcated stereotype image, and that inculcation may properly be seen in some circumstances as a restraint, just as one might view the inculcation of exclusive sex roles in child rearing. These restraints should be lifted or modified and the duties of child rearing shared equitably by men, the liberal believes. But is the capacity to bear children, or the incapacity, itself a restraint? If we stretch the word "restraint" or "unfree" to include the existence or nonexistence of such natural capacities, then clearly anything could be counted as a restraint or unfreedom to someone or something, and the concept of restraint or unfreedom would be functionless, at least in the sense of permitting the attribution of responsibility for restraints or unfreedoms. Justified or unjustified complaints about restraints or inabilities presuppose and require that those restraints or inabilities be due to social and legal arrangements controlled (or controllable) by human beings. Consequently, the biological inequalities or differences between men and women cannot be viewed as restraints in the responsibility-attributing sense. They may be viewed as restraints in the sense that they are natural conditions which limit possibilities and which are present in contexts in which there is male domination and oppression of women. One can hardly say, however, that the biological inequalities or differences are

---

[9] I would not write off entirely the Marxist analysis of the oppression of women, but I am not at all convinced that private property is the root of all social evils. If we look at historical realities, unfreedom and oppression (including that of women) are at least as possible under socialist systems as they are under capitalist ones.

[10] Firestone, *The Dialectic of Sex*, p. 226.

[11] Ibid., p. 235.

[12] Ibid., pp. 236–237.

responsible for the social inequalities. Granted, if there were no biological differences between men and women there would be no social inequalities between them. This is tautologically true, because there would be no women (or no men, however one wishes to state this). But it is an extreme solution to the problem of unjust discrimination against women to obliterate either the biological differences between men and women (which Firestone does not propose) or the different biological functions of men and women (which Firestone does propose). Even if freedom could be purchased only at the cost of one's sexuality—which is certainly not the case—this would be a terrible price to pay and, in fact, would vitiate a basic purpose for which social and political systems are devised, namely, self-preservation and the fulfillment of each person's interests. For surely a "self" and "interests" cannot be defined completely apart from sex, sexuality, or biological traits—at least not in the world we know. Perhaps they could in some possible world, and Shulamith Firestone may be urging on us this other possible world—in which case we must be prepared to calculate the advantages and disadvantages of that world as compared with our own. In our world, the key factors responsible for oppression are not biological traits but social, economic, political, and legal options or choices. The oppression due to such choices could exist even under conditions in which some biological differences are minimized (strength, for example) or in which certain biological functions (childbearing) are not performed by women but by machines. Rather than desexualize or asexualize our world through technology (if indeed this is possible), we need to change social and legal systems which discriminate irrelevantly on the basis of sex.

A second radical feminist thesis which is questionable is that freedom for women requires "freedom from sexual classification altogether." As with any claim, everything hangs on its interpretation. If what is meant is that laws and policies which discriminate solely and arbitrarily on the basis of sex (and not on the basis of capacities or abilities to do or become something) are unjust and that a society which has such laws oppresses women (and men), this claim is quite acceptable and follows from the basic democratic commitment to equal rights and equal freedom for all.

However, "freedom from sexual classification altogether" may mean much more than freedom from irrelevant classification based on sex or freedom from unjustified differential treatment based on sex. It may require that sex or sexual characteristics be totally ruled out as ever being relevant to the differential treatment of persons or to according equality of treatment. It may require a system of social justice in which sex and sexually associated characteristics (if they exist and whatever they may be) cannot in principle be invoked. Such a system would increase some freedoms by ridding us of some injustices, for there are many institutionalized practices which discriminate arbitrarily on the basis of sex. At the same time, it would lead to some social injustice *if* there were some differences between the sexes which in certain contexts justified differential treatment. The liberal feminist does not want to rule out such possible differences. Abilities or inabilities due to natural capacities (physical strength or weakness, high or low IQ, blindness, and so on) justify differential treatment in our egalitarian ethic. Firestone rules out such differential treatment with respect to gender in the very name of egalitarianism. Her position on this point would be correct only if all relevant facts, characteristics, or circumstances which could in principle justify differential treatment were independent of gender. One must admit that not all the data are in—perhaps very little which can be trusted—and further that many differences between men and women are enculturated. One might go further and agree that most of the relevant grounds for the differential treatment of persons are independent of gender. But I am leery about prejudging the question before a great deal more research is conducted, and in fact there seem to be differences between men and women (which hold in general) which, whether genetically or culturally caused, justify differential treatment (I am thinking primarily of physical strength).

A third radical feminist thesis which seems to me to be mistaken is that freedom for women requires the utter abolition of the traditional institutions of marriage and the family. There is no doubt that these institutions have oppressed women and continue to do so. But Firestone argues that a free society must preclude the traditional sex-differentiated role for women as a possible option.

However, even if technology will one day permit test-tube babies, even if the state could adequately serve as the custodian of all children, and even if society could function without marriage and the family, the ruling out of traditional options decreases freedom to that extent. Even if freedom were kept as a value (in the sense of the total range of options) distinct from social justice (the proper distribution of goods and services) as a value (though, of course, these values are related), her type of society would limit the range of human options in certain directions and expand it in others. An assessment of her type of society would require a comparative assessment of the range of the options given up and those acquired and the social justice or equality purchased at the cost of limiting human options in her way. Here the liberal feminist's response to the radical is that both social justice for women and the expanded range of options can be had without the preclusion (though not without some alternation) of traditional options (marriage and the family). Marriage and role divisions within marriage are not inherently exploitive and oppressive, though they may be oppressive if predicated on psychological, social, and economic oppression and exploitation (and, of course, many marriages and role divisions are). There is, in other words, no necessary conflict between freedom to choose from a range of options, including traditional roles, and equality or social justice for women. And, with proper modification, the family as an institution need not be a perpetuator of sexist discrimination—though other sorts of inequalities perpetuated by the family as an institution (those stressed in literature from Plato's *Republic* to the Coleman report on *Equality of Educational Opportunity*)[13] are not as easily modified.[14]

[13] James S. Coleman et al., *Equality of Educational Opportunity* (Washington, D.C.: Government Printing Office, 1966).
[14] See my "Human Rights, Equality, and Education," *Educational Theory*, vol. 19, no. 3 (1969), for discussion.

Social Structure and Sexual Oppression

JULIET MITCHELL

Juliet Mitchell (1941–   ) is the author of *Woman's Estate* (1971). She has taught English at the University of Reading, England, and is active in the women's liberation movement in England. She currently teaches at the State University of New York at Buffalo.

The situation of women is different from that of any other social group. This is because they are not one of a number of isolable units, but half a totality: the human species. Women are essential and irreplaceable; they cannot therefore be exploited in the same way as other social groups can. They are fundamental to the human condition, yet in their economic, social and political roles, they are marginal. It is precisely this combination—fundamental and marginal at one and the same time—that has been fatal to them. Within the world of men their position is comparable to that of an oppressed minority: but they also exist outside the world of men. The one state justifies the other and precludes protest. In advanced industrial society, women's work is only marginal to the total economy. Yet it is through work that man changes natural conditions and thereby produces society. Until there is a revolution in production, the labour situation will prescribe women's situation within the world of men. But women are offered a universe of their own: the family. Like woman herself, the family appears as a natural object, but it is actually a cultural creation. There is nothing inevitable about the form or role of the family any more than there is about the character or role of women. It is the function of ideology to present these given social types as aspects of Nature itself. Both can be exalted paradoxically, as ideals. The 'true' woman and the 'true' family are images of peace and plenty: in actuality they may both be sites of violence and despair. The apparently natural condition can be made to appear more attractive than the arduous advance of human beings towards culture. But what Marx wrote about the bourgeois myths of the Golden Ancient World describes precisely women's realm: ". . . in one way the child-like world of the ancients appears to be superior, and this is so, insofar as we seek for closed shape, form and established limitation. The ancients provide a narrow satisfaction, whereas the modern world leaves us unsatisfied or where it appears to be satisfied with itself, is vulgar and mean."

. . .

Source: Juliet Mitchell, "The Longest Revolution," *New Left Review,* Vol. 40 (1966), pp. 1, 5–24. Copyright © 1966 by Juliet Mitchell. Reprinted by permission of Deborah Rogers Ltd., London.

The Second Sex

The contrary is true of De Beauvoir's massive work *The Second Sex*—to this day the greatest single contribution on the subject. Here the focus is the status of women through the ages. But socialism as such emerges as a curiously contingent solution at the end of the work, in a muffled epilogue. De Beauvoir's main theoretical innovation was to fuse the "economic" and "reproductive" explanations of women's subordination by a psychological interpretation of both. Man asserts himself as subject and free being by opposing other consciousnesses. He is distinct from animals precisely in that he creates and invents (not in that he reproduces himself), but he tries to escape the burden of his freedom by giving himself a spurious "immortality" in his children. He dominates woman both to imprison another consciousness which reflects his own and to provide him with children that are securely his (his fear of illegitimacy). The notions obviously have a considerable force. But they are very atemporal: it is not easy to see why socialism should modify the basic "ontological" desire for a thing-like freedom which De Beauvoir sees as the motor behind the fixation with inheritance in the property system, or the enslavement of women which derived from it. In fact she has since criticized this aspect of her book for idealism: "I should take a more materialist position today in the first volume. I should base the notion of woman as *other* and the Manichean argument it entails not on an idealistic and *a priori* struggle of consciences, but on the facts of supply and demand. This modification would not necessitate any changes in the subsequent development of my argument."[1] Concurrent, however, with the idealist psychological explanation, De Beauvoir uses an orthodox economist approach. This leads to a definite evolutionism in her treatment in Volume 1, which becomes a retrospective narrative of the different forms of the feminine condition in different societies through time—mainly in terms of the property system and its effects on women. To this she adds various suprahistorical themes—myths of the eternal feminine, types of women through the ages, literary treatments of women —which do not modify the fundamental structure of her argument. The prospect for women's liberation at the end is quite divorced from any historical development.

Thus, the classical literature on the problem of woman's condition is predominantly economist in emphasis, stressing her simple subordination to the institutions of private property. Her biological status underpins both her weakness as a producer, in work relations; and her importance as a possession, in reproductive relations. The fullest and most recent interpretation gives both factors a psychological cast. The framework of discussion is an evolutionist one which nevertheless fails noticeably to project a convincing image of the future, beyond asserting that socialism will involve the liberation of women as one of its constituent "moments."

What is the solution to this impasse? It must lie in differentiating woman's condition, much more radically than in the past, into its separate structures,

[1] Simone de Beauvoir: *Force of Circumstance* (1965), p. 192.

which together form a complex—not a simple—unity. This will mean rejecting the idea that woman's condition can be deduced derivatively from the economy or equated symbolically with society. Rather, it must be seen as a *specific* structure, which is a unity of different elements. The variations of woman's condition throughout history will be the result of different combinations of these elements—much as Marx's analysis of the economy in *Precapitalist Economic Formations* is an account of the different combinations of the factors of production, not a linear narrative of economic development. Because the unity of woman's condition at any one time is the product of several structures, it is always "overdetermined."[2] The key structures can be listed as follows: Production, Reproduction, Sex and Socialization of children. The concrete combination of these produces the "complex unity" of her position; but each separate structure may have reached a different 'moment' at any given historical time. Each then must be examined separately in order to see what the present unity is and how it might be changed. The discussion that follows does not pretend to give a historical account of each sector. It is only concerned with some general reflections on the different roles of women and some of their interconnections.

. . .

Production

The assumption behind most classical discussion is that the crucial factor starting the whole development of feminine subordination was women's lesser capacity for demanding physical work. But, in fact, this is a major oversimplification. Even within these terms, in history it has been woman's lesser capacity for violence as well as for work that has determined her subordination. In most societies woman has not only been less able than man to perform arduous kinds of work, she has also been less able to fight. Man not only has the strength to assert himself against nature, but also against his fellows. *Social coercion* has interplayed with the straightforward division of labour, based on biological capacity, to a much greater extent than generally admitted. Of course, it may not be actualized as direct aggression. In primitive societies women's physical unsuitability for the hunt is evident. In agricultural societies where women's inferiority is socially instituted they are given the arduous task of tilling and cultivation. For this coercion is necessary. In developed civilizations and more complex societies woman's physical deficiencies again become relevant. Women are no use either for war or in the construction of cities. But with early

[2] See Louis Althusser, *Contradiction et Surdétermination* in *Pour Marx* (1965). Althusser advances the notion of a complex totality in which each independent sector has its own autonomous reality but each of which is ultimately, but only ultimately, determined by the economic. This complex totality means that no contradition in society is ever simple. As each sector can move at a different pace, the synthesis of the different time-scales in the total social structure means that sometimes contradictions cancel each other out and sometimes they reinforce one another. To describe this complexity, Althusser uses the Freudian term "overdetermination." The phrase *"unité de rupture"* (mentioned below) refers to the moment when the contradictions so reinforce one another as to coalesce into the conditions for a revolutionary change.

industrialization coercion once more becomes important. As Marx wrote: "Insofar as machinery dispenses with muscular power, it becomes a means of employing labourers of slight muscular strength, and those whose bodily development is incomplete, but whose limbs are all the more supple. The labour of women and children was, therefore, the first thing sought for by capitalists who used machinery."[3]

René Dumont points out that in many zones of tropical Africa today men are often idle, while women are forced to work all day.[4] This exploitation has no "natural" source whatever. Women may perform their 'heavy' duties in contemporary African peasant societies not for fear of physical reprisal by their men, but because these duties are 'customary' and built into the role structures of the society. A further point is that coercion implies a different relationship from coercer to coerced than exploitation does. It is political rather than economic. In describing coercion, Marx said that the master treated the slave or serf as the "inorganic and natural condition of its own reproduction." That is to say, labour itself becomes like other natural things—cattle or soil: "The original conditions of production appear as natural prerequisites, *natural conditions of the existence of the producer,* just as his living body, however reproduced and developed by him, is not originally established by himself, but appears as his *prerequisite.*"[5] This is preeminently woman's condition. For far from woman's physical weakness removing her from productive work, her social weakness has in these cases evidently made her the major slave of it.

This truth, elementary though it may seem, has nevertheless been constantly ignored by writers on the subject, with the result that an illegitimate optimism creeps into their predictions of the future. For if it is just the biological incapacity for the hardest physical work which has determined the subordination of women, then the prospect of an advanced machine technology, abolishing the need for strenuous physical exertion would seem to promise, therefore, the liberation of women. For a moment industrialization itself thus seems to herald women's liberation. Engels, for instance, wrote: "The first premise for the emancipation of women is the reintroduction of the entire female sex into public industry . . . And this has become possible only as a result of modern large-scale industry, which not only permits of the participation of women in production in large numbers, but actually calls for it and, moreover strives to convert private domestic work also into a public industry."[6] What Marx said of early industrialism is no less, but also *no more* true of an automated society: ". . . it is obvious that the fact of the collective working group being composed of individuals of both sexes and all ages, must necessarily, *under suitable conditions,* become a source of human development; although in its spontaneously devel-

[3] Karl Marx: *Capital* I 394.

[4] 'The African woman experiences a three-fold servitude: through forced marriage; through her dowry and polygamy, which increases the leisure time of men and simultaneously their social prestige; and finally through the very unequal division of labour.' René Dumont: *L' Afrique Noire est Mal Partie* (1962), p. 210.

[5] Karl Marx: *Precapitalist Economic Formations* op. cit. p. 87.

[6] Friedrich Engels, op. cit. 11 233 & 311.

oped, brutal, capitalistic form, where the labourer exists for the process of production, and not the process of production for the labourer, that fact is a pestiferous source of corruption and slavery."[7] Industrial labour and automated technology both promise the preconditions for woman's liberation alongside man's—but no more than the preconditions. It is only too obvious that the advent of industrialization has not so far freed women in this sense, either in the West or in the East. In the West it is true that there was a great influx of women into jobs in the expanding industrial economy, but this soon levelled out, and there has been relatively little increase in recent decades. De Beauvoir hoped that automation would make a decisive, qualitative difference by abolishing altogether the physical differential between the sexes. But any reliance on this in itself accords an independent role to technique which history does not justify. Under capitalism, automation could possibly lead to an ever-growing structural unemployment which would expel women—the latest and least integrated recruits to the labour force and ideologically the most expendable for a bourgeois society—from production after only a brief interlude in it. Technology is mediated by the total social structure and it is this which will determine woman's future in work relations.

Physical deficiency is not now, any more than in the past, a sufficient explanation of woman's relegation to inferior status. Coercion has been ameliorated to an ideology shared by both sexes. Commenting on the results of her questionnaire of working women, Viola Klein notes: "There is no trace of feminist egalitarianism—militant or otherwise—in any of the women's answers to our questionnaire; nor is it even implicitly assumed that women have a 'Right to Work.' "[8] Denied, or refusing, a role in *production,* woman does not even create the *pre*-conditions of her liberation.

Reproduction

Women's absence from the critical sector of production historically, of course, has been caused not just by their physical weakness in a context of coercion—but also by their role in reproduction. Maternity necessitates periodic withdrawals from work, but this is not a decisive phenomenon. It is rather women's role in reproduction which has become, in capitalist society at least, the spiritual "complement" of men's role in production.[9] Bearing children, bringing them up, and maintaining the home—these form the core of woman's natural vocation, in this ideology. This belief has attained great force because of the seeming universality of the family as a human institution. There is little doubt that Marxist

[7] Karl Marx: *Capital* I. 394.

[8] Viola Klein: *Working Wives,* Institute of Personnel Management Occasional Papers, No. 15 (1960), p. 13.

[9] Maternity is *the* distinctive feature on which both sexes base their hopes: for oppression or liberation. The notion of woman's potential superiority on account of her procreative function reaches the absurd in Margherita Repetto: *Maternità e Famiglia, Condizióni per la Libertà della Donna, Rivista Trimestrale* 11-12 (1964) but it is found even in Evelyne Sullerot: *Demain les Femmes* (1965).

analyses have underplayed the fundamental problems posed here. The complete failure to give any operative content to the slogan of "abolition" of the family is striking evidence of this (as well as of the vacuity of the notion).

The biological function of maternity is a universal, atemporal fact, and as such has seemed to escape the categories of Marxist historical analysis. From it follows—apparently—the stability and omnipresence of the family, if in very different forms.[10] Once this is accepted, women's social subordination—however emphasized as an honourable, but different role (cf. the equal but "separate" ideologies of Southern racists)—can be seen to follow inevitably as an *insurmountable* bio-historical fact. The causal chain then goes: Maternity, Family, Absence from Production and Public Life, Sexual Inequality.

The lynch-pin in this line of argument is the idea of the family. The notion that "family" and "society" are virtually co-extensive terms, or that an advanced society not founded on the nuclear family is now inconceivable, is widespread. It can only be seriously discussed by asking just what the family is— or rather what women's role in the family is. Once this is done, the problem appears in quite a new light. For it is obvious that woman's role in the family— primitive, feudal or bourgeois—partakes of three quite different structures: reproduction, sexuality, and the socialization of children. These are historically, not intrinsically, related to each other in the present modern family. Biological parentage is not necessarily identical with social parentage (adoption). It is thus essential to discuss: not the family as an unanalysed entity, but the separate *structures* which today compose it, but which may tomorrow be decomposed into a new pattern.

Reproduction, it has been stressed, is a seemingly constant atemporal phenomenon—part of biology rather than history. In fact this is an illusion. What is true is that the "mode of reproduction" does not vary with the "mode of production"; it can remain effectively the same through a number of different modes of production. For it has been defined till now, by its uncontrollable, natural character. To this extent, it has been an unmodified biological fact. As long as reproduction remained a natural phenomenon, of course, women were effectively doomed to social exploitation. In any sense, they were not masters of a large part of their lives. They had no choice as to whether or how often they gave birth to children (apart from repeated abortion), their existence was essentially subject to biological processes outside their control.

Contraception

Contraception which was invented as a rational technique only in the nineteenth century was thus an innovation of world-historic importance. It is only now just beginning to show what immense consequences it could have, in the form of the pill. For what it means is that at last the mode of reproduction could potentially be transformed. Once child-bearing becomes totally voluntary

---

[10] Philippe Aries in *Centuries of Childhood* (1962) shows that though the family may in some form always have existed it was often submerged under more forceful structures. In fact according to Aries it has only acquired its present significance with the advent of industrialization.

(how much so is it in the West, even today?) its significance is fundamentally different. It need no longer be the sole or ultimate vocation of woman; it becomes one option among others.

. . .

The fact of overwhelming importance is that easily available contraception threatens to dissociate sexual from reproductive experience—which all contemporary bourgeois ideology tries to make inseparable, as the *raison d'être* of the family.

REPRODUCTION AND PRODUCTION

At present, reproduction in our society is often a kind of sad mimicry of production. Work in a capitalist society is an alienation of labour in the making of a social product which is confiscated by capital. But it can still sometimes be a real act of creation, purposive and responsible, even in conditions of the worst exploitation. Maternity is often a caricature of this. The biological product —the child—is treated as if it were a solid product. Parenthood becomes a kind of substitute for work, an activity in which the child is seen as an object created by the mother, in the same way as a commodity is created by a worker. Naturally, the child does not literally escape, but the mother's alienation can be much worse than that of the worker whose product is appropriated by the boss. No human being can create another human being. A person's biological origin is an abstraction. The child as an autonomous person inevitably threatens the activity which claims to create it continually merely as a *possession* of the parent. Possessions are felt as extensions of the self. The child as a possession is supremely this. Anything the child does is therefore a threat to the mother herself who has renounced her autonomy through this misconception of her reproductive role. There are few more precarious ventures on which to base a life.

Furthermore even if the woman has emotional control over her child, legally and economically both she and it are subject to the father. The social cult of maternity is matched by the real socioeconomic powerlessness of the mother. The psychological and practical benefits men receive from this are obvious. . . .

Unlike her nonproductive status, her capacity for maternity *is* a definition of woman. But it is only a physiological definition. So long as it is allowed to remain a substitute for action and creativity, and the home an area of relaxation for men, women will remain confined to the species, to her universal and natural condition. . . .

Sexuality

Sexuality has traditionally been the most tabooed dimension of women's situation. The meaning of sexual freedom and its connexion with women's freedom is a particularly difficult subject which few socialist writers have cared to broach. Yet it is obvious that throughout history women have been appropriated as sexual objects, as much as progenitors or producers. Indeed, the sexual relation can be assimilated to the statute of possession much more easily and completely than the productive or reproductive relationship. Contemporary sexual vocabulary bears eloquent witness to this—it is a comprehensive lexicon of reification. Later Marx was well aware of this, of course: "Marriage . . . is incontestably a form of exclusive private property."[11] But neither he nor his successors ever tried seriously to envisage the implications of this for socialism, or even for a structural analysis of women's condition. Communism, Marx stressed in the same passage, would not mean mere "communalization" of women as common property. Beyond this, he never ventured.

Some historical considerations are in order here. For if socialists have said nothing, the gap has been filled by liberal ideologues. A recent book, *Eros Denied* by Wayland Young, argues that Western civilization has been uniquely repressive sexually and in a plea for greater sexual freedom today compares it at some length with Oriental and Ancient societies. It is striking, however, that his book makes no reference whatever to women's status in these different societies, or to the different forms of marriage-contract prevalent in them. This makes the whole argument a purely formal exercise—an obverse of socialist discussions of women's position which ignores the problem of sexual freedom and its meanings. For while it is true that certain oriental or ancient (and indeed primitive) cultures were much less puritan than Western societies, it is absurd to regard this as a kind of "transposable value" which can be abstracted from its social structure. In effect, in many of these societies sexual openness was accompanied by a form of polygamous exploitation which made it in practice an expression simply of masculine domination. Since art was the province of man, too, this freedom finds a natural and often powerful expression in art—which is often quoted as if it were evidence of the total quality of human relationships in the society. Nothing could be more misleading. What is necessary, rather than this naïve, hortatory core of historical example, is some account of the co-variation between the degrees of sexual liberty and openness and the position and dignity of women in different societies. Some points are immediately obvious. The actual history is much more dialectical than any liberal account presents it. Unlimited juridical polygamy—whatever the sexualization of the culture which accompanies it—is clearly a total derogation of woman's autonomy, and constitutes an extreme form of oppression. Ancient China is a perfect illustration of this. Wittfogel describes the extraordinary despotism of the Chinese *paterfamilias*— "a liturgical (semiofficial) policeman of his kin group."[12] In the West, however, the advent of monogamy was in no sense an *absolute* improvement. It certainly did not create a one-to-one equality—far from it. Engels commented accurately: "Monogamy does not by any means make its appearance in history as the reconciliation of man and woman, still less as the highest form of such a reconciliation. On the contrary, it appears as the subjugation of one sex by the other, as the proclamation of a conflict between the sexes entirely unknown hitherto in prehistoric times."[13] But in the Christian era, monogamy took on a very specific form in the West. It was allied with an unprecedented régime of general sexual repression. In its Pauline version, this had a markedly antifeminine bias, inherited from Judaism. With time this became diluted—feudal

[11] Karl Marx: *Private Property and Communism,* op. cit., p. 153.
[12] Karl Wittfogel: *Oriental Despotism* (1957), p. 116.
[13] Friedrich Engels, op. cit., II 224.

society, despite its subsequent reputation for asceticism, practised formal monogamy with considerable actual acceptance of polygamous behaviour, at least within the ruling class. But here again the extent of sexual freedom was only an index of masculine domination. In England, the truly major change occurred in the 16th century with the rise of militant puritanism and the increase of market relations in the economy.

. . .

For the situation today is defined by a new contradiction. Once formal conjugal equality (monogamy) is established, sexual freedom as such—which under polygamous conditions was usually a form of exploitation—becomes, conversely, a possible force for liberation. It then means, simply, the freedom for both sexes to transcend the limits of present sexual institutions.

Historically, then, there has been a dialectical movement, in which sexual expression was 'sacrificed' in an epoch of more-or-less puritan repression, which nevertheless produced a greater parity of sexual roles, which in turn creates the precondition for a genuine sexual liberation, in the dual sense of equality *and* freedom—whose unity defines socialism.

This movement can be verified within the history of the "sentiments." The cult of *love* only emerges in the 12th century in opposition to legal marital forms and with a heightened valorization of women (courtly love). It thereafter gradually became diffused, and assimilated to marriage as such, which in its bourgeois form (romantic love) became a *free* choice for *life*. What is striking here is that monogamy as an institution in the West anticipated the idea of love by many centuries. The two have subsequently been officially harmonized, but the tension between them has never been abolished. There is a formal contradiction between the voluntary contractual character of "marriage" and the spontaneous uncontrollable character of "love"—the passion that is celebrated precisely for its involuntary force. The notion that it occurs only once in every life and can therefore be integrated into a voluntary contract becomes decreasingly plausible in the light of everyday experience—once sexual repression as a psycho-ideological system becomes at all relaxed.

Obviously, the main breach in the traditional value-pattern has so far been the increase in premarital sexual experience. This is now virtually legitimized in contemporary bourgeois society. But its implications are explosive for the ideological conception of marriage that dominates this society: that of an exclusive and permanent bond. A recent American anthology *The Family and the Sexual Revolution* reveals this very clearly: "As far as extra-marital relations are concerned, the anti-sexualists are still fighting a strong, if losing, battle. The very heart of the Judeo-Christian sex ethic is that men and women shall remain virginal until marriage and that they shall be completely faithful after marriage. In regard to premarital chastity, this ethic seems clearly on the way out, and in many segments of the populace is more and more becoming a dead letter."[14]

The current wave of sexual liberalization, in the present context, could become

[14] Albert Ellis: *The Folklore of Sex,* in *The Family and the Sexual Revolution* ed. E. M. Schur (1964), p. 35.

conducive to the greater general freedom of women. Equally it could presage new forms of oppression. The puritan-bourgeois creation of woman as "counterpart" has produced the *precondition* for emancipation. But it gave statutory legal equality to the sexes at the cost of greatly intensified repression. Subsequently—like private property itself—it has become a brake on the further development of a free sexuality. Capitalist market relations have historically been a precondition of socialism; bourgeois marital relations (contrary to the denunciation of the *Communist Manifesto*) may equally be a precondition of women's liberation.

Socialization

Woman's biological destiny as mother becomes a cultural vocation in her role as socializer of children. In bringing up children, woman achieves her main social definition. Her suitability for socialization springs from her physiological condition; her ability to lactate and occasionally relative inability to undertake strenuous work loads. It should be said at the outset that suitability is not inevitability. Lévi-Strauss writes: "In every human group, women give birth to children and take care of them, and men rather have as their speciality hunting and warlike activities. Even there, though, we have ambiguous cases: of course, men never give birth to babies, but in many societies . . . they are made to act as if they did."[15] Evans-Pritchard's description of the Nuer tribe depicts just such a situation. And another anthropologist, Margaret Mead, comments on the element of wish-fulfilment in the assumption of a *natural* correlation of femininity and nurturance: "We have assumed that because it is convenient for a mother to wish to care for her child, this is a trait with which women have been more generously endowed by a careful teleological process of evolution. We have assumed that because men have hunted, an activity requiring enterprise, bravery, and initiative, they have been endowed with these useful aptitudes as part of their sex-temperament."[16] However, the cultural allocation of roles in bringing up children—and the limits of its variability—is not the essential problem for consideration. What is much more important is to analyse the nature of the socialization process itself and its requirements.

. . .

FAMILIAL PATTERNS

The ideology corresponds in dislocated form to a real change in the pattern of the family. As the family has become smaller, each child has become more important; the actual *act* of reproduction occupies less and less time and the socializing and nurturance process increase commensurately in significance.

---

[15] Claude Lévi-Strauss: *The Family*, in *Man, Culture and Society*, ed. H. L. Shapiro (1956), p. 274.

[16] Margaret Mead: *Sex and Temperament*, in *The Family and The Sexual Revolution*, op. cit., pp. 207–208.

Bourgeois society is obsessed by the physical, moral and sexual problems of childhood and adolescence.[17] Ultimate responsibility for these is placed on the mother.

The present situation is then one in which the qualitative importance of socialization during the early years of the child's life has acquired a much greater significance than in the past—while the quantitative amount of a mother's life spent either in gestation or child-rearing has greatly diminished. It follows that socialization cannot simply be elevated to the woman's new maternal vocation. Used as a mystique, it becomes an instrument of oppression. Moreover, there is no inherent reason why the biological and social mother should coincide. The process of socialization is, in the Kleinian sense, invariable —but the person of the socializer can vary.

. . .

Conclusion

The lesson of these reflections is that the liberation of women can only be achieved if *all four* structures in which they are integrated are transformed. A modification of any one of them can be offset by a reinforcement of another, so that mere permutation of the form of exploitation is achieved. The history of the last 60 years provides ample evidence of this. In the early 20th century, militant feminism in England or the USA surpassed the labour movement in the violence of its assault on bourgeois society, in pursuit of suffrage. This political right was eventually won. Nonetheless, though a simple completion of the formal legal equality of bourgeois society, it left the socio-economic situation of women virtually unchanged. The wider legacy of the suffrage was nil: the suffragettes proved quite unable to move beyond their own initial demands, and many of their leading figures later became extreme reactionaries. The Russian Revolution produced a quite different experience. In the Soviet Union in the 1920's, advanced social legislation aimed at liberating women above all in the field of sexuality: divorce was made free and automatic for either partner, thus effectively liquidating marriage; illegitimacy was abolished, abortion was free, etc. The social and demographic effects of these laws in a backward, semi-literate society bent on rapid industrialization (needing, therefore, a high birth-rate) were—predictably—catastrophic. Stalinism soon produced a restoration of iron traditional norms. Inheritance was reinstated, divorce inaccessible, abortion illegal, etc. "The State cannot exist without the family. Marriage is a positive value for the Socialist Soviet State only if the partners see in it a lifelong union. So-called free love is a bourgeois invention and has nothing in common with the

---

[17] David Riesman, while correctly observing this, makes a rather vain criticism of it: 'There has been a tendency in current social research influenced as it is by psychoanalysis, to over-emphasize and over-generalize the importance of very early childhood in character formation . . . It is increasingly recognized, however, that character may change greatly after this early period . . . Cultures differ widely not only in their timing of the various steps in character formation but also in the agents they rely on as each step.' *The Lonely Crowd* (1950), pp. 38–39.

principles of conduct of a Soviet citizen. Moreover, marriage receives its full value for the State only if there is progeny, and the consorts experience the highest happiness of parenthood," wrote the official journal of the Commissariat of Justice in 1939.[18] Women still retained the right and obligation to work, but because these gains had not been integrated into the earlier attempts to abolish the family and free sexuality no general liberation has occurred. In China, still another experience is being played out today. At a comparable stage of the revolution, all the emphasis is being placed on liberating women in *production*. This has produced an impressive social promotion of women. But it has been accompanied by a tremendous repression of sexuality and a rigorous puritanism (currently rampant in civic life). This corresponds not only to the need to mobilize women massively in economic life, but to a deep cultural reaction against the corruption and prostitution prevalent in Imperial and Kuo Ming Tang China (a phenomenon unlike anything in Czarist Russia). Because the exploitation of women was so great in the *ancien régime* women's participation at village level in the Chinese Revolution, was uniquely high. As for reproduction, the Russian cult of maternity in the 1930's and 1940's has not been repeated for demographic reasons: indeed, China may be one of the first countries in the world to provide free State authorized contraception on a universal scale to the population. Again, however, given the low level of industrialization and fear produced by imperialist encirclement, no allround advance could be expected.

It is only in the highly developed societies of the West that an authentic liberation of women can be envisaged today. But for this to occur, there must be a transformation of all the structures into which they are integrated, and an *"unité de rupture."*[19] A revolutionary movement must base its analysis on the uneven development of each, and attack the weakest link in the combination. This may then become the point of departure for a general transformation. What is the situation of the different structures today?

1. PRODUCTION. The long-term development of the forces of production must command any socialist perspective. The hopes which the advent of machine technology raised as early as the 19th century have already been discussed. They proved illusory. Today, automation promises the *technical* possibility of abolishing completely the physical differential between man and woman in production, but under capitalist relations of production, the *social* possibility of this abolition is permanently threatened, and can easily be turned into its opposite, the actual diminution of woman's role in production as the labour force contracts.

.   .   .

2. REPRODUCTION. Scientific advance in contraception could, as we have seen, make involuntary reproduction—which accounts for the vast majority of births in the world today, and for a major proportion even in the West—a

---

[18] *Sotsialisticheskaya Zakonnost* (1939. No. 2), cit. N. Timasheff: *The Attempt to Abolish the Family in Russia,* in *The Family,* ed. N. W. Bell and E. F. Vogel (1960), p. 59.

[19] See Louis Althusser: op. cit. See note 13.

phenomenon of the past. But oral contraception—which has so far been developed in a form which exactly repeats the sexual inequality of Western society—is only at its beginnings. It is inadequately distributed across classes and countries and awaits further technical improvements. Its main initial impact is, in the advanced countries, likely to be psychological—it will certainly free women's sexual experience from many of the anxieties and inhibitions which have always afflicted it.[20] It will definitely divorce sexuality from procreation, as necessary complements.

. . .

3. SOCIALIZATION. The changes in the composition of the work-force, the size of the family, the structure of education, etc.—however limited from an ideal standpoint—have undoubtedly diminished the societal function and importance of the family. As an organization it is not a significant unit in the political power system, it plays little part in economic production and it is rarely the sole agency of integration into the larger society; thus at the macroscopic level it serves very little purpose.

. . .

Indeed, the attempt to focus women's existence exclusively on bringing up children, is manifestly harmful to children. Socialization as an exceptionally delicate process requires a serene and mature socializer—a type which the frustrations of a *purely* familial role are not liable to produce. Exclusive maternity is often in this sense "counter-productive." The mother discharges her own frustrations and anxieties in a fixation on the child. An increased awareness of the critical importance of socialization, far from leading to a restitution of classical maternal roles, should lead to a reconsideration of them—of what makes a good socializing agent, who can genuinely provide security and stability for the child.

The same arguments apply, *a fortiori,* to the psycho-social role of the family for the couple. The beliefs that the family provides an impregnable enclave of intimacy and security in an atomized and chaotic cosmos assumes the absurd—that the family can be isolated from the community, and that its internal relationships will not reproduce in their own terms the external relationships which dominate the society. The family as refuge in a bourgeois society inevitably becomes a reflection of it.

4. SEXUALITY. It is difficult not to conclude that the major structure which at present is in rapid evolution is sexuality. Production, reproduction, and socialization are all more or less stationary in the West today, in the sense that they have not changed for three or more decades. There is moreover, no widespread *demand* for changes in them on the part of women themselves—the governing ideology has effectively prevented critical consciousness. By contrast, the dominant sexual ideology is proving less and less successful in regulating

[20] Jean Baby records the results of an enquiry carried out into attitudes to marriage, contraception and abortion of 3,191 women in Czechoslovakia in 1959: 80 per cent of the women had limited sexual satisfaction because of fear of conception. Op. cit., p. 82n.

spontaneous behaviour. Marriage in its classical form is increasingly threatened by the liberalization of relationships before and after it which affects all classes today. In this sense, it is evidently the weak link in the chain—the particular structure that is the site of the most contradictions. The progressive potential of these contradictions has already been emphasized. In a context of juridical equality, the liberation of sexual experience from relations which are extraneous to it—whether procreation or property—could lead to true inter-sexual freedom. But it could also lead simply to new forms of neocapitalist ideology and practice. For one of the forces behind the current acceleration of sexual freedom has undoubtedly been the conversion of contemporary capitalism from a production-and-work ethos to a consumption-and-fun ethos.

. . .

Bourgeois society at present can well afford a play area of premarital *non*-procreative sexuality. Even marriage can save itself by increasing divorce and remarriage rates, signifying the importance of the institution itself. These considerations make it clear that sexuality, while it presently may contain the greatest potential for liberation—can equally well be organized against any increase of its human possibilities. New forms of reification are emerging which may void sexual freedom of any meaning. This is a reminder that while one structure may be the *weak link* in a unity like that of woman's condition, there can never be a solution through it alone. The utopianism of Fourier or Reich was precisely to think that sexuality could inaugurate such a general solution. Lenin's remark to Clara Zetkin is a salutary if over-stated corrective: "However wild and revolutionary (sexual freedom) may be, it is still really quite bourgeois. It is, mainly, a hobby of the intellectuals and of the sections nearest them. There is no place for it in the Party, in the class conscious, fighting, proletariat."[21] For a general solution can only be found in a strategy which affects *all* the structures of women's exploitation. This means a rejection of two beliefs prevalent on the left:

Reformism. This now takes the form of limited ameliorative demands: equal pay for women, more nursery-schools, better retraining facilities, etc. In its contemporary version it is wholly divorced from any fundamental critique of women's condition or any vision of their real liberation (it was not always so). Insofar as it represents a tepid embellishment of the *status quo*, it has very little progressive content left.

Voluntarism. This takes the form of maximalist demands—the abolition of the family, abrogation of all sexual restrictions, forceful separation of parents from children—which have no chance of winning any wide support at present, and which merely serve as a substitute for the job of theoretical analysis or practical persuasion. By pitching the whole subject in totally intransigent terms, voluntarism objectively helps to maintain it outside the framework of normal political discussion.

What, then, is the responsible revolutionary attitude? It must include both immediate and fundamental demands, in a single critique of the *whole* of women's situation, that does not fetishize any dimension of it. Modern industrial

[21] Clara Zetkin: *Reminiscences of Lenin* (1925, trans. 1929), pp. 52–53.

development, as has been seen, tends towards the separating out of the originally unified function of the family—procreation, socialization, sexuality, economic subsistence, etc.—even if this "structural differentiation" (to use a term of Parsons') has been checked and disguised by the maintenance of a powerful family ideology. This differentiation provides the real historical basis for the ideal demands which should be posed: structural differentiation is precisely what distinguishes an advanced from a primitive society (in which all social functions are fused *en bloc*).[22]

[22] (See Ben Brewster: *Introduction to Lukács on Bukharin, New Left Review* No. 39, p. 25.) The capitalist mode of production separates the family from its earlier immediate association with the economy, and this marginality is unaffected directly by the transformation of the relations of production from private to public ownership in the transition to a socialist society. As the essence of woman's contemporary problem derives from this marginality, for this problem, *but for this problem only,* the distinction between industrial and preindustrial societies is the significant one. Categories meaningful for one element of the social totality may well be irrelevant or even pernicious if extended to the whole of historical development. Similar arguments, but principally lack of space in a short article must excuse the total neglect of problems arising from class distinctions in the functions and status of women.

Sexual Liberation

Female Sexual Alienation

LINDA PHELPS

Linda Phelps (1900–   ) lives in Kansas City, Missouri, and publishes in the area of women's liberation.

In the last few years, the so-called sexual revolution has turned sour. The end of inhibition and the release of sexual energies which have so often been documented as the innovation of the revolutionary culture are now beginning to be seen as just another fraud. After the gang-rapes at Altamont and Seattle, after the demands raised at People's Park for "Free Land, Free Dope, Free Women," after the analyses of (male) rock culture, women are beginning to realize that nothing new has happened at all. What we have is simply a new, more sophisticated (and thus more insidious) version of male sexual culture. Sexual freedom has meant more opportunity for men, not a new kind of experience for women. And it has been precisely our own experience as women which has been decisive in developing the Women's Liberation critique of the sexual revolution. I am concerned here with only one aspect of female sexuality—that between women and men. The generation of women who only a few years ago saw themselves as the vanguard of a sexual revolution between women and men suddenly find themselves plagued with all the problems of their grandmothers—loss of interest in sex, hatred of sex, disgust with self. This turn-about happened very fast for some of us and I think it happened because we opened ourselves up in consciousness-raising and a lot of bad feeling we thought we'd gotten rid of floated to the top. It has been good to get these feelings out and look at them. But can we *explain* them, can we understand what has happened to us in the last five years?

I would like to suggest that we can understand the destruction of female sexuality if we conceptualize it as a special case of alienation, understood as a political phenomenon. If alienation is the destruction of self which ultimately leads to schizophrenia, the widespread alienation of females from their own sexuality is a kind of rampant mental illness at the base of our experience which we must recognize for what it is.

Alienation is a much used and little explained term. Put simply, it refers to the disintegration of our very selves and personalities which occurs when we are powerless. The opposite of powerlessness is self-actualization; and the healthy, self-actualizing human being is one who moves through the world as an auton-

Source: Linda Phelps, "Female Sexual Alienation," *Women: A Journal of Liberation,* Vol. 3, No. 1 (October 1972), pp. 12–15. Copyright © 1972 by Women: A Journal of Liberation, 3028 Greenmount Avenue, Baltimore, Md. 21218. Reprinted by permission.

omous source of action. As Ernest Becker put it in an important essay on alienation:[1]

> People break down when they aren't "doing"—when the world around them does not reflect the active involvement of their own creative powers . . . Alienated man is man separated from involvement with and responsibility for the effective use of his *self-powers.*

What is more difficult to understand is precisely *how* alienation comes about in certain individuals. Becker suggests three ways: (1) Alienation occurs along the dimension of time. As children we learn certain patterns of behavior which bring us approval. As we grow older, however, we must constantly adapt to new situations. If our early childhood training has been too rigid, we are unable to make the necessary adjustments and become increasingly unable to handle our experiences. (2) Alienation also occurs in terms of the roles we play. This problem affects both men and women, but we are particularly familiar with the female version. Not only are females confined to a few narrow roles, but they are also subject to contradictory messages about the roles they play. Motherhood, for example, is viewed as a sacred task, but mothers are not taken seriously when they act outside their kitchens and homes. (3) The third dimension of alienation is more complex: breakdown of self occurs when the gap between thought and action, theory and practice, mind and body becomes too great. The classic and extreme example of this form of alienation is the schizophrenic, living totally in a thought world of her/his own creation with no relation to reality.

This three-dimensional model of alienation is complex but I think it can help us understand our own experience of sex between women and men. What I am about to say about female sexuality as schizophrenic will make more sense, however, if I digress for a moment to describe some attributes of schizophrenia. This extreme form of alienation, you will recall, is produced by a split between mind and body. Such an odd condition is possible in human beings as opposed to animals because we are self-conscious beings. We have an "inner self" of reflection and thought but our body is part of the world "out there" of experience and material objects. This mind-body dualism is at the base of human power—our ability to reflect upon and then act upon the material world. Such power becomes destructive—as in schizophrenia—when the mind turns in on itself and never tests its perceptions in concrete reality.

In this reverse process, the schizophrenic fails to develop the necessary unity between mind and body, takes refuge in a world of *symbols,* and thereby forfeits *experience.* In other words, a schizophrenic is someone who becomes accustomed to relating to symbol-objects rather than person-objects and in doing so loses all self-powers.

[1] Ernest Becker, "Mills' Social Psychology and the Great Historical Convergence on the Problem of Alienation," in Irving Horowitz, *The New Sociology, Essays in Social Science and Social Theory in Honor of C. Wright Mills* (New York, Oxford University Press, 1964), pp. 108–133.

I would argue that as females we are sexually schizophrenic, relating not to ourselves as self-directed persons, not to our partners as sexual objects of our desire, but to a false world of symbols and fantasy. This fantasy world of sex which veils our experience is the world of sex as seen through male eyes. It is a world whose eroticism is defined in terms of female powerlessness, dependency, and submission. It is the world of sado-masochistic sex. If you don't know what I mean by sado-masochism, think of the erotic themes of all the novels, comic books, movies, jokes, cartoons, and songs you've ever experienced. The major sexual theme which appears over and over again is the drama of conquest and submission: the male takes the initiative and the female waits, waits in a thousand variations on a single theme—eagerly, coyly, shyly, angrily, and at the outer edge of pornography and fantasy, is taken against her will. Usually it is more subtle. The female stands in awe of the hero's abilities, his powers; she is willing when he takes the initiative, guides her by the elbow, puts his arm around her waist, manoevres her into the bedroom. What is it that makes such descriptions arousing? Not a mere run-down of anatomy but the tension in the social situation as male advances on female, whether she is willing or not.

Such submission is acceptable in our culture if the man 'is superior, and this leads to the search for the man who is smarter, taller, more self-confident—someone to look up to and thus worthy of giving in to.

> In each of our lives, there was a first man for whom we were prepared like lambs for the slaughter. My fantasy of him was a composite of Prince Valiant, Gary Cooper, and my father. Trained in submission, in silence, I awaited him through a series of *adolescent boyfriends who were not masterful enough to fit the dream* . . . because I would not really graduate to the estate of womanhood until I had been taken by a strong man.[2]

Trained in submission, women instinctively look for the strong men who will continue the loving benevolence of the father. That this pattern of sexual relations is our society's model is confirmed by psychologist Abraham Maslow.[3] In a study of sexual behavior, Maslow reported that women who find a partner more dominant than they usually make the best sexual adjustment. On the other hand, a very sexually active woman in his study failed to reach orgasm with several male partners because she considered them weaker than herself and thus could not "give in to them." Thus, 'normal' sexual adjustment occurs in our society when the male plays the dominant role.

If we come to view male-dominated sexual relations as by definition healthy sex, the mechanism of this learning process is the bombardment of sexual fantasy that we experience long before we experience sex itself. Sexual images of conquest and submission pervade our imagination from an early age and lay the basis for how we will later look upon and experience sex. Through the television set and the storybook, we live out in imagination society's definition of sex and love.

[2] *Motherlode,* Vol. i, no. i, p. i.

[3] A. H. Maslow, "Self-Esteem (Dominance-Feeling) and Sexuality in Women," in Hendrik M. Ruttenbeck, *Psychoanalysis and Female Sexuality* (New Haven, Conn., College and University Press, 1966), pp. 161–197.

Rapunzel waits in her tower for years in hopes of the young prince who will free her body from its imprisonment. Sleeping Beauty's desires slumber until they are awakened and fulfilled by the kiss of the young prince. These fairy tale princesses are not unusual. There are few women, no matter how intelligent, no matter how dedicated to the pursuit of a goal, who will not finally be conquered —and like it. And if they are not conquered, it is understood that no man desired them anyway.

By experiencing such sexual fantasies at an early age, we become alienated along Becker's first dimension of time. Locked early into a set of fantasy images which define female sexual roles as passive, women are constantly denying feelings which don't fit the cultural definitions. And so all pervasive is the male bias of our culture that we seldom notice that the fantasies we take in, the images that describe to us how to act, are *male* fantasies about females. In a male world, female sex is from the beginning unable to get a clear picture of itself.

And from the beginning, women experience Becker's second dimension of alienation: the role of woman as sexual being is subject to contradictory evaluations by society. Young girls quickly become attuned to society's ambivalent view of their sexuality. Women come to see themselves as synonymous with sex yet female sexuality is seen as valid only under certain conditions such as marriage. Even as such narrow restrictions break down in more permissive ages like our own and the limits of female sexuality expand, we still run up against those limits at the point where a female can be labelled promiscuous. And women who initiate and direct sexual activity on a regular basis find that they have gone beyond the limits of the possible and are termed castrating. Male sexual desires, on the other hand, are affirmed throughout and are associated with prowess, power, and man(self)hood.

As females, then, we relate to symbol-objects rather than person-objects. Like the schizophrenic, we are alienated from our own experience and from our own self-powers of initiation. This form of alienation has to do with sex in a very direct way because women do not often take the initiative in relation to men.

> Schizophrenic passivity is a direct reflex of the abrogation of one's powers in the face of the object . . . If you relate to an object under your own initiatory powers, then it becomes an object which enriches your own nature. If you lack initiatory powers over the object, it takes on a different value, for it then becomes an in- dividual which crowds your own nature . . . A girl really comes to exist as a feminine sex object for the adolescent only as he learns to exercise active courtship powers in relation to her.[4]

If women become objects of sexual desire for men in the social process of male-initiated relationships, how does the male become an object of sexual desire for the female? It is not clear, in fact, that the male body *per se* is deemed erotic by women, certainly not in the same way that the female body is for men. In fact, since women are bombarded with the same sex stimuli of the female body as is a man, females often respond in a narcissistic way to their own body and

---

[4] Becker, op. cit., p. 125.

what is being *done* to it rather than projecting sexual desire out onto the male. The female is taught to be the object of sexual desires rather than to be a self-directed sexual being oriented toward another; she is taught to be adored rather than adoring. Is it surprising then that so many women find the male body ugly, that so many women see the drama of sex in what is done *to* them?

Two things happen to women's sexual lives. Many women have no sexual fantasies at all (since there is little male sexual imagery available in this culture). Masters and Johnson found that many women who could not focus on sexual imagery had difficulty having orgasm. The good doctors have tried to encourage sexual fantasy (by reading arousing material!) to enable women to experience orgasm.

Females that do have fantasies often have the same sado-masochistic fantasies that men do. As Shulamith Firestone points out in *The Dialectic of Sex.*

> Cultural distortion of sexuality also explains how female sexuality gets twisted in narcissism: women make love to themselves vicariously through the man rather than directly making love to him.[5]

In these fantasy episodes, the female does not always play the masochistic role. The female who is focusing on sexual imagery can take the part either of the male, the female, or an onlooker, but in any case eroticism is still dealing in female powerlessness.

How do women tolerate a situation in which men control and define the experience of sex? I believe we solve our problem in the same way the schizophrenic does. A woman's sexuality is experienced in symbolic terms at the expense of active physical involvement. Sex is re-presented to her by society in symbolic messages of passivity and conquest. Like the symbolic world of the schizophrenic, a woman's fantasy life—her desire to be taken, overpowered, mastered—allows her to play the passive role and perhaps even to enjoy it *if she fully accepts the world as defined by men.* Caught between the demands of a male-dominated society and the demands of our own self-definition, we survive by fully accepting the masochistic symbol-world given to us by male society at the expense of our own experience. In fact, our physical experience has been denied and distorted for so long that most of us aren't even aware of the sacrifice we have made. We are only uneasy that all is not well.

Yet ultimately in the lives of those women for whom fantasy and reality become too far apart, a crisis occurs. The mechanism of crisis in some cases may be merely the demystification of the male through years of marriage. It is hard to keep intact fantasies of male power when confronted with the reality of a pot-bellied, lethargic husband. Such a crisis may result either in a transfer of fantasy to a new male or in a loss of interest in sex altogether. For women in Women's Liberation the whole fragile structure of fantasy and power often falls along with the myth of male supremacy. Males are subject to the same fantasies of conquest, yet their fantasy life is an expression of their own active powers (albeit in a false way) and does not separate them from their own experience.

Women, then, are alienated from their sexuality along several dimensions.

[5] Shulamith Firestone. *The Dialectic of Sex* (New York, William Morrow, 1970), p. 178.

From an early age, we are alienated from ourselves as sexual beings by a male society's ambivalent definition of our sexuality: we are sexy but we are pure; we are insatiable but we are frigid; we have beautiful bodies but we must shave and anoint them. We are also alienated because we are separated from our own experience by the prevailing male cultural definition of sex—the male fantasy of active man and passive woman. From an early age, our sexual impulses are trained to turn back onto ourselves in the narcissistic counterpart of the male fantasy world. In social relations with men, we are alienated from ourselves as initiating, self-directed persons. Some women hold all these contradictory parts together; most women, I suspect, have given up on sex, whether or not they have informed their husbands and lovers.

Calling into question our traditional female role has meant calling into question more and more layers of our experience. With this questioning has come the discovery that there is not much left that is valid in male-female relations as we have known them. Kate Millet showed us in *Sexual Politics* that fascism—the relations of dominance and submission that begin with sex and extend throughout our society—is at the very core of our cultural experience. So it is with little joy and much sadness that we peel back the layers of our consciousness and see our sexual experience for what it really is. And it is also with much sadness that we admit that there is no easy answer. It is too easy to say that we have been merely the victims of male power plays. The sado-masochistic content of sex is in the heads of women too. As long as female powerlessness is the unspoken underlying reality of sexual relations, women will want to be conquered. As long as our cultural vision is the projection of solely male experience, women will not be able to understand even their own alienation.

To say this is to suggest some ways out of our cultural and sexual alienation. Yet it is also too easy to blithely assume, as we often do, that all this sexual distortion is going to be easily changed in some new culture in the future. We have pushed beyond the economic revolution and the cultural revolution to come face to face with the real sexual revolution and we are not sure what we have left in the way of hope and affirmation.

Perhaps the most courageous and in the long run the most positive statement we can make is to acknowledge the pain we feel now and the perhaps irreparable damage that we have sustained. But saying this is not totally to despair. Sometimes it is necessary to touch rock bottom before we can find the strength to push up for air.

Sexual Love and Human Expression

ROBERT SOLOMON

Robert Solomon (1942–   ), associate professor of philosophy at the University of Texas, is the author of *From Rationalism to Existentialism* (1972) and co-author of *The Myth of the Passions* (1975).

It is a cocktail lounge, well-lit and mirrored, not a bar, martinis and not beer, two strangers—a furtive glance from him, shy recognition from her. It is 1950's American high comedy: boy arouses girl, both are led through ninety minutes of misunderstandings of identity and intention, and, finally, by the end of the popcorn, boy kisses girl with a clean-cut fade-out or panned clip of a postcard horizon. It is one of the dangers of conceptual analysis that the philosopher's choice of paradigms betrays a personal bias, but it is an exceptional danger of sexual conceptual analysis that one's choice of paradigms also betrays one's private fantasies and personal obsessions.[1] No doubt that is why, despite their extraprofessional interest in the subject, most philosophers would rather write about indirect discourse than intercourse, the philosophy of mind rather than the philosophy of body.

In Tom Nagel's pioneering effort[2] there are too many recognizable symptoms of liberal American sexual mythology. His analysis is cautious and competent, but absolutely sexless. His Romeo and Juliet exemplify at most a romanticized version of the initial phases of (hetero-)sexual attraction in a casual and innocent pick-up. They "arouse" each other, but there is no indication to what end. They "incarnate each other as flesh," in Sartre's awkward but precise terminology, but Nagel gives us no clue as to why they should indulge in such a peculiar activity. Presumably a pair of dermatologists or fashion models might have a similar effect on each other, but without the slightest hint of sexual intention. What makes this situation paradigmatically sexual? We may assume, as we would in a Doris Day comedy, that the object of this protracted arousal is sexual intercourse, but we are not told this. Sexuality without content. Liberal sexual mythology takes this Hollywood element of "leave it to the imagination" as its starting point and adds the equally inexplicit suggestion that whatever activities two consenting adults choose as the object of their arousal and its gratification is "their business." In a society with such secrets, pornography is

---

[1] I confess, for example, that certain male biases infiltrate my own analysis. I thank Janice Moulton for pointing this out to me.

[2] "Sexual Perversion," this JOURNAL, LXVI, 1, Jan. 16, 1969, 15–17.

Source: Robert Solomon, "Sexual Paradigms," *The Journal of Philosophy,* Vol. LXXI, No. 11 (June 13, 1974), pp. 336–345.

bound to serve a radical end as a vulgar valve of reality. In a philosophical analysis that stops short of the very matter investigated, a bit of perverseness may be necessary just in order to refocus the question.

Sexual desire is distinguished, like all desires, by its aims and objects. What are these peculiarly sexual aims and objects? Notice that Nagel employs a fairly standard "paradigm case argument" in his analysis; he begins,

> . . . certain practices will be perversions if anything is, such as shoe fetishism, bestiality and sadism; other practices, such as unadorned sexual intercourse will not be (5).

So we can assume that the end of Romeo and Juliet's tryst will be intercourse—we do not know whether "adorned" or not. But what it is that makes intercourse the paradigm of sexual activity—its biological role in conception, its heterosexuality, its convenience for mutual orgasm? Would Nagel's drama still serve as a sexual paradigm if Juliet turns out to be a virgin, or if Romeo and Juliet find that they are complementarily sado-masochistic, if Romeo is in drag, if they are both knee-fetishists? Why does Nagel choose two *strangers*? Why not, as in the days of sexual moralism, a happily married couple enjoying their seventh anniversary? Or is not the essence of sex, as Sartre so brutally argues, Romeo and Juliet's mutual attempts to possess each other, with each's own enjoyment only a secondary and essentially distracting effect? Are we expected to presume the most prominent paradigm, at least since Freud, the lusty ejaculation of Romeo into the submissive, if not passive, Juliet? Suppose Juliet is in fact a prostitute, skillfully mocking the signs of innocent arousal: is this a breach of the paradigm, or might not such subsequent "unadorned" intercourse be just the model that Nagel claims to defend?

To what end does Romeo arouse Juliet? And to what end does Juliet become affected and in turn excite Romeo? In this exemplary instance, I would think that "unadorned" intercourse would be perverse, or at least distasteful, in the extreme. It would be different, however, if the paradigm were our seven-year married couple, for in such cases "adorned" intercourse might well be something of a rarity. In homosexual encounters, in the frenzy of adolescent virginal petting, in cases in which intercourse is restricted for temporary medical or political reasons, arousal may be no different, even though intercourse cannot be the end. And it is only in the crudest cases of physiological need that the desire for intercourse is the sole or even the leading component in the convoluted motivation of sexuality. A nineteen-year-old sailor back after having discussed nothing but sex on a three-month cruise may be so aroused, but that surely is not the nature of Juliet's arousal. Romeo may remind her of her father, or of her favorite philosophy professor, and he may inspire respect, or fear, or curiosity. He may simply arouse self-consciousness or embarrassment. Any of these attitudes may be dominant, but none is particularly sexual.

Sexuality has an essential bodily dimension, and this might well be described as the "incarnation" or "submersion" of a person into his body. The end of this desire is interpersonal communication; but where Sartre gives a complex theory of the nature of this communication, Nagel gives us only an empty notion of "multi-level interpersonal awareness." Presumably the mutual arousal that is the means to this awareness is enjoyable in itself. But it is important that Nagel resists the current (W.) Reichian-American fetish for the wonders of the genital orgasm, for he does not leap to the facile conclusion that the aim of sexual activity is mutual or at least personal orgasm. It is here that Nagel opens a breach with liberal sexual mythology, one that might at first appear absurd because of his total neglect of the role of the genitalia and orgasm in sexuality. But we have an overgenitalized conception of sexuality, and, if sexual satisfaction involves and even requires orgasm, it does not follow that orgasm is the goal of the convoluted sexual games we play with each other. Orgasm is the "end" of sexual activity, perhaps, but only in the sense that swallowing is the "end" of tasting a Viennese torte.

There was a time, and it was not long ago and may come soon again, when sexuality required defending. It had to be argued that we had a right to sex, not for any purpose other than our personal enjoyment. But that defense has turned stale, and sexual deprivation is no longer our problem. The "swollen bladder" model of repressed sexuality may have been convincing in sex-scared bourgeois Vienna of 1905, but not today, where the problem is not sexual deprivation but sexual dissatisfaction. The fetishism of the orgasm, now shared by women as well as men, threatens our sex lives with becoming antipersonal and mechanical, anxiety-filled athletic arenas with mutual muliple orgasm its goal. Behind much of this unhappiness and anxiety, ironically, stands the liberal defense of sexuality as enjoyment. It is one of the virtues of Nagel's essay that he begins to overcome this oppressive liberal mythology. But at the same time he relies upon it for his support and becomes trapped in it, and the result is an account which displays the emptiness we have pointed out and the final note of despair with which he ends his essay.

Liberal sexual mythology appears to stand upon a tripod of mutually supporting platitudes: (1) and foremost, that the essential aim (and even the sole aim) of sex is enjoyment; (2) that sexual activity is and ought to be essentially private activity, and (3) that any sexual activity is as valid as any other. The first platitude was once a radical proposition, a reaction to the conservative and pious belief that sexual activity was activity whose end was reproduction, the serving of God's will or natural law. Kant, for example, always good for a shocking opinion in the realm of normative ethics, suggests that sexual lust is an appetite with an end intended by nature, and that any sexual activity contrary to that end is "unnatural and revolting," by which one "makes himself an object of abomination and stands bereft of all reverence of any kind."[3] It was Sigmund Freud who destroyed this long-standing paradigm, in identifying sexuality as "discharge of tension" (physical and psychological), which he simply equated with "pleasure," regardless of the areas of the body or what activities or how many people happened to be involved. Sex was thus defined as self-serving, activity for its own sake, with pleasure as its only principle. If Freud is now accused of sexual conservatism, it is necessary to remind ourselves that he introduced the radical paradigm that is now used against him. Since Freud's classic efforts, the conception of sexuality as a means to other ends, whether

[3] *Metaphysics of Ethics,* trans. Scmple (Edinburgh: Clark, 1971) IV, pt. I, ch. I, sec. 7.

procreation or pious love, has become bankrupt in terms of the currency of opinion. Even radical sexual ideology has confined its critique to the social and political *abuses* of this liberal platitude without openly rejecting it.

The second platitude is a hold-over from more conservative days, in which sexual activity, like defecation, menstruation, and the bodily reactions to illness, was considered distasteful, if not shameful and to be hidden from view. Yet this conservative platitude is as essential as the first, for the typically utilitarian argument in defense of sexuality as enjoyment is based on the idea that sex is private activity and, when confined to "consenting adults," should be left as a matter of taste. And sex is, we are reminded by liberals, a natural appetite, and therefore a matter of taste.

The platitude of privacy also bolsters the third principle, still considered a radical principle by many, that any sexual activity is as valid as any other. Again, the utilitarian argument prevails, that private and mutually consented activity between adults, no matter how distasteful it might be to others and no matter how we may think its enthusiasts to be depraved, is "their own business."

Nagel's analysis calls this tri-part ideology to his side, although he clearly attempts to go beyond it as well. The platitude of enjoyment functions only loosely in his essay, and at one point he makes it clear that sexuality need not aim at enjoyment. ["It may be that . . . perfection *as sex* is less enjoyable than certain perversions; and if enjoyment is considered very important, that might outweigh considerations of sexual perfection in determining rational preference" (16/17).] His central notion of "arousal," however, is equivocal. On the one hand, arousal is itself not necessarily enjoyable, particularly if it fails to be accompanied with expectations of release. But on the other hand, Nagel's "arousal" plays precisely the same role in his analysis that "tension" (or "cathexis") plays in Freud, and though the arousal itself is not enjoyable, its release is, and the impression we get from Nagel, which Freud makes explicit, is that sexual activity is the intentional arousal both of self and other in order to enjoy its release. On this interpretation, Nagel's analysis is perfectly in line with post-Freudian liberal theory.

Regarding the second platitude, Nagel's analysis does not mention it, but rather it appears to be presupposed throughout that sexuality is a private affair. One might repeat that the notion of privacy is more symptomatic of his analysis itself. One cannot imagine J. L. Austin spending a dozen pages describing the intentions and inclinations involved in a public performance of making a promise or christening a ship without mentioning the performance itself. Yet Nagel spends that much space giving us the preliminaries of sexuality without ever quite breaching the private sector in which sexual activity is to be found.

The third platitude emerges only slowly in Nagel's essay. He begins by chastising an approach to that same conclusion by a radical "skeptic," who argues of sexual desires, as "appetites,"

Either they are sexual or they are not; sexuality does not admit of imperfection, or perversion, or any other such qualification (7).

Nagel's analysis goes beyond this "skepticism" in important ways, yet he does conclude that "any bodily contact between a man and a woman that gives them sexual *pleasure* [italics mine], is a possible vehicle for the system of multi-level interpersonal awareness that I have claimed is the basic psychological content of sexual interaction" (15). Here the first platitude is partially employed to support the third, presumably with the second implied. Notice again that Nagel has given us no indication what distinguishes "sexual pleasure" from other pleasures, whether bodily pleasures or the enjoyment of conquest or domination, seduction or submission, sleeping with the president's daughter or earning thirty dollars.

To knock down a tripod, one need kick out only one of its supporting legs. I for one would not wish to advocate, along with several recent sexual pundits, an increased display of fornication and fellatio in public places, nor would I view the return of "sexual morality" as a desirable state of affairs. Surprisingly, it is the essential enjoyment of sex that is the least palatable of the liberal myths.

No one would deny that sex is enjoyable, but it does not follow that sexuality is the activity of "pure enjoyment" and that "gratification," or "pure physical pleasure," that is, orgasm, is its end. Sex is indeed pleasurable, but, as Aristotle argued against the hedonists of his day, this enjoyment accompanies sexual activity and its ends, but is not that activity or these ends. We enjoy being sexually satisfied; we are not satisfied by our enjoyment. In fact, one might reasonably hypothesize that the performance of any activity, pleasurable or not, which is as intensely promoted and obsessively pursued as sex in America would provide tremendous gratification. [One might further speculate on the fact that recent American politics shows that "every (white, male Christian) American boy's dream of becoming President" seems to encourage the exploitation of all three sexual platitudes of enjoyment, privacy, and "anything goes." (Cf. H. Kissinger, "Power is the ultimate aphrodisiac.")]

If sexuality does not essentially aim at pleasure, does it have any purpose? Jean-Paul Sartre has given us an alternative to the liberal theory in his *Being and Nothingness,* in which he argues that our sexual relations with others, like all our various relationships with others, are to be construed as *conflicts,* modeled after Hegel's parable of master and slave. Sexual desire is not desire for pleasure, and pleasure is more likely to distract us from sexuality than to deepen our involvement. For Sartre, sexual desire is the desire to possess, to gain recognition of one's own freedom at the expense of the other. By "incarnating" and degrading him/her in flesh, one reduces him/her to an object. Sadism is but an extension of this domination over the other. Or one allows himself to be "incarnated" as a devious route to the same end, making the other his/her sexual slave. Sexual activity concentrates its attention on the least personal, most inert parts of the body—breasts, thighs, stomach, and emphasizes awkward and immobile postures and activities. On this model, degradation is the central activity of sex, to convince the other that he/she is a slave, to persuade the other of one's own power, whether it be through the skills of sexual technique or through the passive demands of being sexually served. Intercourse has no privileged position in this model, except that intercourse, particularly in these liberated times in which it has become a contest, is ideal for this competition for power and recognition. And no doubt Sartre, who, like Freud, adopts a paradigmatically male perspective, senses that intercourse is more likely to be degrading to the woman, who thus begins at a disadvantage.

Sartre's notion of sexuality, taken seriously, would be enough to keep us out of bed for a month. Surely, we must object, something has been left out of account, for example, the two-person *Mitsein* that Sartre himself suggests in the same book. It is impossible for us to delve into the complex ontology that leads Sartre into this pessimistic model, but its essential structure is precisely what we need to carry us beyond the liberal mythology. According to Sartre, sexuality is interpersonal communication with the body as its medium. Sartre's mistake, if we may be brief, is his narrow constriction of the message of that communication to mutual degradation and conflict. Nagel, who accepts Sartre's communication model but, in line with the liberal mythology, seeks to reject its pessimistic conclusions, makes a mistake in the opposite direction. He accepts the communication model, but leaves it utterly without content. What is communicated, he suggests, is arousal. But, as we have seen, arousal is too broad a notion; we must know arousal of what, for what, to what end. Nagel's notion of "arousal" and "interpersonal awareness" gives us an outline of the grammar of the communication model, but no semantics. One might add that sexual activity in which what is aroused and intended are pleasurable sensations alone is a limiting and rare case. A sensation is only pleasurable or enjoyable, not in itself, but in the context of the meaning of the activity in which it is embedded. This is as true of orgasm as it is of a hard passion-bite on the shoulder.

This view of sexuality answers some strong questions which the liberal model leaves a mystery. If sex is pure physical enjoyment, why is sexual activity between persons far more satisfying than masturbation, where, if we accept recent physiological studies, orgasm is at its highest intensity and the post-coital period is cleansed of its interpersonal hassles and arguments? On the Freudian model, sex with other people ("objects") becomes a matter of "secondary process," with masturbation primary. On the communication model, masturbation is like talking to yourself; possible, even enjoyable, but clearly secondary to sexuality in its broader interpersonal context. (It is significant that even this carnal solipsism is typically accompanied by imaginings and pictures; "No masturbation without representation," perhaps.) If sex is physical pleasure, then the fetish of the genital orgasm is no doubt justifiable, but then why in our orgasm-cluttered sex lives are we so dissatisfied? Because orgasm is not the "end" of sex but its resolution, and obsessive concentration on reaching climax effectively overwhelms or distorts whatever else is being said sexually. It is this focus on orgasm that has made Sartre's model more persuasive; for the battle over the orgasm, whether in selfish or altruistic guise ("my orgasm first" or "I'll *give* you the best ever") has become an unavoidable medium for conflict and control. "Unadorned sexual intercourse," on this model, becomes the ultimate perversion, since it is the sexual equivalent of hanging up the telephone without saying anything. Even an obscene telephone caller has a message to convey.

Sexual activity consists in speaking what we might call "body language." It has its own grammar, delineated by the body, and its own phonetics of touch and movement. Its unit of meaningfulness, the bodily equivalent of a sentence, is the *gesture*. No doubt one could add considerably to its vocabulary, and perhaps it could be possible to discuss world politics or the mind-body problem by an appropriate set of invented gestures. But body language is essentially expressive, and its content is limited to interpersonal attitudes and feelings— shyness, domination, fear, submissiveness and dependence, love or hatred or indifference, lack of confidence and embarrassment, shame, jealousy, possessiveness. There is little value in stressing the overworked point that such expressions are "natural" expressions, as opposed to verbal expressions of the same attitudes and feelings. In our highly verbal society, it may well be that verbal expression, whether it be poetry or clumsy blurting, feels more natural than the use of our bodies. Yet it does seem true that some attitudes, e.g., tenderness and trust, domination and passivity, are best expressed sexually. Love, it seems, is not best expressed sexually, for its sexual expression is indistinguishable from the expressions of a number of other attitudes. Possessiveness, mutual recognition, "being-with," and conflict are expressed by body language almost essentially, virtually as its deep structure, and here Sartre's model obtains its plausibility.

According to Nagel, "perversion" is "truncated or incomplete versions of the complete configuration" (13). But again, his emphasis is entirely on the form of "interpersonal awareness" rather than its content. For example, he analyzes sadism as "the concentration on the evocation of passive self-awareness in others . . . which impedes awareness of himself as a bodily subject of passion in the required sense." But surely sadism is not so much a breakdown in communication (any more than the domination of a conversation by one speaker, with the agreement of his listener, is a breach of language) as an excessive expression of a particular content, namely the attitude of domination, perhaps mixed with hatred, fear, and other negative attitudes. Similarly, masochism is not simply the relinquishing of one's activity (an inability to speak, in a sense), for the masochist may well be active in inviting punishment from his sadistic partner. Masochism is excessive expression of an attitude of victimization, shame, or inferiority. Moreover, it is clear that there is not the slightest taint of "perversion" in homosexuality, which need differ from heterosexuality only in its mode of resolution. Fetishism and bestiality certainly do constitute perversions, since the first is the same as, for example, talking to someone else's shoes, and the second is like discussing Spinoza with a moderately intelligent sheep.

This model also makes it evident why Nagel chose as his example a couple of strangers; one has far more to say, for one can freely express one's fantasies as well as the truth, to a stranger. A husband and wife of seven years have probably been repeating the same messages for years, and their sexual activity now is probably no more than an abbreviated ritual incantation of the lengthy conversations they had years before. One can imagine Romeo and Juliet climbing into bed together each with a spectacular set of expectations and fantasies, trying to overwhelm each other with extravagant expressions and experiments. But it may be accordingly, that they won't understand each other, or, as the weekend plods on, sex, like any extended conversation, tends to become either more truthful or more incoherent.

Qua body language, sex admits of at least two forms of perversion: one deviance of form, the other deviance in content. There are the techniques of sexuality, overly celebrated in our society, and there are the attitudes that these techniques allegedly express. Nagel and most theorists have concentrated on perversions in technique, deviations in the forms of sexual activity. But it seems to me that the more problematic perversions are the semantic deviations, of which the most serious are those involving insincerity, the bodily equivalent of the lie. Entertaining private fantasies and neglecting one's real sexual partner is thus an innocent semantic perversion, while pretended tenderness and affection that reverses itself soon after orgasm is a potentially vicious perversion. However, again joining Nagel, I would argue that perverse sex is not necessarily bad or immoral sex. Pretense is the premise of imagination as well as of falsehood, and sexual fantasies may enrich our lives far more than sexual realities alone. Perhaps it is an unfortunate comment on the poverty of contemporary life that our fantasies have become so confined, that our sexuality has been forced to serve needs which far exceed its expressive capacity. That is why the liberal mythology has been so disastrous, for it has rendered unconscious the expressive functions of sex in its stress on enjoyment and, in its platitude of privacy, has reduced sexuality to each man's/woman's private language, first spoken clumsily and barely articulately on wedding nights and in the back seats of Fords. It is thus understandable why sex is so utterly important in our lives, and why it is typically so unsatisfactory.

The Morality of Homosexual Behavior

RONALD ATKINSON

Ronald Atkinson (1928–   ) teaches philosophy at the University of Keele in England. He is the author of *Sexual Morality* (1965).

The Wolfenden Committee did not spend much time on the question of morality of homosexual behaviour. Possibly they felt that in any way to question its immorality would only arouse opposition to their recommendation concerning the attitude to be taken to it by the law. They are emphatic that, in staking a claim for a sphere of private morality and immorality beyond the reach of the law, they do not wish to be understood as condoning private immorality. Moreover, in so far as the concern is with *positive* morality, the received code of behaviour such as it is, there is no doubt at all that homosexual activity is immoral. But can one avoid asking the question whether positive morality is

Source: Ronald Atkinson, *Sexual Morality* (New York, 1965). Copyright © 1965 by Ronald Atkinson. Reprinted by permission of Harcourt Brace Jovanovich, Inc., and Hutchinson Publishing Group Ltd.

right on this matter? Suppose, as the Wolfenden Committee thought, that there may be homosexual acts which do no harm to non-consenting non-adults, and which, being private, are no affront to public decency—on what grounds could they be held to be morally wrong?

Not on utilitarian grounds, obviously; nor, leaving out of account the present state of the law and public opinion, on prudential grounds either. People do not choose to become homosexuals, they rather find that they are: and even if they should then want to change the direction of their sexual inclinations, which they may not, there would at present seem to be no certainty that this can be successfully accomplished. To deny one's sexual nature all physical expression, still ignoring the consequences homosexuals may suffer from law and public opinion, goes beyond, if not contrary to, the demands of prudence.

It may be that, in fact, many homosexual relationships present morally objectionable features: they may involve seduction, and exploitation of the young. But the evidence noticed above suggests that most do not, and that the risk of a homosexual who practices with fellow adults turning to boys is comparatively small. It is, moreover, relevant to the assessment of the moral importance of such risk as there is to point out that the harm done by seduction, or even assault, to young boys can easily be exaggerated—as can the damage done by heterosexual interference with small girls. In both cases the extreme reactions of parents, understandable though they may be, tend to increase the harm. And the likelihood of a boy being turned into a homosexual by seduction would not seem to be very great, as home influences are more important than outside encounters in determining one's sexual orientation. Most men who engage in homosexual activity in special circumstances—school, prison, the army—appear to abandon it when heterosexual opportunities become available. Some, much, even most homosexual activity may be morally exceptionable: so too is a good deal of heterosexual activity. In neither case is this necessarily so. Nor does it appear that homosexual relationships in themselves are necessarily more objectionable than heterosexual ones. I can see no good reason to doubt that it is possible for a homosexual to conduct his sexual life with prudence, beneficence, fairness and responsibility. If he does, there is no ground for moral complaint.

Another claim that is often made is that homosexual relationships are apt to be morally worthless or of little worth, to fall very far short of the ideal form of human relationship. (It is important to distinguish this complaint from the previous one. *That* was to the effect that they offended against, so to say, "basic morality": *this* is to the effect that they are not ideal. . . .) Homosexual relations seem normally to be of brief duration, and homosexual promiscuity to be common. They seem, that is to say, to resemble those heterosexual relationships which are held to be least worth while. This sort of contention has great rhetorical force. It purports to make a lavish concession, to allow, as, of course, many people do not, that homosexual relationships are to be judged on the *same footing* as heterosexual ones, and yet still contrives to find them objectionable. How far must we go along with it?

Two comments are in place. The first, and less important one, is that the unworthwhile features manifested by some homosexual relationships may largely be the result of the public attitude to them. The result of, and hence not the justification for, that attitude. Stable relationships are hardly possible when all homosexual associations are condemned out of hand. The more important point is that, low though casual sexual encounters may be on the heterosexual's scale of preference, they may still be the best or only form of sexual association available to the homosexuals involved. The basic morality of avoiding harm and unfairness to others we may reasonably demand of everybody: our ideals in so far as they go beyond this are for the guidance of our own, not other people's, conduct. In general we do not blame people, or hold them to be wicked or immoral, for not sharing our ideals; at worst we may hold them misguided or mistaken, or that they are 'missing something.' It is doubtful, in fact, whether even such mild criticisms or commiserations fit the case of the homosexual, who has not chosen his condition and probably cannot change it.

It may further be noted that from the point of view of the morality of personal relationships, which was considered in a different connexion above . . . , homosexual associations as such cannot be held to be immoral. The authors of the Quaker pamphlet recognise this with characteristic candour:

> . . . we see no reason why the physical nature of a sexual act should be the criterion by which the question whether it is moral should be decided. An act which (for example) expresses true affection between two individuals and gives pleasure to them both, does not seem to us to be sinful by reason *alone* of the fact that it is homosexual. The same criteria seem to us to apply whether a relationship is heterosexual or homosexual [p. 36].

I expressed some doubt above about the responsibility of viewing heterosexual associations exclusively from the agent-centred ethic of personal relationships. This seemed to me to take insufficient account of the possibility of children being conceived. This consideration does not arise where homosexual associations are concerned.

It is true, of course, that many people find the thought of homosexual practice deeply disgusting. It is sometimes suggested that this is the result of over-compensation for their own latent homosexuality, but whatever the explanation of it, the fact remains. One cannot, however, allow any simple inference from the disgusting to the immoral. In fact, surely, in this case the movement of thought is the other way. Homosexual practices are felt to be peculiarly disgusting because they are held to be exceptionally sinful or immoral. They disgust because they are 'unnatural.'

No one who thinks like this will be induced to improve his view of homosexual activity by such claims as that made by Chesser (*Live and Let Live*, pp. 30–1) that the most abominated homosexual act, anal intercourse, is probably commoner among married than homosexual couples. The act is felt to be abominable whenever and between whomsoever it occurs. What puts homosexuals utterly beyond the pale is that *all* their physical sexual activities are necessarily unnatural in some degree, even if not in the very highest.

It is, as already suggested . . . , a matter of great difficulty to grasp the rationale of this way of thinking, to make sense of the notions of *nature* and *the natural* involved. As a beginning one has to suppose that the purpose or function of sex is mainly procreation. It would seem to follow that heterosexual intercourse which is intended to be fertile is the ideally natural sexual act. This is not, however, exactly the conclusion usually desired, for such intercourse clearly could take place outside marriage or even a loving relationship. Consequently sex has to be allowed a second, non-procreative, "relational" or companionate purpose, which may then be held to be achievable only within marriage. Provided not too much is made of the relational purpose, provided that it is kept firmly subordinate to the procreational one, homosexual activity is still bound to come out as unnatural—it cannot fulfil procreational purposes at all. But, as we shall see in connexion with contraception in the next chapter, there are snags in emphasising the importance of the procreational purpose. Suppose we want to allow deliberately infertile heterosexual intercourse within marriage. Even in this case it is still possible to pay some regard to the claims of procreation by insisting that couples should not refuse to have children altogether, even though they may use contraceptives for a large proportion of their married life. This is a typically Anglican attitude, expressed for instance by Dr. D. S. Bailey in his "Homosexuality and Christian Morals" (in Rees & Usill). From this point of view homosexual activity can still consistently be held to be unnatural. I do not, however, see how it can be by anyone prepared to allow permanently childless marriages, or intentionally infertile heterosexual relationships outside marriage.

It is, in my opinion, *possible* consistently to hold homosexual activity to be unnatural. Much care and ingenuity are, however, required, and I suspect that many people who do regard it as unnatural are, in fact, inconsistent at one point or another. Nor, rare though it is, is consistency enough. The *truth* of the premises concerning the purposes of sex, and the relative importance of the purposes assigned, is crucial too. And yet, as observed above, it is very difficult to see how it is to be ascertained. They are not empirical premises, of which the truth could be assessed by some sort of morally neutral scientific enquiry— biological, psychological, sociological, or whatever it might be. The relevant form of enquiry is, perhaps, theological—but whether there is a subject-matter for theology is itself a controversial question. There is no ground, even in principle, for expecting reasonable men to agree on matters of theology, as there is on matters of biology, psychology and sociology. The credentials of theology as a subject are in dispute. And the propositions of natural theology are just as uncertain as those of revealed.

Accordingly, to the unbeliever, arguing to moral conclusions from theologically based premises about the nature or purpose of sex seems to be little more than a matter of arbitrarily selecting those premises which yield the moral conclusions desired. If you want to condemn contraception and homosexuality you have to emphasise the procreational purpose. If you want to permit contraception you must give greater weight to non-procreational purposes. To the believer, on the other hand, it does not seem like this at all. He must believe that questions about the nature and purpose of sex related to matters of (non-empirical) fact. He will not see himself as arbitrarily choosing answers that are in line with moral judgments he has reached on other grounds, but rather, when he differs from his predecessors in moral theology, as correcting their mistakes of emphasis. These mistakes he may see as the result of prejudices resulting from local and temporary features of his predecessors' situation. If they attributed undue importance to procreation this will be because they did not write from the vantage point of a potentially over-populated world. The truth will never change, but our view of it does, perhaps getting nearer to it all the time.

I have myself no enthusiasm at all for appraising human conduct as natural or unnatural. I have, however, tried to draw attention to the *complexity* of the notion of the natural employed by moral theologians, mainly in order to show how different it is from that implicit in the popular condemnation of homosexual behaviour as unnatural. In the popular view the unnatural and the disgusting are closely connected, and judging something to be unnatural is felt to be the simple, direct, inevitable reaction of the 'healthy' mind to it. But there can be nothing simple in any notion of the natural which will admit of application over the whole range of sexual behaviour, which will serve as the key idea in a comprehensive sexual morality. Nor will there be any necessary connexion between the corresponding notion of the *un*natural and the disgusting.

Abortion and the Nature of Persons

WILLIAM E. MAY

William E. May (1927–   ) is Program Chairman of Religious Studies at the University of Indiana. He has published many articles and books, including *A Catalogue of Sins* (1967) and *Perspectives on Death* (1969).

. . .

Our purpose now is to examine the meaning of abortion as a human activity and to offer reasons why a sound moral philosophy should judge that abortion, understood as an activity that has as its direct intent the death of a fetus, as a wrongful act. In his important essay on abortion Noonan observed that "the teaching of a religious body may invoke revelation, claim authority, employ symbolism, which make the moral doctrine it teaches binding for believers in the religion but of academic concern to those outside its boundaries." Or it may, he continued, "embody insights, protect perceptions, exemplify values, which concern humanity."[1] My belief, as a human being and as a philosopher, is that

---

[1] John T. Noonan, Jr., "An Almost Absolute Value in History," in *The Morality of Abortion*, edited by John T. Noonan, Jr. (Cambridge, Mass.: Harvard University Press, 1970), p. 3.

Source: William E. May, "Abortion and Man's Moral Being," in *Abortion: Pro and Con* (Cambridge, Mass., 1974), pp. 17–31, 32–35. Reprinted by permission of Schenkman Publishing Company.

the teaching of the Roman Catholic Church on abortion is of the latter variety. The question of abortion is *not* a "religious" issue in any narrow sense. It is a question that touches deeply the meaning of human existence and the character of human existence as a moral existence. If abortion is a wrongful human act, it is so not because it is judged to be so by a religious authority but because of what it means as a human deed. Consequently, before examining the important questions of the status of fetal life and the conditions under which the killing of one human being by another or others is morally permissible, I want to sketch briefly a general moral framework for evaluating human acts.

To be a human being is to be an animal; but it is, as René Dubos has so beautifully put it, to be so *human* an animal. It is to be an animal *with a difference*. The difference can be expressed in various ways, but one major and critically important way of putting this difference is to say that man, and man alone of all animals, is a *moral* being. That man, and man alone, is a moral being is illustrated in common speech. It is meaningful, for instance, to speak about making human life human. Yet to speak in this way is paradoxical. We would find it odd, indeed absurd, were someone to speak of making bovine life bovine or simian life simian. A cow, after all, is a cow and an ape is an ape. Yet it is not absurd or meaningless to speak about making human life human. Since it does make sense to speak in this fashion, it follows that man is indeed a unique kind of animal, and it also follows that the word *human* must be used in two quite distinct ways when we talk about making human life human. The second use of the term implies that a human being is not totally "human" when he comes into existence. Certainly no one who uses the term *human* in this second sense wants to deny that all men are equally human beings simply from the fact that they are all identifiably men, i.e., members of the same biological species. Yet he is affirming that "being human" is not something factually given but is rather a process, a growth. To use the term in this second sense is to imply that there is something or some set of things (what we can call the "human good" or *bonum humanum*) "perfective" of a human being precisely as a human being and that human beings are summoned, individually and as members of the human community, to struggle to achieve these goods that are perfective of them. In addition, to distinguish between two meanings of the term *human* is to affirm that not everything that men do and can do is really human. It is to distinguish between *is* and *ought,* between what men actually are and do and what men ought to be and ought to do.[2]

In common with many moralists in what can be termed the natural law tradition, I conceive the human good to be a totality composed of individual goods each of which corresponds to some basic human need, so that we can truthfully

---

[2] On this matter it is useful to note a passage from Roger L. Shinn in his book *Man: The New Humanism* (Philadelphia: Westminster, 1968). Shinn distinguishes between the *empirical* human and the *normative* human, and writes: "the word 'human' has both an empirical and a normative sense, and the gap between the two is immense. In the empirical sense any thing that men do is human. Human behavior is a mixed bag, containing all that the newspapers report or suppress, all that priests and psychiatrists hear in clerical or secular confessionals, all that people think or do. In this sense humanization is unnecessary. Men are already humanized. . . . In the normative sense, the human is assumed to be good."

say that each is a good *of* man, not *for* man, that each is a good to be *prized*, not *priced*. Among such real goods may be included life itself, health, justice, friendship, peace, truth. These goods, which are constitutive of the *bonum humanum*, define aspects of our personal being. They are common insofar as they are not *my* goods or *your* goods but rather human personal goods capable of being communicated to and shared by every human being.[3] Because they are real goods corresponding to real needs existing in every human being just because he is human, they generate real rights: each human being has a right to them, a claim on them, precisely because he is a human being and because they are the realities that make a human being more human.[4]

Each of these goods, moreover, can serve as a purposeful goal of human activity. They are what the Scholastics termed "principles of practical reason" and what we can call "principles of intelligent activity." They shape our activity from within inasmuch as each can function as a choiceworthy purpose for doing anything. Each of these goods, moreover, is incommensurable with the others: how can one, for instance, compare a friend to his health, or his life to a just order among men? Because of this, none of these goods is the absolute good in the sense of the *summum bonum;* none is the be-all and end-all of human existence to which the others must be subordinated. Although none of these goods is the absolute human good, "none is so relative," Grisez observes, "that it does not resist submergence."[5] That is, each of the particular goods comprising the *bonum humanum* is a real human good and demands to be recognized as such and respected as such. To repudiate one of these goods by declaring it to be evil and to be willing to destroy it in oneself and in others is to repudiate a meaningful dimension of human existence, to reject one's humanity, to act irrationally.

Man's supreme or absolute good, at least from the perspective of moral philosophy, consists in his goodness precisely as a human being, that is, as the moral being capable of distinguishing between *is* and *ought* and of acting responsibly in accordance with his judgments of what he ought to do if he is to become more fully human. Man makes his moral being in and through his deeds, because it is in and through them that he both discloses his moral identity to himself and to others and achieves this moral identity. In and through his deeds he reveals his attitudes toward the goods constitutive of the *bonum humanum,* whether he respects them for what they are, real goods intended for and perfective of all human beings, just because they are human beings; or whether he pursues them for himself and his friends alone, ready to destroy them in others, or irrationally erects one into an absolute to which he is ready to sacrifice all others and for which he is ready to repudiate all others.

[3] In developing the ideas set forth in the preceding two paragraphs I have been immeasurably aided by reflecting on the way in which this ethical tradition has been articulated by Germain G. Grisez. See in particular his *Contraception and the Natural Law* (Milwaukee: The Bruce Publishing Company, 1964), pp. 60–72, his book on abortion (n. 1), pp. 307–321, and his article on killing (n. 9).

[4] On the question of real goods generating real rights see Mortimer Adler, *The Time of Our Lives* (New York: Holt, Rinehart, and Winston, 1970), pp. 137–156.

[5] Grisez, *Contraception and the Natural Law,* p. 69.

As a moral being, moreover, man is the animal who is not only capable of distinguishing between *is* and *ought* and of acting responsibly in the light of his judgments of what he ought and ought not to do, he is also the animal of moral worth or value. Because he is this kind of being, he surpasses or transcends the world about him. Each of us is, as an *individual* human being, a part of a larger whole, of the society of which we are members; but each of us is, as an individual *human* or *moral* being, related to this society not simply as a part to a whole but as a whole to a whole. By this I mean that every human being, because he is a moral entity and a being of moral worth, has moral rights that are his because of what he is. It is for this reason that we abhor totalitarianism, which would subordinate individual human beings completely to the good of the state (i.e., of those in power) and crush their rights in order to achieve goals worthwhile in themselves. Because men are moral beings the common good of human societies, as noted previously, must flow back to and be sharable by all the members of those societies.[6]

In acting to pursue the real goods constitutive of the *bonum humanum* each of us, as a moral being, is obliged to respect these goods for what they are, that is, goods meriting our love because they are the goods that are indeed perfective of ourselves and of all other human beings, that is, of all those who have, with us, *equal* claims on or titles toward these goods. Although we may at times, because of the situations in which we are placed, be compelled to do something that results in the destruction of one of these goods either in ourselves or in others, this does not mean that we can repudiate or deny their goodness or the value of the human beings in whom they are destroyed. For instance, we may be called upon to forego our health in order to care for the sick; in doing this we do not repudiate health as a human good. We willingly, although reluctantly, allow our health to be destroyed while we are engaged in activities that *of themselves* are directly aimed at serving some other human good (e.g., friendship or justice). We may, in order to protect a person being viciously assaulted, deliver a mortal blow to his assailant. In doing this we do not necessarily repudiate or reject the life of the assailant as a human good, but rather willingly perform a deed of itself directed to saving his victim and properly describable as an act of defense that we foresee will have as one of its consequences the death of the assailant. To make the destruction of one of these goods, however, the precise point of our deed, even if this deed is itself ordered to serving some other human good, is to act immorally. It is to declare ourselves ready to accept, as part of our moral identity, the identity of a destroyer of some basic human good. We shall return later to this point, for it requires fuller exposition, but for the present the basic thrust of the position I am developing should be clear.

We are now ready to reflect on the important questions of the status of fetal life and the conditions under which the killing of one human being by another is morally permissible. The status of fetal life (and I use this term in an inclusive

---

[6] On this whole issue of man as a being of moral or personal worth and as being related to human society not simply as a part but as a whole, see Jacques Maritain, *The Person and the Common Good* (New York: Charles Scribner's, 1947), chapter 3.

manner to refer to the unborn organism from conception until birth[7]) is central to the abortion debate, a factor recognized by the Supreme Court in its decisions of Roe v. Wade and Doe v. Bolton. The Court, it may be noted, expressly declared that it had no intent to "resolve the difficult question of when life begins."[8] Yet it may likewise be noted that the Court did, in fact, pronounce judgment on this difficult question, inasmuch as it found that the fetus is not, prior to viability, a being to be protected and that the fetus, even after viability, is only the "potentiality of human life," or "potential life."[9] Obviously if the fetus is only "potential life" or the "potentiality of human life" it is *not* itself life. If a being is only potentially something, then it is not now that something which it *can* become. My oldest boy is a potential father, but he is not now a father, nor could he be a *potential* father if, in fact, he actually were a father. Thus one must conclude that the Supreme Court did, in truth, resolve the question of when life begins: it begins when one is born.[10]

There are many different attitudes toward the status of fetal life. They range from the view, expressed by Philip Wylie, that the fetus is "protoplasmic rubbish" or a "gobbet of meat,"[11] through the views that it is simply "gametic materials" (Joseph Fletcher),[12] a "blueprint" (Garrett Hardin),[13] a "part of the mother" (Havelock Ellis),[14] to the views that it is alive and human although not the subject of protectable rights (Daniel Callahan, Michael Tooley),[15] that it is indeed an individual human being and the subject of protectable rights (Germain Grisez).[16] I submit that the views regarding the fetus as non-human are indefensible in view of *reality-making* factors disclosed by contemporary biomedical research. As C. G. Goodhart of the zoology department of Cambridge University remarked in an exchange with Malcolm Potts:

> Dr. Potts has argued that human development is a continuous process . . . and that it is in principle impossible to define when a new human individual comes into

[7] Here a word about terminology may be useful. *Zygote* refers to the unicellular organism resulting from the fertilization of an egg by a sperm; *embryo* in the strict sense refers to the developing organism from implantation until the end of the sixth or eighth week; *fetus* in the narrow sense refers to the developing organism from the sixth or eighth week of development until the end of the seventh month. In ordinary language both fetus and embryo are used synonymously and are used to refer to the developing being from the time of conception until birth.

[8] Roe v. Wade, X, *The United States Law Week* 41 LW (1–23–73) 4227.

[9] Ibid., X and XI, 4228, 4229.

[10] On this point the perceptive comments of John T. Noonan, Jr., in *The National Catholic Reporter* of February 3, 1973 are pertinent.

[11] Philip Wylie, *The Magic Animal* (New York: Doubleday, 1968), p. 272, a particularly virulent passage filled with invective against the notion of the "sanctity" of human life.

[12] Joseph Fletcher, "New Beginnings of Life," in William Hamilton, editor, *The New Genetics and the Future of Man* (Grand Rapids, Mich.: Eerdmans, 1972), pp. 76–91.

[13] Garrett Hardin, "Abortion—or Compulsory Pregnancy?" *Journal of Marriage and the Family*[30] (May, 1968), 250.

[14] Havelock Ellis, *Studies in the Psychology of Sex* (New York, 1924) 6, 607.

[15] Callahan, op. cit., note 21, pp. 378–409. Michael Tooley, "Abortion and Infanticide," *Philosophy and Public Affairs* (Fall, 1972), 37–65.

[16] Grisez, op. cit., note 1, pp. 273–286, 410–423.

existence. May I with great respect suggest that this is a view which is contradicted by biological knowledge? For there is a real discontinuity at fertilization, or to be pedantic, at the "activation" of the ovum which is not necessarily always the same thing. This is the point after, but not before, it becomes capable of completing its development without any further stimulus from outside. Once activated, the organism will carry on its development until it dies. That is what most of us would have called the moment of conception, however else the British Council of Churches may now have decided to define the word. But whatever we call it, it occurs at a specific point in time, after, but not before which, development can proceed; and that is a real *discontinuity* marking the coming into existence of a new biological organism.[17]

Calling a human fetus "protoplasmic rubbish," "gametic materials," a "blueprint," or a "part of the mother" is to engage in rhetoric and to evade the issues raised by abortion. The fetus, and we are here concerned with the human fetus, is obviously an entity that is living, that is individuated at least with respect to its parents if not (prior to segmentation) with respect to any possible twins it might have, and that is human. There is an identity *in being* between the zygote, the fetus, the neonate, the child, the adolescent, the adult, the senior citizen. The central issue in the abortion debate, as Paul Ramsey forcefully notes, is not when does human life begin, but "When does equally protectable life begin?"[18] My life, as yours, began "as a minute informational speck, drawn at random from many other minute informational specks [my] parents possessed out of the common human gene pool. This took place at the moment of impregnation,"[19] or, to use Goodhart's terminology, at the moment of "activation." But was I then—and were *you* then—a being possessed of rights that ought to be acknowledged by other men?

If, in order to be a being possessing moral rights, it is necessary to pass the criteria set forth by Joseph Fletcher in his list of "indicators of humanhood" (an I.Q. of at least 20 and probably 40, self-awareness, self-control, a sense of time, the capability to relate to others, etc.)[20] or the criterion stipulated by Michael Tooley that one possess "the concept of a self as a continuing subject of experiences and other mental states" and believe "that it is itself such a continuing entity,"[21] it is obvious that neither I nor you nor any other human being was the subject of moral rights during the fetal stage of our development. But on these criteria we possessed no rights for a considerable period after birth either, and according to these criteria we might rightfully dismiss significant

[17] C. B. Goodhart, "Reply to Dr. Potts," in *Biology and Ethics,* edited by F. C. Ebling (New York/London: Academic Press, 1969), pp. 101-103. Potts' position is developed in ibid., pp. 74-75.

[18] Ramsey, "Abortion: A Review Article," loc. cit., 182.

[19] Ramsey, "The Morality of Abortion," in *Moral Problems,* edited by James Rachel (New York: Harper & Row, 1971), pp. 4-5. This essay is a revised version of a paper that first appeared in *The Dublin Review* (Spring, 1967) 1-27 and then in *Life or Death: Ethics and Options,* edited by Daniel H. Labby (Seattle, Wash.: University of Washington Press, 1968).

[20] See Joseph Fletcher, "Indicators of Humanhood: A Tentative Profile of Man," in *The Hastings Center Report* 2.5 (November, 1972), 1-4.

[21] Michael Tooley, art. cit. (note 40), 44.

numbers of individuals readily numbered among the human race as of no moral significance or worth. Common to the thought of Fletcher, Tooley and those who would agree with them is the belief that "membership in a species is of no moral significance."[22] This belief is warranted *only* if one is capable of showing that man's significance as a *moral* being (for this is one crucial way in which he differs from other animals) is ultimately explicable fully and adequately in terms of a difference in the degree of development of man (or some men) over the development that has taken place in other animals and is *not* rooted in man's being a different *kind* of animal from all other animals. My position is that our belief that a human being is a moral being and thus the subject of moral rights is based on a belief that human beings differ radically in kind from other animals: men are moral beings not because of something that they achieve or do but because of what they are. My point may be made clearer, perhaps, if we cite a passage from Mortimer Adler. According to Adler, if men differ from other animals only in degree, that is, by doing something that other animals do not do but do not do only because they have not attained the stage of development that men have attained, then:

> those who now oppose injurious discrimination on the moral ground that all human beings, being equal in their humanity, should be treated equally in all those respects that concern their common humanity, would have no solid basis in fact to support their normative principle. A social and political ideal that has operated with revolutionary force in human history could be validly dismissed as a hollow illusion that should become defunct . . . We can now imagine a future state of affairs in which a new global division of mankind replaces all the old parochial divisions based upon race, nationality, or ethnic group . . . a division that separates the human elite at the top of the scale from the human scum at the bottom, a division based on accurate scientific measurement of human ability and achievement and one, therefore, that is factually incontrovertible . . . .[23]

Put another way, I believe that the major area of disagreement between those who defend abortion and those who oppose abortion over the status of fetal life comes down to the question: Is humanity, in the sense of being an entity that is the subject of rights, an endowment or an achievement? Those who accept abortion accept, with Ashley Montagu,[24] Joseph Fletcher,[25] Gerald Leach,[26] and Michael Tooley,[27] and others, the assumption that humanity or being human in a significant moral sense, is an achievement. In order to be a human being for whom society should be concerned, one must *do* something or actually be capable of doing something that will enhance or promote human welfare (e.g., be capable of actually entering into meaningful human relations). There are, in

[22] See Tooley, ibid., 48, 55.

[23] Mortimer Adler, *The Difference of Man and the Difference It Makes* (New York: Meridan, 1968), pp. 264–265.

[24] Ashley Montagu, in a letter to *The New York Times,* March 3, 1967, in which he rejected the use that some who oppose abortion had put to a statement in his *Life Before Birth* (New York: Signet, 1965) in which he had stated that life began at conception.

[25] See the way Fletcher develops his position in his "Indicators of Humanhood," loc. cit., note 45.

[26] Gerald Leach, *The Biocrats* (Baltimore: Penguin, 1972), p. 104f.

[27] Tooley, loc. cit., note 40.

other words, some kinds of tests, variously described by various authors, that one must pass before he is entitled to be called a human being in a meaningful sense. For those, on the contrary, who oppose what could be called an ethic of abortion, being human is not primarily a matter of achievement; rather it is a gift, an endowment that one has not because he has already done something worthwhile or is actually capable of doing something worthwhile but simply because he is and is present (even if hidden in the womb) to his fellow men. On this latter view I am—and you are—a being of moral worth not because of anything that I have done or actually can do but simply because I am. On this latter view each of us holds our humanity as a gift, a gift (for those who are religiously motivated) from God, a gift (for those motivated by a humanistic spirit) from our fellow men. On this latter view the words of Ralph Potter—if not those of Jeremiah who wrote: "Before I formed thee in the belly I knew thee" (1:5)—carry weight: "the fetus symbolizes you and me and our tenuous hold upon a future here at the mercy of our fellow men."[28]

I realize that in the foregoing I have not offered any kind of irrefutable scientific or philosophical "proof" for the humanity (i.e. moral worth) of the fetus, although the consideration of man's difference as a moral animal from other animals as being a difference *in kind* and not *in degree* gives a general indication of the type of argument that could be developed.[29] Nonetheless those who oppose the humanity of fetal life must either explain away considerable scientific evidence that human fetuses are alive and humanly alive (in the sense of being specifiably biologically human in their life rather than non-human) or evolve arguments that go counter to the democratic and humane tendency to extend the protection of human society to secure the basic human rights of those human beings who are defenseless and incapable of claiming and asserting the rights that are theirs by reason of their humanness, and not by reason of some accomplishments that they have made by reason of their own efforts.

What of the morally permissible taking of the life of one human being by another? This, I believe in company with Paul Ramsey[30] and Germain Grisez,[31] is *the* issue at stake in the abortion controversy. What are the conditions under which the doing of the deadly deed is permissible? One way of answering this question is adopted by those who endorse a situational, consequentialistic, or utilitarian approach to solving conflict situations. The ethical position defended is what can be called an *ethics of intended consequences* or an *ethics of intent*. Those who espouse this approach, and I would include here those Catholic moralists mentioned previously who reject the principle of double effect as a

[28] Ralph Potter, "The Abortion Debate," in *The Religious Situation 1968*, edited by Donald Culter (Boston: Beacon, 1968), p. 157.

[29] My basic point is that *being* a human being *does* make a significant moral difference because the difference between man and other animals demands, for its sufficient explanation, the presence within man's makeup, that is, within his being, of an element not found at all in other animals, namely spirit. I believe that the most coherent and logically structured argument in defense of this position is that developed by Adler in his *The Difference of Man and the Difference It Makes*.

[30] Ramsey, "Abortion: A Review Article," loc. cit., p. 211.

[31] Grisez, *Abortion: The Myths, the Realities and the Arguments*, p. 321ff.

matter of casuistic quibbling, are primarily interested in what our deeds as human beings *do,* that is, in their results. They urge that the ultimate criterion in evaluating human acts is the net balance of good over evil, or what some, like Van der Poel, call "its impact upon the well-being of the individual and the human society,"[32] or what others, like Van der Marck, describe as its ability to "build up community."[33] This way of evaluating human deeds can make the claim of being a compassionate ethic; one concerned to help suffering human beings, to provide support and dignity to women who become pregnant when they really do not want to and when the birth of a child will cause serious hardships and threaten the attainment of real human goods. This is a claim sincerely advanced by many who adopt this ethical approach, and it ought to be recognized that many who defend abortion as a human act and social practice do so because of a burning sense of justice, of compassion, of human concern. Their intention or what they have in view in their activity, is to do good and to promote human welfare.

Yet it must be pointed out that this way of justifying the deadly deed *is* a consequentialistic ethics or an ethics of intent as related to consequences and not what can be called an *ethics of intent + content.* The ethics of intent justifies the destruction of fetal life because of the beneficial consequences that will result from this destruction. It justifies this act precisely because, in the judgment of those who defend it, it will bring about a net balance of good over evil; it will contribute to the building up of the community and will lead to the well-being of the pregnant woman and of society at large by preventing the birth of a child who is not wanted for one reason or another. This type of ethics, it should be clear, is an ethics primarily concerned with ends, not means; it is an ethics that sees the significance of human acts in what they *do* and not in what they *say.*

The ethics that I have termed an ethics of intent + content, on the other hand, is concerned with means as well as ends; it is interested in the results of our acts, to be sure, but in addition to being interested in what our acts *do* it is also imensely interested in what they *say,* in what they disclose or reveal about us as human beings and about the meaning of human existence.[34] In this type of ethics, consequences are, of course, important in judging the morality of our deeds, but there are reality-making factors *other than consequences* or results that simply must be taken into account. The activity in question is one of these factors, and it is one precisely because it is a *human* activity and is thus a revelation or disclosure of human identity. In addition, one's intentions or what one "has in view" and seeks to effect through his activity include not only the larger goals or ends one wishes to achieve but also the activity that one chooses to use as a way toward their attainment.[35]

If we now look at the activity (and practice) that we call abortion we realize

[32] Van der Poel, *The Search for Human Values,* p. 56.

[33] Van der Marck, *Toward a Christian Ethic,* pp. 60–69.

[34] On this see the perceptive work by Herbert McCabe, *What Is Ethics All About?* (Washington: Corpus, 1969), in particular pp. 90–94.

[35] On willing the means as well as the needs see, among other sources, Thomas Aquinas, *Summa Theologica,* I–II, 6–10.

that for an ethics of intent + content (and this is the ethics that is behind the thinking that gave rise to the principle of double effect) it is necessary to take into account not only the real goods that can be realized if an abortion is performed but also the character of the abortion itself as an expression of human identity. And direct abortion as a human activity inescapably, inevitably, requires as *one* of its purposes, as one of the elements unavoidably and necessarily within the scope of one's intentions, the death of the fetus, the destruction, within the fetus, of the life that it has. This death is an ineluctable part both of the intent and the content of the act. It is so in *direct* abortion because, in acts properly describable as directly abortive, the death of the fetus is itself the *means* to attaining the desired results *and* is the *terminus or end of the action* itself; that is, the destruction of the fetus is what an older, Scholastic terminology called the *finis operis* (end of the act) in contradistinction to the *finis operantis* (end of the agent) or *subjective motives* of the agent, or it is what a contemporary writer, Paul Ramsey, calls the "primary thrust" of the activity itself.[36] In direct abortion, and this is the kind of activity involved when abortion is undertaken to prevent the birth of babies unwanted either because of fetal defects, socioeconomic factors, or other reasons, the purpose of the activity (its "primary thrust" or direction, the *finis operis*, the "intention" of the action) is necessarily directed to the death of the human fetus.

It may be suggested (and indeed *is* argued by some) that many women who have abortions and that many people who may be disposed to accept abortion as an acceptable human solution to some agonizing human problems, do not really *want* to destroy fetal life. They see the activity in question as being something other than the destruction of a fetus; they see it in terms of the good that is sought through the abortion itself. By this I mean that these persons are not really ready to accept, as part of their own personal identity, the identity of persons responsible for feticide. They are not willing, deep in their own consciousness, to endorse and ratify the wrong that their act is causing to the developing human existent that is the fetus. This, I believe, is why abortion is so frequently described in euphemistic terms as the removal of the products of conception or as the elimination from the womb of genetic materials or tissue or protoplasm. There is, in other words, an attempt to conceal the nature of the activity. There is operative, as Eric D'Arcy has noted, a human propensity to *redescribe* the act in question in terms of its intended consequences.[37] But, as D'Arcy also noted, it is simply not truthful to reality to redescribe acts in this manner when doing so "conceal(s), or even fail(s) to reveal, the nature of the act itself."[38] And, in cases properly describable as acts of direct abortion, the nature of the *act itself* is such that its primary thrust, direction, or whatever one may wish to term it, is to destroy the life of the fetus. This is precisely what is meant by the expression *direct abortion*.

[36] Ramsey, "The Morality of Abortion," in Rachels, op. cit., pp. 16–17.

[37] Eric D'Arcy, *Human Acts: An Essay on Their Moral Evaluation* (Oxford: Oxford University Press, 1963), p. 25. See Ramsey's expansion of D'Arcy's ideas in his Deeds and Rules in Christian Ethics (New York: Charles Scribner's, 1967), pp. 192–200.

[38] D'Arcy, op. cit., p. 18.

What are instances when an abortive act, that is an act resulting in the death of the fetus, can be described properly as an act of *indirect abortion?* The principle of double effect was developed by moralists who wanted both to be truthful in their way of describing moral reality and to provide a philosophically intelligent justification of doing deeds that inevitably and unavoidably caused injury or evil as well as good. They recognized that frequently in life we are put in situations when no matter what we do some evil is going to result. Their purpose was not, as Callahan suggests,[39] to devise a clever way for insuring "clean" consciences, but was rather, as Ramsey observes,[40] a desire to explicate the requirements for judging the objective conditions under which actions can rightfully be done. An accurate statement of the principle involves four points, and these are well stated by Grisez as follows:

One may perform an act having two effects, one good and the other bad, if four conditions are fulfilled simultaneously.

1. The act must not be wrong in itself, even apart from consideration of the bad effects . . .

2. The agent's intention must be right . . .

3. The evil effect must not be the means to the good effect, for then evil would fall within the scope of one's intention, and evil may not be intended even for the sake of an ulterior good purpose . . .

4. There must be a proportionately grave reason for doing such an act, since there is a general obligation to avoid evil so far as possible . . .[41]

The principle was meant to clarify in specific ways the critically important distinction between the "indirectly voluntary" and the "directly voluntary." This key distinction and its relevance to the principle of double effect have been accurately stated by Philippa Foot:

The doctrine of the double effect is based on a distinction between what a man foresees as a result of his voluntary action and what, in the strict sense, he intends. He intends in the strictest sense both those things that he aims at as ends [e.g., in abortion, the avoidance of the socioeconomic and personal costs entailed in caring for a mongoloid child] and those that he aims at as means to his ends [e.g., the abortion of a child discovered through amniocentesis to be mongoloid]. The latter may be regretted in themselves but nevertheless desired for the sake of the end. . . . By contrast a man is said not strictly, or directly, to intend the foreseen consequences of his voluntary actions where these are neither the end at which he is aiming nor the means to this end.[42]

Controversy over the principle has focused primarily on the third requirement in Grisez's list, and it can surely be admitted that the principle, as developed and employed by Roman Catholic manuals of moral theology in the past, did frequently give rise to disputatious "quibbling" and that the principle,

---

[39] Callahan, op. cit., p. 429.
[40] Ramsey, "Abortion: A Review Article," loc. cit., 208.
[41] Grisez, *Abortion: The Myths, The Realities, and The Arguments*, p. 329.
[42] Philippa Foot, "Abortion and the Doctrine of the Double Effect," in Rachels, ed. *Moral Problems*, p. 29.

as interpreted, at times unnecessarily restricted the evil that one could right-fully do in pursuit of good. Classic examples center on cases when the life of the mother-to-be is in danger and an abortive act could save her. One such case is that cited by Jonathan Bennett and involves the situation of a woman who will surely die unless an operation is performed in which the head of her unborn child is crushed or dissected, whereas if the act is not undertaken the child may be safely delivered alive by post-mortem Caesarian section.[43] Most Roman Catholic moralists of the past, seeking to apply the principle of double effect to situations of this kind, held that it was wrong to abort the child in this way because this would be to violate the third condition of the principle of double effect and would constitute doing evil in order that good might result.

Although this type of situation (and others can be and have been brought forward of similar character) raises serious difficulties for those who believe that the principle of double effect embodies a significant effort to be faithful to reality-making factors in determining objectively what men may rightfully do, the response required is *not* to abandon the principle and, even more im-portantly, the critical distinction between the directly voluntary and the in-directly voluntary upon which it is based, but rather to think more deeply about what the directly voluntary and indirectly voluntary *mean*. I believe that a proper moral analysis of the type of situation described above will lead one to the conclusion that in instances of this nature the activity in question does not constitute "direct" killing; it is not a matter of the "directly voluntary" destruc-tion of fetal life but rather an "indirectly voluntary" deed so far as the death of the fetus is concerned. Here Germain Grisez and Paul Ramsey, despite real differences between them,[44] help us to understand the moral realities at stake. Although Ramsey, in one essay (even as revised),[45] believes that some of the

[43] Jonathan Bennett, "Whatever the Consequences," in Rachels, op. cit., p. 43.

[44] Grisez, in reinterpreting the principle of double effect, insists that the evil caused through our actions must be *one* aspect of an act that itself brings about good. One of his tests for determining whether an act *is* in fact of this kind is whether any other human act, one's own or another, need intervene or could intervene to bring about the good effect (see his *Abortion. . . ,* p. 333). Ramsey (in "Abortion: A Review Article," p. 215f) believes that this is too stringent a requirement and offers cases that he thinks justifiable but that he be-lieves could not be justified if this requirement is demanded. For Ramsey the "crucial test" is not . . . whether the death-dealing act may precede the life-saving component of the same human action . . . but whether in (justifiably) doing the deadly deed, the target is upon that life or upon what it is doing to another life" (221). I would like to note here that I think Ramsey, in his article (224–226) erroneously concludes that Grisez's position on abortion, because of Grisez's way of describing the nature of "indirect intent," is, quite para-doxically, similar to that of Judith Thompson in her "Defense of Abortion" in *Philosophy and Public Policy* (Fall, 1971), 47–66. My reasons for saying this is that I think Ramsey fails to pay serious enough attention to Grisez's insistence that an abortion properly described as "indirect" might nevertheless be an immoral act.

[45] "The Morality of Abortion," in Rachels, op. cit., pp. 3–27. As noted in note 44 this article originally appeared in *The Dublin Review* in 1967, was revised for Labby's 1968 anthology, and revised again for Rachels' 1971 anthology. Ramsey himself notes, in this "Abortion: A Review Article" (219) that Richard A. McCormick in the article cited in our note 1, had argued that Ramsey's analysis of what he had termed *direct* abortion "could, if correct, be readily brought under the meaning of the indirectly voluntary." McCormick, I believe, is correct in his appraisal and the justice of his appraisal is effectively acknowledged

acts resulting in the death of the fetus in situations of this kind can properly be called "direct abortion," he agrees ultimately with Grisez "that any killing of man by man must be 'indirect.' "[46] His point is that, in acts that do kill the fetus but are undertaken *only* because the abortion in question is necessary to save the life of the mother-to-be (a condition that satisfies the fourth requirement of the principle of double effect), "the intention of the action, and in this sense its direction, is not upon the *death* of the fetus." He continues by stating:

> The intention of the action is directed toward the *incapacitation* of the fetus from doing what it is doing to the life of the mother, and is not directed toward the death of the fetus, as such, even in the killing of it. The child, of course, is only doing what comes naturally, i.e., growing and attempting to be born. But he is, objectively and materially, aggressing upon the life of the mother. Her life, which alone can be saved, can be saved only if this is stopped; and to incapacitate the fetus from doing this can be done only . . . by a direct [?] act of killing nascent life. Still, in this situation, it is correct to say that the intention of the action is not the killing, nor the death of the fetus, but the incapacitation of it from carrying out the material aggression that it is effecting upon the life of the mother.[47]

In sum, in instances when an act that results in the death of the fetus and is foreseen to issue in this consequence, the abortion is "indirectly voluntary" and not directly so if, and *only* if, the trust of the action—*its* "intention" or direction or what used to be called the *finis operis*—is itself targeted, not upon the life of the fetus, but upon countering the injurious effect that the fetus, simply by its presence, is causing its mother. The case here is parallel to the taking of the life of one human being by another in an act properly describable as an act of self-defense.[48] The justification of the deadly deed is not based upon consequentialistic factors as such. The good consequences do enter in as providing a "proportionate reason" for undertaking the activity in question, but they do not, just by themselves, sufficiently ground the rightness of the deed. In order for the act to be justified as one in which human beings may rightfully engage, it is also necessary that the *activity itself,* considered from the perspective of its content or meaningful intelligibility, be truthfully describable as primarily an act of what Aquinas called a "measured force" countering a force directed against the life that is being imperiled. The act of abortion, in such instances when the death of the fetus is "indirectly voluntary" and is only *one* aspect of an act that in its totality can properly be said to be directed to saving the life of the mother-to-be, is justifiable. But it is critically significant, I believe, to the meaning of human existence as a moral existence, to show that it is justifiable not because of factors extrinsic to the activity itself (e.g., the good

---

by Ramsey in his most recent essay on the subject ("Abortion: A Review Article") particularly by his agreement with Grisez that any taking of the life of one human being by another must, if it is to be justifiable, be indirect (220).

[46] Michael Tooley, "Abortion and Infanticide," *Philosophy and Public Affairs* (Fall 1972), p. 44.

[47] Ramsey, "The Morality of Abortion," in Rachels, op. cit., pp. 20–21.

[48] On this see Thomas Aquinas, *Summa Theologica,* II–II, 164, 7, and the comment on this by Grisez in his "Toward a Consistent Natural-Law Ethics of Killing," loc. cit., note 9. It should be noted that both Grisez and Ramsey appeal to this article in developing their positions.

that will come about as a result of the deed) but because of the inherent intelligibility of the deed itself as an expression of man's moral being, because of factors intelligently discernible within the activity itself.

In concluding this paper, in which I hope I have articulated the reasons why I believe it wrong directly to destroy fetal life and under what conditions this destruction may rightfully be permitted to happen as a result of one's activities, I want to affirm my conviction that a truly human ethics, one opposed to what can be called an ethic of abortion, must be just as concerned with alleviating the terrible human problems for which abortion is proposed as is the consequentialist ethics that defends abortion—only more so. Too frequently those who decry abortion as inhuman ignore the agonizing personal and social suffering for which it is intended as a remedy. Abortion is not the right way to meet these real human needs, but neither is the refusal to see them and to do something about them.

Seven

Self and Personal Identity: A Metaphysical Quest

> But I did not stop to consider what the soul was, or if I did stop, I imagined that it was something extremely rare and subtle like a wind, a flame, or an ether, which was spread throughout my grosser parts.
>
> —René Descartes

Introduction

In this chapter our essays deal with the self. The first section considers the self as a part of the larger universe and what a human self's relation is to the rest of the universe. The second section deals with the integrity of the self, which appears to be a complex entity. How is this complex held together to make the self a single, unified integrated entity? Does our consciousness play any role in unifying ourselves? These are two central questions for which answers are proposed by the authors of the essays in the second section.

We are dealing with metaphysical issues here, suggesting rather rarefied, abstract, remote, unfamiliar, and wholly theoretical issues. However, as will become clear to you, they have important, essential links to practical moral life.

Persons: Determined and/or Free

Most of us think there is one universe, and, since the advent of the ecological movement, we have been conscious of the universe as interconnected in all its parts and aspects, which seems fairly obvious at first thought. It becomes less obvious as soon as we remind ourselves that we also take it as obvious that humans are unique, totally different in some part or aspect from everything else in nature. Is the desire to be at one with nature ultimately incapable of achievement because we are irreducibly different from the rest of nature? A monistic view is that the universe is one; a dualistic view is that there are two universes. Dualism is the proper view for persons who consider humans distinct from other parts of the universe.

One distinctive feature of human beings that dualists have emphasized is their "free will." Only human beings have it; all other things in the universe (excepting God and the angels for those who believe they exist) are without free will. The nature of human beings differs from the nature of the rest of the universe if only human beings have free will. The stakes are high. This metaphysical dualism has dualist moral consequences. Moral praise, blame, obligation, value, according to conventional wisdom, is applicable only to creatures with free will; the rest of the universe does not fall within the "moral universe." Many of those who believe that preservation of the moral universe is important believe that we have to preserve metaphysical dualism; one way of doing this is to show that human beings have free will and that only human beings have free will. If we do not differ in terms of free will, human beings are sunk into the metaphysical monism of nature; this is a metaphysical leveling many persons find repugnant. These are the stakes over which the essays in this section contend.

To get a background for the essays, we first talk about the notion of a universe and what conditions must be satisfied to say there is only one universe. Following that, we will indicate in more detail how the contrast between human beings and the rest of nature is made in order to support a metaphysical and moral dualism.

We might start by asking: How many universes are there? It won't do to answer: One, that's the very meaning of *uni*verse. And it won't do because there are many things that are one, a point we could gain cheaply by a linguistic trick: we could talk of a unichicken, a unitable, a unimarble, and so forth. Just as it is obvious that there are many unichickens, unitables, and unimarbles, it is also obvious that there may be many universes.

This forces us to consider what a universe is. Let us say that a universe is (1) a whole that either has or does not have parts, and (2) a whole that is not itself a part of any other whole. Let us concede that our universe does have parts, being a complex universe. This notion of a universe leads us to say that if there is one and only one universe, then anything that exists is a part of a complex whole, and everything that is a part is a part of the same whole.

The operative question now is: Under what conditions would we be willing to say of anything that it is a part of the same whole as some other part? We can conjecture two conditions, a static one and a dynamic one. The static condition requires that two parts belong to the same whole if and only if they share at least one property. The dynamic condition requires that two parts belong to the same whole if and only if one has been acted on by the other directly, or indirectly through an intervening series of direct actions.

Consider, first, the static requirement and how a popular theory of man on that requirement leads us to conclude that there are two universes, not one. Man, in a popular view, has both a mind and a body. In Descartes' formulation of this (see his essay in this chapter), he notes that the nature of mind is that it thinks but is not spatial, whereas matter is spatial but does not think. Mental substance and material substance share no properties. Not sharing any properties, according to the static universe requirement, these two substances cannot be parts of the same whole; therefore, there is not one universe, but two universes. This frustrates monists.

If we identify human essence with the human mind, we exalt the mind; our mind makes us unique. Matter is usually identified as nature, and it is what natural science studies and hopes to understand by discovering the laws that govern matter's behavior. Man and nature, in the static view, constitute two universes.

If we identify human essence with the human mind, we exalt the mind; our mind makes us unique. Matter is usually identified as nature, and it is what natural science studies and hopes to understand by discovering the laws that govern matter's behavior. Man and nature, in the static view, constitute two universes.

Consider also the dynamic requirement and how our popular moral notions again lead us to conclude that there are two universes, not one. Our understanding of nature is ideally expressed in laws, preferably mathematical laws. These laws formulate regular relations between natural events, often stated as causal relations and causal laws. Two parts belong to the same universe, then, according to the dynamic condition, if one of them has been causally acted on by the other. If every event in the universe is a natural event, every event involving a part must directly or indirectly have been acted on by some other event involving some other part. But if this were so, there would be no acts of free will. An act of free will must be one that has not been caused by some other act; thus, by escaping the dynamic requirement, whatever entity acts freely cannot be part of nature.

If the universe is "dynamically" one, then natural science has everything for its subject matter, including human beings, who become objects of natural science. All knowledge becomes one. However, if we have a dual universe, because human actions are freely willed and not caused, we have two kinds of knowledge: scientific knowledge and moral knowledge; and two sciences: natural science and moral science.

Immanuel Kant struggled with the problems inherent in dualism. He had respect for the natural sciences, on the one hand, and for the moral sciences, on the other. He wanted to preserve both. He distinguished, as we saw in Chapter One, between things and persons; the first we may use as means, the latter we may never use as means but should treat as ends only. (See Kant's essay in Chapter One and our introduction to him in that chapter.)

Immanuel Kant accepts the aim of natural science and law that we sketched; he also affirms that free will is a necessary condition for being able to praise or blame someone for his actions; for Kant, free will is a necessary condition for the possibility of morals. But these ideas of natural science and morals appear to be in conflict, events in nature being governed by causal laws while willed events escape them. How can man both be an object of science and a moral agent? Kant solves this conflict by distinguishing the sensible nature of man, that aspect of him that we can observe through our senses (science), from his intelligible nature, that aspect of man that we can grasp only through our "Reason" (morals). Kant says,

"Our problem was this only: whether freedom and natural necessity can exist without conflict in one and the same action; and this we have sufficiently answered. [They can.] We have shown that since freedom may stand in relation to a quite different kind of conditions from those of natural necessity, the law of the latter does not affect the former, and that both may exist, independently of one another and without interfering with each other." Notice that Kant saves the possibility of morals at a cost; Kant has "solved" himself into two universes. We seem to be caught between two sets of alternatives, neither of which is very palatable. Either we give up morals to inherit one universe or we embrace two universes to save morals.

"Determinism" is the name of the view that the dynamic interconnectedness of the universe consists of cause-and-effect relations; a cause of another thing consists of the necessary and sufficient conditions that bring about an effect-event. When the sufficient conditions are present, the effect will occur; when the necessary conditions are absent, the effect will not occur; when both are present, the effect *must* occur. According to determinism, every event in the universe has a cause; we are able to predict which events will occur because of this. Scientists search for the necessary and sufficient conditions; they attempt to state them as precisely as possible, hence, their use of mathematics and arithmetical quantification in stating laws; and they seek to systematize the knowledge of these conditions into a single, logically coherent whole. Determinists view the universe as a mechanism.

Baron Holbach's essay (the first in this section) is a paradigm example of just how far pure mechanism can carry our issue. Holbach has contempt for anyone who holds the view that man has free will. He grants that there is the illusion that we have free will but that it is due entirely to our ignorance. Holbach is direct. "Man is being purely physical; in whatever manner he is considered, he is connected to universal nature, and submitted to the necessary and immutable laws that she imposes on all the beings she contains, according to their peculiar essences." Notice that Holbach's physicalism yields him a single universe. And how are we to account for human actions that some attribute to will? "The will . . . is a modification of the brain, by which it is disposed to action, or prepared to give play to the organs." The brain, as we all know, is physical.

"Libertarianism" is the name of the view that **Jean-Paul Sartre** advocates. Sartre believes that humans are wholly free; none of their acts are caused; to suppose they are is only to hide from yourself because you are unwilling to accept responsibility for your moral failure. To aver that your act was caused is evidence of "bad faith."

Sartre escapes the determinist's argument because Sartre, unlike the determinist, does not believe that human beings have a "nature." Not having a nature, we are not subject to natural laws. Human beings are not part of the facts of the universe. Human beings, unlike other entities in the universe, are conscious of nothingness, of a lack, of an absence of something; people conceive negation. We act to bring about a fact in the universe because we note a lack in the universe; I proceed to act to cook my meat because I notice that it is *not* cooked and I want it cooked; the meat is not merely raw; being raw it is also *not* cooked.

One of the facts missing from the universe is what we will be. Each of us has to notice what about ourselves that is not that we would have be. Then we may act to bring it about, and, in doing so, create ourselves and adopt an essence. "Man is condemned to be free. . . . The existentialist . . . thinks that man, with no support and no aid, is condemned every moment to invent man."

Robert Olson argues that neither the determinist nor the libertarian has the correct view of man's freedom or lack of it. He does not think we are forced to choose between their views as if there were an incompatibility between determinism and human freedom. "Freedom is not only compatible with determinism, it is a product of determinism."

Olson thinks that the essence of the libertarian position is "that the self is an autonomous being that chooses or generates its own values and that in tracing the causal antecedents of a free act one must come to a full stop when one finally encounters this autonomous activity of the moral self." He thinks this view is attributable both to Kant and Sartre. Olson agrees with the first part of the libertarian's position but not with the second part.

As to the first part, that the self is autonomous, he says, and agrees with the libertarian, "The moral self, the higher self, the self as agent can only be defined as the rational self . . . We are morally responsible agents only to the extent that deliberation or forethought is capable of influencing choice and that choices once made can be successfully implemented."

Olson disagrees with the second part, that there are no causal antecedents to this choice and action autonomy, which are the two conditions for freedom of the moral self. He agrees with the determinist; "If our concrete desires were manifestations of a purely spontaneous choice by ourselves as nonempirical agents, then it would certainly seem that predictions based upon empirical correlations between felt desires or character traits, on the one hand, and natural or social circumstances, on the other, would be altogether unreliable—which is contrary to fact." Our free rational choices and decisions do have, for Olson, causal antecedents.

"It might be objected that if a man's behavior is wholly determined by his past experience and external circumstances, then he could not be free since freedom implies that he is the author of his behavior. But this objection cannot be allowed. If an individual's choices are among the causal antecedents of his behavior, then he *is* the author of that behavior. If B is the cause of C, B remains the cause of C even though A is the cause of B." Suppose that C is a choice, and B is deliberation that is the cause of C, and A is the antecedent cause or causes of that deliberation, B. The agent's deliberation, B, is the source of the agent's choice, C; this deliberation, being the agent's, means that the agent is the author of his choice just as the libertarian requires; hence, the agent is free in the libertarian sense. Yet, Olson can agree with the determinist because deliberation, B, does have causal antecedents, A; his deliberation is not outside the natural order of things. For Olson, the natural and moral may constitute parts of a single, unified, universe.

The important move that Olson makes to get freedom and determinism to lie down peacefully together is to make rationality rather than the will the instrument of human freedom. "I reject the notion of will because I am unaware of any evidence for the existence of anything corresponding to it." Were you to follow Olson's analysis of freedom, and were you to seek the maximum degree of freedom, you would have to maximize your rationality. To the extent that philosophy is a rational enterprize, it is, then, an instrument for freedom. Think on.

The Natural Determinism of Persons

BARON HOLBACH

Baron Holbach (1723–1789) was the most outspoken materialist during the Enlightenment. In addition to contributing to Diderot's *Encyclopedia,* he wrote *The System of Nature* (1770) and *Good Sense* (1772).

Man is a being purely physical; in whatever manner he is considered, he is connected to universal nature, and submitted to the necessary and immutable laws that she imposes on all the beings she contains, according to their peculiar essences or to the respective properties with which, without consulting them, she endows each particular species. Man's life is a line that nature commands him to describe upon the surface of the earth, without his ever being able to swerve from it, even for an instant. He is born without his own consent; his organization does in nowise depend upon himself; his ideas come to him involuntarily; his habits are in the power of those who cause him to contract them; he is unceasingly modified by causes, whether visible or concealed, over which he has no control, which necessarily regulate his mode of existence, give the hue to his way of thinking, and determine his manner of acting. He is good or bad, happy or miserable, wise or foolish, reasonable or irrational, without his will being for any thing in these various states. Nevertheless, in despite of the shackles by which he is bound, it is pretended he is a free agent, or that independent of the causes by which he is moved, he determines his own will, and regulates his own condition.

Source: Baron Holbach, *The System of Nature,* Vol. i, trans. by H. D. Robinson (1853), Chap. ii.

However slender the foundation of this opinion, of which every thing ought to point out to him the error, it is current at this day and passes for an incontestable truth with a great number of people, otherwise extremely enlightened; it is the basis of religion, which, supposing relations between man and the unknown being he has placed above nature, has been incapable of imagining how man could either merit reward or deserve punishment from this being, if he was not a free agent. Society has been believed interested in this system; because an idea has gone abroad, that if all the actions of man were to be contemplated as necessary, the right of punishing those who injure their associates would no longer exist. At length human vanity accommodated itself to a hypothesis which, unquestionably, appears to distinguish man from all other physical beings, by assigning to him the special privilege of a total independence of all other causes, but of which a very little reflection would have shown him the impossibility.

As a part subordinate to the great whole, man is obliged to experience its influence. To be a free agent, it were needful that each individual was of greater strength than the entire of nature; or that he was out of this nature, who, always in action herself, obliges all the beings she embraces to act, and to concur to her general motion. . . .

The will . . . is a modification of the brain, by which it is disposed to action, or prepared to give play to the organs. This will is necessarily determined by the qualities, good or bad, agreeable or painful, of the object or the motive that acts upon [man's] senses, or of which the idea remains with him, and is resuscitated by his memory. In consequence, he acts necessarily, his action is the result of the impulse he receives either from the motive, from the object, or from the idea which has modified his brain, or disposed his will. When he does not act according to this impulse, it is because there comes some new cause, some new motive, some new idea, which modifies his brain in a different manner, gives him a new impulse, determines his will in another way, by which the action of the former impulse is suspended: thus, the sight of an agreeable object, or its idea, determines his will to set him in action to procure it; but if a new object or a new idea more powerfully attracts him, it gives a new direction to his will, annihilates the effect of the former, and prevents the action by which it was to be procured. This is the mode in which reflection, experience, reason, necessarily arrests or suspends the action of man's will: without this he would of necessity have followed the anterior impulse which carried him towards a then desirable object. In all this he always acts according to necessary laws, from which he has no means of emancipating himself.

If when tormented with violent thirst, he figures to himself an idea, or really perceives a fountain, whose limpid streams might cool his feverish want, is he sufficient master of himself to desire or not to desire the object competent to satisfy so lively a want? It will no doubt be conceded, that it is impossible he should not be desirous to satisfy it; but it will be said—if at this moment it is announced to him that the water he so ardently desires is poisoned, he will, notwithstanding his vehement thirst, abstain from drinking it: and it has, therefore, been falsely concluded that he is a free agent. The fact, however, is that the motive in either case is exactly the same: his own conservation. The same necessity that determined him to drink before he knew the water was deleterious, upon this new discovery equally determined him not to drink; the desire of conserving himself either annihilates or responds the former impulse; the second motive becomes stronger than the preceding, that is, the fear of death, or the desire of preserving himself, necessarily prevails over the painful sensation caused by his eagerness to drink: but, it will be said, if the thirst is very parching, an inconsiderate man without regarding the danger will risk swallowing the water. Nothing is gained by this remark: in this case, the anterior impulse only regains the ascendency; he is persuaded that life may possibly be longer preserved, or that he shall derive a greater good by drinking the poisoned water than by enduring the torment, which, to his mind, threatens instant dissolution: thus the first becomes the strongest and necessarily urges him on to action. Nevertheless, in either case, whether he partakes of the water, or whether he does not, the two actions will be equally necessary; they will be the effect of that motive which finds itself most puissant; which consequently acts in the most coercive manner upon his will.

This example will serve to explain the whole phenomena of the human will. This will, or rather the brain, finds itself in the same situation as a bowl, which, although it has received an impulse that drives it forward in a straight line, is deranged in its course whenever a force superior to the first obliges it to change its direction. The man who drinks the poisoned water appears a madman; but the actions of fools are as necessary as those of the most prudent individuals. The motives that determine the voluptuary and the debauchee to risk their health, are as powerful, and their actions are as necessary, as those which decide the wise man to manage his. But, it will be insisted, the debauchee may be prevailed on to change his conduct: this does not imply that he is a free agent; but that motives may be found sufficiently powerful to annihilate the effect of those that previously acted upon him; then these new motives determine his will to the new mode of conduct he may adopt as necessarily as the former did to the old mode. . . .

Choice by no means proves the free agency of man: he only deliberates when he does not yet know which to choose of the many objects that move him, he is then in an embarrassment, which does not terminate until his will is decided by the greater advantage he believes he shall find in the object he chooses, or the action he undertakes. From whence it may be seen, that choice is necessary, because he would not determine for an object, or for an action, if he did not believe that he should find in it some direct advantage. That man should have free agency it were needful that he should be able to will or choose without motive, or that he could prevent motives coercing his will. Action always being the effect of his will once determined, and as his will cannot be determined but by a motive which is not in his own power, it follows that he is never the master of the determination of his own peculiar will; that consequently he never acts as a free agent. It has been believed that man was a free agent because he had a will with the power of choosing; but attention has not been paid to the fact that even his will is moved by causes independent of himself; is owing to that which is inherent in his own organization, or which belongs to the nature of the beings acting on him.[1] Is he the master of willing not to withdraw his hand from the fire when he fears it will be burnt? Or has he the power to take away from fire the property which makes him fear it? Is he the master of not choosing a dish of meat, which he knows to be agreeable, or analogous to his palate; of not preferring it to that which he knows to be disagreeable or dangerous? It is always according to his sensations, to his own peculiar experience, or to his suppositions, that he judges of things, either well or ill; but whatever may be his judgment, it depends necessarily on his mode of feeling, whether habitual or accidental, and the qualities he finds in the causes that move him, which exist in spite of himself. . . .

In despite of these proofs of the want of free agency in man, so clear to unprejudiced minds, it will, perhaps be insisted upon with no small feeling of triumph, that if it be proposed to any one, to move or not to move his hand, an action in the number of those called *indifferent,* he evidently appears to be the master of choosing; from which it is concluded that evidence has been offered of his free agency. The reply is, this example is perfectly simple; man in performing some action which he is resolved on doing, does not by any means prove his free agency: the very desire of displaying this quality, excited by the dispute, becomes a necessary motive, which decides his will either for the one or the other of these actions: what deludes him in this instance, or that which persuades him he is a free agent at this moment, is, that he does not discern the true motive which sets him in action, namely, the desire of convincing his opponent: if in the heat of the dispute he insists and asks, "Am I not the master of throwing myself out of the window?" I shall answer him, no; that whilst he preserves his reason there is no probability that the desire of proving his free agency, will become a motive sufficiently powerful to make him sacrifice his life to the attempt: if, notwithstanding this, to prove he is a free agent, he should actually precipitate himself from the window, it would not be a sufficient warranty to conclude he acted freely, but rather that it was the violence of his temperament which spurred him on to his folly. Madness is a state, that depends upon the heat of the blood, not upon the will. A fanatic or a hero, braves death as necessarily as a more phlegmatic man or a coward flies from it.[2] . . .

---

[1] Man passes a great portion of his life without even willing. His will depends on the motive by which he is determined. If he were to render an exact account of every thing he does in the course of each day—from rising in the morning to lying down at night—he would find that not one of his actions have been in the least voluntary; that they have been mechanical, habitual, determined by causes he was not able to foresee; to which he was either obliged to yield, or with which he was allured to acquiesce: he would discover, that all the motives of his labours, of his amusements, of his discourses, of his thoughts, have been necessary; that they have evidently either seduced him or drawn him along.

[2] There is, in point of fact, no difference between the man that is cast out of the window by another, and the man who throws himself out of it, except that the impulse in the first instance comes immediately from without, whilst that which determines the fall in the second case, springs from within his own peculiar machine, having its more remote case also exterior. When Mucius Scaevola held his hand in the fire, he was as much acting under the influence of necessity (caused by interior motives) that urged him to this strange action, as if his arm had been held by strong men: pride, despair, the desire of braving his enemy, a wish to astonish him, an anxiety to intimidate him, etc., were the invisible chains that held his hand bound to the fire. . . .

To be undeceived on the system of his free agency, man has simply to recur to the motive by which his will is determined; he will always find this motive is out of his own control. It is said: that in consequence of an idea to which the mind gives birth, man acts freely if he encounters no obstacle. But the question is, what gives birth to this idea in his brain? was he the master either to prevent it from presenting itself, or from renewing itself in his brain? Does not this idea depend either upon objects that strike him exteriorly and in despite of himself, or upon causes, that without his knowledge, act within himself and modify his brain? Can he prevent his eyes, cast without design upon any object whatever, from giving him an idea of this object, and from moving his brain? He is not more master of the obstacles; they are the necessary effects of either interior or exterior causes, which always act according to their given properties. A man insults a coward, this necessarily irritates him against his insulter, but his will cannot vanquish the obstacle that cowardice places to the object of his desire, because his natural conformation, which does not depend upon himself, prevents his having courage. In this case, the coward is insulted in despite of himself; and against his will is obliged patiently to brook the insult he has received.

The partisans of the system of free agency appear ever to have confounded constraint with necessity. Man believes he acts as a free agent, every time he does not see any thing that places obstacles to his actions; he does not perceive that the motive which causes him to will, is always necessary and independent of himself. A prisoner loaded with chains is compelled to remain in prison; but he is not a free agent in the desire to emancipate himself; his chains prevent him from acting, but they do not prevent him from willing; he would save himself if they would loose his fetters; but he would not save himself as a free agent; fear or the idea of punishment would be sufficient motives for his action.

Man may, therefore, cease to be restrained, without, for that reason, becoming a free agent: in whatever manner he acts, he will act necessarily, according to motives by which he shall be determined. He may be compared to a heavy body that finds itself arrested in its descent by any obstacle what ever: take away this obstacle, it will gravitate or continue to fall; but who shall say this dense body is free to fall or not? Is not its descent the necessary effect of its own specific gravity? The virtuous Socrates submitted to the laws of his country, although they were unjust; and though the doors of his jail were left open to him, he would not save himself; but in this he did not act as a free agent; the invisible chains of opinion, the secret love of decorum, the inward respect for the laws, even when they were iniquitous, the fear of tarnishing his glory, kept him in his prison; they were motives sufficiently powerful with this enthusiast for virtue, to induce him to wait death with tranquility; it was not in his power to save himself, because he could find no potential motive to bring him to depart, even for an instant, from those principles to which his mind was accustomed.

Man, it is said, frequently acts against his inclination, from whence it is falsely concluded he is a free agent; but when he appears to act contrary to his inclination, he is always determined to it by some motive sufficiently efficacious to vanquish this inclination. A sick man, with a view to his cure, arrives at conquering his repugnance to the most disgusting remedies: the fear of pain, or the dread of death, then becomes necessary motives; consequently this sick man cannot be said to act freely.

When it is said, that man is not a free agent, it is not pretended to compare him to a body moved by a simple impulsive cause: he contains within himself causes inherent to his existence; he is moved by an interior organ, which has its own peculiar laws, and is itself necessarily determined in consequence of ideas formed from perceptions resulting from sensations which it receives from exterior objects. As the mechanism of these sensations, of these perceptions, and the manner they engrave ideas on the brain of man, are not known to him; because he is unable to unravel all these motions; because he cannot perceive the chain of operations in his soul, or the motive principle that acts within him, he supposes himself a free agent; which, literally translated, signifies, that he moves himself by himself; that he determines himself without cause: when he rather ought to say, that he is ignorant how or for why he acts in the manner he does. It is true the soul enjoys an activity peculiar to itself: but it is equally certain that this activity would never be displayed, if some motive or some cause did not put it in a condition to exercise itself: at least it will not be pretended that the soul is able either to love or to hate without being moved, without knowing the objects, without having some idea of their qualities. Gunpowder has unquestionably a particular activity, but this activity will never display itself, unless fire be applied to it; this, however, immediately sets it in motion.

It is the great complication of motion in man, it is the variety of his action, it is the multiplicity of causes that move him, whether simultaneously or in continual succession, that persuades him he is a free agent: if all his motions were simple, if the causes that move him did not confound themselves with each other, if they were distinct, if his machine were less complicated, he would perceive that all his actions were necessary, because he would be enabled to recur instantly to the cause that made him act. A man who should be always obliged to go towards the west, would always go on that side; but he would feel that, in so going, he was not a free agent: if he had another sense, as his actions or his motion, augmented by a sixth, would be still more varied and much more complicated, he would believe himself still more a free agent than he does with his five senses.

It is, then, for want of recurring to the causes that move him; for want of being able to analyze, from not being competent to decompose the complicated motion of his machine, that man believes himself a free agent: it is only upon his own ignorance that he founds the profound yet deceitful notion he has of his free agency; that he builds those opinions which he brings forward as a striking proof of his pretended freedom of action. If, for a short time, each man was willing to examine his own peculiar actions, search out their true motives to discover their concatenation, he would remain convinced that the sentiment he has of his natural free agency, is a chimera that must speedily be destroyed by experience. . . .

Man either sees or believes he sees much more distinctly the necessary relation of effects with their causes in natural philosophy than in the human heart: at least he sees in the former sensible causes constantly produce sensible effects, ever the same, when the circumstances are alike. After this he hesitates not to look upon physical effects as necessary; whilst he refuses to acknowledge necessity in the acts of the human will: these he has, without any just foundation, attributed to a motive-power that acts independently by its own peculiar energy, which is capable of modifying itself without the concurrence of exterior causes, and which is distinguished from all material or physical beings. Agriculture is founded upon the assurance, afforded by experience, that the earth, cultivated and sown in a certain manner, when it has otherwise the requisite qualities, will furnish grain, fruit and flowers, either necessary for subsistence or pleasing to the senses. If things were considered without prejudice, it would be perceived, that in morals, education is nothing more than *the agriculture of the mind:* that, like the earth, by reason of its natural disposition, of the culture bestowed upon it, of the seeds with which it is sown, of the seasons, more or less favourable that conduct it to maturity, we may be assured that the soul will produce either virtue or vice—*moral fruit,* that will be either salubrious for man or baneful to society. *Morals* is the science of the relations that subsist between the minds, the wills, and the actions of men, in the same manner that geometry is the science of the relations that are found between bodies. Morals would be a chimera and would have no certain principles, if it was not founded upon the knowledge of the motives which must necessarily have an influence upon the human will, and which must necessarily determine the actions of human beings. . . .

In spite of the gratuitous ideas which man has formed to himself on his pretended free agency; in defiance of the illusions of this supposed intimate sense, which, maugre his experience, persuades him that he is master of his will; all his institutions are really founded upon necessity: on this, as on a variety of other occasions, practice throws aside speculation. Indeed, if it was not believed that certain motives embraced the power requisite to determine the will of man, to arrest the progress of his passions; to direct them towards an end, to modify him, of what use would be the faculty of speech? What benefit could arise from education, from legislation, from morals, even from religion itself? What does education achieve, save give the first impulse to the human will; make man contract habits; oblige him to persist in them; furnish him with motives, whether true or false, to act after a given manner? When the father either menaces his son with punishment, or promises him a reward, he is not convinced these things will act upon his will? What does legislation attempt except it be to present to the citizens of a state those motives which are supposed necessary to determine them to perform some actions that are considered worthy; to abstain from committing others that are looked upon as unworthy? What is the object of morals, if it be not to show man that his interest exacts he should suppress the momentary ebullition of his passions, with a view to promote a more certain happiness, a more lasting well-being, than can possibly result from the gratification of his transitory desires? Does not the religion of all countries suppose the human race, together with the entire of nature, submitted to the irresistible will of a necessary being who regulates their condition after the eternal laws of immutable wisdom? Is it not this divine being who chooses and who rejects? The anathemas fulminated by religion, the promises it holds forth, are they not founded upon the idea of the effects these chimeras will necessarily produce upon ignorant and timid people? Is not man brought into existence by this kind Divinity without his own knowledge? Is he not obliged to play a part against his will? Does not either his happiness or his misery depend on the part he plays?[3]

Education, then, is only necessity shown to children: legislation, is necessity shown to the members of the body politic: morals, is the necessity of the relations subsisting between men, shown to reasonable beings: in short, man grants necessity in every thing for which he believes he has certain unerring experience: that of which he does not comprehend the necessary connexion of causes with their effects he styles probability: he would not act as he does, if he was not convinced, or, at least, if he did not presume that certain effects will necessarily follow his actions. . . .

From all that has been advanced in this chapter, it results, that in no one moment of his existence is man a free agent. He is not the architect of his own conformation, which he holds from nature; he has no control over his own ideas, or over the modification of his brain; these are due to causes, that, in despite of him, and without his own knowledge, unceasingly act upon him; he is not the master of not loving or coveting that which he finds amiable or desirable; he is not capable of refusing to deliberate, when he is uncertain of the effects certain objects will produce upon him; he cannot avoid choosing that which he believes will be most advantageous to him; in the moment when his will is determined by his choice he is not competent to act otherwise than he does. In what instance, then, is he the master of his own actions? In what moment is he a free agent?[4]

---

[3] Every religion is evidently founded upon fatalism. Among the Greeks they supposed men were punished for their *necessary* faults—as may be seen in Orestes, in Œdipus, etc., who only committed crimes predicted by the oracles. Christians have made vain efforts to justify God Almighty in throwing the faults of men on their *free will,* which is opposed to *Predestination,* another name for *fatalism.* However, their system of *Grace* will by no means obviate the difficulty, for God gives grace only to those whom he pleases. In all countries religion has no other foundation than the fatal decrees of an irresistible being who arbitrarily decides the fate of his creatures. All theological hypotheses turn upon this point; and yet those theologians who regard the system of fatalism as false or dangerous, do not see that the Fall of Angels, Original Sin, Predestination, the System of Grace, the small number of the Elect, etc., incontestably prove that religion is a true system of fatalism.

[4] The question of *Free Will* may be reduced to this:—Liberty, or Free Will, cannot be associated with any known functions of the soul; for the soul, at the moment in which it acts, deliberates, or wills, cannot act, deliberate, or will otherwise than it does, because a thing cannot exist and not exist at the same time. Now, it is my will, such as it is, that makes me deliberate; my deliberation, that makes me choose; my choice that makes me act; my determination that makes me execute that which my deliberation has made me choose, and I have only deliberated because I have had motives which rendered it impossible for me not to be willing to deliberate. Thus liberty is not found either in the will, in the deliberation, in the choice, or in the action. Theologians must not, therefore, connect liberty with these operations of the soul, otherwise there will be a contradiction of ideas. If the soul is not free when it wills, deliberates, chooses, or acts, will theologians tell us when it can exercise its liberty?

It is evident that the system of liberty, or free will, has been invented to exonerate God

(Continued)

The Natural Determinism of Persons 525

That which a man is about to do, is always a consequence of that which he has been—of that which he is—of that which he has done up to the moment of the action: his total and actual existence, considered under all its possible circumstances, contains the sum of all the motives to the action he is about to commit; this is a principle the truth of which no thinking being will be able to refuse accrediting: his life is a series of necessary moments; his conduct, whether good or bad, virtuous or vicious, useful or prejudicial, either to himself or to others, is a concatenation of action, as necessary as all the moments of his existence. To *live* is to exist in a necessary mode during the points of that duration which succeed each other necessarily; *to will* is to acquiesce or not in remaining such as he is; *to be free* is to yield to the necessary motives he carries within himself.

If he understood the play of his organs, if he was able to recall to himself all the impulsions they have received, all the modifications they have undergone, all the effects they have produced, he would perceive that all his actions are submitted to that *fatality,* which regulates his own particular system, as it does the entire system of the universe: no one effect in him, any more than in nature, produces itself by *chance;* this . . . is a word void of sense. All that passes in him; all that is done by him; as well as all that happens in nature, or that is attributed to her, is derived from necessary causes, which act according to necessary laws, and which produce necessary effects from whence necessarily flow others.

Fatality is the eternal, the immutable, the necessary order, established in nature; or the indispensable connexion of causes, that act, with the effects they operate. Conforming to this order, heavy bodies fall; light bodies rise; that which is analogous in matter reciprocally attracts; that which is heterogeneous mutually repels; man congregates himself in society, modifies each his fellow; becomes either virtuous or wicked; either contributes to his mutual happiness, or reciprocates his misery; either loves his neighbour, or hates his companion necessarily, according to the manner in which the one acts upon the other. From whence it may be seen, that the same necessity which regulates the physical, also regulates the moral world, in which every thing is in consequence submitted to fatality. Man, in running over, frequently without his own knowledge, often in despite of himself, the route which nature has marked out for him, resembles a swimmer who is obliged to follow the current that carries him along: he believes himself a free agent, because he sometimes consents, sometimes does not consent, to glide with the stream, which, notwithstanding, always hurries him forward; he believes himself the master of his condition, because he is obliged to use his arms under the fear of sinking. . . .

The false ideas he has formed to himself upon free agency, are in general thus founded: there are certain events which he judges *necessary;* either because he sees that they are effects constantly and invariably linked to certain causes,

---

from the evil that is done in this world. But is it not from God man received this liberty? Is it not from God he received the faculty of choosing evil and rejecting the good? If so, God created him with a determination to sin, else liberty is essential to man and independent of God.

which nothing seems to prevent; or because he believes he has discovered the chain of causes and effects that is put in play to produce those events: whilst he contemplates as *contingent* other events of whose causes he is ignorant, and with whose mode of acting he is unacquainted: but in nature, where every thing is connected by one common bond, there exists no effect without a cause. In the moral as well as in the physical world, every thing that happens is a necessary consequence of causes, either visible or concealed, which are of necessity obliged to act after their peculiar essences. *In man, free agency is nothing more than necessity contained within himself.*

The Existential Person

JEAN-PAUL SARTRE

Jean-Paul Sartre (1905–   ), French existentialist, was professor of philosophy at Lyceé Condorcet from 1935 to 1942. A successful playwright and novelist as well as a philosopher, Sartre has given up teaching to devote his time to writing. His major works include *Being and Nothingness* (1943) and *Existentialism and Humanism* (1946).

What is meant by the term *existentialism?*

Most people who use the word would be rather embarrassed if they had to explain it, since, now that the word is all the rage, even the work of a musician or painter is being called existentialist. . . . It seems that for want of an advance-guard doctrine analogous to surrealism, the kind of people who are eager for scandal and flurry turn to this philosophy which in other respects does not at all serve their purposes in this sphere.

Actually, it is the least scandalous, the most austere of doctrines. It is intended strictly for specialists and philosophers. Yet it can be defined easily. What complicates matters is that there are two kinds of existentialists; first, those who are Christian, among whom I would include Jaspers and Gabriel Marcel, both Catholic; and on the other hand, the atheistic existentialists, among whom I class Heidegger, and then the French existentialists and myself. What they have in common is that they think that existence precedes essence, or, if you prefer, that subjectivity must be the starting point.

Just what does that mean? Let us consider some object that is manufactured, for example, a book or a paper-cutter: here is an object which has been made by an artisan whose inspiration came from a concept. He referred to the concept of what a paper-cutter is and likewise to a known method of production, which is part of the concept, something which is, by and large, a routine. Thus, the paper-cutter is at once an object produced in a certain way and, on the other hand, one having a specific use; and one cannot postulate a man who produces a paper-cutter but does not know what it is used for. Therefore, let us say that,

Source: Jean-Paul Sartre, *Existentialism,* trans. by Bernard Frechtman (New York, 1947). Reprinted by permission of the Philosophical Library, Inc.

for the paper-cutter, essence—that is, the ensemble of both the production routines and the properties which enable it to be both produced and defined—precedes existence. Thus, the presence of the paper-cutter or book in front of me is determined. Therefore, we have here a technical view of the world whereby it can be said that production precedes existence.

When we conceive God as the Creator, He is generally thought of as a superior sort of artisan. Whatever doctrine we may be considering, whether one like that of Descartes or that of Leibnitz, we always grant that will more or less follows understanding or, at the very least, accompanies it, and that when God creates He knows exactly what He is creating. Thus, the concept of man in the mind of God is comparable to the concept of paper-cutter in the mind of the manufacturer, and, following certain techniques and a conception, God produces man, just as the artisan, following a definition and a technique, makes a paper-cutter. Thus, the individual man is the realization of a certain concept in the divine intelligence.

In the eighteenth century, the atheism of the *philosophes* discarded the idea of God, but not so much for the notion that essence precedes existence. To a certain extent, this idea is found everywhere; we find it in Diderot, in Voltaire, and even in Kant. Man has a human nature; this human nature, which is the concept of the human, is found in all men, which means that each man is a particular example of a universal concept, man. In Kant, the result of this universality is that the wild-man, the natural man, as well as the bourgeois, are circumscribed by the same definition and have the same basic qualities. Thus, here too the essence of man precedes the historical existence that we find in nature.

Atheistic existentialism, which I represent, is more coherent. It states that if God does not exist, there is at least one being in whom existence precedes essence, a being who exists before he can be defined by any concept, and that this being is man, or, as Heidegger says, human reality. What is meant here by saying that existence precedes essence? It means that, first of all, man exists, turns up, appears on the scene, and, only afterwards, defines himself. If man, as the existentialist conceives him, is indefinable, it is because at first he is nothing. Only afterward will he be something, and he himself will have made what he will be. Thus, there is no human nature, since there is no God to conceive it. Not only is man what he conceives himself to be, but he is also only what he wills himself to be after this thrust toward existence.

Man is nothing else but what he makes of himself. Such is the first principle of existentialism. It is also what is called subjectivity, the name we are labeled with when charges are brought against us. But what do we mean by this, if not that man has a greater dignity than a stone or table? For we mean that man first exists, that is, that man first of all is the being in the future. Man is at the start a plan which is aware of itself, rather than a patch of moss, a piece of garbage, or a cauliflower; nothing exists prior to this plan; there is nothing in heaven; man will be what he will have planned to be. Not what he will want to be. Because by the word "will" we generally mean a conscious decision, which is subsequent to what we have already made of ourselves. I may want to belong to a political party, write a book, get married; but all that is only a manifestation of an earlier, more spontaneous choice that is called "will." But if existence really does precede essence, man is responsible for what he is. Thus, existentialism's first move is to make every man aware of what he is and to make the full responsibility of his existence rest on him. And when we say that a man is responsible for himself, we do not only mean that he is responsible for his own individuality, but that he is responsible for all men.

The word subjectivism has two meanings, and our opponents play on the two. Subjectivism means, on the one hand, that an individual chooses and makes himself; and, on the other, that it is impossible for man to transcend human subjectivity. The second of these is the essential meaning of existentialism. When we say that man chooses his own self, we mean that every one of us does likewise; but we also mean by that that in making this choice he also chooses all men. In fact, in creating the man that we want to be, there is not a single one of our acts which does not at the same time create an image of man as we think he ought to be. To choose to be this or that is to affirm at the same time the value of what we choose, because we can never choose evil. We always choose the good, and nothing can be good for us without being good for all.

If, on the other hand, existence precedes essence, and if we grant that we exist and fashion our image at one and the same time, the image is valid for everybody and for our whole age. Thus, our responsibility is much greater than we might have supposed, because it involves all mankind. If I am a workingman and choose to join a Christian trade-union rather than be a communist, and if by being a member I want to show that the best thing for man is resignation, that the kingdom of man is not of this world, I am not only involving my own case—I want to be resigned for everyone. As a result, my action has involved all humanity. To take a more individual matter, if I want to marry, to have children; even if this marriage depends solely on my own circumstances or passion or wish, I am involving all humanity in monogamy and not merely myself. Therefore, I am responsible for myself and for everyone else. I am creating a certain image of man of my own choosing. In choosing myself, I choose man.

This helps us understand what the actual content is of such rather grandiloquent words as anguish, forlornness, despair. As you will see, it's all quite simple.

First, what is meant by anguish? The existentialists say at once that man is anguish. What that means is this: the man who involves himself and who realizes that he is not only the person he chooses to be, but also a law-maker who is, at the same time, choosing all mankind as well as himself, cannot help escape the feeling of his total and deep responsibility. Of course, there are many people who are not anxious; but we claim that they are hiding their anxiety, that they are fleeing from it. Certainly, many people believe that when they do something, they themselves are the only ones involved, and when someone says to them, "What if everyone acted that way?" they shrug their shoulders and answer, "Everyone doesn't act that way." But really, one should always ask himself, "What would happen if everybody looked at things that way?" There is no escaping this disturbing thought except by a kind of double-dealing. A man who lies and makes excuses for himself by saying "not everybody does that," is someone with an uneasy conscience, because the act of lying implies that a universal value is conferred upon the lie.

Anguish is evident even when it conceals itself. This is the anguish that Kierkegaard called the anguish of Abraham. You know the story: an angel has ordered Abraham to sacrifice his son; if it really were an angel who has come and said, "You are Abraham, you shall sacrifice your son," everything would be all right. But everyone might first wonder, "Is it really an angel, and am I really Abraham? What proof do I have?" . . .

Now, I'm not being singled out as an Abraham, and yet at every moment I'm obliged to perform exemplary acts. For every man, everything happens as if all mankind had its eyes fixed on him and were guiding itself by what he does. And every man ought to say to himself, "Am I really the kind of man who has the right to act in such a way that humanity might guide itself by my actions?" And if he does not say that to himself, he is masking his anguish.

There is no question here of the kind of anguish which would lead to quietism, to inaction. It is a matter of a simple sort of anguish that anybody who has had responsibilities is familiar with. For example, when a military officer takes the responsibility for an attack and sends a certain number of men to death, he chooses to do so, and in the main he alone makes the choice. Doubtless, orders come from above, but they are too broad; he interprets them, and on this interpretation depend the lives of ten or fourteen or twenty men. In making a decision he cannot help having a certain anguish. All leaders know this anguish. That doesn't keep them from acting; on the contrary, it is the very condition of their action. For it implies that they envisage a number of possibilities, and when they choose one, they realize that it has value only because it is chosen. We shall see that this kind of anguish, which is the kind that existentialism describes, is explained, in addition, by a direct responsibility to the other men whom it involves. It is not a curtain separating us from action, but is part of action itself.

When we speak of forlornness, a term Heidegger was fond of, we mean only that God does not exist and that we have to face all the consequences of this. The existentialist is strongly opposed to a certain kind of secular ethics which would like to abolish God with the least possible expense. About 1880, some French teachers tried to set up a secular ethics which went something like this: God is a useless and costly hypothesis; we are discarding it; but meanwhile, in order for there to be an ethics, a society, a civilization, it is essential that certain values be taken seriously and that they be considered as having an *a priori* existence. It must be obligatory, *a priori,* to be honest, not to lie, not to beat your wife, to have children, etc., etc. So we're going to try a little device which will make it possible to show that values exist all the same, inscribed in a heaven of ideas, though otherwise God does not exist. In other words—and this, I believe, is the tendency of everything called reformism in France—nothing will be changed if God does not exist. We shall find ourselves with the same norms of honesty, progress, and humanism, and we shall have made of God an outdated hypothesis which will peacefully die off by itself.

The existentialist, on the contrary, thinks it very distressing that God does not exist, because all possibility of finding values in a heaven of ideas disappears along with Him; there can be no longer an *a priori* Good, since there is no infinite and perfect consciousness to think it. Nowhere is it written that the Good exists, that we must be honest, that we must not lie; because the fact is we are on a plane where there are only men. Dostoievsky said, "If God didn't exist, everything would be possible." That is the very starting point of existentialism. Indeed, everything is permissible if God does not exist, and as a result man is forlorn, because neither within him nor without does he find anything to cling to. He can't start making excuses for himself.

If existence really does precede essence, there is no explaining things away by reference to a fixed and given human nature. In other words, there is no determinism, man is free, man is freedom. On the other hand, if God does not exist, we find no values or commands to turn to which legitimize our conduct. So, in the bright realm of values, we have no excuse behind us, no justification before us. We are alone, with no excuses.

That is the idea I shall try to convey when I say that man is condemned to be free. Condemned, because he did not create himself, yet, in other respects is free; because, once thrown into the world, he is responsible for everything he does. The existentialist does not believe in the power of passion. He will never agree that a sweeping passion is a ravaging torrent which fatally leads a man to certain acts and is therefore an excuse. He thinks that man is responsible for his passion.

The existentialist does not think that man is going to help himself by finding in the world some omen by which to orient himself. Because he thinks that man will interpret the omen to suit himself. Therefore, he thinks that man, with no support and no aid, is condemned every moment to invent man. Ponge, in a very fine article, has said, "Man is the future of man." That's exactly it. But if it is taken to mean that this future is recorded in heaven, that God sees it, then it is false, because it would really no longer be a future. If it is taken to mean that, whatever a man may be, there is a future to be forged, a virgin future before him, then this remark is sound. But then we are forlorn.

To give you an example which will enable you to understand forlornness better, I shall cite the case of one of my students who came to see me under the following circumstances: his father was on bad terms with his mother, and, moreover, was inclined to be a collaborationist; his older brother had been killed in the German offensive of 1940, and the young man, with somewhat immature but generous feelings, wanted to avenge him. His mother lived alone with him, very much upset by the half-treason of her husband and the death of her older son; the boy was her only consolation.

The boy was faced with the choice of leaving for England and joining the Free French Forces—that is, leaving his mother behind—or remaining with his mother and helping her to carry on. He was fully aware that the woman lived only for him and that his going-off—and perhaps his death—would plunge her into despair. He was also aware that every act that he did for his mother's sake was a sure thing, in the sense that it was helping her to carry on, whereas every effort he made toward going off and fighting was an uncertain move which might run aground and prove completely useless; for example, on his way to England he might, while passing through Spain, be detained indefinitely in a Spanish camp; he might reach England or Algiers and be stuck in an office at a desk job. As a result, he was faced with two very different kinds of action: one, concrete, immediate, but concerning only one individual; the other concerned an incomparably vaster group, a national collectivity, but for that very reason was dubious, and might be interrupted en route. And, at the same time, he was wavering between two kinds of ethics. On the one hand, an ethics of sympathy, of personal devotion; on the other, a broader ethics, but one whose efficacy was more dubious. He had to choose between the two.

Who could help him choose? Christian doctrine? No. Christian doctrine says, "Be charitable, love your neighbor, take the more rugged path, etc., etc." But which is the more rugged path? Whom should he love as a brother? The fighting man or his mother? Which does the greater good, the vague act of fighting in a group, or the concrete one of helping a particular human being to go on living? Who can decide *a priori*? Nobody. No book of ethics can tell him. The Kantian ethics says, "Never treat any person as a means, but as an end." Very well, if I stay with my mother, I'll treat her as an end and not as a means; but by virtue of this very fact, I'm running the risk of treating the people around me who are fighting, as means; and, conversely, if I go to join those who are fighting, I'll be treating them as an end, and, by doing that, I run the risk of treating my mother as a means.

If values are vague, and if they are always too broad for the concrete and specific case that we are considering, the only thing left for us is to trust our instincts. That's what this young man tried to do; and when I saw him, he said, "In the end, feeling is what counts. I ought to choose whichever pushes me in one direction. If I feel that I love my mother enough to sacrifice everything else for her—my desire for vengeance, for action, for adventure—then I'll stay with her. If, on the contrary, I feel that my love for my mother isn't enough, I'll leave."

But how is the value of a feeling determined. What gives his feeling for his mother value? Precisely the fact that he remained with her. I may say that I like so-and-so well enough to sacrifice a certain amount of money for him, but I may say so only if I've done it. I may say, "I love my mother well enough to remain with her" if I have remained with her. The only way to determine the value of this affection is, precisely, to perform an act which confirms and defines it. But, since I require this affection to justify my act, I find myself caught in a vicious circle. . . .

As for despair, the term has a very simple meaning. It means that we shall confine ourselves to reckoning only with what depends upon our will, or on the ensemble of probabilities which make our action possible. When we want something, we always have to reckon with probabilities. I may be counting on the arrival of a friend. The friend is coming by rail or street-car; this supposes that the train will arrive on schedule, or that the street-car will not jump the track. I am left in the realm of possibility; but possibilities are to be reckoned with only to the point where my action comports with the ensemble of these possibilities, and no further. The moment the possibilities I am considering are not rigorously involved by my action, I ought to disengage myself from them, because no God, no scheme, can adapt the world and its possibilities to my will. When Descartes said, "Conquer yourself rather than the world," he meant essentially the same thing.

The Marxists to whom I have spoken reply, "You can rely on the support of others in your action, which obviously has certain limits because you're not going to live forever. That means: rely on both what others are doing elsewhere to help you, in China, in Russia, and what they will do later on, after your death, to carry on the action and lead it to its fulfillment, which will be the revolution. You even *have* to rely upon that, otherwise you're immoral." I reply at once that I will always rely on fellow fighters insofar as these comrades are involved with me in a common struggle, in the unity of a party or a group in which I can more or less make my weight felt; that is, one whose ranks I am in as a fighter and whose movements I am aware of at every moment. In such a situation, relying on the unity and will of the party is exactly like counting on the fact that the train will arrive on time or that the car won't jump the track. But, given that man is free and that there is no human nature for me to depend on, I cannot count on men whom I do not know by relying on human goodness or man's concern for the good of society. I don't know what will become of the Russian revolution; I may make an example of it to the extent that at the present time it is apparent that the proletariat plays a part in Russia that it plays in no other nation. But I can't swear that this will inevitably lead to a triumph of the proletariat. I've got to limit myself to what I see.

Given that men are free, and that tomorrow they will freely decide what man will be, I cannot be sure that, after my death, fellow fighters will carry on my work to bring it to its maximum perfection. Tomorrow, after my death, some men may decide to set up Fascism, and the others may be cowardly and muddled enough to let them do it. Fascism will then be the human reality, so much the worse for us.

Actually, things will be as man will have decided they are to be. Does that mean that I should abandon myself to quietism? No. First, I should involve myself; then, act on the old saw, "Nothing ventured, nothing gained." Nor does it mean that I shouldn't belong to a party, but rather that I shall have no illusions and shall do what I can. For example, suppose I ask myself, "Will socialization, as such, ever come about?" I know nothing about it. All I know is that I'm going to do everything in my power to bring it about. Beyond that, I can't count on anything. Quietism is the attitude of people who say, "Let others do what I can't do." The doctrine I am presenting is the very opposite of quietism, since it declares, "There is no reality except in action." Moreover, it goes further, since it adds, "Man is nothing else than his plan; he exists only to the extent that he fulfills himself; he is, therefore, nothing else than the ensemble of his acts, nothing else than his life."

SUGGESTED READINGS

1. AYER, A. J., "Freedom and Necessity," in *Philosophical Essays* (London: Macmillan & Co., Ltd., 1954), pp. 271–284.
2. CAMPBELL, C. A., "Is 'Free Will' a Pseudo-Problem?" *Mind*, Vol. 60 (1951), pp. 446–465.

3. Darrow, Clarence, *Plea in Defense of Loeb and Leopold* (Gerard, Kan.: Little Blue Books, 1926), pp. 40–43.
4. Desan, Wilfrid, *The Tragic Finale* (New York: Harper, 1960).
5. Lehrer, Keith, "Can We Know That We Have Free Will by Introspection?" *Journal of Philosophy*, Vol. 57 (1960), 145–157.
6. Wood, Ledger, "The Free-Will Controversy," *Philosophy*, Vol. 16 (1941), pp. 396–397.

Freedom, Selfhood, and Moral Responsibility

ROBERT OLSON

Robert G. Olson (1924–   ) is a professor of philosophy at University College, Rutgers. Among his books are *An Introduction to Existentialism* (1962), *The Morality of Self-Interest* (1965), and *Meaning and Argument* (1969).

By a chain of inferences, each of them appearing at first sight irrefutable, one easily arrives at a conclusion that strikes at the heart of my position. If, it is said, an individual is morally responsible for an act, that act must be performed freely; if the act is performed freely, the individual must himself be its author; and if the individual is himself its author, then the act can be causally explained neither in terms of external circumstances nor in terms of biological inheritance. In other words, to the extent that the individual is a morally responsible agent, he is free; and to the extent that he is free, he transcends the biological, physical, and social conditions of his being. Consequently my position must be false. It cannot be that the moral development of the individual is largely a matter of social circumstance, nor can it be that the individual's primary moral responsibility is to add to the sum of human well-being. The autonomy of the free moral agent is a gift of God which transports him into the society of angels— not a natural debt which the individual must discharge in the mundane world of human affairs. In this chapter I shall try to show that this argument, despite its initial plausibility, rests upon highly dubious assumptions about the nature of the moral self and of human freedom. I shall also try to show how a proper understanding of moral selfhood and freedom confirms my own views. Freedom is not only compatible with determinism, it is a product of determinism.

Libertarianism

The essence of libertarianism, as the position against which I am arguing is ordinarily called, is not that a free act is totally uncaused or undetermined,

Source: Robert G. Olson, *The Morality of Self-Interest* (New York: Harcourt Brace Jovanovich, Inc., 1965), pp. 135–156. Reprinted by permission of the author.

although critics of libertarianism frequently tend to give this impression. The essence of the position is rather that the moral self is an autonomous being that chooses or generates its own values and that in tracing the causal antecedents of a free act one must come to a full stop when one finally encounters this autonomous activity of the moral self. The most famous as well as the most able of the libertarians are Immanuel Kant and Jean-Paul Sartre. Kant refers to the moral agent as a self-legislating *noumenal* self independent of external influences and opposes it to the empirical, or phenomenal, self, the latter a creature of desire and passion that *is* subject to determination by external influences. The noumenal self issues moral commands; it is for the phenomenal self to obey. Sartre dispenses with the concept of the noumenal self, arguing that the individual as moral agent is a pure nothingness that spontaneously manifests itself by directly creating its empirical, or phenomenal, needs and desires.

Against the libertarian view of selfhood and freedom, whether Kantian or Sartrean, I have three principal objections.

1. It is extremely difficult to conceive at all concretely the libertarian self and at least as difficult to establish its actual existence. Kant freely admits that we have no knowledge of the noumenal self and that its existence is simply a postulate that he believes necessary to the moral life. At best it might be said that the noumenal self is an hypothesis needed to explain that elementary and actually observable fact of moral experience, the conflict between duty and desire. As I have already shown in Chapter II, however, the conflict between duty and desire can be quite adequately explained without recourse to any unobservable entities of this kind. Sartre, for his part, claims that our existence as a nothingness that spontaneously chooses its own values can be established through an intuitive insight coming to us in the experience of anguish. But knowledge revealed in this manner is no more reliable than knowledge revealed to the religious mystic, and if we accept such alleged insights as valid we shall have almost as many different accounts of the nature of the self as there are persons who claim to know the self in this way.

2. Both the Kantian and the Sartrean views of moral selfhood raise problems to which no satisfactory answer appears forthcoming. Kant, for instance, must explain how the noumenal self actually influences the conduct of the phenomenal self, since most of us subscribe to the Spinozistic view that a desire can be combatted only with the aid of another desire and do not, therefore, see how a command issued by an affectless noumenal self can by itself counteract such phenomenal affects as self-love. Kant would sometimes have us understand that this takes place through the intermediary of "the will." But nowhere does he clearly describe the will. What is it? Is it an empirical phenomenon? If so, why is its existence so widely contested, especially by empirical psychologists? Or is it a nonempirical phenomenon whose existence Kant merely postulates along with the noumenal self? If so, the problem has been displaced, not solved. Sartre's problem is to explain how our empirical desires correlate so consistently with other empirical facts, especially social circumstances. If our concrete desires were manifestations of a purely spontaneous choice by ourselves as nonempirical agents, then it would certainly seem that predictions based upon empirical cor-

relations between felt desires or character traits, on the one hand, and natural or social circumstances, on the other, would be altogether unreliable—which is contrary to fact.

3. Finally, libertarian selfhood and freedom, even if they were *vera causa,* could not possibly be an adequate explanation of moral responsibility for two distinct but related reasons.

a. To say that a person is morally responsible for an act is to say that he may properly be praised or blamed by other persons for that act. But it is generally agreed that a person may not properly be praised or blamed for his past or present behavior and cannot consequently be held morally responsible for it unless there is reason to believe that praise or blame is likely to have some effect upon his future behavior. If, for instance, we believed that a man were drinking to excess and that moral censure by a well-disposed friend might have the effect of curbing overindulgence in the future, we would in all probability recognize the legitimacy of moral censure. If, however, we were convinced that the man's drinking had reached the stage where moral censure would be totally ineffective, as it would be if his drinking were thoroughly compulsive, we would almost certainly consider the use of moral censure improper. In this latter case the man would cease to be an agent in the proper sense of that term, *viz.,* a person who acts of his own volition. He would be instead a patient, someone acted upon by circumstances over which he has no control. To censure him would be a useless act of cruelty. The point is that no matter how wrong an act may be considered objectively in terms of its consequences for the well-being of the person involved or for the well-being of others, an act is not wrong in the sense that it may properly elicit blame unless blame will serve a useful purpose. Similarly, we do not proportion the praise that a man receives simply to the moral value of his behavior as judged by its consequences. Let us say that two men have performed acts of kindness of equal objective value but that whereas the first of these men is known to have previously performed few acts of kindness, the second is known to have performed many such acts. Surely it is the first who will receive the warmest accolades. Here again the explanation is that we regard it as improper to distribute praise and blame without taking into account the effect it is likely to have upon the future conduct of the persons concerned, and it is clear that the probable effect of praise upon the first man's future conduct would be greater than upon that of the second man, whose generous dispositions are already deeply entrenched. Now, if so much is granted, what follows with respect to the contention that a man cannot be held morally responsible for his behavior unless it is free in the sense that it has not been determined by external circumstances? Clearly that contention will have to be rejected. The foregoing argument implies that to be morally responsible the individual's behavior must be subject to determination by moral suasion from other persons, *i.e.,* by external causal factors.

b. It is generally agreed that we cannot hold an individual morally responsible for his behavior unless we know the empirical circumstances of his behavior. Killing, for instance, is wrong when considered objectively in terms of its consequences. But before praising or blaming a man for a particular act of killing we must know the concrete circumstances. Was it in self-defense, for the sake of gain, in the line of duty, etc.? Now, what could be clearer than that in determining the circumstances of an individual's behavior we treat them as partial causes? Once again we see that causality by external circumstances, far from being a reason for withholding ascriptions of moral responsibility, is, in fact, a necessary condition of such ascriptions.

Freedom and Moral Responsibility

Nothing in the preceding section was intended to suggest that "freedom" and "moral selfhood" are empty terms. What I disputed was merely one, almost exclusively philosophical, use of these expressions—a use that I believe to be not only irrelevant to moral experience but also far removed from the meaning that these terms are usually given and by right ought to be given in actual moral discourse. As will be seen, the terms "freedom" and "moral responsibility" have two distinguishable popular uses. One of the popular uses of the term "freedom" is directly related to the use of the term "moral responsibility" when the latter is employed neutrally to signify legitimate liability to praise or blame. The other—and larger—use of the term "freedom" is less directly related to "moral responsibility" so defined; its proper correlate is the honorific use of the term "moral responsibility," as when we say that a man behaved in a thoroughly responsible way in the face of a very trying situation. In the present section, however, the term "moral responsibility" will be used in the neutral sense, as it has been up to this point, my first task being to analyze the meaning of the term "freedom" where freedom is said to be a necessary condition for ascriptions of praise or blame.

My contention is that freedom as a condition of moral responsibility implies with respect to any given act (a) that if an individual *chose* to perform it he could do so and (b) that deliberation could be causally efficacious in causing the individual to choose or not to choose to perform it. The import of (a) and (b) can best be seen by considering what each excludes from the sphere of free behavior. By (a) we see that an individual's freedom is restricted by physical disability and by psychological compulsion. A cripple is obviously not free to walk. Nor is the hopeless alcoholic free to quit drinking, though typically he is free to choose or resolve to do so at frequent intervals. By (b) we see that an individual's freedom is restricted by personality traits so deeply rooted that he cannot seriously consider acting in a manner that runs counter to them. An example would be the man whose sense of duty or spirit of benevolence is so strong that no amount of reflection with regard to the advantages to be gained by betraying a friend or the hardships to be undergone as a consequence of remaining loyal could possibly have any bearing upon his choices. Another example would be the individual who is so thoroughly selfish that no considerations that might be brought to his attention would induce him to remain loyal to his associates if by acting otherwise he could reasonably expect private advantage.

It should be carefully noted that condition (b) is wholly distinct from condition (a). This is a point that can be easily overlooked, condition (b) often being assimilated to condition (a). The person whose freedom is restricted by condition (a) is someone who can choose to behave differently than he in fact does but who cannot execute his choice. The person whose freedom is restricted by condition (b), on the other hand, is someone who could execute a choice but who cannot make that choice. The difference between the two cases is that the man who suffers from a physical disability or who acts compulsively can be made to see and frequently does see that his actual behavior is undesirable; whereas the man who cannot be moved to choose otherwise than he does as a result of deliberation cannot be so moved precisely because it is impossible for him, given his character, actually to believe that behavior of a different kind would be desirable. For him there is no live option; he has no genuine alternatives. He can, of course, envisage the consequences of a different pattern of conduct, but that alternative pattern of conduct either makes no appeal to his affective nature or else arouses strong negative reactions.

Although (a) and (b) are both necessary conditions of moral responsibility, they do not even jointly constitute a sufficient condition. To be legitimately liable to praise or blame the act in question must also be determinable as right or wrong. This third condition of moral responsibility does not, however, play any role in our use of the term "freedom." When we say that freedom is a necessary condition of moral responsibility all that we normally mean, and all that we ought to mean, is that conditions (a) and (b) have both been met. If an individual has genuine alternatives between which deliberation might decide and if a choice made after deliberation could be executed, the individual is free in the requisite sense. And this is the case even though the individual's decision to deliberate, as well as the outcome of the deliberation, is wholly determined by his past experience and external circumstances. We do, of course, often and rightly withhold praise or blame when an individual's choice is known to be determined. But this is not *because* the choice was determined; it is because the determining factors are too powerful to be counteracted by moral sanctions. If, for instance, the conditions of a man's life have led him to choose a criminal career and also to respond with bitterness and hatred to moral censure, we would do well to withhold blame—not, however, because his choice was determined but because he has been determined to react negatively to blame. Besides, what difference can it make to us that a man's choices are wholly determined if our actions and his deliberations both figure among the possible determining factors? We do not live for the past; we live for the future. And to bend the future to our will we must rely upon causal laws.

It might be objected that if a man's behavior is wholly determined by his past experience and external circumstances, then he could not be free since freedom implies that he is the author of his behavior. But this objection cannot be allowed. If an individual's choices are among the causal antecedents of his behavior, then he *is* the author of that behavior. If B is the cause of C, B remains the cause of C even though A is the cause of B. If a man is led to deliberate and to act differently than he would otherwise have done because of our intervention, his behavior must none the less be credited to him. Similarly, if because of favorable childhood experiences a man is extraordinarily benevolent, it is none the less he who is benevolent. The real threat to the moral dignity of the individual is not determinism, but determination by factors that develop weak or morally deficient personalities instead of strong and morally wholesome ones.

Some libertarians will also object because in my definition of freedom I have omitted any reference to the will. In considering the question of the will, let us picture a man who, though not a confirmed alcoholic, is in danger of becoming one. This man is aware that his drinking causes hardship to his family and embarrassment to his friends, and these are facts to which he is not indifferent. He also suffers from a loss of self-esteem and is disturbed by the adverse judgments of others. However, he finds it difficult to get through a normal workday of difficult business conferences without a substantial number of drinks. He dreads going home to a nagging wife and querulous children. He enjoys the warm camaraderie of old friends from college days who regularly get together for drinks at the end of the day. And spending big sums in public places helps satisfy his ego drives. This man is thus torn between the specifically moral motives of benevolence, duty, and desire for moral approval that incline him to abandon drinking and a set of motives without special moral relevance that dispose him to continue. Now, according to most libertarians a favorable outcome of this struggle will depend largely upon the strength of the man's will. According to my view a favorable resolution will depend largely upon rational discipline, especially the accuracy and concreteness with which the individual analyzes the motives at work and represents to himself the consequences of the possible courses of conduct open to him.

As already stated, I reject the notion of will because I am unaware of any evidence for the existence of anything corresponding to it. I also reject the concept because no one to my knowledge has ever offered a satisfactory criterion by which it can be decided whether a man who succumbs to temptation has done so through weakness of will or as a result of the strength of the temptation. Moreover, it is very difficult to see how anyone *could* provide a satisfactory criterion. I ask the reader to imagine that the man in the example given becomes a hopeless alcoholic. How would you even go about deciding whether he was overcome by psychological forces and external circumstances beyond his control or whether he was simply weak-willed? I do not, of course, claim that it would always be easy to determine whether such a man fell prey to the compulsion of drink because of a failure properly to deliberate, but certainly this is a far less forbidding task. And certainly there is more reason to hope that moral suasion would lead the man to an accurate appraisal of his situation and consequently to a desirable resolution of his problem than to hope that moral suasion would produce a movement of this dubious entity called the will. That deliberation could bring into play what we have called the moral motives and cause these motives to prevail over others can be easily understood; for motives usually operate only when we believe that the circumstances are appropriate, and it is by deliberation that we decide what the circumstances are. How the will could bring the moral motives into play is for me a mystery.

It might be countered that I have misrepresented the libertarian position and falsely located the problem. The libertarian view, it might be said, is not so irrationalist as suggested, for libertarians do recognize that reason must decide how the individual ought to behave. And the problem is not to determine how the will brings moral motives into play, but how the will implements rational choice. Assume, for instance, that the man in our example has decided that the right thing to do is to quit drinking. Suppose further that, though he has decided to quit drinking, the empirical moral motives—the sense of duty, benevolence, and the desire for approval—are still weaker than the nonmoral motives. How is he to execute his decision? It is to explain that men do frequently execute decisions under circumstances like these, so the objection continues, that the notion of the will was invoked. I will not quarrel with this interpretation of libertarianism; some libertarians do hold this position. But I will quarrel with the contention that a rational decision about right behavior ever does cause us to act unless it enlists the support of empirical motives.

To say, for instance, that the incipient alcoholic has decided that the right thing for him to do is to quit drinking could only mean that he has come to believe one or some combination of four things: (a) that it is in his best interests to quit, (b) that to quit is to act in accordance with a moral rule, (c) that to quit is beneficial to others, or (d) that not quitting will lead to moral disapproval. If (a) is the basis of the decision then there is no problem as to how it is translated into action. If (b) is the basis of the decision, it will be effective only if the individual has actually committed himself to the rule and would suffer loss of self-esteem by not observing it. If (c) is the basis of the decision, it will be translated into action only to the extent that the individual actually cares about the welfare of others. If, finally, (d) is the basis, the decision will result in action only to the extent that the individual in fact fears moral disapproval.

Of course, the generalizations about human motivation that I have just offered cannot be proved in any strict sense. Nor can I in any strict sense of the term prove that the person who claims to introspect an entity properly called will, which sometimes tips the scales in favor of right and reason, is wrong. I can only say that for myself I have never been able to introspect in any instance of moral struggle elements other than those indicated here, nor have I felt the need to introduce additional elements to account for the moral behavior of others.

There is still another objection to my position that I feel called upon to answer, and once again I find it advisable to state that objection with reference to a concrete example. Suppose that a man were required to betray another person or else submit to torture and possible death. Now, consistently with the position I have just outlined this man would not be subject to praise for submitting to torture and possible death if one of his moral motives, such as the sense of duty, were so strongly developed that the other possibility was not for him a genuine alternative. Similarly, a man would not be subject to blame for betraying his friend under these circumstances if his moral motives were so weakly developed that self-love would necessarily prevail. Moreover, if moral motives inclining him to abstain were genuinely competitive with other motives inclining him to betray, then consistent with the thesis maintained in Chapter I the individual probably ought in deliberating to give full weight to all motives concerned and finally to act after having decided what constitutes his own best long-range interests. The pertinent point in this third case is that in deliberating men can, and no doubt some men do, dwell more or less exclusively upon motives inclining them to act according to their ideas of moral right, shutting out of mind considerations that tend to bring other motives into play. According to the view maintained in this book, however, to do so would be not only irrational but in all likelihood morally wrong. Can anyone, so the objection goes, seriously maintain such utterly paradoxical theses?

Now, it will not be gainsaid that my position with respect to these three cases has an air of paradox. Intellectually, we are all natural conservatives; old and familiar views die hard. None the less, however paradoxical these views may seem, we cannot logically reject them without embracing views that are even more paradoxical.

Consider the first case. A man has submitted to torture and possible death rather than betray another person. By hypothesis his motive was a strongly developed sense of duty—a sense of duty so strongly developed that no matter how long or how concretely he fixed in mind the advantages of acting differently he would not be able to do so. Why is he not legitimately to be praised? Because, I answer, he was not free to act otherwise than he did; because as he himself would be the first to tell us he had no choice in the matter; and because praise for this act would be as little likely to affect his behavior in similar future situations as blame would be likely to cure the confirmed dope addict. One could not consistently maintain that this man ought to be praised without at the same time denying that freedom is a necessary condition of moral responsibility and affirming that moral approval ought to be expressed even though it cannot serve a useful purpose.

The air of paradox in the position I have adopted will be further dispelled if we bear in mind the following points: (1) Although this man cannot be legitimately praised, he can be admired. For the same reasons that admiration rather than praise is appropriate with respect to physical beauty or native intelligence, so admiration rather than praise is appropriate with respect to established moral traits that have become second nature. (2) Although praise is something that almost all men covet, praise from one's moral inferiors is a matter of relative indifference and under many circumstances may properly be regarded as presumptuous. To praise another man implies that one is, if not his moral superior, at least his moral equal. And how many of us are the moral equal of our hypothetical hero? (3) There is something highly artificial about this hypothetical case. To simplify the argument I assumed that the sole motive operating in favor of the hero's actual behavior was a sense of duty and that it was so strongly developed that of itself it guaranteed a desirable outcome. In fact, however, it is almost always the case, even where we are witness to the most exalted moral fervor, that many motives are at work and that few of them are so strong that they could not conceivably be reinforced by praise. My criterion for deciding when praise is due will not, therefore, exclude many cases in which a man has acted nobly.

Consider the second case. A man has betrayed another rather than submit to torture and possible death himself. By hypothesis his motives were selfish, the moral motives being too weak effectively to compete even though they all are given due consideration. Why is this man not to be legitimately blamed?

Again, the answer is: because he was not free to act differently than he did; because, though not compelled to act as he did, he was none the less constrained to choose as he did; and because blame would be useless. It might be objected here that blame would not be useless. The moral motives include not only the sense of duty and the spirit of benevolence but also the fear of social disapprobation, and by blaming the man we might actually influence the balance of factors determining his behavior. But this objection rests upon the false assumption that we blame people for their behavior before they have acted. It is true that before acting the man will if he chooses rationally make a fair estimate of the amount of disapprobation he is likely to encounter as a result of his behavior. But the crucial factor here is not the disapprobation that actually follows; the crucial factor is his *estimate* of the disapprobation that is likely to ensue, and this estimate can only be based upon generalizations from past experience.

I would be quite willing to rest my argument on the points just made; but, as before, I shall adduce a few considerations that may help to overcome resistance. (1) Although we are not entitled to blame this man, we are entitled to feel offended by the baseness of his character. Physical ugliness offends the eye, and the man who is not offended by it no doubt lacks aesthetic sensibility. Similarly, moral ugliness offends persons of moral character. But to blame a man for moral ugliness that cannot be corrected by blame is as useless and cruel as to blame a man who has had the misfortune of being born with three eyes and two noses. (2) To blame a man generally implies that the most effective cause of his behavior lies within him and that the most effective remedy is effort on his part; but in cases of the kind illustrated by this example these implications are false, and by blaming the agent we simply divert attention from the true cause and true remedy. The true cause in the illustrative example is this man's living in a society where individuals have not been given adequate moral training and where they can be terrorized into performing base acts. The true remedy is social action. An analogy may make this clearer. Someone, noting comparative statistics on homicide, illegitimacy, venereal disease, absenteeism from work, desertions from military forces, etc., may issue a moral condemnation of the Negro race. To do so is clearly to give a false impression about the effective causes of the moral weaknesses to which these statistics point and to discourage efforts to eliminate discrimination. (3) Finally, as noted above, the motives of our behavior are usually far more complex than in the hypothetical cases we are considering; and since among them there are almost always some that might be favorably altered by moral censure the person with an incurable itch to blame his fellow men for wrong-doing will not be so sorely frustrated if he adopts my criterion for the distribution of blame as he might at first sight suppose.

Consider now the third case, that of the man who has a genuine choice between the two possible lines of conduct, who can by guiding the course of deliberation and dwelling more or less exclusively upon the advantages of acting in accord with the established moral rules persuade himself to choose "rightly" but whose best interests when all relevant factors are considered require that he act "wrongly." My thesis is that this man ought not to be blamed for acting "wrongly." The probability is that it would be socially desirable if he were to be guided by rational appraisal of his best interests even though his best interests required him to violate established moral rule and even though he was free to follow them. Now, it is not my intention to repeat the whole of Chapter I, the principal object of which was to defend this very thesis. It will, however, be worthwhile briefly to restate and in some respects to elaborate upon the arguments of that chapter with the example that presently concerns us in mind.

1. A reasonably well-ordered moral society is one in which care has been taken to instill in its members a spirit of benevolence and a sense of duty and in which there prevails a system of rewards and punishments, including moral as well as economic and penal sanctions, such that most individuals will find it in their best interests to observe the established moral rules in most cases. This is in fact the kind of society we live in, and in a society of this kind the consistent practice of rationality as we defined it in Chapter IV will have a generally beneficial effect, since wrongdoing defined in terms of violation of conventional moral rules will normally be due to ignorance of true self-interest. The question then is whether we ought to encourage others to desist from the practice of rationality in those special cases where they have good reason to believe that it will dispose them to violate established moral rules. My answer is that we ought not to do so. And the first of my three reasons is that rationality consists of a set of habitual dispositions that must be strengthened through practice and that will be weakened to the extent that they are violated. My point here is similar to one that could no doubt be used against me. I am in effect saying that a general rule of conduct that has proved its worth ought to be observed even in cases where it does not have its normal consequences, since by authorizing exceptions we tend to bring the rule into disrepute and to weaken a valuable habitual disposition. This line of reasoning has been used by moral philosophers for approximately twenty-five centuries in support of consistent observance of such moral rules as truth-telling and promise-keeping—rules of conduct that I insist the individual be permitted to violate without censure in those special cases where he has rationally determined that they are contrary to his true over-all interests. Note, however, that if my reasoning is correct, the rational pursuit of self-interest is a higher-order rule than rules of truth-telling, promise-keeping, etc., in the sense that the rule applies to a wider range of conduct and that action based upon it has on the whole more advantageous consequences. Also bear in mind the generally established principle that where a higher-order rule conflicts with lower-order rules, the higher-order rule ought to prevail.

Fortunately for society, persons with a strongly developed sense of duty or spirit of benevolence will rarely find themselves in situations where the higher-order rule dictating rational pursuit of self-interest conflicts with lower-order rules. The person with a strong sense of duty has chosen to realize his personal well-being by consistent adherence to lower-order rules and will suffer in self-esteem if he violates them. Violations are not, therefore, likely to be in his own interests. Similarly, since the person with a strong spirit of benevolence will be personally distressed by the thought of possible suffering to others attending violation of lower-order rules, self-interest itself will usually require that he observe them. Conflicts of the kind that we are discussing arise most frequently only when the sense of duty or spirit of benevolence is absent or very poorly developed, and in these cases the only effective instrument of social control is the use of sanctions appealing to the individual's self-love. If, however, we fail consistently to encourage rational pursuit of self-interest, the effectiveness of this one remaining instrument of social control will be impaired.

2. As pointed out in Chapter I and again in discussing the case of the man who was not free not to betray, to blame someone for his behavior is to imply that he is chiefly responsible for it and that the most effective remedy is largely within his personal power. Where, however, a man finds it in his interests to betray another, I do not believe that he is chiefly responsible or that corrective action on his part is very likely to be of avail. The chief culprit would be society and the most effective means of preventing further violations would be concerted social action. To blame individuals in cases of this kind is to perpetuate that sharp distinction between personal morality and social policy and to encourage that baseless optimism with respect to the value of mere moralizing that have been the bane of the Christian era in Western civilization.

3. By blaming a man for acting contrary to his best interests we shall either embitter him if he believes that blame is unjustified or else implant a disrespect for rationality and an unwholesome sense of guilt if he believes that it is justified. In either case we have deprived ourselves of whatever help the individual might otherwise have been able to offer in creating a better and happier society. That blame will embitter an offender of the established code if he believes it unjustified will probably not be disputed. My reasons for fearing disrespect for rationality if the individual is made to believe in the legitimacy of blame in these circumstances were presented in Chapter I and will not be repeated. It will, however, probably be asked why the sense of guilt over acting contrary to one's best interests is unwholesome. I reply that the sense of guilt is unwholesome unless its ultimate effect is to strengthen or enrich the individual's personality, thereby giving him cause for legitimate pride in the future, and that feelings of guilt under the circumstances described cannot be expected to have this effect. It is true that feelings of guilt under these circumstances could lead the individual to act in the future so as to win greater respect from others and that the sense of self-worth in fact often depends upon the respect of others. But legitimate pride, the warranted sense of our own worth, does not depend upon the attitudes of others. No thoroughly self-respecting, autonomous moral agent will feel guilty simply because others disapprove of him, however unhappy or displeased he may be over their disapprobation. A genuine sense of worth derives exclusively from the individual's personal conviction that he has acted rightly and from the active exercise of his native capacities with the feeling of self-expansion and power that accompanies it.

These last observations bring me to the problem of the moral self and freedom in that larger sense of which I spoke at the beginning of this section.

Freedom and Moral Selfhood

When we say that an individual is not morally responsible for his behavior unless *he* is the author of that behavior, what do we mean by the word "he"?

It is clear that we do not mean the physical self, and upon reflection it becomes equally clear that we do not mean the totality of the psychological self. An individual who is motivated by instinct is not to that extent the moral author of his behavior, nor is the man who acts from habit, desire, or impulse. Instincts, habits, desires, and impulses are no doubt properties of individuals, parts of their psychological make-up that must be included in any adequate description of their several selves. But the moral self, the self as an agent, as a causal factor in the genesis of behavior that may properly be called free, cannot be equated with the whole of the psychological self. This is not only because the moral self exercises a certain power over many of these motivational factors but also because the moral self is a higher self, a source of dignity and worth that cannot be ascribed to these other elements in our make-up. This does not mean, however, that the moral self must be regarded as a nothingness or as a transcendent, noumenal reality. The inadequacy of these conceptions has already been shown. What it means is that the moral self will have to be regarded as a limited aspect of the total psychological self. What aspect?

It would be tempting to answer that the moral self is identical with the moral motives, especially the spirit of benevolence and the sense of duty. I have myself suggested that an individual does not have great moral stature unless these motives are highly developed. Yet this answer will not do. If the moral self were defined in this way, then we could not appeal to the higher selves of persons in whom these motives remain undeveloped or regard these persons as moral agents—which in fact we do. Furthermore the moral motives themselves require guidance and direction by a moral agent. The moral self, the higher self, the self as agent can only be defined as the rational self: that ensemble of capacities, disciplines, and habitual dispositions that permits us to arbitrate among competing desires or other empirical motives and to achieve our chosen goals. We are morally responsible agents only to the extent that deliberation or forethought is capable of influencing choice and that choices once made can be successfully implemented.

But here a distinction is in order. The possession of rational capacities marks man as superior to the beasts, and it is to this that his existence as a free and morally responsible moral agent must be attributed. But there is a difference between the man who rightly exercises those capacities and the man who does not. Although in one sense of these terms a man is free and morally responsible simply because he possesses these capacities and regardless of how he uses them, in another sense of these terms he is free and morally responsible only if he actually uses them and, moreover, uses them rightly. Hitler, for instance, was a moral agent; he was substantially free in that much of his behavior was or could have been a consequence of deliberation; and he was morally responsible in that for many of his actions he could not properly have claimed exemption from blame. But it is most unlikely that he was free and morally responsible in the sense of these terms I am about to explicate.

When in any ordinary nonmoral context a man says that he is free to do something, he does of course mean that if he chooses to do it, he will be able to do it. To the extent that a man cannot achieve a chosen goal, he is frustrated by external obstacles or in bondage to his ignorance of the means by which these obstacles may be overcome. He also means that he is free to choose, that deliberation or reflection might influence his decision, that there are for him genuine alternatives. We are obviously not free to follow a course of action that we can only envisage with an invincible and overpowering distaste. But he means more than these two things. He means that it lies within his power to reconcile or harmonize conflicting desires so as to take the sting out of choice; for to the extent that a man cannot reconcile or harmonize his desires—as opposed to merely being able to choose between them—he is burdened with a nasty problem of choice, and whatever choice he finally makes will be more or less unsatisfactory.

"I am free to go to Europe," for instance, means that if I apply for a passport, ask for a vacation from work, attempt to purchase a ticket, etc., the passport will be granted, my employer will give me the necessary vacation time, the travel bureau will give me a reservation, etc. If I cannot persuade the State Department to give me a passport or my employer to give me a vacation, if it is a busy tourist season and I cannot book passage, etc., then I am not free to go to Europe. "I am free to go to Europe" also means that I can conceive of not going and that deliberation might have a bearing upon my choice. But, in addition, it means that I have found a way of harmonizing the desire to go to Europe with the main body of my other desires and that the satisfaction of this desire does not involve agonizing and painful sacrifices.

In this larger sense of the term no one, of course, is ever fully free. Few of us make major choices that do not involve painful sacrifice; and in ordinary discourse we accommodate ourselves to this fact of life, saying simply in a given situation that we are free, although strictly speaking we are only partially free. None the less it is evident that freedom as an ideal toward which we strive involves a measure of ease and psychological comfort, as well as the ability to choose and to act as we choose. And it is no less evident that the exercise of rationality is the principal condition of whatever measure of freedom we actually possess. This is not only because the rational man is better equipped than the nonrational man to make the best possible choice in any given situation and to overcome external obstacles but also because the rational man is better equipped satisfactorily to resolve internal conflicts and to harmonize competing desires. I repeat, however, that no man is wholly free and that the individual practice of rationality cannot guarantee even a relatively high measure of freedom. There are adverse environmental circumstances that would defeat even the most rational of us, and there are persons suffering from inner conflicts caused by early experiences that the most persistent rational effort will fail fully to resolve. Individual rational discipline will be an adequate guarantee of individual freedom only if and when society at large becomes a community of rational men.

Let us now inquire into the honorific meaning of moral responsibility. In praising a man for being morally responsible we do not necessarily imply that his behavior conforms to the accepted moral rules. There are, after all, morally responsible persons who not only violate some of the accepted moral rules but who do so from a sense of duty. Neither do we mean merely that the man has a strongly developed sense of duty or spirit of benevolence. The man who does not possess these traits may be morally responsible within certain limits, and even the man who possesses them must, if he is to be fully responsible, guide and direct them. To praise a man for his moral responsibility is fundamentally to declare that he is guided by reason, that he is a true agent who acts only after proper reflection and who can be trusted to act according to rational choice. The difference between moral responsibility in the restricted sense implying merely liability to praise or blame and moral responsibility in the larger and honorific sense lies wholly in the fact that the latter entails more than the former, *viz.*, *rational* deliberation as opposed to simple capacity for deliberation. To be subject to moral sanctions it suffices that one be capable of deliberation, but a fully responsible moral agent must actually exercise that capability and exercise it rightly. The parallel between freedom in the large sense of the term and moral responsibility in the honorific sense is in this respect complete.

The upshot of the argument in this section is, then, that where freedom is regarded as the ultimate idea of human striving and where moral responsibility is regarded as a singular token of high human achievement, the exercise of rationality is a condition of both. Whereas, however, freedom is the reward of rationality, moral responsibility is its price. The practice of rationality gives us power, and power is often a burden as well as a privilege. No one is so likely to be subject to moral censure by the voice of his conscience as the rational man, for no one is so conscious of the consequences of his acts, for evil as for good. And no one is so likely to be subjected to moral censure by his fellow man, for no one is more inclined to be impatient with popular prejudice and intellectual sloth. Should he withdraw into himself, he is the prey of his conscience; should he disturb the quiet sleep of his fellows, he must fight their resentment. The rational man lives not by a code that society has bequeathed him, but by a code which he has forged in the heat of intense personal experience. He knows the exacting demands of reflection, the torment of not being able always to justify his behavior, the pain of having to let go of comfortable prejudices, the suspicion of many natural impulses, the sometimes desperate need to articulate, and the stubborn, often willful, incomprehension of others. But he does not lead a dull and colorless life of quiet desperation; he does not trade dignity for security; and when he collapses, if he does, it is not through personal weakness. Like Socrates, Spinoza, Marx, and Freud, he knows the joys of creativity, and, feeling the weight of his own self, he cannot be indifferent to the potentialities of other human personalities. He will not, therefore, cynically exploit other persons' weaknesses nor sentimentally minister to their prejudices. He abhors all that cheapens human contacts, reducing human beings to tools for the satisfaction of one another's sordid needs for security, social privilege, professional advancement, or mere escape from neurotic loneliness. And if he is contemptuous of others, his contempt springs less from a sense of personal superiority than from the exhilarating awareness of what it would be like were human relationships based upon the sense of personal dignity and inner strength that can only be purchased through the exercise of reason.

There are, of course, especially in this age of maudlin sentimentality and irresponsible flight from freedom, those who would rather be pitied than blamed and who would rather that their adult behavior be determined by early toilet training or external authorities than by mature, individual reflection. It must, however, be borne in mind that if moral responsibility is the fate of the strong, contempt is the fate of the weak. And it must also be borne in mind that the man who trades his dignity and individuality for security, eschewing the labor of rationality, more often than not strikes a bad bargain; the security that he purchases so dearly is a false security.

To be sure, selfhood is a difficult achievement, and, to be sure, a world without compassion and sympathy, a world in which the individual finds no support or guidance from the community, would be intolerable. But very often pity is an affront to human dignity, as many young social workers afire with the idea that *tout comprendre c'est tout pardonner* have soon discovered. Frequently blame is not only more appropriate but more welcome. And, as many a conformist has discovered to his chagrin, exclusive reliance upon the community has as its consequence, not the sense of solid well-being he had hoped to find, but merely an obliteration of his sense of personal identity. Spinoza once remarked that there are men who, having renounced their role as rational moral agents, are merely acted upon and that when they cease to be acted upon they cease to be. This remark is not strictly correct. These men cease to be, not when they cease to be acted upon, but from the moment they cease to act. For it is the distinguishing mark of a person as opposed to a beast that his very being lies in the exercise of his rational powers. The person as moral agent cannot be less than an autonomous rational being.

Self, Substance, and Identity

FOOL: What is it which everything that ever was, is, or will be has, yet which nothing that ever was, is, or will be has in common with anything else?

KING: I know thee for a fool for certain, if thou knowest not the answer to that riddle.

FOOL: Nay, but I know it.

KING: If thou knowest it, why do you ask me?

FOOL: But to see if Kings may be Fools!

KING: Well, then, since that would be 'gainst all sense, 'tis necessary that you answer it.

FOOL: (Aside—The King may be no fool, but I'll wager he would be a Fool.) Self-identity.

KING: That was, is, and will be the obvious answer, for if it were not, then Kings would be Fools and Fools Kings, and I would have your head, Fool, before allowing this kingdom to be blast against all Nature. I would have self-identity to be a monarchical principle.

FOOL: I yield, Sire; I know thee for my King, for thou art the King of Fools.

The fool and the king have said they are self-identical. Let us take it that each thing is identical with itself. And now we may ask, as so many before have asked: "What is it about myself that is self-identical?"

Before we consider this metaphysical question about the self, it will be instructive to lay some groundwork by considering some metaphysical questions about things in general.

1. *Individuation.* Is there more than one thing in the universe? It seems obvious that there is, for if we get past the number "one" in counting things, there must be more than one thing. A student sits at his desk with a piece of paper in front of him. He hears a song coming from his radio as he inhales the smoke from his cigar and tastes the flavor. If we consider the paper, the song, and the flavor of the cigar, there are at least three things, three individuals. Individuation is the process of dividing the world into a number of things.

Counting is the process of putting individuals and numerals in a one-to-one relationship. Each individual is to be assigned one and only one numeral. The piece of paper is assigned the numeral "one," the song "two," the cigar flavor "three," and so forth. Counting depends on individuating. Then what is the criterion for individuating, for deciding that something is an individual and may be assigned a numeral? Why is it that when one looks at the piece of paper he decides it is a separate thing, not, for example, merged with the song? Because a piece of paper is one kind of thing and a song is another; they are different kinds. Difference is the basis for individuating. And what about counting things of the same kind, for example, two pieces of paper? A person counts two things because there is difference; perhaps they have different colors or perhaps different relations, one being to the left of the typewriter and the other to the right.

2. *Unity.* When one looks at the piece of paper or listens to the song, he assigns the piece of paper one number, not, for example, two. The same for the song. They are one although they are many; the paper has many areas, the song has many notes. How does one decide that there is a single piece of paper and a single song? There is one piece of paper because it is all of one piece. If he cuts it, there are two pieces; lifting one of them does not lift the other. Physical connections of the fibers hold the many areas together and make them one thing. However, this will not do as a way of explaining the unity of a song. The song has an early part and a late part. Why does a person count the song as one thing rather than as two things? Not because they are connected by fibers. Think of a class of schoolchildren. Why should a person count the class of children as one thing, even though there are many children?

In counting the contents of the universe we must be able to see individuals as one thing, and we have seen that different kinds of things have different principles of unity. The unity of pieces of paper is achieved by different means than the unity of songs; musical notes are not held together by fibers.

3. *Identity.* Suppose that at one time a person counts N number of things in the universe and at another time counts M number of things. How many of the Ms were Ns? Generally we recognize individuals as being numerically the same at one time as at another time. Hence, we say they maintain their identity through time, even though many of the individuals have changed. The student has now typed on that piece of paper; this time the song is played with a piano instead of a guitar.

What criteria do we use to decide that the piece of paper with the writing on it is identical with the piece of paper that did not have writing on it? We said before that we use differences to individuate and to count things as distinct individuals. Now there is a difference between the paper at one time and at a later time; by the criterion of difference, they should be counted as numerically distinct rather than as numerically identical. Clearly, in order to say things keep their identity through time, we shall have to say that some changes do not alter identity.

Which changes do not alter identity? Suppose the student burns the paper so that it changes into ash. Are the paper and the ash to be counted as one identical thing despite having such radically different properties? One cannot burn songs, although he can burn printed notations of songs; so a song's principle of identity through time must be considered independently from that of a piece of paper. Suppose that we use exactly the same notes that are in the song and rearrange them? Do we have the identical song, or should we say that now there are two songs rather than one?

4. *Creation and destruction.* Some changes are so drastic that we say a thing cannot hold its identity. For most people, burning the piece of paper would be such a change; they would say the piece of paper was destroyed. It is out of existence; it is not something we count anymore.

Some changes are so drastic that we say something exists that we never counted before. Thus, we may say that rearranging the notes of a song creates a new song. It has come into existence.

Now we are ready to consider the self in terms of these concepts—individuation, unity, identity, creation, and destruction.

If you do not yet feel the need for a metaphysical investigation of the concept of self, perhaps you are blissfully unaware that many writers have made it the prime victim of our modern, perilous social conditions. They have said we are empty, dehumanized, depersonalized, full of dread, anxious, and full of despair. This news is bound to reach you sooner or later, so we hope to prepare you for the worst!

Our first essay is by **René Descartes,** because he made the topic of self of prime importance in Western philosophy and cultural consciousness. Notice the elaborate, earnest, deeply felt doubts about all he had learned at the university. Adrift on a sea of doubt, the one anchorage he finds is in the self; the one thing he cannot doubt is that he exists. He makes a key remark about the self: "But I do not yet know clearly enough what I am, I who am certain that I am." From this statement, Descartes can be interpreted as an existentialist, emphasizing the primacy of the self's existence over the self's whatness or nature. Descartes' first knowledge is that he knows he exists (which is why he might be interpreted as an existentialist); his second knowledge will be of what he is, of his essence.

Another reason Descartes is of special interest to us is because he stood within two overlapping phases of thought. One phase we shall call "theological" and the other "humanistic." The theological phase relates to the concept of the self because it introduces special difficulties about counting. How many human selves are there in the universe? How do we individuate selves? According to Christian theology, a person is a dual entity consisting of a body and a soul. In counting human selves, which are we to count? The body or the soul?

In counting human selves, we probably count people; and the way we count people, as in a crowd at a rally, is to count the number of human bodies present. In short, we use the body as a principle for individuating selves. If we do, in fact, individuate by bodies, we are not very good Christians —for a Christian, it is the soul that is the important member of the pair. One reason that it is important is, of course, that Christian doctrine claims man to be immortal. However, the body is obviously destructible; it loses its continuity and hence its identity through time. So, the immortal person cannot be identified with his body; he must be identified with something that is not destructible, which, for a dualist, must be the soul, because that is the only candidate for immortality he has left after denying that a person is the body.

Descartes was a devout Christian, or so he professed, and stood in the theological phase because he maintained the dual-substance view of man, one of man's parts being the immortal soul. But Descartes also stands in the humanistic phase because he honestly faced the metaphysical questions about the soul self. Suppose that the self's existence is assured. What is the self? What is its nature, its essence? The kind of thing it is, as we saw earlier, will have important bearings on the criteria for individuation, unity, identity, creation, and destruction. If the self is a soul, and the soul is not a body—not "a wind, a flame, or an ether," as Descartes imagined in unreflective moments —then we cannot use physical criteria to individuate or identify souls. How do we count souls? We cannot answer that question until we know what kind of a thing the soul is, until we discover the nature of souls.

Descartes took a modern turn toward the humanistic phase by the way he characterized the soul. Although he did say that the soul was a mental substance, he gave it empirical content by saying that he was a "thing which thinks. What is a thing which thinks? It is a thing which doubts, understands, conceives, affirms, denies, wills, refuses, which also imagines and feels."

This brings us to a crucial point in trying to understand the metaphysics of the self. Notice that Descartes says the soul is a "thing." It is a thing that does something. It is a "thing which thinks." He does not say the soul *is* (identical to) thinking. Obviously, the soul is conceived by Descartes as an object, analogous to a ball, for example. The ball is not just rolling, any more than the soul is just thinking. There is a *soul* thinking, as there is a *ball* rolling. The concept of an object is deeply rooted in our commonsense thinking. Descartes is moving in the groove here. Commonsensical or not, we can raise an interesting question that suggests a criticism of Descartes' position. Can we have any knowledge of the nature of this soul thing or substance apart from our understanding of its doings (its thinking, doubting, denying, imagining, and so forth)? A positive answer to this question will not be satisfactory if it does not enable us to say how we individuate souls or account for their unity, their identity through time, or their creation and destruction or their immortality.

The author of the second essay in this section, **David Hume,** gave a negative answer to this question and effectively erased the theological phase. He took Descartes' humanistic phase seriously. He tried to make direct acquaintance with the self as a thing by introspecting. However, what he found was not anything he could label a "self thing" or "soul thing"; all he found were thoughts, doubts, and so on. "For my part, when I enter most intimately into what I call *myself,* I always stumble on some particular perception or other, of heat or cold, light or shadow, love or hatred, pain or pleasure. I never can catch *myself* at any time without a perception, and never can observe anything but the perception." Hume finds, then, no way to talk about the self's individuation or identity other than in terms of thinking, perceiving, feeling, and so forth. If there is a self, it is not something over and above experience itself; hence, it must be identical to each thought itself or must be constructed out of the series of thoughts. The first alternative would leave one with as many selves as there are thoughts; this is an extreme form of individuation that seems to vary too much from our usual individuation practice to be acceptable. The alternative is to specify ways of constructing a self from the series of thoughts. Individuation of selves, following this alternative, does not seem particularly difficult, because two series with different thoughts give a way of individuating each of the two series, hence of individuating each of the two selves constructed from the two series. To provide for the unity of the series, a way of relating the thoughts to each other must be found; of course, it cannot be done by relating each thought to *oneself* because one cannot assume a "oneself" that stands outside the series, the "oneself" being the series itself. As to how one can provide for the self's continuity or identity through time, we leave you to glean that from Hume's essay, the bulk of it directed at that question. Since a series may be finite (have a beginning and an end), the creation and destruction of selves is easily accounted for.

Descartes' and Hume's thoughts about the self ran toward the individualistic strain. From Descartes' discussion, it would appear that the self or soul's existence and nature are completely independent of other persons, social organization, and human exchange. Hume, too, conceives of the self as constructing itself out of a string of private experiences. When we come to **A. K. Bierman**'s essay, we see a shift toward a social rather than an individualistic point of view. For Bierman, the concept of persons is more basic than the concept of self; until we become persons, we do not become selves. To be a human self is to become a person; the process of creation of a self does not occur somewhere beyond our ken, suddenly yielding a product we call the self, then delivered to ourself with appropriate introductions, "Jack meet Jack," ourself surprised. It is a process in which we come gradually to participate. A body becomes a person by taking on relations to other things and other persons; these relations are established by learning behavior patterns similar to the behavior patterns of already existing persons; we do not blindly, unconsciously learn these patterns; rather, we learn them in consort with learning what others expect of us and what we expect of them, learning that each of us is conscious of the other's expectation, and that each of us becomes conscious of the consciousness of each other's expectations. Acquiring behavior patterns with the accompanying mutual and reciprocal consciousness of our knowledge of these patterns is the process of creating a self. The self does not come into being in quiet isolation.

Bierman suggests that in thinking about the self we think about persons, and that in thinking about persons we think about cognitive bodies in a social network. To become a self is to take consciously a place in that network. A metaphysics of the self that places an emphasis on the social nature of persons does, Bierman argues, make it possible to understand persons' mutual stake in fulfilling moral obligations better than an atomistic metaphysics of the self.

Keith E. Davis, working in the kind of metaphysical framework outlined by Bierman, provides some concrete remarks about how the establishment of a person's identity depends upon social, historical, and cultural relations. He shows how successful and thwarted identity efforts occur, each depending, respectively, on learning, and participating in, and affirming social practices and not learning, not participating in, and rejecting social practices. Of special importance is the shift in identity that occurs with different social commitments. Both Davis and Bierman draw the conclusion that a social conception of the self and one's identity leads one to appreciate that the goal of becoming another, better self cannot be accomplished by individual effort or will alone; social practices, too, must change.

The Self as Substance

RENÉ DESCARTES

René Descartes (1595–1658) was the first outstanding French philosopher and the father of modern philosophy. He was educated at the Jesuit college of La Fleche, where he first developed his interest in mathematics, and at the University of Poitiers, from which he received a law degree. Although he spent some time traveling and as a mercenary in a foreign army, he eventually returned to study and to do scientific research. His most important writings include *Discourse on the Method of Properly Guiding the Reason in the Search for Truth in the Sciences* (1637), *Meditations on First Philosophy in Which the Existence of God and the Distinction Between Mind and Body Are Demonstrated* (1641), *Principles of Philosophy* (1644), and *The Passions of the Soul* (1649).

Meditation I: Of the Things Which May Be Brought Within the Sphere of the Doubtful

It is now some years since I detected how many were the false beliefs that I had from my earliest youth admitted as true, and how doubtful was everything I had since constructed on this basis; and from that time I was convinced that I must once for all seriously undertake to rid myself of all the opinions which I had formerly accepted, and commence to build anew from the foundation, if I wanted to establish any firm and permanent structure in the sciences. But as this enterprise appeared to be a very great one, I waited until I had attained an age so mature that I could not hope that at any later date I should be better fitted to execute my design. This reason caused me to delay so long that I should feel that I was doing wrong were I to occupy in deliberation the time that yet remains to me for action. Today, then, since very opportunely for the plan I have in view I have delivered my mind from every care [and am happily agitated by no passions] and since I have procured for myself an assured leisure in a peaceable retirement, I shall at last seriously and freely address myself to the general upheaval of all my former opinions.

Now for this object it is not necessary that I should show that all of these are false—I shall perhaps never arrive at this end. But inasmuch as reason already persuades me that I ought no less carefully to withhold my assent from matters which are not entirely certain and indubitable than from those which appear to me manifestly to be false, if I am able to find in each one some reason to doubt, this will suffice to justify my rejecting the whole. And for that end it will not be requisite that I should examine each in particular, which would be an endless undertaking; for owing to the fact that the destruction of the foundations of necessity brings with it the downfall of the rest of the edifice, I shall only in the first place attack those principles upon which all my former opinions rested.

Source: The Philosophical Works of Descartes, trans. by E. S. Haldane and G. R. T. Ross (New York, 1911), pp. 69–80. Reprinted by permission of Cambridge University Press.

All that up to the present time I have accepted as most true and certain I have learned either from the senses or through the senses; but it is sometimes proved to me that these senses are deceptive, and it is wiser not to trust entirely to any thing by which we have once been deceived.

But it may be that although the senses sometimes deceive us concerning things which are hardly perceptible, or very far away, there are yet many others to be met with as to which we cannot reasonably have any doubt, although we recognise them by their means. For example, there is the fact that I am here, seated by the fire, attired in a dressing gown, having this paper in my hands and other similar matters. And how could I deny that these hands and this body are mine, were it not perhaps that I compare myself to certain persons, devoid of sense, whose cerebella are so troubled and clouded by the violent vapours of black bile, that they constantly assure us that they think they are kings when they are really quite poor, or that they are clothed in purple when they are really without covering, or who imagine that they have an earthenware head or are nothing but pumpkins or are made of glass. But they are mad, and I should not be any the less insane were I to follow examples so extravagant.

At the same time I must remember that I am a man, and that consequently I am in the habit of sleeping, and in my dreams representing to myself the same things or sometimes even less probable things, than do those who are insane in their waking moments. How often has it happened to me that in the night I dreamt that I found myself in this particular place, that I was dressed and seated near the fire, whilst in reality I was lying undressed in bed! At this moment it does indeed seem to me that it is with eyes awake that I am looking at this paper; that this head which I move is not asleep, that it is deliberately and of set purpose that I extend my hand and perceive it; what happens in sleep does not appear so clear nor so distinct as does all this. But in thinking over this I remind myself that on many occasions I have in sleep been deceived by similar illusions, and in dwelling carefully on this reflection I see so manifestly that there are no certain indications by which we may clearly distinguish wakefulness from sleep that I am lost in astonishment. And my astonishment is such that it is almost capable of persuading me that I now dream.

Now let us assume that we are asleep and that all these particulars, e.g. that we open our eyes, shake our head, extend our hands, and so on, are but false delusions; and let us reflect that possibly neither our hands nor our whole body are such as they appear to us to be. At the same time we must at least confess that the things which are represented to us in sleep are like painted representations which can only have been formed as the counterparts of something real and true, and that in this way those general things at least, i.e. eyes, a head, hands, and a whole body, are not imaginary things, but things really existent. For, as a matter of fact, painters, even when they study with the greatest skill to represent sirens and satyrs by forms the most strange and extraordinary, cannot give them natures which are entirely new, but merely make a certain medley of the members of different animals; or if their imagination is extravagant enough to invent something so novel that nothing similar has ever before been seen, and that their work represents a thing purely fictitious and absolutely false, it is certain all the same that the colours of which this is composed are necessarily real. And for the same reason, although these general things, to wit, [a body], eyes, a head, hands, and such like, may be imaginary, we are bound at the same time to confess that there are at least some other objects yet more simple and more universal, which are real and true; and of these just in the same way as with certain real colours, all these images of things which dwell in our thoughts, whether true and real or false and fantastic, are formed.

To such a class of things pertains corporeal nature in general, and its extension, the figure of extended things, their quantity or magnitude and number, as also the place in which they are, the time which measures their duration, and so on.

That is possibly why our reasoning is not unjust when we conclude from this that Physics, Astronomy, Medicine and all other sciences which have as their end the consideration of composite things, are very dubious and uncertain; but that Arithmetic, Geometry and other sciences of that kind which only treat of things that are very simple and very general, without taking great trouble to ascertain whether they are actually existent or not, contain some measure of certainty and an element of the indubitable. For whether I am awake or asleep, two and three together always form five, and the square can never have more than four sides, and it does not seem possible that truths so clear and apparent can be suspected of any falsity [or uncertainty].

Nevertheless I have long had fixed in my mind the belief that an all-powerful God existed by whom I have been created such as I am. But how do I know that He has not brought it to pass that there is no earth, no heaven, no extended body, no magnitude, no place, and that nevertheless [I possess the perceptions of all these things and that] they seem to me to exist just exactly as I now see them? And, besides, as I sometimes imagine that others deceive themselves in the things which they think they know best, how do I know that I am not deceived every time that I add two and three, or count the sides of a square, or judge of things yet simpler, if anything simpler can be imagined? But possibly God has not desired that I should be thus deceived, for He is said to be supremely good. If, however, it is contrary to His goodness to have made me such that I constantly deceive myself, it would also appear to be contrary to His goodness to permit me to be sometimes deceived, and nevertheless I cannot doubt that He does permit this.

There may indeed be those who would prefer to deny the existence of a God so powerful, rather than believe that all other things are uncertain. But let us not oppose them for the present, and grant that all there is here said of a God is a fable; nevertheless in whatever way they suppose that I have arrived at the state of being that I have reached—whether they attribute it to fate or to accident, or make out that it is by a continual succession of antecedents, or by some other method—since to err and deceive oneself is a defect, it is clear that the greater will be the probability of my being so imperfect as to deceive myself ever, as is the Author to whom they assign my origin the less powerful. To these reasons I have certainly nothing to reply, but at the end I feel constrained to confess that there is nothing in all that I formerly believed to be true, of which I cannot in some measure doubt, and that not merely through want of thought or through levity, but for reasons which are very powerful and maturely considered; so that henceforth I ought not the less carefully to refrain from giving credence to these opinions than to that which is manifestly false, if I desire to arrive at any certainty [in the sciences].

But it is not sufficient to have made these remarks, we must also be careful to keep them in mind. For these ancient and commonly held opinions still revert frequently to my mind, long and familiar custom having given them the right to occupy my mind against my inclination and rendered them almost masters of my belief; nor will I ever lose the habit of deferring to them or of placing my confidence in them, so long as I consider them as they really are, i.e. opinions in some measure doubtful, as I have just shown, and at the same time highly probable, so that there is much more reason to believe in than to deny them. That is why I consider that I shall not be acting amiss, if, taking of set purpose a contrary belief, I allow myself to be deceived, and for a certain time pretend that all these opinions are entirely false and imaginary, until at last, having thus balanced my former prejudices with my latter [so that they cannot divert my opinions more to one side than to the other], my judgment will no longer be dominated by bad usage or turned away from the right knowledge of the truth. For I am assured that there can be neither peril nor error in this course, and that I cannot at present yield too much to distrust, since I am not considering the question of action, but only of knowledge.

I shall then suppose, not that God who is supremely good and the fountain of truth, but some evil genius not less powerful than deceitful, has employed his whole energies in deceiving me; I shall consider that the heavens, the earth, colours, figures, sound, and all other external things are nought but the illusions and dreams of which this genius has availed himself in order to lay traps for my credulity; I shall consider myself as having no hands, no eyes, no flesh, no blood, nor any senses, yet falsely believing myself to possess all these things; I shall remain obstinately attached to this idea, and if by this means it is not in my power to arrive at the knowledge of any truth, I may at least do what is in my power [i.e. suspend my judgment], and with firm purpose avoid giving credence to any false thing, or being imposed upon by this arch deceiver, however powerful and deceptive he may be. But this task is a laborious one, and insensibly a certain lassitude leads me into the course of my ordinary life. And just as a captive who in sleep enjoys an imaginary liberty, when he begins to suspect that his liberty is but a dream, fears to awaken, and conspires with these agreeable illusions that the deception may be prolonged, so insensibly of my own accord I fall back into my former opinions, and I dread awakening from this slumber, lest the laborious wakefulness which would follow the tranquility of this repose should have to be spent not in daylight, but in the excessive darkness of the difficulties which have just been discussed.

Meditation II: Of the Nature of the Human Mind; And That It Is More Easily Known Than the Body

The Meditation of yesterday filled my mind with so many doubts that it is no longer in my power to forget them. And yet I do not see in what manner I can resolve them; and, just as if I had all of a sudden fallen into very deep water, I am so disconcerted that I can neither make certain of setting my feet on the bottom, nor can I swim and so support myself on the surface. I shall nevertheless make an effort and follow anew the same path as that on which I yesterday entered, i.e. I shall proceed by setting aside all that in which the least doubt could be supposed to exist, just as if I had discovered that it was absolutely false; and I shall ever follow in this road until I have met with something which is certain, or at least, if I can do nothing else, until I have learned for certain that there is nothing in the world that is certain. Archimedes, in order that he might draw the terrestrial globe out of its place, and transport it elsewhere, demanded only that one point should be fixed and immovable; in the same way I shall have the right to conceive high hopes if I am happy enough to discover one thing only which is certain and indubitable.

I suppose, then, that all the things that I see are false; I persuade myself that nothing has ever existed of all that my fallacious memory represents to me. I consider that I possess no senses; I imagine that body, figure, extension, movement and place are but the fictions of my mind. What, then, can be esteemed as true? Perhaps nothing at all, unless that there is nothing in the world that is certain.

But how can I know there is not something different from those things that I have just considered, of which one cannot have the slightest doubt? Is there not some God, or some other being by whatever name we call it, who puts these reflections into my mind? That is not necessary, for it is not possible that I am capable of producing them myself? I myself, am I not at least something? But I have already denied that I had senses and body. Yet I hesitate, for what follows from that? Am I so dependent on body and senses that I cannot exist without these? But I was persuaded that there was nothing in all the world, that there was no heaven, no earth, and there were no minds, nor any bodies: was I not then likewise persuaded that I did not exist? Not at all; of a surety I myself did exist since I persuaded myself of something [or merely because I thought of something]. But there is some deceiver or other, very powerful and very cunning, who ever employs his ingenuity in deceiving me. Then without doubt I exist also if he deceives me, and let him deceive me as much as he will, he can never cause me to be nothing so long as I think that I am something. So that after having reflected well and carefully examined all things, we must come to the definite conclusion that this proposition: I am, I exist, is necessarily true each time that I pronounce it, or that I mentally conceive it.

But I do not yet know clearly enough what I am, I who am certain that I am; and hence I must be careful to see that I do not imprudently take some other object in place of myself, and thus that I do not go astray in respect of this knowledge that I hold to be the most certain and most evident of all that I have formerly learned. That is why I shall now consider anew what I believed myself to be before I embarked upon these last reflections; and of my former opinions I shall withdraw all that might even in a small degree be invalidated by the reasons which I have just brought forward, in order that there may be nothing at all left beyond what is absolutely certain and indubitable.

What then did I formerly believe myself to be? Undoubtedly I believed myself to be a man. But what is a man? Shall I say a reasonable animal? Certainly not, for then I should have to inquire what an animal is, and what is reasonable; and thus from a single question I should insensibly fall into an infinitude of others more difficult; and I should not wish to waste the little time and leisure remaining to me in trying to unravel subtleties like these. But I shall rather stop here to consider the thoughts which of themselves spring up in my mind, and which were not inspired by anything beyond my own nature alone when I applied myself to the consideration of my being. In the first place, then, I considered myself as having a face, hands, arms, and all that system of members composed of bones and flesh as seen in a corpse which I designated by the name of body. In addition to this I considered that I was nourished, that I walked, that I felt, and that I thought, and I referred all these actions to the soul: but I did not stop to consider what the soul was, or if I did stop, I imagined that it was something extremely rare and subtle like a wind, a flame, or an ether, which was spread throughout my grosser parts. As to body I had no manner of doubt about its nature, but thought I had a very clear knowledge of it; and if I had desired to explain it according to the notions that I had then formed of it, I should have described it thus: By the body I understand all that which can be defined by a certain figure: something which can be confined in a certain place, and which can fill a given space in such a way that every other body will be excluded from it; which can be perceived either by touch, or by sight, or by hearing, or by taste, or by smell: which can be moved in many ways, not, in truth, by itself, but by something which is foreign to it, by which it is touched [and from which it receives impressions]: for to have the power of self-movement, as also of feeling or of thinking, I did not consider to appertain to the nature of body: on the contrary, I was rather astonished to find that faculties similar to them existed in some bodies.

But what am I, now that I suppose that there is a certain genius which is extremely powerful, and, if I may say so, malicious, who employs all his powers in deceiving me? Can I affirm that I possess the least of all those things which I have just said pertain to the nature of body? I pause to consider, I revolve all these things in my mind, and I find none of which I can say that it pertains to me. It would be tedious to stop to enumerate them. Let us pass to the attributes of soul and see if there is any one which is in me? What of nutrition or walking [the first mentioned]? But if it is so that I have no body it is also true that I can neither walk nor take nourishment. Another attribute is sensation. But one cannot feel without body, and besides I have thought I perceived many things during sleep that I recognised in my waking moments as not having been experienced at all. What of thinking? I find here that thought is an attribute that belongs to me; it alone cannot be separated from me. I am, I exist, that is certain. But how often? Just when I think; for it might possibly be the case if I ceased entirely to think, that I should likewise cease altogether to exist. I do not now admit anything which is not necessarily true: to speak accurately I am not more than a thing which thinks, that is to say a mind or a soul, or an understanding, or a reason, which are terms whose significance was formerly unknown to me. I am, however, a real thing and really exist; but what thing? I have answered: a thing which thinks.

And what more? I shall exercise my imagination [in order to see if I am not something more]. I am not a collection of members which we call the human body: I am not a subtle air distributed through these members, I am not a wind, a fire, a vapour, a breath, nor anything at all which I can imagine or conceive; because I have assumed that all these were nothing. Without changing that supposition I find that I only leave myself certain of the fact that I am somewhat. But perhaps it is true that these same things which I supposed were non-existent because they are unknown to me, are really not different from the self which I know. I am not sure about this, I shall not dispute about it now; I can only give judgment on things that are known to me. I know that I exist, and I inquire what I am, I whom I know to exist. But it is very certain that the knowledge of my existence taken in its precise significance does not depend on things whose existence is not yet known to me; consequently it does not depend on those which I can feign in imagination. And indeed the very term *feign* in imagination[1] proves to me my error, for I really do this if I imagine myself a something, since to imagine is nothing else than to contemplate the figure or image of a corporeal thing. But I already know for certain that I am, and that it may be that all these images, and, speaking generally, all things that relate to the nature of body are nothing but dreams [and chimeras]. For this reason I see clearly that I have as little reason to say, "I shall stimulate my imagination in order to know more distinctly what I am," than if I were to say, "I am now awake, and I perceive somewhat that is real and true: but because I do not yet perceive it distinctly enough, I shall go to sleep of express purpose, so that my dreams may represent the perception with greatest truth and evidence." And, thus, I know for certain that nothing of all that I can understand by means of my imagination belongs to this knowledge which I have of myself, and that it is necessary to recall the mind from this mode of thought with the utmost diligence in order that it may be able to know its own nature with perfect distinctness.

But what then am I? A thing which thinks. What is a thing which thinks? It is a thing which doubts, understands, [conceives], affirms, denies, wills, refuses, which also imagines and feels.

Certainly it is no small matter if all these things pertain to my nature. But why should they not so pertain? Am I not that being who now doubts nearly everything, who nevertheless understands certain things, who affirms that one only is true, who denies all the others, who desires to know more, is averse from being deceived, who imagines many things, sometimes indeed despite his will, and who perceives many likewise, as by the intervention of the bodily organs? Is there nothing in all this which is as true as it is certain that I exist, even though I should always sleep and though he who has given me being employed all his ingenuity in deceiving me? Is there likewise anyone of these attributes which can be distinguished from my thought, or which might be said to be separated from myself? For it is so evident of itself that it is I who doubts, who understands and who desires, that there is no reason here to add anything to explain it. And I have certainly the power of imagining likewise; for although it may happen (as I formerly supposed) that none of the things which I imagine are true, nevertheless this power of imagining does not cease to be really in use, and

---

[1] Or "form an image" (effingo).

it forms part of my thought. Finally, I am the same who feels, that is to say, who perceives certain things, as by the organs of sense, since in truth I see light, I hear noise, I feel heat. But it will be said that these phenomena are false and that I am dreaming. Let it be so; still it is at least quite certain that it seems to me that I see light, that I hear noise and that I feel heat. That cannot be false; properly speaking it is what is in me called feeling; and used in this precise sense that is no other thing than thinking.

From this time I begin to know what I am with a little more clearness and distinction than before; but nevertheless it still seems to me, and I cannot prevent myself from thinking, that corporeal things, whose images are framed by thought, which are tested by the senses, are much more distinctly known than that obscure part of me which does not come under the imagination. Although really it is very strange to say that I know and understand more distinctly these things whose existence seems to me dubious, which are unknown to me, and which do not belong to me, than others of the truth of which I am convinced, which are known to me and which pertain to my real nature, in a word, than myself. But I see clearly how the case stands: my mind loves to wander and cannot yet suffer itself to be retained within the just limits of truth. Very good, let us once more give it the freest rein, so that, when afterwards we seize the proper occasion for pulling up, it may the more easily be regulated and controlled.

Let us begin by considering the commonest matters, those which we believe to be the most distinctly comprehended, to wit, the bodies which we touch and see; not indeed bodies in general, for these general ideas are usually a little more confused, but let us consider one body in particular. Let us take, for example, this piece of wax: it has been taken quite freshly from the hive, and it has not yet lost the sweetness of the honey which it contains; it still retains somewhat of the odour of the flowers from which it has been culled; its colour, its figure, its size are apparent; it is hard, cold, easily handled, and if you strike it with the finger, it will emit a sound. Finally all the things which are requisite to cause us distinctly to recognise a body, are met with in it. But notice that while I speak and approach the fire what remained of the taste is exhaled, the smell evaporates, the colour alters, the figure is destroyed, the size increases, it becomes liquid, it heats, scarcely can one handle it, and when one strikes it, no sound is emitted. Does the same wax remain after this change? We must confess that it remains; none would judge otherwise. What then did I know so distinctly in this piece of wax? It could certainly be nothing of all that the senses brought to my notice, since all these things which fall under taste, smell, sight, touch, and hearing are found to be changed, and yet the same wax remains.

Perhaps it was what I now think, viz. that this wax was not that sweetness of honey, nor that agreeable scent of flowers, nor that particular whiteness, nor that figure, nor that sound, but simply a body which a little while before appeared to me as perceptible under these forms, and which is now perceptible under others. But what, precisely, is it that I imagine when I form such conceptions? Let us attentively consider this, and, abstracting from all that does not belong to the wax, let us see what remains. Certainly nothing remains excepting a certain extended thing which is flexible and movable. But what is the meaning of flexible and movable? Is it not that I imagine that this piece of wax being round is capable of becoming square and of passing from a square to a triangular figure? No, certainly it is not that, since I imagine it admits of an infinitude of similar changes, and I nevertheless do not know how to compass the infinitude by my imagination, and consequently this conception which I have of the wax is not brought about by the faculty of imagination. What now is this extension? Is it not also unknown? For it becomes greater when the wax is melted, greater when it is boiled, and greater still when the heat increases; and I should not conceive [clearly] according to truth what wax is, if I did not think that even this piece that we are considering is capable of receiving more variations in extension than I have ever imagined. We must then grant that I could not even understand through the imagination what this piece of wax in particular is, for as to wax in general it is yet clearer. But what is this piece of wax which cannot be understood excepting by the [understanding or] mind? It is certainly the same that I see, touch, imagine, and finally it is the same which I have always believed it to be from the beginning. But what must particularly be observed is that its perception is neither an act of vision, nor of touch, nor of imagination, and has never been such although it may have appeared formerly to be so, but only an intuition of the mind, which may be imperfect and confused as it was formerly, or clear and distinct as it is at present, according as my attention is more or less directed to the elements which are found in it, and of which it is composed.

Yet in the meantime I am greatly astonished when I consider [the great feebleness of mind] and its proneness to fall [insensibly] into error; for although without giving expression to my thoughts I consider all this in my own mind, words often impede me and I am almost deceived by the terms of ordinary language. For we say that we see the same wax, if it is present, and not that we simply judge that it is the same from its having the same colour and figure. From this I should conclude that I knew the wax by means of vision and not simply by the intuition of the mind; unless by chance I remember that, when looking from a window and saying I see men who pass in the street, I really do not see them, but infer that what I see is men, just as I say that I see wax. And yet what do I see from the window but hats and coats which may cover automatic machines? Yet I judge these to be men. And similarly solely by the faculty of judgment which rests in my mind, I comprehend that which I believed I saw with my eyes.

A man who makes it his aim to raise his knowledge above the common should be ashamed to derive the occasion for doubting from the forms of speech invented by the vulgar; I prefer to pass on and consider whether I had a more evident and perfect conception of what the wax was when I first perceived it, and when I believed I knew it by means of the external senses or at least by the common sense[2] as it is called, that is to say by the imaginative faculty, or whether my present conception is clearer now that I have most carefully examined what it is, and in what way it can be known. It would certainly be absurd to doubt as to this. For what was there in this first perception which was distinct? What was there which might not as well have been perceived by any

[2] *Sensus communis.*

of the animals? But when I distinguish the wax from its external forms, and when, just as if I had taken from it its vestments, I consider it quite naked, it is certain that although some error may still be found in my judgment, I can nevertheless not perceive it thus without a human mind.

But finally what shall I say of this mind, that is, of myself, for up to this point I do not admit in myself anything but mind? What then, I who seem to perceive this piece of wax so distinctly, do I not know myself, not only with much more truth and certainty, but also with much more distinctness and clearness? For if I judge that the wax is or exists from the fact that I see it, it certainly follows much more clearly that I am or that I exist myself from the fact that I see it. For it may be that what I see is not really wax, it may also be that I do not possess eyes with which to see anything; but it cannot be that when I see, or (for I no longer take account of the distinction) when I think I see, that I myself who think am nought. So if I judge that the wax exists from the fact that I touch it, the same thing will follow, to wit, that I am; and if I judge that my imagination, or some other cause, whatever it is, persuades me that the wax exists, I shall still conclude the same. And what I have here remarked of wax may be applied to all other things which are external to me [and which are met with outside me]. And further, if the [notion or] perception of wax has seemed to me clearer and more distinct, not only after the sight or the touch, but also after many other causes have rendered it quite manifest to me, with how much more [evidence] and distinctness must it be said that I now know myself, since all the reasons which contribute to the knowledge of wax, or any other body whatever, are yet better proofs of the nature of my mind! And there are so many other things in the mind itself which may contribute to the elucidation of its nature, that those which depend on body such as these just mentioned, hardly merit being taken into account.

But finally here I am, having insensibly reverted to the point I desired, for, since it is now manifest to me that even bodies are not properly speaking known by the senses or by the faculty of imagination, but by the understanding only, and since they are not known from the fact that they are seen or touched, but only because they are understood, I see clearly that there is nothing which is easier for me to know than my mind. But because it is difficult to rid oneself so promptly of an opinion to which one was accustomed for so long, it will be well that I should halt a little at this point, so that by the length of my meditation I may more deeply imprint on my memory this new knowledge.

There Is No Substantial Self

DAVID HUME

David Hume (1711–1776), an outstanding British empiricist, not only wrote on philosophical subjects but also became famous as a historian. Among his major works are *A Treatise of Human Nature* (1739–1740), *Essays, Moral and Political* (1741–1742), and *The History of England* (1754–1762).

There are some philosophers who imagine we are every moment intimately conscious of what we call our Self; that we feel its existence and its continuance in existence; and are certain, beyond the evidence of a demonstration, both of its perfect identity and simplicity. The strongest sensation, the most violent passion, say they, instead of distracting us from this view, only fix it the more intensely, and make us consider their influence on *self* either by their pain or pleasure. To attempt a farther proof of this were to weaken its evidence; since no proof can be derived from any fact, of which we are so intimately conscious; nor is there any thing, of which we can be certain, if we doubt of this.

Unluckily all these positive assertions are contrary to that very experience, which is pleaded for them, nor have we any idea of *self*, after the manner it is here explained. For from what impression could this idea be derived? This question it is impossible to answer without a manifest contradiction and absurdity; and yet it is a question, which must necessarily be answered, if we would have the idea of self pass for clear and intelligible. It must be some one impression, that gives rise to every real idea. But self or person is not any one impression, but that to which our several impressions and ideas are supposed to have a reference. If any impression gives rise to the idea of self, that impression must continue invariably the same, through the whole course of our lives; since self is supposed to exist after that manner. But there is no impression constant and invariable. Pain and pleasure, grief and joy, passions and sensations succeed each other, and never all exist at the same time. It cannot, therefore, be from any of these impressions, or from any other, that the idea of self is derived; and consequently there is no such idea.

But farther, what must become of all our particular perceptions upon this hypothesis? All these are different, and distinguishable, and separable from each other, and may be separately considered, and may exist separately, and have no need of any thing to support their existence. After what manner, therefore, do they belong to self; and how are they connected with it? For my part, when I enter most intimately into what I call *myself*, I always stumble on some particular perception or other, of heat or cold, light or shade, love or hatred, pain or pleasure. I never can catch *myself* at any time without a perception, and never can observe any thing but the perception. When my perceptions are removed for any time, as by sound sleep; so long am I insensible of *myself*, and may truly

Source: David Hume, *A Treatise of Human Nature*, Book I, Part 4 (London, 1739).

be said not to exist. And were all my perceptions removed by death, and could I neither think, nor feel, nor see, nor love, nor hate after the dissolution of my body, I should be entirely annihilated, nor do I conceive what is farther requisite to make me a perfect non-entity. If any one upon serious and unprejudiced reflexion, thinks he has a different notion of *himself,* I must confess I can reason no longer with him. All I can allow him is, that he may be in the right as well as I, and that we are essentially different in this particular. He may, perhaps, perceive something simple and continued, which he calls *himself;* though I am certain there is no such principle in me.

But setting aside some metaphysicians of this kind, I may venture to affirm of the rest of mankind, that they are nothing but a bundle or collection of different perceptions, which succeed each other with an inconceivable rapidity, and are in a perpetual flux and movement. Our eyes cannot turn in their sockets without varying our perceptions. Our thought is still more variable than our sight; and all our other senses and faculties contribute to this change; nor is there any single power of the soul, which remains unalterably the same, perhaps for one moment. The mind is a kind of theatre, where several perceptions successively make their appearance; pass, re-pass, glide away, and mingle in an infinite variety of postures and situations. There is properly no *simplicity* in it at one time, nor *identity* in different; whatever natural propension we may have to imagine that simplicity and identity. The comparison of the theatre must not mislead us. They are the successive perceptions only, that constitute the mind; nor have we the most distant notion of the place, where these scenes are represented, or of the materials, of which it is composed.

What then gives us so great a propension to ascribe an identity to these successive perceptions, and to suppose ourselves possest of an invariable and uninterrupted existence through the whole course of our lives? . . .

We have a distinct idea of an object, that remains invariable and uninterrupted through a supposed variation of time; and this idea we call that of *identity* or *sameness.* We have also a distinct idea of several different objects existing in succession, and connected together by a close relation; and this to an accurate view affords as perfect a notion of *diversity,* as if there were no manner of relation among the objects. But though these two ideas of identity, and a succession of related objects be in themselves perfectly distinct, and even contrary, yet it is certain, that in our common way of thinking they are generally confounded with each other. The action of the imagination, by which we consider the uninterrupted and invariable object, and that by which we reflect on the succession of related objects, are almost the same to the feeling, nor is there much more effort of thought required in the latter case than in the former. The relation facilitates the transition of the mind from one object to another, and renders its passage as smooth as if it contemplated one continued object. This resemblance is the cause of the confusion and mistake, and makes us substitute the notion of identity, instead of that of related objects. However at one instant we may consider the related succession as variable or interrupted, we are sure the next to ascribe to it a perfect identity, and regard it as invariable and uninterrupted. Our propensity to this mistake is so great from the resemblance abovementioned, that we fall into it before we are aware; and though we incessantly correct ourselves by reflexion, and return to a more accurate method of thinking, yet we cannot long sustain our philosophy, or take off this bias from the imagination. Our last resource is to yield to it, and boldly assert that these different related objects are in effect the same, however interrupted and variable. In order to justify to ourselves this absurdity, we often feign some new and unintelligible principle, that connects the objects together, and prevents their interruption or variation. Thus we feign the continued existence of the perceptions of our senses, to remove the interruption; and run into the notion of a *soul*, and *self*, and *substance*, to disguise the variation. But we may farther observe, that where we do not give rise to such a fiction, our propension to confound identity with relation is so great, that we are apt to imagine[1] something unknown and mysterious, connecting the parts, beside their relation; and this I take to be the case with regard to the identity we ascribe to plants and vegetables. And even when this does not take place, we still feel a propensity to confound these ideas, though we are not able fully to satisfy ourselves in that particular, nor find any thing invariable and uninterrupted to justify our notion of identity.

Thus the controversy concerning identity is not merely a dispute of words. For when we attribute identity, in an improper sense, to variable or interrupted objects, our mistake is not confined to the expression, but is commonly attended with a fiction, either of something invariable and uninterrupted, or of something mysterious and inexplicable, or at least with a propensity to such fictions. . . .

We now proceed to explain the nature of *personal identity*, which has become so great a question in philosophy, especially of late years in *England*, where all the abstruser sciences are studied with a peculiar ardour and application. . . .

It is evident, that the identity, which we attribute to the human mind, however perfect we may imagine it to be, is not able to run the several different perceptions into one, and make them lose their characters of distinction and difference, which are essential to them. It is still true, that every distinct perception, which enters into the composition of the mind, is a distinct existence, and is different, and distinguishable, and separable from every other perception, either contemporary or successive. But, as, notwithstanding this distinction and separability, we suppose the whole train of perceptions to be united by identity, a question naturally arises concerning this relation of identity; whether it be something that really binds our several perceptions together, or only associates their ideas in the imagination. That is, in other words, whether in pronouncing concerning the identity of a person, we observe some real bond among his perceptions, or only feel one among the ideas we form of them. This question we might easily decide, if we would recollect what has been already proved at large, that the understanding never observes any real connexion among objects, and that even the union of cause and effect, when strictly examined, resolves itself into a customary association of ideas. For from thence it evidently follows, that identity is nothing really belonging to these different perceptions, and

---

[1] If the reader is desirous to see how a great genius may be influenced by these seemingly trivial principles of the imagination, as well as the mere vulgar, let him read my Lord Shaftsbury's reasonings concerning the uniting principle of the universe, and the identity of plants and animals. See his *Moralist:* or, *Philosophical Rhapsody.*

uniting them together; but is merely a quality, which we attribute to them, because of the union of their ideas in the imagination, when we reflect upon them. Now the only qualities, which can give ideas an union in the imagination, are these three relations above-mentioned. These are the uniting principles in the ideal world, and without them every distinct object is separable by the mind, and may be separately considered, and appears not to have any more connexion with any other object, than if disjoined by the greatest difference and remoteness. It is, therefore, on some of these three relations of resemblance, contiguity and causation, that identity depends; and as the very essence of these relations consists in their producing an easy transition of ideas; it follows, that our notions of personal identity, proceed entirely from the smooth and uninterrupted progress of the thought along a train of connected ideas, according to the principles above-explained.

The only question, therefore, which remains, is, by what relations this uninterrupted progress of our thought is produced, when we consider the successive existence of a mind or thinking person. And here it is evident we must confine ourselves to resemblance and causation, and must drop contiguity, which has little or no influence in the present case.

To begin with *resemblance*; suppose we could see clearly into the breast of another, and observe that succession of perceptions, which constitutes his mind or thinking principle, and suppose that he always preserves the memory of a considerable part of past perceptions; it is evident that nothing could more contribute to the bestowing a relation on this succession amidst all its variations. For what is the memory but a faculty, by which we raise up the images of past perceptions? And as an image necessarily resembles its object, must not the frequent placing of these resembling perceptions in the chain of thought, convey the imagination more easily from one link to another, and make the whole seem like the continuance of one object? In this particular, then, the memory not only discovers the identity, but also contributes to its production, by producing the relation of resemblance among the perceptions. The case is the same whether we consider ourselves or others.

As to *causation*; we may observe, that the true idea of the human mind, is to consider it as a system of different perceptions or different existences, which are linked together by the relation of cause and effect, and mutually produce, destroy, influence, and modify each other. Our impressions give rise to their correspondent ideas; and these ideas in their turn produce other impressions. One thought chases another, and draws after it a third, by which it is expelled in its turn. In this respect, I cannot compare the soul more properly to anything than to a republic or commonwealth, in which the several members are united by the reciprocal ties of government and subordination, and give rise to other persons, who propagate the same republic in the incessant changes of its parts. And as the same individual republic may not only change its members, but also its laws and constitutions; in like manner the same person may vary his character and disposition, as well as his impressions and ideas, without losing his identity. Whatever changes he endures, his several parts are still connected by the relation of causation. And in this view our identity with regard to the passions serves to corroborate that with regard to the imagination, by the making our distant perceptions influence each other, and by giving us a present concern for our past or future pains or pleasures.

As memory alone acquaints us with the continuance and extent of this succession of perceptions, it is to be considered, upon that account chiefly, as the source of personal identity. Had we no memory, we never should have any notion of causation, nor consequently of that chain of causes and effects, which constitute our self or person. But having once acquired this notion of causation from the memory, we can extend the same chain of causes, and consequently the identity of our persons beyond our memory, and can comprehend times, and circumstances, and actions, which we have entirely forgot, but suppose in general to have existed. For how few of our past actions are there, of which we have any memory? Who can tell me, for instance, what were his thoughts and actions on the first of *January* 1715, the 11th of *March* 1719, and the 3d of *August* 1733? Or will he affirm, because he has entirely forgot the incidents of these days, that the present self is not the same person with the self of that time; and by that means overturn all the most established notions of personal identity? In this view, therefore, memory does not so much *produce* as *discover* personal identity, by shewing us the relation of cause and effect among our different perceptions. It will be incumbent on those, who affirm that memory produces entirely our personal identity, to give a reason why we can thus extend our identity beyond our memory.

The whole of this doctrine leads us to a conclusion, which is of great importance in the present affair, *viz.*, that all the nice and subtle questions concerning personal identity can never possibly be decided.

Persons and Relational Beings

A. K. BIERMAN

> I am marryed tew apparentcy?
> —Fanebius Perlyng

Persons should not be thought of as if they were objects. To think of them as objects is pernicious because it generates an individualistic conception of man and thereby hinders the establishment of moral relations between persons. It is a metaphysical view of the self that leads to moral and social atomism.

Individualism, I have said, is a defense mechanism employed when persons realize they have been abandoned by their society. That is its pitiful side. Individualism also encourages bravado, which is its rugged side. "Rugged" individualism is a clarion summons to gird up your muscles and to act vigorously to gain your goals; anyone caught hesitating to go roughshod in the world is spiked as a pallid, callow, sentimental bleedingheart; assertions of human inter-

Source: A. K. Bierman, *The Philosophy of Urban Existence* (Athens, Ohio: Ohio University Press, 1973), pp. 54–66, 71–79.

dependency are seen as admissions of weakness; competing is the great thing and the winner's reward is control over the losers; social welfare programs, medical aid, unemployment benefits, bankruptcy laws, and special help programs in the public schools are regarded as evidence of the victims' moral fiberlessness and failure rather than as evidence of a crippling social system; it is man heroically matching himself against a perpetually present, rugged frontier, self-interest is all; glory be to Daddy Warbucks!

Rugged individualism flies the proud banner of self-reliance and self-confidence. It also runs up the banner of freedom, of autonomy. In relying on and confiding in yourself alone, you can avoid buckling yourself to others. Any dependency relation you have with another person is unwelcome because it restricts your choices and actions, and, therefore, restricts your freedom. The other becomes as a millstone around your neck. In order to achieve maximum freedom—according to the ethics of rugged individualism—you should be the sole source of the energy required to achieve your goals. Human alliances are undertaken under the pressure of circumstances, and always reluctantly, because the acid of each alliance destroys a bit more of your freedom. It is assumed that human aid can be purchased only at the cost of freedom.

Given that the supreme value of rugged individualism is personal freedom, human relations are to be avoided except when you cannot accomplish your goals without help from others. The conditions which account for social relations, therefore, are those in which we look on other persons as means to our ends. The perfect relation to have with another person if we are absolutely forced to resort to using him as a means—according to individualism—is a one-way relation: You get help from him and he asks nothing in return, for, by asking for nothing, he does not restrict your freedom. The closest we come to this one-way relation between humans is in the master-slave relationship. The ideal logical outcome of rugged individualism when forced to operate in a world where we need others is slavery. The ideal outcome when persons are not forced to rely on the help of others is a "society" of personal atoms, each doing his own thing independently of others. This kind of society is essentially an aggregate of atoms, since there are no mutual relations tying the atoms together; it is a Many that shuns Oneness. If we were to picture an extreme form of alienation, we would picture the unrelated aggregate of personal atoms which rugged individualism projects as its ideal.

Of course, the person committed to rugged individualism does not want to be the slave of another because a slave suffers a minimum state of freedom. To avoid becoming another's slave, a person must either have the power to be a master or he must live in splendid isolation. Among a group of persons, it is not logically possible for everyone to be a master; masters cannot be masters without someone being a slave. Given that no rugged individualist willingly becomes a slave, a power struggle to determine who shall be masters and who slaves is another logical outcome of rugged individualism. Might doesn't make right, it makes Masters. To be caught in the toils of the ethics of rugged individualism is to be caught permanently in the toils of war.

There is a way out of this permanent state of war that is becoming more and more a practical possibility. With advances in technology, we can replace slaves with machines. This makes possible the perfect one-way relationship because machines help us accomplish our goals without asking for anything in return. Technology perfected would enable us to live in complete freedom from others without struggle. The bliss of living with machines would be chilled only by their lack of love, respect, care, admiration, praise, encouragement, and concern. This chill might be removed by programming the machines to show by their behavior that they do love, respect, care for, admire, praise, encourage, and are concerned for us. Of course, our programming these human attitudes into the machines would be the ultimate act of rugged individualism because they would, in effect, then be attitudes of self-love, self-respect, self-care, self-admiration, self-praise, self-encouragement, and self-concern.

The ethic of rugged individualism logically results, then, in alienation, slavery, war, and self-glorification. These results should be enough reason to reject it as our ideal ethical system. The fact that the results are exactly our present moral situation makes the philosophical task of fashioning an alternative more than an academic exercise.

I don't suppose anyone would willingly opt for rugged individualism if faced with these logical results. He might suicidally resign himself to this fate, however, if he thought that it was an unavoidable "human condition." Unfortunately, this seems to be exactly what many do think. I believe that most of our contemporaries are resigned to some form of the ethic of rugged individualism because they believe that the nature of persons leaves us with no alternative. I do not have in mind an appraisal of the moral nature of persons but, rather, a view of the metaphysical nature of persons. The metaphysical view of persons that underwrites rugged individualism is the view that a person is an object kind of thing called a substance.

I shall show how, in thinking that persons are substances, we are led to think of them as self-contained entities, atoms of existence, fundamentally isolated from each other because relations between them affect only the surface and not the core of each other's reality. In short, to think of persons as substances is to think of them as metaphysically alienated. This metaphysical alienation underwrites a form of moral and political alienation such as rugged individualism because it imposes a particular image of society on us. The image is that society is a collection of atoms, each atom being a person. Atoms are morally isolated from each other because moral and political relations between them fail to tie their core realities together into an integrated society; they tie only the surface appearance of persons together. This view of persons and their moral relations leaves us barren of any other than prudential reasons why we should treat others morally because nothing more profound than their appearance is at stake. Substance thinking makes a mystery of morality and of a commitment to social ideals.

We are like BB's scattered randomly on a plane; we touch only on the surface, if we touch at all.

Let us proceed to draw out what it is to think of a person as a substance, as, I suspect, you do.

The concept of substance is given its marching orders by our common sense notion of a physical object, so that to think of a person, a self, as a substance is to think of him on the model of a physical object. To be sure, not everyone who holds a substance theory of persons believes that the substance of persons is physical matter; they may hold that a person is a mental substance, a soul. Still, even as a mental substance, the person is thought of as a thing, an object, albeit a mental thing.

I have often noticed that at the mention of the word "metaphysics" or of metaphysical words such as "substance," people's eyes glaze over, they start acting slightly shifty, and you know they are wondering how they ever got themselves into such a situation. They are perfectly willing to leave metaphysics to the philosophers who apparently find some use for it, little knowing that they themselves are metaphysicians. People generally have too great a reverence and/or fear of Madame Metaphysics. Let us escort her from the study to the kitchen where we may comfortably consort with her.

A Metaphysical Interlude

The scene is Andrea and Homer's kitchen. They are engaged in their usual sort of after-dinner conversation.

ANDREA: I've been reading Descartes' *Meditations* again, Homer, and thinking about substance.

HOMER: That's swell, Andrea.

ANDREA: Why are your eyes glazing over?

HOMER: They always do that when you mention "substance."

ANDREA: You've simply got to get over that. You embarrass me in front of our friends.

HOMER: Can you help me?

ANDREA: I hope so. Look, Homer, suppose all your concepts were laid out before you. You'd find that they presented a cluster pattern. There would be a cluster of concepts that we use to think about economics, another we use to think about botany, another we use to think about food, another we use to think about law and so forth.

HOMER: I would?

ANDREA: Yes, and you would also notice that some concepts occur in every cluster. These concepts saturate all your thinking. You use them to think about anything. These pervasive concepts are metaphysical concepts.

HOMER: That doesn't sound complicated. Can you give me some examples?

ANDREA: Sure, and all of them perfectly familiar to you. Beginning and end, individual, character, unity, change, identity, and interaction. Oh, good, you're beginning to unglaze a little.

HOMER: And my breathing is getting more normal, too.

ANDREA: I think you're ready for substance.

HOMER: I'm starting to feel shifty, though.

ANDREA: Relax, dear, nothing could be simpler to explain. Substance is simply a concept you use in thinking, for example, about physical objects. You do think about physical objects, you know.

HOMER: Oh, yes, all the time, but I don't think I use substance all the time. Do I?

ANDREA: I think so. You think physical objects have a beginning and an end, don't you?

HOMER: Of course. Even the world has a beginning and an end.

ANDREA: Do you think things, or the world, are made out of nothing?

HOMER: You can't make something out of nothing. Even good fairies can't do that. The good fairy had to make Cinderella's horses out of mice and her carriage out of a pumpkin.

ANDREA: You agree with the first Greek philosophers, then. They thought there is a primary stuff out of which everything is made. Now listen to this: They called that primary stuff "substance."

HOMER: Am I unglazing just a little?

ANDREA: I think so. Now, Homer, you think that this substance is divisible because you think there are individual things.

HOMER: Absolutely. Here is an individual candle, there another one. And they are different individuals from the table they're sitting on. They're separate from each other.

ANDREA: Good. And don't you distinguish between a thing and its character? Don't you think that a character is something different from the thing that has the character?

HOMER: I suppose so, if you mean by a thing's character its properties or qualities.

ANDREA: That is what I mean. Roses are red, violets are blue. Now suppose that a thing's character were taken away from it. What would you have left? Suppose you take the taste, odor, color, shape, size, and so forth away from a piece of wax. What would you have left?

HOMER: I would have left whatever has those qualities.

ANDREA: Very clever. What should we call it?

HOMER: Substance?

ANDREA: Right. Substance and shadow, the thing and its appearance.

HOMER: Huh?

ANDREA: The character is the outward appearance, the show of the underlying reality which is substance. The character, the complex of qualities, inheres in the substance.

HOMER: What's this "inheres" bit? Is it as if the substance were some sticky stuff to which qualities stick, or what?

ANDREA: A visual and tactile metaphor won't do because even a "sticky stuff" is substance with a sticky character rather than "pure" substance. Substance is not something that can be observed by the senses; only its character appearance is sensible. Substance is the child of theory. It is an entity known only by reason. Descartes, in his *Second Meditation,* observes a piece of wax fresh from the beehive. When fresh from the hive it has a given character but, when he puts it by fire, it melts and changes its character completely. It tastes and smells different; it changes color and shape and size. Still we say it is the identical wax.

HOMER: I do. The wax didn't go out of existence just because its character changed.

ANDREA: Why do you suppose you can say it is the identical wax even though it has completely changed its character?

HOMER: Substance, again. The substance is the same before and after the wax melted; the substance did not go out of existence.

ANDREA: You see how marvelous you are at metaphysics, darling?

HOMER: Thanks. But I'm not yet wholly unglazed. I still don't understand how character inheres in substance.

ANDREA: There are some things you just have to accept. The mind must come to rest somewhere. Substance, being a child of reason, has whatever nature our mind needs in order to organize our experience of physical objects. For example, here is another use for substance. The character of an object is complex; it is made up of several qualities such as taste, smell, size, shape. Though the qualities are Many, the character is One. How is it possible that a character may have this unity?

HOMER: Like the good fairy, I utter a magic word: Substance! Since each of the characteristics inheres in the same substance, they are held together as a single character.

ANDREA: Excellent: More brandsey, please. Your eyes are getting quite unglazed now. Things change. Let me tell you how substance helps us unnerstand shange. A thing shanges when one of its qualities gets disinherited and nother inheres in ish playsh. Simple.

HOMER: Drunken qualities replace sober qualities.

ANDREA: That's because of the brandsey. One thing has an effect on another when they interact; it makesh a substance lose one characteristic and gain another.

HOMER: That makes me sad.

ANDREA: Poor Homer. Tell me all about it.

HOMER: You said a thing's character is only an appearance, an outward show. If interaction between things changes only the world's appearance but not its substance, reality never changes. Reality is static; it stays the same forever. That means our personal relations don't really change anything of our reality; we are doomed to affect only each other's appearance.

ANDREA: What a terribly sobering thought.

HOMER: You are beyond the hand of change even when it is the hand of someone who loves you very much. We are locked in our substances. There is an unbridgeable gulf between our substances. Our souls—

ANDREA: Souls?

HOMER: Yes, our souls. They are our substance, our reality. After all, I am not my body. Our souls are like BB shot lying on the plane of existence. Society amounts to no more than an aggregate of unconnected BB-souls. There is no true, profound interpenetration of one human substance by another.

ANDREA: But what makes you think . . .

HOMER: Andrea, I don't want you to ever read Descartes again. Look what his foul substance has done. Our personal character, sometimes so hard won, is vain foppery, the soul's dress, subject to fashion's whims, forever concealing our real, naked self from others. Do you realize what this means? I'll tell you. You may have the brains, but I've got the heart. What it means is that we are never able to reach beyond our own to another's reality. That means all our moral aspirations must sink to a base, rugged individualism or some similar stupid ethic, a kind of BB version of our moral condition. To a rugged individualist, only a featherbrained idealist could raise expectations for genuine relations and obligations between people.

ANDREA: But what makes you think . . .

HOMER: Don't stop me now. Thinking of humans as substances is merely a metaphysical version of human BB-hood; it is a metaphysical basis for yielding to belief in ultimate, unavoidable alienation; it is a metaphysical prop for a BB-ethic. According to your substance-cretins, we live a life of pretense if we think we can lay an obligation on somebody else because, in effect, our realities are sealed off from each other. As substances we are existentially independent; only our appearances are affected by human relations. Life is a series of transmigrations, which is just a series of transmogrifications of persons' appearance. In actuality, our hermetically sealed souls drift in eternal isolation, unperturbed, unruffled, unchanged, essentially uninvolved, shedding one appearance after another like a snake shucking last year's dead skin. Weep for them, Andrea. Weep.

ANDREA: Come, come, dear, the slough of despair doesn't suit you. We can escape this dreadful metaphysical fate. What makes you think that we have to think of persons as substances, as if they were like physical objects?

HOMER: You don't deny that we think of them that way, do you? After all, we do apply all the metaphysical concepts to humans that we apply to physical objects. Persons have beginnings and ends, birth and death; we distinguish one individual person from another; persons have character, personality; their character belongs to them and no one else, and may have a unity; persons change, the child and the adult are as different as the wax is before and after melting; persons maintain their identity even though their character changes completely; I remember a poem Bob Kennedy gave me, a Hindu poem, he said:

> Death is only matter dressed
>   in some new form,
> A varied vest:
> From tenement to tenement
>   though tossed,
> The Soul does not change.
> Only the figure is lost!

And you won't deny that persons interact.

ANDREA: What is all that supposed to prove?

HOMER: That the metaphysical concepts—beginning and end, individual, character, unity, change, identity, and interaction—apply to persons as well as to physical objects.

ANDREA: Just because they apply to persons doesn't by itself prove that persons are substances. Substance happens to be part of a particular metaphysical theory designed to 'explain how metaphysical concepts apply to physical objects. But, those concepts apply to every field. Remember?

HOMER: Sure, I remember. That's what makes them metaphysical concepts. So they do apply. So what? Brandy, Andrea?

ANDREA: At least the glaze is gone, but you're still too damn shifty, Homer. Those metaphysical concepts apply to economics. Take the idea of a market. Markets come and go; the surrey market is kaput, dead. We distinguish the tobacco market from the hair spray market. Markets have a character; just read the *Wall Street Journal*. Markets have a unity; if they didn't, we couldn't financially "grab" "the market"; there has to be something you control when you control it. Markets change; they rise and fall. And they have to have an identity or we couldn't say the market has fallen. Today the market is 783; yesterday it was 785. One number is lower than the other; but if the two numbers don't describe the same entity (it, the market) at two different times, we couldn't say that *it* had fallen. Finally, markets interact; the auto market affects the steel market.

Here comes the big question, Homer. When you think of the market, do you think there is a substance that is its underlying reality?

HOMER: That's an easy one. No.

ANDREA: Well, there you are, we don't always need substance to explain how the metaphysical concepts apply. What makes you think we need it to explain how they apply to persons?

HOMER: To tell you the truth, I'm not sure.

ANDREA: The existence and nature of substance is entirely dependent on theory. It is a theoretical entity. We can keep it as long as it plays a necessary part in a good theory. But as soon as we reject the theory, we can reject substance. Substance becomes a useless piece of baggage that is best dropped. Don't you agree?

HOMER: I think I do. Some biologists once thought there was a life-force. They needed it to explain how "inert" matter could be alive, but now that we have more advanced chemical and physical theories to explain life, we don't need such an entity as "life-force" anymore. Good.

ANDREA: Do you think the substance theory of persons is a good one?

HOMER: You must not have taken my tirade seriously. Any metaphysical theory that leads to a bad ethic such as rugged individualism has got to be bad.

ANDREA: Why don't you throw it out, then?

HOMER: I don't know. Maybe I still think it's true.

ANDREA: You don't have to believe in the existence of substance in the way that you have to believe in the existence of candles. You can see, feel, smell, and taste candles, but you can't see, feel, smell, or taste substance. It's an entity invented by the mind to explain how we apply metaphysical concepts. You admit you don't use it—so, you don't need it—to explain your talk about markets. Maybe the concept of a person is more like the concept of a market than it is like the concept of a physical object. If it is, then substance is a superfluous theoretical entity. Give up your old metaphysical habits; they only lead to rotten moral theories. You've got metaphysical freedom, sweetie. Reorganize your thought about persons.

HOMER: Freedom from substance! What a slogan! I like it. Do you mean we might think of a different theory of persons? I'd like one that makes a decent human society possible, a theory in which it is possible for human relations to affect the essence of each other's being. I'd like a theory that helps us understand how our very existence and nature are dependent upon the achievement of a set of moral relations to each other. We wouldn't have to live like BB's, then.

ANDREA: That's what I've always found dear in you, Homer, that streak of nobility, your hunger for moral dignity. It becomes you.

HOMER: Thanks, Andrea, but, tell me, what kind of a theory of persons would give us what I want, really?

ANDREA: You've been too generous with the brandy. I can't figure that one out tonight. It will just have to wait, Homer.

> And Godde sayd, "Lett ther bee rybs and realatyons."
> —Fanebius Perlyng

A person is a collection of relatents. His existence and his nature are dependent upon his relations to others. Since a person is by nature a relational being, man's social and communal nature receives a metaphysical foundation.

By eavesdropping on Andrea and Homer's conversation, we learned that we not only don't have to think of persons as substances, but that we don't want to think of them as substances because a substance theory of persons is a metaphysical version of alienation that supports the moral isolation of rugged individualism. With her comments on an economic market, Andrea taught us that we have the theoretical freedom to recast our metaphysical notion of a person. In this chapter, I take advantage of that freedom to suggest another theory of what a person is.

. . .

Andrea suggested to Homer that a person may be more like a market than like a physical object. We know that Andrea had had too much brandy when she said that. Of course, it may be a ridiculous idea, but just on the chance that she was putting us on the trail of a vein we might profitably prospect, let's think about the notion of a market for a bit.

Here we are on a flying carpet, scooting over the world, peering down through its rents. We dip down toward the world to have a closer look. Below we see some things: two men, some pieces of silver, and a ham. The men are talking: "I'll give you five pieces of silver for the ham." "It's a deal. It's cheap, but a deal." We are witnessing an exchange which is a portion of a market.

An exchange is a banal occurrence that holds something of interest to us. The occurrence takes place amongst correlatives. A correlative is something—for example, a buyer—that stands in some relation to something else—for example, a seller—that stands in a relation to the buyer. Something that is a buyer is a correlative; it is a correlative to a seller. A parent and child are correlatives. A valley and a mountain are correlatives. Correlatives are tied with bonds of necessity. There cannot be a buyer unless there is a seller; and *vice versa*. There cannot be a parent unless there is a child; and *vice versa*. There cannot be a valley without a mountain; and *vice versa*.

Just as a seller and a buyer are correlatives, so a seller and his goods are correlatives. One cannot be a seller unless he has goods to sell. Similarly, a buyer and his coin are correlatives. Also, a seller and the buyer's coin are correlatives because if the seller doesn't get something for his goods he has either given his goods as a gift or his goods have been stolen. Further, a buyer and the seller's goods are correlatives; you can't be a buyer if you haven't bought something.

The banal occurrence we call an exchange does not take place unless there are at least four things in a complex network of co-relations. A market such as the stock market is a set of such exchanges actual or potential.

One more step and then we will be ready to grasp a new vision of persons.

What makes silver (or seashells) money? Not the fact that it is silver, for something may be silver and not be money. Nor that it is valuable, for many things are valuable that are not money. What makes ham (or shoes) goods? It isn't always goods because sometimes it is food. What makes a person a buyer? Not that he is a person, for persons are not always buyers; sometimes they are sellers. Clearly, what makes silver money, ham goods, and persons buyers and sellers are their being in correlative relations to each other. It is not the silver's physical nature nor the ham's physical nature that makes one money and the other goods; their natures may make them silver and ham, but it is their co-realtions that make them money and goods. (Hint: The concept of person is like the concepts of goods and money, not like the concept of ham or silver.)

In the spirit that we ask what makes an object such as ham a piece of goods, or what makes an object such as silver money, we ask what makes a body a person. We approach our answer to this question through an analogy. What makes a piece of wood a spear and a support and a part of a picture frame and a handle? The same piece of wood may be a spear to a boy playing Hercules, a part of a picture frame to an artist, a support for plants to the gardener, or a placard handle to a picketer.

Which of them the piece of wood is depends upon the situation it is in; it depends upon the relations it has to other things. Buyers, sellers, money, goods, spears, supports, picture frame parts, and handles are not things-in-themselves. They are what they are because of the other things to which they are related and because of the way they are related to those other things.

We can make this clearer by means of a generalization: xRy. We will let x and y stand for objects and R stand for a relation. Suppose y is a sheet of cardboard, x is the stick, and the relation R is "tacked to," so that the stick is tacked to the cardboard. That relation and the cardboard object to which the stick is related make the stick into a handle.

Suppose, again, that y is a willowy plant and the relation R is "tied to," so that the stick is tied to the plant. That relation and the plant to which the stick is related make the stick into a support.

x is a relatent, so I call it. What it is (a handle, a support, etc.) varies with and depends on R and y in xRy. y, too, I call a relatent.

Spears, supports, handles, picture frame parts, buyers, sellers, money, goods are relational entities, or what, in short, I call relatents. Let us call $"xRy,"$ as a whole, a relationship. x and y, considered together, I call correlatents; why I do so should be clear from my discussion of correlatives. In applying these notions to persons, I will call x the inner correlatent and y the outer correlatent.

Suppose that a piece of wood could simultaneously be a spear, a support, a picture frame part, a handle. It would be possible to give a name to the collection of these things; we could call the collection, for example, a ridotto. A person is like a ridotto. "Person" is the word we use to refer to a collection of relatents. Consider some of our relatents. There are familial relations that make us into sons, daughters, wives, fathers, uncles, and cousins. There are occupational relations that make us into bosses, employees, foremen, actors, salesman, assistant professors, longshoremen, journalists, executives, and lawyers. There are neighborhood relations that make us into neighbors, volunteers, Neighborhood Council members, Civic Affairs chairmen, monthly newsletter editors and writers, and boosters. There are city relations that make us taxpayers, voters, supervisors, citizens, mayors, witnesses, judges, Democrats, Republicans, jury members, and petitioners. A relatent is not the same concept as a role. I shall distinguish later between a factual- and a moral-relatent, which get confused in the concept of role.

Just as a piece of wood becomes a handle because relatents are created, that is, because it becomes related to other things in specific ways, so out of human bodies persons are created because their bodies become related to other bodies, families, occupations, neighborhoods, cities, and so forth. To be a person is to be many of the kinds of relatents of which I gave a sample list above. "Person" is the word we use to designate a collection of relatents. You are a collection of such relatents as son, husband, uncle, employee, musician, citizen, Democrat, voter, and many, many others.

This notion of person is theoretically useful because it helps us to understand what it means to say that man is a social being. Each person is a self; the self is a correlative being, a set of inner correlatents. Since a self is a collection of correlatents, and, since correlatents' existence and nature logically depend upon the existence of others and the nature of their relations to others, we see why the existence and nature of the self is logically dependent upon other persons; since other persons, too, are sets of correlatents, they, too, logically depend upon relations to your self and other selves.

You must not confuse this point with a commonplace psychological doctrine. It is a truism to say that our social environment influences the kind of attitudes, dreams, emotions, fears, ambitions, and conscience we have. My point is not a psychological one; it is a logical point. I am talking about the conditions necessary for your existence; and I am talking about the conditions necessary for your having the nature of a person at all, not about the psychological conditions that make you this kind of person rather than that kind of person.

This notion of person is theoretically useful, again, because it helps us to reinterpret our notion of society. We no longer have to think of a society as a collection of atoms, as a collection of hermetically sealed substances. A society is to self and others as a topography is to a mountain and a valley. A topography is a variation in land levels described relationally as mountains, valleys, and plains; a society is an organization of human bodies described relationally as sets of relatents. It is an arrangement that creates persons; some arrangements are good, others bad, because some make good persons possible and others do not.

The following two reality diagrams show us the contrast between a substance picture of social reality and a relatent picture of social reality.

Substance Picture of Society   Relatent Picture of Society

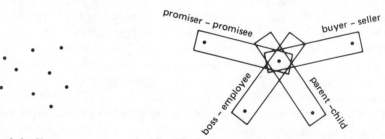

In the left diagram, a person is identified as a substance, represented by a dot. It is a picture of a reality composed of isolated substances. On the right, a person is identified as a set of inner correlatents—promisee, employee, parent, and buyer. The outer correlatents in the picture are promiser, boss, child, and seller. It is a picture of a reality composed of persons. To picture a person in that diagram, we necessarily have to draw moral and social co-relations between the dots, which represent bodies. We can have relations out of the substance picture of reality, however, because they are mere appearances in that world, whereas in the relatent world they are the reality of persons.

The substance picture underwrites the rugged individualist, who aims at self-sufficiency and maximum autonomy in pursuit of his self-interest. That picture posits the substance-dot as the moral center; all moral treasures are located there in the fortress self; and therein resides the autonomous, self-activating moral tyrant we call the will. The substance-dot defines the perspective from which he views the world; it affords him a personal point of view of the social landscape. From the safe battlements of the self, the tyrant directs his foraging forces of appearance in their raids on other appearances. Though his point of view is provincial, and though he is doomed to moral solipsism, he is happy enough because his vantage point is metaphysically autonomous, secure, and impregnable.

When we conceive of a person as a collection of relatents, it is impossible to locate the moral center in a dot. Since each inner correlatent requires an outer correlative entity, a person and his moral treasures are spread throughout the social landscape. A person cannot remain provincial in his point of view; he must take up the perspective of the other as well as himself because his existence and nature are logically related to the existence and nature of others. If, for example, you wish to be a seller, you must also concern yourself with the existence of a buyer; you must help some other to retain his buyer nature if you are to retain your seller nature. It is logically impossible to define a person's interests in terms of self-interest alone according to a relatent theory of persons; it is logically impossible to conceive of your interests apart from the interests of others; thus, the relatent theory is morally useful because it razes the rugged fortress walls of the substance-self.

The relatent notion of a person is morally useful also because it erases the distinction between a person's reality and his appearance, a distinction which is central to the substance notion of a person. In ranking the value of reality and appearance, reality takes chief place; appearance is "mere" appearance, illusion, the world's seeming, not its being. According to the substance theory, our character, including the social and moral aspects of our character, belong to appearance; our obligations to others and theirs to us are of secondary importance. This relegation of the social and moral aspects of our life to secondary importance gives free license to the rugged individualist who seizes the opportunity to pursue his "self-interest" with maximum autonomy. Restraint on one's action by others is to be avoided; obligations are a burden, not an opportunity—an obstacle, not a necessity.

With the relatent notion of a person, on the other hand, we can discern that our moral and social relations are both a necessity and an opportunity first, because they are necessary to our existence as persons, and secondly, because they are the material out of which we form our nature in accord with our ideal.

Perhaps another image might help you to grasp the concept of a person that I am advocating. Picture a net. Let the net represent a society, the net knots—not the string of the knots—represent persons, and the string between the net knots represent relations. If we were to cut the strings that lead from a net knot to other net knots, what was a net knot would become a detached, knotted string, but it would no longer be a net knot. (Moral: If you cut all a body's relations to other bodies, you have made relatents impossible for it and, thereby, destroyed a person [and injured the society]. Alienation is a form of murder.) What made the knotted string a net knot was its stringy relations to other net knots.

If I pull on a net knot some distance from a given net knot, the latter will be affected. (Moral: What is done to others in your society, whether done by you or someone else, is done to you.) Also, if someone pulls on a given net knot, it will affect the other net knots. (Moral: What is done to or by you is done to others in your society.)

And I will make you fishers of men.

Identity, Alienation, and Ways of Life

KEITH E. DAVIS

Keith E. Davis (1936–   ) received his Ph.D. from Duke University in 1961 and has written on the problem of personal interaction.

. . .

The aim of this final section is to remove some of the mystery from a set of related concepts—*identity, alienation, commitment*—that are bandied about in both popular and scholarly discussions of man's place in contemporary society. Of necessity, these concepts extend beyond purely psychological considerations because the phenomena are social, historical, and cultural. Thus our starting place is the social reality that gives substance to personal identities.

What Holds a Society Together?

If society is held together by more than fear, then the positive basis must consist in some *appreciation* by the individual of his own place in it and of what everyone is getting out of the society's practices and institutions—a sense that the arrangement benefits those taking part in it. Actually, in most complex societies, there may be few who appreciate the full range of society's practices and many for whom certain practices are unacceptable. In the actual case then, the social fabric must be held together by a narrower perspective. Probably the rock bottom requirement is that a person appreciate his own options and his own place in society. Such an appreciation gives one a reason to accept norms and rules that do not confer immediate personal advantage.

When this condition is not met for a sufficient number of persons, there is widespread social chaos and pervasive identity confusion and alienation. When

Source: Michael Wertheimer, *Confrontation* (Glenview, Ill.: Scott, Foresman, 1970), pp. 51–56.

people cease to think that their interests and their values are being protected by the larger social pattern, then each significant social subgroup is tempted to take the enforcement of norms or the protection of its own interests into its own hands. Witness the recent concern for "law and order."

Many conditions can foster social disorganization. Perhaps the most critical one is the existence of genuine contradictions in the social system. A self-contradictory system cannot in fact be understood: thus it can hardly be fully appreciated.

A particularly pernicious form of self-contradiction has been labeled *value-access disjunction* by sociologists (Merton, 1957). To the degree that people come to cherish values and strive for goals that are not in fact open to them (or, in the case of values, are not adhered to by those in power), one has the conditions for *anomie*—a sense of social chaos and individual confusion of self and values. In a very concrete sense, the members of the society are being taught to live a way of life that cannot be lived, and this state of affairs has serious implications for psychological functioning—particularly with respect to the kinds of identities that can be developed.

Contradictions in a social system are likely to be a matter of degree, in that some contradictions affect more people than others, and affect them more severely. For example the contradiction between our ideal of equality before the law and the actual absence of effective legal services for the poor has its greatest detrimental effect on the poor—others in the society do not feel the impact of the contradiction and may even be unaware of it. The same is true of the discrepancy between our ideals of freedom and equality and the systematic, unthinking anti-Negro policies that have been so prevalent in our society.

When a person does not appreciate his options and his place in society, it may be because he is inadequate or pathological in some way, so that he suffers a *reduced ability to appreciate a way of life*. This personal pathology interpretation is reflected in Keniston's "Inburn." There we see a person who distrusts men, who anticipates only harm, injustice, and abuse from his fellow men. He wishes to return to the womb. He rejects society, has no definite plans; he is unable to relate to women of his own age. In short, he has no appreciation for what the society has to offer in the way of ideals, careers, and personal satisfaction, nor does he appreciate his place in society. The opportunities and possibilities of youth and adulthood have no zest for him. Rather they are nothing more than uncertainties and difficulties when he compares them to his special relationship with his mother.

But another general possibility is that the person's society has offered him a *reduced opportunity to participate meaningfully in its practices*. On this view, there is nothing to appreciate: one's place in the society really *is* unacceptable. Again, it is Keniston who most clearly articulates the relevance of this alternative. There he shows conditions which are conducive to social pathology. In his analysis, rapid, chronic social change is the key, for it contributes to the irrelevance of parents as sources of positive identities, and to a cult of the present. Also produced by these kinds of social changes are (1) a fragmentation of work and of communities in ways that make the development of a stable identity more difficult, and (2) family tensions which are reflected in the difficulty that men have in reconciling the demands of career and family and that women have in the severe frustrations of their artistic and intellectual strivings because of the sheer fact of motherhood.

With rapid social change, the potential for self-contradiction increases. It is a commonplace idea of sociological theory that social change will have unanticipated consequences. Because any change, planned or not, has this potential to produce results that conflict with other practices or values of the society, we sometimes must live with our new practices for a generation or more to know just what they will bring. An example of unintended and undesired consequences of a new practice is described in Bettelheim's *Children of the Dream* (1969), which deals with what the second- and third-generation children of the Israeli kibbutzim are like. While the intent of the communal child-rearing was to reduce the extremely close family ties and the subtle controlling power of the family (now almost a cliché in the form of the "Jewish-mother" stereotype), Bettelheim has found evidence that the collective child rearing has resulted in a person who is less guilt-ridden and less psychologically disturbed but also more shallow and less complex.

In Keniston's view the prevalence of alienation and protest among those students in the best social positions—from affluent backgrounds, at the best colleges and universities—argues for the social pathology thesis. The depth of the alienation, identity crises, and despair are such that the society itself must be contributing to the problem. In a recent article on student drug use (1969) he says:

> Political and historical events do not have a direct, one-to-one relationship with drug use: the war in Vietnam does not *cause* students to smoke marijuana or experiment with LSD. But the political climate of the past few years has created a negative view of the possibility of meaningful involvement within the established institutions of the society, at the same time that it has convinced many students that society is in desperate need of reform. This climate of opinion in turn contributes to the assumption that if meaning, excitement, and dignity are to be found in the world, they must be found within one's own cranium. Drug use can indeed be a kind of cop-out, not from perverstiy or laziness, but simply because there seems to be no other alternative. Student drug use is indeed a commentary upon American society, but it is above all an indirect criticism of our society's inability to offer the young exciting, honorable and effective ways of using their intelligence and idealism to reform our society.

While the relative contribution of the two sources—personal and societal—is unclear, we have a situation in which too few people appreciate what the society actually does have to offer them, and in which our society, to some extent, really does offer bitterly conflicting values and social practices. And it is just this situation that shows us the relationship of *alienation* and *commitment* to each other and to a way of life. To be alienated from one's way of life is to go through the motions of participating in some (or all) of its practices while seeing no meaning or value in them. For example, the individual gets a job and works not because work is a human good containing the possibility of self-realization, productivity, and service to others but simply because he must live.

The commitments normally associated with one's work are nonexistent, or they are held only mechanically. Alienation is, therefore, a distinctive kind of identity confusion that has its roots jointly in the individual's experience and capacities and in the society's structuring of his experience and opportunities.

Sense of Identity and One's Place in Society

It is a commonplace finding in research on the self-concept that for most people, status concepts such as age, sex, religion, career, and the like play a central role in their concepts of themselves—of "who they are." A person tends to think of himself in terms of the positions he occupies and the roles he has in the society. Such a fact raises a number of interesting questions: (1) What is the relation between self-concept and sense of identity? (2) What is the role of ideology in identity development? (3) What explains the dramatic changes of identity that occasionally occur? Let us deal with these in order.

IDENTITY AND SELF-CONCEPT. In many respects the notions of self-concept and identity have the same conceptual implications, but in one important way they differ. The self-concept—how a particular person views himself and how he treats himself—can be reproduced by a list of characteristics and statuses. An identity, however, involves a unity of the self as object and actor. In the same way that a physical object is a unity—not a fragment, part, or incomplete element of another structure—the self has a unity and completeness. So conceptually a sense of identity includes the idea of the unified totality, which no list of characteristics could ever capture.

One of the favorite assessment devices for self-concept involves having the person answer the question, "Who am I?" by listing 20 items. One of the common complaints by persons taking this instrument is, "But I am more than a list of the 20 most important things about me." And of course the complaint is justified. But though the list structure is inappropriate to capture that sense of unity, it is needed for specifying what identity crisis the person is suffering or in what respect he is alienated; thus the classic self-concept research can be useful in understanding identities.

IDEOLOGY AND IDENTITY. One might wonder whether a person at the bottom of the social order—say, an untouchable in nineteenth-century India—could have anything but a negative view of himself. The answer is that, even though his position is the lowest in the society, he may yet have a partially positive self-image and identity through sharing his society's ideology. In fact, one might argue that only brute force could hold together a society with severe inequities if an ideology did not exist which justified the social order and which was accepted by most of its members. In the case of the untouchable, the Hindu religious way of life contains the possibility of reincarnation in animal and human forms. Thus the lowly untouchable was still a person with the possibility, in the next life, of a much higher social station and the ultimate possibility of perfection or oneness with God and nature (Nirvana).

Also important is the fact that a social order, too, is a totality. Just as the lowest position on any team is still an intrinsic part of the team, so even the lowest social position is required by the society for it to exist in its current form. An ideology or religion that justifies the entire way of life will, then, contain a justification for even the lowest social position and a statement of its importance.

But just as an ideology provides the resources for reconciling people to the social order, so it can provide the resources for rebellion, protest, and reform. It is the youth who take the values of justice, equality, and moral commitment seriously who are most likely to protest the discrepancies they see between what is preached and what is practiced.

Erikson, in his studies of Luther and Gandhi, has shown how the creative resolution of identity crises can be the source of significant alterations of a way of life. Luther's innovation was the idea of the freedom of the human spirit and the pre-eminence of the individual conscience over the structure of the Church—ideas which were to fuel the fires both of the reformation and, later, of liberalism. Gandhi's innovation was the idea of militant nonviolence as a tool of social revolution by the weak. In both cases, the ideas, when acted upon, were to lead to significant political and social change.

CONVERSIONS AND DRAMATIC IDENTITY CHANGES. Perhaps no other aspect of identity is more puzzling than the dramatic changes of the convert to a new way of life. Malcolm X (1964), a hustler, drug addict, and thief, down and out in jail, was converted to Black Muslimism and became a Puritan in his gratification of physical pleasures and an extraordinarily adept preacher, proselytizer, and political debater. Furthermore, he had the psychological flexibility to profit from his experiences in Mecca and with white student audiences to begin to rethink the Muslim separatist doctrine. Bertrand Russell, after devoting ten years to intense intellectual work (with Whitehead) on the *Principia Mathematica,* largely withdrawn from society and for most of the period without any intimate relations (emotional or sexual) with his first wife, came out of his isolation into a love affair and into an active life of political, social, and moral combat. In his autobiography, Russell (1968) comments on some of the changes he underwent as a result.

> Ottoline had a great influence upon me, which was almost wholly beneficial. She laughed at me when I behaved like a don or a prig, and when I was dictatorial in conversation. She gradually cured me of the belief that I was seething with appalling wickedness which could only be kept under by an iron self-control. She made me less self-centered, and less self-righteous. Her sense of humour was very great, and I became aware of the danger of rousing it unintentionally. She made me much less of a Puritan, and much less censorious than I had been. And of course the mere fact of happy love after the empty years made everything easier. Many men are afraid of being influenced by women, but as far as my experience goes, this is a foolish fear. It seems to me that men need women, and women need men, mentally as much as physically. For my part, I owe a great deal to women whom I have loved, and without them I should have been far more narrow-minded.

Identity changes can range all the way from the major sort experienced by Malcolm X and Martin Luther through the moderate changes described by Russell to minor changes such as the giving up of a bad habit or vice like cigarette smoking or profanity.

Anthony Wallace (1961), the cultural anthropologist, described the general features of a case of identity change that is typical. The focus in this excerpt is not an individual, as in the illustrations we have used so far, but an entire people.

The severe disorganization of a sociocultural system may be caused by the impact of any one or combination of a variety of forces which push the system beyond the limits of equilibrium. Some of these forces are: climatic or faunal changes which destroy the economic basis of its existence; epidemic disease which grossly alters the population structure; wars which exhaust the society's resources of manpower or result in defeat or invasion; internal conflict among interest groups which results in extreme disadvantage for at least one group; and, very commonly, a position of perceived subordination and inferiority with respect to an adjacent society. The latter, by the use of more or less coercion (or even no coercion at all, as in situations where the mere example set by the dominant society raises too-high levels of aspiration), brings about uncoordinated cultural changes. Under conditions of disorganization, the system, from the standpoint of at least some of its members, is unable to make possible the reliable satisfaction of certain values which are held to be essential to continued well-being and self-respect. The [world view] of a culturally disillusioned person, accordingly, is an image of a world that is unpredictable, or barren in its simplicity, or both. His mood (depending on the precise nature of the disorganization) will be one of panic-stricken anxiety, shame, guilt, depression, or apathy.

An example of the kind of disorganization to which we refer is given by the two thousand or so Seneca Indians of New York at the close of the eighteenth century. Among these people, a supreme value attached to the conception of the absolutely free and autonomous individual, unconstrained by and indifferent to his own and others' pain and hardship. This individual was capable of free indulgence of emotional impulses but, in crises, freely subordinated his own wishes to the needs of his community. Among the men, especially, this ego-ideal was central in personality organization. Men defined the roles of hunting, of warfare, and of statesmanship as the conditions of achievement of this value; thus, the stereotypes of "the good hunter," the brave warrior," and "the forest statesman" were the images of masculine success. But the 43 years from 1754, when the French and Indian War began, to 1797, when the Seneca sold their last hunting grounds and became largely confined to tiny, isolated reservations, brought with them changes in their situation which made achievement of these ideals virtually impossible. The good hunter could no longer hunt; the game was scarce, and it was almost suicidally dangerous to stray far from the reservation among the numerous hostile white men. The brave warrior could no longer fight, being under-supplied, abandoned by his allies, and his women and children threatened by growing military might of the United States. The forest statesman was an object of contempt, and this disillusionment was perhaps more shattering than the rest. The Iroquois chiefs, for nearly a century, had been able to play off British and French, then Americans and British, against one another, extorting supplies and guarantees of territorial immunity from both sides. They had maintained an extensive system of alliances and hegemonies among surrounding tribal groups. Suddenly they were shorn of their power. White men no longer spoke of the League of the Iroquois with respect; their western Indian dependents and allies regarded them as cowards for having made peace with the Americans.

The initial Seneca response to the progress of sociocultural disorganization was quasi-pathological: many became drunkards; the fear of witches increased; squabbling factions were unable to achieve a common policy. But a revitalization movement developed in 1799, based on the religious revelations reported by one of the disillusioned forest statesman, one Handsome Lake, who preached a code of patterned religious and cultural reform. The drinking of whiskey was proscribed; witchcraft was to be stamped out; various outmoded rituals and prevalent sins were to be abandoned. In addition, various syncretic cultural reforms, amounting to a reorientation of the socioeconomic system, were to be undertaken, including the adoption of agriculture (hitherto a feminine calling) by the men, and the focusing of kinship responsibilities within the nuclear family (rather than in the clan and lineage). The general acceptance of Handsome Lake's Code, within a few years, wrought seemingly miraculous changes. A group of sober, devout, partly literate, and technologically up-to-date farming communities suddenly replaced the demoralized slums in the wilderness.

Such dramatic transformations are, as a matter of historical fact, very common in human history, and probably have been the medium of as much culture change as the slower equilibrium processes. (pp. 144–146)[1]

In the more dramatic cases of identity change, the change is a matter of adopting (Malcolm X) or creating a new way of life (Handsome Lake and Luther) with a basis for self-respect. Wallace continues.

Revitalization depends on the successful completion of the following functions:

1. *Formulation of a code.* An individual, or a group of individuals, constructs a new, utopian image of sociocultural organization. This model is a blueprint of an ideal society or "goal culture." Contrasted with the goal culture is the existing culture, which is presented as inadequate or evil in certain respects. Connecting the existing culture and the goal culture is a transfer culture: a system of operations which, if faithfully carried out, will transform the existing culture into the goal culture. Failure to institute the transfer operations will, according to the code, result in either the perpetuation of the existing misery or the ultimate destruction of the society (if not of the whole world). Not infrequently the code, or the core of it, is formulated by one individual in the course of a hallucinatory revelation; such prophetic experiences are apt to launch religiously oriented movements, since the source of the revelation is apt to be regarded as a supernatural being. Nonhallucinatory formulations usually are found in politically oriented movements. In either case, the formulation of the code constitutes a reformulation of the author's own [world view], and often brings to him a renewed confidence in the future and a remission of the complaints. . . .

2. *Communication.* The formulators of the code preach the code to other people in an evangelistic spirit. The aim of the communication is to make converts. The code is offered as the means of spiritual salvation for the individual and of cultural salvation for the society. Promises of benefit to the target population need not be immediate or materialistic, for the basis of the code's appeal is the attractiveness of identification with a more highly organized system, with all that this implies in the way of self-respect. Indeed, in view of the extensiveness of the changes in values often implict in such codes, appeal to currently held values would often be pointless.

[1] From *Culture and Personality* by Anthony Wallace, pp. 144–146 and 148–149. Copyright © 1961 by Random House, Inc. Reprinted by permission of the publisher.

Religious codes offer spiritual salvation, identification with God, elect status; political codes offer honor, fame; the respect of society for sacrifices made in its interest. But refusal to accept the code is usually defined as placing the listener in immediate spiritual, as well as material, peril with respect to his existing values. In small societies, the target population may be the entire community; but in more complex societies, the message may be aimed only at certain groups deemed eligible for participation. . . .

Wallace's other characteristics of a successful revitalization movement need not be given here in detail. They deal with conversions, social organization, and the eventual routinization of the code. A very useful source for the study of identity change specifically in college students is Madison's *Personality Development in College* (1969).

Conclusion

A central theme here has been the connection between one's sense of identity and the ways of life available to him. The development of a sense of identity requires not only inner values and a sense of selfhood but a commitment to certain social practices and to the implications of certain standards of performance and evaluation. To appreciate these practices is to be inclined to participate in the way of life that embodies them. If a significant minority does not appreciate the practices of the larger society, then the conditions are ripe for social disorganization and identity confusion. When these conditions exist, one of the possible results is ideological change and the creation of new identities. Whether or how generally we are now at that stage in our society is difficult to say.

Eight

God, Evil, and the Meaning of Life

> Do we not smell the divine putrefaction? for even Gods putrefy! God is dead! God remains dead! And we have killed him! How shall we console ourselves, the most murderous of all murderers?
>
> —Friedrich Nietzsche

Introduction

Why is there such a thing as religion at all? What accounts for its longevity? Why are Eastern religions and the teachings of Don Juan attractive? Is it because the Judeo-Christian God is dead as Nietzsche proclaims and the gods are still alive in the East and in the hovels and the mountains?

But what have gods to do with religion? Would a set of doctrines or attitudes or a posture be "religious" if it excluded gods? To answer such questions would seem easier if we could only fix on a definition of "religion" and "the religious." But, unfortunately, it seems as difficult to define these terms as it is to answer these questions. Perhaps we should not look for common characteristics shared by all movements that have been called "religions"; there may be only a family resemblance among them, an overlapping of some but not all characteristics. Thus, although Buddhism and Christianity do not share the characteristic of requiring a God, they are both deeply concerned with suffering.

In this chapter, our three sections deal with three overlapping features: God, evil, and man's relation to the cosmos.

On God's Existence

Some religions emphasize the attitude of faith toward their central tenets; a Christian is expected to believe that a certain kind of God exists; this belief need not be based on empirical proof or deductive argument; for Christian theology, belief in God taken as an article of faith is as qualified a belief as if it were based on rational grounds. This contrasts with belief about ordinary matters of fact such as the amount of money in my checking account or the existence of Number 17 Bus on Jones Street. Usually we would consider a person rather irrational and a mite peculiar, if not downright unreliable, should he or she take it as an article of faith rather than evidence that there is money in the checking account; such people need bringing up short; you "just can't operate that way."

Why should we tolerate persons taking such an important belief as belief in God on faith when we will not allow it with checking accounts? Are we just more tolerant about religion? Or is that this belief is acknowledgedly irrational and, therefore, beyond empirical or deductive proof for its truth? **Søren Kierkegaard** finds it vain for Reason to attempt to prove the existence of God, our name for the Unknown. It is also paradoxical that Reason should try to prove the Unknown, for by its very nature Reason can deal only with that which is knowable. Kierkegaard wonders "And how does God's existence emerge from the Proof? . . . As long as I keep my hold on the proof, i.e., continue to demonstrate, the existence does not come out, if for no other reason than that I am engaged in proving it; but when I let the proof go, the existence is there. But this act of letting go is surely also something; it is indeed a contribution of mine. Must not this also be taken into account, this little moment, brief as it may be—it need not be long, for it is a *leap*." This "contribution" is ours, something we give rather than being the gift of Reason, although Reason paradoxically wishes to muscle in on the act. "The paradoxical passion of the Reason thus comes repeatedly into collision with the Unknown, which does indeed exist, but is unknown, and insofar does not exist. The Reason cannot advance beyond this point, and yet it cannot refrain in its paradoxicalness from arriving at this limit and occupying itself therewith."

While Kierkegaard recommends giving up Reason's project for proving God's existence, there are Christian divines who think that God's existence need not be taken on faith alone because it is not irrational to believe in God; they think there are rational proofs of God's existence. One qualifies as a Christian if God's existence is taken on faith; but this does nothing for bringing the non-Christian to belief because the non-Christian will not accept God's existence on faith alone. Theology and philosophy may join hands; what theology says can be taken on faith alone and what philosophy says can be believed only if rational grounds are supplied need not exclude one another; faith and reason do not lead us in opposite directions according to St. Anselm, St. Thomas Aquinas, and William Paley, who offer different arguments for God's existence.

The argument from **St. Anselm** (the first essay in this section) is very short yet elusive for the student, who too frequently casually dismisses it. We urge you to give the argument considerable thought. The best way to do this is to frame a refutation of it and then let one of your friends, the class, or your mentor show you why you have not got a refutation after all. Ironically, your refutation is likely to be embarrassingly longer than Anselm's argument.

St. Thomas Aquinas (the second essay) recognized that some people do not accept Christianity because they lack faith. One cannot give people faith as one would give them instruction; and it does not do much good to exhort or threaten them; and spellbinding generally has only a short-term effect. The most one can do is prepare the unbeliever and take away the obstacles that have stunted the flower of faith. One of these obstacles could be rational doubt that the object of faith and worship exists. It may seem to the unbeliever that belief in the existence of God is a rag of mythological nonsense woven by the imagination of the insecure and frightened who need reassurance in a wicked world. If so, then anyone who feels it their duty to help as many unbelievers to salvation as they can will formulate arguments that rationally prove the existence of God. This duty calls for theologians to become philosophers, to supplement the "revealed truth" with philosophic reason.

William Hamilton has remarked that his son, who has become a technological man, does not feel the same awe that Hamilton felt as a youth when he looked into the sky. This feeling of awe has been called natural piety. The emotional experience of fully realizing the incredible complexity of the world may be so overwhelming that our breast fills with it and our mind says to our heart, "Yes, this is the religious experience." This natural piety may increase with an increase in knowledge; the natural piety of men took a sharp leap after Isaac Newton's great works were published, because they yielded additional knowledge and evidence of the universe's incredible order, an order marvelously matching the universe's incredible complexity. **William Paley,** in the third essay of this section, uses a watch as an example of designed order. That in itself would not seem relevant to a proof of God's existence, but it becomes pregnant with relevance if one is able to show that the universe has an order similar to the watch. That was precisely what people believed Newton had shown. Until then, the premise about nature's order was relatively weak; Newton gave it muscle. The divines praised Newton because he showed them that the glory of physics rests in its theological service. A vast structure of natural theology was erected on the basis of the strengthened design argument, neatly presented here by Paley.

The Ontological Argument

ST. ANSELM

St. Anselm (1033–1109) was made Archbishop of Canterbury in 1093. Anselm's name will forever be associated with the ontological argument for the existence of God. During his years in the abbey, he wrote two works for which he is best known: *The Monologium* and *The Proslogium.*

Truly there is a God, although the fool hath said in his heart, There is no God.

And so, Lord, do thou, who dost give understanding to faith, give me, so far as thou knowest it to be profitable, to understand that thou art as we believe; and

Source: St. Anselm: Basic Writings, 2nd ed., trans. by S. N. Deane, with Introduction by Charles Hartshorne (La Salle, Ill., 1961). Reprinted by permission of The Open Court Publishing Co.

that thou art that which we believe. And, indeed, we believe that thou art a being than which nothing greater can be conceived. Or is there no such nature, since the fool hath said in his heart, there is no God? (Psalms xiv. 1). But, at any rate, this very fool, when he hears of this being of which I speak—a being than which nothing greater can be conceived—understands what he hears, and what he understands is in his understanding; although he does not understand it to exist.

For, it is one thing for an object to be in the understanding, and another to understand that the object exists. When a painter first conceives of what he will afterwards perform, he has it in his understanding, but he does not yet understand it to be, because he has not yet performed it. But after he has made the painting, he both has it in his understanding and he understands that it exists, because he has made it.

Hence, even the fool is convinced that something exists in the understanding, at least, than which nothing greater can be conceived. For, when he hears of this, he understands it. And whatever is understood, exists in the understanding. And assuredly that, than which nothing greater can be conceived, cannot exist in the understanding alone. For, suppose it exists in the understanding alone: then it can be conceived to exist in reality; which is greater.

Therefore, if that, than which nothing greater can be conceived, exists in the understanding alone, the very being, than which nothing greater can be conceived, is one, than which a greater can be conceived. But obviously this is impossible. Hence, there is no doubt that there exists a being, than that which nothing greater can be conceived, and it exists both in the understanding and in reality.

God cannot be conceived not to exist—God is that, than which nothing greater can be conceived.—That which can be conceived not to exist is not God.

And it assuredly exists so truly, that it cannot be conceived not to exist. For, it is possible to conceive of a being which cannot be conceived not to exist; and this is greater than one which can be conceived not to exist. Hence, if that, than which nothing greater can be conceived, can be conceived not to exist, it is not that, than which nothing greater can be conceived. But this is an irreconcilable contradiction. There is, then, so truly a being than which nothing greater can be conceived to exist, that it cannot even be conceived not to exist; and this being thou art, O Lord, our God.

So truly, therefore, dost thou exist, O Lord, my God, that thou canst not be conceived not to exist; and rightly. For, if a mind could conceive of a being better than thee, the creature would rise above the Creator; and this is most absurd. And, indeed, whatever else there is, except thee alone, can be conceived not to exist. To thee alone, therefore, it belongs to exist more truly than all other beings, and hence in a higher degree than all others. For, whatever else exists does not exist so truly, and hence in a less degree it belongs to it to exist. Why, then, has the fool said in his heart, there is no God (Psalms xiv. 1), since it is so evident, to a rational mind, that thou dost exist in the highest degree of all? Why, except that he is dull and a fool?

How the fool has said in his heart what cannot be conceived.—A thing may be conceived in two ways: (1) when the world signifying it is conceived; (2) when the thing itself is understood. As far as the word goes, God can be conceived not to exist; in reality he cannot.

But how has the fool said in his heart what he could not conceive; or how is it that he could not conceive what he said in his heart? since it is the same to say in the heart, and to conceive.

But, if really, nay, since really, he both conceived, because he said in his heart; and did not say in his heart, because he could not conceive; there is more than one way in which a thing is said in the heart or conceived. For, in one sense, an object is conceived, when the word signifying it is conceived; and in another, when the very entity, which the object is, is understood.

In the former sense, then, God can be conceived not to exist; but in the latter, not at all. For no one who understands what fire and water are can conceive fire to be water, in accordance with the nature of the facts themselves, although this is possible according to the words. So, then, no one who understands what God is can conceive that God does not exist; although he says these words in his heart, either without any, or with some foreign signification. For God is that than which a greater cannot be conceived. And he who thoroughly understands this, assuredly understands that this being so truly exists, that not even in concept can it be non-existent. Therefore, he who understands that God so exists, cannot conceive that he does not exist.

I thank thee, gracious Lord, I thank thee; because what I formerly believed by thy bounty, I now so understand by thine illumination, that if I were unwilling to believe that thou dost exist, I should not be able not to understand this to be true.

Five Proofs of the Existence of God

ST. THOMAS AQUINAS

St. Thomas Aquinas (1225–1274) devoted his life to the clarification of Christian doctrine and its integration with Aristotle's metaphysics. He was the greatest medieval Catholic philosopher and wrote more than a hundred volumes of philosophy.

Whether God Exists?

Objection 1. It seems that God does not exist; because if one of two contraries be infinite, the other would be altogether destroyed. But the name *God*

Source: Basic Writings of St. Thomas Aquinas, ed. by Anton C. Pegis (New York, 1945). Copyright © 1945 by Random House, Inc. Reprinted by permission of the publisher and Ian Hislop, O.P., St. Dominic's Priory, London.

means that He is infinite goodness. If, therefore, God existed, there would be no evil discoverable; but there is evil in the world. Therefore God does not exist.

Obj. 2. Further, it is superfluous to suppose that what can be accounted for by a few principles has been produced by many. But it seems that everything we see in the world can be accounted for by other principles, supposing God did not exist. For all natural things can be reduced to one principle, which is nature; and all voluntary things can be reduced to one principle, which is human reason, or will. Therefore there is no need to suppose God's existence.

On the contrary, It is said in the person of God: *I am who am* (Exod. iii. 14).

I answer that, The existence of God can be proved in five ways.

The first and more manifest way is the argument from motion. It is certain, and evident to our senses, that in the world some things are in motion. Now whatever is moved is moved by another, for nothing can be moved except it is in potentiality to that towards which it is moved; whereas a thing moves inasmuch as it is in act. For motion is nothing else than the reduction of something from potentiality to actuality. But nothing can be reduced from potentiality to actuality, except by something in a state of actuality. Thus that which is actually hot, as fire, makes wood, which is potentially hot, to be actually hot, and thereby moves and changes it. Now it is not possible that the same thing should be at once in actuality and potentiality in the same respect but only in different respects. For what is actually hot cannot simultaneously be potentially hot; but it is simultaneously potentially cold. It is therefore impossible that in the same respect and in the same way a thing should be both mover and moved, *i.e.,* that it should move itself. Therefore, whatever is moved must be moved by another. If that by which it is moved be itself moved, then this also must needs be moved by another, and that by another again. But this cannot go on to infinity, because then there would be no first mover, and, consequently, no other mover, seeing that subsequent movers move only inasmuch as they are moved by the first mover; as the staff moves only because it is moved by the hand. Therefore it is necessary to arrive at a first mover, moved by no other; and this everyone understands to be God.

The second way is from the nature of efficient cause. In the world of sensible things we find there is an order of efficient causes. There is no case known (neither is it, indeed, possible) in which a thing is found to be the efficient cause of itself; for so it would be prior to itself, which is impossible. Now in efficient causes it is not possible to go on to infinity, because in all efficient causes following in order, the first is the cause of the intermediate cause, and the intermediate is the cause of the ultimate cause, whether the intermediate cause by several, or one only. Now to take away the cause is to take away the effect. Therefore, if there be no first cause among efficient causes, there will be no ultimate, nor any intermediate, cause. But if in efficient causes it is possible to go on to infinity, there will be no first efficient cause, neither will there be an ultimate effect, nor any intermediate efficient causes; all of which is plainly false. Therefore it is necessary to admit a first efficient cause, to which everyone gives the name of God.

The third way is taken from possibility and necessity, and runs thus. We find in nature things that are possible to be and not to be, since they are found to be generated, and to be corrupted, and consequently, it is possible for them to be and not to be. But it is impossible for these always to exist, for that which can not-be at some time is not. Therefore, if everything can not-be, then at one time there was nothing in existence. Now if this were true, even now there would be nothing in existence, because that which does not exist begins to exist only through something already existing. Therefore, if at one time nothing was in existence, it would have been impossible for anything to have begun to exist; and thus even now nothing would be in existence—which is absurd. Therefore, not all beings are merely possible, but there must exist something the existence of which is necessary. But every necessary thing either has its necessity caused by another, or not. Now it is impossible to go on to infinity in necessary things which have their necessity caused by another, as has been already proved in regard to efficient causes. Therefore we cannot but admit the existence of some being having of itself its own necessity, and not receiving it from another, but rather causing in others their necessity. This all men speak of as God.

The fourth way is taken from the gradation to be found in things. Among beings there are some more and some less good, true, noble, and the like. But *more* and *less* are predicated of different things according as they resemble in their different ways something which is the maximum, as a thing is said to be hotter according as it more nearly resembles that which is hottest; so that there is something which is truest, something best, something noblest, and, consequently, something which is most being, for those things that are greatest in truth are greatest in being, as it is written in [Aristotle's] *Metaphysics* ii. Now the maximum in any genus is the cause of all in that genus, as fire, which is the maximum of heat, is the cause of all hot things, as is said in the same book. Therefore there must also be something which is to all beings the cause of their being, goodness, and every other perfection; and this we call God.

The fifth way is taken from the governance of the world. We see that things which lack knowledge, such as natural bodies, act for an end, and this is evident from their acting always, or nearly always, in the same way, so as to obtain the best result. Hence it is plain that they achieve their end, not fortuitously, but designedly. Now whatever lacks knowledge cannot move towards an end, unless it be directed by some being endowed with knowledge and intelligence; as the arrow is directed by the archer. Therefore some intelligent being exists by whom all natural things are directed to their end: and this being we call God.

Reply Obj. 1. As Augustine says: *Since God is the highest good, He would not allow any evil to exist in His works; unless His omnipotence and goodness were such as to bring good even out of evil.* This is part of the infinite goodness of God, that He should allow evil to exist, and out of it produce good.

Reply Obj. 2. Since nature works for a determinate end under the direction of a higher agent, whatever is done by nature must be traced back to God as to its first cause. So likewise whatever is done voluntarily must be traced back to some higher cause other than human reason and will, since these can change and fail; for all things that are changeable and capable of defect must be traced back to an immovable and self-necessary first principle, as has been shown.

The Teleological Argument

WILLIAM PALEY

William Paley (1743–1806) wrote many apologetic works, including *Evidences of Christianity* (1794) and *Appearances of Nature* (1802).

Statement of the Argument

In crossing a heath, suppose I pitched my foot against a *stone*, and were asked how the stone came to be there, I might possibly answer, that, for anything I knew to the contrary, it had lain there forever; nor would it, perhaps, be very easy to show the absurdity of this answer. But suppose I found a *watch* upon the ground, and it should be inquired how the watch happened to be in that place, I should hardly think of the answer which I had before given—that, for anything I knew, the watch might have always been there. Yet why should not this answer serve for the watch as well as for the stone? why is it not as admissible in the second case as in the first? For this reason, and for no other, viz., that, when we come to inspect the watch, we perceive (what we could not discover in the stone) that its several parts are framed and put together for a purpose, e.g. that they are so formed and adjusted as to produce motion, and that motion so regulated as to point out the hour of the day; that, if the different parts had been differently shaped from what they are, if a different size from what they are, or placed after any other manner, or in any other order than that in which they are placed, either no motion at all would have been carried on in the machine, or none which would have answered the use that is now served by it. To reckon up a few of the plainest of these parts, and of their offices, all tending to one result:—We see a cylindrical box containing a coiled elastic spring, which, by its endeavor to relax itself, turns round the box. We next observe a flexible chain (artificially wrought for the sake of flexure) communicating the action of the spring from the box to the fusee. We then find a series of wheels, the teeth of which catch in, and apply to, each other, conducting the motion from the fusee to the balance, and from the balance to the pointer, and at the same time, by the size and shape of those wheels, so regulating that motion as to terminate in causing an index, by an equable and measured progression, to pass over a given space in a given time. We take notice that the wheels are made of brass, in order to keep them from rust; the springs of steel, no other metal being so elastic; that over the face of the watch there is placed a glass, a material employed in no other part of the work, but in the room of which, if there had been any other than a transparent substance, the hour could not be seen without opening the case. This mechanism being observed (it requires indeed an examination of the instrument, and perhaps some previous knowledge of the subject, to perceive and understand it; but being once, as we

Source : William Paley, *Natural Theology* (1802).

have said, observed and understood), the inference, we think, is inevitable, that the watch must have had a maker; that there must have existed, at some time, and at some place or other, an artificer or artificers who formed it for the purpose which we find it actually to answer; who comprehended its construction, and designed its use.

I. Nor would it, I apprehend, weaken the conclusion, that we had never seen a watch made; that we had never known an artist capable of making one; that we were altogether incapable of executing such a piece of workmanship ourselves, or of understanding in what manner it was performed; all this being no more than what is true of some exquisite remains of ancient art, of some lost arts, and, to the generality of mankind, of the more curious productions of modern manufacture. Does one man in a million know how oval frames are turned? Ignorance of this kind exalts our opinion of the unseen and unknown artist's skill, if he be unseen and unknown, but raise no doubt in our minds of the existence and agency of such an artist, at some former time, and in some place or other. Nor can I perceive that it varies at all the inference, whether the question arise concerning a human agent, or concerning an agent of a different species, or an agent possessing, in some respect, a different nature.

II. Neither, secondly, would it invalidate our conclusion, that the watch sometimes went wrong, or that it seldom went exactly right. The purpose of the machinery, the design, and the designer, might be evident, and, in the case supposed, would be evident, in whatever way we accounted for the irregularity of the movement, or whether we could account for it or not. It is not necessary that a machine be perfect, in order to show with what design it was made; still less necessary, where the only question is, whether it were made with any design at all.

III. Nor, thirdly, would it bring any uncertainty into the argument, if there were a few parts of the watch, concerning which we could not discover, or had not yet discovered, in what manner they conduced to the general effect; or even some parts, concerning which we could not ascertain whether they conduced to that effect in any manner whatever. For, as to the first branch of the case, if by the loss, or disorder, or decay of the parts in question, the movement of the watch were found in fact to be stopped, or disturbed, or retarded, no doubt would remain in our minds as to the utility or intention of these parts, although we should be unable to investigate the manner according to which, or the connection by which, the ultimate effect depended upon their action or assistance; and the more complex is the machine, the more likely is this obscurity to arise. Then, as to the second thing supposed, namely, that there were parts which might be spared without prejudice to the movement of the watch, and that he had proved this by experiment, these superfluous parts, even if we were completely assured that they were such, would not vacate the reasoning which we had instituted concerning other parts. The indication of contrivance remained, with respect to them, nearly as it was before.

IV. Nor, fourthly, would any man in his senses think the existence of the watch, with its various machinery, accounted for, by being told that it was one out of possible combinations of material forms; that whatever he had found in the place where he found the watch, must have contained some internal configuration or other; and that this configuration might be the structure now exhibited, viz., of the works of a watch, as well as a different structure.

V. Nor, fifthly, would it yield his inquiry more satisfaction, to be answered, that there existed in things a principle of order, which had disposed the parts of the watch into their present form and situation. He never knew a watch made by the principle of order; nor can he even form to himself an idea of what is meant by a principle of order, distinct from the intelligence of the watch-maker.

VI. Sixthly, he would be surprised to hear that the mechanism of the watch was no proof of contrivance, only a motive to induce the mind to think so:

VII. And not less surprised to be informed, that the watch in his hand was nothing more than the result of the laws of *metallic* nature. It is a perversion of language to assign any law as the efficient, operative cause of anything. A law presupposes an agent; for it is only the mode according to which an agent proceeds; it implies a power; for it is the order according to which that power acts. Without this agent, without this power, which are both distinct from itself, the *law* does nothing, is nothing. The expression, "the law of metallic nature," may sound strange and harsh to a philosophic ear; but it seems quite as justifiable as some others which are more familiar to him such as "the law of vegetable nature," "the law of animal nature," or, indeed, as "the law of nature" in general, when assigned as the cause of phenomena in exclusion of agency and power, or when it is substituted into the place of these.

VIII. Neither, lastly, would our observer be driven out of his conclusion, or from his confidence in its truth, by being told that he knew nothing at all about the matter. He knows enough for his argument: he knows the utility of the end: he knows the subserviency and adaptation of the means to the end. These points being known, his ignorance of other points, his doubts concerning other points, affect not the certainty of his reasoning. The consciousness of knowing little need not beget a distrust of that which he does know. . . .

Application of the Argument

Every indication of contrivance, every manifestation of design, which existed in the watch, exist in the works of nature; with the difference, on the side of nature, of being greater and more, and that in a degree which exceeds all computation. I mean the contrivances of nature surpass the contrivances of art, in the complexity, subtilty, and curiosity of the mechanism; and still more, if possible, do they go beyond them in number and variety; yet in a multitude of cases, are not less evidently mechanical, not less evidently contrivances, not less evidently accommodated to their end, or suited to their office, than are the most perfect productions of human ingenuity. . . .

The Leap to God

SØREN KIERKEGAARD

Søren Kierkegaard (1813–1855), the father of modern existentialism, has also had a keen influence upon the widespread twentieth-century theological movement associated with the name of Karl Barth. In his *Philosophical Fragments* (1936) and *Concluding Unscientific Postscript* (1942), Kierkegaard attacked the rationalist desire for proofs as an evasion of the claim of revelation.

But what is this unknown something with which the Reason collides when inspired by its paradoxical passion, with the result of unsettling even man's knowledge of himself? It is the Unknown. It is not a human being, insofar as we know what man is; nor is it any other known thing. So let us call this unknown something: *God*. It is nothing more than a name we assign to it. The idea of demonstrating that this unknown something (God) exists could scarcely suggest itself to the Reason. For if God does not exist it would of course be impossible to prove it; and if he does exist it would be folly to attempt it. For at the very outset, in beginning my proof, I will have presupposed it, not as doubtful but as certain (a presupposition is never doubtful, for the very reason that it is a presupposition), since otherwise I would not begin, readily understanding that the whole would be impossible if he did not exist. But if when I speak of proving God's existence I mean that I propose to prove that the Unknown, which exists, is God, then I express myself unfortunately. For in 'that case I do not prove anything, least of all an existence, but merely develop the content of a conception. Generally speaking, it is a difficult matter to prove that anything exists; and what is still worse for the intrepid souls who undertake the venture, the difficulty is such that fame scarcely awaits those who concern themselves with it. The entire demonstration always turn into something very different from what it assumes to be, and becomes an additional development of the consequences that flow from [our] having assumed that the object in question exists. Thus I always reason from existence, not toward existence, whether I move in the sphere of palpable sensible fact or in the realm of thought. I do not, for example, prove that a stone exists, but that some existing thing is a stone. The procedure in a court of justice does not prove that a criminal exists, but that the accused, whose existence is given, is a criminal. Whether we call existence an *accessorium* or the eternal *primus*, it is never subject to demonstration. Let us take ample time for consideration. We have no such reason for haste as have those who from concern for themselves or for God or for some other thing, must make haste to get its existence demonstrated. Under such circumstances there may indeed be need for haste, especially if the prover sincerely seeks to ap-

Source: Søren Kierkegaard, *Philosophical Fragments or A Fragment of Philosophy,* 2nd ed., original translation and introduction by David Swenson, new introduction and commentary by Niels Thulstrup, translation revised and commentary translated by Howard V. Hong (Princeton, N.J., 1962), pp. 31–36. Copyright © 1936, 1962 by Princeton University Press; Princeton paperback, 1967. Reprinted by permission of Princeton University Press.

preciate the danger that he himself, or the thing in question, may be non-existent unless the proof is finished; and does not surreptitiously entertain the thought that it exists whether he succeeds in proving it or not.

If it were proposed to prove Napoleon's existence from Napoleon's deeds, would it not be a most curious proceeding? His existence does indeed explain his deeds, but the deeds do not prove his existence, unless I have already understood the word "his" so as thereby to have assumed his existence. But Napoleon is only an individual, and insofar there exists no absolute relationship between him and his deeds; some other person might have performed the same deeds. Perhaps this is the reason why I cannot pass from the deeds to existence. If I call these deeds the deeds of Napoleon, the proof becomes superfluous, since I have already named him; if I ignore this, I can never prove from the deeds that they are Napoleon's, but only in a purely ideal manner that such deeds are the deeds of a great general, and so forth. But between God and his works there exists an absolute relationship; God is not a name but a concept. Is this perhaps the reason that his *essentia involvit existentiam* [essence involves existence]? The works of God are such that only God can perform them. Just so, but where then are the works of God? The works from which I would deduce his existence are not immediately given. The wisdom of God in nature, his goodness, his wisdom in the governance of the world—are all these manifest, perhaps, upon the very face of things? Are we not here confronted with the most terrible temptations to doubt, and is it not impossible finally to dispose of all these doubts? But from such an order of things I will surely not attempt to prove God's existence; and even if I began I would never finish, and would in addition have to live constantly in suspense, lest something so terrible should suddenly happen that my bit of proof would be demolished. From what works then do I propose to derive the proof? From the works as apprehended through an ideal interpretation, i.e., such as they do not immediately reveal themselves. But in that case it is not from the works that I prove God's existence. I merely develop the ideality I have presupposed, and because of my confidence in *this* I make so bold as to defy all objections, even those that have not yet been made. In beginning my proof I presuppose the ideal interpretation, and also that I will be successful in carrying it through; but what else is this but to presuppose that God exists, so that I really begin by virtue of confidence in him?

And how does God's existence emerge from the proof? Does it follow straightway, without any breach of continuity? Or have we not here an analogy to the behaviour of these toys, the little Cartesian dolls? As soon as I let go of the doll it stands on its head. As soon as I let it go—I must therefore let it go. So also with the proof for God's existence. As long as I keep my hold on the proof, i.e., continue to demonstrate, the existence does not come out, if for no other reason than that I am engaged in proving it; but when I let the proof go, the existence is there. But this act of letting go is surely also something; it is indeed a contribution of mine. Must not this also be taken into account, this little moment, brief as it may be—it need not be long, for it is a *leap*. However brief this moment, if only an instantaneous now, this "now" must be included in the reckoning. If anyone wishes to have it ignored, I will use it to tell a little anecdote, in order to show that it really does exist. Chrysippus was experimenting with a sorites to see if he could not bring about a break in its quality, either progressively or retrogressively. But Carneades could not get it in his head when the new quality actually emerged. Then Chrysippus told him to try making a little pause in the reckoning, and so—so it would be easier to understand. Carneades replied: "With the greatest pleasure, please do not hesitate on my account; you may not only pause, but even lie down to sleep, and it will help you just as little; for when you awake we will begin again where you left off. Just so; it boots as little to try to get rid of something by sleeping as to try to come into the possession of something in the same manner."

Whoever therefore attempts to demonstrate the existence of God (except in the sense of clarifying the concept, and without the *reservatio finalis* noted above, that the existence emerges from the demonstration by a leap) proves in lieu thereof something else, something which at times perhaps does not need a proof, and in any case needs none better; for the fool says in his heart that there is no God, but whoever says in his heart or to men: "Wait just a little and I will prove it"—what a rare man of wisdom is he![1] If in the moment of beginning his proof it is not absolutely undetermined whether God exists or not, he does not prove it; and if it is thus undetermined in the beginning he will never come to begin, partly from fear of failure, since God perhaps does not exist, and partly because he has nothing with which to begin. A project of this kind would scarcely have been undertaken by the ancients. Socrates at least, who is credited with having put forth the physico-teleological proof for God's existence, did not go about it in any such manner. He always presupposes God's existence, and under this presupposition seeks to interpenetrate nature with the idea of purpose. Had he been asked why he pursued this method, he would doubtless have explained that he lacked the courage to venture out upon so perilous a voyage of discovery without having made sure of God's existence behind him. At the word of God he casts his net as if to catch the idea of purpose; for nature herself finds many means of frightening the inquirer, and distracts him by many a digression.

The paradoxical passion of the Reason thus comes repeatedly into collision with the Unknown, which does indeed exist, but is unknown, and insofar does not exist. The Reason cannot advance beyond this point, and yet it cannot refrain in its paradoxicalness from arriving at this limit and occupying itself therewith. It will not serve to dismiss its relation to it simply by asserting that the Unknown does not exist, since this itself involves a relationship. But what then is the Unknown, since the designation of it as God merely signifies for us that it is unknown? To say that it is the Unknown because it cannot be known, and even if it were capable of being known, it could not be expressed, does not satisfy the demands of passion, though it correctly interprets the Unknown as a limit; but a limit is precisely a torment for passion, though it also serves as an incitement. And yet the Reason can come no further, whether it risks an issue *via negationis* or *via eminentia*.[2]

---

[1] What an excellent subject for a comedy of the higher lunacy!

[2] I.e., by the method of making negative statements about God or by the method of attributing known qualities to God in a higher degree (ED.).

What then is the Unknown? It is the limit to which the Reason repeatedly comes, and insofar, substituting a static form of conception for the dynamic, it is the different, the absolutely different. But because it is absolutely different, there is no mark by which it could be distinguished. When qualified as absolutely different it seems on the verge of disclosure, but this is not the case; for the Reason cannot even conceive an absolute unlikeness. The Reason cannot negate itself absolutely, but uses itself for the purpose, and thus conceives only such an unlikeness within itself as it can conceive by means of itself; it cannot absolutely transcend itself, and hence conceives only such a superiority over itself as it can conceive by means of itself. Unless the Unknown (God) remains a mere limiting conception, the single idea of difference will be thrown into a state of confusion, and become many ideas of many differences. The Unknown is then in a condition of dispersion διασπορά and the Reason may choose at pleasure from what is at hand and the imagination may suggest (the monstrous, the ludicrous, etc.).

But it is impossible to hold fast to a difference of this nature. Every time this is done it is essentially an arbitrary act, and deepest down in the heart of piety lurks the mad caprice which knows that it has itself produced its God. If no specific determination of difference can be held fast, because there is no distinguishing mark, like and unlike finally become identified with one another, thus sharing the fate of all such dialectical opposites. The unlikeness clings to the Reason and confounds it, so that the Reason no longer knows itself and quite consistently confuses itself with the unlikeness. On this point paganism has been sufficiently prolific in fantastic inventions. As for the last-named supposition, the self-irony of the Reason, I shall attempt to delineate it merely by a stroke or two, without raising any question of its being historical. There lives an individual whose appearance is precisely like that of other men; he grows up to manhood like others, he marries, he has an occupation by which he earns his livelihood, and he makes provision for the future as befits a man. For though it may be beautiful to live like the birds of the air, it is not lawful, and may lead to the sorriest of consequences: either starvation if one has enough persistence, or dependence on the bounty of others. This man is also God. How do I know? I cannot know it, for in order to know it I would have to know God, and the nature of the difference between God and man; and this I cannot know, because the Reason has reduced it to likeness with that from which it was unlike. Thus God becomes the most terrible of deceivers, because the Reason has deceived itself. The Reason has brought God as near as possible, and yet he is as far away as ever.

On Evil

Many experiences and considerations lead persons to belief in God's existence. The arguments for God's existence are probably the least influential of all. Similarly, the refutation of the arguments probably play less of a role in causing persons to doubt God's existence than their suffering does. It is difficult for a person who has suffered deeply to reconcile the suffering with the existence of an all-good, all-powerful (omnipotent), all-knowing (omniscient) God. The classic argument from evil goes as follows: If God is all-good, He/She will not wish there to be evil in the world, suffering and pain being evil; if God is all-powerful, He/She will be able to prevent the occurrence of evil; if God is all-knowing, He/She knows there is evil in the world, and being all-good will will to do away with evil, and being all-powerful will be able to do away with evil. But there is evil in the universe. Therefore, God, conceived as all-good, -powerful, and -knowing must not exist. But if God does exist, then He/She cannot have all these omniproperties as Christians claim that God does. **John Hick** tries to reconcile the presence of evil and the existence of the typical Christian deity. To do so, one or more of the premises in the above argument from evil must be denied.

Two kinds of evil exist at present in our society, causing much suffering, degradation, humiliation, and pain; these evils are sexism and racism. What makes these evils of particular interest to persons concerned with the Christian religion is that great doers of these evils profess to be Christians.

George D. Kelsey goes beyond the usual psychological, sociological, or economic accounts of racism. According to him, it is essentially a metaphysical issue, an issue about being. "Racial alienation stands alone among the forms of human conflict as the one form of collective hostility founded in the question of human being as such." Further, Kelsey finds that Christians who are racists are idolaters. He uses H. Richard Niebuhr's definition of faith, as "trust in that which gives value to the self" and "it is loyalty to what the self values." Kelsey then points out that the racist relies on race as the source of personal value and as a Christian also relies on God as a value center. This double life makes the Christian an idolator, a follower of the false idol of race, insofar as he or she is a Christian. "Thus a Christian racist may think he lives under the requirements of the God of biblical faith in most areas of his life, but whenever matters of race impinge on his life, in every area affected, the idol of race determines his attitude, decision, and action."

Evil lies within the very heart of Christian theology according to **Mary Daly.** "The myths and symbols of Christianity are essentially sexist. . . . The myth of feminine evil, expressed in the story of the Fall, is reinforced by the myth of salvation/redemption by a single human being of the male sex." These myths are responsible for the degradation of women in our culture; to rid ourselves of this evil, we must have a theological revolution. "The women's revolution is not only Antichurch. It is a postchristian spiritual revolution. The ethos of Judeo-Christian culture is dominated by The Most Unholy Trinity:

Rape, Genocide, and War. . . . The women's revolution is concerned with the transvaluation of values, beyond the ethics dominated by The Most Unholy Trinity." For those who agree with Hick that God is not responsible for evil in the universe, but that humans are, there is no other course for Western religious persons to follow than to commit themselves to rooting out the evil of sexism in the very heart of their belief structures; that is, if they would end the evil of sexism, they must remythologize Christianity. A major deterrent to this remythologizing revolution is the fear that the revolutionary result will no longer be "Christian." "The result might be a better religion but will it be Christian?" is a question that more conservative persons might ask. Is a desexed God a Christian God? How necessary to the concept of a Christian God is its male sex? Daly questions the need for anthropomorphic symbols as tools for describing God's reality; if they are superfluous, then demythologizing Christianity by erasing the connection between God and maleness would not eliminate anything necessarily distinctive about Christian doctrine.

Solutions to the Problem of Evil

JOHN HICK

John Hick (1922–   ) is Lecturer in Divinity, Cambridge University. He was formerly Stuart professor of Christian philosophy at Princeton Theological Seminary. He received his M.A. degree from the University of Edinburgh and his D.Phil. from Oxford University. His works include *Faith and Knowledge* (1957), *Philosophy of Religion* (1963), *The Existence of God* (1964), and *Faith and the Philosophers* (1964).

To many, the most powerful positive objection to belief in God is the fact of evil. Probably for most agnostics it is the appalling depth and extent of human suffering, more than anything else, that makes the idea of a loving Creator seem so implausible and disposes them toward one or another of the various naturalistic theories of religion.

As a challenge to theism, the problem of evil has traditionally been posed in the form of a dilemma: if God is perfectly loving, he must wish to abolish evil; and if he is all-powerful, he must be able to abolish evil. But evil exists; therefore God cannot be both omnipotent and perfectly loving.

Certain solutions, which at once suggest themselves, have to be ruled out so far as the Judaic-Christian faith is concerned.

To say, for example (with contemporary Christian Science), that evil is an illusion of the human mind, is impossible within a religion based upon the stark realism of the Bible. Its pages faithfully reflect the characteristic mixture

Source: John Hick, *Philosophy of Religion* (Englewood Cliffs, N.J., 1963), pp. 40–47. Copyright © 1963. Reprinted by permission of Prentice-Hall, Inc.

of good and evil in human experience. They record every kind of sorrow and suffering, every mode of man's inhumanity to man and of his painfully insecure existence in the world. There is no attempt to regard evil as anything but dark, menacingly ugly, heart-rending, and crushing. In the Christian scriptures, the climax of this history of evil is the crucifixion of Jesus, which is presented not only as a case of utterly unjust suffering, but as the violent and murderous rejection of God's Messiah. There can be no doubt, then, that for biblical faith, evil is unambiguously evil, and stands in direct opposition to God's will.

Again, to solve the problem of evil by means of the theory (sponsored, for example, by the Boston "Personalist" School)[1] of a finite deity who does the best he can with a material, intractable and co-eternal with himself, is to have abandoned the basic premise of Hebrew-Christian monotheism; for the theory amounts to rejecting belief in the infinity and sovereignty of God.

Indeed, any theory which would avoid the problem of the origin of evil by depicting it as an ultimate constituent of the universe, coordinate with good, has been repudiated in advance by the classic Christian teaching, first developed by Augustine, that evil represents the going wrong of something which in itself is good.[2] Augustine holds firmly to the Hebrew-Christian conviction that the universe is *good*—that is to say, it is the creation of a good God for a good purpose. He completely rejects the ancient prejudice, widespread in his day, that matter is evil. There are, according to Augustine, higher and lower, greater and lesser goods in immense abundance and variety; but everything which has being is good in its own way and degree, except in so far as it may have become spoiled or corrupted. Evil—whether it be an evil will, an instance of pain, or some disorder or decay in nature—has not been set there by God, but represents the distortion of something that is inherently valuable. Whatever exists is, as such, and in its proper place, good; evil is essentially parasitic upon good, being disorder and perversion in a fundamentally good creation. This understanding of evil as something negative means that it is not willed and created by God; but it does not mean (as some have supposed) that evil is unreal and can be disregarded. Clearly, the first effect of this doctrine is to accentuate even more the question of the origin of evil.

Theodicy,[3] as many modern Christian thinkers see it, is a modest enterprise, negative rather than positive in its conclusions. It does not claim to explain, nor to explain away, every instance of evil in human experience, but only to point to certain considerations which prevent the fact of evil (largely incomprehensible though it remains) from constituting a final and insuperable bar to rational belief in God.

In indicating these considerations it will be useful to follow the traditional division of the subject. There is the problem of *moral evil* or wickedness: why does an all-good and all-powerful God permit this? And there is the problem of

[1] Edgar Brightman's *A Philosophy of Religion* (Englewood Cliffs, N.J.: Prentice-Hall, Inc., 1940), Chaps. 8–10, is a classic exposition of one form of this view.

[2] See Augustine's *Confessions,* Book VII, Chap. 12; *City of God,* Book XII, Chap. 3; *Enchiridion,* Chap. 4.

[3] The word "theodicy" from the Greek *theos* (God) and *dike* (righteous) means the justification of God's goodness in the face of the fact of evil.

the *non-moral evil* of suffering or pain, both physical and mental: why has an all-good and all-powerful God created a world in which this occurs?

Christian thought has always considered moral evil in its relation to human freedom and responsibility. To be a person is to be a finite center of freedom, a (relatively) free and self-directing agent responsible for one's own decisions. This involves being free to act wrongly as well as to act rightly. The idea of a person who can be infallibly guaranteed always to act rightly is self-contradictory. There can be no guarantee in advance that a genuinely free moral agent will never choose amiss. Consequently, the possibility of wrongdoing or sin is logically inseparable from the creation of finite persons, and to say that God should not have created beings who might sin amounts to saying that he should not have created people.

This thesis has been challenged in some recent philosophical discussions of the problem of evil, in which it is claimed that no contradiction is involved in saying that God might have made people who would be genuinely free and who could yet be guaranteed always to act rightly. A quotation from one of these discussions follows:

> If there is no logical impossibility in a man's freely choosing the good on one, or on several occasions, there cannot be a logical impossibility in his freely choosing the good on every occasion. God was not, then, faced with a choice between making innocent automata and making beings who, in acting freely, would sometimes go wrong: there was open to him the obviously better possibility of making beings who would act freely but always go right. Clearly, his failure to avail himself of this possibility is inconsistent with his being both omnipotent and wholly good.[4]

A reply to this argument is suggested in another recent contribution to the discussion.[5] If by a free action we mean an action which is not externally compelled but which flows from the nature of the agent as he reacts to the circumstances in which he finds himself, there is, indeed, no contradiction between our being free and our actions being "caused" (by our own nature) and therefore being in principle predictable. There is a contradiction, however, in saying that God is the cause of our acting as we do but that we are free beings in relation to God. There is, in other words, a contradiction in saying that God has made us so that we shall of necessity act in a certain way, and that we are genuinely independent persons in relation to him. If all our thoughts and actions are divinely predestined, however free and morally responsible we may seem to be to ourselves, we cannot be free and morally responsible in the sight of God, but must instead be his helpless puppets. Such "freedom" is like that of a patient acting out a series of posthypnotic suggestions; he appears, even to himself, to be free, but his volitions have actually been predetermined by an-

---

[4] J. L. Mackie, "Evil and Omnipotence," *Mind* (April, 1955), p. 209. A similar point is made by Anthony Flew in "Divine Omnipotence and Human Freedom," *New Essays in Philosophical Theology*. An important critical comment on these arguments is offered by Ninian Smart in "Omnipotence, Evil and Supermen," *Philosophy* (April, 1961), with replies by Flew (January, 1962) and Mackie (April, 1962).

[5] Flew, in *New Essays in Philosophical Theology*.

other will, that of the hypnotist, in relation to whom the pateint is not a free agent.

A different objector might raise the question of whether or not we deny God's omnipotence if we admit that he is unable to create persons who are free from the risks inherent in personal freedom. The answer that has always been given is that to create such beings is logically impossible. It is no limitation upon God's power that he cannot accomplish the logically impossible, since there is nothing here to accomplish, but only a meaningless conjunction of words[6]—in this case "person who is not a person." God is able to create beings of any and every conceivable kind; but creatures who lack moral freedom, however superior they might be to human beings in other respects, would not be what we mean by persons. They would constitute a different form of life which God might have brought into existence instead of persons. When we ask why God did not create such beings in place of persons, the traditional answer is that only persons could, in any meaningful sense, become "children of God," capable of entering into a personal relationship with their Creator by a free and uncompelled response to his love.

When we turn from the possibility of moral evil as a correlate of man's personal freedom to its actuality, we face something which must remain inexplicable even when it can be seen to be possible. For we can never provide a complete causal explanation of a free act; if we could, it would not be a free act. The origin of moral evil lies forever concealed within the mystery of human freedom.

The necessary connection between moral freedom and the possibility, now actualized, of sin throws light upon a great deal of the suffering which afflicts mankind. For an enormous amount of human pain arises either from the inhumanity or the culpable incompetence of mankind. This includes such major scourges as poverty, oppression and persecution, war, and all the injustice, indignity, and inequity which occur even in the most advanced societies. These evils are manifestations of human sin. Even disease is fostered to an extent, the limits of which have not yet been determined by psychosomatic medicine, by moral and emotional factors seated both in the individual and in his social environment. To the extent that all of these evils stem from human failures and wrong decisions, their possibility is inherent in the creation of free persons inhabiting a world which presents them with real choices which are followed by real consequences.

We may now turn more directly to the problem of suffering. Even though the major bulk of actual human pain is traceable to man's misused freedom as a sole or part cause, there remain other sources of pain which are entirely independent of the human will, for example, earthquake, hurricane, storm, flood, drought, and blight. In practice, it is often impossible to trace a boundary between the suffering which results from human wickedness and folly and that which falls upon mankind from without. Both kinds of suffering are inextricably mingled together in human experience. For our present purpose, however, it is important

---

[6] As Aquinas said, ". . . nothing that implies a contradiction falls under the scope of God's omnipotence," *Summa Theologica,* Part I, Question 25, article 4.

to note that the latter category does exist and that it seems to be built into the very structure of our world. In response to it, theodicy, if it is wisely conducted, follows a negative path. It is not possible to show positively that each item of human pain serves the divine purpose of good; but, on the other hand, it does seem possible to show that the divine purpose as it is understood in Judaism and Christianity could not be forwarded in a world which was designed as a permanent hedonistic paradise.

An essential premise of this argument concerns the nature of the divine purpose in creating the world. The skeptic's assumption is that man is to be viewed as a completed creation and that God's purpose in making the world was to provide a suitable dwelling-place for this fully-formed creature. Since God is good and loving, the environment which he has created for human life to inhabit is naturally as pleasant and comfortable as possible. The problem is essentially similar to that of a man who builds a cage for some pet animal. Since our world, in fact, contains sources of hardship, inconvenience, and danger of innumerable kinds, the conclusion follows that this world cannot have been created by a perfectly benevolent and all-powerful deity.[7]

Christianity, however, has never supposed that God's purpose in the creation of the world was to construct a paradise whose inhabitants would experience a maximum of pleasure and a minimum of pain. The world is seen, instead, as a place of "soul-making" in which free beings grappling with the tasks and challenges of their existence in a common environment, may become "children of God" and "heirs of eternal life." A way of thinking theologically of God's continuing creative purpose for man was suggested by some of the early Hellenistic Fathers of the Christian Church, especially Irenaeus. Following hints from St. Paul, Irenaeus taught that man has been made as a person in the image of God but has not yet been brought as a free and responsible agent into the finite likeness of God, which is revealed in Christ.[8] Our world, with all its rough edges, is the sphere in which this second and harder stage of the creative process is taking place.

This conception of the world (whether or not set in Irenaeus' theological framework) can be supported by the method of negative theodicy. Suppose, contrary to fact, that this world were a paradise from which all possibility of pain and suffering were excluded. The consequences would be very far-reaching. For example, no one could ever injure anyone else: the murderer's knife would turn to paper or his bullets to thin air; the bank safe, robbed of a million dollars, would miraculously become filled with another million dollars (without this device, on however large a scale, proving inflationary); fraud, deceit, conspiracy, and treason would somehow always leave the fabric of society undamaged. Again, no one would ever be injured by accident; the mountain-climber, steeplejack, or playing child falling from a height would float unharmed to the ground; the reckless driver would never meet with disaster. There would be no need to work, since no harm could result from avoiding work; there would be no

[7] This is the nature of David Hume's argument in his discussion of the problem of evil in his *Dialogues*, Part XI.

[8] See Irenaeus' *Against Heresies*, Book IV, Chaps. 37 and 38.

call to be concerned for others in time of need or danger, for in such a world there could be no real needs or dangers.

To make possible this continual series of individual adjustments, nature would have to work by "special providences" instead of running according to general laws which men must learn to respect on penalty of pain of death. The laws of nature would have to be extremely flexible: sometimes gravity would operate, sometimes not; sometimes an object would be hard and solid, sometimes soft. There could be no sciences, for there would be no enduring world structure to investigate. In eliminating the problems and hardships of an objective environment, with its own laws, life would become like a dream in which, delightfully but aimlessly, we would float and drift at ease.

One can at least begin to imagine such a world. It is evident that our present ethical concepts would have no meaning in it. If, for example, the notion of harming someone is an essential element in the concept of a wrong action, in our hedonistic paradise there could be no wrong actions—nor any right actions in distinction from wrong. Courage and fortitude would have no point in an environment in which there is, by definition, no danger or difficulty. Generosity, kindness, the *agape* aspect of love, prudence, unselfishness, and all other ethical notions which presuppose life in a stable environment, could not even be formed. Consequently, such a world, however well it might promote pleasure, would be very ill adapted for the development of the moral qualities of human personality. In relation to this purpose it would be the worst of all possible worlds.

It would seem, then, that an environment intended to make possible the growth in free beings of the finest characteristics of personal life, must have a good deal in common with our present world. It must operate according to general and dependable laws; and it must involve real dangers, difficulties, problems, obstacles, and possibilities of pain, failure, sorrow, frustration, and defeat. If it did not contain the particular trials and perils which—subtracting man's own very considerable contribution—our world contains, it would have to contain others instead.

To realize this is not, by any means, to be in possession of a detailed theodicy. It is to understand that this world, will all its "heartaches and the thousand natural shocks that flesh is heir to," an environment so manifestly not designed for the maximization of human pleasure and the minimization of human pain, may be rather well adapted to the quite different purpose of "soul-making."[9]

These considerations are related to theism as such. Specifically, Christian theism goes further in the light of the death of Christ, which is seen paradoxically both (as the murder of the divine Son) as the worst thing that has ever happened and (as the occasion of Man's salvation) as the best thing that has ever happened. As the supreme evil turned to supreme good, it provides the paradigm for the distinctively Christian reaction to evil. Viewed from the stand-

---

[9] This brief discussion has been confined to the problem of human suffering. The large and intractable problem of animal pain is not taken up here. For a discussion of it, see, for example, Nels Ferré, *Evil and the Christian Faith* (New York: Harper & Row, Publishers, Inc., 1947), Chap. 7; and Austin Farrer, *Love Almighty and Ills Unlimited* (New York: Doubleday & Company, Inc., 1961), Chap. 5.

point of Christian faith, evils do not cease to be evils; and certainly, in view of Christ's healing work, they cannot be said to have been sent by God. Yet, it has been the persistent claim of those seriously and wholeheartedly committed to Christian discipleship that tragedy, though truly tragic, may nevertheless be turned, through a man's reaction to it, from a cause of despair and alienation from God to a stage in the fulfillment of God's loving purpose for that individual. As the greatest of all evils, the crucifixion of·Christ, was made the occasion of man's redemption, so good can be won from other evils. As Jesus saw his execution by the Romans as an experience which God desired him to accept, an experience which was to be brought within the sphere of the divine purpose and made to serve the divine ends, so the Christian response to calamity is to accept the adversities, pains, and afflictions which life brings, in order that they can be turned to a positive spiritual use.[10]

At this point, theodicy points forward in two ways to the subject of life after death.

First, although there are many striking instances of good being triumphantly brought out of evil through a man's or a woman's reaction to it, there are many other cases in which the opposite has happened. Sometimes obstacles breed strength of character, dangers evoke courage and unselfishness, and calamities produce patience and moral steadfastness. But sometimes they lead, instead, to resentment, fear, grasping selfishness, and disintegration of character. Therefore, it would seem that any divine purpose of soul-making which is at work in earthly history must continue beyond this life if it is ever to achieve more than a very partial and fragmentary success.

Second, if we ask whether the business of soul-making is worth all the toil and sorrow of human life, the Christian answer must be in terms of a future good which is great enough to justify all that has happened on the way to it.

[10] This conception of providence is stated more fully in John Hick, *Faith and Knowledge* (Ithaca: Cornell University Press, 1957), Chap. 7, from which some sentences are incorporated in this paragraph.

Racism as Christian Idolatry

GEORGE D. KELSEY

George D. Kelsey (1910–   ) is an American theologian. He received his Ph.D. at Yale University and now teaches at Drew University Theological School. Among his books is *Racism and the Christian Understanding of Man* (1965).

Racism is a faith. It is a form of idolatry. It is an abortive search for meaning. In its early modern beginnings, racism was a justificatory device. It did not

Source: George D. Kelsey, *Racism and the Christian Understanding of Man* (New York, 1965), pp. 19–30, 36–38, 86, 114. Copyright © 1965 by George D. Kelsey. Reprinted by permsision of Charles Scribner's Sons.

emerge as a faith. It arose as an ideological justification for the constellations of political and economic power which were expressed in colonialism and slavery. But gradually the idea of the superior race was heightened and deepened in meaning and value so that it pointed beyond the historical structure of relation, in which it emerged, to human existence itself. The alleged superior race became and now persists as a center of value and an object of devotion. Multitudes of men gain their sense of the "power of being" from their membership in the superior race. Accordingly, the most deprived white man, culturally and economically, is able to think of himself as "better'n any nigger."

The purpose of this book [from which this essay is taken] is to provide a Christian criticism of racism as a faith system in all of its facets and tendencies. By and large, Christians have failed to recognize racism as an idolatrous faith, even though it poses the problem of idolatry among Christians in a way that no other tendency does. Racism is especially problematical not only because of the peculiar nature of the racist faith, but because it is a "Trojan horse" within organized Christianity and Christian civic communities.

The procedure which is followed in this book is that of correlating the questions implied in the racist situation with the relevant answers of the Christian message. The search for meaning is first pursued from the side of racism. This is followed by the elaboration of Christian answers which are related to the situation. The use of the expression "the Christian . . ." in this book is done in full acknowledgment that a particular theological point of view is represented.

The Christian faith is brought into dialogue with racism for two reasons. First, I am convinced that Christian faith provides authentic answers to the questions which racism poses but to which racism is able to provide only false answers. Second, racism is a phenomenon of modern Christian civilization. By and large, the people who have been the racists of the modern world have also been Christians or the heirs of Christian civilization. Among large numbers of Christians, racism has been the other faith or one of the other faiths.

The phrase "in-race" refers to the race of the speaker who makes the racist pronouncements or the actor who implements racist aims. The "out-race" is the ethnic group which is vilified, discriminated against, segregated, exterminated, or is to be exterminated in the great "eschatological event." The terms "aggressive racism" or "imperialistic racism" are used to describe white racism or racism in power. Black racism or Black Muslimism is referred to as "counter-racism" because it arises as a racist answer to white "imperialistic racism."

Racism has the character of faith in both its imperialistic and counter-racist forms, but an important distinction between the two must be noted. Imperialistic racism is full-bodied. It can walk on its feet and strike with its fists because its spirit permeates the institutions of power. A race as such lacks centeredness. The racist faith must therefore find its life through the use of political, military, economic, and cultural institutions. White men control the political, military, economic, and cultural institutions. Black men do not. Racism among the former is accordingly imperialistic and aggressive. They are able to project and implement concrete programs of political action while the Black Muslims must substitute eschatology for political action. Black Muslimism is racism out of power.

This difference is important to the analysis found in this book. The form of racism is a naturalistic ontology, but its vital principle is the will to power expressed in a political plan of action. Since Black Muslimism lacks power, it is not full-bodied racism. It lacks feet to walk on and fists with which to strike. The spirit is present; the hope is compelling; but the will to power cannot find the institutions of power through which it can express itself. The result of this distinction for this book is the fact that Black Muslimism provides no illustrative material for the study of racism in its most important facet—the plan of political action.

Racism—Modern Phenomenon

Racism is a modern phenomenon. It is a product of modern world conditions. It is a system of meaning and value that could only have arisen out of the peculiar conjunction of modern ideas and values with the political, economic, and technological realities of colonialism and slavery. Various forms of groupism appeared on the stage of history prior to the modern period, but none of them was racist.[1] In the late 1880's, the French racist philosopher Vacher de Lapouge wrote, "I am convinced that in the next century millions will cut each other's throats because of one or two degrees more or less of cephalic index."[2] In this statement, Lapouge gave a strictly modern reason for the mutual slaughter of men.

It is often said that racism has been a perennial problem in human history. But those who make this claim employ the concept of race erroneously. They loosely identify the idea of race with tribal, territorial, national, religious, and cultural groups. It is true that ethnocentrism—the belief in the unique value and rightness of one's own group—is universal as well as perennial. But ethnocentrism does not always take the form of racism.

While the late medieval and early modern Church granted the right of conquest and enslavement of the heathen, it nevertheless imposed a responsibility with that right. In the fifteenth century Nicholas V issued a papal bull authorizing the Portuguese "to attack, subject, and reduce to perpetual slavery the Saracens, pagans, and other enemies of Christ southward of Cape Bojador and Non, including all the coast of Guinea."[3] The condition attached to this authorization was that the captives must be converted to Christianity, and conversion must be followed by manumission. About a century after the bull of Nicholas V, a memorial of the Archbishop of Valencia was issued to Philip III of Spain. This memorial reaffirms the "Christian justification for conquest and enslavement," but it also reflects a new motive. The memorial explicitly affirms the

[1] The Hindu caste system of India is frequently identified with the caste practices of modern racism because it maintains itself primarily by direct blood relationship. But the Indian caste order is not based on color or physical characteristics in the sense that its objective is "purity of blood." The aim of the caste order is to preserve the sacred style of life. Sacred duties and ritualistic requirements are correlated with status and rank, and the community is accordingly preserved.

[2] Quoted in Ruth Benedict, *Race: Science and Politics* (rev. ed.; New York, 1947), p. 3.

[3] Quoted in Ina Corinne Brown, *Race Relations in a Democracy* (New York, 1949), p. 41.

economic motive in addition to that of conversion to Christianity as a justification for slavery.

> . . . Your majesty may, without any scruple of conscience, make slaves of all the Moriscos and may put them into your own galleys or mines, or sell them to strangers. And as to their children they may be all sold at good rates here in Spain, which will be so far from being a punishment, that it will be a mercy to them; since by that means they will all become Christians. . . . By the holy execution of which piece of Justice, a great sum of money will flow into your majesty's treasury.[4]

Since men are never willing to justify their behavior on the simple claim that might makes right or that their conduct satisfies their interests and desires, a new justification for colonialism and slavery was necessary. A ready-made explanation was at hand. The conquered and enslaved people were dark-skinned. The conquerors were white. Since the white people possessed a superior economic and military technology and were therefore able to conquer and enslave the people of color, it was a simple matter to explain the superiority of the cultural apparatus in terms of a superior human endowment. In other words, the exploiters read from right to left—from a cultural effect to a natural or congenital cause. Thus modern racism emerged as a sort of afterthought, a by-product of the ideological justification of European political and economic power arrangements over colored peoples—the justification of a set of advantages that medieval religious sanctions could no longer sustain.

For this reason, and because racial hostility is most potently manifest on the political and economic planes, many observers mistakenly assume that racism is nothing more than a device by which political, economic, and cultural interests are defended and expanded. Although racism did have its beginnings in a particular constellation of political and economic events in the early modern world, it has developed into an independent phenomenon, possessing meaning and value in itself and giving character to all the institutions of some societies. The cultural phenomenon that made its appearance in modern history as a form of self-justification and a defense of political and economic interests eventually became a complete system of meaning, value, and loyalty.

The fact that racism exists alongside other faiths does not make it any less a faith. Rather, this fact is testimony to the reality of polytheism in the modern age. In its maturity, racism is not a mere ideology that a political demagogue may be expected to affirm or deny, depending upon the political situation in which he finds himself. Racism is a search for meaning. The devotee of the racist faith is as certainly seeking self-identity in his acts of self-exaltation and his self-deifying pronouncements as he is seeking to nullify the selfhood of members of out-races by acts of deprivation and words of vilification.

Human Alienation Purely and Simply

It is this faith character of racism which makes it the final and complete form of human alienation. Racism is human alienation purely and simply; it is the

---

[4] Ibid., p. 42.

prototype of all human alienation. It is the one form of human conflict that divides human beings as human beings. That which the racist glorifies in himself is his being. And that which he scorns and rejects in members of out-races is precisely their human being. Although the racist line of demarcation and hostility inevitably finds expression through the institutions of society, it is not primarily a cultural, political, or economic boundary. Rather, it is a boundary of estrangement in the order of human being as such.

Accordingly, the basic racist affirmation of superiority, on the one hand, and inferiority, on the other, is not an empirical generalization as is commonly supposed. Rather, it is an affirmation concerning the fundamental nature of human beings. It is a declaration of faith that is neither supported nor weakened by any objective body of fact. Racism is an expression of the will to believe. The fundamental racist affirmation is that the in-race is glorious and pure as to its being, and out-races are defective and depraved as to their being. Any statement the racist makes concerning the cultural and political achievement, or potential, of the in-race or the out-races is based on this prior judgment concerning human being.

The claim of the racist that he studies the facts of history and arrives inductively at his generalizations is contradicted by his consistently negative response to contrasting situations. For example, when the racist asserts that Negroes cannot learn to operate complicated machinery or that all Jews are dishonest, instances to the contrary do not disturb his confidence in the truth of these generalizations. His confidence is not disturbed because his assertions are not empirical generalizations. The "facts" which the racist claims to be reading from Negro and Jewish character and behavior are in reality "faith" facts. Declarations of faith do not need to be proved from evidences in the objective world of facts. They do not need to be proved because the devotee of a faith is convinced that his faith assertions are reflections of the fundamental order of reality.

Thus when the racist sees Negroes actually operating complicated machinery he dismisses the meaning of what he sees by pointing out that these particular Negroes are "different." He believes that the place of the Negro is fixed in the fundamental order of reality: his status is not a matter of the accidents of history. And when the racist sees Jews who are honest by every objectively discernible standard available, he is still convinced that Jews are dishonest because the honesty of the Jew is Jewish honesty. To the anti-Semitic consciousness, the honesty of the Jew is not the same as the honesty of the Christian or non-Jew. The honesty of the Jew inheres in the Jewish being. Even the virtue of the Jew is therefore vice because it is his because it inheres in defective being.

The claim that racism is human alienation purely and simply may be clarified by comparing racial alienation with other forms of human conflict. All other forms of collective hostility are expressions of conflict over some value or interest that exists *between* men. Human groups contend with each other because they cannot agree on the appropriate relationship each has to some value or values. For example, capital and labor struggle over the definition of their respective shares in the distribution of income from a product or a service.

They also contend over their respective rights to power of decision in certain areas of economic process. The nations compete and contend against each other for land, minerals, markets, spheres of influence, and political hegemony. Organized religious bodies struggle with each other over the issues of who possesses the truth, of the proper means for its communication, and of the right to propagate it. Racial alienation stands alone among the forms of human conflict as the one form of collective hostility founded in the question of human being as such. A particular conflict among races may involve political or economic interest, but it is not the political or economic interests that make the conflict racial. The conflict is racial because of the racist faith present in the society involved. Numerous political and economic conflicts occur in one and the same society, but they have a racial character only when two or more racially related groups of that society are in contention. Furthermore, racial antipathy exists and persists in the hearts of men who have no contact whatsoever with the objects of their hostility. A popular saying in many suburbs and small towns of America is, "We do not have the problem because we do not have any of them here." The damaging nature of this claim to the very people who utter it is completely overlooked. It means that if any of *them* do show up, we are ready spiritually and politically to send them reeling back where they came from.

Christian Racism Implies a Pejorative Judgment Concerning the Action of God

Since racism assumes some segments of humanity to be defective in essential being, and since for Christians all being is from the hand of God, racism alone among the idolatries calls into question the divine creative action. The central claim of the racist is fundamentally a proposition concerning the nature of creation and the action of God rather than a doctrine concerning the nature of man. By implication, one part of the primary racist affirmation is the idea that God has made a creative error in bringing out-races into being. For Christians, the only possible theological alternative to the implication that God has made a creative error is the doctrine that out-races are the victims of a double fall. If the doctrine of the Demiurge had triumphed in Christianity, a third theological ground for explaining the existence of out-races would be available. But in the Gnostic controversies of the early Church the concept of the Demiurge was relegated to the limbo of heresy. In accounting for the origin of out-races, the Black Muslims enjoy a decided advantage over Christian racists. The creation mythology of the Black Muslims contains a Demiurge as the creator of the white man.

While Christian racists never appeal to the notion of the Demiurge to account for the nature of the existence of out-races, the doctrine of a second fall is explicitly enunciated in some naïve and obscurantist circles. The usual form of this theological proposition is the assertion that God himself has condemned Negroes to be "the hewers of the wood and drawers of the water now henceforth and forever" under the curse of Ham. A variation of the doctrine is the notion that Negroes are the descendants of Cain's union with an ape whom Cain, the first criminal, saw fit to marry "in the land of Nod."[5] This means that while the Negro shares the universal condemnation of the human race in Adam, he also bears the added condemnation of God in a special, racial fall. Since no promise of renewal and redemption is ever correlated with this second, special, racial fall, the Negro is a permanent victim of history and ultimately without hope. Whether the defectiveness in the humanity of out-races be an implication of the nature of creation or an explicit affirmation concerning a special, racial fall, the conclusion cannot be avoided that the action of God is the primary point of reference for Christian racists.

The Faith Character of Racism

As a doctrine concerning the fundamental nature of human beings and a way of life elaborated on that doctrine, racism is a faith. H. Richard Niebuhr defines faith as "trust in that which gives value to the self," on the one hand; and on the other, "it is loyalty to what the self values."[6] It is in this sense that we speak of the racist faith.

In the experience of faith, the devotee has a double relation to the object of faith. He trusts in it as the source of his personal value, and at the same time he is loyal to the object of his faith for the value it possesses independent of himself. Niebuhr illustrates this double relation in the life of the patriot whose faith is nationalism. The experience of the racist corresponds to that of the patriot, with the difference that the racist deifies his own being rather than an objective historic structure. The racist relies on the race as the source of his personal value. His life has meaning and worth because it is a part of the racial context. It fits into and merges with a valuable whole, the race. As the value-center, the race is the source of value, and it is at the same time the object of value. No questions can be raised about the rightness or wrongness of the race; it is the value-center which throws light on all other value. Criminals, degenerates, and even enemies have worth and goodness if they are members of the in-race. They have a goodness and worth which is not found in the most noble character of members of out-races, for goodness and worth are only secondarily qualities of behavior and character. Primarily they are qualities of being. Goodness and worth inhere in being that is worthy. If noble character inheres in a racially defective being, that person of noble character is nonetheless depraved, for the nobility he has achieved inheres in his unalterably corrupt humanity.

When the racist is also a Christian, which is often the case in America, he is frequently a polytheist. Historically, in polytheistic faiths, various gods have controlled various spheres of authority. Thus a Christian racist may think he

---

[5] The idea of a racial fall is also ascribed to the Jews. It is the view, held by some Christians, that since the Jews are the chosen people, God has punished them and will continue to punish them until they acknowledge the Messiah. Thus the persecutions of Jews by Christians are preordained.

[6] H. Richard Niebuhr, *Radical Monotheism and Western Culture* (New York, 1960), p. 16.

lives under the requirements of the God of biblical faith in most areas of his life, but whenever matters of race impinge on his life, in every area so affected, the idol of race determines his attitude, decision, and action.

Polytheistic faith has been nowhere more evident than in that sizable group of Christians who take the position that racial traditions and practices in America are in no sense a religious matter. These people assert that the whole field of race relations is an area with which religion has nothing to do. When pressed for a positive statement of the matter, they say that segregationist racial practices are merely amoral expressions of private preference. They completely overlook the fact that race relations are structured as a system which is not only enforced by the social mores but by institutional policy over all the country, and in some sections of the country, by law and public policy as well. The judgment that race relations involve amoral forms of behavior means in effect that interracial attitudes and practices are beyond the reach of Christian moral ideas and norms. The presence of polytheism among the adherents of the greatest monotheistic religion is not shocking in view of the insights of that very religion concerning original sin. The Old Testament provides ample historical evidence of man's continuous effort to restrict the Covenant of the Lord so that he may pursue certain interests and values as he sees fit. The prophetic tradition makes it equally clear that the only alternative to the worship of and obedience to the Lord God Jehovah is devotion to the Baals of the Canaanites.

It is an anomaly that morally concerned Christian leaders have rarely understood racism for what it really is. For a long time racist ideas and practices were viewed by morally sensitive Christians as nothing more than expressions of cultural lag and as products of ignorance. Since racial hostility is one of the forms of human conflict, many Christians have sought to understand racism wholly in terms of political, economic, and cultural factors. They have not seen the faith character of racist devotion and commitment, nor that racial antipathy is conflict in the order of humanity. A probable explanation of this peculiar state of affairs is that modern Christianity and Christian civilization have domesticated racism so thoroughly that most Christians stand too close to assess it properly.

The Meaning of Racism

The faith character of racism may be fully disclosed by an analysis of its various facets. In her *Race: Science and Politics*, Ruth Benedict defines racism as

> the dogma that one ethnic group is condemned by Nature to hereditary inferiority and another group is destined to hereditary superiority. It is the dogma that the hope of civilization depends upon eliminating some races and keeping others pure. It is the dogma that one race has carried progress throughout human history and can alone ensure future progress.[7]

[7] Benedict, op. cit., p. 98.

From this definition, it may be seen first of all that racism is a form of naturalism. Man owes his existence to nature and nature controls his destiny. Nature has condemned inferior races and blessed the superior race. This means that the fundamental thing about a man is his body, specifically his genetic structure. Mental and spiritual qualities depend upon the natural quality, and are, in fact, but expressions of it.

This naturalistic view of man is diametrically opposed to the biblical doctrine of the creation of man in the image of God; it is also opposed to the main tendencies in the development of Western philosophy. One of the great anomalies of our time is the fact that the racist ideology has taken so firm a grasp upon the heirs of both traditions, and has emerged in the modern world which is precisely that world wherein philosophy and theology broke their esoteric bonds, and became widely available, at least in their main ideas, through popular education.

It must be observed that not all people who understand man naturalistically in the context of race relations subscribe to the naturalistic doctrine in general. Some Christians would be horrified to discover that they really believe in a naturalistic view of man when race relations call for decision and action. If told that this is the case, they will vigorously deny it. Many of them are quite orthodox in their theology and even literalistic in their approach to the Bible. In the abstract, they constantly repeat the phrase that God has created all men in His own image. In the abstract, they believe that the essence of man is spirit. But when they actually view the races in relation to each other, or make social and political decisions concerning race, they bring judgments to bear upon the situation which clearly indicate their belief that the races are poles apart in the order of humanity and that the ground of the great human differences lies in the genes.

The fact that racist claims are affirmations concerning the fundamental nature of humanity, rather than empirical generalizations as they are popularly thought to be, may be made more evident by a few illustrations. During the last war, General J. L. DeWitt was in charge of the evacuation of naturalized Japanese from California. General DeWitt made the following statement concerning Japanese Americans: "A Jap's a Jap. . . . It makes no difference whether he is an American citizen or not. . . . I don't want any of them here. . . . They are a dangerous element. . . . There is no way to determine their loyalty."[8] In another statement, General DeWitt made it unqualifiedly clear that the element which he regarded as evil within the Japanese character is incorrigible because it is rooted in the genetic structure. "The Japanese race is an enemy race and while many second and third generation Japanese born on United States soil, possessed of United States citizenship, have been 'Americanized' the racial strains are undiluted."[9]

[8] U.S. Army, Western Defense Command and Fourth Army, Final Report, Japanese Evacuation from the West Coast, 1942 (Washington, D.C., Government Printing Office, 1943), p. 34; quoted in Charles Abrams, *Forbidden Neighbors* (New York, 1955), p. 41.

[9] Ibid.

Knowledge of the Self in Antithetical
Relation to the Other

The racist consciousness operates in what Martin Buber has called "the World of It."[10] The World of It is the world of objects and things. In this world there is a single center of consciousness. This single subject, the "I," experiences, arranges, and appropriates. It does not enter into relationship with other, different beings. It experiences human beings racially different from itself only as "the other," as antithetical to the self in the order of humanity. The "I" self "knows" itself as pure being while it "knows" the other as depraved being. The "I" self does not enter into communion with the other, for the other is not known as "Thou." The other is first, last, and always "It." The other is an object to be used, manipulated, or eliminated. But since the other in fact belongs to the order of human being, and not merely to the animal kingdom, the relation of the self to the other is on a different plane than the relation of the self to the worlds of animality and nature. The self is aware that the other is in some sense a center of consciousness. The fact that the other in some way belongs on the same plane with the self will not down. The radical contrast between the self and the other can therefore be expressed only in polar terms. The racist consciousness knows itself in contrast, in polarity with and opposition to the racially contemptible object. This means that in the racial context, the racist cannot know himself until he first knows the other. The racist is completely dependent upon the antithetical correlation. When the other is properly experienced, appropriated, and arranged, the racist consciousness can know itself as the other pole in a structure of human contrasts.

The idea that the Negro appears in the anti-Negro consciousness as a contrast conception was ably presented by Lewis Copeland about a generation ago, but very little has been made of this notion in the literature of race relations. Copeland found the social opposition between Negroes and whites so sharp as to give rise to a conceptual dichotomy "somewhat analogous to that between God and the devil in popular religion."[11] And just as in popular religion the contrast between God and the devil introduces a dichotomy which is conceived as running through the whole universe, dividing both the natural world and the social order, the counterconcepts of the racist consciousness "form the basis for the interpretation of human nature and society."[12]

The idea of the contrast conception as a basic constituent of the racist self-consciousness seems to have originated with Erich Voegelin. In his *Rasse und Staat,* Voegelin develops the thesis that Judaism in Christian Germany is a counterconception. Likewise, Jean-Paul Sartre, writing on French anti-Semitism, designates the Jew as a contrast conception. When the anti-Semite speaks of Jewish avarice, says Sartre, he means there is a "Jewish" avarice, an avarice determined by that synthetic whole, the Jewish person. This avarice is different

[10] Martin Buber, *I and Thou,* trans. Ronald Gregor Smith (New York, 1937).
[11] Lewis C. Copeland, "The Negro as a Contrast Conception," in Edgar T. Thompson, ed., *Race Relations and the Race Problem* (Durham, N.C., 1939), p. 152.
[12] Ibid.

from Christian avarice. It is not the universal, human trait of avarice, but an avarice which emerges from a unique synthesis, the Jewish being.

In popular thought in America, black and white have become conceptual opposites.

> The black man and his appurtenances stand at the antithesis of the character and properties of the white man. The conception makes of the Negro a counter-race. The black race serves as a foil for the white race, by which the character of the latter is made all the more impressive.[13]

The antipodal positions of the two races are often verbalized in the phrase "the opposite race." In its fullest meaning, the word "opposite" is a reference to more than the extremes of color. It suggests the two opposites of human being. An examination of the counter-racist consciousness discloses the same element. Eric Lincoln writes:

> To a great extent the Muslims define their movement by negative contrast to their most important audiences; Negroes, Jews, the orthodox Moslems in America and the hated whites. They assert their strength and purity by castigating the weakness and depravity they claim to see among these strangers.[14]

To the Black Muslim, knowledge of the self has its corollary in "the truth about the white man."[15] The Black Muslim therefore cannot "know" himself until he first "knows" the white man. Knowledge of "the truth about the white man" produces knowledge of the self as the opposite in the order of human being.

The Christian Doctrine of Equality

The Christian doctrine of equality is an affirmation of faith. It is not a perception of sight. It is an affirmation of faith because it relates solely to the action of God, and not to the achievements of men or to any intrinsic quality which men may possess. Men are equal because God has created them in His own image and called them to sonship. The Christian doctrine of equality does not draw at all upon measurements of talent and merit. It is a doctrine concerning the creative gift of God.

There is ample evidence in history that men are unequal in knowledge, skill, power, and cultural achievements in general. Most of life is organized and proceeds on the assumption of these inequalities. Men of sight, rather than faith, are obviously much more impressed and influenced by historically conditioned and structured inequalities than by any doctrines of equality, philosophical or theological. But the conviction that men are equal in some fundamental sense has not been destroyed in the West, despite the ideological claims to the contrary or widespread practices that belie the idea. The Western democracies have developed a relatively high degree of political equalitarianism at the very moment in history when disproportions of power, wealth, knowledge, and skill are

---

[13] Copeland, op. cit., p. 153.

[14] Eric Lincoln, *The Black Muslims in America* (Boston, 1961), p. 135.

[15] Ibid., p. 190.

great and numerous as never before. An important influence in this development has been Christian teaching concerning man.

When Christian faith speaks of equality, it refers to the action and purpose of God. God has created all men in His own image and called all men to the same destiny. The decision as to whether or not men are equal cannot be made by looking at men; he who would decide must look at God. God alone is the source of human dignity. All men are equal because God has bestowed upon all the very same dignity. He has created them in His own image and herein lies their dignity. Human dignity is not an achievement, nor is it an intrinsic quality; it is a gift, a bestowal. Christian faith asserts that men are equally human; all are creatures and all are potentially spiritual sons of God. Variations in the talents and skills of culture rest upon this fundamental humanness.

Thus Christian faith affirms the unity of mankind. The idea of the unity of mankind is another way of expressing the essential likeness of man. Modern science supports the claim of biblical faith that mankind is a unity, but it is not upon empirical evidence that the biblical conviction is based. The conviction of faith is independent of all scientific results because creation stands above the historical and empirical planes.

> The religious belief in the unity of the human race through the Creation, in and for the Divine image, is completely independent of all biological, palaeontological, scientific results. The story of Adam in Genesis expresses, in historical form, it is true, a fact which in itself is super-empirical and super-historical; the biological genealogical question has very little to do with belief in the unity of the creation. . . . The unity of the divine creation of man lies upon a quite different plane. Humanity is not necessarily a unity from a zoological point of view; it may indeed be composed of different species of differing origin or it may not. It is, however, beyond all doubt a unity, a humanitas, "through" the humanum, its one origin and its one destiny in God's creative Word and plan of salvation, spiritually given to man by God himself.[16]

It is upon the foundation of the equal humanness of men that democratic rights are established. The American Declaration of Independence asserts that "all men are created equal." This proposition was never intended to mean that all men are equal in capacity, knowledge, and skill. Yet it does have concrete political significance. It means that there are some rights that belong to persons as persons, as creatures of God. These rights are said to be inalienable for the very reason that they belong to every person as a person. They can no more be transferred from one person to another than personhood itself can be transferred. And to deny these rights is identical with denying the reality of the person. Inalienable rights are primal. They exist prior to the performance of any function, and are the foundation upon which all secondary and derived rights are elaborated. The rights of the individual as man are primary and unique. All particularized rights are secondary and derived. They derive from the social organization of life and belong to persons only in the exercise of their particular technical, professional, and institutional functions.

[16] Emil Brunner, *Man in Revolt*, trans. Olive Wyon (London, 1939), p. 333.

Not only does the idea of equal human dignity place the stress on the likeness and unity of mankind and thus constitute the foundation for all assessment of human rights; it also combines harmoniously with unlikeness and inequality. The essential rights of the individual are primary and universal; but individual rights combine harmoniously with derived and differentiated rights relating to historic function because individuality and community are equally original in God's creative act. Man is the covenant-partner of God and of man from the creation. But each man is also created a unique being, with his own individuality. Thus equal dignity and likeness are united with individuality and unlikeness in the Christian doctrine of creation.

The Christian doctrine of individuality and unlikeness is radically opposed to racist particularism. In the Christian idea, individuality means unlikeness and inequality in community. But in the racist idea, individuality does not exist: the individual is made faceless in a homogenized collectivity. Unlikeness and inequality are alleged to be characteristics of racial collectivities rather than individuals. While even the racist is obliged to admit the reality of inequality and unlikeness within races, it is only the alleged inequalities between races that have significance for him. Christian faith knows of unlikeness and inequality only as between individuals. But since individuality is always related to community which is also original in God's plan for man, inequality and equality are harmoniously combined.

The Christian conception of equality is inseparable from the idea of person in community. The two elements of equality and inequality, of equal dignity and different function, are both fully expressed. They are brought together in the Christian idea of communion. The fact that men are different from each other means that they are dependent on each other. In a Christian community, men will to serve each other in their mutual dependence. The one recognizes his dependence upon the other, no matter how lowly the occupation of the other may be in the eyes of the world. There are so many respects in which one man may be superior or inferior to another that there is probably no man who is superior or inferior to another in every respect. The unity of mankind is made the more manifest by the inequalities which have their basis in individuality.

The Christian idea of the unity of mankind finds concrete expression in societies of mutual cooperation and helpfulness. Differences of function create of necessity variations in status and role in institutional structures. But the roles and statuses in these institutions are assigned on the strength of real individual differences. They are not, as in racism, based upon hostile power arrangements, upon the results of previous discriminations, or upon invidious comparisons that falsify the nature of man as a creature of God.

Desegregation and Integration

In the field of race relations, American society is in a state of flux. Within the last decade, social change in this field has reached revolutionary proportions. Since American society is, and has been to a great degree, a color-caste society, the terms "desegregation" and "integration" are now in constant use. These terms belong together, but they do not mean the same thing. Desegregation refers to a process—the elimination of compulsory segregation. Desegregation may be voluntary or involuntary. It is voluntary when those who administer and make the policies of an institution freely decide to change its policy from one of racial exclusivism to one of racial inclusivism. It is involuntary when law, judicial decision, or public pressure requires such a change. Integration refers to a realized condition of community, involving mutuality, reciprocity, and respect among persons. Integration is voluntary and spiritual. The two terms belong together because in a racially segregated society, by and large, people of different racial groups lack the simple conditions and experience of togetherness upon which integration can exist without the prior process of desegregation.

Desegregation is referred to as a prior process because the mere "mixing" of the races is not integration. There is much desegregation in the United States outside the South but little integration. Integration requires more of persons than the mere removal of the external barriers and distances that separate them. But the transition from a segregated to an integrated society cannot be made without the process of removing the external barriers. The simple experiences of doing things together, such as working, playing, learning, etc., provide the foundation upon which genuine community can grow.

A society may be referred to as integrated when it has become a community of persons.

In the deepest sense, integration has taken place only when those of another race or class are accepted as full and equal partners in a common task. It is based on mutual respect and on a sense of the dignity and worth of the human person.[17]

An integrated society is one in which there is both a sense of and a will toward the common good. The common good is received through and communicated by persons. This means that an integrated society is one in which the individual person comes alive. It is not really the group which accepts or respects another group; it is, rather, a community of persons who accept and respect each other. In such a society, all definitions of function and opportunity presuppose the equal dignity of persons. Men are thus able in defining tasks to focus on those qualities of the individual person which are really related to performance; namely talent, training, knowledge, and skill. Extraneous issues, such as the question, "Who is your mother?" do not enter into the decision as to whether a man shall be permitted to study law in the state university. His admission to the law school rests on such criteria as his individual character, ability, and the quality of his prelegal training. And these are precisely the same criteria which every other person must individually meet in the society.

An integrated society in no sense reduces the individual. It is the one society in which a person can at all times be a person. In racially segregated society, parochialism and prideful separation are normative values. Lest some people fail to interiorize these values, they are forced by law and custom to "keep step" in their external behavior. Thus a white man is required by law to relate to a Negro as a white man; he is not permitted to relate to him as a creature of God or as a religiously committed person. Obviously, the same law regulates the

[17] Maston, op. cit., p. 63.

goings, comings, and doings of the Negro, except that it specifies that he remain "outside" or "beneath," in all matters pertaining to the larger society. To dare to act in a legally segregated society as a member of a more universal community of love than a racial community can provide is often to court imprisonment. An integrated society is, on the contrary, a community in which persons have become persons. They remain persons in all their relationships, for even professional and technical functions are exercised by persons.

The objection may rightly be raised that an authentic community of persons does not exist anywhere on a large scale; and accordingly, a truly integrated society, with or without a history of racial alienation, is an ideal. But to say this is not to dismiss such a society as a human and Christian requirement. Man never fully achieves any of his ideals that have the quality of the transcendent, but they are nevertheless incumbent upon him. In truth, an authentic community of persons would be a society of pure persons in which "the good of society and the good of each person would be one and the same good."[18] Although such a society is never fully realized, nevertheless it can be in process of realization if its ideal of the common good is informed and urged by that which transcends itself.

A society is integrated and is a genuine community of persons when it exists under God in fact. The community of persons is found in the common bond of the Spirit. The common good of society escapes every form of particularism— racial, class, religious, or otherwise—because the center of meaning and value transcends the society.

[18] Jacques Maritain, *The Person and the Common Good* (New York, 1947), p. 50.

The Qualitative Leap Beyond Patriarchal Religion

MARY DALY

Mary Daly (1938–   ) teaches at Boston College and is one of the organizers of the Catholic Women's Caucus. She holds several degrees in theology and philosophy and is the author of *The Church and the Second Sex* (Harper & Row, 1968), which explores sexism in the history of the church.

The writing of this article presents a minor dilemma. I do not wish simply to rewrite ideas which I have presented elsewhere. Yet there is a background, or frame of reference, or context, out of which the present article is written. To resolve this I am setting forth in very skeletal form, in the form of twenty-

Source: Mary Daly, "The Qualitative Leap Beyond Patriarchal Religion," *Quest,* Vol. 1, No. 4 (Spring 1975), pp. 20–22, 24–40. Copyright © 1975 by Mary Daly. Reprinted by permission of the author.

three statements, a context discussed at length in a number of articles and in two books.[1]

Prolegomena

1. There exists a planetary sexual caste system, essentially the same in Saudi Arabia and in New York, differing only in degree.

2. This system is masked by sex role segregation, by the dual identity of women, by ideologies and myths.

3. Among the primary loci of sexist conditioning is grammar.

4. The "methods" of the various "fields" are not adequate to express feminist thought. Methodolatry requires that women perform Methodicide, an act of intellectual bravery.

5. All of the major world religions function to legitimate patriarchy. This is true also of the popular cults such as the Krishna movement and the Jesus Freaks.

6. The myths and symbols of Christianity are essentially sexist. Since "God" is male, the male is God. God the Father legitimates all earthly Godfathers, including Vito Corleone, Pope Paul, President Gerald Ford, the Godfathers of medicine (e.g. the American Medical Association), of science (e.g. NASA), of the media, of psychiatry, of education, and of all the -ologies.

7. The myth of feminine evil, expressed in the story of the Fall, is reinforced by the myth of salvation/redemption by a single human being of the male sex. The idea of a unique divine incarnation in a male, the Godman of the "hypostatic union," is inherently sexist and oppressive. Christolatry is idolatry.

8. A significant and growing cognitive minority of women, radical feminists, are breaking out from under the sacred shelter of patriarchal religious myths.

9. This breaking out, facing anomy when the meaning structures of patriarchy are seen through and rejected, is a communal, political event. It is a revelatory event, a creative, political ontophany.

10. The bonding of the growing cognitive minority of women who are radical feminists, commonly called *sisterhood*, involves a process of new naming, in which words are wrenched out of their old semantic context and heard in a new semantic context. For example, the "sisterhoods" of patriarchy, such as religious congregations of women, were really mini-brotherhoods. *Sisterhood* heard with new ears is bonding for women's own liberation.

11. There is an inherent dynamic in the women's revolution in Judeo-Christian society which is Antichurch, whether or not feminists specifically concern ourselves with churches. This is so because the Judeo-Christian tradition legitimates patriarchy—the prevailing power structure and prevailing world view—which the women's revolution leaves behind.

12. The women's revolution is not only Antichurch. It is a postchristian spiritual revolution.

---

[1] *Beyond God the Father: Toward a Philosophy of Women's Liberation* (Boston: Beacon Press, 1973) ; *The Church and the Second Sex*, With a New Feminist Post-Christian Introduction by the Author (New York: Harper Colophon, 1975).

13. The ethos of Judeo-Christian culture is dominated by The Most Unholy Trinity: Rape, Genocide, and War. It is rapism which spawns racism. It is gynocide which spawns genocide, for sexism (rapism) is fundamental socialization to objectify "the other."

14. The women's revolution is concerned with transvaluation of values, beyond the ethics dominated by The Most Unholy Trinity.

15. The women's revolution is not merely about equality within a patriarchal society (a contradiction in terms). It is about *power* and redefining power.

- 16. Since Christian myths are inherently sexist, and since the women's revolution is not about "equality" but about power, there is an intrinsic dynamic in the feminist movement which goes beyond efforts to reform Christian churches. Such efforts eventually come to be recognized as comparable to a Black person's trying to reform the Ku Klux Klan.

17. Within patriarchy, power is generally understood as power *over* people, the environment, things. In the rising consciousness of women, power is experienced as *power of presence* to ourselves and to each other, as we affirm our own being against and beyond the alienated identity (non-being) bestowed upon us within patriarchy. This is experienced as *power of absence* by those who would objectify women as "the other," as magnifying mirrors.

18. The presence of women to ourselves which is *absence* to the oppressor is the essential dynamic opening up the women's revolution to human liberation. It is an invitation to men to confront non-being and hence affirm their be-ing.

19. It is unlikely that many men will accept this invitation willingly, or even be able to hear it, since they have profound vested (though self-destructive) interest in the present social arrangements.

20. The women's movement is a new mode of relating to the self, to each other, to men, to the environment—in a word—to the cosmos. It is self-affirming, refusing objectification of the self and of the other.

21. Entrance into new feminist time/space, which is moving time/space located on the boundaries of patriarchal institutions, is active participation in ultimate reality, which is de-reified, recognized as Verb, as intransitive Verb with no object to block its dynamism.

22. Entrance into radical feminist consciousness involves recognition that all male-dominated "revolutions," which do not reject the universally oppressive reality which is patriarchy, are in reality only reforms. They are "revolutions" only in the sense that they are spinnings of the wheels of the same senescent system.

23. Entrance into radical feminist consciousness implies an awareness that the women's revolution is the "final cause" (pun intended) in the radical sense that it is the cause which can move the other causes. It is the catalyst which can bring about real change, since it is the rising up of the universally and primordially objectified "Other," discrediting the myths which legitimate rapism. Rapism is by extension the objectification and destruction of all "others" and inherently tends to the destruction of the human species and of all life on this planet.

Radical feminism, the becoming of women, is very much an Otherworld Journey. It is both discovery and creation of a world other than patriarchy.

Some observation reveals that patriarchy is "everywhere." Even outer space and the future have been colonized. As a rule, even the more imaginative science fiction writers (seemingly the most foretelling futurists) cannot/will not create a space and time in which women get far beyond the role of space stewardess. Nor does this situation exist simply "outside" women's minds, securely fastened into institutions which we can physically leave behind. Rather, it is also internalized, festering inside women's heads, even feminist heads.

The journey of women *becoming*, then, involves exorcism of the internalized Godfather, in his various manifestations (His name is legion). It involves dangerous encounters with these demons. Within the Christian tradition, particularly in medieval times, evil spirits have sometimes been associated with the Seven Deadly Sins, both as personifications and as causes.[2] A "standard" and prevalent listing of the Sins is, of course, the following: pride, avarice, anger, lust, gluttony, envy, and sloth.[3] I am contending that these have all been radically misnamed, that is, inadequately and even preversely "understood" within Christianity. These concepts have been used to victimize the oppressed, particularly women. They are particularized expressions of the overall use of "evil" to victimize women. The feminist journey involves confrontations with the demonic distortions of evil.

Why has it seemed "appropriate" in this culture that a popular book and film (*The Exorcist*) center around a Jesuit who "exorcises" a girl-child who is "possessed"? Why is there no book or film about a woman who exorcises a Jesuit?[4] Within a culture possessed by the myth of feminine evil, the naming, describing, and theorizing about good and evil has constituted a web of deception, a Maya. The journey of women becoming is breaking through this web— a Fall into free space. It is reassuming the role of subject, as opposed to object, and naming good and evil on the basis of our own intuitive intellection.

Breaking through the web of the Male Maya is both exorcism and ecstasy. These are two aspects of the same journey. Since women have been prohibited from real journeying, that is, from encountering the strange, the unknown, the women's movement is movement into uncharted territory. The process involves removal of the veils which prevent confrontation with the unknown. Let it be noted that "journey" is a multidimensional word and that the various meanings and images conjured up by the word are not sharply distinguishable. One thinks of mystical journeys, quests, adventurous travel, advancement in skills, in sports, in intellectual probing, in psychological integration and transformation. So also the "veils," the insulations against the unknown imposed upon women by male mediators, are multidimensional and intertwined. The veils are woven of religious myths (for example, the myth of the "good woman," the Virgin Mother who has only a Son, not a Daughter), legal restrictions, social customs, medical and psychoanalytic ideologies and practices, academic restrictions (withholding of

---

[2] An elaborate historical study of the Sins is to be found in Morton W. Bloomfield, *The Seven Deadly Sins* (Michigan State University Press, 1952, 1967).

[3] Bloomfield gives a variety of "listings" of Deadly Sins in different periods and cultures, with useful contextual information.

[4] See Dolores Bargowski's review of the film in *Quest: A Feminist Quarterly* I, No. 1, (Summer, 1974), pp. 53–57.

access to "higher" education, to certain professions), grammatical conditioning ("he" supposedly includes "she"), economic limitations. The very process of exorcism, of casting off the blinding veils, is movement outside the patriarchally imposed sense of reality and identity. This demystification process, standing/moving outside The Lie, *is* ecstasy.

The process of encountering the unknown, of overcoming the "protection" racket, also involves a continual conversion of the previously unknown into the familiar.[5] This requires the use of tools and instruments now in the possession of women's captors. Amazon expeditions into the male-controlled "fields" such as law, medicine, psychology, philosophy, theology, literature, history, sociology, biology, and physics, are necessary in order to leave the Fathers' cave and live in the sun. A crucial problem has been to learn how to plunder righteously while avoiding being caught too long in the cave. In universities, and in virtually all of the professions, there are poisonous gases which are almost invisible and odorless, and which gradually stifle women's minds and spirits. Those who carry out the necessary expeditions run the risk of shrinking into the mold of the mystified Athena, the twice-born who forgets and denies her Mother and Sisters. "Reborn" from the Father, she becomes Daddy's Girl, the mutant who serves the master's purposes. The token woman, who in reality is enchained, possessed, "knows" that she is free. She is a useful tool of the patriarchs, particularly against her sister Artemis who knows better, respects her womanself, bonds with her sisters, and refuses to sell her freedom, her original birthright, for a mess of respectability.

Exorcism, Processions, and Remythologization

What clues can we find concerning the "nature" and direction of the Otherworld journey of radically feminist (i.e. conscious) women? Some important hints can be discovered in *Three Guineas,* an astonishing book published in the 1930s by a prophetic foremother. In that book Virginia Woolf links processions (e.g. academic, churchly, military, judicial) with professions and processions. She asks:

What are these ceremonies and why should we take part in them? What are these professions and why should we make money out of them? Where, in short, is it leading us, the procession of the sons of educated men?[6]

Clearly, they are leading us to destruction of the human species and of the planet. The rigid, stylized, hierarchical, gynocidal and genocidal processions of male-controlled professions—of church, state, university, army—are all intimately interconnected. These processions capture and reify process. They are deadly. It is important to understand them in order to understand what feminist process/journeying is *not.*

Patriarchal processions both generate and reflect the archetypal image of

---

[5] This idea is developed in a remarkable article. See Peggy Allegro, "The Strange and the Familiar," *Amazon Quarterly,* I, 1, pp. 29–41.

[6] Virginia Woolf, *Three Guineas* (New York: Harcourt, Brace, and World, Inc., 1938, 1966), p. 63.

"procession" from and return to God the Father. In Christian myth, this is a cyclic pattern: separation and return. Christians participate in the procession— they join the parade—through Baptism, which explicitly contains a rite of exorcism. This mythic symbolic procession toward "God," then, begins with belief in possession by evil forces ("possession" technically in a broad sense, of course), release from which requires captivity by the church. What is ultimately sought is reconciliation with the Father.

Clearly, the ultimate symbol of "procession" is the All Male Trinity itself. In various abstruse ways theologians have elaborated upon the "mystery," or as some would say, the "symbol," of the Trinity. What is of great significance here is the fact that this is a myth of Father and Son (no Mother or Daughter involved) in total unity, so total that this "love" is expressed by the Third Person, the Holy Spirit. This is the epitome of male bonding, beyond the wildest dreams of Lionel Tiger. It is (almost?) erotic male homosexual mythos, the perfect All Male Marriage, the All Male Divine Family. It is asymmetric patriarchy carried to the sublime absurdity of contradiction, christened "mystery." To the timid objections sometimes voiced by Christian women, the classic answer has been: "You're included. The Holy Spirit is feminine." The conclusion of this absurd logic arrives quickly if one asks: How then, did "he" impregnate the Virgin Mary?

Mere human males, of course, cannot fully identify with the divine Son. Perfect consubstantiality with the Father, therefore, cannot be achieved. The earthly processions of the sons of men have as their basic paradigm an attempted identification with the Father. (God the Father, the Godfather, the Oedipal Father). The junior statesman dreams of becoming The President. The academic junior scholar (disciple) dreams of becoming The Professor (Master). The acolyte dreams of becoming The Priest. And, as Woolf recognized, the death-oriented military processions reveal the real direction of the whole scenario, which is a funeral procession of the human species. God the Father requires human sacrifice.

Women becoming must indeed recognize the fact of having been possessed by the structures of evil. However, the solution is not "rebirth" or Baptism by the Father's surrogates, for it is this socialized "rebirth" which is the captivity from which we are trying to escape. Radical feminism is *not* reconciliation with the Father. It begins with saying "No" to the Father, who attempts to eradicate our Mother and to transform us into mutants by forcing "rebirth" (whether from the head of Zeus or from the rib of Adam or from baptismal "grace"). More than this: radical feminism means saying "Yes" to our original birth, the original movement—surge toward life. This is both a remembering and a rediscovering. Athena remembers and rediscovers her Mother. That which is generated between us is Sisterhood. We are then no longer confined by our identities as "Mother" or "Daughter." The Daughter is *not* obedient to the Mother "unto death." The Mother does not send her forth to be crucified for the sins of women or of men. Rather, they go forth as Sisters. Radical feminism releases the inherent dynamic in the Mother-Daughter relationship toward Sisterhood, which is thwarted within the Male-mastered system. The Mother does *not* demand self-sacrifice of the Daughter. Rather, both demand of each other affirmation of the self and of each other in an on-going personal/ political process which is mythic in its depths—which is both exorcising and remythologizing process. The "sacrifice" that is required is not mutilation at the hands of men, but rather the discipline needed for action together, for self-defense and self-actualization on a planet dominated by the Reign of Terror which is the Reign of the Godfathers. It is important that we consider the actual conditions of this terrain through which we must make our journey.

The Land of the Fathers

As Phyllis Chesler has pointed out, the story of the Virgin Mary, impregnated by God to bring forth his only Son, is classic patriarchal rape-incest myth. The Madonna has no Divine Daughter. Moreover, as the same author perceptively says, she foregoes sexual pleasure, physical prowess, and economic and intellectual power in order to become a "mother" for her "divine" son.[7] And this is the primary role-model for women in our culture. This is the life that women are condemned to live out—an alienation which is personal, social, mythic—and which is all the deeper because unrecognized, unacknowledged.

In a society in which women are in fact *robbed* of physical prowess, of economic and intellectual power, we live in a State of Siege.[8] As Jeanne Lafferty and Evelyn Clark wrote:

Every female person knows the humiliation of being constantly harassed and solicited by males. Having her person talked at, whistled at, yelled at, grunted at, hooted and howled at, visually dismembered or stared and winked at by males everywhere— on the street, at work, at school, at home—everywhere.[9]

This is the very real condition of women in a rapist society. Moreover, the dismemberment is not always only visual. Male fetishism concerning women's bodies, the cutting into objectified parts which is the prime material of advertising and pornography, has as its logical outcome the brutal rape murders and actual physical dismemberments which take place in such a society. In a world ruled by God the Father this is not considered a serious problem. A feminist author wrote:

Rape is too personal and too terrible a crime to be left to the punishment of indifferent male law.[10]

In a society possessed by the sexual caste system, that is, in a rapist society, there is a deep struggle on the part of those designated "victims" to cast out the deception that warps the soul. The deception inflicted upon women is a kind of mindbinding comparable to the footbinding procedure which mutilated

[7] Phyllis Chesler, *Women and Madness* (New York: Doubleday, 1972), pp. 24–26.

[8] This expression was used by Emily Culpepper in an unpublished paper entitled "Reflections on Ethics and Self Defense: Establishing a Firm Stance."

[9] "Self Defense and the Preservation of Females," in *The Female State: A Journal of Female Liberation,* Issue 4 (April, 1970), p. 96.

[10] Elizabeth Gould Davis, author of *The First Sex* (New York: G. P. Putnam's Sons, 1971) wrote this in an article about her own devastating rape in *Prime Time,* June, 1974, p. 3.

millions of Chinese women for a thousand years.[11] Just as footbinding destroyed the capacity for physical movement—walking, running, dancing—mindbinding damages the capacity for autonomous creativity, action, thinking, imagining, willing. Stripping away the mindbindings of lies that reduce women to the status of physical, mental, and spiritual rapes is the basic loving act in such a society.

The Qualitative Leap

Creative, living, political hope for movement beyond the gynocidal reign of the Fathers will be fulfilled only if women continue to make qualitative leaps in living our transcendence. A short-circuited hope of transcendence has caused many to remain inside churches, and patriarchal religion sometimes has seemed to satisfy the hunger for transcendence. The problem has been that both the hunger and the satisfaction generated within such religions have to a great extent alienated women from our deepest aspirations. Spinning in vicious circles of false needs and false consciousness, women caught on the patriarchal wheel have not been able to experience women's own experience.

I suggest that what is required is *ludic cerebration,* the free play of intuition in our own space, giving rise to thinking that is vigorous, informed, multidimensional, independent, creative, tough. *Ludic cerebration* is thinking out of experience. I do not mean the experience of dredging out All That Was Wrong with Mother, or of instant intimacy in group encounters, or of waiting at the doctoral dispensary, or of self-lobotomization in order to publish, perish, and then be promoted. I mean the experience of being. *Be-ing* is the verb that says the dimensions of depth in all verbs, such as intuiting, reasoning, loving, imaging, making, acting, as well as the couraging, hoping, and playing that are always there when one is really living.

It may be that some new things happen within patriarchy, but one thing essentially stays the same: women are always marginal beings. From this vantage point of the margin it is possible to look at what is between the margins with the lucidity of The Compleat Outsider. To change metaphors: the systems within the System do not appear so radically different from each other to those excluded by all. Hope for a qualitative leap lies in *us* by reason of that deviance from the "norm" which was first imposed but which can also be *chosen* on our own terms. This means that there has to be a shift from "acceptable" female deviance (characterized by triviality, diffuseness, dependence upon others for self-definition, low self-esteem, powerlessness) to deviance which may be unacceptable to others but which is acceptable to the self and *is* self-acceptance.

For women concerned with philosophical/theological questions, it seems to me, this implies the necessity of some sort of choice. One either tries to avoid "acceptable" deviance ("normal" female idiocy) by becoming accepted as a

---

[11] The horrors of footbinding are recounted by Andrea Dworkin, *Woman Hating* (New York: Dutton, 1974), pp. 95–117. These "tiny feet" were malodorous, mutilated humps. Women fell from one to the other. These stumps were described in fantastically deceptive euphemistic language and were the objects of sadistic male fetishism.

male-identified professional, or else one tries to make the qualitative leap toward self-acceptable deviance as ludic cerebrator, questioner of everything, madwoman, and witch.

I do mean witch. The heretic who rejects the idols of patriarchy is the blasphemous creatrix of her own thoughts. She is finding her life and intends not to lose it. The witch that smolders within every woman who cared and dared enough to become a philosophically/spiritually questing feminist in the first place seems to be crying out these days: "Light my fire!" The qualitative leap, the light of those flames of spiritual imagination and cerebral fantasy can be a new dawn.

On "Androgyny"

Feminists have searched for a word to express the concept/reality of psychic wholeness, of integration, which we are just beginning to glimpse intuitively, experientially, as realizable. In this search for the right word we have experienced the poverty of the language bequeathed to us, and we have recognized the manner in which it constricts and even distorts our thought. In my book *Beyond God the Father,* I frequently use the word "androgyny" to express this intuition and incipient experience of wholeness, which transcends sex-role stereotyping—the societally imposed "eternal feminine" and "eternal masculine." Feminist ethicist Janice Raymond has written perceptively of an "intuition of androgyny" as identical with the intuition of being.[12] Two young theologians, graduates of Harvard Divinity School, used the term to convey a feminist understanding of wholeness in a much discussed jointly published article.[13] Feminist poet Adrienne Rich used the word in her poem *The Stranger,* which concludes with the following lines:

> I am the androgyne
> I am the living mind you fail to
>   describe
> in your dead language
> the lost noun, the verb surviving
> only in the infinitive
> the letters of my name are written
>   under the lids
> of the newborn child.[14]

All of these authors now experience some hesitancy about using the word "androgyny" to express our vision(s). This hesitancy is at least in part due to an increasing understanding of the political use and abuse of language. This

---

[12] "Beyond Male Morality," in *Women and Religion,* Revised Edition, edited by Judith Plaskow and Joan Romero, (Missoula, Montana: American Academy of Religion and The Scholars' Press, 1974), pp. 115–125.

[13] Linda L. Barufaldi and Emily E. Culpepper, "Androgyny and the Myth of Masculine/ Feminine," *Christianity and Crisis,* April 16, 1973, pp. 69–71.

[14] Adrienne Rich, *Diving into the Wreck, Poems 1971–72* (New York: W. W. Norton, 1973).

increased sophistication has resulted from some distressing misinterpretations of the word.

In speaking to audiences, I have sometimes had the impression that people hearing this term vaguely envisage two distorted halves of a human being stuck together—something like John Wayne and Brigitte Bardot scotchtaped together —as if two distorted "halves" could make a whole. That is, there is a kind of reification of wholeness, instead of recognition that what is being described is continual process. This non-understanding of "androgyny," which feminists have used when attempting to describe the *process* of integration, is also reflected in the assumption on the part of some women (and men) that a woman who is successful in a career on male terms (for example, a successful business executive) and at the same time a model housewife has achieved "androgyny." In fact, this career housewife as described fails to criticize radically either the "masculine" or the "feminine" roles/worlds. She simply compartmentalizes her personality in order to function within both, instead of recognizing/rejecting/ transcending the inherent oppressiveness of such institutions as big business and the nuclear family.

When one becomes conscious of the political usages of language, she recognizes also that the term "androgyny" is adaptable to such mystifying usage as the expression "human liberation" has been subjected to. That is, it can easily be used to deflect attention from the fact that women and men at this point in history cannot simply "get together and work it out," ignoring the profound differences in socialization and situation within the sexual caste system. Both "androgyny" and "human liberation" function frequently to encourage false transcendence, masking—even though unintentionally—the specific content of the oppression of women, and suggesting that wholeness depends upon identification with men. Some of us do still use the term "androgyny," of course, but less frequently, more circumspectly, and with some apprehension that we will be misunderstood.

Some feminists began to feel somewhat less comfortable with the word "androgyny" when the implications of a small terse fact surfaced to consciousness. That fact is etymological: the first part of the word obviously is derived from the Greek *aner, andros* (man), while the second part is from *gyne* (woman). This, of course, carries its own message. A first reaction was to employ the word "gynandry," which, from the perspective of women's becoming, is more appropriate. But it soon became evident that the priority problem in the etymology of the word was really symptomatic of deeper problems.

In fact, the term "androgyny" comes to us heavily fraught with traditional associations, that is, associations of male-centered tradition(s). The image conveyed by the word is that of a "feminized" male. This fact has been brought home to me in public discussions with male Christian theologians who, confronted with the problem of the inherent oppressiveness of Christolatry, have responded earnestly that there really is no problem since "Jesus was androgynous." Whatever this may mean, it has little relevance to the problem of women's becoming *now,* and in fact it distracts from the real issues confronting us. Dressing up old symbols just will not work for women who are conscious of sexist religiosity.

"Gynandry" helps to shift images away from the traditional biases, but only to a limited degree. Placing the female part of the word first does not dissolve the inherent dependency of the word itself upon stereotypes in order that there be any meaningful content at all. To put it another way, in an "androgynous" or "gynandrous" society it would be senseless to speak of "androgyny" or "gynandry" since people would have no idea of the sex-stereotyped characteristics and/or roles referred to by the components of the terms. Use of these terms at this point in history is dysfunctional to the extent that it encourages on some level a perpetuation of stereotypes (as is the case with Jungian ideology of the "anima" and "animus"). "Gynandry" or "androgyny" *can* function in a liberating way if they are seen as "transitional" words, or, more precisely, as self-liquidating words. They should be understood as having a built-in planned obsolescence.[15]

Wanted: "God" or "The Goddess"?

Feminist consciousness is experienced by a significant number of women as ontological becoming, that is, being. This process requires existential courage, courage to be and to *see*, which is both revolutionary and revelatory, revealing our participation in ultimate reality as Verb, as intransitive Verb.

The question obviously arises of the need for anthropomorphic symbols for this reality. There is no inherent contradiction between speaking of ultimate reality as Verb and speaking of this as personal. The Verb is more personal than a mere static noun. However, if we choose to *image* the Verb in anthropomorphic symbols, we can run into a problematic phenomenon which sociologist Henri Desroche calls "crossing." "Crossing" refers to a notable tendency among oppressed groups to attempt to change or adapt the ideological tools of the oppressor, so that they can be used *against* him and *for* the oppressed. The problem here is the fact that the functioning of "crossing" does not generally move far enough outside the ideological framework it seeks to undermine. In the "Black theology" of James Cone, for example, we find a Black God and a Black Messiah, but this pigmentation operation does not significantly alter the behavior of Jahweh & Son. Cone's Black God is as revengeful and sexist as his White prototype. For feminist eyes it is clear that this God is at least as oppressive as the old (for black women as well as for white women). The message in the alteration of symbol is simply about *which* male-ruled racial group will be on top and which will be on the bottom. The basic presupposition of *hierarchy* remains unaltered: that is, the presupposition that there must be an "us" or a "them" on top, and a corresponding "them" or "us" on the bottom.

Some women religious leaders within Western culture in modern times have performed something like a "crossing" operation, notably such figures as Mary Baker Eddy and Ann Lee, in stressing the "maternal" aspect of the divinity. The result has been mixed. Eddy's "Father-Mother God" is, after all, the

---

[15] In a speech delivered at the Modern Languages Association Forum, December, 1973, Cynthia Secor noted that there is no "Androgyne Quarterly"—most probably because there are no androgynes around to publish it.

Christian God. Nor does Ann Lee really move completely outside the Christian framework. It is interesting that their writings lack the thirst for vengeance that characterizes Cone's all too Christian Black theology, which is certainly in their favor. But it is also necessary to note that their theologies lack explicit relevance to the concrete problems of the oppression of women. Intellection and spirituality remain cut off from creative political movement. In earlier periods also there were women within the Christian tradition who tried to "cross" the Christian all-male God and Christ to some degree. An outstanding example was Juliana of Norwich, an English recluse and mystic who lived in the last half of the fourteenth century. Juliana's "God" and "Jesus" were—if language conveys anything—hermaphroditic constructs, with the primary identity clearly male. While there are many levels on which I could analyze Juliana's words about "our beloved Mother, Jesus, (who) feeds us with himself,"[16] suffice it to say here that this hermaphroditic image is somewhat less than attractive. The "androgynous" God and Jesus present problems analogous to and related to those problems which occur in connection with the use of the term "androgyny" to describe the direction of women's becoming. There is something like a "liberation of the woman within" the (primarily male) God and Jesus.

Indeed, it is harder to perform a transsexual operation on the Judeo-Christian divinity than a mere pigmentation operation. This is one reason, no doubt, why Cone is able to achieve a purely Black God and Black Messiah, rather than a Mulatto, whereas the Christian women mentioned brought forth hermaphrodites, with emphasis upon maleness. Indeed, they did something on the symbolic level which is analogous to "liberating the woman within the man." Since they went only this far, they accomplished little or nothing, in social or mythic terms, toward the genuine liberation of women.

One fact that stands out here is that these were women whose imaginations were still partially controlled by Christian myth. My contention is that they were caught in a contradiction (which is not the case in the work of Black *male* theologians). I am saying that there is a profound contradiction between the inherent logic of radical feminism and the inherent logic of the Christian symbol system. I would not have said this ten years ago, at the time of writing the original edition of *The Church and the Second Sex,* which expressed hope for reform of Christianity in general and Roman Catholicism in particular. Nor would some women today say this—women who still perceive their identity as both Christian and feminist.

Both the reformers and those who leave Judaism and Christianity behind are contributing and will contribtue in different ways to the process of the becoming of women. The point here is not to place value judgments upon individual persons and their efforts—and there are heroic efforts at all points of the feminist spectrum. Rather, it is to disclose an inherent logic in feminism. The courage which some women have in affirming this logic comes in part from having been on the feminist journey for quite awhile. Encouragement comes also from

---

[16] Juliana of Norwich, *Revelations of Divine Love,* edited by Clifton Walters (Baltimore, Maryland: 1966), Ch. 61.

knowing increasing numbers of women who have chosen the route of the logical conclusion. Some of these women have "graduated" from Christianity or religious Judaism, and some have never even been associated closely with church or synagogue, but have discovered spiritual and mythic depths in the women's movement itself. What we share is a sense of becoming in cosmic process, which I prefer to call the Verb, Be-ing, and which some would still call "God."

For some feminists concerned with the spiritual depth of the movement, the word "God" is becoming increasingly problematic, however. This by no means indicates a movement in the direction of "atheism" or "agnosticism" or "secularism," as these terms are usually understood. Rather, the problem arises precisely because of the spiritual and mythic quality perceived in feminist process itself. Some use expressions such as "power of being." Some reluctantly still use the word "God" while earnestly trying to divest the term of its patriarchal associations, attempting to think perhaps of the "God of the philosophers" rather than the overtly masculist and oppressive "God of the theologians." But the problem becomes increasingly troublesome, the more the "God" of the various Western philosophers is subjected to feminist analysis. "He"—"Jahweh" still often hovers behind the abstractions, stunting our own thought, giving us a sense of contrived double-think. The word "God" just may be inherently oppressive.

Indeed, the word "Goddess" has also been problematic, but for different reasons. Some have been worried about the problem of "crossing." However, that difficulty appears more and more as a pseudo-difficulty when it is recognized that "crossing" is likely to occur only when one is trying to work *within* a sexist tradition. For example, Christian women who in their "feminist liturgies" experiment with referring to "God" as "she" and to the Trinity as "The Mother, the Daughter, and the Holy Spirit," are still working within all the boundaries of the same symbolic framework and the same power structure. Significantly, their services are at the same place and time as "the usual," and are regarded by most of the constituency of the churches as occasional variations of "business as usual."

As women who are outside the Christian church inform ourselves of evidence supporting the existence of ancient matriarchy and of evidence indicating that the Gods of patriarchy are indeed contrived, pale derivatives and reversals of the Great Goddess of an earlier period, the fear of mere "crossing" appears less appropriate and perhaps even absurd. There is also less credibility allowable to the notion that "Goddess" would function like "God" in reverse, that is, to legitimate an oppressive "female-dominated" society, if one is inclined to look seriously at evidence that matriarchal society was not structured like patriarchy, that it was non-hierarchical.[17]

Would "Goddess" be likely to function oppressively, like "God"? Given the present situations of women, the danger is not imminent. "Would it function that way in the future?" My inclination is to think not, but it is not my in-

[17] See Robert Briffault, *The Mothers,* (New York: Macmillan, 1927), Vol. I. See also J. J. Bachofen, *Myth, Religion and Mother-Right,* trans. by Ralph Manheim (Princeton: Princeton University Press, 1967).

tention to attempt to "prove" this point at this time. The question has a quality of "abstraction" and remoteness from the present social realities and it is, it seems to me, diversionary. When it is raised, and it is usually raised by men, one senses an "atmosphere" about the question, an aroma of masculine hysteria, a fear of invading hordes of "matriarchs" (read: female patriarchs) taking over The Man's world.

There are, however, two points concerning the symbol "Goddess" which I think *are* relevant to the existing situation. First, it can at the very least be pointed out that whenever the pendulum has swung extremely in one direction (and it *has*—for millennia), it is psychologically/socially/ethically important to emphasize "the other side." The hermaphroditic image hardly seems satisfactory for anyone. For an increasing minority of women—and even for some men[18]—"Goddess" is becoming more functional, meaningful, and loaded with healing associations. As this minority grows, Western society will be shaken by the presence of gynarchic symbolism in a new and potent way. It should be noted that women are inclined to speak and write of "The Goddess," whereas one seldom says "The God." In our culture it has been assumed that "goddesses" are many and trivial, whereas the "real" divinity *is* "God," who does not even require the definite article. The use of the expression, "The Goddess," is a way of confronting this trivialization, of exorcising the male "God," and of affirming a different myth/reality.

A second, and related, point has to do with the fact that the "self-transcending immanence," the sense of giving birth to ourselves, the sense of power of being within, which is being affirmed by many women, does not seem to be denoted, imaged, adequately pointed to, or perhaps even associated with the term "God." With her permission, I will relate a story told to me by a theologian for those insights I have the greatest respect. This woman told me that in the past when riding in planes (and feeling fearful about the situation) she often conjured up images remembered from childhood of "God" as "having the whole world in his hands." Later, this image/prayer? became meaningless. When she was on a plane recently, the ride suddenly became extremely "bumpy" and rough. It occurred to her to "try on" the name/image "Goddess." The result, as she described it, was immediate, electrifying, consoling. She sensed a presence and had/heard? the thought: "Just let go. Just sit on the seat and sit on the air waves and ride." The ride, though as rough as before, became a joyful experience.[19]

Clearly, it would be inappropriate and arrogant to try to "explain" or "interpret" this experience of another person. I can only comment that many women I know are finding power of being within the self, rather than in "internalized" father images. As a philosopher, my preference has been for abstractions. Indeed I have always been annoyed and rather embarrassed by "anthropomorphic" symbols, preferring terms such as "ground and power of being" (Tillich), "beyond subjectivity and objectivity" (James), "the Encompassing" (Jaspers), or

[18] Kenneth Pitchford chooses Goddess imagery, which occurs frequently in his more recent poems.

[19] The story was told by Professor Nelle Morton of Drew Theological Seminary, and paraphrased by myself.

the commonly used "Ultimate Reality," or "cosmic process." More recently I have used the expression "Intransitive Verb." Despite this philosophical inclination, and also because of it, I find it impossible to ignore the realm of symbols, or to fail to recognize that many women are experiencing and participating in a remythologizing process, which is a new dawn.

It is necessary to add a few remarks about the functioning of the confusing and complex "Mary" symbol within Christianity. Through it, the power of the Great Goddess symbol is enchained, captured, used, cannibalized, tokenized, domesticated, tranquillized. In spite of this, I think that many women and at least some men, when they have heard of or imaged the "Mother of God," have, by something like a selective perception process, screened out the standardized, lobotomized, dull, derivative and dwarfed Christian reflections of a more ancient symbol; they have perceived something that might more accurately be described as the Great Goddess, and which, in human terms, can be translated into "the strong woman who can relate because she can stand alone." A woman of Jewish background commented that "Mother of God" has always seemed strange and contradictory to her. Not having been programmed to "know" about the distinctions between the "divine" and the "human" nature of "Christ," or to "know" that the "Mother of God" is less than God, this woman had been able to hear the expression with the ears of an extraenvironmental listener. It sounded, she said, something like "infinite plus one."[20] When this symbolic nonsense is recognized, it is more plausible simply to *think* "infinite," and to *image* something like "Great Mother," or "Goddess."

It may appear that the suffix "-ess" presents a problem, when one considers other usages of that suffix, for example, in "poetess," or in "authoress." In these cases, there is a tone of depreciation, a suggestion that women poets and authors are in a separate and "inferior" category to be judged by different standards than their male counterparts. However, the suffix does not always function in this "diminishing" way. For example, there appear to be no "diminuitive" overtones suggested by the word "actress." So also it seems that the term "Goddess"—or "The Goddess"—*is not only non-diminuitive, but very strong.* Indeed, it calls before the mind images of a powerful and ancient tradition before, behind, and beyond Christianity. These are multi-dimensional images of women's present and future becoming/be-ing.

"Priests" or "Priestesses"?

I would suggest that "priestess" has diminuitive connotations if it is applied within the framework of Christianity (Episcopalian priestesses?), since of course within the limitations of that framework the role "acted out" by women has to be seen as derivative. It is only when one considers the possibility that the Christian tradition is itself derivative from a far more ancient and woman-centered tradition, that one's perception of priesthood changes. For women to be priestesses then is no longer perceived simply as a derivative phenomenon, but as primary and authentic. But then neither is it a Christian phenomenon. The

[20] Comment of Linda Franklin, Boston College student.

priesthood of women need not seek legitimation within Christian churches. Nor need it be seen as a title or office conferred upon certain officially designated women to the exclusion of others.

Moreover, there are impossible contradictions in the idea of woman-identified Christian priests. While it may be possible for a twice-born Athena to "say Mass," or to commit baptism "in the name of the Father and of the Son and of the Holy Ghost," this sort of behavior presents incredible problems, that is, problems of credibility. Moreover, as I have said, it is inconsistent simply to try to fit a "feminine" symbolism into these sclerotic vessels. The "form" would still be the message, with some alterations in "content."

Is it true, as Malcolm Boyd has recently argued, that "when the (Christian) priest is a woman, even God is no longer a male?"[21] At one time, some years ago, I might have agreed with this. However, it is important to look at Protestant churches which have been ordaining women for years. Clearly, their God (and Gods) are still male. Large patriarchal institutions are still male. Large patriarchal institutions are still quite capable of absorbing a few tokens and in fact of profiting from this, appearing "liberal" while at the same time attracting women who are doubly devoted to the task of serving male Gods. I say "doubly devoted" because, as the cliche goes, a woman has to be twice as "good" as a man to get half as much recognition.

It is instructive to read the list of 110 Catholic signers who have called for the ordination of women "to the priesthood of the universal church."[22] Having read some writings of some of them, I question 1) whether they can possibly understand what the logic of feminism is all about (i.e., leaving behind and thus leaving to die the inherently oppressive structures of patriarchal religions); 2) whether they *do* "understand" what the logic of feminism is about and see "containment" as an important tactic for holding women in bondage as long as possible.

The women's movement *is* about refusal to be merely contained as well as refusal to be mere containers. It is about saying "Yes" to ourselves, which is the deepest way of saying "Yes" to others. At some point in her history a woman may sincerely see ordination to the Christian priesthood as her way of saying this "Yes." It is my hope that such women will *continue* their journey. Ambition to "ordination" perhaps reaches a respectable altitude for the jet age, but it does not reach very far, I think, into feminist space/time. It is my hope that these sisters will raise their ambitions and their self-respect higher, immeasurably higher, that they will one day outgrow their books of common prayer and dream less common dreams.

[21] *Ms.,* December, 1974.
[22] Reported in *National Catholic Reporter,* November 8, 1974, p. 5.

On the Meaning of Life

In his book *The Varieties of Religious Experience,* William James uses a distinction he learned from Francis W. Newman: that between the once-born and the twice-born. The once-born are healthy minded, optimistic, cheerful, assured, without metaphysical doubts, confident of a harmonious, friendly world, and congenitally happy. James cites Walt Whitman as a supreme example of the once-born consciousness. He says, "In some individuals optimism may become quasipathological. The capacity for even a transient sadness or a momentary humility seems cut off from them as by a kind of congenital anaesthesia."

In their first life, the twice-born are dark thinkers, often in despair, pessimistic, appalled at life's transiency, metaphysically inclined, perceptive of the falsity of beguiling goods and successes, sensitive to the presence of evil, and persuaded of its pervasiveness. The twice-born cannot shuck this fearsome baggage without being born again to a new life. A religious conversion is often hailed as the end of an old life and the beginning of a new life, a rebirth that signals an awakening to the meaningfulness of life. The twice-born communicant is freshly launched again after his or her travail in the slough of despair.

Moods of pessimism and optimism are not to be confused with the feelings of depression and elation. Feelings are relatively momentary compared to the more permanent moods. Presumably, our moods are subject to rational manipulation. If we have no well-founded reason for pessimism, the mood should lift. The question "What is the meaning of life?" could be construed as a plea for a rational explanation of why life is worth living, a plea for a rational shield against the corrosive effects of the pessimistic mood that, when buttressed by a feeling of despair, may wear down the will to live. As a plea, the question about the meaning of life seems, as it seemed to Camus, to be the most important philosophical question we humans must wrestle with. It seems to be so, at least, to the twice-born before his or her second birth.

Perhaps some thinkers' congenital optimism might be blamed for the disdain they have for the question about life's meaningfulness, but that is not the sole reason. Some philosophers doubt that the question itself is meaningful. For many of them, mostly contemporary, the question is as nonsensical as, to use John Wisdom's example, "What is bigger than the largest thing in the world?" Not every set of words that is grammatically a sentence and ends with a question mark is answerable. Some questions cannot be answered, not because they are difficult, but because logically they cannot have an answer. A question that can have no answer can hardly be construed as a real question. Wisdom, however, suggests that because there are different kinds of answers to "What is the meaning of . . . ?" there are different kinds of questions lying beneath the sentence form "What is the meaning of . . . ?" "But with the words "What is the meaning of it all?" we are trying to find the order in the drama of Time." The question about the meaning of life is comparable to the question about the meaning of a play, the characters, the significance of this act in the whole. Just as with our answer to the question about the meaning of a drama, so, too, with the answer about the meaning of life, "We must not anticipate that the answer can be given in a word or in a neat list."

"What is the meaning of life?" has a passive feel to it. Its form suggests that an answer to it is something we find after a proper investigation, as if the answer were ready for the taking even before the question was asked. Contrast the passive form with a more active question: "What meaning can we give to life?" In the active form, the meaning of life depends upon us and our own efforts, individually and collectively, rather than upon a kindly or demonic cosmos. In the passive form, the moods of optimism or pessimism are justified, depending upon our conception of the cosmos. The twice-born may be religious converts who lose their pessimism and gain their optimism because they have discovered that the cosmos is in the good hands of a kindly patriarch and/or matriarch or of a whole family of gods. Of course, the discovery can go the other way, too, with pessimism as the payoff. In the active form, the moods of optimism or pessimism may be justified, depending upon one's appraisal of the nature of man. If you think human beings are by nature selfish and that our nature is not alterable, the likelihood of changing your fortunes and the world line is too bleak to support the mood of optimism. On the other hand, confidence in yourself and the goodness of your fellow human beings would support an optimistic answer to the active question.

Albert Camus, in this section's first essay, represents the agnostic existentialist position on the meaning of life. His agnosticism leads him to say, "I don't know whether this world has a meaning that transcends it. But I know that I do not know that meaning and that it is impossible for me just now to know it." That is why he calls the world absurd. It is only in "this unintelligible and limited universe" that "Man's fate henceforth assumes its meaning." Although this absurd world guarantees no future, this has the advantage that it provides the opportunity for the existential human being to be free. In an absurd world, one is free to become what one wishes. A life can have meaning even if the world does not. Thus, Camus is an agnostic about the passive question but finds advantages for us when we come to answer the active form of the question about life's meaning. For Camus, the meaning of life is cast in terms of two existentialist values: the *revolt* against conformity and the absurd, and the *freedom* felt through existentially free choices. We refer you to Jean-Paul Sartre's essay in Chapter Seven for further elaboration on man's existential freedom.

Camus's outlook can be contrasted with a religious view of the human situation. Consider the Christian outlook, one designed to answer the passive form of our question: The Christian view of the human situation emerges from its account of the creation, purpose, direction, and destiny of the cosmos; we are all born into the same cosmic situation and are subject to all its vicissitudes and glories. In the Christian view, death is neither a basis for despair nor the ground of absurdity, because death is not the end of life but the beginning of its best phase, the phase during which one's immortal soul enters into contemplation and communion with God. Rebirth through a realization of God's plan, love, and care is possible on earth and allows escape from the melancholy attacks to which those who have not hitherto grasped the meaningfulness of life on earth are subject. Other religions present different cosmic pictures and characterizations of the human situation, but, for all their variety, they all aim at the generality that qualifies their answer to the question about life's meaning as being a philosophical answer.

It is the generality of an answer to the question "What is the meaning of life?" that makes it philosophical rather than psychological. For example, psychological counseling is tailormade for each person's special circumstance. Philosophical answers, on the other hand, are fitting regardless of the person or his personal conditions.

This importance of general applicability has usually been recognized by those who believe that life has a meaning and who try to say what it is. This has led to talk of such things as the "human condition," the "human situation," "the place of man in the scheme of things," "the purpose of human existence," and "the destiny of man." Here there is no discussion of this human being or that human being (Manuel, Neil, Bess, or Grace) but of "human." Whatever is said of "human" is said of you (and Manuel and Bess) as well, for, being human, you too have the "condition" or are in the "situation," even though, if you are a once-born type, you may not be aware of it.

One such condition to which all human beings are subject is death. Furthermore, human beings are apparently the only form of life on earth conscious of their mortality. The universal concern with death makes it eligible for philosophical attention, and its concomitant *Angst* can be addressed in a philosophical theory of life's meaningfulness, or meaninglessness.

Neither Camus nor **K. E. M. Baier** accept the Christian or any other religious characterization of the human situation. Baier believes that the cosmic picture that science provides replaces the Christian picture; however, this need not give us cause for despair, because our lives can still have meaning in one sense of that term. Our lives can be made worthwhile without the Christian machinery. He suggests that human life can be made meaningful because we can give purpose to our lives through moral commitments and efforts. Baier achieves philosophical generality by giving a general *prescription* of how human beings are to make their lives worthwhile rather than by giving a *description* of the human condition, or human situation, or human destiny.

W. D. Joske remarks that Baier's optimism about the meaningfulness of life depends upon a confidence that our efforts to make our lives meaningful will succeed. Joske contrasts his position to Baier's: "I want to argue that life may be meaningless for reasons other than that it does not contribute to a worthwhile goal, so that the failure to find meaning in life can be due to the nature of the world and not simply to failure of adequate commitment by an agent." Life's meaningfulness is analogous to an activity's meaningfulness; Joske thinks there are four elements in the meaningfulness of an activity, and life: The activity should be worthwhile for its own sake; it should have point, not be trivial or futile. The nature of the world may make our life meaningless because our activities are futile, because we are frustrated from achieving the desired end due to the an inhospitable world; in this case, pessimism rather than Baier's optimism, seems justified.

The other main contention of Joske's that you should note is his claim that "certain commonly held and rationally defendable philosophical views can be seen as threatening human life with futility." He cites four such views.

The Absurdity of Human Existence

ALBERT CAMUS

Albert Camus (1913–1960), born in Algeria, became one of the foremost existential writers and won the Nobel prize in literature. Among his books are *The Stranger* (1942) and *The Fall* (1957).

Absurdity and Suicide

There is but one truly serious philosophical problem, and that is suicide. Judging whether life is or is not worth living amounts to answering the fundamental question of philosophy. All the rest—whether or not the world has three dimensions, whether the mind has nine or twelve categories—comes afterwards. These are games; one must first answer. And if it is true, as Nietzsche claims, that a philosopher, to deserve our respect, must preach by example, you can appreciate the importance of that reply, for it will precede the definitive act. These are facts the heart can feel; yet they call for careful study before they become clear to the intellect.

If I ask myself how to judge that this question is more urgent than that, I reply that one judges by the actions it entails. I have never seen anyone die for the ontological argument. Galileo, who held a scientific truth of great importance, abjured it with the greatest of ease as soon as it endangered his life. In a certain sense, he did right.[1] That truth was not worth the stake. Whether the earth or the sun revolves around the other is a matter of profound indifference. To tell the truth, it is a futile question. On the other hand, I see many people die because they judge that life is not worth living. I see others paradoxically getting killed for the ideas or illusions that give them a reason for living (what is called a reason for living is also an excellent reason for dying). I therefore con-

---

[1] From the point of view of the relative value of truth. On the other hand, from the point of view of virile behavior, this scholar's fragility may well make us smile.

Source: Albert Camus, *The Myth of Sisyphus and Other Essays,* trans. by Justin O'Brien (New York, 1955), pp. 3–7, 12–13, 51–53, 57–58, 60–62, 88–91. Copyright © 1955 by Alfred A. Knopf, Inc. Reprinted by permission of the publisher.

clude that the meaning of life is the most urgent of questions. How to answer it? On all essential problems (I mean thereby those that run the risk of leading to death or those that intensify the passion of living) there are probably but two methods of thought: the method of La Palisse and the method of Don Quixote. Solely the balance between evidence and lyricism can allow us to achieve simultaneously emotion and lucidity. In a subject at once so humble and so heavy with emotion, the learned and classical dialectic must yield, one can see, to a more modest attitude of mind deriving at one and the same time from common sense and understanding.

Suicide has never been dealt with except as a social phenomenon. On the contrary, we are concerned here, at the outset, with the relationship between individual thought and suicide. An act like this is prepared within the silence of the heart, as is a great work of art. The man himself is ignorant of it. One evening he pulls the trigger or jumps. Of an apartment-building manager who had killed himself I was told that he had lost his daughter five years before, that he had changed greatly since, and that that experience had "undermined" him. A more exact word cannot be imagined. Beginning to think is beginning to be undermined. Society has but little connection with such beginnings. The worm is in man's heart. That is where it must be sought. One must follow and understand this fatal game that leads from lucidity in the face of existence to flight from light.

. . .

But if it is hard to fix the precise instant, the subtle step when the mind opted for death, it is easier to deduce from the act itself the consequences it implies. In a sense, and as in melodrama, killing yourself amounts to confessing. It is confessing that life is too much for you or that you do not understand it. Let's not go too far in such analogies, however, but rather return to everyday words. It is merely confessing that that "is not worth the trouble." Living, naturally, is never easy. You continue making the gestures commanded by existence for many reasons, the first of which is habit. Dying voluntarily implies that you have recognized, even instinctively, the ridiculous character of that habit, the absence of any profound reason for living, the insane character of that daily agitation, and the uselessness of suffering.

What, then, is that incalculable feeling that deprives the mind of the sleep necessary to life? A world that can be explained even with bad reasons is a familiar world. But, on the other hand, in a universe suddenly divested of illusions and lights, man feels an alien, a stranger. His exile is without remedy since he is deprived of the memory of a lost home or the hope of a promised land. This divorce between man and his life, the actor and his setting, is properly the feeling of absurdity. All healthy men having thought of their own suicide, it can be seen, without further explanation, that there is a direct connection between this feeling and the longing for death.

The subject of this essay is precisely this relationship between the absurd and suicide, the exact degree to which suicide is a solution to the absurd. The principle can be established that for a man who does not cheat, what he believes to be true must determine his action. Belief in the absurdity of existence must then dictate his conduct. It is legitimate to wonder, clearly and without false pathos, whether a conclusion of this importance requires forsaking as rapidly as possible an incomprehensible condition. I am speaking, of course, of men inclined to be in harmony with themselves.

Stated clearly, this problem may seem both simple and insoluble. But it is wrongly assumed that simple questions involve answers that are no less simple and that evidence implies evidence. *A priori* and reversing the terms of the problem, just as one does or does not kill oneself, it seems that there are but two philosophical solutions, either yes or no. This would be too easy. But allowance must be made for those who, without concluding, continue questioning. Here I am only slightly indulging in irony: this is the majority. I notice also that those who answer "no" act as if they thought "yes." As a matter of fact, if I accept the Nietzschean criterion, they think "yes" in one way or another. On the other hand, it often happens that those who commit suicide were assured of the meaning of life. These contradictions are constant. It may even be said that they have never been so keen as on this point where, on the contrary, logic seems so desirable. It is a commonplace to compare philosophical theories and the behavior of those who profess them. . . . Schopenhauer is often cited, as a fit subject for laughter, because he praised suicide while seated at a well-set table. This is no subject for joking. That way of not taking the tragic seriously is not so grievous, but it helps to judge a man.

In the face of such contradictions and obscurities must be conclude that there is no relationship between the opinion one has about life and the act one commits to leave it? Let us not exaggerate in this direction. In a man's attachment to life there is something stronger than all the ills in the world. The body's judgment is as good as the mind's, and the body shrinks from annihilation. We get into the habit of living before acquiring the habit of thinking. In that race which daily hastens us toward death, the body maintains its irreparable lead. In short, the essence of that contradiction lies in what I shall call the act of eluding because it is both less and more than diversion in the Pascalian sense. Eluding is the invariable game. The typical act of eluding, the fatal evasion that constitutes the third theme of this essay, is hope. Hope for another life one must "deserve" or trickery of those who live not for life itself but for some great idea that will transcend it, refine it, give it a meaning, and betray it.

Absurdity and Meaning

All great deeds and all great thoughts have a ridiculous beginning. Great works are often born on a street-corner or in a restaurant's revolving door. So it is with absurdity. The absurd world more than others derives its nobility from that abject birth. In certain situations, replying "nothing" when asked what one is thinking about may be pretense in a man. Those who are loved are well aware of this. But if that reply is sincere, if it symbolizes that odd state of soul in which the void becomes eloquent, in which the chain of daily gestures is broken, in which the heart vainly seeks the link that will connect it again, then it is as it were the first sign of absurdity.

It happens that the stage sets collapse. Rising, streetcar, four hours in the office or the factory, meal, streetcar, four hours of work, meal, sleep, and Monday Tuesday Wednesday Thursday Friday and Saturday according to the same rhythm—this path is easily followed most of the time. But one day the "why" arises and everything begins in that weariness tinged with amazement. "Begins"—this is important. Weariness comes at the end of the acts of a mechanical life, but at the same time it inaugurates the impulse of consciousness. It awakens consciousness and provokes what follows. What follows is the gradual return into the chain or it is the definitive awakening. At the end of the awakening comes, in time, the consequence: suicide or recovery. In itself weariness has something sickening about it. Here, I must conclude that it is good. For everything begins with consciousness and nothing is worth anything except through it.

At the heart of all beauty lies something inhuman, and these hills, the softness of the sky, the outline of these trees at this very minute lose the illusory meaning with which we had clothed them, henceforth more remote than a lost paradise. The primitive hostility of the world rises up to face us across millennia. For a second we cease to understand it because for centuries we have understood it in solely the images and designs that we had attributed to it beforehand, because henceforth we lack the power to make use of that artifice. The world evades us because it becomes itself again. That stage scenery masked by habit becomes again what it is. It withdraws at a distance from us. Just as there are days when under the familiar face of a woman, we see as a stranger her we had loved months or years ago, perhaps we shall come even to desire what suddenly leaves us so alone. But the time has not yet come. Just one thing: that denseness and that strangeness of the world is the absurd.

Men, too, secrete the inhuman. At certain moments of lucidity, the mechanical aspect of their gestures, their meaningless pantomine makes silly everything that surrounds them. A man is talking on the telephone behind a glass partition; you cannot hear him, but you see his incomprehensible dumb show: you wonder why he is alive. This discomfort in the face of man's own inhumanity, this incalculable tumble before the image of what we are, this "nausea," as a writer of today calls it, is also the absurd. Likewise, the stranger who at certain seconds comes to meet us in a mirror, the familiar and yet alarming brother we encounter in our own photographs is also the absurd. . . .

I come at last to death and to the attitude we have toward it. On this point everything has been said and it is only proper to avoid pathos. Yet one will never be sufficiently surprised that everyone lives as if no one "knew." This is because in reality there is no experience of death. Properly speaking, nothing has been experienced but what has been lived and made conscious. Here, it is barely possible to speak of the experience of others' deaths. It is a substitute, an illusion, and it never quite convinces us. That melancholy convention cannot be persuasive. The horror comes in reality from the mathematical aspect of the event. If time frightens us, this is because it works out the problem and the solution comes afterward. All the pretty speeches about the soul will have their contrary convincingly proved, at least for a time. From this inert body on which a slap makes no mark the soul has disappeared. This elementary and definitive aspect of the adventure constitutes the absurd feeling. Under the fatal lighting of that destiny, its uselessness becomes evident. No code of ethics and no effort are justifiable *a priori* in the face of the cruel mathematics that command our condition. . . .

Understanding the world for a man is reducing it to the human, stamping it with his seal. The cat's universe is not the universe of the anthill. The truism "All thought is anthropomorphic" has no other meaning. Likewise, the mind that aims to understand reality can consider itself satisfied only by reducing it to terms of thought. If man realized that the universe like him can love and suffer, he would be reconciled. If thought discovered in the shimmering mirrors of phenomena eternal relations capable of summing them up and summing themselves up in a single principle, then would be seen an intellectual joy of which the myth of the blessed would be but a ridiculous imitation. That nostalgia for unity, that appetite for the absolute illustrates the essential impulse of the human drama. But the fact of that nostalgia's existence does not imply that it is to be immediately satisfied. . . .

With the exception of professional rationalists, today people despair of true knowledge. If the only significant history of human thought were to be written, it would have to be the history of its successive regrets and its impotences.

Of whom and of what indeed can I say: "I know that!" This heart within me I can feel, and I judge that it exists. This world I can touch, and I likewise judge that it exists. There ends all my knowledge, and the rest is construction. For if I try to seize this self of which I feel sure, if I try to define and to summarize it, it is nothing but water slipping through my fingers. I can sketch one by one all the aspects it is able to assume, all those likewise that have been attributed to it, this upbringing, this origin, this ardor of these silences, this nobility or this vileness. But aspects cannot be added up. This very heart which is mine will forever remain indefinable to me. Between the certainty I have of my existence and the content I try to give to that assurance, the gap will never be filled. Forever I shall be a stranger to myself. . . .

Hence the intelligence, too, tells me in its way that this world is absurd. . . . In this unintelligible and limited universe, man's fate henceforth assumes its meaning. A horde of irrationals has sprung up and surrounds him until his ultimate end. In his recovered and now studied lucidity, the feeling of the absurd becomes clear and definite. I said that the world is absurd, but I was too hasty. This world in itself is not reasonable, that is all that can be said. But what is absurd is the confrontation of this irrational and the wild longing for clarity whose call echoes in the human heart. The absurd depends as much on man as on the world. . . .

I don't know whether this world has a meaning that transcends it. But I know that I do not know that meaning and that it is impossible for me just now to know it. What can a meaning outside my condition mean to me? I can understand only in human terms. What I touch, what resists me—that is what I understand. And these two certainties—my appetite for the absolute and for unity and the impossibility of reducing this world to a rational and reasonable principle—I also know that I cannot reconcile them. What other truth can I admit without lying, without bringing in a hope I lack and which means nothing within the limits of my condition?

If I were a tree among trees, a cat among animals, this like would have a meaning, or rather this problem would not rise, for I should belong to this world. I should *be* this world to which I am now opposed by my whole consciousness and my whole insistence upon familiarity. This ridiculous reason is what sets me in opposition to all creation. I cannot cross it out with a stroke of the pen. What I believe to be true I must therefore preserve. What seems to me so obvious, even against me, I must support. And what constitutes the basis of that conflict, of that break between the world and my mind, but the awareness of it? If therefore I want to preserve it, I can through a constant awareness, ever revived, ever alert. This is what, for the moment, I must remember. . . .

Let us insist again on the method: it is a matter of persisting. At a certain point on his path the absurd man is tempted. History is not lacking in either religions or prophets, even without gods. He is asked to leap. All he can reply is that he doesn't fully understand, that it is not obvious. Indeed, he does not want to do anything but what he fully understands. He is assured that this is the sin of pride, but he does not understand the notion of sin; that perhaps hell is in store, but he has not enough imagination to visualize that strange future; that he is losing immortal life, but that seems to him an idle consideration. An attempt is made to get him to admit his guilt. He feels innocent. To tell the truth, that is all he feels—his irreparable innocence. This is what allows him everything. Hence, what he demands of himself is to live *solely* with what he knows, to accommodate himself to what is, and to bring in nothing that is not certain. He is told that nothing is. But this at least is a certainty. And it is with this that he is concerned: he wants to find out if it is possible to live *without appeal*. . . .

Before encountering the absurd, the everyday man lives with aims, a concern for the future or for justification (with regard to whom or what is not the question). He weighs his chances, he counts on "someday," his retirement or the labor of his sons. He still thinks that something in his life can be directed. In truth, he acts as if he were free, even if all the facts make a point of contradicting that liberty. But after the absurd, everything is upset. That idea that "I am," my way of acting as if everything has a meaning (even if, on occasion, I said that nothing has)—all that is given the lie in vertiginous fashion by the absurdity of a possible death. Thinking of the future, establishing aims for oneself, having preferences—all this presupposes a belief in freedom, even if one occasionally ascertains that one doesn't feel it. But at that moment I am well aware that that higher liberty, that freedom *to be,* which alone can serve as basis for a truth, does not exist. Death is there as the only reality. . . .

But at the same time the absurd man realizes that hitherto he was bound to that postulate of freedom on the illusion of which he was living. In a certain sense, that hampered him. To the extent to which he imagined a purpose to his life, he adapted himself to the demands of a purpose to be achieved and became the slave of his liberty. Thus I could not act otherwise than as the father (or the engineer or the leader of a nation, or the post-office subclerk) that I am preparing to be. . . .

The absurd enlightens me on this point: there is no future. Henceforth, this is the reason for my inner freedom. . . .

But what does life mean in such a universe? Nothing else for the moment but indifference to the future and a desire to use up everything that is given. Belief in the meaning of life always implies a scale of values, a choice, our preferences. Belief in the absurd, according to our definitions, teaches the contrary. But this is worth examining.

Knowing whether or not one can live *without appeal* is all that interests me. I do not want to get out of my depth. This aspect of life being given me, can I adapt myself to it? Now, faced with this particular concern, belief in the absurd is tantamount to substituting the quantity of experiences for the quality. If I convince myself that this life has no other aspect than that of the absurd, if I feel that its whole equilibrium depends on that perpetual opposition between my conscious revolt and the darkness in which it struggles, if I admit that my freedom has no meaning except in relation to its limited fate, then I must say that what counts is not the best of living but the most living. . . .

On the one hand the absurd teaches that all experiences are unimportant, and on the other it urges toward the greatest quantity of experiences. How, then, can one fail to do as so many of those men I was speaking of earlier—choose the form of life that brings us the most possible of that human matter, thereby introducing a scale of values that on the other hand one claims to reject?

But again it is the absurd and its contradictory life that teaches us. For the mistake is thinking that that quantity of experiences depends on the circumstances of our life when it depends solely on us. Here we have to be over-simple. To two men living the same number of years, the world always provides the same sum of experiences. It is up to us to be conscious of them. Being aware of one's life, one's revolt, one's freedom, and to the maximum, is living, and to the maximum. Where lucidity dominates, the scale of values becomes useless.

. . .

The gods had condemned Sisyphus to ceaselessly rolling a rock to the top of a mountain, whence the stone would fall back of its own weight. They had thought with some reason that there is no more dreadful punishment than futile and hopeless labor.

If one believes Homer, Sisyphus was the wisest and most prudent of mortals. According to another tradition, however, he was disposed to practice the profession of highwayman. I see no contradiction in this. Opinions differ as to the reasons why he became the futile laborer of the underworld. To begin with, he is accused of a certain levity in regard to the gods. He stole their secrets. Ægina, the daughter of Æsopus, was carried off by Jupiter. The father was shocked by that disappearance and complained to Sisyphus. He, who knew of the abduction, offered to tell about it on condition that Æsopus would give water to the citadel of Corinth. To the celestial thunderbolts he preferred the benediction of water. He was punished for this in the underworld. Homer tells us also that Sisyphus had put Death in chains. Pluto could not endure the sight of his deserted, silent empire. He dispatched the god of war, who liberated Death from the hands of her conqueror.

It is said also that Sisyphus, being near to death, rashly wanted to test his wife's love. He ordered her to cast his unburied body into the middle of the public square. Sisyphus woke up in the underworld. And there, annoyed by an obedience so contrary to human love, he obtained from Pluto permission to return to earth in order to chastise his wife. But when he had seen again the face of this world, enjoyed water and sun, warm stones and the sea, he no longer wanted to go back to the infernal darkness. Recalls, signs of anger, warnings were of no avail. Many years more he lived facing the curve of the gulf, the sparkling sea, and the smiles of earth. A decree of the gods was necessary. Mercury came and seized the impudent man by the collar and, snatching him from his joys, led him forcibly back to the underworld, where his rock was ready for him.

You have already grasped that Sisyphus is the absurd hero. He *is,* as much through his passions as through his torture. His score of the gods, his hatred of death, and his passion for life won him that unspeakable penalty in which the whole being is exerted toward accomplishing nothing. This is the price that must be paid for the passions of this earth. Nothing is told us about Sisyphus in the underworld. Myths are made for the imagination to breathe life into them. As for this myth, one sees merely the whole effort of a body straining to raise the huge stone, to roll it and push it up a slope a hundred times over; one sees the face screwed up, the cheek tight against the stone, the shoulder bracing the clay-covered mass, the foot wedging it, the fresh start with arms outstretched, the wholly human security of two earth-clotted hands. At the very end of his long effort measured by skyless space and time without depth, the purpose is achieved. Then Sisyphus watches the stone rush down in a few moments toward that lower world whence he will have to push it up again toward the summit. He goes back down to the plain.

It is during that return, that pause, that Sisyphus interests me. A face that toils so close to stones is already stone itself! I see that man going back down with a heavy yet measured step toward the torment of which he will never know the end. That hour like a breathing-space which returns as surely as his suffering, that is the hour of consciousness. At each of those moments when he leaves the heights and gradually sinks toward the lairs of the gods, he is superior to his fate. He is stronger than his rock.

If this myth is tragic, that is because its hero is conscious. Where would his torture be, indeed, if at every step the hope of succeeding upheld him? The workman of today works every day in his life at the same tasks, and this fate is no less absurd. But it is tragic only at the rare moments when it becomes conscious. Sisyphus, proletarian of the gods, powerless and rebellious, knows the whole extent of his wretched condition: it is what he thinks of during his descent. The lucidity that was to constitute his torture at the same time crowns his victory. There is no fate that cannot be surmounted by scorn.

If the descent is thus sometimes performed in sorrow, it can also take place in joy. This word is not too much. Again I fancy Sisyphus returning toward his rock, and the sorrow was in the beginning. When the images of earth cling too tightly to memory, when the call of happiness becomes too insistent, it happens that melancholy rises in man's heart: this is the rock's victory, this is the rock itself. The boundless grief is too heavy to bear. These are our nights of

Gethsemane. But crushing truths perish from being acknowledged. Thus, Œdipus at the outset obeys fate without knowing it. But from the moment he knows, his tragedy begins. Yet at the same moment, blind and desperate, he realizes that the only bond linking him to the world is the cool hand of a girl. Then a tremendous remark rings out: "Despite so many ordeals, my advanced age and the nobility of my soul make me conclude that all is well." Sophocles' Œdipus, like Dostoevsky's Kirilov, thus gives the recipe for the absurd victory. Ancient wisdom confirms modern heroism.

One does not discover the absurd without being tempted to write a manual of happiness. "What! by such narrow ways—?" There is but one world, however. Happiness and the absurd are two sons of the same earth. They are inseparable. It would be a mistake to say that happiness necessarily springs from the absurd discovery. It happens as well that the feeling of the absurd springs from happiness. "I conclude that all is well," says Œdipus, and that remark is sacred. It echoes in the wild and limited universe of man. It teaches that all is not, has not been, exhausted. It drives out of this world a god who had come into it with dissatisfaction and a preference for futile sufferings. It makes of fate a human matter, which must be settled among men.

All Sisyphus' silent joy is contained therein. His fate belongs to him. His rock is his thing. Likewise, the absurd man, when he contemplates his torment, silences all the idols. In the universe suddenly restored to its silence, the myriad wondering little voices of the earth rise up. Unconscious, secret calls, invitations from all the faces, they are the necessary reverse and price of victory. There is no sun without shadow, and it is essential to know the night. The absurd man says yes and his effort will henceforth be unceasing. If there is a personal fate, there is no higher destiny, or at least there is but one which he concludes is inevitable and despicable. For the rest, he knows himself to be the master of his days. At that subtle moment when man glances backward over his life, Sisyphus returning toward his rock, in that slight pivoting he contemplates that series of unrelated actions which becomes his fate, created by him, combined under his memory's eye and soon sealed by his death. Thus, convinced of the wholly human origin of all that is human, a blind man eager to see who knows that the night has no end, he is still on the go. The rock is still rolling.

I leave Sisyphus at the foot of the mountain! One always finds one's burden again. But Sisyphus teaches the higher fidelity that negates the gods and raises rocks. He too concludes that all is well. This universe henceforth without a master seems to him neither sterile nor futile. Each atom of that stone, each mineral flake of that night-filled mountain, in itself forms a world. The struggle itself toward the heights is enough to fill a man's heart. One must imagine Sisyphus happy.

The Meaning of Life:
Christianity Versus Science

K. E. M. BAIER

K. E. M. Baier (1917–   ) was president of the Australian Association of Philosophy in 1961. He now teaches philosophy at the University of Pittsburgh. He wrote *Moral Point of View* (1958).

Tolstoy, in his autobiographical work, "A Confession," reports how, when he was fifty and at the height of his literary success, he came to be obsessed by the fear that life was meaningless.

> At first I experienced moments of perplexity and arrests of life, as though I did not know what to do or how to live; and I felt lost and became dejected. But this passed, and I went on living as before. Then these moments of perplexity began to recur oftener and oftener, and always in the same form. They were always expressed by the questions: What is it for? What does it lead to? At first it seemed to me that these were aimless and irrelevant questions. I thought that it was all well known, and that if I should ever wish to deal with the solution it would not cost me much effort; just at present I had no time for it, but when I wanted to, I should be able to find the answer. The questions however began to repeat themselves frequently, and to demand replies more and more insistently; and like drops of ink always falling on one place they ran together into one black blot.[1]

A Christian living in the Middle Ages would not have felt any serious doubts about Tolstoy's questions. To him it would have seemed quite certain that life had a meaning and quite clear what it was. The medieval Christian would picture assigned to man a highly significant, indeed the central part in the grand scheme of things. The universe was made for the express purpose of providing a stage on which to enact a drama starring Man in the title role.

To be exact, the world was created by God in the year 4004 B.C. Man was the last and the crown of this creation, made in the likeness of God, placed in the Garden of Eden on earth, the fixed centre of the universe, round which revolved the nine heavens of the sun, the moon, the planets and the fixed stars, producing as they revolved in their orbits the heavenly harmony of the spheres. And this gigantic universe was created for the enjoyment of man, who was originally put in control of it. Pain and death were unknown in paradise. But this state of bliss was not to last. Adam and Eve ate of the forbidden tree of knowledge, and

---

[1] Count Leo Tolstoy, "A Confession," reprinted in *A Confession, The Gospel in Brief, and What I Believe*, No. 229, The World's Classics (London: Geoffrey Cumberlege, 1940).

Source: K. E. M. Baier, "The Meaning of Life," Inaugural Lecture delivered at the Canberra University College (1957), pp. 3–29. Reprinted by permission of the author.

life on this earth turned into a death-march through a vale of tears. Then, with the birth of Jesus, new hope came into the world. After He had died on the cross, it became at least possible to wash away with the purifying water of baptism some of the effects of Original Sin and to achieve salvation. That is to say, on condition of obedience to the law of God, man could now enter heaven and regain the state of everlasting, deathless bliss, from which he had been excluded because of the sin of Adam and Eve.

To the medieval Christian the meaning of human life was therefore perfectly clear. The stretch on earth is only a short interlude, a temporary incarceration of the soul in the prison of the body, a brief trial and test, fated to end in death, the release from pain and suffering. What really matters, is the life after the death of the body. One's existence acquires meaning not by gaining what this life can offer but by saving one's immortal soul from death and eternal torture, by gaining eternal life and everlasting bliss.

The scientific world picture which has found ever more general acceptance from the beginning of the modern era onwards is in profound conflict with all this. At first, the Christian conception of the world was discovered to be erroneous in various important details. The Copernican theory showed up the earth as merely one of several planets revolving around the sun, and the sun itself was later seen to be merely one of many fixed stars each of which is itself the nucleus of a solar system similar to our own. Man, instead of occupying the centre of creation, proved to be merely the inhabitant of a celestial body no different from millions of others. Furthermore, geological investigations revealed that the universe was not created a few thousand years ago, but was probably millions of years old.

Disagreements over details of the world picture, however, are only superficial aspects of a much deeper conflict. The appropriateness of the whole Christian outlook is at issue. For Christianity, the world must be regarded as the "creation" of a kind of Superman, a person possessing all the human excellences to an infinite degree and none of the human weakness, Who has made man in His image, a feeble mortal, foolish copy of Himself. In creating the universe, God acts as a sort of playwright-cum-legislator-cum-judge-cum-executioner. In the capacity of playwright, He creates the historical world process, including man. He erects the stage and writes, in outline, the plot. He creates the *dramatis personae* and watches over them with the eye partly of a father, partly of the law. While on stage, the actors are free to extemporise, but if they infringe the divine commandments, they are later dealt with by their creator in His capacity of judge and executioner.

Within such a framework, the Christian attitudes towards the world are natural and sound: it is natural and sound to think that all is arranged for the best even if appearances belie it; to resign oneself cheerfully to one's lot; to be filled with awe and veneration in regard to anything and everything that happens; to want to fall on one's knees and worship and praise the Lord. These are wholly fitting attitudes within the framework of the world view just outlined. And this world view must have seemed wholly sound and acceptable because it offered the best explanation which was then available of all the observed phenomena of nature.

As the natural sciences developed, however, more and more things in the universe came to be explained without the assumption of a supernatural creator. Science, moreover, could explain them better, that is, more accurately and more reliably. The Christian hypothesis of a supernatural maker, whatever other needs it was capable of satisfying, was at any rate no longer indispensable for the purpose of explaining the existence or occurrence of anything. In fact, scientific explanations do not seem to leave any room for this hypothesis. The scientific approach demands that we look for a natural explanation of anything and everything. The scientific way of looking at and explaining things has yielded an immensely greater measure of understanding of, and control over, the universe than any other way. And when one looks at the world in this scientific way, there seems to be no room for a personal relationship between human beings and a supernatural perfect being ruling and guiding men. Hence many scientists and educated men have come to feel that the Christian attitudes towards the world and human existence are inappropriate. They have become convinced that the universe and human existence in it are without a purpose and therefore devoid of meaning.[2]

1. The Explanation of the Universe

Such beliefs are disheartening and unplausible. It is natural to keep looking for the error that must have crept into our arguments. And if an error has crept in, then it is most likely to have crept in with science. For before the rise of science, people did not entertain such melancholy beliefs, while the scientific world picture seems literally to force them on us.

There is one argument which seems to offer the desired way out. It runs somewhat as follows. Science and religion are not really in conflict. They are, on the contrary, mutually complementary, each doing an entirely different job. Science gives provisional, if precise, explanations of small parts of the universe, religion gives final and over-all, if comparatively vague, explanations of the universe as a whole. The objectionable conclusions, that human existence is devoid of meaning, follows only if we use scientific explanations where they do not apply, namely, where total explanations of the whole universe are concerned.[3]

After all, the argument continues, the scientific world picture is the inevitable outcome of rigid adherence to scientific method and explanation, but scientific, that is, causal explanations from their very nature are incapable of producing real illumination. They can at best tell us *how* things are or have come about, but never *why*. They are incapable of making the universe intelligible, comprehensible, meaningful to us. They represent the universe as meaningless, not because it *is* meaningless, but because scientific explanations are not designed to yield answers to investigations into the why and wherefore, into the meaning, purpose, or point of things. Scientific explanations (this argument continues)

---

[2] See e.g. Edwyn Bevan, *Christianity*, pp. 211–227. See also H. J. Paton, *The Modern Predicament* (London: George Allen and Unwin Ltd., 1955), pp. 103–116, 374.

[3] See for instance, L. E. Elliott-Binns, *The Development of English Theology in the Later Nineteenth Century* (London: Longmans, Green & Co., 1952), pp. 30–33.

began, harmlessly enough, as partial and provisional explanations of the movement of material bodies, in particular the planets, within the general framework of the medieval world picture. Newton thought of the universe as a clock made, originally wound up, and occasionally set right by God. His laws of motion only revealed the ways in which the heavenly machinery worked. Explaining the movement of the planets by these laws was analogous to explaining the machinery of a watch. Such explanations showed *how* the thing worked, but not *what it was for* or *why* it existed. Just as the explanation of how a watch works can help our understanding of the watch only if, in addition, we assume that there is a watchmaker who has designed it for a purpose, made it, and wound it up, so the Newtonian explanation of the solar system helps our understanding of it only on the similar assumption that there is some divine artificer who has designed and made this heavenly clockwork for some purpose, has wound it up, and perhaps even occasionally sets it right, when it is out of order.

Socrates, in the Phaedo, complained that only explanations of a thing showing the good or purpose for which it existed could offer a *real* explanation of it. He rejected the kind of explanation we now call "causal" as no more than mentioning "that without which a cause could not be a cause," that is, as merely a necessary condition, but not the *real* cause, the real explanation.[4] In other words, Socrates held that *all* things can be explained in two different ways: either by mentioning merely a necessary condition, or by giving the *real* cause. The former is not an elucidation of the explicandum, not really a help in understanding it, in grasping its "why" and "wherefore."

This Socratic view, however, is wrong. It is not the case that there are two kinds of explanation for everything, one partial, preliminary, and not really clarifying, the other full, final, and illuminating. The truth is that these two kinds of explanation are equally explanatory, equally illuminating, and equally full and final, but that they are appropriate for different kinds of explicanda.

When in an uninhabited forest we find what looks like houses, paved streets, temples, cooking utensils, and the like, it is no great risk to say that these things are the ruins of a deserted city, that is to say, of something man-made. In such a case, the appropriate explanation is teleological, that is, in terms of the purposes of the builders of that city. On the other hand, when a comet approaches the earth, it is similarly a safe bet that, unlike the city in the forest, it was not manufactured by intelligent creatures and that, therefore, a teleological explanation would be out of place, whereas a causal one is suitable.

It is easy to see that in some cases causal, and in others teleological, explanations are appropriate. A small satellite circling the earth may or may not have been made by man. We may never know which is the true explanation, but either hypothesis is equally explanatory. It would be wrong to say that only a teleological explanation can *really* explain it. Either explanation would yield complete clarity although, of course, only one can be true. Teleological explanation is only one of several that are possible.

It may indeed be strictly correct to say that the question *"Why* is there a satellite circling the earth?" can only be answered by a teleological explanation.

[4] See "Phaedo" (*Five Dialogues* by Plato, Everyman's Library No. 456), para. 99, p. 189.

It may be true that "Why?"-questions can really be used properly only in order to elicit *someone's reasons for* doing something. If this is so, it would explain our dissatisfaction with causal answers to "Why?"-questions. But even if it is so, it does not show that "Why is the satellite there?" *must be answered by a teleological explanation.* It shows only that either it must be so answered or it must not be asked. The question "Why have you stopped beating your wife?" can be answered only by a teleological explanation, but if you have never beaten her, it is an improper question. Similarly, if the satellite is not man-made, "Why is there a satellite?" is improper since it implies an origin it did not have. Natural science can indeed only tell us *how* things in nature have come about and not *why*, but this is so not because something else can tell us the *why* and *wherefore*, but because there is none.

What, then, does all this amount to? Merely to the claim that scientific explanations are no worse than any other. All that has been shown is that all explanations suffer from the same defect: all involve a vicious infinite regress. In other words, no type of human explanation can help us to unravel the ultimate, unanswerable mystery. Christian ways of looking at things may not be able to render the world any more lucid than science can, but at least they do not pretend that there are no impenetrable mysteries. On the contrary, they point out untiringly that the claims of science to be able to elucidate everything are hollow. They remind us that science is not merely limited to the exploration of a tiny corner of the universe but that, however far our probing instruments may eventually reach, we can never even approach the answers to the last questions: "Why is there a world at all rather than nothing?" and "Why is the world such as it is and not different?" Here our finite human intellect bumps against its own boundary walls.

Is it true that scientific explanations involve an infinite vicious regress? Are scientific explanations really only provisional and incomplete? The crucial point will be this. Do *all* contingent truths call for explanation? Is the principle of sufficient reason sound? Can scientific explanations never come to a definite end? It will be seen that with a clear grasp of the nature and purpose of explanation we can answer these questions.[5]

Explaining something to someone is making him understand it. This involves bringing together in his mind two things, a model which is accepted as already simple and clear, and that which is to be explained, the explicandum, which is not so. Understanding the explicandum is seeing that it belongs to a range of things which could legitimately have been expected by anyone familiar with the model and with certain facts.

There are, however, two fundamentally different positions which a person may occupy relative to some explicandum. He may not be familiar with any model capable of leading him to expect the phenomenon to be explained. Most

---

[5] In what follows I have drawn heavily on the work of Ryle and Toulmin. See for instance G. Ryle, *The Concept of Mind* (London: Hutchinson's University Library, 1949), pp. 56–60 &c. and his article, "If, So, and Because," in *Philosophical Analysis* by Max Black, and S. E. Toulmin, *Introduction to the Philosophy of Science* (London: Hutchinson's University Library, 1953).

of us, for instance, are in that position in relation to the phenomena occurring in a good seance. With regard to other things people will differ. Someone who can play chess, already understands chess, already has such a model. Someone who has never seen a game of chess has not. He sees the moves on the board but he cannot understand, cannot follow, cannot make sense of what is happening. Explaining the game to him is giving him an explanation, is making him understand. He can understand or follow chess moves only if he can see them as conforming to a model of a chess game. In order to acquire such a model, he will, of course, need to know the constitutive rules of chess, that is, the permissible moves. But that is not all. He must know that a normal game of chess is a competition (not all games are) between two people, each trying to win, and he must know what it is to win at chess: to manoeuvre the opponent's king into a position of check-mate. Finally, he must acquire some knowledge of what is and what is not conducive to winning: the tactical rules or canons of the game.

A person who has been given such an explanation and who has mastered it—which may take quite a long time—has now reached understanding, in the sense of the ability to follow each move. A person cannot in that sense understand merely one single move of chess and no other. If he does not understand any other moves, we must say that he has not yet mastered the explanation, that he does not really understand the single move either. If he has mastered the explanation, then he understands all those moves which he can see as being in accordance with the model of the game inculcated in him during the explanation.

However, even though a person who has mastered such an explanation will understand many, perhaps most, moves of any game of chess he cares to watch, he will not necessarily understand them all, as some moves of a player may not be in accordance with his model of the game. White, let us say, at his fifteenth move, exposes his queen to capture by Black's knight. Though in accordance with the constitutive rules of the game, this move is nevertheless perplexing and calls for explanation, because it is not conducive to the achievement by White of what must be assumed to be his aim: to win the game. The queen is a much more valuable piece than the knight against which he is offering to exchange.

An onlooker who has mastered chess may fail to understand this move, be perplexed by it, and wish for an explanation. Of course he may fail to be perplexed, for if he is a very inexperienced player he may not *see* the disadvantageousness of the move. But there is such a need whether anyone sees it or not. The move *calls for* explanation because to anyone who knows the game it must appear to be incompatible with the model which we have learnt during the explanation of the game, and by reference to which we all explain and understand normal games.

However, the required explanation of White's 15th move is of a very different kind. What is needed now is not the acquisition of an explanatory model, but the removal of the real or apparent incompatibility between the player's move and the model of explanation he has already acquired. In such a case the perplexity can be removed only on the assumption that the incompatibility between the model and the game is merely apparent. As our model includes a presumed aim of both players, there are the following three possibilities: (a) White has made a mistake: he has overlooked the threat to his queen. In that case, the explanation is that White thought his move conducive to his end, but it was not. (b) Black has made a mistake: White set a trap for him. In that case, the explanation is that Black thought White's move was not conducive to White's end, but it was. (c) White is not pursuing the end which any chess player may be presumed to pursue: he is not trying to win his game. In that case, the explanation is that White has made a move which he knows is not conducive to the end of winning his game because, let us say, he wishes to please Black who is his boss.

Let us now set out the differences and similarities between the two types of understanding involved in these two kinds of explanation. I shall call the first kind "model" understanding and explaining, respectively, because both involve the use of a model by reference to which understanding and explaining is effected. The second kind I shall call "unvexing," because the need for this type of explanation and understanding arises only when there is a perplexity arising out of the incompatibility of the model and the facts to be explained.

To sum up. The question, "Why is there anything at all?" looks like a perfectly sensible question modelled on "Why does *this* exist?" or "How has *this* originated?" It looks like a question about the origin of a thing. However, it is not such a question, for the universe is not a thing, but the totality of things. There is therefore no reason to assume that the universe has an origin. The very assumption that it has is fraught with contradictions and absurdities. If, nevertheless, it were true that the universe has originated out of nothing, then this would not call either for an unvexing or a model explanation. It would not call for the latter, because there could be no model of it taken from another part of our experience, since there is nothing analogous in our experience to origination out of nothing. It would not call for the former, because there can be no perplexity due to the incompatibility of a well-established model. If, on the other hand, as is more probable, the universe has not originated at all, but is eternal, then the question why or how it has originated simply does not arise. There can then be no question about why anything at all exists, for it could not mean how or why the universe had originated, since ex hypothesi it has no origin. And what else could it mean?

Lastly, we must bear in mind that the hypothesis that the universe was made by God out of nothing only brings us back to the question who made God or how God originated. And if we do not find it repugnant to say that God is eternal, we cannot find it repugnant to say that the universe is eternal. The only difference is that we know for certain that the universe exists, while we have the greater difficulty in even making sense of the claim that God exists.

2. The Purpose of Man's Existence

Our conclusion in the previous section has been that science is in principle able to give complete and real explanations of every occurrence and thing in the universe. This has two important corollaries: (i) Acceptance of the scientific world picture cannot be *one's reason for* the belief that the universe is unintelligible and therefore meaningless, though coming to accept it, after having been taught the Christian world picture, may well have been, in the case of many individuals, *the only or the main cause* of their belief that the universe and human existence are meaningless. (ii) It is not in accordance with reason to reject this pessimistic belief on the grounds that scientific explanations are only provisional and incomplete and must be supplemented by religious ones.

In fact, it might be argued that the more clearly we understand the explanations given by science, the more we are driven to the conclusion that human life has no purpose and therefore no meaning. The science of astronomy teaches us that our earth was not specially created about 6,000 years ago, but evolved out of hot nebulae which previously had whirled aimlessly through space for countless ages. As they cooled, the sun and the planets formed. On one of these planets at a certain time the circumstances were propitious and life developed. But conditions will not remain favourable to life. When our solar system grows old, the sun will cool, our planet will be covered with ice, and all living creatures will eventually perish. Another theory has it that the sun will explode and that the heat generated will be so great that all organic life on earth will be destroyed. That is the comparatively short history and prospect of life on earth. Altogether it amounts to very little when compared with the endless history of the inanimate universe.

Biology teaches us that the species man was not specially created but is merely, in a long chain of evolutionary changes of forms of life, the last link, made in the likeness not of God but of nothing so much as an ape. The rest of the universe, whether animate or inanimate, instead of serving the ends of man, is at best indifferent, at worst savagely hostile. Evolution to whose operation the emergence of man is due is a ceaseless battle among members of different species, one species being gobbled up by another, only the fittest surviving. Far from being the gentlest and most highly moral, man is simply the creature best fitted to survive, the most efficient if not the most rapacious and insatiable killer. And in this unplanned, fortuitous, monstrous, savage world man is madly trying to snatch a few brief moments of joy, in the short intervals during which he is free from pain, sickness, persecution, war or famine until, finally, his life is snuffed out in death. Science has helped us to know and understand this world, but what purpose or meaning can it find in it?

Complaints such as these do not mean quite the same to everybody, but one thing, I think, they mean to most people is that science shows life to be meaningless, because life is without purpose. The medieval world picture provided life with a purpose, hence medieval Christians could believe that life had a meaning. The scientific account of the world takes away life's purpose and with it its meaning.

There are, however, two quite different senses of "purpose." Which one is meant? Has science deprived human life of purpose in both senses? And if not, is it a harmless sense, in which human existence has been robbed of purpose? Could human existence still have meaning if it did not have a purpose in that sense?

What are the two senses? In the first and basic sense, purpose is normally attributed only to persons or their behavior as in "Did you have a purpose in leaving the ignition on?" In the second sense, purpose is normally attributed only to things, as in "What is the purpose of that gadget you installed in the workshop?" The two uses are intimately connected. We cannot attribute a purpose to a thing without implying that someone did something, in the doing of which he had some purpose, namely, to bring about the thing with the purpose. Of course, *his* purpose is not identical with *its* purpose. In hiring labourers and engineers and buying materials and a site for a factory and the like, the entrepreneur's purpose, let us say, is to manufacture cars, but the purpose of cars is to serve as a means of transportation.

There are many things that a man may do, such as buying and selling, hiring labourers, ploughing, felling trees, and the like, which are foolish, pointless, silly, perhaps crazy, to do if one has no purpose in doing them. A man who does these things without a purpose is engaging in inane, futile pursuits. Lives crammed full with such activities devoid of purpose are pointless, futile, worthless. Such lives may indeed be dismissed as meaningless. But it should also be perfectly clear that acceptance of the scientific world picture does not force us to regard our lives as being without a purpose in this sense. Science has not only not robbed us of any purpose which we had before, but it has furnished us with enormously greater power to achieve these purposes. Instead of praying for rain or a good harvest or offspring, we now use ice pellets, artifical manure, or artificial insemination.

By contrast, having or not having a purpose, in the other sense, is value neutral. We do not think more or less highly of a thing for having or not having a purpose. "Having a purpose," in this sense, confers no kudos, "being purposeless" carries no stigma. A row of trees growing near a farm may or may not have a purpose: it may or may not be a windbreak, may or may not have been planted or deliberately left standing there in order to prevent the wind from sweeping across the fields. We do not in any way disparge the trees if we say they have no purpose, but have just grown that way. They are as beautiful, made of as good wood, as valuable, as if they had a purpose. And, of course, they break the wind just as well. The same is true of living creatures. We do not disparage a dog when we say that it has no purpose, is not a sheep dog or a watch dog or a rabbiting dog, but just a dog that hangs around the house and is fed by us.

Man is in a different category, however. To attribute to a human being a purpose in that sense is not neutral, let alone complimentary: it is offensive. It is degrading for a man to be regarded as merely serving a purpose. If, at a garden party, I ask a man in livery, "What is your purpose?" I am insulting him. I might as well have asked, "What are you *for*?" Such questions reduce him to the level of a gadget, a domestic animal, or perhaps a slave. I imply that *we* allot to *him* the tasks, the goals, the aims which he is to pursue; that *his* wishes and desires and aspirations and purposes are to count for little or nothing. We are treating him, in Kant's phrase, merely as a means to our ends, not as an end in himself.

The Christian and the scientific world pictures do indeed differ fundamentally on this point. The latter robs man of a purpose in this sense. It sees him as a being with no purpose allotted to him by anyone but himself. It robs him of any goal, purpose, or destiny appointed for him by any outside agency. The Christian world picture, on the other hand, sees man as a creature, a divine artifact, something halfway between a robot (manufactured) and an animal (alive), a homunculus, or perhaps Frankenstein, made in God's laboratory, with a purpose or task assigned him by his Maker.

However, lack of purpose in this sense does not in any way detract from the meaningfulness of life. I suspect that many who reject the scientific outlook because it involves the loss of purpose of life, and therefore meaning, are guilty of a confusion between the two senses of "purpose" just distinguished. They confusedly think that if the scientific world picture is true, then their lives must be futile because that picture implies that man has no purpose given him from without. But this is muddled thinking, for, as has already been shown, pointlessness is implied only by purposelessness in the other sense, which is not at all implied by the scientific picture of the world. These people mistakenly conclude that there can be no purpose *in* life because there is no purpose *of* life; that *men* cannot themselves adopt and achieve purposes because *man*, unlike a robot or a watchdog, is not a creature with a purpose.[6]

However, not all people taking this view are guilty of the above confusion. Some really hanker after a purpose of life in this sense. To some people the greatest attraction of the medieval world picture is the belief in an omnipotent, ominscient, and all-good Father, the view of themselves as His children who worship Him, of their proper attitude to what befalls them as submission, humility, resignation in His will, and what is often described as the "creaturely feeling."[7] All these are attitudes and feelings appropriate to a being that stands to another in the same sort of relation, though of course on a higher plane, in which a helpless child stands to his progenitor. Many regard the scientific picture of the world as cold, unsympathetic, unhomely, frightening, because it does not provide for any appropriate object of this creaturely attitude. There is nothing and no one in the world, as science depicts it, in which we can have faith or trust, on whose guidance we can rely, to whom we can turn for consolation, whom we can worship or submit to—except other human beings. This may be felt as a keen disappointment, because it shows that the meaning of life cannot lie in submission to His will, in acceptance of whatever may come, and in worship. But it does not imply that life can have *no* meaning. It merely implies that it must have a different meaning from that which it was thought to have. Just as it is a great shock for a child to find that he must stand on his own feet, that his father and mother no longer provide for him, so a person who has lost his faith in God must reconcile himself to the idea that he has to stand on his own feet, alone in the world except for whatever friends he may succeed in making.

Let us, however, for argument's sake, waive all these objections. There re-

[6] See e.g. "Is Life Worth Living?" B.B.C. Talk by the Rev. John Sutherland Bonnell in *Asking Them Questions,* Third Series, ed. by R. S. Wright (London: Geoffrey Cumberlege, 1950).

[7] See e.g. Rudolf Otto, *The Idea of the Holy,* pp. 9–11. See also C. A. Campbell, *On Selfhood and Godhood* (London: George Allen & Unwin Ltd., 1957), p. 246, and H. J. Paton, *The Modern Predicament,* pp. 69–71.

mains one fundamental hurdle which no form of Christianity can overcome: the fact that it demands of man a morally repugnant attitude towards the universe. It is now very widely held[8] that the basic element of the Christian religion is an attitude of worship towards a being supremely worthy of being worshipped and that it is religious feelings and experiences which apprise their owner of such a being and which inspire in him the knowledge or the feeling of complete dependence, awe, worship, mystery, and self-abasement. There is, in other words, a bi-polarity (the famous "I-Thou relationship") in which the object, "the wholly-other," is exalted whereas the subject is abased to the limit. Rudolf Otto has called this the "creature-feeling"[9] and he quotes as an expression of it, Abraham's words when venturing to plead for the men of Sodom: "Behold now, I have taken upon me to speak unto the Lord, which am but dust and ashes" (Gen. XVIII. 27). Christianity thus demands of men an attitude inconsistent with one of the presuppositions of morality: that man is not wholly dependent on something else, that man has free will, that man is in principle capable of responsibility. We have seen that the concept of grace is the Christian attempt to reconcile the claim of total dependence and the claim of individual responsibility (partial independence), and it is obvious that such attempts must fail. We may dismiss certain doctrines, such as the doctrine of original sin or the doctrine of eternal hellfire or the doctrine that there can be no salvation outside the Church as extravagant and peripheral, but we cannot reject the doctrine of total dependence without rejecting the characteristically Christian attitude as such.

3. The Meaning of Life

Perhaps some of you will have felt that I have been shirking the real problem. To many people the crux of the matter seems as follows. How can there be any meaning in our life if it ends in death? What meaning can there be in it that our inevitable death does not destroy? How can our existence be meaningful if there is no after-life in which perfect justice is meted out? How can life have any meaning if all it holds out to us are a few miserable earthly pleasures and even these to be enjoyed only rarely and for such a piteously short time?

I believe this is the point which exercises most people most deeply. Kirilov, in Dostoevsky's novel, *The Possessed*, claims, just before committing suicide, that as soon as we realize that there is no God, we cannot live any longer, we must put an end to our lives. One of the reasons which he gives is that when we discover that there is no paradise, we have nothing to live for.

". . . there was a day on earth, and in the middle of the earth were three crosses. One on the cross had such faith that He said to another, 'To-day thou shalt be with me in paradise.' The day came to an end, both died, and they went, but they found neither paradise nor resurrection. The saying did not come true.

---

[8] See e.g. the two series of Gifford Lectures most recently published: *The Modern Predicament* by H. J. Paton (London: George Allen & Unwin Ltd., 1955), pp. 69ff., and *On Selfhood and Godhood* by C. A. Campbell (London: George Allen & Unwin Ltd., 1957), pp. 231–250.

[9] Rudolf Otto, *The Idea of the Holy*, p. 9.

Listen: that man was the highest of all on earth. . . . There has never been any one like Him before or since, and never will be. . . . And if that is so, if the laws of Nature did not spare even *Him*, and made even Him live in the midst of lies and die for a lie, then the whole planet is a lie and is based on a lie and a stupid mockery. So the very laws of the planet are a lie and a farce of the devil. What, then, is there to live for?"[10] And Tolstoy, too, was nearly driven to suicide when he came to doubt the existence of God and an after-life.[11] And this is true of many.

What, then, is it that inclines us to think that life is to have a meaning, there would be an after-life? It is this. The Christian world view contains the following three propositions. The first is that since the Fall, God's curse of Adam and Eve, and the expulsion from Paradise, life on earth for mankind has not been worth while, but a vale of tears, one long chain of misery, suffering, unhappiness, and injustice. The second is that a perfect after-life is awaiting us after the death of the body. The third is that we can enter this perfect life only on certain conditions, among which is also the condition of enduring our earthly existence to its bitter end. In this way, our earthly existence which, in itself, would not (at least for many people if not all) be worth living, acquires meaning and significance: only if we endure it, can we gain admission to the realm of the blessed.

Our disappointment therefore arises out of these two propositions, that the earthly life is not worth living, and that there is another perfect life of eternal happiness and joy which we may enter upon if we satisfy certain conditions. We can regard our lives as meaningful, if we believe both. We cannot regard them as meaningful if we believe merely the first and not the second. It seems to me inevitable that people who are taught something of the history of science, will have serious doubts about the second. If they cannot overcome these, as many will be unable to do, then they must either accept the sad view that their life is meaningless or they must abandon the first proposition: that this earthly life is not worth living. They must find the meaning of their life in this earthly existence. But is this possible?

A moment's examination will show us that the Christian evaluation of our earthly life as worthless, which we accept in our moments of pessimism and dissatisfaction, is not one that we normally accept. Consider only the question of murder and suicide. On the Christian view, other things being equal, the most kindly thing to do would be for everyone of us to kill as many of our friends and dear ones as still have the misfortune to be alive, and then to commit suicide without delay, for every moment spent in this life is wasted. On the Christian view, God has not made it that easy for us. He has forbidden us to hasten others or ourselves into the next life. Our bodies are his private property and must be allowed to wear themselves out in the way decided by Him, however painful and horrible that may be. We are, as it were, driving a burning car. There is only one way out, to jump clear and let it hurtle to destruction.

[10] Fyodor Dostoyevsky, *The Devils* (London: The Penguin Classics, 1953), pp. 613–614.
[11] Leo Tolstoy, *A Confession, The Gospel in Brief, and What I Believe,* The World's Classics, p. 24.

But the owner of the car has forbidden it on pain of eternal tortures worse than burning. And so we do better to burn to death inside.

On this view, murder is a less serious wrong than suicide. For murder can always be confessed and repented and therefore forgiven, suicide cannot—unless we allow the ingenious way out chosen by the heroine of Graham Greene's play, *The Living Room*, who swallows a slow but deadly poison and, while awaiting its taking effect, repents having taken it. Murder, on the other hand, is not so serious because, in the first place, it need not rob the victim of anything but the last lap of his march in the vale of tears, and, in the second place, it can always be forgiven. Hamlet, it will be remembered, refrains from killing his uncle during the latter's prayers because, as a true Christian, he believes that killing his uncle at that point, when the latter has purified his soul by repentance, would merely be doing him a good turn, for murder at such a time would simply despatch him to undeserved and everlasting happiness.

These views strike us as odd, to say the least. They are the logical consequence of the official medieval evaluation of this our earthly existence. If this life is not worth living, then taking it is not robbing the person concerned of much. The only thing wrong with it is the damage to God's property, which is the same both in the case of murder and suicide. We do not take this view at all. Our view, on the contrary, is that murder is the most serious wrong because it consists in taking away from some one else against his will his most precious possession, his life. For this reason, when a person suffering from an incurable disease asks to be killed, the mercy killing of such a person is regarded as a much less serious crime than murder because, in such a case, the killer is not robbing the other of a good against his will. Suicide is not regarded as a real crime at all, for we take the view that a person can do with his own possessions what he likes.

However, from the fact that these are our normal opinions, we can infer nothing about their truth. After all, we could easily be mistaken. Whether life is or is not worthwhile, is a value judgment. Perhaps all this is merely a matter of opinion or taste. Perhaps no objective answer can be given. Fortunately, we need not enter deeply into these difficult and controversial questions. It is quite easy to show that the medieval evaluation of earthly life is based on a misguided procedure.

Let us remind ourselves briefly of how we arrive at our value judgments. When we determine the merits of students, meals, tennis players, bulls, or bathing belles, we do so on the basis of some criteria and some standard or norm. Criteria and standards notoriously vary from field to field and even from case to case. But that does not mean that we have *no* idea about what are the appropriate criteria or standards to use. It would not be fitting to apply the criteria for judging bulls to the judgment of students or bathing belles. They score on quite different points. And even where the same criteria are appropriate as in the judgment of students enrolled in different schools and universities, the standards will vary from one institution to another. Pupils who would only just pass in one, would perhaps obtain honours in another. The higher the standard applied, the lower the marks, that is, the merit conceded to the candidate.

The same procedure is applicable also in the evaluation of a life. We examine it on the basis of certain criteria and standards. The medieval Christian view uses the criteria of the ordinary man: a life is judged by what the person concerned can get out of it: the balance of happiness over unhappiness, pleasure over pain, bliss over suffering. Our earthly life is judged not worthwhile because it contains much unhappiness, pain, and suffering, little happiness, pleasure, and bliss. The next life is judged worthwhile because it provides eternal bliss and no suffering.

I have so far only spoken of the worthwhileness, only of what a person can get out of a life. There are other kinds of appraisal. Clearly, we evaluate people's lives not merely from the point of view of what they yield to the persons that lead them, but also from that of other men on whom these lives have impinged. We judge a life more significant if the person has contributed to the happiness of others, whether directly by what he did for others, or by the plans, discoveries, inventions, and work he performed. Many lives that hold little in the way of pleasure or happiness for its owner are highly significant and valuable, deserve admiration and respect on account of the contributions made.

It is now quite clear that death is simply irrelevant. If life can be worthwhile at all, then it can be so even though it be short. And if it is not worthwhile at all, then an eternity of it is simply a nightmare. It may be sad that we have to leave this beautiful world, but it is so only if and because it is beautiful. And it is no less beautiful for coming to an end. I rather suspect that an eternity of it might make us less appreciative, and in the end it would be tedious.

It will perhaps be objected now that I have not really demonstrated that life has a meaning, but merely that it can be worthwhile or have value. It must be admitted that there is a perfectly natural interpretation of the question, "What is the meaning of life?" on which my view actually proves that life has no meaning. I mean the interpretation discussed in section 2 of this lecture, where I attempted to show that, if we accept the explanations of natural science, we cannot believe that living organisms have appeared on earth in accordance with the deliberate plan of some intelligent being. Hence, on this view, life cannot be said to have a purpose, in the sense in which man-made things have a purpose. Hence it cannot be said to have a meaning or significance in that sense.

However, this conclusion is innocuous. People are disconcerted by the thought that *life as such* has no meaning in that sense only because they very naturally think that it entails that no individual life can have meaning either. They naturally assume that *this* life or *that* can have meaning only if *life as such* has meaning. But it should by now be clear that your life and mine may or may not have meaning (in one sense) even if life as such has none (in the other). Of course, it follows from this that your life may have meaning while mine has not. The Christian view guarantees a meaning (in one sense) to every life, the scientific view does not (in any sense). By relating the question of the meaningfulness of life to the particular circumstances of an individual's existence, the scientific view leaves it an open question whether an individual's life has meaning or not. It is, however, clear that the latter is the important sense of "having a meaning." Christians, too, must feel that their life is wasted and meaningless if they have not achieved salvation. To know that even such lost lives have a meaning in another sense is no consolation to them. What matters is not that life should have a guaranteed meaning, whatever happens here or here-after, but that, by luck (Grace) or the right temperament and attitude (Faith) or a judicious life (Works) a person should make the most of his life.

"But here lies the rub," it will be said. "Surely, it makes all the difference whether there is an after-life. This is where morality comes in." It would be a mistake to believe that. Morality is not the meting out of punishment and reward. To be moral is to refrain from doing to others what, if they followed reason, they would not do to themselves, and to do for others what, if they followed reason, they would want to have done. It is, roughly speaking, to recognize that others, too, have a right to a worthwhile life. Being moral does not make one's own life worthwhile, it helps others to make theirs so.

Conclusion

I have tried to establish three points: (i) that scientific explanations render their explicanda as intelligible as pre-scientific explanations; they differ from the latter only in that, having testable implications and being more precisely formulated, their truth or falsity can be determined with a high degree of probability; (ii) that science does not rob human life of purpose, in the only sense that matters, but, on the contrary, renders many more of our purposes capable of realization; (iii) that common sense, the Christian world view, and the scientific approach agree on the criteria but differ on the standard to be employed in the evaluation of human lives; judging human lives by the standards of perfection, as Christians do, is unjustified; if we abandon this excessively high standard and replace it by an everyday one, we have no longer any reason for dismissing earthly existence as not worthwhile.

On the basis of these three points I have attempted to explain why so many people come to the conclusion that human existence is meaningless and to show that this conclusion is false. In my opinion, this pessimism rests on a combination of two beliefs, both partly true and partly false: the belief that the meaningfulness of life depends on the satisfaction of at least three conditions, and the belief that this universe satisfies none of them. The conditions are, first, that the universe is intelligible, second, that life has a purpose, and third, that all men's hopes and desires can ultimately be satisfied. It seemed to medieval Christians and it seems to many Christians to-day that Christianity offers a picture of the world which can meet these conditions. To many Christians and non-Christians alike it seems that the scientific world picture is incompatible with that of Christianity, therefore with the view that these three conditions are met, therefore with the view that life has a meaning. Hence they feel that they are confronted by the dilemma of accepting either a world picture incompatible with the discoveries of science or the view that life is meaningless.

I have attempted to show that the dilemma is unreal because life can be meaningful even if not all of these conditions are met. My main conclusion, therefore, is that acceptance of the scientific world picture provides no reason for saying that life is meaningless, but on the contrary every reason for saying that there are many lives which are meaningful and significant. My subsidiary conclusion is that one of the reasons frequently offered for retaining the Christian world picture, namely, that its acceptance gives us a guarantee of a meaning for human existence, is unsound. We can see that our lives can have a meaning even if we abandon it and adopt the scientific world picture instead. I have, moreover, mentioned several reasons for rejecting the Christian world picture: (i) the biblical explanations of the details of our universe are often simply false; (ii) the so-called explanations of the whole universe are incomprehensible or absurd; (iii) Christianity's low evaluation of earthly ·existence (which is the main cause of the belief in the meaninglessness of life) rests on the use of an unjustifiably high standard of judgment.

SUGGESTED READINGS

1. BRITTON, KARL, *Philosophy and the Meaning of Life* (Cambridge: Cambridge University Press, 1969).
2. HEPBURN, R. W. "Questions About the Meaning of Life," *Journal of Religious Studies*, Vol. 1 (1967), pp. 125–140.
3. DILMAN, IHLAM, "Professor Hepburn on Meaning in Life," *Journal of Religious Studies*, Vol. 3 (1967), pp. 547–554.
4. FLEW, ANTONY, "Tolstoi and the Meaning of Life," *Ethics*, Vol. LXXIII (1963), pp. 110–118.
5. NIELSEN, KAI, "Linguistic Philosophy and the 'Meaning of Life,'" *Cross Currents* (Summer 1964), pp. 313–334.
6. TAYLOR, RICHARD, *Good and Evil* (New York: Macmillan, 1970), Ch. 18.

Philosophy and the Meaning of Life

W. D. JOSKE

W. D. Joske (1928–   ) is professor of philosophy at the University of Tasmania. Among his publications is *Material Objects* (1967).

Most intelligent and educated people take it for granted that philosophers concern themselves with the meaning of life, telling us whether or not life has a meaning, and, if it has, what that meaning is. In this sense questions about the meaning of life are thought to be the direct concern of the philosopher. Philosophy is also believed to concern itself indirectly with the meaning of life, for it is thought that many purely philosophical disputes, about such topics as the existence of God, the truth or falsity of determinism, and the nature of moral

Source: W. D. Joske, "Philosophy and the Meaning of Life," *Australasian Journal of Philosophy,* Vol. 52, No. 2 (August 1974), pp. 93–104. Reprinted by permission of the Journal and the author.

judgments, can render certain attitudes to life more or less appropriate. In particular, many people are afraid of philosophy precisely because they dread being forced to the horrifying conclusion that life is meaningless, so that human activities are ultimately insignificant, absurd and inconsequential.

Although philosophy has had its great pessimists the prevailing mood among linguistic philosophers is one of qualified optimism. The mood is optimistic in so far as it is widely argued that philosophical positions cannot demonstrate the insignificance of life; but it is qualified by a caveat reminding us that if philosophical views cannot justify pessimism, they are equally incapable of providing a secure foundation for optimism. Life, it is claimed, cannot be shown to be either significant or insignificant by philosophy. In this paper I wish to argue that the contemporary attempt to establish the bland neutrality of philosophical views is not successful; philosophy is indeed dangerous stuff, and it is fitting that it should be approached with fear.

Of course the question 'What is the meaning of Life?' is notoriously vague, and its utterance may be little more than an expression of bewilderment and anxiety or a shy request for help and illumination. In addition to being vague it is ambiguous. The questioner may be seeking or doubting the significance of life in general, of human life or of his own particular life. In this paper I will restrict myself to considering the significance of human life, and will not raise the questions concerning the significance of biological life or of individualistic and idiosyncratic life styles.

However, even if we restrict our concern to human life we have not removed all ambiguity. Many philosophers who have written about the meaning of human life have dealt with the significance of the course of history or the totality of human deeds, and sought to discover whether or not there was some goal which unified and made sense of all the individual and social strivings of mankind. They investigated the significance of the existence of *homo sapiens*. Yet others have wanted not the purpose of history, but a justification of the typical features of human existence, of what is fashionably called the human condition. They have asked whether or not the typical human life style can be given significance, and it is this question that I shall be concerned with. This is not to deny that there may well be connections between the two senses of the question 'What is the meaning of human life?', for it may be argued that the human life style derives its significance by enabling the totality of human deeds to bring into being some valuable end. Scholastic philosophers thus see a life lived in accordance with human nature as deriving its meaning from the part which such a life will play in the fulfilment of eternal law.

If the ambiguity of our question stems from different meanings of the word 'life', the vagueness grows out of the obscurity of the word 'meaning'. It is the vagueness of 'meaning' which has enabled contemporary philosophers to dismiss pessimistic fears as unwarranted. Aware of the confusion and uncertainty that surrounds the word, they attempt to give the question 'What is the meaning of life?' respectability by reading 'meaning' in a precise sense borrowed from some context in which it is used with comparatively rigorous propriety. It is then discovered that the question makes no sense when interpreted in this way, so that our worries about life's meaning are shown to be pseudo-worries.

The fact that somebody asks the question shows that he has not thought seriously about the meanings of the words which make it up. Nobody need live in dread of discovering that life is meaningless, just as a prudish person need not fear the vulgarity of a fraction.

The simplest and crudest example of this rejection of the legitimacy of the question is given by those philosophers who insist that only words, sentences or other conventional symbols can have meaning. Life is not a conventional symbol and is therefore neither meaningful or meaningless. Pessimism is inappropriate, and so too is optimism, but we should be cured of the desire for optimism when we realise the conceptual absurdity which it presupposes.

I do not think that any contemporary philosopher would be guilty of such a crude dismissal of the question. Intellectual fashion has changed, and in addition, we are considerably more subtle about our theories of language than we used to be. However, there is a currently popular view which, although more sophisticated and less condescending in its willingness to admit that people who puzzle about the meaning of life may be puzzling about something real, is ultimately as disparaging of the intelligence of the questioner and the seriousness of his problem as the crude argument of the past.

It is nowadays conceded that 'meaning' when it occurs in the phrase 'the meaning of life' is not used in the sense of conventional meaning. Things other than conventional signs may have meaning—things such as activities. A contemporary philosopher is therefore prepared to grant that a questioner may be asking if human life is meaningful in the way in which activities can be meaningful.

What is it that makes activities meaningful? It is argued that a meaningful activity is one which has significance or importance, and that the significance of an activity may either be *intrinsic,* coming from the value of a performance in itself, or *derivative,* stemming from the part which it plays in the achievement of some worthwhile end. Now it does not require much reflection to discover that people who ask about the meaning of life are not simply asking whether the standard pattern of human life is worth following for its own sake, for they are asking a question which relates both to the world and to life. They wish to know whether the world is the sort of place which justifies and gives significance to what might otherwise seem to be the drudgery of a typical human existence. In other words, they are asking whether or not the world confers derivative meaning upon life.

At this point it is easy to argue that an activity can only possess derivative value if it can be seen as bringing nearer some end which is itself worthwhile. If, as Kurt Vonnegut speculates in *The Sirens of Titan,*[1] the ultimate end of human activity is the delivery of a small piece of steel to a wrecked space ship wanting to continue a journey of no importance whatsoever, the end would be too trivial to justify the means. It is therefore appropriate to ask how the end from which life might derive its value gains its own value, and the answer which is commonly given is that even the value of this ultimate end, must, if it is to be effective, be given to it by human agents. Even if there are objective and non-

[1] K. Vonnegut: *The Sirens of Titan* (1962).

natural value facts, the most worthwhile end will not satisfy an agent unless he subscribes to the value of the end, unless he commits himself to it and makes it *his* end. Even the purposes of God are useless until a man makes them his own.

It follows from this that one cannot seek the fundamental justification of human life from the nature of the world. We fail to understand the nature of meaning if we attempt to do so. The world is neutral and cannot give meaning to men. If someone wants life to be meaningful he cannot discover that meaning but must provide it himself. How we go about giving meaning to life seems to depend upon the society we accept as our own; a Frenchman might leap into the dark, an American go to a psycho-analyst, and an Englishman cease asking embarrassing questions.

The seeker after the meaning of life is thus shown to be confused, even if his confusion about the relation between fact and value is excusable. He is not however left without consolation, for if the world cannot produce meaning it cannot produce triviality. In addition, the diagnosis of his confusion directs him to the way out of his bewilderment. He must examine his own life and undertake his own commitments, even if, in order to commit himself, he may have to turn himself into a different kind of person.

An interesting variant of this contemporary optimism is proposed by Kurt Baier in his *The Meaning of Life*.[2] Baier attempts to demonstrate that any attempt to show that life is intrinsically worthless must be false, for it will depend upon criteria that are both unreasonably high and inappropriate to the evaluation of life. He argues that a worthwhile life is simply one that is above the average of the kind in respect to such things as 'the balance of happiness over unhappiness, pleasure over pain, and bliss over suffering.' The mere fact of its being human cannot make a life worthless, for it is necessarily true that we cannot all be below average.

It should be noted that Baier's dissolution of utter pessimism tells against the popular view that life is itself intrinsically valuable, for we cannot all be above average any more than we can all be below it. If we can assume a normal distribution of hedonic values among mankind, Baier's criteria condemn approximately half of us to lives that are not worthwhile. I would not accuse a man of undue concern if he deplored this state of affairs. However, Baier's account of the criteria of evaluation is clearly implausible. We should not describe as intrinsically worthwhile a life in which unhappiness, pain and suffering outweighed happiness, pleasure and bliss if it turned out to be the case that such a life was above the average of our kind. Again, Baier's account of evaluation has the paradoxical consequence that a man can raise himself above the average and so make his life worthwhile, not only by improving himself, but also by increasing the balance of misery in the lives of other people. Clearly, the value of a life cannot be measured simply by comparing it to the average of its kind.

In spite of the plausibility of contemporary optimism I think that most of those people who question the meaning of life would not be happy with the diagnosis they have been offered. They would feel that it belittled their perplexity. All that agonising about a conceptual muddle! Perhaps their dissatisfaction

---

[2] K. Baier: *The Meaning of Life* (1957) esp. pp. 25–27.

is no more than pique. A neurotic who requested psychotherapy and was promptly and successfully treated with pills might well feel chagrin. He wanted to be cured, but he also wanted the adventure and discovery and struggle that are part and parcel of the sort of cure he had anticipated. He would feel less of a human being because he and his troubles were not considered worthy of analysis. Yet I do not think that the questioner's dissatisfaction is so completely unjustified. The diagnosis which he had been offered is too simple, so that the therapy suggested is not suited to the affliction from which he suffers.

I want to argue that life may be meaningless for reasons other than that it does not contribute to a worthwhile goal, so that the failure to find meaning in life can be due to the nature of the world and not simply to failure of adequate commitment by an agent. Discoveries about the world can force us to the conclusion that a committed life spent in pursuing worthwhile ends lacks meaning.

Our contemporary optimists are correct in taking the meaning of life to be analogous to the meaning of an activity, but their account of activities has been too simple. I want to argue that the significance of an activity can be challenged on grounds other than that the activity lacks intrinsic or derivative worth. To be precise, I shall claim that there are at least four elements of the meaningless, which I shall label worthlessness, pointlessness, triviality, and futility. To forestall unnecessary criticism, I must emphasise that I am not attempting to analyse the meanings of these terms as they occur in everyday discourse; I am, rather, stipulating uses of these terms which will I believe help clarify our problem.

I shall call an activity 'worthless' if it lacks intrinsic merit, so that its performance needs justification by reference to some external purpose. An activity which is mere drudgery would thus be a worthless activity. Most of us would find the practice of parsing and analysing sentences worthless, and would need some extra reason for indulging in its exercise. We find ourselves bewildered by the school master in Guthrie Wilson's[3] novel, *The Incorruptibles* who devotes his life to parsing and analysing every sentence of *Paradise Lost*.

An activity can, of course, be meaningful even if worthless provided it is performed for some worthwhile end. An activity which is not directed towards the fulfilment of an end I shall call 'pointless'. A person who hits a ball against a wall without hoping to improve his health or to earn money would thus be indulging in a pointless activity. If the activity is not worthless, there is nothing absurd about it. Indeed, the very pointlessness of an activity can contribute to its pleasure, making it more truly play.

In contrast to worthless and pointless activities, an activity is trivial if, although it has a point, the purpose lacks sufficient worth to justify its performance. These are cases where the end fails to justify the means.

If lack of worth, pointlessness, and triviality were the only shortcomings which could be used to support the claim that a certain activity lacked meaning, we might indeed find it difficult to see how states of affairs outside the values of the agent could make an activity meaningless. The contemporary optimist has, however, neglected the category of the futile. This is surprising in view of

[3] Guthrie Wilson: *The Incorruptibles* (1960).

the fact that so many existentialists have exalted futility into a paradigm of their beloved absurdity.

I shall call an activity 'futile' if, although it has a point or needs a point in order to make it fully meaningful, the world prevents the achievement of the required end. One extreme type of futility would be an attempt to achieve some goal which is necessarily unobtainable. When we try to square the circle or solve Euler's puzzle we are guilty of such extreme futility. At the other extreme, accidental features of the world can happen to produce futility. Normally we can find uses for estimates of future population based upon current statistics and life tables, yet the task could be made futile by the unexpected disaster. In between these two extremes we find cases where the futility is neither necessary nor unpredictable. Thomas Nagel gives us the example of the man who delivers a brilliant and persuasive speech in support of a motion which has already been passed. Another case from Nagel is that of the impassioned declaration of love to a recorded announcement.[4]

The examples given above are all cases in which the world prevents the actor from realising his consciously intended end. In other cases an action may be futile although it has no consciously intended end, provided that it is the sort of activity which normally requires an end if it is to be considered worthwhile. The classical example of this sort of futility is that of Sisyphus—condemned to spend eternity pushing his stone to the top of a hill in order that it might roll down so that it could again be pushed to the top. A parallel case is found in the alleged practice of military prisons. A prisoner is given a small spoon and a large heap of sand. He is instructed to move the heap from one place to another, and when the task is completed to move it back again. In both these cases the punishment is peculiarly degrading because the actor is aware of the futility of the performance, and is compelled to act in accordance with desires which he cannot make his own.

We have then four different elements of the meaningful, four different ways in which we can criticise an activity for lacking in meaning.

I shall say that an activity is *fully meaningful* if it suffers from none of these defects, so that it is valuable in itself, directed towards an end which is not trivial, and is not futile. Many people who seek a short answer to the question 'What is the meaning of life?' are, I suspect, looking for some simple fact or vision which will enable a human being who knows the secret to so organise his life that all of his activities will be fully meaningful. The meaning of life is thought to be the fact which makes such re-direction possible. However, few of us have such high expectations, and we are content to perform tasks that are not fully meaningful. We will endure drudgery if we can accomplish something worthwhile, and we are happy playing pointless games.

At the other extreme, I shall say that an action is *valueless* if it lacks all four elements of the meaningful, so that, from the point of view of the agent, there is no internal reason why it should be undertaken. The performance of a valueless activity is rational only if the agent is compelled to undertake it.

[4] T. Nagel: 'The Absurd,' *Journal of Philosophy* LXVIII No. 20 (Oct. 4 1971), pp. 716–727.

In between the valueless and the fully meaningful, we have those activities which are worth performing even though they fall short of the fully meaningful, such activities I shall call *valuable*.

How do our four elements of the meaningful determine the value of an action? I do not wish to explore this problem fully, but merely to make a few points. In the first place, it is clearly a tautology that if an action has worth then it is valuable. Even the performance of a futile task is justified if it is fun, and Sisyphus would have defeated the intentions of the Gods if he had happened to like rolling rocks up hills. However, it is not unnatural to hold that worth alone does not make an action completely satisfying. Many people have an incurable desire to cast a shadow across the future and affect the world so that it is for-ever modified by their intentions. They would find an activity which possessed only worth not nearly as rewarding as one which possessed some additional value. Those who protest concerning the irrationality of such desires should re-member how we expect the activities of parents, politicians and public servants to be, in part at least, directed towards the production of benefits which will be enjoyed only by people yet unborn.

In the second place, while it is clear that triviality prevents an activity which has point gaining any additional value from that point, it is not so clear that this is the case with futility. Does an activity which is directed towards a non-trivial end, gain significance from that end if the activity is futile so that the goal can never be reached? My tentative answer is that we are each of us justified in striving for an unattainable end, provided we do not realise that the end *is* unattainable. However, when we do become aware of the futility of an activity, the goal loses its power to add meaning to the performance.

That is why the fear of futility is peculiarly haunting. We can never rid our-selves of the possibility of discovering that the world has doomed us to frustra-tion. The altruistic project which is intended to increase the well-being of man-kind may produce effects that run counter to our intentions. Subjectively, it seems that ignorance is at least near to bliss, for the ignorant man can gain satisfaction from the pursuit of the impossible, and he can derive that satisfac-tion only because he is ignorant.

I want now to show that certain commonly held and rationally defendable philosophical views can be seen as threatening human life with futility. I have said that I would use the phrase 'human life' to refer to 'the typical human life style,' and this vague phrase now needs elucidation.

We expect a member of a biological species to develop in a manner which is both typical of and distinctive to the species to which it belongs. The life style of a species is the pattern of behaviour which an animal follows because it is a member of the species. When we say that cats are predatory and carnivorous we are claiming that certain types of behaviour are part of the life style of the cat. Unfortunately, if we treat human beings as a biological species, we encounter difficulties when we seek the human life style. The physiological phases of our development are clear enough, the human being will inevitably develop from childhood through adolescence to maturity and senescence, but in contrast to other animals human behaviour is pliable. There are no fixed courting rituals, no common habits of nest building, and not even any common practices of child rearing. Moreover, the variety of human practices is not akin to the variety of life styles which would be found in a collection of many different kinds of animals. *Homo sapiens* is not an assortment of species. We each of us know that if we had chosen otherwise or been brought up differently we might be enjoying or enduring a way of life very different from that which we are now living. We might have had more or fewer spouses, have left school earlier, be working in a different profession or be aiming at some achievement towards which we at present have no sympathy whatsoever.

Yet it is the very diversity of individual lives which enables us to sketch in the fundamentals of the human life style. The peculiarity of the human animal is that he can rationalise, reflect and criticise, so that he is not like a bird which cannot help but build a nest instead of a cocoon. We are creatures who pursue very general ends imposed upon us by the brute facts of physiology, and who must choose patterns of life in accordance with these general ends. The human life style thus involves critical and reflective activity, and requires the use of practical and theoretical reason directed, among other things, towards the discovery and achievement of ends which will not be seen to be futile when we learn more about our own natures and the world.

How strong is the analogy between the human life style and straightforward activities? Is there any point in assessing that life style by criteria derived from the assessment of action? It might seem not, for we do not choose either our fundamental drives or our intellectual pretensions. We find ourselves with them, rather than adopt them. A man criticising the human life style might seem as absurd as a caterpillar speculating about the value of building cocoons. We do not undertake living in the way in which we deliberately decide to do something.

Nevertheless, there is point in evaluating human life as if it were an activity. In the first place, we are not as helpless as nesting birds or metamorphosing insects. Even if the fundamentals of human life are given, there is always the choice of not living, which is why philosophers who have worried about the meaning of life have so often been obsessed by the thought of suicide. In the second place it is by no means clear that human nature cannot be changed through the interference of man. Koestler, who finds certain elements of our nature anachronistic, looks for chemicals to alter this nature.[5] Finally, even if we are only playing a game of let's pretend when we construe human life as if it were a deliberately chosen activity, many people find satisfaction in playing the game. They would find intellectual or aesthetic delight in discovering that if human life were a voluntary activity it could justifiably be chosen by a rational creature.

Having argued that there is sufficient analogy between human life and an activity to warrant our assessing them by common criteria, I want to show how philosophical views about the world may give us reason for believing in the futility of that life.

Case 1. The Naked Ape

If the speculations of some popularisers of biological theories are correct, there is good reason for holding that human life possesses the anachronistic

[5] A. Koestler: *The Ghost in the Machine* (1968).

futility exemplified by the speaker who declaims brilliantly after the motion has been passed.[6] They claim that many bewildering human activities such as our common aversion and hostility towards members of out groups, and our propensity to become violent and quarrelsome when huddled too close to our fellows, represent biological survivals which, although they once served our needs, are inappropriate to the modern environment. If our lives are necessarily an accommodation to these primitive leftovers there is a good deal of pointless struggle and torment; but the salt has yet to be rubbed into the wound.

If we see people as naked apes, we cannot but be cynical concerning the superstructure of justification associated with many of the most memorable human enterprises. Once we accept that many of our political and military endeavours are the working out of a primitive instinct of territoriality, we can no longer regard as fully meaningful the gloss of reasoning and argument which men use in an attempt to show that their undertakings are reasonable. The words of debate become mere persiflage; the talk a mere epiphenomenon of creatures ignorant of the true springs of their actions. We begin to undermine our faith in the capacity of human beings to know the truth, discover what causes what, and learn, through self-examination, about the integrity of their own motives.

Case 2. Moral Subjectivism

I do not believe that moral subjectivism necessarily produces a lack of accord between the world and our activities. If we were lucky, the universe and a man's attitudes could be in harmony. However, it seems that, in fact, the moral stances which people take are often of such a kind that they are futile in the face of the world. People not uncommonly sacrifice their happiness, and even their lives, for hopeless causes. Even odder than this is the fact that men who do not share a martyr's attitudes frequently admire him for standing up for truth, and the integrity of his personality. Good motives do not provide complete absolution, but the man who suffers in vain for his morality is commonly admired.

If we hold that ultimate value judgments can possess objective truth or falsity, and that this truth or falsity is not determined by the desires and attitudes of man, we can lend sense both to the act of self-sacrifice and to our reverence for it. The martyr is a martyr not simply for integrity but also for truth. Yet if relativistic subjectivism is true, the self-sacrifice is vain, for truth is not at stake. The martyr for the lost cause becomes, not silly, but pitiful. He accomplishes nothing and is simply a person who would have been better off had his ultimate desires been other than they were.

It will undoubtedly be said that I have missed the point of relativism. A man can have no better reason, it will be argued, for acting in a certain way than the excellent reason that what he does accords with his innermost being. It may well be the case that no reason could be better, but if this is so it is an ironic

---

[6] See, for example, K. Lorenz: *On Aggression* (1967); Desmond Morris: *The Naked Ape: a zoologist's study of the human animal* (1967); and Robert Ardrey: *The Territorial Imperative: a personal inquiry into the animal origins of property and nations* (1967).

misfortune. The best reason a man has may fail to fit the nature of the universe, so that the rational act is futile.

Case 3. Ultimate Contingency

I think it is still true that, among professional philosophers, the orthodox view concerning the explanation of natural phenomena is modified Humeanism. It is believed that our ability to discover the laws of nature, and to utilise them in order to both explain and cope with the world about us, depends upon the occurrence of ultimate regularities which are contingent and inexplicable. They are not inexplicable because we lack the intellectual capacity to explain, rather they are inexplicable because they have no explanation. Of course, the regularities which we encounter and recognise in our everyday dealings with the world are almost certainly not inexplicable, for we can justify our reliance upon them if we can show that they are the products of more fundamental regularities, but ultimately, it is held, the edifice of science rests upon brute and inexplicable regularities—the fundamental laws of nature.

Yet here we have a paradox. In ordinary life when we come to accept that a regularity has no explanation we regard it as a mere coincidence. If, for example, we find that all the books on a particular shelf are between 200 and 250 pages long, and we cannot discover any causal connection between their being on the shelf and their having that length, we dismiss the regularity as a mere coincidence. When we do this we acknowledge that we have no right to make any inference concerning the number of pages of the next book that might be put upon the shelf. Yet according to Humeanism, the basic regularities which we hold to be laws of nature have no explanation. If we were to be consistent it seems that we should dismiss them as merely coincidental. Yet of course we label them laws of nature precisely because we do not wish to surrender our right to make inductive inferences concerning natural phenomena. If the world view of the Humean is correct, it seems we cannot be consistent in our attempt to construct rational models of the world. Yet reason demands consistency, so that science becomes futile; a game which cannot be won unless the rules are broken.

Case 4. Atheism

The relationship between belief in God and the meaning of life is notoriously complex. Traditionally God has been used as a guarantee of objective values to provide justification for holding that certain activities are worthwhile in themselves, and also, in his capacity as designer of the universe, to justify our hope that there is point to our lives, the point deriving from the part which human existence plays in the fulfilment of the divine purpose. Unfortunately for the theist, I do not believe that anyone has been able to adequately ground objective values in the nature of God. The question which Plato asked in 'The Euthyphro,' 'Why do the Gods value what is just?' cannot be evaded. Similarly, the attempt to give indirect value to human life by deriving that value from the purpose of God is open to the argument already mentioned, that the purposes of God are irrelevant unless we accept them as valuable in themselves and adopt them as our own. In addition, many philosophers find degrading the very idea of our lives being ordered by a superior being for the production of an end determined by the nature of that being. Thus, Kurt Baier has written, 'To attribute to a human being a purpose in that sense is not neutral, let alone complimentary: it is offensive. It is degrading for a man to be regarded as merely serving a purpose.'[7]

In spite of this, many people do feel that without God human life becomes meaningless. In part, the explanation of this is obvious. In most societies it is common to indoctrinate children with the belief that everything that matters derives from God. Yet what is surprising is that the view that unless there is a God life has no meaning is still proclaimed not just by children but by the sophisticated. Thus, Paul Ramsey, Professor of Religion at Princeton, is still able to claim in his *Modern Moralists* that 'suicide is an inner logical consequence of *vital* atheism.'[8] If Ramsey is correct I and many others have started people along the road to suicide. Of course he is not correct, and shows a surprising lack of awareness of the traditional arguments concerning the relation between God and morality. Nevertheless, although it does not follow from atheism that a person has no reason to continue living or to regard any activity as worthwhile, I think that atheism does open the possibility of discovering that human life possesses an extra element of absurdity. The traditional religions do claim that because the world is designed, and because a rational nature plays a part in this design, human activities cannot be futile. Although we cannot know how our desires accord with the nature of the world, the theist claims that it would be contrary to the nature of a perfect and omnipotent being to have given us desires that were not in principle capable of being acted upon and fulfilled, or to have imposed upon us life-patterns which could not be held consistent and justifiable. In this sense, I believe that although atheism does not render life meaningless, it *opens* for us the possibility of discovering that it is futile. Perhaps Descartes should not be lightly dismissed when he claims that only the theist has reason to trust his intellectual powers.

I have used these four cases to demonstrate that philosophical positions are not neutral in the conflict between pessimism and optimism, and in particular I have argued that certain widely held views lend strength to the claim that there are strong analogies between human life and a futile activity. I have not of course established that life is futile, but merely that there are *prima facie* analogies between pointless activities and many of the goal-directed undertakings that are part of the human life style. What are the practical consequences which we should draw?

In the first place, we are not justified in rejecting a philosophical view simply because if that view is true, valued life styles can no longer be uncritically accepted. We are not entitled, for example, to believe in God simply to protect our species against the charge that its activities are futile. On the other hand, views which demonstrate the futility of the procedures of reasoning which we rely upon in order to establish that futility may be queried. Perhaps the scepticism

---

[7] K. Baier: *The Meaning of Life* (1957) p. 20.
[8] P. Ramsey: *Modern Moralists* (1970) p. 26.

which follows from Humeanism is a ground for holding that Humeanism must be false.

In the second place, the futility of human life does not warrant too profound a pessimism. An activity may be valuable even though not fully meaningful, and we have seen that Sisyphus would have frustrated the Gods if he could have given worth to his eternal task. We, too, can value life even if we believe that it is futile, and an active life may be fruitful in that it is productive of unexpectedly valuable consequences.[9] In addition, the pessimist is not by his pessimism exempted from all responsibility for his individual decisions; he is still faced with choices, and with giving meaning to the life which is the outcome of those choices.

Yet in spite of these consolations, it seems to me that it would be a matter of regret if we did discover that the basic capacities which make us human were incapable of being fulfilled. Human life would be flawed, tarnished and ultimately unreasonable; a second-best existence. When we remember that we do not choose to be human, the analogy between our lot and that of Sisyphus, the eternal prisoner, becomes grim. A philosopher, even though he enjoys living, is entitled to feel some resentment towards a world in which the goals that he must seek are forever unattainable.

[9] I owe this suggestion to Professor D. A. T. Gasking.